THE TRIAL

THE TRIAL

*A History from Socrates
to O. J. Simpson*

SADAKAT KADRI

HarperCollins*Publishers*

HarperCollins*Publishers*
77–85 Fulham Palace Road
Hammersmith, London, W6 8JB

www.harpercollins.co.uk

Published by HarperCollins*Publishers* 2005

1

Copyright © Sadakat Kadri 2005

Sadakat Kadri asserts the moral right to
be identified as the author of this work

A catalogue record for this book
is available from the British Library

ISBN: 0 00 711121 5

Set in Minion
Typeset by Terence Caven

Printed and bound in Great Britain by
Clays Ltd, St Ives plc

For my mum and dad, with love.

Contents

Acknowledgements

Hats off to my agent, Derek Johns at A.P. Watt, for talking me up and calming me down so wisely over the last few years, and to Arabella Pike and Will Murphy, my UK and US editors, for all the encouragement, enthusiasm and good humour that they have lent this book. Much respect also to the HarperCollins team who helped me wrap things up for the UK edition: Kate Hyde for sassiness and *sang froid* in the face of my ever more unreasonable demands, Caroline Hotblack for hunting down the book's pictures, Annabel Wright for being there whenever everyone else disappeared, Julian Humphries for the cover, Terence Caven for the book design, Marcella Edwards and Caroline Michel for cordiality beyond the call of duty, copy-editor Michael Cox, indexer Christine Bernstein, and Carol Anderson for her formidable proofreading skills. Belated thanks are due to Dr Boyd Hilton for giving me the chance to study history at Cambridge in the first place; to Felicity Rubinstein, whose appreciation of my guide to Prague set me thinking about many of the ideas pursued in this book; and to Anjali Pratap of A.P. Watt, who was the first person to read and like my proposal. I overshot so many deadlines that plenty of people had moved on by the time I was done. Jon Karp at Random House US made sure that the manuscript did not fall into a black hole when I lost my original American editor. Philip Gwyn Jones deserves three particularly resounding cheers: after encouraging me to get my literary act together for a decade, he went all out to help when I finally did, and his support helped win me the backing of Ann Godoff and Courtney Hodell who were then at Random House US. The trio collectively gave me the confidence and means to write at the pace and place that I thought I needed. I can only hope that I have done my subject justice, but I know that the attempt would have been considerably more meagre had it not been for everyone mentioned.

Countless others have contributed at a personal level. My clerks and colleagues at Doughty Street Chambers are inspirational. I thank them one and all for their cameraderie, bow to their brilliance, apologise to any whose ideas I have stolen, and hope that they enjoy the book. Thanks to Marjorie Heins, with whom I interned at the ACLU in 1994, who gave me my first practical experience of US law; and to Berlin lawyer Nicolas Becker for introducing me to the modern German legal system. Natasha Walter and Paul Moss both read early draft chapters, and for their sympathetic feedback and relentless encouragement, I'm deeply grateful. On an unprofessional level, I'm obliged to countless friends in London and Prague for steering me off the straight and narrow as and when my well-being needed recalibration: a collective thanks to you all, and a specific one to Kate Lissanevitch, living proof – as if such were needed – that lawyers too can be fun. I wrote in New York during interesting times, and many others helped keep my American dream alive as the country staggered from the awfulness of September 11 into the madness of 2003: Shazia Ahmad, Clarice Annegers and Zed Ettinger, Audrey Baker, Jan Baracz, Zack, Elliott and Jane Barowitz, Chris Beneke and Sasha Rodriguez, Josh Cody, Allison de Frees, Blake Ferris, Melissa Fox, Sean Fuller, Tom Gross, Ellen Harvey and Tom Campbell, Henrietta Hill, Mark Jolly, Craig Karmin, Amitav Kaul, Mandy Keifetz, Anna Kuyomcuoglu, Mark Kuzmack, Stephen Powles and Shaun Waterman. More thanks to Aaron and Juliette Adams, Asla Bâli, Isaac Flatteau, Gaelle Laroque, Jonathan Huston and Silvia Danailov, Jeremy Pam and Partha Chattoraj – and above all, to Rupa Mitra, whose friendship and wit ensured that even amidst the doomiest gloom, New York never quite lost the glitz, the ritz, the razzle and the dazzle. Thanks, Rupa. The final debt, in many ways the biggest of them all, is owed to the staff of the New York Public Library, the British Library, the Institute of Advanced Legal Studies and the Northcote Road library in Wandsworth, London: I raise my pass to you all.

Introduction

In August 1792, as the French Revolution hurtled towards its years of Terror, Paris was seized by panic. Armies from Prussia and Austria were marching on the capital to restore King Louis XVI to the throne, and radicals had responded by slaughtering several hundred of his Swiss guards and placing the royal household under arrest. To the sound of boots and drums and bells, the capital mobilized, aware that the commander of the invading forces had sworn vengeance on every Parisian if the king's person was violated. When the Germans reached Verdun, just a hundred miles east, the possibility of a bloodbath became imminent. As fear mounted, the pamphleteers and propagandists of the Revolution identified a threat even closer to home than the Prussians: the thousand or so royalists and clerics who were being held in the municipal jails. 'You have traitors in your bosom,' warned Danton. '[W]ithout them the fight would have been soon over.' 'The prisons are full of conspirators,' thundered the *Orateur du peuple*. 'The first battle we shall fight will be inside the walls of Paris.' The prescription of Marat was most precise of all. '[T]he people's duty,' he wrote, was to 'run [the traitors] through with a sword'.

It soon became clear that many Parisians were inclined to agree. As a train of cabs carrying some twenty captive priests inched its way through the seething capital on 2 September, one of the passengers, deluded or desperate, lashed out with a stick. It was a bad move. The man struck by his assault leapt onto the carriage step, thrust a sabre three times through its open door, and raised the glistening blade to the roaring crowd. The passengers in the cab were cut to pieces and at the convoy's destination, a prison called the Abbaye, a mob broke down the doors and turned pikes and bayonets onto those who had survived. The murders set off a holocaust. Some twelve hundred prisoners were killed over the next four days and nights, despatched inside prisons that echoed with their screams and then stacked high on streets and bridges that ran with their blood. It was the deadliest single atrocity in a Revolution that never lacked for violence – but it was distinguished by more than its scale. Almost as soon as it had begun, the Parisian authorities despatched an urgent instruction to those carrying it out. The people's enemies were not to be killed so quickly, it warned. They had to be tried first.

One of those who faced the revolutionary music was army officer François Jourgniac de Saint-Méard, who was taken from his cell in the Abbaye during the early hours of 4 September and led into a darkened chamber. About a dozen men were present. Some stood around in bloody shirts and aprons, machetes hanging limp from their waists; others dozed on the sidelines. Behind a bench at the far end, his gaunt features illuminated by the smoky flames of two torches, was the tall, dark, and tubercular figure of Stanislas Maillard, a 29-year-old veteran of the storming of the Bastille who had assumed the status of tribunal president. Saint-Méard was detained behind crossed sabres as a soused sansculotte handed up a reference for the 70-year-old man whose trial was reaching its conclusion. Maillard waved it aside. 'They are useless, these appeals for traitors,' he grumbled. 'My hands are washed of it; take [him] away.' As the old man was dragged to the back of the room, he struggled furiously with his captors. 'It is frightful!' he protested. 'Your judgment is murder!' Maillard scribbled into his files as the doors were opened onto the street. Men and women outside, skulking like dogs around an abattoir, suddenly galvanized into a pack. It swallowed its prey with a great roar. Maillard continued to leaf through his papers. 'Another!' he called.

Saint-Méard's guards tugged him to the centre of the room. Shadows leapt as defendant and judges peered at each other across a table littered with pipes, inkstands, and half-drained bottles of liquor. Why had he been arrested, demanded Maillard. Saint-Méard replied that he was thought, wrongly, to have edited a royalist newspaper. A single lie, snapped another voice, would mean instant death. If he was innocent, why had he been charged?

He had begun to reply when a priest was suddenly hauled into the room. A stupefied Saint-Méard watched as the cleric was bombarded with a flurry of questions, sentenced to death, and then pulled away, pleading for mercy. His judges invited him to continue. How could they be sure that documents he had handed up were not forgeries? Saint-Méard suggested, very hopefully, that they should adjourn his case while they checked – only to be interrupted again. A jailer, pale with fear, burst into the room to report that a prisoner was clambering up the chimney. Maillard warned grimly that if he made good his getaway, the turnkey would pay with his life. Everyone's attention switched to the new drama, as pistols were fired up the flue and a heap of straw was lit in the fireplace. Only when the would-be fugitive dropped into the hearth – where, stunned and ablaze, he was beaten to death – did the trial resume. You have told us many times what you were *not*, noted one of the judges, but what is it that you *are*? Saint-Méard desperately replied that he was a patriot and explained that, far from plotting against the Revolution, he had considered it too timid. The claim, addressed to men who were diligently murdering in said Revolution's name, was an audacious one. None of his judges looked convinced. Most appeared unmoved. Some seemed asleep. But their inscrutability masked one final surprise.

'I am for granting him his liberty,' declared Maillard. His fellow judges expressed their agreement, with joy rather than reluctance, and an astonished Saint-Méard was embraced by his jailers. And as he was escorted into the street between the torches of an honour guard, the mob that had just torn a man limb from limb parted to let him through, with cries of '*Vive la nation!*'

Saint-Méard's experience was far from unique. Around one in seven of those at the Abbaye were spared, and the acquittals were repeatedly greeted with jubilation or tears from judges, guards, and citizenry alike. Historians have typically characterized the trials as shams but, understandable as that is, it begs an obvious question – who was being fooled? Saint-Méard struggled to believe that the proceedings were something more exalted and succeeded to the extent that his life was saved. His judges were partners as much as adversaries, from the moment that they asked him to explain his arrest to the point when they freed him. Far from deliberately performing the preamble to a murder, everyone was longing to enact a dream of liberty, equality, and fraternity. And the delusions created their own reality.

The law has become so closely associated with reasoned deliberation that it is sometimes hard to think of criminal trials as anything other than inquiries – but they have always performed a function that goes far beyond that of establishing who did what to whom. The first judges were priests, whose punishments were as sacrificial as they were penal, and the law has ever since asserted the power most proper to gods: the ability to rebalance a cosmos knocked out of kilter. Since the days of ancient Athens, there is no wrong that it has not somewhere claimed to right – even when no human defendant has been available to carry blame. In the courts of early modern Europe, creatures from beetles to bulls were regularly prosecuted, defended, and condemned at public expense. English juries for several centuries returned homicide verdicts against mischievous objects from haystacks to locomotives. Lawyers discovered new categories of criminal, from traitors to werewolves, whenever popular passion or private fear required. The long arm of the legal process even reached into the grave: for well over half a millennium, the bodies of dead criminals were brought into court to be accused by witnesses, defended by advocates and, if convicted, punished by the public executioner.

The cowls have metamorphosed into gowns and the incantations have turned to jargon, but ancient impulses still quiver around every courtroom. Rational concerns and logical argument typify any given case, but the terror of infanticide and Devil worship that once sent witches to their deaths could still be resurrected, in the form of satanic sexual abuse allegations, during the 1980s. Animals and corpses are no longer put on trial, but the urge to punish defendants regardless of their mental state lives on in prosecutions of children and the mentally ill. Perhaps the best example of the continuing faith in legal omnipotence comes from a case that never quite happened. In the spring of 1949, the first president of the Israeli Supreme Court, Moshe Smoira, received dozens of petitions from Christian clerics around the world. His country was less than a year old and had just fought off five Arab armies committed to its destruction, but the writers had few doubts about the urgency of their appeal – and none at all concerning the legitimacy of the Jewish state. Would he please, they asked, reopen the proceedings of the Sanhedrin and overturn the conviction of Jesus Christ?

This book quickened in 2000 in London, where I had been working for seven years as a criminal barrister. Almost a decade before, I had lived in post-revolutionary Prague and had then been struck by the extent to which many Czechoslovakians seemed to be blaming others to avoid tough questions about their own contributions to the communist era. I had vaguely wondered then if such thoughts might stretch into a book on scapegoats and soon decided that they would not. The weird dynamic of naming and shaming continued to interest me, however, as I represented villains, both innocent and guilty and by 2000, I was ready to try again. This time, I had a far clearer structure in mind. By writing a history of the criminal trial, stories rather than theories would drive the book forward.

Events elsewhere would delineate the outlines of the structure further. Before Prague I had studied at Harvard and qualified for the New York Bar, and it seemed a sensible idea – or at least a pleasant one – to relocate to the United States. I reached New York in the summer of 2001. By mid August I was ensconced in a small studio with a splendid view over Manhattan's financial district. Thus it was that on 11 September I watched from my windows as the towers of the World Trade Center burned and collapsed. Over subsequent weeks I wandered a city in mourning, personally unable to write and convinced that little was now of less significance to anything than an analysis of the criminal trial. I would spend another two and a half years in the United States and my mood would pass. But others, many of them in high places, were expressing similarly gloomy conclusions about the redundancy of the criminal process – and in their case, the trauma would have lasting effects. Over the next few months, a landscape familiar to me since law school seemed sometimes to be melting away. Several legal commentators were suggesting that the constitutional right to silence should be abolished. A Harvard law professor whom I had once respected proposed that it might be time to introduce a right to torture in its place. The administration of President George W. Bush, meanwhile, embarked on a policy of deeming entire categories of people, American and foreign, to be subject to indefinite detention without a right of access to courts, let alone a right to public trial.

Emergency powers have been invoked to combat terrible crimes since the days of heresy and witchcraft, and the fact that twenty-first-century commentators were readopting stances that inquisitors had abandoned in the eighteenth soon reassured me that a little historical perspective would not go amiss. But the aftermath of September 11 also sharpened the focus of my book. I had always anticipated that a central theme would be the conflict between reason and emotion – a tension that galvanizes any courtroom – but in the new climate a more fundamental aspect of that link came to the fore: why trials take place at all. For at the same time that hundreds of people were being accused without prosecution, official talk of justice – and even Infinite Justice – was reaching a crescendo. Governments are not the only component of a criminal justice system, but the reasons that they might want to avoid courts increasingly came to seem at least as significant as the reasons that trials occur. The relationship between secrecy, publicity and transparency consequently became central to my book.

From the very outset, I chose not to conduct interviews. Contemporary topics such as capital punishment and the war on terror would have called for a range of views, while trials potentially demanded contributions from participants ranging from the defendant to the judge. Anthropologists, sociologists and political scientists, not to mention historians and lawyers, might all have had other worthwhile things to say. Finding experts to cover every subject evenly would have been beyond my time and inclination. The book quotes from countless chronicles, pamphlets, transcripts and newspaper reports but my own voice is the only one to keep the babble in line.

The task that lay ahead when I began was a daunting one. The tale I intended to trace began more or less at the dawn of time, hopped back and forth between centuries, and demanded that I address subjects as dark as child abuse and terrorism with as light a touch as possible. It was a tall order, and attempting to fulfil it gave the book a very particular structure. Rather than use a straightforwardly chronological approach, which lacked flexibility, or compile a compendium, which would have bored me let alone anyone else, I divided the work into eight thematic chapters that proceed in roughly historical order. They begin with the religious rituals of the classical and barbarian worlds and end in the trial circuses of today, and several address specific aspects of twenty-first-century justice. Each dovetails into the next and with luck, they combine to form more than the sum of their parts.

Several ideas run through the chapters, but one simple theme could be said to link them all: the tension inherent in the criminal process between the desire to punish and the fear of making a mistake. Courts have collectively spilled at least as much blood as the people they condemned, but criminal justice has always aimed at more than violence. The oldest laws yet to be discovered, enacted by Babylon's King Hammurabi in the eighteenth century BC, worried about injustice to the extent that false witnesses were to be punished as harshly as those who were properly convicted. And although the sword of righteousness has been in play since King Solomon, confronted with two women claiming the same child, threatened to slice it in two and wisely surmised that the impostor was the one who agreed, Justice has wielded another tool for even longer. Four and a half thousand years ago, when Hammurabi's dynasty was unknown and Athens' Golden Age shimmered as far in the future as it now lies buried in the past, the priests of Egypt were already venerating the goddess Ma'at – whose scales measured out justice for the dead. In the Hall of Two Truths, watched by a horrid hybrid of cat, crocodile and hippopotamus called Am-Mit, she would place the hearts of those who had just died into one pan, and drop the feather of truth onto the other. If the feather sank, the departed soul would gain entrance to the Kingdom of the Dead. But if it rose, outweighed by the heart's burden of deceit, Am-Mit would be fed – and its owner would be abandoned to oblivion.

The balance remains the most potent image of justice in the Western world. But as it migrated into modern Europe from Egypt and Babylon, via Jews, Greeks, Romans and barbarians, the meaning of its symbolism would be decisively transformed. No story better exemplifies that than one from the career of Sir Edward Marshall Hall, a famous British barrister of the early twentieth century.

Marshall Hall was defending one Edward Lawrence, charged in 1909 with having murdered his lover with a gun. Lawrence entered the dock with one foot already on the scaffold. He had admitted to police that he had shot her, and declared that he was 'glad' to have done so, because she was 'wicked' and 'best dead'. But by the end of the defence case, words that had seemed so damning no longer sounded worse than callous. Lawrence had claimed from the witness box that the victim died accidentally as he was pulling a gun from her. He had re-enacted the struggle three times, so convincingly that even the judge was privately persuaded of his innocence. More than twenty witnesses had told the jury about the victim's ferocious temper and frequent threats against Lawrence. By the time that Marshall Hall came to make his final speech, a case that had seemed black and white was turning very murky – and it was to uncertainty itself that he now appealed. Standing with arms outstretched, he asked the jurors to imagine 'a great statue of justice holding those two scales with equally

honest hands' and began methodically to go through the evidence for and
against his client. First one side, and then the other, he told them –
swaying all the while – might seem lower. It might be almost impossible
to say which side was closer to the ground. And as the jurors watched,
entranced, came the punchline.

> Then in the one scale, in the prisoner's scale, unseen by human
> eye, is placed that overbalancing weight, the weight of the pre-
> sumption of innocence . . . it is your duty to remember the
> invisible weight of that invisible substance.

With those words, he let one arm drop with a thud to the bench. The jury
acquitted after twenty minutes.

The journey from the Hall of Two Truths to the Old Bailey is a vast one.
It crosses from the marbled courtrooms of Athens to the ordeal pits of
Anglo-Saxon England, passing from the torture chambers of the
Inquisition to the judicial theatres of Salem in the 1690s and Moscow in the
1930s. Justice and vengeance, secrecy and spectacle, and superstition and
reason intertwine continually along the way, but this book's trajectory is a
straightforward one. At a time when governments appear increasingly
unsure whether the criminal trial is a dispensable relic or a touchstone of
liberty, it explores why the West came to regard the invisible doubt as a
more reliable guide to justice than the feather of truth.

This book is concerned with only the Western legal tradition, and
although it covers continental law in some detail in the first few chapters,
its modern focus is on the Anglo-American jury trial and the war crimes
trial. Any attempt to broaden its scope would have required either over-
simplification or a work twice as long, and would probably have produced
both. Whether the quality of Western justice is better or worse than that
of other cultures is a question that I have happily ducked. The book's
theme is the brutality or nobility of the West's institutions, and the extent
to which those institutions have honoured or betrayed the ideals for
which they claim to stand.

THE TRIAL

1

From Eden to Ordeals

It is only our conception of time that makes us call the Last Judgment by that name; in fact it is a permanent court-martial.

FRANZ KAFKA, *Aphorisms*

One of the few things that humanity has agreed upon for most of history is that its laws descend directly from the gods. The oldest complete legal code yet discovered, inscribed onto a black cone by the Babylonians almost four thousand years ago, shows Shamash, god of the sun, enthroned and handing down his edicts to a reverential King Hammurabi. Jehovah reportedly did much the same thing a few centuries later, carving ten commandments onto two tablets with His own finger as Moses stood by on fiery Mount Sinai. Coincidentally or otherwise, it was said of Crete's King Minos that he climbed Mount Olympus every nine years to receive legal advice from Zeus. Ancient cultures were equally certain that the power to adjudicate breaches of the law rested ultimately in the hands of the gods. The methods of enforcement were often as terrible as they were mysterious – ranging from bolts of lightning to visitations of boils – but the justice of the punishments was as unquestionable as the law that they honoured.

And yet, for all the insistence that heavenly laws were cast in stone and divine judgments unerring, one question always caused turmoil – namely to whom, down on earth, had the right to judge been delegated? The priests who veiled their various scrolls and statutes invariably argued that only they could interpret their secrets, backing up the claim with further revelations as and when required. Monarchs were no less assertive, and constantly sought to interfere with the religious mysteries

of justice. Some even argued that the power lay elsewhere. Among the Hebrews, for example, an old tradition prescribed that homicides should be tried by common people, and although Judah's priests established something close to a theocracy after 722 BC, their oldest myth of all characterized the ability to tell good from evil as every human being's birthright. The story of the Fall was not, admittedly, a ringing endorsement of the power to judge – Adam and Eve had, after all, paid for their apple with sorrow, sweat, and death – but it was certainly a start.

The Athenians would produce a considerably more robust illustration of humanity's inherent sense of justice: Aeschylus' *Oresteia*, the oldest known courtroom drama in history. The trilogy, first performed in 458 BC, retells the ancient myth of Orestes, scion of the royal house of Atreus – a bloodline as polluted as any that has managed to perpetuate itself on this earth. The corruption had set in when its founding father Tantalus chose, for imponderably mythic reasons, to slaughter his son, boil the body, and serve it up as soup to the gods. Aggrieved Olympians condemned him to an eternity of tantalization, food and drink forever just out of reach, and resolved to visit folly, blindness and pride on his offspring for evermore. Family fortunes began a rapid decline, and by the time that Tantalus' great-great-grandson Orestes reached adulthood, its history of rape, incest, cannibalism, and murder had generated a degree of domestic dysfunction that was pathological even by the standards of Greek mythology.

The play opens with news that Agamemnon, commander of the Greek armies and father of Orestes, has just triumphed at the Trojan Wars. But all is not well. Victory was purchased through the sacrifice of his own daughter, Iphigeneia, and he has abducted Cassandra, the beautiful child of Troy's King Priam, to have as his concubine. His wife, Clytemnestra, has meanwhile taken a lover of her own and sworn to avenge Iphigeneia. When Agamemnon returns to the marital home, as oblivious to the obvious as every tragic protagonist should be, the tension mounts. Cassandra waits at the gates while he enters its portals – and the princess, cursed to know the future but powerless to change it, sees horror ahead. Hopping and screeching on the palace eaves are the Furies, supernatural guardians of cosmic propriety, and throbbing deep within are visions of anguish: torn wombs, a soil that streams blood, a bath swirling red . . . and Agamemnon, dead. 'I know that odour,' intones Cassandra, as she steps up to the threshold. 'I smell the open grave.' Screams engulf her, and the first act closes with Clytemnestra exulting over the bodies of her husband and his prize, a bloody knife in her right hand. Her work, she proclaims, is a masterpiece of justice.

It all leaves Orestes in a pickle. On the one hand, he loves his mother. On the other, he is honour-bound to slaughter her. Urged on by a crazed Chorus, he makes his way to the family palace, where he first cuts down her lover. He then forces Clytemnestra to gaze on the body. Pleading for her life, so desperate that she bares the breasts that once suckled him, she begs her son to accept that destiny played as much of a role in Agamemnon's demise as her dagger. Orestes is torn between the claim of vengeance and the tie of affection, and the drama pivots on a moment of hesitation – before it tips. 'This too,' retorts Orestes, 'destiny is handing you your death.' He hurls his mother to the floor and makes her embrace her lover's corpse, before running her through with his sword. The sated Chorus re-gathers to pronounce that the family's misfortunes have come to an end. Resolution remains an act away, however, and Orestes has of course won no more than his turn to bear the ancestral curse. As it settles, stifling, on his shoulders, he sees the serpent-haired Furies swarming to take revenge and even the Chorus finally begins to waver. 'Where will it end?' its members wail, 'where will it sink to sleep and rest, this murderous hate, this fury?'

Aeschylus' answer comes in the final part of the trilogy. Shadowed by his mother's supernatural avengers, Orestes seeks refuge at Apollo's oracle at Delphi. Apollo, god of justice and healing, reassures him that he did the right thing, but advises him nevertheless to seek the protection of wise Pallas Athena. Orestes duly makes his way to her hilltop citadel on the

Areopagus of Athens. The owl-eyed goddess is rather more equivocal. There are arguments both ways, she points out, and even she cannot resolve a conflict between right and right. Her solution is simple. She will summon ten Athenian citizens, bind them by oath, and make them decide.

The substance of the argument that ensues is less significant than its outcome – for although the jury splits evenly, Athena casts her vote for Orestes and is so impressed by her innovation that she prescribes its use in all future homicide cases. Athens, she pronounces, stands on the verge of unprecedented peace and tranquillity. Only the Furies remain unconvinced, hissing with repulsion at the thought of harmony, but even they are quieted by Athena's assurance that they will have an honoured place in her new court. Their venom has been drawn – and the snake-headed hags, optimistically renamed the Kindly Ones, close the play at the head of a torchlit procession through their blessed city.

Aeschylus intended his work as a celebration of Athens in particular and human potential in general. When it was first performed in 458 BC, some two centuries after the scattered farms and fishing villages of the Attican peninsula had first begun to coalesce, the city was at its zenith. It had just seen off would-be invaders from Persia and transformed itself into a regional superpower, while political reforms were entrusting its male citizens with rights of participation and personal freedom never before seen in the ancient world. In a spirit epitomized by a famous assertion by a thinker called Protagoras that 'man [was] the measure of all things', its poets and philosophers were busily blazing trails that still dazzle more than two millennia later. Aeschylus' brilliance manifested itself in a series of plays, and it was epitomized in the *Oresteia*. Whereas Homer had simply paid homage to Orestes as a righteous avenger, and Euripides would later resolve his anguish by having him acquitted before twelve gods, the playwright's perspective was as radical as it was optimistic. Human honesty, he ventured, might be as sure a guide to the mysteries of justice as the most divine of oracles.

Straightforward though that message appears, it is easy to over-rationalize it. Aeschylus' faith was reflected by reality, in that legal reforms had just transferred the power to judge serious crimes from state officials to ordinary Athenian men, but the ritual that he revered was no fact-finding inquiry. There had been no uncertainty about what Orestes had done: he had deliberately murdered his mother, who had just done the same to his father. And just as the jurors were not convened to find facts, the defendant was not cleared because evidence proved his innocence: he was cleansed of guilt because they decided – by the barest of majorities, tipped by the casting vote of a goddess – that he was not blameworthy. Nor was vengeance removed from the process. Honouring the family by repaying wrongs done to it was still seen as part and parcel of the natural order, and any fifth-century Athenian would have regarded forgiveness as cowardly at best and accursed at worst. Aeschylus had made sure to give the Furies a dignified place in Pallas Athena's court, and the clinching argument that the goddess used to secure their co-operation was a reminder that they had won the votes of half of the jurors. In his play, as in life, vengeance was being idealized and institutionalized, but it was certainly not being abolished.

Aeschylus' stance reflected a tension between two ideas about justice that were always at odds with each other in the ancient world. One assumption, that people were only at fault if they had done evil deliberately, was almost as common in fifth-century Athens as it is today. However, there also existed another, more visceral, belief – that some deeds demanded punishment regardless of the perpetrator's intention, if the rage of the gods was to be forestalled. The view was notoriously prevalent among the ancient Hebrews, who enumerated an entire catalogue of unforgivable abominations, from sodomy to sex with mothers-in-law,* and used scapegoats and turtledoves to bear away the burden of a countless lesser sins. In Greece itself, some three centuries before Aeschylus was born, the poems of a farmer called Hesiod had proposed that entire cities could suffer because of one man's misdeeds. About three decades after he died Sophocles would retell the notorious tragedy of King Oedipus, whose unwitting seduction and slaughter of his mother and father respectively brought shame and pestilence onto his realm. And fifth-century Athenians did not just write about such matters; they regularly visited suffering on a minority to cleanse the majority. An annual festival called the Ostracism allowed Athenian men to banish a fellow citizen by vote, and although they often

---

* To be more precise, the Torah required the burning only of those men who had sex with their mother-in-law and wife *at the same time*: Leviticus 20: 14.

did so for practical reasons, the ritual was widely seen as a way of ridding
the body politic of contamination. Athens, like other Greek cities, also
maintained a stock of human scapegoats known as the *pharmakoi* –
comprising its poorest, lamest, and ugliest inhabitants – whose function
was to be feasted and venerated at public expense, until famine or plague
struck. They would then be dragged from their thrones and paraded about
to the clatter of pans and the squeal of pipes, before being hounded out of
the city gates under a hail of stones.

Trials themselves could operate to shift blame as well as discover it – as
the Athenians also appreciated. Every midsummer up to the third century
AD, they held a festival known as the *bouphonia*, at which an axe-wielding
official would, after sacrificing an ox, discard his weapon and flee the
scene. Someone would then flay the beast, and all present would eat the
meat, re-stitch the hide, stuff the carcass with straw, and yoke it to a plough
– at which point, a trial was convened to establish who, in the absence of
the human killer, was guilty of its death. Accusations were levelled first at
the women who had brought the water to whet the blades. They would
accuse the sharpeners. Those men, questioned in turn, would blame the
people who had taken the axe and the knife from them to the slaughter.
The messengers would accuse the carver, who laid one final charge. The
true shame, he would argue, lay with his blade. And there the buck would
stop. For when the knife damned itself by its silence, the axe was formally
acquitted and the guilty weapon was hurled into the sea.

Although the modern mind tends to picture Greek courtrooms as sun-
bleached temples to debate and deliberation, a similar tension between
reason and unreason characterized the rituals that were used to resolve
actual crimes in fifth-century Athens. Freemen had gained the right to
judge – which they would exercise in groups not of ten, but in assemblies
of up to a thousand and one – but while they were building a fizzing, bab-
bling democracy, seventy silent per cent of the adult population remained
legal nonentities. Women were permitted to litigate only through
guardians, while slaves could not even give evidence except under torture,
on the strength of a theory that they were constitutionally incapable of
telling the truth unless subject to great pain.

Trials for homicide, a touchstone of the social order in any close-knit
community, were not just affected by superstition but founded on it. It
was commonly believed that killers exuded the *miasma*, a vapour so

abhorrent to the gods that the slightest whiff could incite them to rage, so despicable that those around whom it clung were barred from temples, games, and marketplace – and so persistent that only a trial could dispel it. The origins of the *miasma* are as misty as any myth but its existence in fifth-century Athens was a firmly established sociological fact. Murder trials were held outdoors to minimize the risk of infection, and at least one defendant relied on its reality to prove his innocence, pointing out to his judges that he had recently sailed in a ship that had not sunk. Killers sometimes attended court to purge themselves even when there was no one to prosecute them – as might happen if the deceased was a legal cipher like a slave – and one Athenian tribunal, the *prytaneion*, was dedicated to nothing but the prosecution of killer beasts and murderous objects.* Defendants who had been exiled for one murder but wanted to cleanse themselves of a second charge were tried in the most prudent court of all. It convened at a stretch of Athenian shoreline called the Phreatto where the accused addressed his judges from a boat, which bobbed offshore at a suitably circumspect distance.

The superstition played an important role in anchoring the criminal trial in Athenian society. It sharpened the only choice open to most defendants in the ancient world – whether to undergo a trial or enter exile – and at a time when predators human and bestial roamed the countryside, those accused had every reason to take their chances in court. It simultaneously made it more likely that accusers would prosecute, for the *miasma* was also thought to linger around anyone who failed to obtain vengeance. And as it became established that prosecutions were as valid a form of revenge as any other, the premium that was placed throughout the ancient world on life behind a city's walls also generated its own moral basis for the exercise of judicial power. The law codes of Israel and Judah instructed municipal officials to grant sanctuary to killers only if they agreed to stand trial, and in Athens, where idealization of the city ran especially deep, it became established that judgments were binding,

---

* Plato recommended in Book IX of his *Laws* (873d –874a) that relatives should always cleanse themselves in such cases. He advised that any non-human killer, from animals to toppling statues, should be prosecuted and then cast beyond the city walls, and was prepared to make an exception only for lightning bolts. Similar ideas would revive, with force, in late medieval and early modern Europe: see Chapter 5.

whether right or wrong. A willingness to take complaints to court and abide by judicial ruling became, literally, the civilized thing to do.

No ancient trial better illuminates the development than the most famous one of them all: the prosecution of Socrates, charged in 399 BC with having invented new spiritual beings and corrupted Athenian youth. The 70-year-old was a metropolitan fixture at the time of his prosecution: an ugly, acerbic and provocative philosopher who had spent decades haranguing hecklers and debating passersby on the nature of the universe. Through a series of historical accidents, the accusations have entered popular history as the persecution of a sage, condemned by a city that could not bear to hear some harsh truths about itself. The assessment obscures considerably more than it illuminates.

It stems from the eyewitness reports of just two men – Socrates' pupil, Plato, and an acquaintance called Xenophon – and neither is a reliable narrator. Plato produced the more comprehensive account, but the future philosophical colossus, then a mere prodigy of 28, omitted to record much of the crucially important political background to the case. Assumptions of style and relevance undoubtedly played some part in that, but so too did the fact that Plato idolized his teacher and was concerned throughout to portray him in the purest light. One effect has been to consolidate an enduring popular myth that the charges were more irrational than they were. Another has been to blur one of the most important aspects of the trial. Plato's account leaves no doubt that the prosecution pitted the community against the individual, but its outcome illustrated as clearly how Socrates was bound to Athens as it showed his ability to stand up against it.

The Athens that put Socrates on trial was a shadow of the city that Aeschylus had glorified half a century before. Three decades of war with Sparta, its militaristic twin and rival, had recently come to an end. The Spartans had vanquished the Athenian navy and then reduced the city's starving population to unconditional surrender before destroying its fleet and demolishing its walls. The physical collapse was rapidly followed by political disintegration. A despotically inclined citizen called Critias had established a collaborationist oligarchy known as the Thirty, and for eight months Athens became a police state, terrorized by bands of dagger- and whip-wielding thugs who daily murdered opponents of the new dispensation. Around fifteen hundred people were summarily executed – almost as many as had died over the previous ten years of war – before the terror came to an end in 403 BC. The restored democracy declared an amnesty for political offences in the interests of peace – but plenty remained eager to settle accounts.

Socrates was among those who paid, heavily, but he was not chosen at random. No one has ever been entirely sure what ideas he expounded, because he wrote nothing and owes his philosophical footprint to Plato; but among the tenets later attributed to him were plenty that chimed neatly with those of the oligarchs. They included a belief that wise individuals could gain insights into absolute truths – a claim that was well suited to those who subscribed to the 'rule of the best', or *aristokratia*, and who pointed out that democracy could guarantee neither wisdom nor justice. It is also known that Socrates was not only an indirect inspiration to the enemies of democracy. He had taught several men closely associated with Thirty – one of whom was none other than Plato, connected to the aristocrats by a web of social and family connections. Another was a second cousin to Plato – Critias himself. As if that did not make the old man suspect enough, he was widely known to admire Sparta, a fact so notorious that the playwright Aristophanes had mocked him for it throughout his comedy, *The Clouds*.

None of the smears had much substance. Whatever Critias may have taken away from his lessons with Socrates, the older man remained sufficiently independent to disobey an order to arrest an innocent man during Critias' time in power. The single-mindedness of Spartan society certainly appealed to the philosopher in Socrates, very likely because he saw in its rigour a triumph of the human will. The totalitarian shadow of such beliefs is now apparent, but it could not have been to Socrates, and his admiration for Sparta seems to have resembled the rose-tinted feelings that some twentieth-century intellectuals once harboured towards the Soviet Union – symptomatic of idealistic impatience rather than venomous treachery. His ideological flirtations did not, in any event, stop him serving Athens loyally during the war, both as a civic officer and as a soldier.

There is little doubt, however, that the capital charges against Socrates, though framed in moral and religious terms to get round the amnesty for political offences, were effectively ones of treason. Although Plato chose not to record the speeches of the three accusers, the allegation was that he had lent aid and comfort to Athens' enemies at a time of war.

Plato's account of Socrates' trial portrays the older man as a model of integrity, as determined to expose the weaknesses of the case against him as he was resolute not to save himself through flattery. In his record, the snowy-curled philosopher, standing before 501 fellow citizens, began with the traditionally disingenuous plea of the seasoned orator – an apology for his inarticulacy – before launching into a speech that honoured nothing but the truth. He opened by telling his listeners that the Oracle of Apollo at Delphi – the source of wisdom visited by, among others, Orestes in the *Oresteia* – had identified him as the wisest person alive. Although initially puzzled, he had come to realize why – for he more than anyone else appreciated the limits of his own knowledge. The charges against him were however nonsense. They accused him of teaching young people to believe in new gods, and he had never done that. It was true that a spirit whispered in his ear, but it was a travesty to call that spirit a god. Its voice simply told him to speak plainly and ask awkward questions, and although such behaviour had made him unpopular, he would not stop even if acquitted. He was like a horsefly on the lazy beast of Athens. His judges would spare him if they were sensible, but he suspected that they would sleepily swat him down instead.

Despite the uncertainty over what Socrates taught, it has always been known how he taught it – essentially by prodding his listeners to conclusions that theoretically represented truths that they already knew – and there can be no better demonstration of the technique than the performance recorded by Plato. Some people find the speech moving, while others consider it the preaching of a prig; but whatever the best way to characterize Socrates' defiance (and Xenophon claims that he simply wanted to die) it won him few friends. He inspired such hostility that he had to ask for silence several times, and although shouting, clapping and booing were common at Athenian trials, when the judges voted, by dropping pebbles into earthenware jars, about 280 of the 501 were for conviction.

Athenian law required that Socrates propose his own sentence, but his response to conviction was to become even less conciliatory. Xenophon recorded that he refused to suggest anything. Plato has him telling the judges that what he most deserved was maintenance at state expense for the rest of his life, and dismissing exile with the explanation that the judges were too likely to impose it if he proposed it, before condescending to pay a derisory fine. The old man's supporters swiftly multiplied his offer thirtyfold, but the damage was done. When the ballot was counted, at least eighty of those who had supported his acquittal were now voting for his death. Still Socrates remained undaunted. He would not weep or wail to save himself. He looked forward to meeting the immortals. 'Now it is time that we were going, I to die and you to live,' he concluded. '[W]hich of us has the happier prospect is unknown to anyone but God.'

Plato's record, for all its bias, must be largely accurate – not least because his contemporaries would otherwise have written spirited corrections – but Socrates was not condemned simply because he was too honest to deny his genius. The city had just imploded after the most bitter war in its history, eviscerated by a Sparta that he idealized, and those judging him would almost all have been touched by the brutality of the Thirty. When he claimed exalted insights and spoke of a spirit that whispered into his ear, they would have recalled that his wisdom had been taught to traitors. To many of those who heard him, he was neither a harmless crank, nor a seeker after truth. He was an accessory to mass murder.

But the conflict between Socrates and the state would have an unexpected ending. After spending a month in his condemned cell, considerably more jolly than his morose acolytes, he was visited by a pupil called Crito who told him that an escape had been organized. Socrates, however, refused to countenance the idea. He had voluntarily attended his trial instead of exiling himself, he reminded his old friend, and he invited him to contemplate what the laws of Athens would think about the proposal if they were able to speak. As far as Socrates was concerned, they would be horrified. 'Do you imagine that a city can continue to exist and not be turned upside down,' they would ask, 'if the legal judgments which are pronounced in it have no force but are nullified and destroyed by private persons?' Socrates owed it to the city to stay. It was only through its laws that his parents had been able to marry each other and that he and his children had received their education. He had no more right to undermine an Athenian law that was being wrongly enforced than he would have had to retaliate against his father or his employer.

The willingness to yield to judgment after so steadfast a defence was remarkable enough, but Socrates would now bow even lower. For he did not simply submit to punishment – he carried it out. Athenian law allowed some capital offenders to purchase poison from the state, and Socrates did so. Plato records that he drained his glass in one gulp while disciples wept uncontrollably, and took his leave of life by asking Crito to sacrifice a cock to the god of healing. The pain was over. 'Such . . . was the end of our comrade,' observed Plato, 'the bravest . . . wisest and most upright man [of our time].'

As such remarks incessantly remind the reader, Plato was writing in large part to tell Athenians that their verdict had been an awful mistake, but the significance of his account can hardly be overstated. The arguments that he put into Socrates' mouth, idealizing the law while condemning those who misapplied it, would reverberate down the centuries. They would give birth to the notion that rules can be trusted even when humans cannot, inspiring ideals like the rule of law and the notion that some rights are inalienable. They would have a darker side, underpinning the authoritarian vision of a state that knows best and civil liberties that are always contingent. The record also showed, for the first time, how trials can enforce judgment by turning defendants against themselves. It was a development that would be seen again and again, whenever communal values and political institutions grew sufficiently strong to harness the force of the individual conscience. Its significance was summarized by Sigmund Freud in an image that bears repetition, even if the psychoanalytical theories underlying it might not. 'Civilization,' he wrote, 'obtains mastery over the individual's dangerous desire for aggression by weakening and disarming it and by setting up an agency within him to watch over it, like a garrison in a conquered city.'

The conventional bridge from Athens to the modern world is the civilization that conquered Greece in 200 BC – Rome. By then, the Republic had a legal culture that was already some three centuries old and its jurists were on the way to developing complex rules of contractual and property law, but its notions of criminal justice would never become quite as sophisticated. Spectacular treason and conspiracy trials would punctuate Roman history, but they were as political as they were principled: an opportunity for ambitious Romans to rally their supporters, display their power or publicly turn the tables on their rivals through a successful prosecution or defence. As in Athens, citizens facing a capital charge had the choice of departure or submission – required either to exile themselves, or attend court unwashed, unshaven, and in shabby mourning dress – but such ritualism rarely stretched to soldiers and never touched the cases of slaves. Roman law had originated in priestly mysteries just as holy as those of any other culture, but justice in the empire was a tool rather than an ideal, wielded by magistrates whose role was to police an empire rather than to honour a tradition.

The most distinctive feature of Roman penal laws was, unsuprisingly, not the trials they mandated but the punishments they prescribed. Prisoners of war and those convicted of murder, arson, or sacrilege might be executed at the arena – burned alive as a warm-up act, or offered as fodder to hungry beasts while the gladiators took a breather. The most notorious prosecution in Roman history is accordingly remembered not for the perfunctory ritual of condemnation but for the horrors that were reportedly inflicted subsequently: whether Jesus was convicted by the Sanhedrin or Pontius Pilate pales into insignificance against his scourging, whipping, and crucifixion. Other penalties made his fate look almost placid. A debtor, after sixty days in prison, was punishable by execution or enslavement at the election of his creditor – and if the insolvent owed money to more than one person, the plaintiffs could adjust their losses (among other things) by collectively tearing him apart limb from limb. Most rococo of all was the punishment imposed on those who killed a parent. The parricide was beaten with rods until blood was drawn, and then drowned in a sack with a dog, cock, monkey and snake, or some writhing permutation thereof.

The allure of Rome was such that Europe's lawyers would never stop asserting a Latin pedigree for their own legal theories, but a historical firebreak divides the classical and medieval worlds and the claims would very often be wishful ones. Its criminal laws in particular would reach modern Europe only in a highly warped form. There was one aspect of its criminal justice system, however, that was destined to have a lasting

and widespread impact, in the field of criminal law as much as any
other. The Romans, consummate intriguers that they were, had become
fascinated by the Greek art of persuasion, and in the first century BC a
defence lawyer called Marcus Tullius Cicero restated the rules of
rhetoric in a form that has survived to the modern day.

Some of Cicero's theories were very specific to his time and place. He
advised, for example, that anger was best expressed with high-pitched
staccato phrases and that speeches should always be made with the right
hand extended like a weapon. Energetic passages, he felt, ought to be both
introduced and concluded with a vigorous stamp of the feet. But he also
possessed a cynicism that was timeless. Advocacy, he claimed, was about
advancing 'points which look like the truth, even if they do not corre-
spond with it exactly', and he was said to have boasted twice of winning
acquittals by throwing dust into his judges' eyes. His own life encapsulated
the mixture of brutality, efficiency, and superstition that characterized
Roman criminal law – and never more so than when he took leave of it.
He was one of the first people to theorize that laws presupposed the right
to a trial, but he personally arranged for several summary executions in
63 BC, and he himself was assassinated twenty years later on the orders of
Mark Antony, then one of Rome's ruling triumvirate. The posthumous
treatment of the 63-year-old was eloquent comment on the judicial
system that he had come to personify. The rostra of the Roman Forum,
from which he had won so many hearts and minds, was adorned with his
severed head and hands. Mark Antony's wife is said to have taken an even
more symbolic revenge. Cicero had recently attacked her in several vitri-
olic speeches, and according to one Roman historian, she now inflicted
the most poetic injustice of all, driving a hairpin hard through the great
orator's tongue.

Rome formally adopted Christianity as its state religion during the fourth
century AD. The Holy Roman Empire would loom large in Europe's
history over the next millennium, inspiring countless wars between popes
and princes who sought to cloak themselves in its pseudo-legitimacy, but
Roman culture itself would collapse long before the nations of medieval
Europe began to emerge. In the middle of the fifth century, waves of
invaders thundered out of central Asia and set off a chain reaction of hos-
tilities that soon robbed the Empire of its heart, as barbarian incursions

caused the imperial capital to relocate to Constantinople. In the late 520s, Emperor Justinian had his lawyers produce the *Digest*, a codification of virtually every Roman edict and legal theory ever penned, but his honouring of one tradition was accompanied by the evisceration of another. He simultaneously closed Europe's last institutional link with ancient Greek philosophy, the Athenian Academy that Plato had established to perpetuate the teachings of Socrates some nine centuries before. A curtain was falling on the ancient world.

Scientists have recently postulated that the impact of a comet or a volcanic eruption set off catastrophic climatic cooling during the mid 530s and, whether or not they are correct, the decade marked the beginning of four centuries of unprecedented gloom. The Black Death reached Europe for the first time, spreading like an inkblot from its southeast corner, and more marauders were soon storming in from the steppes. By the middle of the next century, an entirely new horde was sweeping out of Arabia behind the standards of Islam, conquering, converting, or killing all in its path. Europe's Vandals, Franks, Goths, and Celts were meanwhile stampeding about like beasts in a forest fire, fleeing disaster one year only to shove their neighbours towards it the next. It was the beginning of the era that the peoples of western and southern Europe would come to call the Dark Ages. As monasteries were abandoned and monks forgot how to read, Christendom dropped the baton of learning that had been passing around the Mediterranean for a millennium. By the time it recovered its wits five centuries later – thanks in large part to translated texts and fresh commentaries preserved by Arab and Persian scholars – Greece would be barely a memory, and Rome's traditions would have been bastardized almost beyond recognition.

Two peoples would clamber towards the top of the heap. The first were the Germans, a cluster of tribes originating somewhere in Asia, who ousted the Celts from a vast chunk of central Europe. While some established the settlements that would eventually coalesce into Germany, others, known as the Franks, settled west of the Rhine in the region known as Gaul. The second group – the Scandinavians – would arguably have an even greater reach. A contingent of Danes invaded Britain during the mid fifth century, accompanied by two north German tribes known as the Angles and the Saxons, and a later wave of emigrants travelled considerably further during the 700s. In search of a little living room, the

Norsemen got as far as America and North Africa, established permanent colonies in Greenland, Iceland, and Russia, and caused so much havoc among their erstwhile cousins in England that the country had to be partitioned in the late 800s. (They would only stop sticking their oars into the island's politics in 1016, when Denmark's King Canute brought the interference to a neat conclusion by taking over entirely.) Viking raids in Gaul led to a compromise no less significant when, in 911, King Charles the Simple persuaded a red-headed raider called Rollo to swear allegiance in return for control over a large region near Rouen. Rollo reportedly displayed little fealty to the Frankish monarch, delegating the job of kissing Charles' foot to a flunky who upended the royal leg. His hairy warriors would, however, become some of the truest sons of feudalism – for as they swapped their longboats for horses, Gaul became France and the Norsemen became the Normans.

The barbarians, whose customs incorporated ingredients from as far afield as Mongolia and India, transformed Europe's notions of justice just as dramatically as they affected every other aspect of continental culture. Although the Romans' concepts of contractual and property law lived on, their pragmatic techniques of dealing with crime expired or mutated beyond recognition as semi-rational inquiries gave way to rituals that relied squarely on the gods. For whereas the deities of Rome and Greece had never interfered directly in the processes of criminal justice, few areas of human endeavour seemed to fascinate those of the barbarians more. Celtic Druids caged troublemakers in mammoth wicker effigies that were periodically set ablaze to propitiate their gods. German priests enjoyed a similar monopoly over judgment and dispensed punishments that were regarded as offerings to the god of war. Scandinavian religion produced one of the most bloodthirsty ceremonies of all. In honour of Odin, criminals were strangled from long wooden beams and stabbed repeatedly while they died. Odin's time was running out, but the ritual that honoured him was destined to last – for the Norse *gálgatré* would come to be known as the gallows tree.

The appeal of vengeance was even stronger among the barbarians than it had been for the Athenians. Few activities were quite as satisfying to German and Scandinavian warriors as the thrill of hunting down and annihilating a kinsman's killer and they did not even theoretically leave the job to the gods. Whereas the Furies of Greece had stood ready to wreak vengeance if a kinsman failed to do so, the closest barbarian equivalent were the German Valkyries, and they were responsible only for hovering over battlefields and transporting fallen warriors to Valhalla. The shame of cowardice and the spur of a fame to outlast death were enough for the barbarians.

The eagerness and moral imperative for revenge finds expression in all the great literature of the era. The epic poem of *Beowulf*, written in the tenth century and composed up to three hundred years earlier, was concerned throughout with justice, and it was owed as much to the dead as to the living. On occasion, the dead even had the prior claim. When King Hrethel's eldest son was accidentally killed by a younger one, the monarch was plunged into despair – not only because his firstborn had died, but also because kinship rules forbade him from killing the survivor.

No less vivid is the Norse myth of Balder the Beautiful. Balder, the god of light, was so beloved that when he dreamed of death, his mother Freya was able to persuade almost every single object on earth not to hurt him. She failed to ask only the mistletoe, a plant so young and feeble that it seemed entirely harmless. The omission would, needless to say, have consequences. As news spread around Asgard that Balder was invulnerable, his fellow gods began playfully to pelt him with battleaxes, clubs, and spears. Only two stood on the sidelines: Loki, god of mischief, and Hodur, the blind, dim twin of brilliant Balder. Loki, unremitting prankster that he was, had made it his business to learn mistletoe's secret, and he asked Hodur why he was not joining in the fun. Hodur explained sadly that he had no missiles, and wouldn't know where to throw them even if he did. Loki offered to assist. He happened in fact to have a bow and a mistletoe dart. And thus it was that while Balder was joyfully bouncing off hardware from every other direction, Loki guided Hodur's aim and a whirring arrow skewered like a stiletto through Balder's beautiful forehead. The god teetered and toppled, and had barely hit the ground before a fellow deity called Wali had sworn neither to comb his hair nor wash his hands until he had sent the guilty party to the underworld. But it was not Loki whom he had in mind. His first concern was with the killer himself – and it was hapless Hodur who was hunted down and despatched to the shadowlands of Hel.

Christianity made steady headway through the new peoples, but the potency of such traditions was such that it was converted almost as much as the pagans were. The idea that the morality of a deed depended on the doer's state of mind, though seen throughout the Bible and common among the Athenians and Romans, steadily gave way to a sense that acts were good or evil, regardless of intention. Christianized rulers often enacted laws based on the Bible but, keenly aware of the fragility of authority, generally did very little to enforce them.

Laws were not, however, abandoned. Although rulers could not make their subjects be good, they began to establish some control over their feuds and squabbles by fixing guidelines for compensation, and asserting that complainants could resort to violence only as a last resort. The tariffs varied depending on the seriousness of the offence. The laws of the Salian Franks, written down towards the end of the fifth century AD, required three shillings from those who defamed someone by calling them a fox or a hare. Abducting a virgin in Kent a century later entitled her owner to fifty shillings. Among the Frisians of the late eighth century, the value of a life ranged from cost price, for a slave, to eighty shillings for a nobleman.

Such codes hardly made for the rule of law, but each reflected the development that Aeschylus had once idealized in the *Oresteia*: the attempt to formulate collective justice as an honourable substitute for private revenge. The same process seems to occur whenever a community becomes sufficiently self-aware to recognize that it has disputes to resolve. Cultures around the world have used countless different methods to contain the violence. Among the Inuit of Greenland, disputants once abused each other in song and proved the superiority of their claims through feats of great athleticism. The Tiv of Nigeria chanted insults at their opponents, and tied them to trees. Massa clans in Cameroon–Chad used to thrash out their differences by fighting huge battles with very small twigs. And the proto-litigants of medieval Europe relied on a very particular technique of their own – the oath.

The oath has probably been guaranteeing truth for as long as humanity has been able to envisage a power more vengeful than itself, and the promise to god has always been a terrible one. Accuser and accused in an Athenian murder trial would swear on their children's heads while standing atop the entrails of a boar, a ram, and a bull. One method of renewing the Covenant among the ancient Hebrews involved walking between the two halves of a bisected calf. Medieval Christendom used tokens of mortality no less fearsome, typically the body parts of saints, and oaths formed the basis for its earliest trials – ceremonies known as compurgation, at which defendants proved their innocence by gathering together people willing to swear to their cause.

The ritual was enshrined in writing in the very first barbarian law codes, and by the seventh and eighth centuries it was being practised across Europe. Under open skies, each member of the team – known collectively as compurgators, conjurors, or jurors – would swear upon a shard of holy shinbone, say, that the defendant had not committed the alleged crime. The number of witnesses required depended on factors that ranged from the status of the suspect to the nature of the offence. Queen Uta of Germany, accused of adultery in 899, was acquitted only after eighty-two knights stepped forward to confirm her chastity. It would have taken six hundred people to acquit an accused poisoner in Dark Age Wales. On the other hand, those lucky enough to be deaf, dumb, aristocratic or pregnant were often accorded special privileges, and anyone accused of crime in seventh- and eighth-century Spain was down-right lucky. Suspects who swore to the baselessness of charges laid against them were not only absolved of guilt, but also awarded compensation at the expense of their accusers.

Such proceedings, though reliant on witnesses, were not inquiries. The oath, far from ensuring the reliability of evidence, was the evidence; and jurors swore to their support of a defendant rather than to what they knew of a case. One consequence was that they were liable in some places to punishment for perjury if they got it wrong. Another was that any formal defect in the ceremony allowed people to lie with impunity. Swearing falsely on a saint's relics was ordinarily a one-way ticket to hell, but if the reliquary was empty – because, for example, the testifier had secretly removed its contents – a person could swear that black was white with no ill effects at all. Similarly, it was a grievous sin to speak falsely to a priest while holding a consecrated cross, but fine to clutch the crucifix and lie blind if the only people present were non-clerical. In medieval Europe, breaking a promise was of little consequence. The fault lay in doing so after God had been asked to watch.

At the end of the first millennium AD, attitudes towards criminal justice in Europe therefore stood at a cusp. Religious and secular authorities were trying to encourage individuals to give courts a chance before taking matters into their own hands, but the belief in vengeance remained alive and well. The passions of the feud were being accommodated rather than ignored, and they were always liable to spill over beyond the institutions designed to contain them. No tale better captures the frailty – and peculiarity – of the attempts to tame gang warfare with the oath than the Icelandic *Saga of Burnt Njal*.

The story was written almost three centuries after the island's conversion to Christianity in AD 1000, but it depicts a land rumbling to rhythms far older: a volcanic place of trolls and sprites, where the earth would more likely shrug its shoulders than a man would turn the other cheek. Feuds erupt and cool throughout the fifty years spanned by the work, but the narrative hinges at a point when men loyal to a chieftain called Flosi burn the eponymous Njal to death in his farmhouse. Njal and his wife steadfastly await the flames from the discomfort of their bed and his immediate family chooses to perish alongside him, but one relative determines to escape. Nephew Kari Solmundarson clambers to the rafters and, treading timbers that are sweating smoke, reaches the edge of the building. Seconds after he leaps from the roof, his hair and clothes ablaze, it crashes to the ground. After dousing his sorrows in a nearby stream, he embarks on the mission that will make his name a byword for good fortune throughout Iceland. In agony though he is, disfigured though he is, and bereaved though he is, Kari is also very, very lucky. He has survived to seek revenge.

Outrage mounts as he moves from kinsman to kinsman with news of Flosi's crime. Thorhall Asgrimsson, a foster son to Njal, is so apoplectic that blood spurts from his ears and he collapses to the ground – a moment of weakness for which he expresses great shame – but he will prove a stalwart ally. For Thorhall Asgrimsson possesses a quality that is hardly less magical than good luck: knowledge of the law. And Njal's friends and kinsmen agree that it is time to exact an awful revenge. They will take the killers to court.

On being given notice of suit, Flosi ponders whether to settle the case, but is persuaded by a fellow arsonist that, having shown such defiance, it would not be proper to back down. He decides instead to engage a lawyer. After ruling out one candidate, a warrior's kinsman, on the basis that whoever takes the job is likely to die, Flosi approaches Eyjolf Bolverksson, one of Iceland's most formidable pleaders. Eyjolf, resplendent in scarlet cloak, gold headband, and silver axe, initially refuses to have anything to do with the case. He is no cats-paw, he declares, ready to meddle in a dispute that has nothing to do with him. Flosi, confronted with a lawyer who speaks of integrity, knows just what to do. He dangles a chunky gold chain from his arm, and Eyjolf rapidly reconsiders. 'It is only proper for me to accept this bracelet in the face of such courtesy,' he purrs. 'And you can fairly expect that I shall take over the defence and do everything that may be required.' It was a bad move. Icelanders, like virtually every people before and since, had contempt for anyone so dishonourable as to require money to plead for someone's rights. Eyjolf's fictional fate was sealed.

The trial takes place on one of Iceland's endless summer days at the Law Rock, a lava cliff overlooking a large valley and a silver river snaking far below. From across the island, jurors, chieftains, and onlookers converge around the booths that contain the legal teams. All the lawyers are, as is traditional, armed to the teeth and in full battle regalia. On the Rock itself stands Skapti Thoroddson, the omniscient Law Speaker, who bears the awesome responsibility of memorizing the law and publicly reciting a third of its provisions every year. Kari's nine jurors are sat on the riverbank, their job not to assess evidence but to swear that procedural steps have been performed correctly. A hush descends, and lawyer Mord Valgardsson steps up to the Rock. In words that echo around the valley, he swears that he will plead according to truth, fairness and law. He calls witnesses to testify that he has been duly appointed and has given the defendants notice of the action. He declares that he had brought nine sworn men to the Law Rock. And do the defendants, he demands, have any objections?

All those watching agree that the performance is a confident one – but Eyjolf Bolverksson, sporting his scarlet cloak and silver axe, then delivers a response that threatens to cripple Mord. Two of the jurors, he contends, should be disqualified because they are related to him. The lawyer, previously so eloquent, is reduced to silence. Consternation spreads across the Rock. The prosecution has barely begun, but seems already to be in ruins.

Only one man can save the day. Thorhall Asgrimsson, bedridden by a monstrous leg inflammation, has been left at home – so upset not to be present that he had waved off his kinsmen with a face as red as beetroot and tears tumbling like hailstones – but his moment of glory has come.

Messengers run to the great jurist's cot with news of the crisis and Thorhall, amused at Bolverksson's audacity, explains what to do. The advice is relayed to Mord, who swiftly resumes his place. The fact that two of the jurors are his kinsmen does not disqualify them, he retorts. Only kinship with the accuser himself would have that effect. It is, by general consensus, a brilliant rejoinder. Thorhall Asgrimsson, from his sickbed, has saved the day.

A chastened Eyjolf admits that he had not anticipated so unerring a counterstroke, but promptly pulls another arrow from his quiver. Two of the jurors, he declares, are ineligible to swear because they do not own a house. As the jurors rise uncertainly, another wave of anticipation ripples through the spectators. The challenge sounds even more excellent than the first – but the messengers who relay it to Thorhall soon return with more advice. Mord strides to the riverbank, his confidence returning like the tide, and invites both men to resume their seats. The objection is nonsense, he booms. A juror need not own a house. It is enough if he possesses a milk cow. Amidst tumultuous excitement, the point is once again referred for adjudication to Skapti Thoroddson. The crowds wait in an atmosphere so tense it could be split with a battleaxe, until the Law Speaker emerges from his booth to announce his ruling. The prosecution is right. It is enough to own a milk cow.

Eyjolf finally lets fly with a plea that many think the most powerful of all. Four of the jurors must stand down, he contends, because there are other men who live closer to the scene of the crime. The point is, Thorhall accepts, a superb one. But not so superb as to be unanswerable. Told what to say, Mord steps forward once again. The four jurors are indeed disqualified, he concedes – but a majority verdict will suffice, and five of the original nine jurors remain. For long minutes, the Law Speaker silently ponders the claim. And then he rules. The point is good – so good, indeed, that he is astonished. Until that moment, he had believed that he was the only man alive who knew it to be the law.

The time has come for Eyjolf Bolverksson to advance Flosi's defence. The case has, he briskly declares, been brought before the wrong division of the Law Rock. He is right, but a new action is swiftly lodged in the correct court and, as the pace of the case accelerates, the arguments become personal. Kari's side has learned about the bracelet that Eyjolf accepted to argue the case, and they now accuse Flosi of bribery and Eyjolf with procedural incorrectness – each a grave offence punishable with outlawry and confiscation. But just as it seems that Kari's team has landed a knockout blow, Mord Valgardsson makes a fatal blunder. Rather than await Thorhall's advice, he impatiently demands that six judges in the new court stand down and that the others award him a verdict. For ineffably complex reasons of Icelandic jurisprudence, he should have asked for twelve judges to be removed instead. The mistake is a serious one. Instead of outlawing Njal's killers, he has paved the way for his kinsmen to be exiled instead.

A messenger takes the news to Thorhall who, saying not a word, heaves his lame leg from his bed, grasps his spear with both hands, and gouges the abscess from his thigh. Oblivious to a stream of blood and pus that pours from the wound, he strides to the Law Rock. The first man he encounters is Grim the Red, a member of Flosi's legal team. Thorhall, great jurist though he is, has tired of pleadings and with a single thrust of his spear, he splits Grim's shoulder blades into two. Several of Thorhall's kinsmen are stricken with shame. That a sick man should be so brave as to murder his enemies while they stand aside disgraces them all.

The next several pages of the saga describe, with great delight, the mayhem that now ensues. Across the Law Rock weapons fly, bones crack, body parts are pierced, and at least one bystander is hurled headlong into his boiling cauldron. When the Law Speaker suggests to Snorri the Priest that they negotiate a cease-fire, he is speared through both calves and Snorri throws his monks into the fray. Lucky Kari himself, zipping through the mêlée like a wasp among bees, parries, pirouettes and slays with sublime assurance, even managing at one point to catch a spear in mid-flight and return it quivering into the body of its owner. The casualties mount until Flosi's dishonourable lawyer is spotted by one of Kari's companions. 'There is Eyjolf Bolverksson,' he roars. 'Reward him for that bracelet.' Snatching a spear from a friend, Kari does just that – and the blade that hurtles clean through the renowned pleader's waist finally resolves the crisis. Each side withdraws in order to treat its injured and bury its dead, and those men still standing return to the Law Rock the following morning. 'There have been harsh happenings here, in loss of life and lawsuits,' observes one of Flosi's team. The time has finally come to bury the hatchet, before matters get out of hand.

The trial is not typical of its era, in that defendants rather than prosecutors were usually the ones required to produce co-swearers, but the *Saga of Burnt Njal* is based on actual events and accurately depicts the hazards of litigation in late medieval Europe. Formalities were an entrenched aspect of legal procedure everywhere – so much so that a word out of place could cost the speaker a fine, the case or his life, until well into the fourteenth century. Across northern Europe it remained customary to attend one's case fully armed until at least the late tenth century, each side ideally signalling compromise by clashing together weapons and shields (a ritual known as the weapon-touch or *wapentake*), and Icelandic trials remained fraught with danger for considerably longer. Violence escalated well into the 1200s, with clubs giving way to small arsenals, until the country's bishops were finally able to persuade enough litigants to leave their weapons at home for peace to take hold.

Compurgation, rough and ready though it was, was never entirely senseless. It could show a divided community where the balance of power lay. At a time when it was common knowledge that perjurers were liable to be frozen rigid, flipped backwards or reduced to dwarfish proportions,* it also encouraged honesty – even if confusion over whether witnesses were swearing to knowledge or belief meant that honesty was never a reliable guide to accuracy. But even in the depths of the Dark Ages, there were sufficient objections to the system that another form of trial process became pre-eminent. As might be expected of an irrational age, the alternative tapped even more deeply into the supernatural. Once a sufficiently large number of people had sworn to someone's guilt, he or she might be subjected to an ordeal, typically using fire or water, at which God was invited to rescue the innocent by way of a miracle. If He did so, the person making the accusation would be punished. If He declined the opportunity, it was the accused who stood condemned – to banishment or death.

---

* Lying fingers were also liable, at least in a later era, to sprout posthumously from the grave: for one such instance, dating from 1624, see Heinrich Roch, *Neue Laußnitz, Böhm und Schlesische Chronica* (Torgau, 1687), p. 267.

The procedures, unknown in the Bible,* probably rested on traditions of elemental worship that the Germans picked up directly or indirectly from India, but the Catholic Church took to them with gusto. As early as the sixth century, a distinguished bishop called Gregory of Tours was informing Christendom that trial by boiling water could be used to disclose God's will. He told how a Catholic deacon and a heretical priest had agreed to settle their doctrinal differences by plucking a ring from a boiling cauldron, and how, moments before the test was due to begin, the Catholic was found to have smeared a magic balm onto his arm. As the honour of the True Church had teetered in the balance, a stranger from Ravenna had stepped from the crowd and plunged his own arm into the seething waters. The newcomer, whose name was Hyacinth, took his time – reportedly telling bystanders as he groped around that the water was a little chilly towards the bottom and pleasantly warm at the top – but within an hour he had the ring safely in his grasp. His rival then tried his luck, but had the flesh boiled off the bones up to his elbow. 'And so', Gregory gravely noted, 'the dispute ended.'

By the ninth century, a similar ceremony was being used to resolve serious accusations in churches across Europe. While a fire burned in the vestibule, mass would be celebrated and the priest, clutching a Bible, would lead a line of cross-bearing and censer-swinging clerics towards the kettle. To the sound of psalms and the scent of myrrh, the water would then be blessed in the name of the Trinity, Resurrection, and Armageddon and God would be implored to illuminate that which had been secret. Onlookers would meanwhile pray for the accused's vindication or destruction according to taste, and he or she would then try to remove a stone from the bubbling waters. The resulting wound would be bandaged and three days later, the priest would remove the dressing and interpret the blister. If he declared it healed, all well and good. But if he pronounced it festering, guilt would be established, and exile or execution would be added to the woes of the accused.

---

* The only parallel is a test for female adulterers proposed by the Book of Numbers (5: 12–31) that a suspect should be made to drink dirty water and then condemned if 'her belly shall swell, and her thigh shall rot'. Far from being irrational, it sounds like a pragmatically merciless instruction that the woman be punished only if her transgression turns out to leave permanent souvenirs in the form of pregnancy and/or infection.

The ordeal of fire switched elements but otherwise followed much the same pattern, requiring defendants to test their flesh against flame and then spend three days praying for a miracle, a merciful priest, or a combination of the two. Glowing iron bars were usually used, but during the eleventh century the mother of Edward the Confessor, Emma of Normandy, was reportedly made to walk barefoot over nine red-hot ploughshares in order to meet charges of an adulterous relationship with the Bishop of Winchester. (If Church chroniclers are to believed, which of course they are not, she was so manifestly innocent that she had already strolled obliviously across the sizzling blades by the time she asked to begin.) A crusading peasant called Peter Bartholomew underwent an even more spectacular form of trial by fire in 1098. While wandering through the rubble of a ruined church in Syria, he identified an iron pole as the lance with which Jesus had been pierced on the cross. Although similar assertions would put countless others on the fast track to canonization, a faction of fellow soldiers alleged, for reasons unknown, that he was lying. If not, they contended, he would make good his claim by passing through two lines of blazing olive branches. He apparently jumped at the chance to prove his piety, pole in hand, but the story then becomes a little murky. According to Raymond of Agiles, a fierce supporter of Peter's bona fides, he ambled between walls of flame that were a foot apart and forty feet high, pausing briefly only to converse with the Lord inside the inferno, before emerging unscathed – at which point a mob of admirers excitedly broke his spine. A second account was considerably more sceptical. A third condemned Peter as an out-and-out fraud. Charity, if nothing else, makes it more pleasant to accept Raymond's recollection, but since even he noted that Peter died twelve days later ('on the hour set by God'), it probably makes little difference either way.

Several other techniques were used to attract God's attention. The ordeal of cold water involved immersing bound suspects in exorcized streams or wells, where priests would prod them with poles to see if they sank or swam. On the strength of a theory that water was so pure that it repelled sin, anyone who floated was convicted; those who sank convincingly enough were vindicated and, with luck, resuscitated. Another type of ordeal, said to be especially popular among the Anglo-Saxons, was the trial by morsel, which required suspects to swear to their innocence and then swallow a piece of blessed bread and cheese without

Ordeal of cold water (12th century). The defendant is tied up to avoid any attempt to pervert justice. The inscription recognises God's omnipresence and requests, abjectly, that He furnish urgent assistance.

choking to death. It sounds like a procedure that would require a miracle to convict rather than to acquit, but no records survive to confirm or question its effectiveness. One incident from the eleventh century suggests, however, that there were at least some medievalists who regarded it as reliable. The tale concerns the Earl Godwin of Wessex, an eleventh-century maker and breaker of monarchs, who is said to have got up to no good in 1036 while playing host to one Prince Alfred, a young pretender to England's hotly contested throne. Chroniclers record that Godwin began the evening pleasantly enough, entertaining Alfred at his castle and promising to support his claims, but ended it considerably less cordially by handing him over to his mortal rival, Harold Harefoot, whose henchmen extracted his eyeballs and let him bleed to death. Godwin soon gathered together the requisite number of cronies to swear to his innocence, but Edward the Confessor harboured a lurking doubt and took the opportunity at an Easter banquet seventeen years later to repeat the accusation of murder. Godwin seized a chunk of bread and raised it to the heavens. 'May God cause this morsel to choke me,' he bellowed, 'if I am guilty in thought or deed.' The chroniclers – none of whom, admittedly, had much time for Godwin – record that he chewed, trembled, and dropped dead.

The notion of God as umpire attained its purest expression in trial by combat. The ritual required plaintiff and defendant to prove that He would take their side in a fight, and after weapons were blessed – to neutralize blade-blunting spells and the like – victory would go to whoever reduced the other to submission or death. There were subtle variations. Women, priests, and cripples generally had to hire professional fighters. German jurisdictions often found other ways to level the odds: a man might be buried waist-deep and armed with a mace, for example, and his female opponent allowed to roam free but given only a rock in a sack. The residents of East Friesland allowed accused murderers to shift the charge onto a third party and prove their innocence by defeating him rather than their accuser. The choices were greatest of all for a defendant in twelfth-century England and France. He could turn the accusation onto innocent bystanders, challenge his own witnesses or, for a few gloriously violent years, appeal a verdict by battling those who had delivered it.

Compurgation and trial by ordeal had little to commend them by modern standards. Although the more blood-curdling ceremonies presumably terrified some guilty people into confessing, only the laws of probability offered any guarantee of occasional efficiency. In an age committed to the notion that a just God was perpetually tinkering with His handiwork, it

German woman with rock in sack litigates against a buried man with a mace. This image is from 1467, but the ritual was far older.

must however have always been considerably easier to assume the rituals' effectiveness than to imagine why they might *not* work. Scepticism was clearly abroad as early as 809, when Charlemagne felt it necessary to bolster ordeals with a law commanding his subjects to believe in them; but even the doubts were generally irrational. Pope Eugene II expressed concerns about perjury during the 820s but he was more worried for the souls of witnesses than the reliability of their evidence – and resolved his misgivings by ordering that defendants undergo the ordeal of cold water instead. Fifty years later, Pope Nicholas I banned trial by combat but he too was no more than suspicious of its value: he replaced it with the ordeal of boiling water, and noted that David's defeat of Goliath proved that judicial duels might sometimes work.

The mood began to change with the turn of the millennium. As the solstice of AD 1000 came and went with no sign of Armageddon, widespread relief was followed by a sense of rebirth across southern and western Europe. Within less than three years, according to the eleventh-century chronicle of the monk Rudolfus Glaber, men everywhere 'began to reconstruct churches . . . It was as if the whole world were shaking itself free, shrugging off the burden of the past, and cladding itself everywhere in a white mantle of churches.' The physical renewal was complemented by an intellectual revival no less palpable. For the wind that had once moved men like Aeschylus and Protagoras, the belief in reason that had been so long stagnant in Europe, started once again to blow.

Muslim scholars in Cordoba and Persia contributed considerably to the new atmosphere, thanks to their possession of Greek texts that had been lost to Latin Europe for centuries, but so too did the rediscovery in around 1170 of a document that was quintessentially European. And the latter work would ensure that lawyers were at the vanguard of the intel-lectual revival. For a brightly coloured envelope emerged in Pisa – found, according to legend by a soldier as he pottered through the ruins of Amalfi – and it contained the core of the vast legal code that the Emperor Justinian had enacted during the dying days of the Western Empire.

The rediscovery of the *Digest* coincided with a major clash between the papacy and Germany's imperial throne, and at a time when no source of authority was quite as compelling as tradition, its impact was immense. Clerics were soon flocking to Italy to trawl its text, and as they did so the first great law school to appear in Europe since the days of the Empire coalesced in Bologna. Students were soon producing inventive, ingenious, and mutually contradictory theses aplenty, but when Justinian's laws were matched against contemporary practice, one fact was stark. They contained not a jot of support for trials by ordeal and oath. The work of canonical scholars, who were simultaneously organizing centuries of papal edicts and saintly pronouncements into systematic compilations for the first time, only made it clearer that the same was true of Scripture. A problem was becoming apparent.

The first generations of scholars hesitated to follow their concerns through, but by the late twelfth century opponents of ordeals were increasingly making themselves heard. One of the most outspoken was Peter the Chanter, a prominent theologian based at the Parisian cathedral of Notre Dame. If trial by battle was so infallible, he wondered, why did people who hired champions invariably prefer seasoned warriors to wizened old men? When three defendants were charged with the same offence, and therefore required to carry the same red-hot iron in turn, was it really divine intervention that made the last in line least likely to show a burn? And what did it mean to say that God was watching over every ordeal if – as Peter knew had occurred – people were sometimes hanged for crimes that had not even taken place? Peter's conclusion, reiterated to room after room of spellbound monks, was as simple as it was revolutionary. The system tempted the Lord to work miracles more than it tested humanity for its sins, and the clergy should have nothing to do with it.

Complementing such principled criticisms were eminently practical ones. Even at its fairest, the system was as likely to free the guilty as to convict the innocent; and in the hands of priests with an axe to grind, it could be even more arbitrary. So great a discretion in the hands of clerics meant that secular rulers were often suspicious of the system but during the twelfth century the problem became acute. For ordeals finally began to operate against the interests of Catholicism itself.

The late medieval Church was corrupt as old cheese, filled with drunks and fornicators who expected congregations to subsidize their sins, and countless reformers had begun to emerge by the twelfth century. From the Church's point of view their prescriptions could only worsen the rot. Henry of Le Mans roused rabbles across eastern France for three decades after 1116, with fervent sermons that condemned rituals ranging from baptism to prayers for the dead – and, implicitly, rejected the need for a clergy at all. Peter of Bruis simultaneously led riotous mobs through the south of the country, urging his followers to munch meat on Fridays and make bonfires of their crucifixes, until outraged opponents burned him alive in one of his blasphemous blazes during the early 1130s. Most ominous of all was a philosophical tradition known as dualism. It had been incubating among Christian communities in the Balkans for several centuries and now began to spread through western Europe via the ports of southern France – and it took issue with the Church on the nature of evil itself.

The dualists called themselves Cathars, after the Greek word for purity, and their challenge to Catholicism was profound. Whereas Catholic scholars would be content to spend lifetimes trying to work out why a benevolent and omnipotent God seemed so tolerant of unpleasantness on earth, the heretics plumped for a very simple explanation: that He had no choice. The world in its entirety, they believed, lay firmly under the control of Satan and life amounted to an unhappy moment of incarceration within a tomb of flesh. The soul's salvation demanded abstention from sex, meat, and dairy products, ideally in person but alternatively through one of the Cathar's abstemious clerics. Those who grasped the truth and confessed their creed at the blissful moment of death could expect an eternity of ethereal perfection.

The Church was not impressed. It took grave exception to the suggestion that its theology was a delusion founded on a mistake. And although it had its own impressive traditions of self-mortification – running from Origen, a founding father who had castrated himself for love of the Lord, through innumerable pillar-squatting and thorn-bush-dwelling hermits – it had by the twelfth century become extremely reconciled to earthly things. Church propagandists were soon recycling hoary myths of cannibalism, bestiality, and promiscuity that Roman authorities had once used against the early Christians, while Pope Lucius III ordered every bishop in 1184 to smoke out the heretics in his diocese by way of an annual dragnet. The unbelievers continued, however, inexorably to advance. By the end of the century, Catharism was running Catholicism a close second across much of northern Italy. In the Languedoc, a politically volatile region of southern France, there were large pockets where it was not so much a heresy as the orthodoxy.

The crisis came to a head with the advent of 37-year-old Lotario de
Conti to the papacy in 1198. The youngish Lotario took the name of
Innocent III and a contemporary fresco painting shows him to have a
ruddy baby-face, but he was in fact about as ruthless
and astute a politician as would ever occupy the
Holy See. Soon after his accession, he wrote that
the relationship between royal and papal authority resembled that of the sun and the moon –
and the papacy did the radiating rather than the
reflecting. He had his eyes on a prize: a world
that owed its primary allegiance not to kings but
to God, and more specifically, to His
earthly representative. In pursuit of his
vision, Innocent would blast seven
kings and two emperors with ex-
communications and interdictions
during his eighteen-year pontificate. But he was also honest
enough to recognize that the Church was as much part of the problem
as its solution. In a series of letters, he condemned his own bishops for
whoring, hunting and gambling while heresy had spawned, slumbering
like dogs too dumb to bark – and at last turned to the challenge that
others had spent decades avoiding.

The first element of the counter-attack was put in place over the winter
of 1205–6, when Innocent granted an audience to a charismatic Castilian
in his mid-thirties called Domingo de Gúzman. The Spaniard, who
dreamt as fervently as any heretic of pain and poverty, had already spent
time preaching against the Cathars and he had come to Rome hoping for
permission to convert infidels on the Mongol fringes of eastern Europe.
Innocent saw in his gleaming eye an energy that was needed closer to
home. The pontiff sent him straight back to the Languedoc. Domingo
arrived to find that monks from the wealthy Cistercian order were
in slothful charge of the Church's anti-heresy drive, and he was soon
co-ordinating a mission that would transform Catholicism as much as it
confronted its heretical opponents. Ostentatiously humble and tirelessly
willing to debate any Cathar into the ground, he inspired an increasing
number of acolytes – the Dominicans – who would become the spiritual

shock troops of Catholic resurgence. The battle for hearts and minds had begun.

At the same time, back in the Eternal City, Innocent was busily exploring the possibilities of a more conventional conflict. Secret requests to King Philip Augustus of France to launch a crusade against the Cathars came to nothing however, the French monarch pleading a prior engagement to destroy King John of England, and Innocent hesitated to sponsor unilateral military action against a nominally Christian region. But Domingo's disputations and Innocent's hesitations then came to a sudden end.

On 13 January 1208, one of Innocent's legates, awaiting a ferryboat on the banks of the Rhône, was murdered by a horse-borne killer. The rider, who ran a sword through his victim's back, instantly galloped back into the anonymity from which he had swooped, but his bull's-eye had consequences as momentous as those of any other homicide in history. A contemporary account describes the crisis council that Innocent now convened. Between the stone pillars of St Peter's, surrounded by a circle of twelve cardinals, he called down a curse upon the assassin and snuffed out a candle, before demanding in the gloom what was to be done. One of his most trusted lieutenants, Arnold of Cîteaux, stood next to a pillar with head bent and then raised his eyes towards Innocent. 'The time for talking is over,' he replied. Innocent, his chin in one hand, nodded – and then declared, for the first time in Christian history, a crusade against an enemy within the Church itself.

Greedy barons, eager to participate in a papally sanctioned rampage through the wealthy Languedoc, contributed thousands of troops to the army that set off from Lyons in June 1209. The fighting would last two decades, but the force faced its first test just a month later, at the Cathar stronghold of Béziers. The city's fate was emblematic of the mentality that had produced trial by ordeal, and constituted a suitably sanguine curtain-raiser to the four centuries of religious zealotry that were about to engulf Europe. While the soldiers prepared for a lengthy siege, setting up their catapults, tents, and latrines on the plains around the city, a group of kitchen boys mounted a quixotic assault on its walls. They somehow broke through. Within minutes, crusaders were pouring into the breach and Arnold of Cîteaux – told that it was impossible to distinguish Catholic from Cathar – was asked for his orders. 'Slay them all,' he reportedly murmured. 'God will know His own.'

The news from Béziers overjoyed Innocent – who postulated that God had deliberately held back from destroying its residents with the breath of His nostrils in order that the crusaders could earn salvation by exterminating them personally – but no Catholic of his intelligence trusted in the sword alone. The Church needed a procedure that could detect the canker before it took hold, and that was a question of law rather than war. Innocent was never likely to think highly of trials that entitled his priests to extort several shillings for boiling a kettle, and having studied law at Bologna and theology at Paris, he would probably have been aware of Peter the Chanter's theological critiques of trial by ordeal. But the most decisive argument was almost certainly a pragmatic one. A suspected heretic would escape punishment if acquitted. Innocent was too hard-nosed a pope to leave the future of his Church to the vagaries of divine intervention.

The papal interest in reform was already evident. Innocent had previously curtailed the use of compurgation in Church disciplinary cases, and in 1199, had approved a novel way of proceeding in criminal cases – *per inquisitionem*. The new technique entitled judges, in suitably clear cases, to launch inquiries of their own motion. That was, pointed out the pontiff, no more than God had done at Sodom and Gomorrah. The reform was a sign of things to come – and they came at the Fourth Lateran Council of November 1215.

The Council, which lasted three weeks, was an assembly of about four hundred bishops and over a thousand abbots, ambassadors, priors, and proxies from every country in the Catholic world. It was one of the grandest gatherings that Europe had ever seen, a fiesta of fireworks and parades so raucous that more than a few visiting pilgrims were trampled to death. But amidst all the excitement, Innocent remained firmly in control. Seventy reforms were presented to the delegates, for approval rather than debate, and they left few abuses unaddressed. As part of a crackdown on clerical misbehaviour, priests were forbidden from throwing dice, watching clowns, and wearing pointy-toed shoes. Princes were instructed to make Muslims and Jews wear unusual clothes, because too many Christians had been having sex with them and then claiming not to have noticed the difference. Every Catholic was required to make confession at least once a year, on pain of excommunication and burial in unhallowed ground. And tucked away in the package was Canon 18, which prohibited priests from blessing ordeals by water and fire. On 30 November, Innocent exposed a chunk of the True Cross for the delegates' adoration and sent them home. It would take several years for the reforms to percolate through the continent, but the deed had been done. Since ordeals could not occur without priestly participation, European criminal justice had been transformed for ever.

A thought-provoking way of appreciating the significance of 1215 is offered by Lewis Carroll's *Alice in Wonderland*. As any once well-read child will recall, the tale concludes with a trial at which the Knave of Hearts is accused of stealing the Queen's tarts on a summer's day and making good his escape. After witnesses testify that jam tarts are made of pepper and accuse the Knave of failing to sign a poem that he did not write, the proceedings culminate in a moment of high drama. The Red Queen, responding to her husband's suggestion that the jurors consider their verdict, splenetically insists that he has it backwards. 'Sentence first –,' she screams, 'verdict afterwards!' The merest infant knows  that she is in fact the one who is wrong; Alice herself is so exasperated by the illogic that she brings down the house of cards, and wakes from Wonderland to boot. But there are many times and places where the distinction between sentence and verdict has been far less clear.

Wrongdoing in non-Western cultures has often been tackled by rituals that have assumed guilt as much as they have investigated it. Among nineteenth-century Angolans, to take just one example, the fact that a woman was eaten by an alligator while her two companions survived could be regarded as a sure sign of sorcery, and a hearing might be held simply to establish which of the survivors had worked the magic. The pre-modern Western world blurred the distinction between investigation and verdict even more comprehensively. Ordeals and compurgation combined them into a single ritual that operated as much to discover if a wrong had occurred as to establish a suspect's responsibility for it. The idea of distinguishing the two issues was so alien to Dark Age thinking that lawyers had not even possessed a term to describe the process of weighing up evidence: the only one in use was *probatio*, or proof. But in the mid 1200s the word *triatio* entered the legal vocabulary of Christian Europe for the first time. Whereas the Dark Ages had tackled mischief with magic, through pleadings that clashed like mighty spells and rites that unlocked the secret will of God, the Western world had recovered the option of holding an inquiry.

The new faith in human scrutiny would also encourage tremendously significant developments in the field of moral philosophy, and few thinkers were more seminal than a pensive fellow called Anselm, some-time Archbishop of Canterbury. In the 1090s, he set to wondering why God had thought it important to manifest Himself in human form. As his inquiries proceeded, he found himself puzzled how it was that humanity could be absolved for murdering Jesus – for although crucifying the Messiah seemed a conclusively evil thing to do, Jesus himself had asked that his killers be forgiven. Anselm, committed like any good eleventh-century scholar to the principle that there was a reason for everything, pondered the text until he realized that the answer was staring him in the face. Christ himself had argued from the cross that his killers deserved mercy 'for they know not what they do'. Although the plea is a reminder that God the Father had regularly exhibited a more draconian stance, the insight set great chains of reasoning rattling through Anselm's mind. 'Had they known it, they would never have crucified the Lord', he mused, before explaining that, '[A] sin knowingly committed and a sin done ignorantly are so different that an evil . . . may be pardonable when done in ignorance.'

The belief that people deserved condemnation only if they understood what they were doing was not new. Adam and Eve had established the moral relevance of knowledge, and peoples from the Babylonians onwards had taken the view that intentional wrongs were at least some-times more enormous than accidental ones. Coming at the end of the Dark Ages, Anselm's distinction between sins deliberate and ignorant was, however, a radical reassertion of the importance of choice. Thinkers around the continent would soon follow his lead, and the consequences would be far-reaching. Theologians would build on it to develop a concept known as the canonical theory of culpability, which held that guilt depended on a sinner's state of mind. Lawyers would then argue on the same basis that justice demanded not just an inquiry, but one that could establish what a person thought.

All the changes, like Innocent III's abandonment of fire and water ordeals, were the product of a tide rather than a tsunami, and their impact on Europe's judicial systems would be correspondingly gradual. Compurgation would linger for several hundred more years as a way of resolving some civil disputes. The belief that God watched over criminal justice would see suspected witches swum in water four centuries after 1215, while trial by battle remained a legal option in England until 1819. The ordeal of the bier, whereby accused murderers touched their supposed victims and faced condemnation if the corpse bled anew, was arguably most tenacious of all. It was last seen in 1869, when two hundred people were paraded past two bodies in Lebanon, Illinois, in the hope that the cadavers – or, perhaps, the killer's own sense of guilt – would identify the murderer.

The response to Innocent's ruling would, however, be both profound and permanent. As Chapter 3 will show, judges on the small island of Britain would simply adapt the old oath-taking rituals and make jurors out of conjurors. On the continent the revival of rationalism and Roman law would lead to root-and-branch renewal of the law. Innocent III had already approved a ruthless model for judicial reform, based on God's activities at Sodom and Gomorrah. The once imponderable power to judge right and wrong was being arrogated on behalf of lawyers, on the assumption that sufficiently rigorous intellectual inquiry would produce both truth and justice. In an age where evidence and intention were becoming increasingly important, they would formulate techniques capable of examining not only what people had done, but also what they had thought. Defendants had been tormented by conscience at least since the time of Socrates, but the idea that judges too could explore the secrets of the criminal heart represented an unprecedented extension of official power. The Inquisition was dawning.

2

The Inquisition

'My position is becoming more and more difficult.' 'You are mis-interpreting the facts of the case', said the priest. 'The verdict is not so suddenly arrived at, the proceedings only gradually merge into the verdict.' 'So that's how it is', said K., letting his head sink.

FRANZ KAFKA, *The Trial*

The disappearance of ordeals created a legal vacuum, but within two decades the papacy that had abandoned them was rushing to fill it. Justice had previously rested on a belief, common to all participants, that the performance of certain rituals would automatically unlock the judgments of God; but the powers to inquire and judge would now be placed firmly in the hands of human officials. In the name of stamping out heresy, the Church also invented ways to explore the minds of those it suspected. At a time when scholars were reasserting a link between the state of those minds and sinfulness, wrongdoers would be made to internalize the reasons for their condemnation and to display in public their obedience to the rules. Communities had expected submission from criminals since the time of Socrates, but willing degradation would now attain a status that it had never previously possessed. The confession was born from the Church's war on heresy – but lawyers soon fetishized it as a mark of official power, and developed techniques to extract it that would outlast by centuries the threat that they were theoretically intended to meet.

The machinery of repression available to the Church in the early 1200s had been extremely lacklustre. Clerics had been too complacent to hunt down its enemies. Trial by ordeal was too irrational to locate them. And even if a bishop got round to convicting a heretic, the only punishment he could impose was excommunication and denial of Catholic burial, a fate unlikely to disturb the repose of any self-respecting apostate. Innocent III had cleared the way for reform by abolishing ordeals and establishing orders of monks who would report directly to the Holy See, but when he died in 1216 the most fundamental problem – the papacy's lack of muscle – remained unresolved.

That was about to change. In 1232, Pope Gregory IX persuaded Emperor Frederick II of Germany that as a good Catholic, he should instruct his judges to burn heretics as and when officers of the Church identified them. He simultaneously advised monks at the recently established Dominican friary at Regensburg to get identifying. Gregory's relationship with Frederick was always precarious, and it collapsed in 1237, when he denounced his erstwhile ally as 'a Beast . . . with the feet of a bear, the mouth of a raging lion, and the [limbs] of a leopard', but by then the dalliance had already borne fruit. And its offspring was the papal Inquisition.

It would be several decades before the system reached maturity, but the template was established within months of Frederick's agreement with Gregory. Conrad of Marburg, a gaunt and zealous priest who rode about on an ass, had been snooping around the Rhineland on Rome's behalf for several years, and he now began to send back some alarming reports. Although the only sectarians present in the region in significant numbers were the Waldensians, whose heresy was essentially to trudge around without shoes and preach that clerics would do well to do the same, Conrad claimed to have encountered practices far more troubling. The region was infested with people who celebrated Lucifer as the true creator, he warned. They believed, among other outlandish things, that the Eucharist should not be swallowed but spat into a latrine. Converts were initiated at meetings attended by the Devil himself, who generally assumed the form of a toad, a pale-skinned man, a goose, or an immense black cat with a very stiff tail. After kissing his anus, the heretics would extinguish the candles, fumble for each other's genitals, and embark upon an orgy that ended only with another hellish manifestation, this time of a character with loins as furry as a feline and chest more radiant than the sun.

The claim replicated rumours that had been circulating about religious deviants since Roman times, and most historians agree that the tales of Luciferan worship and sexual free-for-alls bore about as much relation to reality as the man with the furry loins. But whether it was malice or mistake that inspired Conrad to his discoveries, Gregory was appalled – and, for the first time, in a position to take action. He urged his emissary to gather some evidence, and Conrad threw himself into the task with grim enthusiasm.

Travelling from town to town in the company of two sinister sidekicks – a certain Conrad Torso and a character with one arm and one eye known only as Johannes – he was soon finding heretics wherever he looked. As the baleful trio progressed, shaving the heads of suspects who named their accomplices and incinerating those who did not, accusations ricocheted ever higher up the social scale. In 1233, Germany's bishops and nobles finally realized that if they did not stand together, they would burn separately.

The showdown occurred at Mainz in July, when Conrad of Marburg summonsed Count Henry of Sayn to answer reports that he had been seen riding a giant crab. Sideways motion was, symbolically speaking, a sure sign of heresy and the charge was a grave one; but the city's clerics and aristocrats stiffened their spines and collectively testified to Henry's piety. Conrad's witnesses, sniffing the wind, admitted that they might well have been mistaken about the crab. The inquisitor dropped his case, vowing revenge, but the game was up. As he trotted furiously back to Marburg he was murdered on his ass, and his henchmen only outlasted him by a few months. One-armed Johannes was last seen in Freiburg, oscillating from the end of a lynch mob's noose, while Conrad Torso, evidently more eager than authoritative, was sliced to ribbons in Strasbourg by the first person he summonsed.

Pope Gregory, infuriated with his clergy, raged that Conrad's assassination was a 'thunderclap that had shaken the walls of the Christian sanctuary'. The bishops had, once again, obstructed a papal attempt to get tough on heresy. But their power to do so was about to be drastically curtailed. Conrad's adventures confirmed that an alliance between agents loyal to the pope and secular judges could potentially work wonders, and although Gregory's relationship with Germany's Emperor remained fraught, France was nurturing a monarch with whom the papacy would be able to do far better business. Louis IX had been under papal protection since the death of his father in 1227. By the time he reached his majority in 1235, Conrad of Marburg would have gained a redoubtable successor.

St Louis, as he would one day become, was a gangly, smooth-featured and prematurely balding young man, but the callow physique belied a prodigious faith. He delighted in dining with beggars. Few were the lepers whose feet he did not stoop to wash. And notwithstanding the occasional impulse to abandon his throne for a monastic cell, he wielded the sword of righteousness as surely as he loved his fellow man. It was better to disembowel Jews than dispute with them, he proposed, while blasphemers in his realm were condemned to be branded on the lips or garlanded in pig entrails. It is perhaps little surprise that when Gregory suggested, in the early 1230s, that France could do with some Dominican inquisitors, Louis accepted with enthusiasm.

Louis' eagerness was motivated primarily by piety, but politics also played its part. Forces loyal to the Church had recently won a final military victory in the quarter-century crusade against the Cathars, and the destruction of the Languedoc offered unparalleled opportunities. The heretics, knights, and troubadours of the region had always been a little too lively to be loyal, but the smoking battlefields that remained looked ready for incorporation into France proper. In a deadly *pas de deux* with Gregory IX, Louis therefore despatched his own judges to join Gregory's monks in asserting royal control over southern France.

The consequences would be far-reaching. Louis would always be at least as concerned to crack down on official abuses as to impose his will. Canonical law could be no less humane, with scholars finding the basis for a whole catalogue of defendants' rights in Justinian's *Digest* and the Old Testament. But as the first papal inquisitors arrived in southern France in 1234, lighting execution pyres that were soon roaring as far north as Flanders, the structure of customary and canonical law began to buckle. The squads of young monks, faced with resistance and riots, were soon translating theoretical safeguards into practices of military efficiency. The idea that no one should be forced to incriminate himself or herself, in support of which canonists had pointed to the silence that Jesus permitted Judas, became increasingly illusory. The notion that some matters were best judged by God, exemplified by Joseph's decision not to shame Mary by way of public divorce, similarly eroded. As humility and mercy evaporated, suspects were instead arrested on the strength of anonymous denunciations, denied legal assistance, and made to state on oath what they thought might have been alleged against them. Stings and bugging operations were used, with *agents provocateurs* encouraging malcontents to share their thoughts while hidden scribes jotted down every word. The powers claimed were as much hygenic as they were punitive. Heresy was conventionally regarded as a disease, and just as the Book of Leviticus had once prescribed the destruction of buildings that harboured pestilence, the houses in which heretics had met were soon being demolished as a matter of course.

The effect was to legalize terror, and a whiff of the fear that swept the Languedoc still emanates from a story recounted about Raymond de Fauga, a Dominican appointed to the bishopric of Toulouse in August 1234. Told that the dying matriarch of a leading Cathar family was deliriously calling for a priest to console her, he rose from his lunch and marched to her house. Shocked relatives were pushed aside as he strode to her deathbed, where the feeble woman obliviously recited her beliefs and offered the traditional Cathar prayer that her life come to a good end. On de Fauga's invitation, she then confirmed her creed – whereupon he rose to his feet, declared her an impenitent heretic and sentenced her to death. She was lashed to her bed, which was carried to a meadow outside the city gates and set ablaze. The Dominican chronicler who recorded the episode – with pride – observed that de Fauga and his companions then returned to their refectory and polished off their interrupted lunch 'with rejoicing'.

By the 1240s, inquisitors had reconsolidated Catholic dominance in the cities of the Languedoc, and as their successors spread across the countryside of southern France and northern Italy, Europe's legal tradition began to undergo permanent change. In 1252, Pope Innocent IV published a bull 'On Extirpation' (*Ad Extirpanda*), which authorized the use of torture against ordinary citizens – a practice permitted under Rome's Emperor Justinian, but seen only exceptionally among barbarian tribes in the seven or so centuries subsequent. A lingering sense that the Church ought not to be in the business of bloodshed led Innocent to stipulate that inquisitors should subcontract interrogations to secular authorities, and major haemorrhages, amputations, and death were to be avoided – but the squeamishness would not last. Over the next decade, papal inquisitors were authorized to conduct their own questioning, and to absolve each other if, in their zeal, it generated too much mess. Their unaccountability increased with their discretion, and by 1262 they were almost literally a power unto themselves – capable even of reversing a bishop's sentence of excommunication if God's work so required.

Secrecy simultaneously entered the trial process for the first time. Whereas Roman law, ordeals, compurgation and canonical law had all regarded openness as essential to justice, the first legal manual for Languedoc's papal inquisitors, written in 1248, instructed them to ignore the old rule that witnesses' names be disclosed. Investigators would instead issue blanket summonses to every male over fourteen and female over twelve in a region, who presented themselves for questioning in public, but were questioned in private. As though to compensate for the change, judgment was simultaneously transformed into a magnificent ceremony, usually staged in the square of the largest regional town, at which church officials would broadcast the verdicts reached and penances imposed. Those who had attended a Cathar service might be sent on a pilgrimage, for example, or instructed to sew a large yellow cross onto a pair of overalls and wear it for the rest of their life. More serious offenders would be told to present themselves to their priest with willow switch in hand and ask for a public flogging. Particularly incorrigible hotheads and proselytizers might be sent to close confinement for a decade or two.

At the very end of the list would be those who refused to admit their errors – who were, in the scatological language favoured by the Inquisition, to be 'cut off like an infected limb' because they had 'returned to their heresy, like a dog to its vomit'. The rules that prevented clerics from spilling blood would, even in the war on heresy, have to be observed. The bishop or inquisitor would therefore 'relax' impenitents into the hands of secular courts and 'affectionately request' the court to be 'moderate' in its sentence. The double-talk was as psychotic as it sounds. Moderation involved chaining the convicts to stakes while piling logs up to their chins, burning the bodies for hours, and finally smashing the carbonized skulls and torsos with a poker. And although zealous papal inquisitors would, for long centuries, shelter behind the fiction that the Church longed to re-embrace its naughty children while someone else insisted on killing them, they were swift to ensure that no one misunderstood the meaning of relaxation. Anyone who assisted excommunicated heretics – by, for example, arguing that they were innocent – became personally liable to condemnation. According to a compilation of German laws written in the 1230s, any judge who was too moderate towards a relaxed heretic was liable to 'be judged . . . as he himself should have judged' – or, less euphemistically, to be burned to death.

In view of the Church's institutional psychopathy, it is unsurprising that popular myth, bolstered by several centuries of anti-Catholic propaganda, now recalls the Inquisition as a blood-drenched threshing machine. Uneven record keeping and Vatican secrecy mean that no reliable estimate of its death toll is actually possible, but the total number of certain executions in fact falls no higher than the low thousands. Hundreds of thousands certainly passed through its mill, but it was insidious more than murderous, designed to recover sheep rather than to annihilate them. Anyone who publicly repudiated heresy was given at least one opportunity to return to the fold. Imprisonment was the preferred penalty even for the recalcitrant. At the same time, although it killed relatively few, it released even fewer. Indeed, it barely comprehended the concept of an acquittal. To be suspected of heresy was heretical in itself, and relapse was a capital offence, with the result that arrest in itself was tantamount to a suspended death sentence. Release invariably required a display of repentance, whether the wearing of a cross, the taking of a beating, or departure on an enforced pilgrimage. Even those condemned to death were expected to show their submission. After being compelled to walk to the stake or gallows in a white shift, clutching a candle of penitence, they were offered the last rites – one final opportunity to submit to the Church in whose name they were being killed.

The Inquisition succeeded in the short term. Orthodoxy was stamped back onto the towns of the Languedoc, and rural communities slowly gave up their heretical ways. Die-hard Cathars melted away into the towns of Germany and the mountains of the Savoy, leaving behind only the crenellated ruins that still litter the region. The repression arguably generated considerably more heresy than it ever destroyed, for the refugees maintained a tradition of dissent that would eventually fuel the Protestant Reformation; but the effect of their departure was to defuse the crisis that had brought the Inquisition into being.

Its techniques would not come to an end however. A brood of baby inquisitions would now hatch from its belly as the kings and nobles of Europe realized just how useful the machinery devised by Pope Gregory IX and his successors could be. The Spanish Inquisition has entered history as its truest successor, thanks to the cruelty of its fifteenth-century anti-Jewish persecutions and its more recent activities on *Monty Python's Flying Circus*; but it was neither the first nor the most influential of the offspring. It was instead in the national courts of France and then Germany that the discomforting procedures pioneered by men like Conrad of Marburg would take deepest root.

When King Louis IX agreed with Gregory IX to import Dominican inquisitors into his realm, it was not just the battle against heresy that was transformed. At a time when ordeals had just been abandoned, his own officials needed a new way of deciding cases, and they were soon taking great leaves from the books of the Dominican inquisitors. It was not long before witnesses and defendants were forced to answer questions on oath. In 1254, two years after Pope Innocent IV had authorized the use of torture, Louis followed suit in that regard as well. Like the papal tribunals, his courts would always try to strike a happy medium between maximal pain and minimal bloodshed. Water torture, sleep deprivation and prolonged isolation were always the most popular methods. Some courts preferred to insert hot eggs under suspects' armpits. The strappado, a rope-and-pulley apparatus used to raise and drop a suspect from the roof, would become ubiquitous.

But all the cross-fertilization had a paradoxical effect. As lessons derived from the papal Inquisition fortified France's royal courts the kingdom was becoming one of the most organized states in Europe, but the same process made those courts increasingly likely to tread on papal toes. Conflicts between kings and popes were nothing new, but at a time when national loyalties were strengthening the personal rivalry was escalating into a struggle between Church and State. Thirteenth-century popes fought dirty – most spectacularly in 1268, when papal scheming resulted in the beheading of Conradin Hohenstaufen, the 15-year-old heir to the German Empire, whose death condemned Germany to five centuries of disunity – but in France the papacy would now meet its match. Its nemesis would be Louis IX's grandson, Philip the Fair.

Philip, just seventeen when he assumed the French throne in 1285, dreamed as avidly as his grandfather of eradicating the infidel. Like Louis, he too had visions of a Christian realm that would stretch from Paris to Jerusalem. But a deep temperamental difference distinguished the two men. Whereas Louis had placed both body and country at the service of the pope, Philip saw the Holy See as an obstacle to his ambitions rather than the inspiration for them. It was an attitude that always boded ill for relations between Paris and Rome, and at the end of 1294, the route to Christian harmony became extremely rocky indeed. For the king who would be pope found himself confronted by a pope who would be king – Pope Boniface VIII.

Boniface was a worldly man, as pontiffs go. His fondness for the ladies was such that he married one and fathered another; while his affection for the men was so notorious that rumours of pederasty would follow him far beyond the grave. He assumed the papacy only after encouraging his predecessor, Celestine V, to resign – whereupon he installed the 81-year-old hermit, who had not wanted the job in the first place, into an oubliette to die. He was never going to take kindly to a whippersnapper like Philip, and the tensions began rising almost immediately. The French king, whose realm constantly teetered on the brink of bankruptcy, had begun to extort money from the country's monasteries in order to finance a war with England, and in 1296 Boniface ordained that monarchs who taxed clerics and clerics who paid up were *ipso facto* excommunicated. The bull was meant as a shot across the bows and was reversed a year and a half later, but Boniface followed up by elevating Louis IX into St Louis, canonizing a French king for the first and last time in Christian history. Recognition of the grandfather was no honour to the grandson – and it was not meant to be.

Battle was about to begin – and the weapons of choice would be legal ones. Canonical law of the late thirteenth century was still Church property, its mysteries guarded by monks and arbitrated by bishops, and Boniface was regarded by many, not least himself, as the finest jurist of the age. Allegiances across Europe were switching from papacy to nation, however, and under the patronage of Philip, France's lawyers were emerging as a distinct and powerful social class. The effect was that whereas Louis had borrowed the legal tools developed by the Church, Philip deployed them – and his target was the Holy See itself.

Skirmishes began when he sent Guillaume de Nogaret, the most trusted of all his legists, to attend a jubilee that Boniface held at Rome in 1300. Nogaret, a man of humble and possibly heretical origins who had several anti-papal chips on his shoulder, would prove himself a worthy champion. According to his own account, he took Boniface aside as soon as he arrived and warned him, *sotto voce*, that his simony and extortion – along, presumably, with several more or less unmentionable vices – had to stop for the sake of the Church's good name. An outraged Boniface had challenged Nogaret to repeat his words before witnesses which, on the Frenchman's own proud recollection, he promptly did. Philip himself increased tensions in the following year. Eager to reassert French control over the Languedoc, he had one of its key bishops charged with sexual and spiritual offences – and to compound the insult, informed Boniface that he had been driven to act because the cleric had defamed the pontiff by calling him Satan incarnate. Boniface returned fire with a bull in 1302, in which he 'declare[d], announce[d] and define[d]' that any 'human creature' who refused to submit to papal authority could expect to spend all eternity in hell. Lest there remained doubt about which human creature he meant, he then let it be known that his French ambassador was instructed to excommunicate the French king.

The thunder hung potential throughout the summer of 1303. Aware that a final conflict might be looming, Philip's lawyers drew up an indictment against Boniface in June, packed with every charge that their hostile, fertile minds could generate – from diabolism and sodomy to materialism and the neglect of fasts. Boniface thereupon drafted a formal document of excommunication. If published, it would have released Catholics everywhere to perpetrate treason and war on the French monarch at their pleasure. But against the power to damn a man till the crack of doom, Philip possessed a weapon that was hardly less potent: Guillaume de Nogaret.

Boniface's bull was due to be nailed to the doors of the cathedral at Anagni, a small hill town where he maintained a sumptuous palace, on 8 September. It was early on the morning of the seventh that Nogaret arrived. He was carrying his indictment – and was accompanied by 1300 men. As bells rang and dogs barked, the invaders stormed through its narrow alleys, but it was not until dusk that the heavy oak doors of Boniface's inner chamber were finally broken down. A certain degree of confusion has come to shroud the events that immediately followed. Some say that Boniface was found atop his throne in vestment, crucifix and triple-tiered tiara, defiant and ready to die for the honour of his office. Others suggest he was trembling like a human jelly. All agree, however, that Nogaret eventually strode through the splintered door to inform him that, having failed to mend his sodomitic ways, he was required to attend at Lyons for trial.

Boniface in fact survived to be escorted by his allies back to Rome, but the shock was all too much. The man who had once asserted supremacy over the entire human race shrank into a wraith and lived for just five more weeks. He died in his sleep, crumpled like a foetus with both fists in his mouth. Pursuant to legal theories that will be considered more closely in Chapter 5, Philip thereupon campaigned to have his body put on trial and burned at the stake.

The conflict exemplified by the struggle between Philip and Boniface would recur across western Europe. As inquisitorial methods were adopted by secular rulers, those rulers seized control of the system from its creators. Christianity and canonical law would continue to influence continental legal systems until the late eighteenth century, but kings and princes would already have gained the upper hand over papal inquisitors by the fifteenth. The fact that legal procedures were secularized would not, however, make them any more humane. Just as monks and canonists had redefined the law to pursue the Church's war in the early 1200s, secular lawyers would reinvent it on behalf of their masters to justify use of the rack, the thumb-screw, and the strappado for centuries.

The question of evidence would generate some of the most inventive theories of all. In an era of trials by ordeal and compurgation there had been no need to consider how something should be proved, since the defining event – a miracle or the swearing of sufficient oaths – either took place or it did not. The rediscovery of Justinian's *Digest* in the late eleventh century had, however, shown Europe's lawyers that the Romans had differentiated between proofs and the verdict, and as witnesses entered the scene following the abolition of ordeals, the status of their testimony began to trouble the canonists. The primary problem was that, despite the rationalist aspirations of the age, no one possessed any systematic theory of how contradictory statements were to be weighed up. The *Digest*'s various recommendations – that judges pay heed to a witness' social standing and manner of speech, for example – did not take matters very far. When lawyers then turned to chapters 17 and 19 of the Book of Deuteronomy – which required allegations to be proved by two respectable eyewitnesses – a new problem arose. Since the Bible said nothing about how to differentiate truth from lies, judges interpreted the two-witness rule literally. If two people swore to a fact, it was proved – conclusively. The injustice of that was apparent to many people even in the formality-obsessed thirteenth century, and dissatisfaction increased as inquisitors tried applying the rules to heresy. Eyewitnesses to disbelief were necessarily hard to find, and the most threatening heretics were in any event those who kept themselves to themselves. Proving their thought-crimes would require a theory more imaginative than one that depended on eyewitnesses.

The answer to the riddle would be the confession. Admissions have since become so routine a feature of Western criminal justice that it is hard to appreciate just how radical a shift took place during the mid thirteenth century, but the nature of that shift is well illustrated by Louis IX's laws for southern France. Aware of the deficiencies of the two-witness rule, the king had ordered his judges never to convict on such evidence unless it was backed up by a confession. He was, however, as perturbed by wrongful acquittals as wrongful convictions – and simultaneously allowed judges to torture defendants who had aroused suspicion but refused to provide the confession that would be needed to convict them.

The law that claimed to protect against unreliable convictions consequently became their primary cause. Within decades the confession was
being promoted from a subordinate form of evidence to the *regina proba-*
tionum – 'the queen of proofs' – and self-condemnation would soon come
to be revered as an almost immaculate guarantor of guilt.

The concept of the *regina probationum* owed nothing but its Latin to
Roman law. It was also alien to the Old Testament – so much so that
Maimonides, the foremost Talmudic scholar of the medieval world,
declared conviction on the basis of a bare confession contrary to divine
law. Confessions came to be exalted not because of ancient traditions,
but because of seismic changes: a new confidence among political
rulers that they could know their subjects' secrets, and a new morality
that was beginning to measure a person's culpability according to the
words they uttered.

The tectonic movement occurred on a timescale that is better measured
in generations than moments; but if a single occurrence could be identified as pivotal, it would be the Fourth Lateran Council of 1215. In the
same set of canons that brought ordeals to an end, Pope Innocent III had
commanded that all Catholics annually confess their sins on oath to a
priest. The cleric was simultaneously empowered to forgive those who
observed the obligation, while those who failed to do so were made liable
to excommunication and unhallowed burial. It was a major change.
Church thinkers had long agreed that salvation demanded contrition
and many had even claimed for the Church a power to forgive sin. No
one, however, had ever presumed to suggest that Christians had to ver-
balize their remorse to be saved – let alone that they had to do so in the
presence of a priest.

Innocent's innovation inspired considerable resistance among ordinary Catholics, and over the next few decades concerted efforts were
made to persuade the flock that confession was in their interests. Gregory
IX formally advised all doctors to recommend it to their patients, and
chroniclers were soon extolling the new sacrament's benefits. The most
influential was a Cistercian monk called Caesarius of Heisterbach whose
Dialogue of Miracles, written in the 1220s, would inform popular
Christianity for centuries. Four of its twelve chapters were devoted to
confessions, and they suggested that that their power was prodigious
indeed. A popular legend doing the rounds told how St Norbert had

exorcized someone of a demon that insisted on revealing the adulteries of everyone around it, but Caesarius now turned the story on its head: he knew of one that had buttoned up simply because the adulterer concerned had confessed. Another fiend had positively lied to protect a girl's reputation for chastity, so impressed was it by her decision to divulge her sexual history to a priest. Caesarius told of confessions so timely that they had saved vessels from sinking and rendered murderers fireproof even as the flames of their execution pyres were lapping around them. One ancient demon of which he had heard had been so impressed by the aura of salvation emanating from the confession box that it had insisted on admitting every misdemeanour it had committed since tumbling out of heaven alongside Lucifer. Silence or equivocation, on the other hand, invariably attracted the attentions of less benign apparitions and might even inspire visits from the undead. The message was clear. Blabbing worked wonders, but verbal retention could end in disaster.

There are weighty philosophical arguments to support the belief that expressing responsibilities might lessen them. The insistence on verbalization has always risked robbing speech of its meaning however, and thirteenth-century jurists were soon treating confessions as symbols of guilt rather than methods of establishing facts. The canonical principle that defendants should not be compelled to condemn themselves was watered down to mean only that a forced confession had to be recited in court. It meanwhile became established that torture could be repeated three times. One Dominican inquisitor called Nicolas Eymeric argued in the late fourteenth century that each of the three sessions could itself be 'continued' indefinitely. By 1705, one lawyer would be basing his critique of torture on the magnificently metaphysical grounds that justice, like nature, abhorred

'On the repetition of the question, or torture': from a criminal law textbook published in the Netherlands in 1555. A scribe records the evidence as it emerges.

infinity. Those who managed, despite everything, to hold out, were treated not as innocents but as culprits who had cheated justice, and were typically sent into exile or deprived of an ear on the basis that they deserved punishment for falling under suspicion in the first place. Jean Bouteiller, a jurist of the late 1300s, expressed the prevailing attitude when he advised that a suspect should only ever be released 'conditionally' because otherwise 'it would seem that he had been held prisoner without cause'. His colleagues were evidently of a similar mind. The country's first trial records, which detail over a hundred cases from Paris between 1389 and 1392, show an overwhelming majority of defendants confessing and not a single one winning an outright acquittal.

Few trials better capture the shifting meaning of spoken guilt in early modern Europe than the 1440 prosecution of Gilles de Rais. Gilles, born in 1404 as heir to the fortune of three of the wealthiest families of France, enjoyed a youth that seemed charmed indeed for the troubled fifteenth century. At a time when his country was convulsed by a seemingly perpet-ual war and its nobility torn between those who supported the territorial claims of the English monarchy and the aspirations of the Dauphin, Charles VII, he gambled for high stakes – and won. In May 1429, fighting shoulder to shoulder alongside Joan of Arc, he helped win the victory at Orléans that turned the tide of the Hundred Years War. The triumph allowed the French pretender to be crowned at Reims Cathedral, the site of every previous coronation in French history, and his gratitude knew no bounds. Gilles was invited to carry the amphora of anointing oil – no insignificant honour, given that it had supposedly descended to earth on the wings of a heavenly dove – and Charles VII, weeping copiously, con-cluded the day by appointing him a Marshal of France. At the age of 24, Gilles had reached the top of the tree. The perennial curse of the early achiever is, of course, that all paths from the treetop go down. Even Gilles could hardly have guessed how far he would fall.

Whatever the passions that drove the young hero, they were soon taking him somewhere far from the battlefield. Gilles increasingly neglected his martial duties in favour of the priesthood, and with the war's end in 1435 he endowed a chapel at his favourite Brittany castle of Machecoul – complete with choir, portable organ, and a chapter of clerics outfitted in fur-lined silk and scarlet – and decided to reenact his most magnificent triumph as theatre in Orléans. It was a glittering train of some two hundred choristers, jugglers, pipers, fire-eaters, and astrologers that now snaked across the countryside – but a shadow was sweeping alongside. For as it moved, children vanished in its wake. Some were last seen taking the hand of rosy-cheeked crones. Others climbed onto strangers' horses, never to be seen again. And Gilles was enjoying the road show so much that he then turned it into a rolling tour.

Over the next few years, the darkness fell deepest around the gloomy towers and brackish moats of Machecoul, and never more so than in 1437, when two small skeletons were found inside the castle. Rumours were soon rife. Some claimed that Gilles was kidnapping youths to sell to the English. Others whispered that he was writing a book of spells with human blood. A few may even have begun to wonder why he had chosen to dedicate his chapel to the Holy Innocents – the infants slaughtered in their cradles by King Herod.

Such matters might ordinarily have come to nothing. Scurrilous tittle-tattle about the misfortunes of a few under-age peasants was never likely to touch the reputation of a nobleman in fifteenth-century France. The talk of diabolism was a little more risky, coming at a time when Europe's witch-hunts were warming up, but invocation of demons still remained a popular hobby among French aristocrats. A discreet lord would have had nothing to fear. But discretion had never been Gilles' strong suit – and incontinence would prove to be his downfall.

As he had traveled, staging miracle plays and mysteries and keeping his choirboys supplied with chalices, censers and pyxes, he had churned his way through the fortune that three bloodlines had taken centuries to accumulate. And in May 1440, hubris finally met nemesis. Having recently sold one of his last properties, a fortress at St-Étienne-de-Mermorte, to a certain Geoffrey le Ferron, he decided that he wanted it back. At the head of a posse, he stormed into its church brandishing a double-headed poleaxe and forced its priest – who was also le Ferron's brother – to open the castle gates before tossing him into its dungeon. It is hard to imagine an act of gratuitous violence that would have been better calculated to bring Gilles' impunity to an end. Invasion of a church violated ancient privileges of the Bishop of Nantes. Geoffrey le Ferron was no mere castellan but treasurer to the Duke of Brittany. The Duke was the only man below the French king to whom Gilles owed fealty, and was thus entitled to confiscate what remained of his wealth if he was convicted of a felony. Gilles had finally found a mark to overstep.

By the early fifteenth century, the papal–national conflict had been unequivocally resolved in favour of secular rulers in France, and the bishopric of Nantes would now work loyally alongside the Duke of Brittany's officers. Proceedings were launched in the episcopal court, and covert inquiries produced a secret report in late July. One and a half months later, ducal officers arrested Gilles along with two servants and two priests. Four days after that, on 19 September 1440, he was escorted into the great hall of Nantes Castle to be told that he faced charges of heresy. Gilles had doubtless come to terms with the fact that abducting a priest at poleaxe-point was going to require some penance, but when he was brought back to court almost three weeks later it became clear that the term 'heresy' covered a multitude of sins. Alongside sundry acts of impiety, apostasy, and sacrilege, the indictment alleged that he had made pacts with demons, and that he had sodomized and murdered some 140 children.

Gilles seems to have been unable quite to believe that the court was presuming to judge him for such trifles. He haughtily insisted on appealing, and when the judges told him that the request was frivolous, and ought to have been in writing anyway, he fell into a monstrous sulk. Even when the prosecutor swore four times to the truth of his indictment, he refused to speak. Five days later, the displeasure had hardened. Spitting invective at the bench, Gilles condemned his judges as 'simoniacs and ribalds' and announced that he would rather hang from a rope than plead to their charges. In the face of such defiance, they deployed the most powerful sanction at their disposal. They excommunicated him.

The judges knew their quarry. When Gilles reappeared two days later he was in tears, begging forgiveness for having questioned their right to try him and pleading for readmission to the Church. The clerics duly re-embraced him to the Church's bosom, but made sure simultaneously to have him watch his servants and priests being sworn, in preparation for secret interrogations that were to take place over the next few days. The pressures on Gilles were mounting; but when the indictment was read aloud, he seemed strangely disengaged. He admitted borrowing a book that explained how demons might be persuaded to transmute base metals into gold, but made a point of insisting that he had returned it to its owner. He had employed several alchemists to freeze quicksilver, he accepted, but he was anxious to assert that he had neither invoked evil spirits nor made sacrifices to them. Of lost children, he spoke not a word.

The members of Gilles' household were then interviewed – very probably, under torture – and, five days later, their statements were read to him. All described acts of diabolism and murder in chilling detail, and Gilles declined to challenge any of the evidence – but the court remained unsatisfied. It duly ordered that he be interrogated on the rack 'in order to shed light on and more thoroughly scrutinize the truth'. Gilles, allowed a night to consider his position, decided that that would not be necessary. On the following afternoon, he made a full confession in his cell to four judges and the prosecutor, and was made to repeat it a day later in a packed courtroom. It was an extraordinary performance.

He began by asking that his words be published not just in Latin but also in French, in order that as many people as possible could learn from his mistakes. He implored his listeners to raise their children with good manners and virtuous habits, because he had been undone by an unbridled childhood. And he then confessed to the abduction and murder of 'so many children that he could not determine with certitude the number' in terms that, even six centuries distant, retain their power to appal. Alongside his servants and other companions, he had throttled his victims and hanged them from hooks, sodomized them and 'ejaculated spermatic seed in the most culpable fashion on [their] bellies . . . as much after their deaths as during it'. He had stabbed and battered them, decapitating some, and while they were in their last throes, he had often 'sat on their bellies and . . . laughed at them'. Once dead, he had 'embraced them . . . contemplating those who had the most beautiful heads and members', and had then torn open their bodies to '[delight] at the sight of their internal organs'.

Having dealt with the question of dead children, Gilles then turned to diabolism – a subject on which he seems to have spent about four times as long – and admitted that he had often hired magicians to invoke demons. All were evidently con artists, warning him off at crucial moments and sometimes beating themselves up in locked rooms to prove the risks they were running, but although their dishonesty had eluded Gilles, his participation had been far from passive. He had once used blood from his little finger to write to a demon, he recalled. On another occasion, he had given a magician the hand, heart, and eyes of a young boy in a jar.

Gilles concluded with a plea to all fathers present not to tolerate sloth or fine dressing in their children, and a warning that his crimes were born out of an insatiable appetite for delicacies and mulled wine. By now in tears, there was just one other thing that he wanted to share. Temptation had been strewn across the path of his life, he admitted. It was only by virtue of his steadfast affection for the Church that he had lost neither body nor soul to the Devil.

Any confession made after the threat of torture in response to accusations by imprisoned accomplices has to be suspect, but Gilles' words – oblivious as a psychopath's and naive as a child's – ring so true that they are almost impossible to disbelieve. The portrait draws from life rather than the formulaic fantasies of inquisitors. It does not depict an omnipotent diabolist, but a gullible fool. And the clinical descriptions of murder are not the words of someone who imagined what crime might be like. They are the recollections of a man who had watched children die.

Three days later he was convicted, excommunicated again, and – after another tearful display of genuflecting remorse – formally readmitted to the Church for a second time. Later that morning, he went to the secular court in order to receive his death sentence, and delivered a second public confession at the request of Pierre de l'Hôpital, the senior judge. De l'Hôpital advised him that his shame in this world would precisely alleviate the punishment he was owed in the next, and although there is little indication that Gilles was anticipating much divine retribution, de l'Hôpital was impressed by his contrition. So much so, indeed, that he granted him the greatest boon he could have extended. After pronouncing that Gilles was to be hanged and then burned, he specified that his corpse should be merely 'embraced' by the flames – in order that it could then be interred in Gilles' church of choice.

Gilles, given one last night to make his peace with God, offered a final display of atonement, fifteenth-century style, at the gallows the next morning. Barefoot and clad in white, he exhorted the two servants who had helped him to throttle, disembowel, and sodomize unnumbered children to be strong in the face of temptation. He bade them *au revoir* instead of *adieu*, assuring them that their souls would be reunited at the moment of death, because no sin was unforgivable 'so long as the sinner felt profound regret and great contrition of heart'. All were then hanged and the servants' bodies, in keeping with their humble stations, were reduced to ashes. Gilles' corpse, lightly singed, was borne away by assorted ecclesiastics and aristocrats for its honourable burial at Nantes Cathedral.

Gilles' confidence might strike modern readers as bizarre, repulsive, or even blasphemous, but the scribes and judges who heard him were not just satisfied, but touched, by the piety they detected. A conventional explanation nowadays for their attitude would be that, just as the era was typified by a concern that sinners display signs of their shame, the inquisitorial system regarded the utterance of regret rather than inner remorse as the way to expiate guilt. That assertion does not, however, go very far. It was well-established Catholic doctrine by the fifteenth century that confessions were invalid unless accompanied by contrition, and the trial record itself indicates that at least some of Gilles' judges wanted insights as well as words. While the witness statements were being taken, he was asked twice if he wanted to 'justify' his actions, or set out his 'motives', and at the time of Gilles' first admissions in his prison cell, a particularly telling exchange took place. Pierre de l'Hôpital, Nantes' senior secular judge, asked him at one point to say who had incited and taught him his crimes. Inquisitors routinely asked the question in the hope of identifying accomplices, but de l'Hôpital was after more than names. When Gilles replied that he had been 'following his own feelings, solely for his pleasure and carnal delight', the judge did not only express surprise, but also pressed on. He wanted to know 'from what motives, with what intent, and to what ends' the murders and sexual abuse had occurred. An explanation, he urged, would allow Gilles 'to disburden his conscience, which most likely was accusing him'. The remark inspired indignation. 'Alas!' snapped the nobleman. 'You are tormenting yourself, and me as well.' The judge fired back that he was not tormenting himself, but wanted to know the 'absolute truth', whereupon Gilles brought the exchange to an abrupt end with a bare assurance that, 'Truly, there was no other cause, no other end nor intention.' Even de l'Hôpital was ultimately sufficiently impressed to grant his prisoner the privilege of a mere toasting, but he seems to have been struggling with ideas that are now as common as they were then inchoate: that defendants can reliably reveal their motivations, and that guilt should be measured by their willingness to do so.

The exchange also exemplifies another feature of the modern trial: the way in which it attempts to reconcile those being judged with those doing the judging, and the extent to which that attempt is so often doomed. No matter how much a criminal may want to explain, a court long to understand, and a grieving relative hope for resolution, the gap in most serious cases is all but unbridgeable. The most obvious reason is that no crime can be undone, but another is that no explanation can ever adequately pin down why one person breaks the rules and another does not. The excuses most commonly heard today – whether social deprivation, mental retardation, or pre-menstrual tension – are inherently no more plausible than Gilles' claim that his murders were the fault of Satan, a wild childhood, and a predilection for mulled wine. Making the leap of imagination to empathize with a criminal is of course easy if one sympathizes with the crime concerned, but the mentality of someone who dedicated a chapel to martyred children while slaughtering real ones, say, is for most people about as unreachable as another mind can be. In such cases, the assessment that resonates truest to modern ears is one that Gilles gave long before his trial. He told a servant that he had been born under a star such that 'nobody could know or understand the anomalies or illicit acts of which [I am] guilty'. And it explains nothing at all.

The concern to hear confessions was not the only feature of the Church's battle against heresy that found permanent expression in the secular legal system of France. Its courts also became increasingly secret, just as the tribunals of the papal inquisitors had in the early thirteenth century. Inquisitorial judges opened their doors only when they were ready to present to the public the spectacle of a confessing defendant or, as happened rather more rarely, the mercy of the sovereign. By the close of the fifteenth century, they were interviewing witnesses in the absence of everyone but their clerks. Defendants meanwhile languished in custody except when it became necessary to present them with their accusers or torture them; and defence lawyers, always rare, were formally excluded in 1539 from most stages of a trial, and absolutely barred in all capital cases after 1670.

Excluding the unlettered and the unwashed undoubtedly appealed to many lawyers then for the same reasons that secrecy still does to many people with power; but there was one notable critic. A judge from Angers called Pierre Ayrault, whose writings would influence generations of French lawyers, wrote a long work specifically on the topic in 1588, in which he complained that French justice had become like 'a sacred mystery that is communicated only to the priest'. Its secrecy, which had been adopted out of 'fear of the uproar, shouting and cheering that people ordinarily indulge in', was a recipe for incompetence and error. Statements obtained during closed interrogations reflected the preconceptions of the legal official taking them rather than the meaning of the person being interviewed. Public trials, on the other hand, would serve to display the law at its most majestic. They would also make it more likely that a judge's rulings were honest and reasoned.

The critique, developed at a time when political concepts like freedom of information and checks and balances still lay some distance in the future, was a perceptive one. The inquisitorial process, by concealing its officials from scrutiny, was inherently prone to corruption. The pernicious nature of the secrecy was, however, greater than Ayrault himself knew, for it could cloud the vision of even its greatest critic.

In August 1598, he was called upon to try a dishevelled and long-haired beggar in his mid-thirties called Jacques Roulet. Roulet had been handed into custody by one Symphorien Damon, whose statement set out how he had come to be arrested. Damon's suspicions had been aroused when he saw the man lying on his stomach in a field for, upon being challenged, Roulet had stared at him malevolently and run away. He had seen him again shortly thereafter, alongside the mutilated body of a young boy and in the custody of four villagers. Everything else that Damon reported came from those four men; and if they ever testified, their evidence has been lost. He recounted how the peasants (one of whom was the dead child's father) claimed to have chanced upon the body as it was being eaten by two wolves, and then to have spotted Roulet as they were chasing the beasts away. The coincidence had struck them as sinister, and their hunch was soon confirmed. Asked what he was doing, the beggar had said, 'Not much', but when they demanded that he reveal who had eaten the child, he had apparently confessed that he, his father, and his cousin had all been responsible. They had been wolves at the time. According to Damon, Roulet had even had long nails and bloody hands when arrested.

Attitudes towards lycanthropy in the late 1590s were in a state of flux. Although Christian scholars had insisted for centuries that werewolves were no more than an optical illusion – essentially because only God could turn humans into ravenous beasts and He had better things to do – the orthodoxy was under pressure. Lawyers, as usual, were at the forefront of the debate. The most eminent jurist in all France, Jean Bodin, had just written a witchcraft manual in which he argued that Satan did in fact enjoy the power to transform people into wolves. There is little reason to think that Ayrault subscribed to Bodin's views, which were controversial even among his fellow demonologists, but the judge from Angers had a belief in the value of self-condemnation that was profound. In words that would be cited by French lawyers for the next two centuries, he wrote – in the same work that attacked his country's legal secrecy – that the ultimate goal of criminal law was to 'instil and engrave its fundamental principles on people's hearts'. It was 'not enough that wrongdoers be justly punished' he insisted. 'They must if possible judge and condemn themselves.' And although he elsewhere warned that confessions could be false, he now put that credo into practice.

Ayrault began by asking Roulet to tell him what he had been accused of – a traditional if sneaky opening gambit among inquisitors – and Roulet replied that people thought him to be a villain. Ayrault specified that he wanted to know what he had been accused of at the time of his arrest, whereupon the beggar told him that he had committed an offence against God and that his parents had given him an ointment. When Ayrault hopefully asked if the potion turned him into a wolf Roulet denied it, but further prodding inspired him to admit that he had killed and eaten a child. He then confessed that he had, after all, been a wolf. Questioned in detail about his appearance at the time, he stated that his face and hands had been bloody, that he had had a wolf's paws but a human head, and that he had attacked the boy with his teeth. Ayrault had heard enough. Whatever his attitude towards lycanthropy might have been, he certainly believed in murder. And having heard Roulet's admissions, he now condemned him to death.

Records of the case give no indication why the sentence was not immediately carried out, but they show that the Paris court of appeal quashed the sentence of death three months later. Roulet was more foolish than evil, declared the *parlement*, and the best way to deal with him was to give him compulsory religious instruction in an asylum for two years. The basis for its decision is not set down, but any sixteenth-century court would have been even less likely than its modern counterpart to reprieve a self-confessed murderous cannibal unless absolutely sure of his innocence. Whether the beggar had been framed or simply fell victim to superstition, Ayrault had evidently got it wrong. He saw the risks of secrecy and untested evidence more clearly than anyone else in early modern France, but alone in his court, away from public scrutiny, his belief that prisoners should 'judge and condemn themselves' had led him to encourage a man's delusions – and then to conclude that they were true.

The progress of inquisitorial procedures through German-speaking central Europe was more uneven than in France, but they would become just as dominant. The execution of the heir to the Hohenstaufen dynasty in 1268[*] saw the region dissolve into a collection of several hundred more or less independent towns and principalities however, and older rituals lingered in many areas long after they had disappeared in others. Some jurisdictions required, for example, that a murder victim be borne into court by chanting relatives and assume formal responsibility for prosecuting its killers. A variation on the same theme saw the deceased's hand severed and given to the defendant who, clad in a loincloth, would have to hold it and assert innocence three times. If the judge detected sufficient signs of discomfort, in either the defendant or the hand, guilt would be established.

Judgment in Germany also retained some notably eccentric features. Judges took their seats clutching unsheathed swords and, after proceedings had been called to order three times by a bailiff, the defendant would recite a confession or request an acquittal. It made no difference which. The judges were formally required to have already decided their verdict, and they would follow up his plea by unfurling and reciting a previously prepared decision. If they had elected to convict, the senior of them would snap his wand of office, toss it to his feet, and pronounce the condemned person's doom. 'Your life is over,' he would roar, as a muffled church-bell tolled. '[T]here is no place on this earth for you any more, and in breaking this wand I also break the tie between you and the human race. Only with God may you still find mercy. Woe upon you

---

* See p. 46.

here! Woe! Woe!' The clerk would add three more woes. So too would the bailiff. And when the woeing was over, the prisoner's theoretical expulsion was made practical, as he or she was staked through the heart, burned on a stake, pulped with the rim of a large cartwheel, or strangled from a gallows.

The decentralization meant that German courts would be typified by a relatively freewheeling attitude towards legal technicalities. Far from mitigating the harshness of inquisitorial procedure, however, the flexibility generally made it even more deadly. German judges often enjoyed a particularly broad discretion to pursue obsessions, whether their own or those of their political masters, and all manner of blameless defendants would feel their wrath over the years. Some of the worst injustices came from one particularly dark corner of German jurisprudence: the Jewish ritual murder trial.

The myth that Jews were in the habit of slaughtering young Christians was not born in Germany. The allegation was first recorded in Norwich in 1144, and similar accusations sparked off bloody pogroms in England and France throughout the 1200s. It was only the wholesale expulsion of Jews from both countries (in 1290 and 1306 respectively) that pushed the epicentres of hatred towards Spain and central Europe. But fear and resentment spiralled as the refugees moved and, at a time when the courtroom was becoming the sharp end of political power, Germany's inquisitors were soon ensuring that both lodged deep within the German body politic.

Their *modus operandi* is exemplified by a 1476 case that arose out of the Bishop of Regensburg's discovery that a tortured Jew in Trent had confessed to murdering a Christian child in his diocese. He turned immediately to the local magistrates and in cahoots with the region's duke, they swiftly itemized the property of the city's richest Jews. Seventeen were then arrested. Although the supposed victim was identified in only the vaguest terms, the judges then drew up a list of twenty-five questions that included the following:

> Which Jews brought and purchased the child? Who tortured him? How much money did each Jew give to participate? What was the blood used for? How were the needles used? How were the pincers used? Why was a handkerchief tied around the child's

throat? How was the foreskin on the penis cut off and which Jews cut off the penis and what was done with it? Which Jewesses knew about this and what had they said?

The men, weighed down with stones, were raised and dropped by the rope of a strappado as each question was asked. Within two weeks, six had confessed to the imaginary murder.

The inquisitorial system could also create not just crimes, but entire superstitions. One of the most chilling cases of all, which is also the earliest to be fully recorded, illustrates the process with graphic clarity. In March 1470, workers restoring the charnel house of the small Black Forest town of Endingen reported the discovery of four skeletons, two of which were missing their skulls. It was just a month before Easter, never a high point for Judaeo–Christian harmony in the Middle Ages, and the presence of stray bones in the ossuary sparked panic. Someone soon recalled that, eight years before, Elias the Jew had sheltered a destitute family, and he and his two brothers were swiftly arrested and subjected to repeated sessions on the strappado. Within days, all had accepted not only that they had murdered the beggars, but also that they had beheaded two children and bathed in their blood.

The interrogations were recorded as they took place, and it is that of Mercklin, questioned after both his brothers had given in, which is the most haunting. He began defiantly, asking why he had to say anything at all if his interrogators already knew him to be guilty. They explained that they wanted to hear the truth from his mouth. Torture soon broke him, but after he confessed he was asked why he and his brothers had drained their victims' blood. It was a question too far. He had no idea what his tormentors wanted him to say, and the desperation in his voice, as he trawled through their prejudices while the strappado was hoisted and released, echoes down the centuries.

> To that he answered in many words, saying at first that Jews need Christian blood because it has great healing power. We would not be satisfied with this answer and told him that he was lying, that we knew why they need it because his brother Eberlin had told us already. To this Mercklin said that Jews need Christian blood for curing epilepsy. But we . . . would not be satisfied with

the answer. Mercklin then said further that Jews need Christian
blood for its taste because they themselves stink. But we would
not be satisfied with the answer and told him that he was lying,
and must tell us the truth, because his brother Eberlin told us a
different story; now he must also tell us the truth. To this he
answered badly that he wanted to tell us the truth, that he saw it
cannot be otherwise . . .but that Jews need Christian blood [as a
holy oil] for circumcision.

It was, at last, the answer that the magistrates wanted and, as was routine
for capital offenders in early modern Germany, the brothers were
stripped, wrapped in cowhides, dragged to the stake by their ankles, and
burned alive.

The punishment was – in extremely relative terms – a mild one. A
magistrate elsewhere in Germany might have compounded the humiliation by binding them in pigskin. If they had been thieves, they might
have been made to wear a hat filled with hot pitch before being hanged.

One of the most unpleasant penalties was the one recorded in the
adjoining woodcut – involving sus-
pension by the heels between two
hungry dogs. But even if the
inquisitors of Endingen were not
quite as brutal as they might have
been, the process that had preceded
the penalty was certainly inventive.
For it did not so much reaffirm an
existing superstition as conjure one
into existence. Mercklin's first
answers had regurgitated myths
that were common by the 1470s.
The notion that human blood
could cure epilepsy was so widely
held that Germans, regardless of religious belief, would line up to drink
thimblefuls of it at public beheadings – until well into the 1800s. The
foetor judaicus had been troubling Christian nostrils for centuries,
and Freiburg's councillors had cited Jews' murderous personal hygiene

problems as a reason to expel them as far back as 1401. Mercklin's final explanation seems, however, to have appeared in writing for the very first time at Endingen.

Quite where it came from is unknown. The focus on foreskins might conceivably have been inspired by Catherine of Siena, recently canonized on the strength of a dream that Christ had given her one, by way of a ring of flesh to wear on her finger.* Psychohistorians have, as might be imagined, come up with considerably more involved theories. But whatever the myth's source, it would endure. The brothers' confessions were quickly transmitted to other towns along the Rhine, and a link between circumcision and bloodlust very soon became part of the canon of German Judaeophobia. Within a month, four Jewish men in nearby Pforzheim were executed after confessing that they too had killed for the sake of their penises, and similar admissions were obtained six years later by inquisitors in Baden. An unknown writer then re-scripted the narratives into the *Endinger Judenspiel*, arguably the first trial dramatization of modern European history, which became wildly popular during the seventeenth century and would pack German auditoriums well into the nineteenth. Endingen, meanwhile, celebrated its victory over the eternal Jew by encasing the headless children in a glass cabinet in the town

---

* The fascination with foreskins was far older than either Catherine of Siena or the Regensburg trial, however. The medieval Church officially celebrated Christ's circumcision by way of an annual feast on 1 January, and His foreskin excited such interest that eight different European churches and monasteries were already claiming to own it by the early thirteenth century. (Pope Innocent III refused to decide who was right, pronouncing that only God could know the truth about so delicate a matter, whereupon several more churches asserted ownership.) For the sake of completeness, it should perhaps be noted that the medieval world's pre-eminent Jewish philosophers, Maimonides and Isaac Ben Yedaiah, had each devoted considerable attention to the question of why removal of the foreskin was so delightful to God. Maimonides suggested in around 1190 that it encouraged premature ejaculation and thereby freed up time for prayer. Isaac Ben Yedaiah, writing a century later, explained how the process worked. The uncircumcised man had 'testicles of iron' and 'ejaculated like a horse', he theorized, which caused women to cling to him and long for his continued attentions. His circumcised counterpart, on the other hand, 'emits his seed as soon as he inserts his crown' and was, as a happy result, detained neither by the act of intercourse nor any interest from his partner. For all sources, see p. 379.

church, until one of its priests decided that their display was a source of shame rather than pride. He reached his conclusion in 1967.

The confidence in rationality that had swept across Europe during the eleventh and twelfth centuries had taken continental jurisprudence a long way. Reason had proved capable of bolstering the most visceral fears and building the most bloodthirsty conclusions. Inspired by a belief that justice was a matter of extracting answers to the right questions, lawyers had developed rules capable of condemning beggars as werewolves. In order to protect Christian children, Jewish prisoners had been identified as vampires. The law's sturdiest logic could produce the purest fantasy – as was never more apparent than in the context of inquisitorial rules of proof.

The first systematic works on the question of evidence, written by lawyers from northern Italy during the fifteenth and sixteenth centuries, had warned judges that torture was permissible only if circumstantial evidence reached a certain threshold, characterized as a 'half-proof' or a 'proximate indication'. The safeguard, always optimistic, very soon became illusory – because judges, rather than dispense with torture, simply expanded the range of half-proofs. By the 1590s, for example, a suspected thief could be tortured in most parts of Europe if he or she had been spending more than usual. Suspected witches could be tortured in France by the early seventeenth century if they avoided the gaze of their judge. And the rules about half-proofs were complemented by the notion of the 'perfect proof', whereby circumstantial evidence, when topped up by a confession, positively required a judge to convict. The logic was elaborate, but the effect was simple: arrest virtually guaranteed torture, which virtually guaranteed conviction.

The diversity of German law meant that its procedures became particularly convoluted. The region's princes notionally owed loyalty to a ruler whom they elected, and during the sixteenth century a law was enacted by Emperor Charles V that sought to minimize arbitrariness by establishing ground rules that would apply in every German state. The 1532 code, known as the Carolina, permitted each one to maintain its customary laws however, and it aimed only at ensuring that there were 'legally sufficient' grounds for torture – with the consequence that it spread inquisitorial lunacies as much as it suppressed them. It advised judges, for example, that torture was permissible if a suspect was 'insolent and wanton', or in possession of something similar to something found at the crime scene. Inquisitors soon got the point, and were developing rules of their own. By the seventeenth century, an unnatural pallor was sufficient to justify torture for several crimes in Frankfurt-am-Main. Suspected adulterers were imperilled simply by being found in an attractive woman's house – unless the culprit was a cleric, in which case he could be caught in a clinch and the court would presume that he had been ministering to the woman's spiritual needs.

The code also advised inquisitors to seek confessions even where eyewitness testimony and circumstantial evidence were already overwhelming. Prisoners who withdrew admissions on the scaffold might therefore be rushed back to the rack, on the theory that a miscarriage of justice would otherwise ensue. And although the Carolina had been based on a Bamberg statute that pronounced it 'better to acquit a guilty person than to condemn an innocent one to death', at least some lawyers took a very different view. Fynes Moryson, an Englishman touring Europe in the late sixteenth century, reported that he had met several who justified deaths through torture with 'a strange, yet good, saying . . . namely that it is better one innocent man should dye by triall, then many [guilty] persons should escape for want of [it]'.

It was in eighteenth-century France – a society in which many began to believe that human wisdom was not just improvable but perfectible – that the faith in reason reached its apogee. The spirit of the age was well expressed by the work of an influential jurist called Pierre François Muyart de Vouglans, whose textbooks portrayed French criminal procedure as an almost mathematically precise tool for the discovery of truth. Since crimes were effectively puzzles waiting to be solved, it was positively unjust to hold back when detaining a suspect. '[T]he welfare of humanity demands that crime should not remain unpunished,' he explained. 'It is for that reason that, in the absence of other means of arriving at [a] complete proof, we are obliged to torture the body of the accused.' That said, the absence of such proof was no bar to punishment. It had been established in 1670 that anyone who refused to confess was liable to any penalty short of death, and Muyart de Vouglans now explained why: anyone liable for torture was already more than 'half-convicted' and deserved a suitably proportioned punishment. If someone's refusal to confess made a death sentence inappropriate, a judge might, for example, send him to the galleys for life instead. The flexibility of such a system, adjusting the penalty to fit the amount of evidence, represented for Muyart de Vouglans the acme of judicial sophistication. 'By means of these augmentations and moderations of Penalties,' he declared, 'our Jurisprudence has reached a degree of perfection which distinguishes it among civilized Nations.'

Enlightenment rationalism did, however, have a more benign aspect. Previous assumptions about punishment and crime were called into question, and at a time when political philosophers were arguing for the first time that the exercise of power demanded public scrutiny, systematic criticism of the inquisitorial system was heard for the first time. The greatest single impetus came in 1764, when an Italian called Cesare Beccaria published a powerful attack on the cruel, arbitrary, and brutal nature of European criminal justice – including a damning critique of the continental reliance on torture – that would define the terms of debate in Europe and America for decades.

Muyart de Vouglans was moved to publish a refutation, but many others were persuaded by Beccaria's argument – among them, a judge called François Serpillon whose own textbook, published at Lyons three years later, contained another condemnation of torture – all the more persuasive because Serpillon had inflicted it. He reported that the custom in his hometown of Autun was to strip suspects, bind them to a table, and then question them for two hours while their legs were crushed between boards and slowly scalded with twelve pints of boiling oil. He had been present at interrogations twice – once only as a witness, but once ('compelled' by the evidence) as the torturer – and neither occasion had ended happily. The good news for the men being questioned was that both had been released following their refusals to confess. The bad news was that the legs of the first suspect had caught fire, necessitating amputation, while the second defendant had been so badly burned that the bones of his toes had had to be removed with pincers.

Another critic of the inquisitorial system, equally vociferous but considerably less compromised by its operation than Serpillon, was Voltaire, who campaigned against its inhumanity for a lifetime, but eloquently damned it with just a few lines in a 1766 commentary on Beccaria's work. He reported that the inquisitors of Toulouse used not only half-proofs but also quarters and eighths, and came to their decisions by adding them up. A piece of hearsay amounted to a quarter-proof, while an even vaguer rumour might count for an eighth. The result was that eight doubts could constitute a perfect proof and send a man to his death.

Notwithstanding the pride of lawyers like Muyart de Vouglans, the entire edifice of inquisitorial procedure was already tottering by the time that Voltaire wrote his critique. Several European governments abolished torture during the late eighteenth century, and after 1780 even French courts permitted its use only to identify accomplices after conviction. The revolution that began at the Paris Bastille nine years later then saw the system collapse. Within two years, France's trials had become public and adversarial, defendants had won guarantees against not just torture but oaths, and the power to investigate crimes was at last detached from the duty to judge them.

Enduring reform then came under Napoleon, who enacted a law code in 1808 that would be adopted across Europe and continues to underpin criminal justice systems on the continent today. Although judges can still conduct pre-trial investigations in secret, and dominate the court to an extent that echoes their former role, the malignity of the inquisition is now very much a thing of the past. Later chapters will show that the dangers of unaccountability and torture live on, but those risks are not the relics of any particular legal culture. Abolition of the inquisitorial system did, however, owe much to a very specific rival tradition. For the progressives who campaigned to bring it down modelled their proposals for reform on a criminal process that actually existed on the other side of the English Channel – the jury trial.

Francisco Goya, For Being a Liberal? (1803–24). *Goya, painfully aware of how fragile a barrier separated reason and instinct, repeatedly attacked torture and inquisitorial methods in his art during this period.*

3

The Jury Trial (1)

He considered what he should say to win over the whole audience once and for all, or if that were not possible, at least to win over most of them for the time being.

FRANZ KAFKA, *The Trial*

Innocent III's decision in 1215 to abandon ordeals threw England as much into the lurch as it did the rest of Christendom. For time out of mind, the country's kings had been subcontracting criminal justice to the clergy, who had been happy to to scald and drown suspected sinners for a small fee. Many ordinary folk had even come to trust trials by fire and water, if only because the primary alternative, trial by combat, seemed suspiciously favourable to whichever litigant was able to afford the better weapons and champion. The country's response to the abolition of ordeals would, however, be very different from that adopted on the continent.

Whereas continental rulers would turn to the techniques of the papal Inquisition and the rules of canonical law to fill the legal vacuum, the Church would never gain an equivalent degree of influence over royal justice in England. Its legal pretensions had already taken a heavy blow when knights loyal to Henry II had rid their king of turbulent Thomas Becket by braining him in Winchester Cathedral in 1170. The assassination was followed by important concessions to clerical independence from a penitent Henry, and the English Church of the early thirteenth century was in no mood to rock the boat. While Catholicism's legal traditions spawned across Europe, nurtured by the demands of its war on heresy, representatives of the English Church positively avoided their country's royal courts. Clerics would long retain peculiar privileges: they were, for example, granted an automatic immunity from punishment if they read Psalm 51 of the Bible aloud from the dock, a provision that would mutate into ridiculousness over the years as convicts memorized the 'neck verse' and merciful judges treated them as monks. Bishops would, for another five centuries, retain the right to try religious crimes such as heresy and moral misdemeanours such as adultery. Canonical law would never get to supersede custom and statute however. The irrationalities of England's royal courts would come from sources other than the Good Book.

The authorities initially had little idea what should replace jury trial. Royal judges customarily took the king's justice to jails around the realm every few years, and their coaches had already left London for the provinces in late 1218, when a rather perplexed note from the guardians of 11-year-old Henry III caught up with them. Proof by fire and water was no longer an option, it reminded them, and they might want to deal with minor cases by exacting promises of good behaviour. Exile would often be appropriate for those suspected of slightly more serious crimes. But all that the note could tentatively suggest for offences of violence or dishonesty was imprisonment – and in an era when judges toured dungeons to empty them rather than fill them up, the proposal was a stopgap rather than a solution. And yet, the king's advisors had nothing else to offer. 'For the present,' they concluded forlornly, 'we must rely very much on your discretion to act wisely according to the special circumstances of each case.'

England's judges would rise to the challenge. Their solution was seen for the first time at a trial in Westminster in 1220, when a self-confessed murderer called Alice snitched on five other accused men in the hope of saving her own skin. The charges could not be resolved by battle, because she was a woman, but those she named then agreed to submit 'for good or ill' to the judgment of twelve of their property-owning neighbours. Said neighbours promptly swore that one was a law-abiding man but that four were thieves, whereupon the unlucky quartet was hanged. By the following summer, when seven of the king's judges set out on another circuit of England's prisons, they had begun to use the new system regularly. Trial by twelve good men and true had been born.

The jury trial would generate countless myths over the following centuries, and those claiming to describe its origins have been among the most tenacious. Athens, Rome, and the Magna Carta – an abortive truce signed in 1215 between King John and rebellious barons – have all, in their time, been credited with inventing the institution. In fact, it owed nothing to any of them. Athenians had judged in groups of several hundred at a time, the mythological *Oresteia* notwithstanding, and their civilization was one of which few people in thirteenth-century England would even have heard. The Roman Republic had seen the establishment of courts known as the *iudicia publica*, at which wealthy officers and senators had judged certain offences, but the precedent had no impact at all on English law. The Magna Carta, for its part, established that monarchs had to obey their own laws when dealing with English property owners, and used language that would later support arguments for speedy and fair trials, but it said nothing about how people were to be tried in the first place.

No innovation built on tradition has a single source, but some of the rituals from which Westminster's judges were drawing in 1220 can be identified. England's rulers had been assembling groups of sworn men to furnish them with information for several centuries, and a link between twelve sworn men and criminal justice had been seen as far back as AD 879, when King Alfred the Great signed a peace treaty with King Guthrum of Denmark. Their agreement, which partitioned England as the price for ending decades of Viking raids, established that a killer in either ruler's realm could cleanse himself of blood-guilt by producing twelve sworn men ('if he dares'). Quite where the idea of a *dozen* judges came from would always excite speculation, with later jurists crediting the Apostles, the tribes of Israel, and so on; but although that mystery remains obscure, it is very clear that in 1220 the number had become conventional. And only a short imaginative step would have been required to transform such compurgation rituals into the jury trial. Even in the early eleventh century, defendants in some cases had been required to choose co-swearers from an independent panel of locals rather than their friends, and the only change required was to turn that exception into the norm. Instead of being allowed to produce their own jurors, defendants would challenge those of their neighbours whom they did not trust to judge them fairly.

Just as there was institutional continuity, the extension of the jury's role into the field of criminal justice was not a sudden leap from ritual to reason. A society that in 1215 had been committed to the belief that God healed blisters and zapped perjurers for love of justice did not in the space of five years decide that He had lost interest. The new system still relied squarely on the oath, and witnesses played no more than an occasional role in trials until well into the fifteenth century. The earliest jurors *were* the witnesses and their *veredictum* – or 'spoken truth' – was the only testimony required. God remained the guarantor of justice, and His wisdom was discovered by rituals that treated jurors as ciphers to be cracked rather than as agents of rational inquiry. They were deprived of food, drink, and fire while they deliberated, individually imprisoned if they held out against the majority for longer than a day and a night, and collectively carted from court to court if they swore a verdict that the judge considered perjurious. The crowning absurdity was that, at the same time that jurors were effectively robbed of a right to silence, defendants were formally prohibited from swearing to their innocence – for fear that the guilty among them would otherwise lose their souls.

No thirteenth-century thinker could even have been entirely sure that entrusting the power of life and death to fallible human beings was capable of substituting adequately for divine judgment. The risk that a juror might break his oath would have been as keenly perceived as the hope that he would abide by it, while the few people who pondered such matters would have had little confidence in the ability of jurors to assess evidence. As elsewhere in Europe, the unseen deed, like the hidden motive, was widely perceived as a phenomenon beyond mortal ken, unknowable to all but God. England's first legal writer, Henry Bracton, thus explained in the 1220s or 1230s that it made no sense for jurors to judge a poisoning – the quintessentially secret crime, always associated with sorcery in the pre-modern world – because '[they] can know nothing of the deed'. And whereas continental inquisitors would overcome such riddles by subjecting defendants to the rack and strappado, English law would require anyone suspected of particularly mysterious crimes to undergo trial by combat for at least another century.

To the limited extent that the new system *did* represent a move away from earlier superstitions, it seems to have inspired feelings ranging from trepidation to terror. At one of the first sets of trials, held in Gloucester in June 1221, almost half of the twenty-seven indicted defendants refused to enter a plea. Matilda, accused of murder, declined because she felt that too many people hated her. John explained that he had done far too much evil to want to put his fate in his neighbours' hands. William, suspected of sheep stealing, backed out after seeing a jury send the defendants immediately ahead of him to the gallows. All the concerns sound eminently sensible, but rationality was certainly not the only force at work. For the judges were almost as unsure about their innovation as the defendants. They did not insist that anyone submit to it, and Matilda, John, and William – along with all the other holdouts – escaped execution. Two of the trio were immediately released.

The judges would soon overcome their compunctions, and by the time they reached Warwick, three months after the Gloucester debacle, they were putting their collective foot down. A murderer and a thief who refused to plead to a jury were unceremoniously hanged, and judges were soon requiring that defendants state – on their knees with right hand raised – that they consented to jury trial 'for good or ill'. If they refused to do so they would be spread-eagled under stones or lead and given only bread and water until they submitted or died. The suspicions attaching to the novel system were nevertheless such that resistance was widespread for decades, and sporadic for far longer. As late as the mid eighteenth century there would be people who would refuse trial by jury, and England's authorities retained the right to extract pleas using thumbscrews and millstones until 1772.

Not much is known about the trials that ensued over the next two centuries, but they were certainly very different from their modern counterparts. Although the law's concern for the fate of defendants' souls meant that an accused was denied the opportunity to give sworn testimony, few asserted a right to silence – for in the absence of any right to a lawyer, suspects who knew what was good for them argued for their lives. Their only opponent was the accuser: prosecuting lawyers appeared only in major cases before the seventeenth century, and independent testimony was all but unheard of until the early 1500s. An English lawyer writing in the 1470s, Sir John Fortescue, found the very notion of witnesses downright sinister. In a lengthy explanation of how English trials were the best in the world, he explained that continental inquisitors not only used unpleasantly belly-bursting, tendon-snapping techniques of torture, but brought people to court to say what they knew. They could, he pointed out, be bribed to say anything. Far more sensible, he argued, to have a system under which no one was liable to conviction except on the sworn evidence of twelve unbiased men.

A gulf had begun to yawn between Europe's two systems; and notwithstanding Fortescue's pride, there is little doubt that the courts of the continent had the stronger credentials. Structured around Roman law and inspired by the belief that justice was a matter of clever men applying their minds to a case, they had both tradition and reason on their side. Those of England, on the other hand, rested on a hotchpotch of superstition. Reliance on the ability of unlettered jurors to administer justice was, quite literally, a relic of barbarism.

And yet, for all its irrationality, England was already producing a method of trial considerably more benign. The notion that some matters were simply unknowable was helping to restrain the temptation to torture: against the bloody record of continental Europe, kings and royal officials would issue no more than eighty-one torture warrants over the entire course of England's history. English judges were also in a better position – at least potentially – to appreciate human frailty. Denied the right to seek the truth through force and required to sit alongside ordinary jurors, they could say, as Chief Justice Brian did in the late 1400s, that, 'The thought of man shall not be tried, for the devil himself knoweth not the thought of man.' And whereas continental justice was becoming a secret process, controlled by adepts who kept a lid on its mysteries until the moment of judgment, English trials were already virtually defined by their openness. The need to assemble jurors made it impossible to exclude the public, and although sheriffs and jailers would extort admission fees until the 1700s, large crowds invariably entered in their wake.

The characteristics of English courtrooms were, like all customs, as accidental as they were determined. They would, however, collectively define a notion of justice that would be of lasting significance – in England first, and then far beyond. And the most important accident of all was publicity, which would now turn the trial from an oath-taking ritual into a dynamic contest of fundamental political and social significance.

The background to the transformation was the crisis that tore England apart in the aftermath of Henry VIII's break from the Roman Church in the 1530s. Henry, anxious to secure spiritual approval for sexual relations with Anne Boleyn, spent the late 1520s unsuccessfully lobbying the pope for a divorce, eventually growing so irritable that in 1534 he established his own national Church. It was enough, very temporarily, to resolve his marital difficulties, but it also marked the beginning of a very troubled era in English history. Over the next decade, Henry beheaded and divorced his way through another three marriages, decimating English Catholicism in the process. As traditional bonds of religious and national fidelity snapped, his government sidelined regular legal procedures in favour of the rudiments of a police state. Tribunals like the Privy Council and Star Chamber assumed the power to punish without trial, and the torture chamber of the Tower of London was replenished and used to a greater extent than ever before. Henry simultaneously redefined treason to force his subjects to recognize his new authority or make their opposition apparent. The crime had never been the most tightly defined of offences – capable of penalizing acts ranging from fornication with the royal consort to forgery of a sixpence – but remaining within its parameters now became an almost acrobatic act. The laws that attempted to keep up with Henry's marital shenanigans are a case in point. The 1534 Act of Succession suddenly rendered it treacherous to deny the legitimacy of Elizabeth, his daughter by Anne Boleyn, or to assert that of his firstborn Mary. Two years later, another statute granted free pardon to anyone who had asserted the whoredom of Anne or the bastardy of her child. In 1544, a late burst of paternal pride inspired Henry to rule that anyone who cast aspersions on the birthright of either of his daughters should be hanged, drawn and quartered.

The oscillations only intensified after Henry's death in 1547. Edward VI had barely hit puberty when he died, aged 15, in 1553, and Mary Tudor then threw the ship of state into reverse by restoring English Catholicism and burning some three hundred Protestants to prove it. Her half-sister, Elizabeth, gave the wheel another turn in 1558. Although conciliatory by temperament, she restored Protestantism as the national religion and soon found herself caught between a regrouping papacy, ambitious monarchs in Spain and France, and a realm on the verge of civil war. In pursuit of peace she flirted politically and socially with almost every eligible Catholic on the continent, but her legitimacy, in every sense, depended on the men of Rome – and they were not to be charmed. Pius V excommunicated her in 1570. Ten years later, Gregory XIII's Secretary of State let it be known that an assassin could expect not just forgiveness from God, but positive gratitude.

In reaction to the papal *fatwa*s, Elizabeth's government mounted an increasingly ferocious assault on the Catholic enemy within. The authoritarian machinery that had taken shape under her father swung into action against religious insurgents real and imagined, while an equally threatening surge of ordinary crime inspired the construction in 1571 of a triple-beamed gallows that would soon become a byword for legal cruelty in England – Tyburn. By the 1590s a visiting Duke of Wirtemberg was able to count more than thirty grinning heads as he strolled across the towers and twenty arches of old London Bridge. Punishments did not just increase in number. Since the reign of Henry VIII, their variety had also been propagating,* and they now flowered into a pattern of dizzying complexity. Minor criminals might be dunked or made to wear a placard carrying the name of their crime. Felons often had the initials of their offence inscribed into their flesh, while those who devalued the royal coin were made to pay with the loss of their ears and nostrils. The symbolic amputation once imposed on libellous printers by Mary Tudor was also revived – claiming, among its first victims, the appropriately named John Stubbes, who exuberantly raised his hat and yelled 'God save the Queen' as a mallet was hammered through his right wrist. One case from 1594 can stand as memorial to all the thousands of other butcheries. It concerned five men convicted of a string of felonies ranging from counterfeiting to blackmail: four were sentenced to 'stand on the pillory and lose their ears if they have any' before being branded on the forehead with the letter 'F'. Elizabeth's most trusted judge, Lord

---

* The most inventive of Henry's innovations may have been the punishment imposed on Richard Roose, a cook who threw poison into his master's porridge in 1531. Complex political calculations inspired Henry to have Roose's crime retrospectively defined as high treason – and mysterious symbolic ones caused him to make it punishable by boiling. Roose was duly simmered to death in a large soup tureen on 5 April 1531. See Krista J. Kesselring, 'A Draft of the 1531 "Acte for Poysoning"', 116 *English Historical Review* 894 (September 2001).

Burghley, complained that such burns healed too quickly and proposed to ten of his fellow Privy Councillors that the Fs should instead be carved into the convicts' cheeks and have coloured powder rubbed into them. It seems, thankfully, to have been a proposal too far. According to the lawyer who reported the case, 'the others made no reply to this'.

The spread of corporal punishment was not unusual. Rulers across Europe were relying on the appearance of power to magnify its reality, and in Elizabeth's realm – riddled by spies, convulsed by rebellions and consumed by crime – the need to show subjects who was in control was a pressing one. But English criminal justice underwent a second, unique, transformation – for it did not use just human bodies as billboards for government authority. At the very same time that the rulers of France and Germany were ending the last vestiges of courtroom publicity, the English government embarked on a deliberate policy of using not just punishments but *trials* to show where power lay.

Henry VIII had sown the seeds with condemnations of, for example, Thomas More and Anne Boleyn, but it was during the reign of Elizabeth that the strategy reached fruition. Under the hammerbeam roofs and stone vaults of England's palaces, traitors stood behind solemn pikemen to hear their crimes described and their protestations of innocence ridiculed by some of the finest advocates of Renaissance England. Vast crowds were permitted to attend, and although witnesses were still forbidden to defendants, they increasingly appeared on behalf of the Crown – often very suddenly. At the trial of the Earl of Essex, for example, the Lord Chief Justice stepped down from the benches to testify at the behest of the Attorney-General while a Privy Councillor emerged at one point from a secret listening post to interrupt and contradict the defendant. And when it was all over, convocations of robed judges invited the jurors to consider the question of innocence or guilt. The verdicts rarely surprised. Records of the proceedings, transcribed by squads of stenographers, were then turned into anti-Catholic propaganda and published in English and Latin for the benefit of audiences domestic and European.

The hearings were rituals of condemnation rather than inquiry, and only a handful of acquittals ever occurred – but the insistence on public articulation meant that even the most careful preparations could suddenly go awry. When William Parry appeared at Westminster Hall in 1585 to answer charges of attempting to assassinate Elizabeth, he wearily entered a guilty plea and declared that, 'I desire not life, but desire to die'. But the court was packed with Londoners anxious to see Parry get his comeuppance, and instead of moving directly to sentence his judges ordered that his confession be read aloud, 'that everyone may see that the matter is as bad as the Indictment purporteth'. As Parry heard his words repeated, steel returned to his broken frame. 'Your Honours know . . . how my confession was extorted,' he declared. They fired back that torture had not been used. It had been threatened, he retorted. Charge and counter-charge spiralled, until Parry was denying any intention to kill the queen at all and promising to 'lay his blood' amongst the judges if they condemned him to death. The rattled men of the bench, warning him against such 'dark speeches', ordered that he be hanged, drawn, and quartered. A process that would have remained behind closed doors on the continent ended with the defendant being pulled down the riverside steps past a hooting mob, demanding 'in his rage and passion' that Elizabeth be summonsed 'to answer for my blood before God'.

No trial better illustrated the unpredictable force of publicity than one that occurred under the reign of Elizabeth's successor, King James I, in November 1603: the prosecution for treason of Sir Walter Raleigh. Drama was virtually guaranteed from the outset. Until Elizabeth's death in March 1603, Raleigh had enjoyed a charmed existence. Tall and elegant, he had shimmered like a peacock in a court where looks had mattered. After sponsoring England's first American colony at Roanoke in 1585, he had introduced the court to the pleasures of tobacco, and done more than any man alive to popularize the potato. Most heroic of all were his exploits against Spain, whose fleet he had taken on in battle three times. As England had flexed its maritime muscles he had trespassed even further into the heart of Spanish darkness, returning from one voyage in 1595 with tales of a land called Guyana where the natives' heads grew beneath their shoulders and precious metals veined every rock. El Dorado, he had reported, was just a return trip away.

All the derring-do came with an arrogance that lost friends as easily as it won them, however. Even Elizabeth sent Raleigh to the doghouse for several years when he breached palace protocol by impregnating one of her maids of honour, and the fastidious James took against him almost instantly. Though unequivocally Protestant, the king was always more

concerned to steady his wobbly throne than to fight the old religion, and
was as underwhelmed by Raleigh's anti-Spanish credentials as he was

unimpressed by his fondness for
tobacco. Within months of James
assuming the throne, the monopolies,
patents, and privileges dispensed
by Elizabeth were suspended and
Raleigh had lost his grace-and-favour
mansion. Although inconvenient,
it seemed no more than a routine
shake-up – until in the summer, one
of Raleigh's closest friends, Lord
Cobham, was implicated in a Catholic
plot to overthrow the king. No evidence linked Raleigh to the conspiracy,
but he too found himself under arrest
in mid July on suspicion of treason.

*Walter Raleigh, a year before
his trial.*

The rogue of the old dispensation was about to turn into the whipping
boy of the new.

In November 1603, with a plague epidemic claiming two thousand
lives a week in London, the entire court decamped to the ancient city of
Winchester for the trials. The city traced its history back to Rome and its
mythology back to Camelot, but this was the grandest show that it had
seen in a long while. Scholars were thrown out of their cathedral lodgings
to accommodate the jurists, James set up field headquarters at a nearby
mansion, and carriages laden with judges, jurors, lawyers, and defendants
were soon streaming through its gates. Raleigh took up residence at the
castle dungeon on 15 November, and arrived to the news that several of
the Catholics charged with conspiring against James had just been tried,
and that all but one had been sentenced to death. Although Raleigh's own
interrogators had never sought to link him to a broader plot, it was not a
good sign.

Early in the morning of 17 November Raleigh was escorted by pike-
wielding guards down to the Bishop's Palace, and led into its sepulchral
courtroom. His plummeting fortunes had been entertaining the country
for months, and popular interest in his anticipated destruction was
immense. On the five-day journey from London, his carriage had been

received with abuse, rocks and showers of clay pipes throughout (inspiring Raleigh laconically to observe that '[d]ogs do always bark at those they know not'), and the pillars, bays, and benches were now filled. Aristocrats and commoners sat cheek to cheek, exhaling large clouds of tobacco smoke if other trials of the time are a guide, as they waited for the show to begin. Almost all would have been hoping to see the final act of an epic life.

All seemed set fair to sink Raleigh. A phalanx of eleven royal commissioners, all of whom had helped investigate the plot against James, sat at the front of the court, four wearing the scarlet robes and black cornercaps of high judicial office. Local legend tells that the king himself was concealed in a cubbyhole, his ear to a listening hole, and although unlikely (because James had specifically sent reporters to court) it would not have been out of character; he secretly eavesdropped at many other major trials that occured during his reign. And at the prosecution benches, flanked by his fellow lawyers, was the most feared advocate of the day: Attorney-General Sir Edward Coke.

The lawyer, in his early fifties like Raleigh, was in many ways the mirror image of his adversary. Equally imposing physically and no less confident personally, he epitomized just as Raleigh did a social type that was emerging for the first time in England: the self-made man. Each was born into comfortable but non-aristocratic families; and although they had frequented different types of court, both had clambered up the hierarchy with a judicious combination of back-stabbing, fawning, and charm. Like many Elizabethans on the make, both were also masterful rhetoricians. In a fluid society where a commoner could no longer become a monk but could be appointed Attorney-General or mount a search for El

Edward Coke, soon after Raleigh's trial

Dorado if he sounded convincing enough, the ability to persuade was becoming an essential skill. Raleigh was a talented poet and writer while Coke, though always more likely to censor England's theatres than to attend them, had an eloquence renowned even among contemporaries who were rarely tongue-tied. Elizabethan grammar schoolboys were all taught adoxography, the art of eruditely praising worthless things.* Coke mastered a converse skill – and with his words, he sent scores of men careening to their deaths.

The power was one that he exercised with pleasure. When the Earl of Essex told his treason jury in 1600 that Coke was 'play[ing] the orator' and displaying 'the trade and talent of those who value themselves upon their skill in pleading innocent men out of their lives', the remarks contained the soupçon of an aristocratic sneer. But the trade and talent of the boy from Norwich Grammar School was enough to persuade twelve peers to despatch Essex to the chopping block, and Coke would only have taken the complaint as a compliment. For he prosecuted with a passion that went beyond the call of professional duty. It was a quality exemplified in his verbal duel with Raleigh, which has good claim to be the most abusive courtroom battle in England's history.

As was usual, Raleigh had not seen the indictment before coming into court, and he now heard for the first time that he had supposedly agreed with Cobham to raise rebellion on behalf of Spain's king and hand James's crown to a Catholic pretender. That came as little surprise, but Coke then continued, apropos of nothing very much, with lurid accounts of the conspiracies of which the other plotters had been convicted two days before. Raleigh listened in silence for several minutes, before pointing out that their crimes had nothing to do with him. Coke did not deign to reply directly. '[L]ike Sampson's foxes, [the treasons] were joined in the tails though their heads were severed,' he pronounced, before stitching together several non sequiturs of his own. Treason, he explained to the jury, had its root, bud, blossom and fruit, and this was treachery so radical that it had not even been put into effect. The others had already been convicted of plotting against 'the [king] and his cubs', he pointed out, before swivelling towards Raleigh. 'But to whom, Sir Walter, did you bear malice? To the royal children?' As though accosted by a drunkard with a knife,

---

* The first English treatise on the subject appeared in 1593 and contained essays celebrating deformity, ugliness, poverty, blindness, drunkenness, sterility, and stupidity. Its preface claimed that it would be particularly useful to lawyers. See Anthony Munday, *The Defence of Contraries* (London, 1593).

Raleigh's reply was nervous courtesy itself. 'Mr. Attorney, I pray you to whom, or to what end speak you all this? . . . What is the treason of [the others] to me?'

Oozing a vitriol that still hisses from the page, Coke finally homed in on his quarry. 'I will then come close to you. I will prove you to be the most notorious traitor that ever came to the bar.' Raleigh replied that if the lawyer could prove anything at all, he would admit not just that he was a traitor but that he was 'worthy to be crucified with a thousand torments'. 'Nay, I will prove all,' growled Coke. '[T]hou art a monster; thou hast an English face, but a Spanish heart.' He continued with another sustained attack on various betrayals supposedly committed by Lord Cobham, who was awaiting his own trial in a dungeon below the court. 'What is that to me?' Raleigh demanded. 'If my Lord Cobham be a traitor, what is that to me?' Coke erupted with anger. 'All that he did was by thy instigation thou viper, for I *thou* thee, thou traitor!' All the thouing, a form of address conventionally used for children, servants, and animals, threatened to turn the exchange into a slanging match, but Raleigh's retaliation remained restrained. '[Y]ou may call me a traitor at your pleasure, yet it becomes not a man of quality and virtue to do so,' he replied, 'but I take comfort in it, it is all that you can do.' Lord Chief Justice Sir John Popham – a massive presence in a blood-red gown – stepped in to separate the men. 'Mr. Attorney speaks out of the zeal of his duty for the service of the King; and you for your life,' he told Raleigh, 'be patient on both sides.'

Any hope of a clean fight was, however, doomed from the start – for it very soon emerged that the combatants did not even agree on the contest's rules. In particular, they had diametrically opposed ideas about what constituted evidence. When Coke responded to Raleigh's challenge by declaring that he would turn to his proofs, he read aloud an unsigned statement in which Lord Cobham was said to have confessed, four months earlier, that Raleigh had incited him to serve Spain. Raleigh, after reminding the jurors that he had done more than most to subvert Spanish interests, asked that Cobham make the claim to his face. Every defendant, he argued, had the right to confront his accuser. The law of England, like the Book of Deuteronomy, guaranteed that no one could be convicted of treason unless publicly charged by at least two witnesses.

The claim caused consternation among the judges; and although one reason was that Raleigh was simply wrong under the law of the time, the discombobulation reflected more than disagreement over the technicalities of treason. It was still just a few decades since witnesses had first begun to appear in trials – and the judges thought it preposterous to propose that criminal allegations required testimony at all. 'I marvel, Sir Walter, that you, being of such experience and wit, should stand on this point,' said Justice Warburton, 'for many horse-stealers should escape if they may not be condemned without witnesses.' When Raleigh insisted that the whole purpose of a trial was to allow a jury to weigh up the prosecution's evidence, Lord Popham hoisted his bulky frame back into the fray. He had already told the jury that he could personally vouch for the truth of Cobham's confession, having taken it himself, and his intervention was as predictable as it was decisive. No, he declared abruptly, trials did not require witnesses. A person could be convicted on the strength of confessions and statements that had been recorded before the hearing. 'I know not, my Lord, how you conceive the law,' responded Raleigh, 'but if you affirm it, it must be a law to all posterity.' 'Nay, we do not conceive the law,' boomed Popham. 'We know the law.'*

Any doubts that Coke might ever have had about his case were finally dispelled. He returned to the attack, now reciting from statements made by the men already convicted, in which they repeated rumours, second- and third-hand, about Raleigh's willingness to betray England. 'O barbarous!' exploded Raleigh. 'Do you bring the words of these hellish spiders against me? . . . I find not myself touched, scarce named; and the course of proof is strange; if witnesses are to speak by relation to one another, by this means you may have any man's life in a week; and I may be massacred by mere hearsay.' He pleaded again for Cobham to be produced in court but Popham held firm, pointing out – plausibly, if unhelpfully – that he might recant and confuse the jury.

As if to taunt Raleigh, Coke then produced a second statement from Cobham in which he apparently claimed that Raleigh had written to tell him that traitors were immune from punishment in the absence of two accusers. When Raleigh vehemently denied writing such a letter, the prosecutor announced that he would, after all, call a live witness. All heads

---

* Popham's pretensions were destined to become dogma. According to William Blackstone, writing almost two centuries after the trial, judges never made up law but simply discovered a truth that had been there all along: *Commentaries on the Laws of England*, 3rd edn, 4 vols (Oxford, 1768–9), 1: 70.

turned – to see an unknown character step forward. The man identified himself as a sailor called Dyer, and told the jurors that someone in Lisbon had once told him that James would never be crowned king of England because Don Raleigh and Don Cobham would slit his throat first. He then drifted away as mysteriously as he had arrived. A flabbergasted Raleigh inquired how the supposed ramblings of an unknown person in Portugal could possibly implicate him. 'Your treason', snarled Coke, 'had wings.'

As the hearing neared its conclusion and Raleigh pleaded with the jury to judge him as they would want to be judged, Coke demanded 'the last word for the King'. 'Nay, I will have the last word for my life,' replied Raleigh. 'Go to,' exploded the Attorney-General. ' I will lay thee upon thy back for the confidentest traitor that ever came to the bar!' Even the judges now sided with Raleigh until Coke sat down and petulantly accused them of encouraging treachery. They relented, like bad parents with a worse child, and begged him to carry on – which he did, at length. His summary of all the statements that everyone had already heard elicited yet another protest, and Coke let loose with one final spray of abuse. Addressing Raleigh to his face, he condemned him as 'the most vile and execrable traitor that ever lived', 'an odious fellow' whose 'name is hateful to all the realm of England for thy pride'. As cool as his opponent was incontinent, Raleigh wondered which of them deserved the superlatives. 'It will go near to prove a measuring cast between you and me, Mr. Attorney.'

The sympathies of the spectators had indeed shifted. One of James's courtiers later told the king that 'he would have gone a thousand miles to have seen [Raleigh] hanged' at the beginning of the trial, but 'would . . . have gone a thousand to save his life' by its end. 'In half a day', another observer reported, 'the mind of all the company was changed from the extremest hate to the greatest pity.' Coke's attacks inspired such hostility among bystanders, wrote someone else, that 'calling hym base trash [they] begann to hyss' while Coke himself looked 'to be something daunted'. But the lawyer also had the thick skin of a seasoned showman – and the nous to save the best till last. Like a knife thrower with one final trick, Coke now pulled a scroll from his pocket, and the crowd hushed.

He had in his hand, he announced, a signed letter that Cobham had written just the day before. The prisoner had been so troubled by a guilty conscience that he had been unable to sleep and he had now chosen finally to unburden himself. 'I have thought it fit', recited Coke in his powerful voice, 'to write nothing but what is true; for I am not ignorant of my present condition, and now to dissemble with God is no time.' Raleigh, the letter continued, had written to him in his jail cell – not just once, but twice – and urged him to withdraw his accusations of treason. But Cobham would not do so. Indeed, 'craving humble pardon' for his 'double dealing', he now claimed that Raleigh had solicited an annual payment of £1500 from the Spanish government in exchange for his services as a spy.

Raleigh was visibly shaken. He eventually handed up a letter, smuggled out of Cobham's cell, in which the prisoner said precisely the opposite, protesting Raleigh's innocence, but it came as a damp squib after Coke's pyrotechnics. Raleigh admitted also that he had indeed written twice to his old friend, that he had been offered £1500 to be a spy and that he had been wrong to conceal that fact from the court. '[B]ut for attempting or conspiring any treason against the King or the State,' he insisted, 'I still deny it to the death, and it can never be proved against me.' It was all too late. Even if Cobham was a double-dealer on his own admission, Raleigh's own words suddenly sounded like those of a man with secrets to hide.

After the jurors were told by one of Coke's colleagues that the defendant had to prove his innocence, a common view in the seventeenth century, it took them just fifteen minutes to return a guilty verdict. Lord Popham then delivered the standard sentence for traitors, ordering that Raleigh be dragged to the scaffold and half-hanged, before being made to watch while his intestines and penis were tossed into a fire. He was then to be decapitated and cut into quarters, each flank to be disposed of at the king's pleasure.

Such a sight would have made a lot of people very happy in 1603, but Raleigh's life had further to run. He was spared by James and spent more than a decade confined to quarters in the Tower of London, conducting chemistry experiments, writing a history of the world and imagining lands and times far away. Then, in 1616, opportunity knocked. James, ruminating on Raleigh's claims to have stumbled upon the route to El Dorado, had decided that a little unfathomable wealth would be no bad thing. He could, declared the king, set off to find the fabled city – a fifth of all receipts to go to the Crown. Raleigh, presented with one last glimpse of glory, set sail on 12 June 1617. By the time he returned a year later, the dream had turned to dust. Skirmishes and smallpox had devastated his crew. Among the scores of men that he had left buried on the banks of the Orinoco were his lifelong servant and his eldest son. And instead of cargoes of bounty, he trailed in his wake only furious complaints from Spain's ambassador that he had attacked one of that country's colonial outposts.

James, deeply unimpressed with his fifth of nothing, now judged it politic to appease the national enemy. The man who had been condemned for serving Spain was about to pay a heavy price for having offended it, for instead of giving Raleigh another trial the king decided simply to enforce the penalty that he had stayed fifteen years before. Sentence was pronounced at a hearing at which Attorney-General Sir Henry Yelverton delivered a Luciferan epitaph for Raleigh. He had lived 'as a star at which the world hath gazed', he told the judges, 'but stars may fall, nay, they must fall when they trouble the sphere wherein they abide'.

The end came on a chilly morning in late October 1618. The crowd's sympathies were this time squarely with Raleigh. At a time when Elizabethan England was already receding into mythology, his erstwhile arrogance had come to seem fitting to an age of giants, and the doomed quest for El Dorado had tempered its edge with tragedy. The panache with which he now lost his head would propel him into the pantheon of great dead Englishmen. After a long speech that ended with him inviting the spectators to join him in prayer, the sexagenarian, etched and grey, thumbed the blade of the axe that would kill him. It was 'a sharp medicine', he murmured, 'but it will cure all diseases'. He knelt at the block and, told that he was facing westwards – away from the traditionally presumed direction of the Last Judgment – declined to switch direction. 'What matter how the head lie, so [long as] the heart be right?' he asked. His last words, refusing the headsman's offer of a blindfold, were suitably swashbuckling: 'Think you I fear the shadow of the axe, when I fear not the axe itself?' The show was over – and with a final flourish, Raleigh threw his arms above his shoulders to call down the curtain.

Whether Raleigh was in fact innocent of the treason charges laid against him in 1603 is as questionable today as it was four centuries ago. He certainly had reason to fear that his influence would decline after Elizabeth's death, and although his score sheet against Spain was impressive, he lived in an age when allegiances were honoured in the breach as much as in the observance. For what it was worth, Cobham reasserted Raleigh's guilt at his own trial and maintained the accusation 'upon the hope of his soul's resurrection' as he stood upon his scaffold.

Raleigh's trial was important, however, for reasons that transcended the truth or falsity of the charges. The sight of him struggling for his life against a phantom accuser, damned by documents that were dealt out like a blackjack hand, was so palpably unfair that it almost immediately became a model for how things ought not to be done. Several of the king's advisers – including Edward Coke – urged James in 1618 to give him a second trial, with witnesses; and although the monarch remained ruthless as ever, reminding them that Raleigh had 'by his wit . . . turned the hatred of men into compassion,' the proceedings would fall ever deeper into disrepute. Raleigh himself claimed at his condemnation that one of the judges had repented of his role at Winchester from his deathbed. By 1656, an anonymous pamphleteer was swearing that Coke had privately expressed shock at the jury's verdict, while another writer recorded that the jurors had knelt to beg Raleigh's forgiveness after convicting him. All the stories were as incredible as they sound, but the speed with which they were recounted and believed is a sign of just how emblematic the trial had become. The myths would in time contribute to ideas even more far-reaching: that courts were there to limit state power as much as to express it; that prosecutions could be unfair even if a defendant was guilty; and that justice was done only if seen to be done. And they did so simply because transparency had made the unfairness of the alternative so manifest.

An ironic postscript is that few people did more to promote the vision of liberty that would accompany the sanctification of Raleigh's trial than Sir Edward Coke himself. In 1606, King James promoted his Attorney-General to Chief Justice of Common Pleas, at which point the erstwhile lapdog clenched his teeth around the hand that had fed him and bit – hard. For the two decades that remained of his life, he would not let go. At a time of political turmoil, when thinkers across Europe were pondering the ideal relationship between God, monarch, and subject, James had written a treatise arguing that kings were above human laws and followed them voluntarily, if at all. Coke, by way of several court rulings, case reports and a monumental textbook, begged to differ, insisting that rulers obeyed because they had to. To cut a very long story extremely short, his arguments won. The Puritan rebels who chopped off the head of James's son, Charles I, cited him as their legal authority in 1649. Towards the end of the next century, his work would enjoy an even more lasting impact –

inspiring American revolutionaries from John Adams to Thomas Jefferson, when they too concluded that it was time to cut their rulers down to size.

Raleigh's claim that criminal trials were public arguments over the meaning of testimony would, of course, be vindicated, but a crucial issue remained unresolved. The ancient notion that jurors themselves were somehow witnesses had always made for a certain tension as to their proper role. It was widely agreed that juries decided questions of fact, but those decisions could be regarded as statements so sacrosanct as to be unquestionable. They might alternatively be seen as lies, tantamount to perjury. Which view prevailed depended simply on whether judges would presume to decide that jurors had breached their oaths to God.

The chances that judges would do so had built throughout the 1500s, as England's expanding middle class grew ever more likely to stand up to their social superiors. By the end of the century, it was becoming increasingly common for judges to fine jurors – sometimes for returning a supposedly corrupt verdict, and sometimes simply for breaching the ancient rules requiring that they deliberate without food, drink, and fire. John Mucklow was imprisoned and fined twenty shillings in the mid 1570s after being caught smuggling preserved barberries, sugar candy, and liquorice into the jury room. A decade later, several jurors who were taking too long over their verdicts were searched and again found to be in possession of contraband: two who confessed to eating figs were fined £5 apiece, and three who admitted possession, but not consumption, of apples, had to pay forty shillings. Such disputes turned on fruit, but they reflected an issue that was anything but trifling: the ancient question of who in the community wielded the ultimate power to judge.

The case that brought the conflict to a head – the prosecution of two Quaker activists in 1670 – could hardly have been more perfectly designed to do so. In a country still rolling with the aftershocks of a civil war that had seen a monarch executed, the Church abolished, and each institution revived within a dozen years, deference was in short supply. Nonconformists such as the Puritans had led the revolt against King Charles I, while countless other sects had thrived during the subsequent eclipse of Anglicanism, and few had been friendly towards the notion of secular rule. Several had theological objections to tax. Some had a problem with human law in its entirety. All were anathema to the restored forces of royalism.

Almost as soon as it took power, the new government had enacted statutes to reassert the authority of the official Church. The most draconian was the Conventicle Act of 1664, which made it an offence – punishable by death, if repeated – to participate in any act of nonconformist worship involving more than four people. Over the next few years, thousands of prosecutions were launched, and hundreds of dissenters were transported or executed for violating the statute. The Act came up for renewal in 1670, provoking protests across England. One of the demonstrations, staged by Quakers, would give rise to the most significant jury trial in history.

The Quakers were a threatening bunch from the standpoint of the status quo. Founded by a man who claimed a hundred and fifty miracles to his credit and named for their tendency to tremble and yelp while at prayer, adherents rarely met a convention that they did not despise. Some regarded clothes as superfluous and perambulated in the nude. Others went in the opposite direction and kept their hats on in the presence of social superiors – an expression of sartorial independence that sometimes inspired no less distress than the nudity. Several set out to undermine the greatest certainty of all, staging enthusiastic attempts to raise the dead. The eccentricity was accompanied by a dynamism that put them at the front line of resistance during the 1660s, and when word spread in August 1670 that they would be holding a prayer meeting at a hall in London's Gracechurch Street, the authorities took no chances. Would-be worshippers arrived to find the doors padlocked. Among those worshippers, however, were two men who realized that the closure made a protest easier than ever. Turning to a crowd that was perhaps a hundred times the size permitted by the Conventicle Act, a 25-year-old called William Penn began to speak. Within minutes, he and a 42-year old linen draper by the name of William Mead were under arrest.

Battle was joined two weeks later at the Sessions House of the Old Bailey. The Fire of London had reduced much of the capital to waste four years before and its courthouse had been temporarily relocated into a wooden shack; but the surroundings belied the significance of the moment. The people present, who included five aldermen and a hundred or so spectators, were in for a magnificent show.

Presiding over the court were London's two most senior judges – its staunchly royalist* Lord Mayor, Samuel Starling, and Recorder Thomas Howel – and they were resolved from the outset to make an example of the nonconformist troublemakers. Both defendants were kept waiting in the malodorous holding cell for the sitting's entire first day, while the court processed assorted ruffians and cutpurses instead, and when it reconvened two days later, the judges were ready with a second surprise. Aware of the Quaker's touchiness about headgear, Samuel Starling had determined to cite both men for contempt as soon as they entered court – and when an over-eager bailiff accidentally upset his plans, he refused to be denied. 'Sirrah, who bid you put off their hats?' he yelled. 'Put [them] back on again.' The defendants were duly re-hatted, whereupon Thomas Howel fined them forty marks (a sum that could have paid for another hundred hats) for refusing to take them off again.

The authorities had charged both men with addressing a tumultuous assembly, a violation of common-law custom – doubtless concerned that a charge under the Conventicle Act might turn the trial into a direct assault on the statute. But Penn was not someone who could be so easily wrongfooted. A portrait painted some four years earlier shows an elegant and self-possessed young man, and although a committed religious rebel, he was easily the social and intellectual equal of his judges. The son of an admiralty official acquainted with King Charles II, he had studied at Oxford – before, on  his own account, being 'banisht' – and the contrariness that then took him into several jails had not stopped him from picking up a legal education at

---

* Starling had served as a juror at the trials of those involved in the execution of King Charles I, and boasted that eighteen times out of eighteen, he had voted to convict. See S[amuel] S[tarling], *An Answer To the Seditious and Scandalous Pamphlet, Entituled, The Tryal of W. Penn and W. Mead . . .* (London, 1671), p. 6.

Lincoln's Inn. And like any eighteenth-century Quaker, he could talk the talk at least as well as he walked the walk. Told the charges against him, he asked that they be put in writing because they were too long to remember and then demanded to know 'upon what law you ground my indictment'. Thomas Howel replied it was based on 'the common law'. And where, Penn asked, might that be found? The flustered judge took refuge in Latin, declaring that it was *lex non scripta* – or unwritten law – and a thing 'which many have studied thirty or forty years to know'. If it was that hard to understand, countered Penn, it did not sound very common at all.

It was presumably crowd-pleasing stuff, but the trial itself, like most hearings of the period, was a perfunctory affair. Four men trooped through the witness box to state that Mead had been at Gracechurch Street, that Penn had 'preached' words that they could not recall, and that there had been several hundred people on the scene. When the defendants tried to address the jurors – contending that they should not be convicted because they had not incited violence, and pleading with them to remember that their verdicts would affect tens of thousands of lives – they were swiftly dragged into the holding cell. As Penn tried to continue his speech from below the court, Howel told the jury that they had heard evidence proving the indictment and should now return their verdict. There is no doubt what he expected it to be.

But events then took an unexpected turn. The jurors asked for time to consider their decision – a request that was in itself becoming unusual by the late seventeenth century – and it was an hour and a half before they returned. Eight were ready to convict, but four of them, led by a wealthy Puritan sugar merchant named Edward Bushel, were not prepared to do so. Starling declared Bushel 'impudent', and the jurors were sent away to think again. If the rebuke was supposed to fortify the majority, the judges were in for a shock. By the time the jurors returned, Bushel had been elected their foreman, and he now declared that Penn was 'guilty of speaking in Grace-Church Street'. Since speech alone had never been a crime under English law, *non scripta* or otherwise, the finding amounted to a verdict of not guilty. 'Is that all?' snapped Howel. 'You had as good say nothing.' Sent off again, the jurors asked for a pen, ink, and paper and returned with a verdict in writing. Penn was guilty only of speaking, they repeated, and Mead was not guilty, full stop. Howel coldly informed them that they would not be going home until they had reversed both decisions.

The court would meanwhile adjourn for the night. And after reminding the bailiff of his traditional duty to withhold food, drink, and fire from the jurors, he added the novel instruction that they be denied a chamber pot.

The court reassembled at seven the next morning. Hungry, thirsty, and smelly the twelve men in the box may have been, but they were even more resolute. Bushel, asked for a verdict, repeated that Penn was guilty of speaking in Gracechurch Street. 'To an unlawful assembly?' inquired Starling, menacingly. 'No, my Lord,' replied Bushel, 'we give no other verdict than what we gave last night; we have no other verdict to give.' Starling, livid, declared that he would cut Bushel's throat if he ever got the chance. The jurors were sent away again.

They eventually returned to reconfirm that they had nothing to add, and the judges finally snapped. An apoplectic Starling abused them for their choice of foreman, and threatened to slit Bushel's nose. When Penn protested, the Lord Mayor told the jailer to gag him and spluttered that he should also be chained to a stake. Recorder Howel was no happier. 'Till now', he bellowed, 'I never understood the reason of the . . . Spaniards, in suffering the inquisition among them: and certainly it will never be well with us, till something like unto the Spanish Inquisition be in England.' The twelve men, he declared, would either convict or starve. Another night in Newgate's fetid dungeons followed. But the jurors were no longer teetering on the brink. They had hit the bottom and bounced. On the following morning, they formally returned not guilty verdicts against both defendants.

Thomas Howel imposed swingeing fines on everyone, with indefinite jail terms for those who would not pay – and Bushel, along with three of his colleagues, chose jail. Their resilience was remarkable. Typhoid and dysentery were so endemic in prisons of the time that around one in ten inmates died awaiting trial, and no judge had ever before entertained a complaint against another's decision to punish his jurors. But after they had spent ten weeks in Newgate's excremental gloom, Lord Chief Justice Vaughan agreed to hear their request to be released – and he then freed them by way of the most significant legal ruling in the history of the jury trial. Two people, he insisted, could honestly disagree even when bound by oath. After almost half a millennium, the idea that a juror swore to what he knew rather than to what he believed was finally laid to rest. '[T]he Verdict of a Jury, and Evidence of a Witness are very different things,' explained Vaughan. '[A] witness swears but to what he hath heard or seen . . . [b]ut a jury-man swears to what he can infer and conclude from the testimony of such witnesses by the act and force of his understanding . . . .'

Vaughan's assertion of a power to clamp down on oppressive judges, made in a ruling known to lawyers ever since as Bushel's Case, was soon being complemented by political changes on a broader front. Less than two decades after he handed down his judgment, the 'Glorious Revolution' of 1689 reasserted Parliamentary control of the British monarchy, finally putting paid to its ancient claims of absolute prerogatives. In the new climate, the judicial advantages previously guaranteed to the executive were steadily eroded. Accused traitors, and then felons in general, were given the right to call witnesses in the early 1700s and judges increasingly permitted prisoners to instruct counsel over the next few decades.

The consequences for criminal justice would be dramatic. Trials had for several centuries been free-for-alls, at which lawyers appeared only to represent the state and only in the most serious cases, while judges, jurors and defendants argued amongst themselves in the large majority. But the arrival of defence counsel, which was complemented by the professionalization of prosecution, turned trials into structured disputes over the meaning of legal history – or 'precedent', as the lawyers called it. As they cited from their tomes and cross-referred to each other's cases, countless rules and conclusions were soon being firmed up. By the middle of the eighteenth century, the customary suspicion of certain types of evidence such as hearsay was being formalized into rules of admissibility and exclusion. Towards its end, an even more far-reaching change took place as the presumption of innocence, previously little more than an aspiration, was promoted to axiom.

The jury was simultaneously propelled into the moral stratosphere. The myth of justice that had been gripping England since the time of Walter Raleigh had found its institutional hero: a body of men so brave it would go to jail for the underdog, and so selfless it would forgo its collective chamber pot for love of liberty. There would always be some controversialists prepared to point out that jurors slept on the job and hanged children as well, but the most influential legal writer of the eighteenth century, William Blackstone, was not one of them. In his mammoth compilation of the criminal law, still annually updated and cited in England's courts, he assured readers during the 1760s that judgment by twelve men 'indifferently chosen, and superior to all suspicion' was the 'sacred bulwark' of the nation's liberties.

The system was also laying down deep roots far beyond Britain. King James had guaranteed jury trials in 1606 to the first emigrants to Virginia, and although settlers' leaders would still try to monopolize power with magistrates' courts, juries soon became commonplace across colonial America. William Penn himself crossed the Atlantic twelve years after his 1670 trial and the founding laws of Pennsylvania, the province that he then founded in honour of his father, promised that twelve men would have 'the final judgment' in every case. By 1735, when a New York jury acquitted a printer called John Peter Zenger in the teeth of a judge's instructions that the truth of his words could be no defence to a charge of sedition, American jurors were flexing their muscles at least as much as their English counterparts. They were also idealized no less than in England. The colonists read Blackstone and devoured the anti-executive arguments of Edward Coke, harbouring hopes and grievances that were virtually defined by England's political struggles, and the right to an open jury trial was close to the top of their wish list. It was the only guarantee contained in all twelve state constitutions that existed in 1776, while the federal constitution that was framed at Philadelphia eleven years later envisaged that the US government would suspend access to courts only in the event of 'rebellion or invasion'.

There were, however, less exalted reasons for the popularity of juries. Trials simply offered a lot to see. Courts were becoming more packed than ever, regularly punctuated by fights and occasionally the scene of gun-shots and murders.* Entire communities could be agitated: perhaps most

---

* Several incidents of courtroom violence are recorded in a 1688 collection of law reports, and an assault committed by a felon called Henry Gillingham, indicted at Salisbury in the summer of 1631, deserves particular mention if only for the eccentricity of the language used to record it. Lawyers of the time traditionally wrote in Law French, a bastardized dialect dating back to the Norman Conquest, and the marginal note of Gillingham's deed – which involved unsuccessfully throwing a missile at his judge – records that he 'ject un Brickbat a le . . . Justice que narrowly mist'. The judge then ordered that he have 'son dexter manus ampute & fix al Gibbet' on which he was 'immediate-ment hange in presence de Court'. See James Dyer, *Les Reports des Divers select Matters & Resolutions des Reverend Judges & Sages del Ley* (aka *Dyers King's Bench Reports*) (London, 1688 edn), p. 188b.

literally when the weight of spectators at East Grinstead in 1684 caused the floor to collapse, and perhaps most metaphorically during the notorious witchcraft prosecutions of Salem eight years later.* Attendance also became an essential part of any respectable person's education during the eighteenth century, as edifying as a trip to the local condemned cells or lunatic asylum. Foreign travellers, hoping to glean lessons about English liberty, became regulars. Gentlemen in the public gallery, eager to contribute to the increasingly legalistic debates, would sometimes interrupt to identify defects in the indictment and advance points in favour of a defendant.

The Old Bailey retained its particular cachet, with one observer complaining by 1786 that 'no one who hath any real business to do can have access', but provincial sittings, or assizes, offered a show that was in many ways even more fascinating. Judges would roll into town twice each year, solemn as sphinxes in their crimson robes and long-bottomed wigs and preceded by up to twenty trumpeters and javelin-wielding officials. As they were wined and dined by the ruddy squires of the county, surrounding dungeons trembled into life. Prisoners clanked their way to the courthouse through the night, and after a sermon and swearing-in ceremony the next morning, the jurors would get to work on their case load – typically deciding within minutes whether to acquit or convict. Anyone found guilty of murder would receive an immediate sentence of death, but other convicts would be holed up to await the assizes' grand finale. The judge would, on the appointed day of judgment, work his way up the ladder of wickedness and close the proceedings with one of two props. If he were leaving with no blood on his hands, he would pull on a pair of white gloves. Rather more often, he would deliver his final sentences wearing the black cap of death.

The media mirrored and magnified the appeal of such occasions. Literacy had been sufficiently prevalent to generate junk journalism since the late sixteenth century, and by the eighteenth, true-crime pamphlets were routinely vying for public attention alongside other staples of the hack printer: recent comets, monstrous births, and so on. Continental writers, excluded from courtrooms and usually subject to censorship,

---

* See pp. 132–40.

could sometimes exploit the sexual scandals that were played out in eccle-siastical courts but were otherwise restricted to writing about the crime that preceded a trial and the punishment that followed it. Their British counterparts faced no such obstacles.

A twenty-four-page booklet had set the ball rolling in August 1566 with an account of the prosecution of Agnes Waterhouse – condemned for witchery with a diabolical dog and a white cat called Satan – and trial reports were soon a fixture on the pedlar's cart. The cut-and-thrust of cross-examination usually offered ready-made dialogue. Even when absent the drama could be gripping: a report from the early seventeenth century, for example, told how the blanched corpses of three children began to bleed reproachfully when their murderous father obeyed a judge's order to call out their name. One popular 1606 story neatly combined speech and silence, telling of a poor little dumb girl who had managed to croak accusingly at the man who had torn out her tongue notwithstanding that the jurors could 'not see so much as [a] stumpe' in her mouth. The evidence evidently spoke no less eloquently: the defendant went to the gallows.

By the 1670s, suitably salacious and brutal trials were being reported within days of a verdict. Eager readers in 1698 might have chosen to con-sider the depravity of Captain Edward Rigby, pilloried for attempted sodomy after picking up William Minton at a firework display in St James's Park. Rigby pleaded guilty in the hope of a quiet life, but the court itself ordered that its proceedings be published. All literate England could soon pay to recoil from the news that he had 'put his Privy Member Erected into Minton's Hand; kist him, and put his Tongue into Minton's Mouth' before expounding on the antiquity of anal intercourse and placing a 'Finger to [his] Fundament'. There were salutary lessons to suit every taste. Someone disinclined to weigh the wages of sin might, for example, have preferred to contemplate the quality of mercy – perhaps by ponder-ing the luck of Mary Price, acquitted of bestiality in 1704 notwithstanding her housemate's claims to have watched through the floorboards as she copulated with a dog.

But although jury trials were offering much to mull over by the eighteenth century, another aspect of criminal justice was still far more visible: the punishments that followed them. Tattooed and maimed con-victs stalked the streets of every city, while lesser deviants sat in stocks and dangled from pillories, braving rotting animals and vegetables if they were lucky and storms of rocks if they were not. The displays were a feature of the landscape from Nuremberg to New York, but they were becoming especially impressive in England. Although a 1718 statute providing for transportation to the colonies removed plenty of convicts from the public gaze, public mutilations continued apace and the number of capital offences also soared – from about fifty in 1688 to well over two hundred in 1810. Few villages lacked for a whipping post, while executions could turn the humblest provincial town into a fairground, drawing thousands of visitors and pumping a fortune into the local economy.

London hosted the grandest spectacle of all, spewing out capital offenders from Newgate every six weeks for transportation across the capital to the Tyburn gallows. The procession had been growing increasingly animated during the seventeenth century, and by the 1720s it was tumultuous indeed. The condemned travelled in open carts, noosed and astride their own coffins, as church bells tolled and crowds cheered them on their way. They wore anything they chose – perhaps velvet, scarlet, and silk with a white cockade to protest their innocence, perhaps a simple burial shroud to acknowledge their guilt – while high-spirited onlookers handed up tankards of ale, asking only that the prisoners buy a round on the way back. The jollity reached a climax under the triangular beams of Tyburn. Convicts who spoke with grace or humour received roars of approbation, while the surly and the sullen were booed and pelted. When the bodies were finally 'turned off' and the souls 'launched into eternity', to use the clichés of the day, chaos would erupt. While acquaintances of the dying tried to shorten their agonies by leaping for the dribbling, jerking legs, hangmen auctioned their clothes and emissaries from London's surgeons' colleges hopped from rope to rope in the hope of scavenging an unwanted cadaver.

The commotion, macabre even by the standards of the time, regularly attracted tens of thousands of spectators and exercised a fascination that spanned class and nationality. César de Saussure, a young Swiss gentleman who whiled away several months in London during the 1720s, was impressed enough to describe it at length in a letter to his mother. 'You see most amusing scenes between the people who do not like the bodies to be cut up and the messengers the surgeons have sent for the bodies,' he enthused. '[B]lows are given and returned before they can be got away, and sometimes in the turmoil the bodies are quickly removed and buried.'

Amusing it may have been, but the increasing frequency and intensifying violence of executions, at a time when juries were being sanctified and courtrooms were formulating rigid rules to guarantee fairness, had a peculiarly paradoxical effect. Trials became almost perverse rituals of cruelty and mercy, at which the dignity afforded the defendant resembled nothing so much as the head start given a fox. Whether a suspect lived or died was in many ways less important than that the chase proceeded by the rules. The responsibility for punishment was meanwhile shuffled around court until it belonged to everyone and no one, and all were free to lament the fate of the person they were killing. At a time when English and American juries were becoming celebrated for their 'pious perjury' – undervaluing stolen goods so as to spare petty thieves the gallows – they continued to convict most capital offenders (a full two-thirds in England, of whom 90 per cent in London were under twenty-one). The role played by judges was no more coherent. While they typically warned juries of the awful consequences of leniency, they simultaneously repaired the damage behind the scenes – recommending so many pardons that three out of four English death sentences were being commuted by the end of the eighteenth century.

It all made for emotional tensions aplenty. After Chief Justice Ryder had to deal with a young woman charged with killing her 6-month-old baby in 1754, he confided to his diary that he had been so affected by his own speech to the jurors 'that the tears were gushing out several times against my will. It was discerned by all the company – which was large – and a lady gave me her handkerchief dipped in lavender water to help me.' He nevertheless encouraged the jury to put aside any doubts about the defendant's sanity, and remained sufficiently stoical to sentence her to death, with an instruction that her body be dissected for the benefit of medical science. Even more lachrymose was the 1777 forgery trial of the Revd Dr William Dodd. 'The judges, the jury, the counsel, the spectators, all the world was bathed in tears,' observed a bemused German visitor. Horrid though it sounds, the jury convicted after ten minutes and Dodd also hanged without a pardon.

For much of the eighteenth century, courtroom and gallows seemed to complement each other. Foreign visitors to England were repeatedly struck by the contrast between the safeguards of English trials and the brutality of its punishments, but in an era of Georgian gentility, when sentimentality and rigour were different sides of the same moral coin, the English rarely seemed to perceive a contradiction. Just as the pamphleteers began their accounts with the foul deed and ended with its just desserts, courtroom spectators were generally no less eager to see the deadly denouements. But towards the century's end, the balance finally began to tilt away from executions, and would continue to tip for several more decades. The reason was not that the courtroom contest became even more thrilling. It was that punishments began literally to disappear.

Eighteenth-century thinkers, convinced that sufficiently rational laws could facilitate progress and possibly even perfection, were always fascinated by crime and punishment, and as each escalated in tandem they could not but wonder what was going wrong. Some argued that the brutality was counter-productive – pointing out, for example, that marking convicts by clipping their ears and slitting their nostrils was not likely to assist their employment prospects. Equally common, if more abstruse, was the belief that penalties had become decoupled from the crimes for which they were imposed, and that the symbolic links needed tightening. Thomas Jefferson was among those who took such a view, and in 1778 he drafted a law for Virginia that would have poisoned poisoners and castrated rapists. The American also believed, for reasons which are sadly not recorded, that it was appropriate to drill half-inch holes through the noses of female polygamists. His attempt to rationalize Virginian law was never enacted.

Capital punishment, which almost everyone agreed was not doing enough to deter crime, inspired particular concern. Some argued that its imposition was so capricious as to be useless, and gazed admiringly towards the proverbially enlightened despotisms of Russia and the Austro-Hungarian Empire, where it had just been abolished. More common was the belief that executions were inherently sound, and that a tad more terror would repair such defects as the system might possess. Britain's Parliament in 1752 accordingly authorized judges to order the posthumous tarring and chaining of criminals' corpses, as and when they thought that that would frighten more people for longer. Others envisaged even more dramatic ways to maximize the fear. James Boswell proposed in 1783 that convicts should be hanged without hoods 'that the distortions may be seen'. In an ideal world, he argued, criminals would have their heads publicly smashed open with an iron mallet, before being jugulated with a machete and hacked apart with an axe.

But at the same time, there were others who felt that the public displays of aggression, no matter how well intentioned, were in fact doing more harm than good. As far back as 1725, one writer had warned that hangings were attended disproportionately by drunks, prostitutes, and pickpockets, and that potential criminals were enjoying the killings far too much to be deterred by them. Over subsequent decades, crowds had become increasingly violent, frequently trying to free prisoners and often launching assaults, up to and including murder, on the executioners and surgeons present. The phenomenon, seen across Europe, inspired British legislators in 1783 to replace the Tyburn processions with stationary executions outside Newgate. But the volatility also gave rise to far more radical proposals for reform. Tinkering with the spectacle was no solution to rising crime, argued some – because publicity itself was the problem.

The reasoning had first been set out in 1751. Henry Fielding, a London magistrate as well as the author of classics such as *Tom Jones*, had set out to explore why London seemed to be experiencing an upsurge in robberies. He assumed, like almost everyone else, that inefficient penalties were the primary cause; but instead of suggesting that their violence be increased, he proposed instead that it be hidden. According to Fielding, it was the delay between trial and execution that created pity for capital offenders, and it was the opportunity granted those offenders to address the gallows crowd that turned them into victims or heroes. Swiftness and secrecy were therefore essential. Prisoners should be hanged in the yard of the court in which they had been tried, within four days of conviction, watched in silence by the robed and bewigged judges who had sentenced them. 'Nothing . . . can be imagined more terrible,' he urged – and writer that he was, he knew that it was imagination rather than sight that produced fear. Shakespeare's *Macbeth* served to illustrate the point. 'A murder behind the scenes', he explained, 'will affect the audience with greater terror than if it was acted before their eyes.' *

Fielding's proposal was a little too avant-garde to be enacted, but it would influence legislators for the next century and heralded an era in which power would be expressed as much by concealment as by

---

* In this context, it is interesting to note that Fielding's half-brother, also a magistrate, was blind.

display. Branding irons, whipping posts, and pillories were being abandoned across the Western world by the late eighteenth century. Do-gooders, inspired by the hope of making convicts work, pray, and see the error of their ways, would soon perfect a new kind of prison – the penitentiary or reformatory – which made its debut in the eastern United States at the turn of the century. The causes driving the change varied considerably from country to country (a major impetus in Britain was the American Revolution of 1776, which robbed the country of its largest penal dustbin overnight), but the shift was seen throughout Europe and America. And during the nineteenth century it began to fuel demands to conceal the most visible punitive spectacle of all – the public execution.

Those who campaigned most strongly for reform were the politicians who most favoured the death penalty – because they feared that the unruliness and unpleasantness of the public ritual was beginning to threaten its continued existence. For precisely opposite reasons, resistance was led by abolitionists – men like Samuel Bowne, a Quaker Assemblyman in New York, who argued against the concealment of public throttlings in 1834 on the grounds that popular disgust would soon lead 'to the entire abolition of capital punishment'. And the supporters of death were soon making the running. Their first success came with a ban on public executions in Rhode Island in 1833 – followed within two years by similar laws in Pennsylvania, New York, New Jersey, and Massachusetts. British opponents of capital punishment fought a similar battle to keep the horror visible, but they too were destined to be out-manoeuvred. On 29 May 1868, three days after one last hanging – before a seething crowd that yelled 'body-snatcher' at the executioner as he cut down the corpse – supporters of the death penalty were able finally to hide it behind prison walls.

Public hangings very probably originated as a sacrificial rite and their concealment in many ways restored the mystery that a century of rationalism had threatened to dispel. For the most immediate effect, just as abolitionists had feared, was to stabilize an institution that had at certain points in the early 1800s begun to seem very wobbly indeed. English hangmen would continue secretly to snap necks for another century. In the United States, where men and women are still poisoned and gassed in hidden chambers, popular support for the death penalty may well be stronger than it was two hundred years ago.

But the change also had another consequence – for as the punishments that had exemplified Western justice for centuries vanished, criminal trials assumed a more prominent position than ever before. New York produced America's first true-crime journal, the *National Police Gazette*, in 1845 – a decade after its legislature did away with public hangings – while the *Illustrated Police News* first hit London's newsstands in 1864, just four years before Britain's Parliament followed suit. A similar shift was seen elsewhere in Europe. In Prussia, the first German state to end public executions, the same statute that relocated the beheadings to prison yards in 1851 opened the kingdom's trials to the public. Equivalent laws did the same throughout the rest of Germany over the next three decades, and by the end of the century day trips to court had become a popular pastime among middle-class families across the country.

In France, the story was a little different. The legal reforms that followed the Revolution of 1789 threw its courts open to the public and guaranteed defendants a right to counsel. They also gave ordinary citizens a role in judging criminal cases, creating a form of the jury that spread, through cultural influence and Napoleonic campaigns, from Madrid to Moscow over the next three-quarters of a century. The country bucked the penal trend by continuing to stage public executions right up to 1939, later than any other country in the Western world, but its experience of publicity also exemplified the growing significance of the criminal trial.

Over the course of the eighteenth century, France's liberal thinkers had developed a deep admiration for the transparency of English criminal justice. '[I]n England no trial is secret,' Voltaire had explained in an impassioned attack on the inquisitorial system in 1762, 'because the punishment of crime is meant to be a lesson to the public . . . and not vengeance for one person. Witnesses testify in open court and any trial of interest is reported in the newspapers.' Attitudes towards the jury itself had always been considerably more equivocal however, and French jurists were very soon having second thoughts about its wisdom.

In 1804, soundings were taken from seventy-five courts across the nation as to whether juries should be retained. The Anglophilia of men like Voltaire was a thing of the past – not least, because France was at war with Britain – and the fifty-two jurisdictions that replied were split precisely in half. One court that expressed an especially firm *non* was that of Doubs. Jury service, argued its judges, was a task that could only appeal to citizens as primitive as those of England. 'At the theatre, the Englishman only cares for ghosts, lunatics, dreadful criminals and drawn-out murders; he scurries to animal fights, and probably regrets the passing of gladiatorial contests,' they observed. '[W]ho can tell if he does not seek the functions of a juror for the pleasure of watching a criminal struggling with his conscience, with the death that awaits him? The Frenchman, on the contrary, is delicate in all his tastes; he flees from any sight which could disagreeably awaken his sensitivity; could he take any pleasure in wielding the bleeding sword of justice?'

The assessment was an audacious one. Frenchmen had just guillotined thousands of their compatriots, and possessed such enthusiasm for the bleeding sword of justice that they would watch its blade rise and fall in public for another 135 years. The sight of squirming criminals was also doing little to repulse them: the world's first newspaper dedicated exclusively to court reporting, the *Gazette des Tribunaux*, was launched within months of the 1791 law that had thrown open the doors of France's trials. But the judges of Doubs were chauvinistic rather than simply wrong. Prurience had always been potential in English trials, even if its source had been publicity rather than juries. And as France moved from inquisitorial secrecy to routine openness, it would take to the voyeuristic pleasures of the courtroom with delight.

The country's cities, like others throughout mainland Europe, were soon making strenuous efforts not merely to accommodate a growing popular interest in courtrooms, but to promote it. 'Palaces of Justice' were built across the country during the nineteenth century: newfangled monuments to open justice, packed to their triforia with crucifixes, statuary, and all the trappings of tradition that its absence could demand. As congregants flocked in, it became increasingly common to issue tickets in order that the classes and sexes could be properly segregated – a development simultaneously seen in England – and the trials of lowlifes were soon pulling in the *haut monde*. The December 1869 prosecution for multiple murder of Jean-Baptiste Troppmann inspired particular interest. His case had been intriguing Parisians from the moment that the six victims had been laid out behind plate glass at the city morgue three months before, and over twenty thousand applications were made for admission passes. Only several hundred were lucky enough to make it into the trial chamber, a magnificent judicial temple inaugurated just a year before, but few who did so would have been disappointed. For three days they trained opera glasses on the dock, perhaps picking up clues from Troppmann's physiognomy, and pondered the table that dominated the room – spread with bloody garments, blades and a jar swimming with the stomach contents of one of the deceased. Aristocrats, socialites and workers attended in force, and so many women were present that *Le Petit journal* marvelled how 'strange' it was that ladies 'raised in velvets, lace and silk' should display such 'mad unbridled passion . . . for the coarse details and repugnant debates' of the case.

That particular concern was widely shared. When Adelaide Bartlett stood trial at the Old Bailey in 1886 for chloroforming her husband – in a case involving a love triangle and liberal condom use – the judge publicly condemned the relish of women in the public gallery for evidence that he and the jurors could hear only with shame. By 1896 one French doctor was expressing not only distaste, but fear. The libertines of *fin-de-siècle* France had developed something of a vogue for throwing acid into their lovers' faces, and Paul Aubry proposed that even reading about a *vitrioleuse* might be enough to launch the female reader (who was 'often not very intelligent') on some passionate mischief of her own. 'What else

The Advocate (Counsel for the Defence)
(Honoré Daumier, c.1860).

does she need to excite [her] imagination?' he asked rhetorically. 'It is easy to throw vitriol at someone [and] one is sure to be acquitted and to be the subject of gossip for forty-eight hours.'

But whatever the other moral consequences of the intensifying court-room drama, the Troppmann trial suggested that the weaker sex was made of rather sterner stuff than their would-be protectors realized. Following the defendant's conviction, several distinguished Parisiennes wrote to *Le Figaro* to complain that the newspaper's correspondent had not acknowledged their presence at court. René de Pont-Just, though as suspicious of female spectators as the next man, was at least capable of irony. He drily explained that the courtroom audience had included 'both ladies and women' and that he had held his tongue for fear of confusing the *dames* with the *femmes*.

Jury trial had come a long way since a desperate murderer called Alice had squealed on five of her co-accused at Westminster in 1220. Just how far was marked, in ways both geographic and historical, by the 1880 publication of Fyodor Dostoevsky's *The Brothers Karamazov*. Juries had been introduced to Russia fourteen years before and the novel concludes with the prosecu-tion of Dmitri Karamazov for the murder of his father, in a courtroom that would have been familiar to readers from Paris to San Francisco. Tickets have been snapped up by luminaries from miles around, lorgnettes twinkle in the audience, and counsel joust across a table stacked with a bloodied silk dressing gown, a blood-stiffened handkerchief, a pistol, a pestle, and a slender pink ribbon. The spectacle, as compelling as it is mysterious, somehow implicates everyone present – and the shared shame is spelled out when Dmitri's brother, Ivan, deliriously characterizes the spectators' lust for bread and circuses as equal to any act of parricide.

Ivan Karamazov had very personal reasons for his distress, but it was shared by right-thinking folk everywhere. French commentators and English hacks rarely reported a trial without tut-tutting at the onlookers. If it was not the fact of their femininity, it might be their eagerness to applaud, their willingness to bring food to court, or their 'morbid curiosity' – attacked, of course, in articles that went on to describe every twitch and tremor of the defendant.

The concerns all echoed those that had been expressed not so long before about public executions. But the bread and circuses of the courtroom constituted a very different diversion from the gallows spectacle. Sobs, applause, and whispers had replaced the howls of hatred. Packed lunches had taken the place of Tyburn's gin-soaked procession. And although the verdict in a high-profile case could still bring traffic to a halt – gridlocking the entire West End of London in the case of one murder acquittal in 1907 – crowds now preferred queueing to rioting. A decision not to issue tickets might cause the lines to form long before sunrise, and spectators might over-flow far beyond the court itself, but attendees always knew their place. When Dr Hawley Harvey Crippen was arraigned for his wife's murder in 1910 – at a trial which saw a shred of her skin passed around on a dish – a multitude of the ticketless swarmed outside the Old Bailey until police steered them into an empty court. Only after several hours of picnicking and chattering did they realize that they had been duped – at which point they drifted home.

The jury trial had further to travel, but by the turn of the twentieth century it had come of age. Born from magical rituals and only tempered by reason, it had always enacted the difference between right and wrong as much as it had decided it. And with the end of public executions, it had become the only judicial show in town: a touch of evil for an era that no longer thought it seemly for crowds to jump at the legs of a dying man.

4

The Witch Trial

I have to fight against countless subtleties in which the Court is likely to lose itself. And in the end, out of nothing at all, an enormous fabric of guilt will be conjured up.

FRANZ KAFKA, *The Trial*

By the fifteenth century, two very different models of criminal justice had established themselves in Europe. On the continent, judges asserted the wisdom of the Romans and the authority of canonical law – and the right to investigate any crime they detected. In England, on the other hand, kings had already delegated considerable responsibility to ordinary men, whose role was only to assess the complaints and defences of people who came before them. The jurists of Europe were honing their inquiries to logical perfection; the jurors of England were entirely unversed in legal theory and so unlikely to be literate that evidence was invariably spoken or shown to them. The history of the witch trials, a saga that lasted two centuries and claimed the lives of between sixty and a hundred thousand people, would encapsulate the differences between the systems. It would begin in the hushed monasteries and torture chambers of central Europe, and would end amidst the high drama of Salem. Subtle doctrines of theology would transform superstitions into denunciations, and the secrecy of the inquisitorial process would generate a vicious cycle of confession and execution. But the publicity of jury trial would produce the most spectacular prosecutions of all.

*   *   *

Medieval Christianity had an instinctive distrust of anyone who dabbled with the supernatural. The Book of Exodus warned against 'suffer[ing] a witch to live', while Leviticus recommended the stoning to death of anyone with 'a familiar spirit', and Christian rulers everywhere were paying lip service to the rules by the end of the first millennium. But anxious though the Church was to kill sorcerers in theory, the practical shortcomings of Dark Age logic always made it hard to define them. Without firm theories of cause and effect, it was impossible to pin down the relationship between a curse and a consequence. The significance of healing was no easier to understand; just as a potion that worked might be magic, a failed doctor could just as well be a magician. To confuse matters further, orthodoxy insisted for centuries that no one but God could bend or suspend the laws of the cosmos. Ever since St Augustine had explained in the fifth century AD, that only He was capable of turning men into beasts and birds, it had taught that sorcery was either ineffective or blessed. The idea that people could actually fly and work evil magic was therefore, in the words of a tenth-century canon, an 'error of the pagans' that wrongly imagined 'some divine power other than the one God'

The late medieval Church consequently had a relatively relaxed attitude towards the forces of darkness. Some demons certainly seemed to be up to no good – flitting through the night as incubi or succubi in search of casual sex perhaps, or cleaning up at a dice table before exiting with a sulphurous whoosh – but chroniclers knew of others far more benign. In the early thirteenth century, an English monk called Roger of Wendover told how Satan had once helped a nun fight off a rapist. Caesarius of Heisterbach reported that he had even lent support to the Church's war on heresy. When the Bishop of Besançon had confidentially invoked him in order to ask how two troublesome preachers were able to walk on water and pass through flames, the Devil had confided that they had infernal charms sewn into their armpits. When the men declined to disclose what lay under their flesh they were flayed by force and burned at the stake. The powers of hell, used wisely, could be extremely helpful indeed.

But at the very same time that both men were writing, the Church's attitude to Satan was undergoing profound change. Catholicism had been at war since 1095, when Pope Urban II had blessed the first crusaders' attempt to capture the Holy Land; and since 1208, when Innocent III launched his attack on the Cathar heretics, its struggle had become one of self-definition as much as survival. The very idea of Catholicism was being challenged – and in the name of combating a heresy that overestimated evil, the Church would itself promote Lucifer from an inferior demon to the Prince of Darkness. The Cathar belief that Satan was slugging it out with God and had the upper hand on earth was already being caricatured as a celebration of wickedness rather than an explanation of it. Church propagandists were asserting that heretics worshipped their savage deity in person, generally by kissing his anus, and the mischievous demons of picaresque tradition were giving ground to diabolical creatures of a far more sinister hue. The stranger at the tavern described by Thomas de Cantimpré in the mid thirteenth century was not a gambler with the luck of the Devil but someone who bought a man's soul for a drink – and unsheathed his talons at closing time to call in his due. By the late 1300s, macabre stories were telling of men who begged from their death-beds to have their right hand amputated, forced *in extremis* to reveal that the limb was pledged to Satan and anxious not to die with the debt unredeemed. Similar stories would one day attach themselves to the exploits of a sixteenth-century conman called Dr Johann Faust – but the pact attributed to his literary reincarnation was already being drafted.

The changing superstitions were transformed into doctrine at the end of the thirteenth century when a Dominican monk called Thomas Aquinas subjected demons – along with the rest of creation – to detailed analysis. The scholar, concerned to establish a rational basis for God's existence in an intellectual climate that demanded proof for every proposition, would establish an orthodoxy that would hold for three more centuries, and his examination of the spiritual world generated some especially alarming conclusions. While recognizing that some people thought demons were illusory, he scrutinized the evidence and showed that they were in fact ubiquitous – and dangerous. Incubi and succubi, for example, were not just cruising whores, but diabolical transsexuals who reaped sperm from men and sowed it into women, generating giants in the process. Although that specific hazard was something from which Aquinas claimed miraculous immunity,* less sanctified individuals faced serious risks. Demons were so malicious that they sought pleasure not for its own sake but only to lead humans to perdition. Magicians were especially liable to be outsmarted by creatures of the netherworld. Indeed, the mere act of invoking a demon meant that a sorcerer was making a deal with death and a pact with hell.

The stock of ritual magic, once the preserve of only the wisest Christians, was plummeting, and a series of events that occurred south of Paris in 1323 offered a vivid indication of how far it was to fall. They began when shepherds driving their flocks past a crossroads noticed two long straws sticking out of the ground and heard a distant miaow. Local inquisitors, summoned to the scene, began digging. It was not long before their spades hit a chest containing a coal-black cat and several vials of consecrated oil and holy water. Inquiries among local carpenters led to the arrest of one Jean Prévost, who explained that he had been trying to assist a group of Cistercian monks from the nearby abbey. They had hired him, along with a magician called Jean Persant, to help recover the abbot's stolen treasury and the plan had been to disinter the cat after three days, skin it alive, make three thongs from its hide, and consume the contents of its stomach. Prévost and Persant anticipated that a demon called Berich would then point them in the direction of the thief. The scheme would have raised few eyebrows just a century earlier, but by the 1320s it was looking distinctly *outré*. The monks were collectively degraded and condemned to lifetime incarceration, while the defendants were burned to ashes. Persant suffered the additional discomfort of having the cat tied around his neck at the stake.

Similar prosecutions proliferated throughout the fourteenth century, but it was reverberations from the longstanding campaigns against heresy

---

* One of the grounds for Aquinas' canonization was a youthful incident that he reportedly recounted in old age to his secretary, Reginald of Priverno. He claimed that his brothers, jealous of his purity, had once tempted him with a comely maiden. Although he had been able to drive her from his cell by brandishing a burning log at her, he had subsequently found himself so troubled by certain thoughts that he had had to pray for deliverance. God's response was to send him two angels who had, in his dreams, bound his genitals so tightly that he had screamed with pain. He was happy to report that, from that day onward, his loins had ceased to stir. See Kenelm Foster (ed.), *The Life of Saint Thomas Aquinas. Biographical Documents* (London and Baltimore, 1959), pp. 29–30, 99–100.

in southern Europe and Germany that finally gave the fears the distinctive shape that is nowadays associated with the witch-hunts. The papal Inquisition, though successful in shattering Catharism, had merely scattered many of its most fervent adherents, and as refugees had poured into Germany and the Savoy, a domino topple of dissent had begun that would set off anti-Catholic movements for centuries. Officials increasingly responded by linking their concerns about magical pacts with the allegations of sexual diabolism that the Church had long been levelling against its enemies, and during the mid fifteenth century all the cross-pollination finally bore fruit. In a series of trials across Burgundy and the Savoy, tortured defendants began to confess to a form of mischief so distinctive as to amount to an entirely new offence. They had, they now admitted, flown on beasts and greased sticks to huge assemblies at which Satan had manifested himself in the form of a lascivious creature like a goat, dog, or monkey. They had repeatedly kissed his rear end. They had also prostituted themselves to demons, raised storms, cast spells against their neighbours and performed acts against nature until cockcrow. It was a crime whose time had come.

There remained just one obstacle to a full-scale crackdown, in that it remained blasphemous to believe that there was anything to crack down on. That was an objection more historical than theological by the late 1400s however, and the Church was about to formulate an intellectual basis for the dread. The breakthrough came in 1484, when Pope Innocent VIII alerted Christendom to the news that satanists in northern Germany were aborting infants, blasting crops, and having congress with demons. He authorized two German Dominican friars, Heinrich Kramer and Jacob Sprenger, to produce a full report. Their findings, primarily written by Kramer, were published two years later in the form of the *Malleus maleficarum*, or 'Hammer of Witches'. The work suddenly turned orthodoxy onto its head. Whereas it had been blasphemous for some five centuries to believe in witchcraft, it now became all but heretical to deny it.

Kramer's reasoning, though held together by little more than the whiff of brimstone and the dazzle of mirrors, managed to neutralize virtually every objection that the Church had ever raised to the reality of sorcery. He began with the premise that the Church had never doubted its existence, and although that was a travesty of the truth he minimized the chances that anyone would say so by warning that the contrary view was itself a heresy. It was correct to say that witchcraft sometimes occurred only in the mind, he accepted, but witches were capable of enjoying and inflicting such hallucinations only because they freely contracted with Satan and sealed the deal with a spot of sexual intercourse. Satan's powers were such that, with the leave of God, he was able to fool every human sense anyway. Even if it was all an illusion, it therefore made no difference.

If the *Malleus* had depended on logic for its fuel, it would not have got very far. But the myths were powered by a force that would send them cascading down the centuries: hatred, and more particularly a hatred of women. Tales of the evil female were nothing new. According to rabbinic legend, the problem was even older than Eve: the very first woman was Lilith, created from sediment and filth, who had spurned God and Adam in favour of communing with demons and killing children. Homer had sung of Circe, ruler of the island of Aeaea, who transformed Ulysses' men into pigs and kept the hero distracted with her charms for a full year. The Romans had bequeathed to their barbarian successors tales of the *strix*, an airborne hag with claws and teeth who spent the hours from dusk till dawn dive-bombing cradles and eating human flesh. But the nightmares were now magnified into a world-view.

Kramer had a personal reason to write his book. He had been a papal inquisitor in Innsbruck who had made fervent attempts to purge the region of female sorcerers but found his efforts repeatedly foiled by conservative bishops. He had been waiting to get his own back – and he now would, in spades. The *Malleus* was a *Mein Kampf* of misogyny, teeming with sluts who would copulate with any passing demon and fall pregnant for the pure pleasure of aborting their foetuses in Satan's honour. It told of midwives who rammed thorn-bushes into wombs and killed infants to procure the fat that, smeared onto chairs and broomsticks, allowed them to fly. Most startling of all was the revelation that female sorcerers could not only magically rob men of their erections – as had been suspected since Roman times – but also steal their penises. 'And what', asked Kramer and Sprenger, 'is to be thought of those witches who collect . . . as many as twenty or thirty members together, and put them in a bird's nest or shut them up in a box, where they move themselves like living members and eat oats and corn?' It is not a question that admits of an easy answer, but the authors had no doubt that it demanded one. They knew someone who claimed to have seen such a nest with his own eyes, after his tormentor had repented of her theft and agreed to restore his organ. She had sent him to the top of a tree with instructions to take whichever one he liked – though 'when he tried to take a big one, the witch said, "You must not take that one . . . because it belongs to a parish priest."' The anecdote suggests that not everyone furnishing information to Kramer and Sprenger was quite as humourless as they were, but the monks' conclusion on the subject of lost genitalia, like those on every other topic they covered, was no laughing matter. The best way to make a witch return her prize was to strangle her until her face turned black.

None of the ideas in the *Malleus* was new and the sexual fears they reflected were pathological even by the standards of witch-hunting monks, but the work crystallized a crime that would persist for two centuries. Published less than thirty years after Europe's first printed book, and reprinted thirteen times over the next four decades, it transformed superstitions into reasons to execute. Kramer's experiences of clerical obstructionism in Innsbruck made him particularly concerned to persuade judges to take the new crime seriously, and a full third of his manual was devoted to the importance of establishing suitably robust legal procedures. He warned that sorceresses often retained their powers after arrest and could blind inquisitors to their guilt simply by looking at them. In order to avoid harm, a judge should therefore discount anything that a defendant did or said while in custody. One sure sign of a true witch was her uncanny ability to maintain her innocence under torture and some particularly effective spells were uttered in the form of pleas and screams. To minimize the risks, inquisitors were therefore advised to strip and shave their suspects from head to toe in order to find the satanic charm that afforded her such power. They also ought to wear magical necklaces of their own and ensure that suspects were brought into court backwards. Such measures were not superstitious, affirmed Kramer. In fact, any judge who failed to take them risked eternal damnation.

The theories of the *Malleus* were soon percolating through Europe's pulpits and universities. Judges never became as likely to consult their work as Kramer might have hoped, but the frequency of prosecutions accelerated rapidly in subsequent decades, and in the west and central European epicentres of the craze, women would constitute about four-fifths of those charged. The persecution did not mount in a single wave but rolled forward in hundreds of discrete campaigns, and showed considerable regional variation. It was almost always milder in regions where strong churches or courts of appeal enforced basic rules of procedure and evidence. On the other hand, the judicial violence intensified in conditions of social and political instability – and sixteenth-century Europe rarely lacked for turmoil.

The Reformation, which tore Europe into two during the mid sixteenth century, ratcheted up kill rates everywhere. Protestant regions generally adopted the theories of the *Malleus* as eagerly as Pope Innocent VIII had once done. In Germany – a chequer-board of sectarianism where armies would battle like red and black ants until the end of the Thirty Years War in 1648 – inquisitors would execute witches at a greater rate and frequency than the rest of the continent combined. It was in France, however, torn by sectarian riots and civil war for three decades after 1562, that Kramer and Sprenger found their true heirs. In 1571, a disgraced conjuror from the court of Charles IX called Trois-Échelles informed his judges that he had more than a hundred thousand accomplices in France and the country was thrown into a panic. And whenever panics erupted in early modern Europe, lawyers were rarely far from the scene. It was time for a new wave of manuals to pick up where the *Malleus* had left off.

Satan adored (1560). The engraving accompanies a description of Satanic rituals that were supposedly current in Calcutta among Brahmin priests, but Satan's pendulous breasts and peculiar genitals more accurately reflect the fears of mid-sixteenth century France.

The first and most authoritative was written by a jurist called Jean Bodin in 1580. Bodin was an apologist for absolutism who was renowned as much for his mastery of political realities as for his grasp of supernatural ones, and his work – *On the Demon-Mania of Sorcerers* – pioneered a legal theory that has appealed to authoritarians ever since: that state interests necessarily take priority over individual liberties. In the face of a crime so threatening to the moral order, he made clear that those aspects of customary law that still protected defendants would simply have to be abandoned. Accomplices' confessions, though traditionally treated as unreliable, were an efficient method of establishing the enormity of witchcraft and should therefore be used wherever possible. Theories of natural law that exempted children and parents from having to testify against each other were no more sacrosanct: it was even more unnatural to permit sorcery than to violate the bonds of the family. Inquisitors should therefore feel free to use entrapment and trickery to obtain confessions, argued Bodin, and the ordinary niceties of torture could have no place. It was in fact advisable to ensure that suspects heard someone shrieking for mercy and saw the instruments of interrogation prior to questioning. Witchcraft was 'so obscure and its mischiefs so hidden', explained Bodin, that 'not one out of a thousand witches would be punished' unless irregularly obtained evidence was allowed to support a conviction.

Other inquisitors duly stepped up their case loads and were soon distilling their experiences into books of their own. Burgundy magistrate Henri Boguet, who drafted a demonology that was updated several times between 1590 and 1611, was alarmed by Trois-Échelles' revelations (having heard that he in fact had anything from thirty to three hundred thousand accomplices in France, 'multiplying upon the earth even as worms in a garden'), but the enemy, though fearsome, fazed him not. Whereas Heinrich Kramer had once felt it necessary to terrify inquisitors into convicting, Boguet had the confidence of a lawyer on top of his game. 'Satan himself holds [judges] in fear and dread', he reassured his readers, and it was superstitious to think that a witch could harm an inquisitor by look or touch alone. There were certainly dangers – but each had its remedy. A defendant who looked at the ground and muttered while being addressed by the judge was probably taking emergency counsel from a demon, for example, but solitary confinement could generally break its hold. There remained scope for small mercies – but only very small ones. Although it was ordinarily right to punish children as adults, which generally meant burning them, he preferred to 'employ . . . some gentler means, such as hanging' if the witch was pre-pubescent.

Others were no less inventive. The Attorney-General of Lorraine, Nicolas Rémy, frankly admitted that he had once thought demons to exist only in fairy tales, but now knew that they often lurked in the corner of his court, and could hide in a defendants' hair or crawl into their throats. Martín Del Rio, a former Attorney-General of Brabant in the Netherlands, warned that they could sabotage torture sessions by loosening ropes and lifting weights. Satan could even send his servants into an insensate slumber while they were undergoing the most excruciating torments.

German experiences also contributed to the debate. Del Rio had been particularly impressed by the resourcefulness of one Westphalian witch-hunter, saddled with a stubborn werewolf who had not only withstood twenty sessions on the rack but beamed with joy throughout. The inquisitor, near wit's end, had slipped his prisoner a cup of drugged wine and the demon within, suddenly helpless, had made full admissions in no time. Other German jurists revived the cold water ordeal, whereby suspects were immersed and condemned if they floated too easily. Given that Pope Innocent III had given it a thumbs-down back in 1215 and Jean Bodin thought the ritual not just superstitious but satanic, the rehabilitation called for subtle reasoning. It came in the form of a 1594 paper by a Cologne judge called Jacob Rickius, who explained that the test had an eminently rational basis. Witches partook of Satan's ethereal essence and were therefore so unnaturally light that they automatically bobbed to the surface of water. Another way of discovering a witch was therefore to weigh her. He personally knew of a sorceress who, though very fat, had tipped the scales at between thirteen and fifteen pounds.

The inquisitorial process, by its nature, generated a dialogue of superstition, in which the fears and credulities of both judge and prisoner fed on each other. Having collectively conducted thousands of interrogations, the new demonologists learned fantastic new details about the crime they were proving. It had become apparent to some, for example, that witches did not just fly on beasts, sticks, and chairs. They also travelled inside clouds. Nicolas Rémy knew of at least one old woman who had crashed into the crown of an oak tree during a thunderstorm. Martín Del Rio had met two sentries at Calais in 1587 who had actually seen a vaporous transport. The soldiers, explaining how a woman with gunshot wounds had come to be in their custody, told inquisitors that they had been minding their own business when a dark cloud filled with voices had scudded towards them across a clear sky. In alarm, one had fired his weapon into the gloom and the injured woman, fat, drunk, and naked, had dropped at their feet.

The inquisitors gathered particularly elaborate descriptions about their suspects' meetings with Satan. Kramer and Sprenger had observed that diabolical sex was a hallmark of witchcraft and early sixteenth-century writers had told of nocturnal ceremonies known as sabbaths, which the Devil would personally attend; but the new writers now elevated the sabbath into one of witchcraft's defining features. It became a carnival of absurdity at which Satan might dispense his urine as an unholy sacrament, guests would gorge on blood and wind, and ordinary rules of engagement were ignored or reversed. Del Rio's account was typical:

> [O]nce a foul, disgusting fire has been lit, an evil spirit sits on a throne as president of the assembly. His appearance is terrifying, almost always that of a male goat or a dog. The witches come forward to worship him in different ways. Sometimes they supplicate him on bended knee; sometimes they stand with their back turned to him . . . They offer candles made of pitch or a child's umbilical cord, and kiss him on the anal orifice as a sign of homage . . . After the feast, each evil spirit takes by the hand the disciple of whom he has charge, and so that they may do everything with the most absurd kind of ritual, each person bends over backwards, joins hands in a circle, and tosses his head as frenzied fanatics do. Then they begin to dance . . . They sing very obscene songs in his [Satan's] honour . . . They behave ridiculously in every way, and in every way contrary to accepted custom. Then their demon-lovers copulate with them in the most repulsive fashion.

Some of the most graphic details came courtesy of an inquisitor called Pierre de Lancre, commissioned by King Henry IV in January 1609 to cleanse the Labourd region of southwestern France. De Lancre was a man of rivalrous temperament and over the course of a four-month investigation that saw him interview hundreds of suspects and send more than fifty to the stake he rarely overlooked an opportunity to outdo the discoveries of his contemporaries. The sabbaths to which his suspects were invited attracted thousands of male and female witches, who danced the night away alongside smoke-wreathed wizards and gyrating lines of fauns, snakes, dragons, and tigers. He agreed with other demonologists that Satan was especially likely to manifest himself as a billy-goat, but the

goat that attended his sabbaths had up to five horns, including an illuminated one at the centre of its forehead. De Lancre also lost himself in
pornographic reveries for paragraphs on end, and although no demo-
nologist lacked for libido, his tales of sodomitic beasts and women shared
between men and demons are in a class of their own. He devoted particular attention to Satan's
penis, and it is probably fair
to say that he gleaned more
information on the topic
than anyone else in history.*
Sixteen-year-old Jeanette
d'Abadie, while trying to
explain to de Lancre just
how depressing and painful
she had found her sexual
experiences with the Devil,
had told him that the organ
in question was over a yard

*From the second edition of De Lancre's
demonology (detail).*

long, coiled like a snake, and covered in scales. Fifteen-year-old Marie de
Marigrane had recalled it to be half-iron and half-flesh. Petry de Linarre
had got the impression that it was made of pure horn, which is why it
made women scream so much. De Lancre's competitive instincts did not
desert him even here. After reporting that a teenager called Marguerite
had found the Devil to be hung like a mule, with an appendage as long
and thick as an arm, he recalled that the demons found by Henri Boguet
in the Franche-Comté rarely had penises larger than a finger. 'The witches
of the Labourd,' mused de Lancre, 'are better served by Satan than those
of the Franche-Comté.'

---

* That is not to say that others lacked interest. As far back in 1521, Sylvester
Prieirias had warned that Satan often appeared with a forked penis to double
his debauchery or a triple-pronged one to maximize it: Robert E. L. Masters,
Eros and Evil. The Sexual Psychopathology of Witchcraft (Baltimore, 1974), p. 17.
Nicolas Rémy noted that the diabolical organ could be as long as a kitchen
utensil, 'even when only half in erection', and as gross as a spindle. Like several
other demonologists, he also commented on the temperature of Satan's semen,
so bitterly cold that women recoiled with shock upon receiving it. See Nicolas
Rémy, *Demonolatry*, tr. E. Allen Ashwin (London, 1930), pp. 12–14.

The dynamics of the call and response sessions that produced such reflections can only be guessed at, but one document allows a glimpse into the darkness. It is a letter smuggled from the cell of Johannes Junius, a burgomaster of Bamberg who found himself accused in 1628 during a witch-hunt that was splitting his town asunder and producing hundreds of executions. In script that spidered across the page, written with hands that had been broken by thumbscrews, the 55-year-old told his daughter Veronica that he had refused to condemn himself on oath until even his torturer had pleaded, 'for God's sake, confess something, whether it be true or not'. He had thereupon admitted that he had made a pact with a beautiful woman, who had turned into a goat and tried to throttle him. His inquisitors had then made him identify numerous fellow citizens as people with whom he had attended a sabbath. When told to specify his own crimes, he initially claimed that, although the goat-maiden had told him to kill his children, he had chosen instead to slaughter a horse. The inquisitors, not impressed, had threatened to return him to the torture chamber – at which point he added that he had also desecrated a communion wafer. That satisfied their Catholic sense of impropriety and Junius was escorted into court, where he repeated the admissions and was condemned to burn. He ended by telling his daughter that the six people who had accused him had already been executed; he had met them before their deaths and forgiven them, because their denunciations had been no more voluntary than his. 'Dear child, pay this man a dollar,' he asked, as he penned his final words. 'I have taken several days to write this: my hands are both lame . . . Good night, for your father Johannes Junius will never see you again.'

The voices of sanity outside the dungeons were almost as lonely. One was Friedrich von Spee, a Jesuit confessor at Würzburg during the 1620s, who kept a detailed record of the lies that sent women and men to their deaths. He noted, for example, that if prisoners gritted their teeth under torture, it was recorded that they had laughed. As and when they fainted, the scribe would note that they had dozed off. Spee also identified the single most insidious feature of the persecutions: their capacity to blind the men who perpetrated them to their own injustice. Every accusation inexorably drove towards conviction, because 'judges think it a disgrace if they acquit, as though they had been too hasty in arresting and torturing the innocent.' He recalled a conversation at which several inquisitors had been asked how an innocent person, if arrested, could ever escape conviction, and their response had not been reassuring. '[T]hey were unable to answer and finally said they would think it over that night.'

Early modern England was no less superstitious than its European neighbours. It was a country where priests pealed church bells to silence thunderstorms and the croaking of frogs and the curdling of milk were thought capable of encrypting cosmic truths; a realm where the birth of a deformed child on earth was freighted with the same mystery as the appearance of a blazing star in the heavens. Its religious divisions were as profound as those elsewhere, and the fear of females may have been even more intense: Englishwomen were nine times more likely than men to be charged with witchcraft, and twice as likely again to be hanged, a bias worse than any country on the continent. And yet the intensity of the English witch-hunt pales by comparison with those elsewhere. Fewer than one in four of all defendants went to the gallows, an execution rate roughly half of the European average. The total put to death was less than a thousand – perhaps a tenth of the French figure and less than a twentieth of the number executed in Germany.

The reasons for the difference lay in the fact that the jury system possessed, almost despite itself, features that operated to keep superstitions in check. Whereas French judges were combining the functions of investigator and assessor as early as the fourteenth century, and those of Germany began to do the same not long after, it was rare in England to have any ordinary criminal offence except treason prosecuted professionally before the late 1600s. Although witchcraft came increasingly to be seen even in England as a crime sufficiently corrosive to demand official intervention, it always remained the case that prosecutions required individuals to identify themselves as victims. Those complainants then had to persuade others of their case – and not just once, but three times. English law had, as part of the process that had brought forth the jury system, developed the grand jury, comprising twenty-three sworn men, whose role was to examine whether accusations should go forward at all. If one did, the judge could stop the case during the trial. If he allowed it to proceed, twelve more men then had to agree on a verdict. In order for an accusation of witchcraft to become a conviction, the stupidity or malice of an accuser therefore had to chime with the credulities of thirty-six men. It did so rather more often than many defendants might have hoped, but the chances that juries would convict were always less than the likelihood that an inquisitor would want to prove the case that he had started. What was more, England only used torture on the direct orders of its monarch or his councillors. Although witchcraft confessions would occur, the admissions inspired by despair, pride, or senility could not match the baroque proportions of those extracted by force.[*]

A witch and her familiars, as imagined by an artist in 1621 England.

The bold conjectures of the continent were, as a result, spindly suppositions by the time they reached England's courtrooms. Many well-read Englishmen came to accept that witchcraft involved a pact with the Devil, but whereas the skies over France and Germany were always thick with witches en route to a night of passionate gyration, Satan always got far less bang for his buck in England. Flying broomsticks and sabbaths each appeared just once at an English trial. A witch's demonic companions were sometimes imagined as monstrous apparitions but were equally likely to manifest themselves as small animals like toads or voles. The complaints of accusers were generally prosaic ones – that, say, a neighbour had supernaturally visited

---

[*] Kramer and Sprenger, always careful to explain that witchcraft's essence lay in a merely mental agreement to serve the Devil, had been keenly aware that over-rigid legal procedures could hinder successful prosecutions. They told of one man in Koblenz who had been so inflamed with lust for an invisible demon that he coupled with her up to four times a day, often in front of his distressed wife. Although he knew perfectly well who had bewitched him, Koblenz retained elements of an older accusatory system and required that she confess spontaneously or that he produce three eyewitnesses – with the result, as the authors bitterly pointed out, that no judge could avenge his suffering. See Heinrich Kramer (aka Institoris) and Jacob Sprenger, *Malleus maleficarum*, tr. Montague Summers (London, 1928), pp. 164–5 [2.2.1].

them with dysentery, or afflicted their cow with a wasting disease. And the stereotypical sorcerer was a misanthropic crone who magicked from home, rarely willing to go further, sexually speaking, than to give suck with a little blood.

Typical was the case of Joan Prentice, charged in 1589 with using witchcraft to kill a neighbour's child. The destitute old woman made partial admissions prior to trial. In particular, she recalled that a tawny brown ferret had leapt onto her lap six years before, before fixing her with fiery eyes and thundering, 'Joan Prentice, give me thy soul!' When she had asked it to identify itself, it had proclaimed: 'I am Satan, feare me not; my comming unto thee is to doe thee no hurt, but to obtaine thy soule.' Prentice had told the ferret that Christ had a prior claim, whereupon it had agreed to make do with a drop of blood from her forefinger. On her account, she then asked it to spoil one neighbour's beer and 'nip but not hurt' the child of another, but broke off all contact when it announced itself set on murder. The confession was, needless to say, enough to take her to the gallows, but one can barely imagine what a man like Pierre de Lancre would have made of Prentice and her ferret.

On the other hand, wherever procedures came to approximate those across the Channel, the deadliness intensified to levels comparable to those of the continent. When regular courts were suspended during the Civil War of the mid 1640s, a posse of freelance witch-hunters strode into the legal limbo, and in the space of just three years took the lives of between 10 and 20 per cent of all the witches ever executed in England. Traipsing from town to town in their high hats, they offered justice at a price – anything from twenty shillings to six pounds per witch – and with the aid of torture and cold-water ordeals they were soon discovering them by the dozen.

The most notorious was Matthew Hopkins. After coming to suspect, for reasons now lost, that several female neighbours had deployed the Devil against him in the form of a bear, he announced in 1644 that he was England's Witchfinder General. He then embarked on his mission by arresting a one-legged widow called Elizabeth Clarke and subjecting her to a test called 'watching', which involved placing her on a stool, depriving her of food, drink, and sleep, and waiting to see if any of her familiars came to visit her. Since they might appear in forms as humble as flies and mice, the test could hardly fail; but Hopkins' claims of success were positively grandiose. He recorded witnessing the arrival of an entire train of imps, including Jarmara, a fat spaniel with no legs, and Vinegar Tom, a greyhound with an ox's head that loped across the room before turning into a headless child and vanishing. On her fourth night without sleep, Clarke finally agreed that she was a witch and set in motion a chain of accusation and arrest that would see about thirty-six women imprisoned, of whom at least nineteen were almost certainly hanged. According to Hopkins, she also identified four more familiars called Elemanzer, Pyewacket, Peckin the Crown, and Grizzel Greedigutt. The names alone proved that she was guilty, he observed, since no mere mortal could have invented them.

Even clearer evidence of the pernicious nature of inquisitorial techniques came from Scotland. Like England, the country had adopted juries during the thirteenth century, but a series of wars with its southern neighbour had made it increasingly sympathetic to continental influence. During the fifteenth century schools devoted to canonical and Roman law were set up at Aberdeen, St Andrews, and Glasgow, and over the next hundred years the country adopted all manner of inquisitorial practices. Instead of requiring that cases begin with a victim's accusation, it allowed a judge to launch investigations on the strength of suspicion alone, tipped off where appropriate by anonymous rumours that could be posted into boxes at any parish church. As the power of judges increased, that of jurors changed, and it became common for them simply to pronounce a verdict after hearing statements recited aloud. It would have been an ominous development at any time, in that the continent was showing just how dangerous it was to amalgamate the powers of criminal accusation and investigation. But the risks that monomania might generate legal precedents became particularly acute during the 1590s – for the king himself became chief promoter of the anti-witchcraft cause.

James VI of Scotland, later James I of England, aroused controversy even at the most basic levels. Some contemporaries record that he was comely of appearance; others say that he was bandy-legged and possessed of a tongue too large for his mouth to accommodate. Some courtiers were impressed by his grace and valour; others characterized him as a dirty, ragged, drooling rogue and a spineless coward. But there was no one, no matter how hostile, who ever doubted his intellectual credentials. James had a wit as sharp as his tongue was gross and an intelligence that would have been rare in anyone, let alone a British monarch. As a child, his idea of fun had been to translate biblical passages from Latin to French to

English, and as an adult he would write tomes on issues ranging from the meaning of monarchy to the evils of nicotine. At a time when no self-respecting Renaissance man could have ignored the advances being made in the art of demonology, it is hardly surprising that his mind wandered to the riddles of the supernatural. Unfortunately for many of his subjects, his interest was never simply academic.

In August 1589, at the age of 23, James married 14-year-old Princess Anne of Denmark. As befitted a busy sixteenth-century monarch, he sent a proxy to go through the motions of betrothal, but when Anne embarked for Scotland on 5 September, in the care of Admiral Peter Munk, the most senior officer in the Danish navy, the outlook for marital bliss seemed fair. As Edinburgh prepared to throw a glorious pageant for the new queen, her flagship set sail at the head of thirteen men-of-war, wending its way in stately procession through the Skagerrak channel. But as the fleet entered the open waters of the North Sea its progress was suddenly checked by a tremendous storm, raging from Norway to Britain. The craft were scattered, while over in Edinburgh a ferry carrying Anne's prospective lady-in-waiting, along with sundry servants and sailors, was sent spiralling to the floor of the Firth of Forth. James, on tenterhooks at Craigmillar Castle, placed the nation on an emergency fast. But as the skies blued and the flotsam cleared, a Danish warship limped into the capital with marvellous news. Admiral Munk, trusty sea dog that he was, had taken shelter in a fjord, and Anne had recovered her wits in the cottage of a kindly farmer. She was now en route, overland this time, for Oslo. The outlook had been grim – but the heavens seemed once again to be smiling.

James, calling off the national fast and giving thanks to God, decided that if Anne could not come to her wedding, the wedding would go to her. Heading for the fjords, three hundred lairds, jugglers, and acrobats in tow, he bedded down respectfully with his wife's saviour for a night and set off for Oslo. There the couple was united in a lavish wedding, marred only by the death from pneumonia of four African dancers whom James made dance naked in the snow, and they then set off for a Copenhagen honeymoon. Amidst his new in-laws, James had the time of his life, hunting, revelling, and ruminating with the cream of Danish society, and it was not until the spring, half a year later, that he and Anne set off again for Scotland. Back through the Skagerrak the royal fleet tacked; but just when it must have seemed safe to be back in the water, the ships re-entered the North Sea. And it began to rain. Admiral Munk had already been telling anyone who would listen back in Denmark that he blamed witches for his maritime misfortunes, and as James's ship tumbled through the gloom, the young monarch doubtless set to thinking. One gale might have been mere misfortune. Two looked downright sinister.

Over the next couple of months, James's suspicions could only have intensified. Over in Copenhagen, six Danish women admitted, presumably after considerable prompting, that they had despatched droves of devils to climb the keel of Anne's ship. One explained, intriguingly, that their motive had been to get back at Admiral Munk after he had thrown a punch at one of their husbands. With a wife to impress and a tempest of his own to explain, James had every reason to take the revelations seriously – and evidence then began to emerge that seemed to confirm the worst.

A servant called Gillis Duncan living just outside Edinburgh had fallen under suspicion of witchcraft – essentially because she treated the sick and sometimes made them better – and her master, the Scottish equivalent of an inquisitor, had subjected her to finger-screws to find out what exactly she was up to. She duly confessed that it was all the Devil's work, identifying several accomplices, and the investigation was soon gusting towards the capital. It might ordinarily have ended with nothing more than a couple of burnings, but high in his castle James was about to embark on some judicial storm-raising of his own. He was a paranoid man – with, admittedly, so many enemies that he had much to be paranoid about – and was growing convinced that one of the several pretenders to his throne, a hare-brained cousin called the Earl of Bothwell, was mobilizing a coven of witches against him. By the end of 1590, he had taken personal charge of the case against Duncan and launched an investigation that would last for almost two years.

Ten defendants were soon produced for pre-trial questioning before James and a court consisting of several senior Scottish nobles. It was an elderly widow called Agnes Sampson, a widely respected Edinburgh midwife, who had been cast in the unhappy role of senior witch presumptive. She steadfastly asserted her innocence and in the truest traditions of inquisitorial procedure, evidence was now created to justify the suspicion. James, who had got fully up to speed on his demonology and was taking 'great delight' in learning what the defendants had to say, informed his colleagues that the Devil often marked his servants by licking them.

Sampson, he commanded, should therefore be stripped and shaved in order to see if there were any signs of Satan's tongue.

The test – similar to one recommended in the *Malleus maleficarum,* but never before seen in Britain – soon proved its worth. Within an hour, the jailers had found a mark on her vagina and Sampson was singing. Satan had instigated her to witchery, she now admitted, because he regarded James as his greatest enemy on earth. In the hope of obstructing his nuptials she had thrown a cat weighed down with human body parts into the Firth of Forth. After initial difficulties caused by the creature scrambling ashore, she had recaptured it, drowned it and sent a ship to the seabed in its wake, raising climatic havoc in the process.

There was more. She also admitted that she had attended an ancient church in North Berwick where Satan himself, sporting black hat and gown, had hosted a sabbath. It had a distinctly Celtic flavour. According to one version of her evidence, she had sailed there in a sieve, swigging wine alongside two hundred other witches, and had arrived to find a swarming horde of sorcerers already present. As midnight neared and waves lashed the lonely churchyard, Gillis Duncan had twanged a ditty on a Jew's harp and the throng had reeled between the graves, adoring the Evil One's ice-cold anus, dancing widdershins around the kirk, and generally violating the natural order of things. The Devil – clawed, hairy, and aquiline – had then addressed them from a pulpit illuminated by black candles, and after making everyone account for their misdeeds, had invited them to desecrate three graves. He had then distributed disinterred fingers, toes, and knees, and after receiving a winding sheet and two human joints, which she had since misplaced, Sampson had given Satan's buttocks one last kiss and returned home.

The first defendant to face a trial after the preliminary inquiry was a young schoolteacher called John Fian. He was accused on 26 December 1590 of twenty separate offences, ranging from the possession of moles' feet and the chasing of cats to allegations that he had sat at Satan's left hand while taking the register at North Berwick. Fian had made extensive admissions after being throttled and having his legs squashed between boards, but he now refused to repeat them in open court. James arranged for needles to be inserted under his fingernails and his legs to be 'crushte and beaten together as small as might bee', but to no avail. Strict inquisitorial theory prescribed that he either be tortured again or released, but the rule was always interpreted liberally and Scottish jurists were even more flexible than their continental counterparts. No one insisted on the letter of the law in Fian's case. He went to his death on Edinburgh's Castle Hill a month later, maintaining innocence of witchcraft but confessing adultery with thirty-two women – a tantalizing hint that he may have made several people very jealous, which might well say more than anything in the record about the reason for his prosecution. Nine others, including Gillis Duncan and Agnes Sampson, were burned at the stake at the same time or very soon thereafter, and over subsequent months the flames billowed into a firestorm as about a hundred of their supposed accomplices were investigated and scores executed.

The destruction of the supposed witches of North Berwick, the first mass witch-hunt in British history, set James off on an intellectual adventure that would match that of any French or German witch-hunter. In October 1591 he established a special commission to safeguard Scotland from sorcery, authorized to use torture against suspects otherwise unwilling to tell the truth, and six years later published an entire treatise on witchcraft, *Daemonologie.* The book, which recycled many of the continent's favourite

superstitions, was reprinted in London when he ascended the English throne in 1603, and it was complemented by a practical change in the law. Witchcraft was redefined to include communications with evil spirits, finally making England's sorcerers punishable whether or not a victim could be found. Four out of every ten accused were hanged over the next four years – as high an execution rate as England would ever see. The swimming of witches would now become increasingly common and suspects would be stripped in search of Satanic signs more often than ever before. In the realm of the King James, even the sabbath made its appearance. Within a decade of his coronation, it formed part of an English prosecution for the first time, and Shakespeare nodded to the new phenomenon in *Macbeth*, first performed before the king and his Danish brother-in-law in the summer of 1606. The play's weird and bearded witches were not the stay-at-homes of English tradition, but gregarious hags who met up over cauldrons of sweltered venom, Tartar's lips, and birth-strangled babes. One even took a tip from Agnes Sampson, going off to sea in a sieve.

James's personal contribution to the witch-hunt is easy to exaggerate, however. The years around 1600 saw witchcraft cases become more frequent throughout Europe, and the last six years of Queen Elizabeth's reign were no less deadly for England's accused than the first four of his own. His critical temperament was in any event as likely to detect the flaws of a prosecution as it was to see the advantages. He reined in his Scottish witch-hunting com-missions as early as 1597, on the basis that innocents were at risk of being condemned by judges with grudges ('particular men, bearing particulars against them'). Nineteen years later, he personally ordered the release of five English suspects after interviewing the 13-year-old victim and concluding that he was a liar – an intervention that heralded a collapse in witchcraft convictions across the country. The factor that most decisively determined the intensity of repression was not individual but institutional. James ruled both sides of the border, but Scotland's judge-dominated courts would burn well over a thousand people for witchcraft – a ratio of executions to popu-lation perhaps twelve times greater than that of England.

The swimming of a witch in Bedford. The defendant, a single mother, floated and was then found to have a satanic teat on her inner thigh. After being told that her young son had denounced her, she confessed and was hanged on 30 March 1613.

After the middle of the seventeenth century, witchcraft prosecutions entered a widespread decline across Europe, but as the frenzy abated a paradox became apparent. Although the closed doors and cloistered minds of inquisitorial courts had been responsible for immeasurably more witch-hunting myths and murders, the jury system now fanned the passions of the hunt even as its fire was cooling elsewhere. The reason was the feature of that system that would always represent its blessing and its curse – publicity. Openness discouraged judicial obsessiveness. But whereas an angry individual on the continent who wanted to legitimize a suspicion could do little more than denounce a neighbour and hope for the worst, the jury court offered a forum in which accusers could vent and amplify them.

England's trials had always seen neighbours, relations, and generations pitted against each other, but by the seventeenth century, the barracking and abuse was becoming so loud that several case records remark on the inability of judges and defendants to hear each other or the evidence. Few prosecutions were more thrilling than one that occurred at Bury St Edmunds in 1664. The case represented the culmination of a dispute that had been simmering in the fishing village of Lowestoft for some seven years. It had begun when an old widow called Amy Duny had tried to breast feed the young son of a neighbour called Dorothy Durent and had given him wind as a result. As their feud had festered, a second widow called Rose Cullender had been identified as Duny's accomplice. Seven years on, four entire families came to court to prosecute the case against them.

Dorothy Durent told the jury that her son had fallen ill as soon as she had made her anger known to Duny. Just a few weeks later she had found a huge toad lurking above his cot and hurled it into the fireplace, where it had exploded like a pistol – and on the following day Duny had seemed to be dishevelled and covered in soot. The old woman, livid and cursing, had warned Durent that she would see some of her children pass away and would herself become lame. Her daughter Elizabeth had indeed died two years later and and – as the jurors could see with their own eyes – she now walked on crutches.

Durent's daughter and two other children also testified. They had been vomiting up crooked pins and seeing visions of the two elderly defendants for months, and from the moment they entered court – when they were struck dumb and assailed by violent fits – the defendants' fate was all but sealed. Ann Durent erupted into convulsions when called to the witness box, while 18-year-old Susan Chandler managed only to scream, 'Burn her! Burn her!' before fainting. Eleven-year-old Elizabeth Pacey made the greatest impact of all. Too indisposed to testify, she was placed on a table at the back of the court where she lay for the entire four days of the trial, her stomach rising and falling like a bellows. Only once did she move – when Sir Matthew Hale, the trial judge, suggested that Amy Duny approach her. As the widow entered within arms' range, the young girl sprang upright and with eyes closed – almost – tore at Duny's face so surely that her fingernails drew blood.

The seventeenth century teetered between tradition and inquisitiveness and Hale – a future Lord Chief Justice of England, whose *History of the Pleas of the Crown* is still occasionally cited in English and American courts – personified the era's contradictions. Like any late seventeenth-century lawyer, he had come to assume the need for evidence prior to conviction and he believed that witchcraft without a victim was not a crime known to English law 'because secret things belong to God', but he never doubted that witches could cause harm. And the theories of cause and effect that could underpin proof in his mind retained a distinctly pre-modern quality – as became apparent when someone in court raised his voice to say that the children might be faking. The judge was sufficiently troubled by the suggestion to ask some legal bystanders to conduct an experiment. They returned in some excitement, informing everyone that one of the girls, made to wear a blindfold, had reacted with equal violence to the touch of a stranger as to that of Amy Duny. A cool current of logic wafted through the courtroom and the cobwebbed superstitions of two centuries quivered – but the moment passed. She might have *believed* that the defendant had touched her, someone pointed out. Hale found the observation so compelling that he allowed the case to proceed. After the jurors were advised to have no doubt about the existence of witches and reminded that acquittal of the guilty was as abominable to the Lord as conviction of the innocent, it took them slightly less than thirty minutes to return guilty verdicts against both defendants.

The drama had been intense, and few felt its cathartic effects as keenly as the supposed victims. Within half an hour of the jury's decision Elizabeth Pacey had emerged from her trance, and all three children were soon well enough to pay a visit to the private lodgings of Sir Matthew

Hale. The effect of the case on Dorothy Durent was even more striking –
indeed, almost miraculous. In the admiring words of the pamphleteer
who wrote up the trial:

> There was one thing very remarkable, that after she had gone
> upon Crutches for upwards of Three Years, and went upon them
> at the time of the Assizes in the Court when she gave her
> Evidence . . . the said Dorothy Durent was restored to the use of
> her Limbs, and went home without making use of her Crutches.

Whether or not the verdict was responsible for Durent's recovery of her
motor functions, it was certainly the reason that the defendants lost theirs:
they were both hanged, refusing to confess, four days after their conviction.

England's last execution for witchcraft took place eighteen years later
at Exeter, where three women went to the gallows led by a senile
Temperance Lloyd, who munched food all the way, unconcerned or
unaware of what awaited her. Sir Francis North, one of Hale's successors
as Lord Chief Justice but a bitter critic of witchcraft prosecutions, made it
his business to learn about the case from the trial judge, and his subsequent report suggests that the drama of the courtroom had yet again
played a crucial role. 'The evidence against them was very full and fanci-
ful', he observed, 'but their own confessions exceeded it. They appeared
not only weary of their lives but to have a great deal of skill to convict
themselves. Their description of the sucking devils with saucer eyes were
[sic] so natural that the jury could not choose but believe them.' But it was
not England that would see the apotheosis of the witch trial as theatre.
That came in 1692, ten years after Temperance Lloyd's execution, in a
small American village near Boston called Salem.

The Puritans of Massachusetts Bay sprang disproportionately from East
Anglia and Essex, regions that produced two of England's deadliest witch-
hunts, but they had been mutating from the moment that the first
colonists sailed from the Isle of Wight in April 1630. As their vessels had
ploughed across the Atlantic their leader and governor, John Winthrop,
had stood on the deck of the flagship *Arbella* and delivered a sermon that
would define their mission. Removed from the corruption of England,
they would be an example to the world, 'as a Citty upon a Hill'. But the
promise of redemption came with a curse. '[I]f wee shall deale falsely with

our god in this worke wee have undertaken,' continued Winthrop, 'wee shall be made a story and a by-word through the world.'

The pressure was on, and from the moment that they had disembarked onto shores thick with forests, not a gleaming turret in sight, the doubts had gathered. Of the thousand or so would-be settlers of the Massachusetts Bay Colony, one in five died during that first winter. Their isolated communities would lurch from crisis to crisis over the next few decades, devastated by smallpox, attacked by natives, and plagued by rival sectarians from the Antinomians to the Quakers. The Puritans' insecurity only intensified after 1660, when their co-religionists in England ceded the power they had won in that country's Civil War to King Charles II – who went on not just to restore gaiety to his realm, but to flirt openly with Catholicism. Someone, it seemed, had it in for the Puritans. And for a community committed to the belief that God had long ago chosen whom to save and whom to damn, the adversary had to be Satan. The alternative – that God Himself had taken against them – was too appalling to contemplate.

It was, nevertheless, by no means predetermined in the 1680s that the colony would host a witch-hunt. Witchcraft had been a capital offence since 1641, when Massachusetts' very first laws had given effect to the biblical injunctions against consulting familiar spirits, but the colonists had always been considerably more likely to pray for possessed individuals than to kill them. In the fifty-eight years that followed the arrival of the *Arbella* they executed only five suspected witches, and although there had been a spate of hangings in nearby Connecticut during the early 1660s none had taken place in Massachusetts since 1656. But as the Puritans' gloom had gathered, so too had the need for explanations. And in 1684 an influential Boston minister called Increase Mather wrote a work devoted to little else.

Mather's *Essay for the Recording of Illustrious Providences* portrayed New England as a land on the verge of Armageddon, where Satan rode lightning bolts, God worked wonders, and nothing was quite as it seemed. It recounted, for example, how at the town of Groton in November 1671 Elizabeth Knap's tongue stuck fast to the roof of her mouth – but a month later, unrolled to a great length and begun uttering monstrous blasphemies. It told of a whole series of mysteries that had perplexed old William Morse of Newberry in 1679. A hog was found to have entered his home, notwithstanding that all the doors had been closed. Household objects, bags of hops, clods of dung, and a cat had moved unpredictably about the premises. An invisible presence had tugged at Morse's beard as he lay in bed one night. At the same time, his young grandson had begun to bark like a hound, eat ashes, and cluck like a hen, and only when he was taken away did calm return to the house. Mather was mystified. 'The true Reason of these strange disturbances is as yet not certainly known,' he observed. Some people, however, 'did suspect Morse's wife to be guilty of Witchcraft'.

Four years after Mather wrote his work, four poorly Boston children named a cantankerous Irish widow as the magical source of their ailments. Following a trial at which she proved unable to say the Lord's Prayer perfectly, she became the first Massachusetts citizen in thirty-two years to be hanged for witchcraft. Increase's son, Cotton Mather, wrote the case up a year later in a treatise of his own, and warned that her crimes were but the smoke of an infernal fire. An invisible army of devils was gathering, intent on devouring human souls, and '[n]othing too vile can be said of, nothing too hard can be done to, such a horrible iniquity as witchcraft is.' A storm was about to break.

The thunder began to roll in February 1692, when two children in the village of Salem – 11-year-old Abigail Williams and 9-year-old Elizabeth Parris – fell into convulsions and were diagnosed as bewitched. The younger girl was a niece of the village's new minister, Samuel Parris; and his Amerindian slave, Tituba, then tried to cure them by feeding the family dog with a cake laced with their urine. The plan, optimistic from the outset, was soon backfiring badly. The spasms intensified, two more girls declared themselves afflicted, and all four began to claim that Tituba herself was one of their three spectral tormentors.

She appeared for pre-trial questioning before magistrates on 1 March. Massachusetts law, following that of England, did not allow suspects to assert their innocence on oath and Tituba, who had already experienced one beating at the hands of Samuel Parris, was in any event disinclined to deny her guilt. Under the high rafters of Salem's meeting house, watched by scores of villagers, she chose instead to spin a fantastic tale. Confirming her accusers' claims that she had haunted them in the company of two other Salemites – an infirm woman called Sarah Osborne and a destitute one called Sarah Good – she told of a great yellow bird that had suckled on Good's fingers, and of broomstick flights she herself had made to Boston. A great winged hairy thing had walked about, its face like a woman but its nose supernaturally long. She had made a pact with the Devil, who had come to her as a hog, a dog, a black cat or a red one, and most often of all as a tall man with white hair and black clothes. She had signed his book with her own blood. There had been nine others who had done just the same. She was not, however, able to say who they were. They could be anyone.

The next to be accused was Martha Corey, a prosperous churchgoer, who was questioned before hundreds of Salem residents on Monday 21 March 1692. The feisty 60-year-old confidently denied that she could or would have hurt anyone by witchcraft, but as she spoke her three accusers, none yet a teenager, began to twitch and moan. One then screamed that she could see a man whispering into Corey's ear. The judges demanded that the defendant reveal what he was saying. 'We must not believe all that these distracted children say,' snorted Corey – but credulity was swiftly becoming the order of the day. Passions mounted, with one of those afflicted hurling her shoe at Corey's head and complaining of a great torment in her bowels. As the accusers grew more confident, the defendant grew more nervous, and the girls then began to synchronize their hysteria according to her own movements. As Corey wrung her hands they begged for mercy; when she bit her lips they screamed with pain. A yellow bird was seen sucking her fingers and a Black Man was whispering into her ear. And why, they shuddered, did she not join her fellow witches who were mustering to drums outside the hall?

The drumbeat would only intensify. The number of people afflicted was increasing daily, and two more suspects were brought to court three days later. The first was 71-year-old Rebecca Nurse. The other was the 4-year-old daughter of Sarah Good. Dorcas Good, her head gripped tightly by court officers to prevent her from casting the evil eye, was jailed after several girls displayed fresh tooth marks on their skin and claimed her spectre had bitten them. Three judges attended in her cell two days later, and found a red spot on her forefinger. Under fierce questioning, the 4-year-old admitted that she had been suckling a small snake. When asked if it had come from the Black Man, she seemed not to understand and named her mother as its source. Sarah Good would be hanged four months later. Dorcas would remain in jail, manacled, for another three months after that, and would emerge so mentally damaged that she needed a carer for the rest of her life.

Over the next two months many more preliminary hearings were held, and they did not so much scrutinize evidence as perform it. Those afflicted often testified with their eyes closed, quivering with fear as they located yellow birds and stalking phantoms, while the Black Man assumed so tangible a form that at one point the entire court attacked him. One magistrate' assault was so vigorous that he broke his cane. Prisoners were meanwhile made to stare fixedly at the bench to minimize the risk of courtroom enchantment. When the gaze of Elizabeth Carey strayed to her accusers, lined up on the floor below her judges, the girls howled and scattered, as though blinded by a lighthouse beam. She was simultaneously being forced to stand with arms outstretched, and when her husband stepped forward to wipe away her tears the judges told him to back away. If she had enough strength to inflict such torment, roared Judge Hathorne, she certainly had the power to remain standing.

One of the most electrifying confrontations of all – an instant that forms a pivotal moment in *The Crucible*, Arthur Miller's dramatization of the Salem witch-hunt – came during 11-year-old Abigail Williams' testimony against the pregnant Elizabeth Proctor. As she shivered, eyes darting upwards, the girl whimpered that Proctor's double was dangling from the timbers – and suddenly made as if to punch the woman in front of her. But her tiny fist slowed and uncurled, as though ploughing through a force field – perhaps of terror, perhaps of shame – and touched down soft as a feather onto Proctor's hood. As it did so, Abigail exploded with an animal scream.

By the end of May there were fifty people in jail. It was already becoming apparent that anyone who, like Tituba, confessed and named accomplices would not face trial. But there were some who continued to insist that they were not witches, and their cases needed resolution. The new governor, Sir William Phipps, who had just arrived from England, set about providing it. One of his first acts was to order that all Salem's prisoners be put in irons, and on 2 June he convened a jury to clear the jail. The same twelve men would sit in judgment at every trial and their first case, against 38-year-old Bridget Bishop, took place on the same day. Over ten Salemites testified to witchery that went back decades – telling of black goblins, muttered curses, supernaturally heavy bags of corn and the like – and a specially appointed jury of women examined her for a Devil's teat – the nipple she used to feed her familiars. They found it in the form of 'a preternathurall Excresence of flesh between the pudendum and Anus'. She was convicted and hanged, refusing to confess, eight days later.

For a moment it seemed as though the execution of Bishop – an unpopular woman who had been arousing hostility for years – might be the exceptional event that would snap the colony back to normalcy. Many orthodox Puritans had been watching events at Salem with growing alarm, deeply unsure whether illusions generated by the Prince of Lies could constitute a reliable basis to send people to their deaths. Increase Mather and several Boston clerics echoed such concerns in a letter they wrote to Governor Phipps, which warned that 'exquisite caution' was required if injustice were to be avoided. But too many people were by now committed to trials for them to be called off and Mather's own letter simultaneously hurled caution to the winds. He 'humbly recommended' that there be 'speedy and vigorous prosecutions' of all those who had made themselves obnoxious to God.

Five women entered the dock on 30 June 1692. The trial that ensued was a proclamation of guilt rather than an investigation of it. There were no defence lawyers, who were banned in Massachusetts on the strength of a theory then prevalent across England and America that judges could be relied upon to defend an accused. That hope reflected reality at Salem even less than usual. The accusers, testifying with eyes closed and convulsing in unison, impressed the bench as much as they did the jurors. When a girl shrieked that Sarah Good's spirit had just stabbed her – and produced a blade to prove it – a young man stepped up to say that it came from a knife he had accidentally broken the day before. He had the handle with him, and passed it to the judges. The senior among them, William Stoughton, placed the two pieces together and, finding them to be a perfect fit, angrily told the witness not to lie. He then invited her to continue her evidence. The jurors went on to return guilty verdicts on everyone except old Rebecca Nurse, and even that glimmer of mercy was snuffed out when Stoughton suggested that they reconsider. After a huddled conference the twelve men changed their minds. To complete the travesty, Governor Phipps issued her a reprieve only to withdraw it after receiving too many complaints.

The defendants were hanged on 19 July. As they stood on Gallows Hill, all maintained their innocence. Clergyman Nicholas Noyes urged Sarah Good to confess, because she was a witch and knew it. 'And you are a liar,' she spat back. 'I am no more a witch than you are a wizard, and if you take away my life, God will give you blood to drink.'

The jury went on to hold two more trials, and by mid September another four men and one woman had been hanged and fifteen others awaited execution. Every single person arraigned had been convicted. But although the chances of acquittal at trial were turning out to be zero, a refusal to submit to the ritual was not something to which Salem's leaders took kindly. Another person indicted was Giles Corey, the 80-year-old husband of Martha, but he declined to enter a plea when brought before the jurors who had just condemned his wife to death. Salem's judges thereupon dusted off the thirteenth-century English statute that pre-scribed pressing under weights for defendants who would not put themselves at the mercy of their neighbours. Corey expired in agony on 19 September, millstones on his chest and Salem's sheriff prodding his tongue back into his mouth with a cane.

Martha Corey, along with six other women and one man, made her own journey from Salem's dungeons to Gallows Hill three days later. All eight had refused to confess in exchange for a reprieve. Mary Easty had made a written plea for clemency but explained that she could not sacrifice her soul by admitting a crime that she had not committed. Samuel Wardwell's honesty was even more remarkable: he did make a confession, but then repented of the lie and chose to take up his place on the scaffold. As smoke from the executioner's pipe rose in clouds around the noosed defendants, all denied their guilt with angry eloquence until the cart was pulled forward and they tumbled into the early morning air. 'What a sad thing it is', declared Nicholas Noyes – sounding, in fact, positively gleeful by the stan-dards of a Puritan divine – 'to see eight firebrands of hell hanging there.'

Accusers now began to fan out to surrounding communities. When a widower from neighbouring Andover asked the victims of Salem to iden-tify who had given his wife her fatal fever, they offered so many leads that one in twelve of the town's inhabitants was soon in custody. The local magistrate eventually chose to flee rather than issue any more warrants – whereupon Salemites themselves turned on his brother and accused him of bewitching a dog. He duly beat a retreat of his own and the hapless hound was put to death; Andover's inhabitants, not wanting to be left out, then killed a cur of their own on suspicion that it possessed the evil eye. But like a pathogen that was too virulent for its own good, the accusations were finally overreaching themselves.

In early October, the wife of John Hale, a pastor from the nearby town of Beverly, fell under suspicion. Convinced until that moment that it was impossible to make a witchcraft accusation unless divinely inspired, Hale changed his mind overnight. Increase Mather, meanwhile, wrote a new tract advising readers that God 'had never intended that all persons guilty of Capital Crimes should be discovered and punished ... in this life', and that it was in fact 'better that ten suspected Witches should escape, than that one innocent Person should be Condemned'. The men of power in Massachusetts were finally realizing what they had unleashed – and according to one contemporary account, Governor Phipps was then informed that his own wife had been accused. Whether true or not, arrests were suddenly suspended. In a letter that all but quivers with panic, Phipps wrote to London on 12 October 'with all imaginable respect' to tell them that he had set up a court because of the 'loud cries and clamours' of others, before leaving for western Massachusetts – only to find on his return that accusations were being levelled against 'severall persons who were doubtlesse inocent and to my certaine knowledge of good reputation'. He had therefore called a halt to the prosecutions, he informed his masters, but felt compelled to write 'because I know my enemys are seeking to turne it all upon mee'. Coming from a man who had not only reprieved Rebecca Nurse but also withdrawn the reprieve, the disingenuity was so craven as to be daring, but the wind in which he was now swivelling was at least benign.

A trial of twenty-six people in early January resulted in not guilty verdicts against all but three, who, unaware that the unwritten rules were changing, had thought it sensible to confess. Phipps pardoned the convicted trio, and by the time of the last court appearances, held in Boston on 25 April 1693, a grand jury refused even to indict a servant called Mary Watkins notwithstanding her own insistence that she was a witch. After nineteen hangings, five deaths in custody, and the pressing to death of an 80-year-old man, the storm at Salem had finally been stilled.

Reactions to the reversal were mixed. The chief judge, William Stoughton, stalked out of his court on hearing the news. '[W]ho it is obstructs the course of Justice I know not,' he fumed, 'the Lord be merciful to the Countrey.' Most were rather more penitent. The colony abolished witchcraft as a crime within two years, and on 14 January 1697 it held a Day of Humiliation during which one judge and all twelve Salem jurors craved forgiveness. Ann Putnam, the driving force behind the first accusations, made a public plea for atonement in Salem's church in 1706.

All, needless to say, laid the blame for their errors squarely on the shoulders of Satan.

The trials have earned the Puritans a reputation as bigoted psychopaths, but the caricature is considerably more misleading than useful. Seventeenth-century Massachusetts never had more than fifteen capital offences – at a time when England's tally was about fifty, with a four-fold increase not far ahead – and the death toll at Salem was probably greater than all previous witchcraft executions in colonial America put together. There were very specific reasons why the prosecutions occurred when and where they did. Conflicts and land disputes fractured Salem village, pitting established families against parvenus, and the ruptures widened in 1689 with the appointment of Samuel Parris as the community's minister. His niece then set the accusations in motion, his slave inflamed them, and other afflicted girls came from families allied to him, while victims were disproportionately drawn from his enemies. Parris himself preached incendiary sermons in which he warned members of his congregation that Satan and the Lamb were warring in Salem and that they themselves were either saints or devils – with the community or against it.

In a community so riven, the persecution of 1692 performed an almost exorcistic role. Obstinacy had always been a sin that Massachusetts judges regarded as particularly blameworthy, and at Salem the desire to see conformity simply reached extreme proportions. Everyone who admitted guilt was spared, while every defendant who refused to do so was condemned to hang. Those who would not humble themselves before the community were spat out from it. The public show of guilt and repentance held Salem together as much as it tore it apart.

But atypical though the trials were, the accusations built on a long history. The dark Devil and fluttering birds of Salem were not conjured into existence by the desperation of Tituba and the shadows of the village's meeting house alone; Temperance Lloyd had seen them both and told the jury so at Exeter ten years before. Spectral evidence and excitable teenagers had sent Amy Duny and Rose Cullender to their deaths at Bury St Edmunds in 1664, after a trial that Salem's judges both studied and relied upon. The less specific features of the Salem panic, a fear of the enemy that refused to reveal itself and a desire to see it confess its nature, had also emerged many times before. They would do so many times again.

*   *   *

Salem was the last great gasp of the Western world's witch frenzy. As professionals and intellectuals increasingly subscribed to philosophies that removed God from the cosmic machine, societies handed to doctors the responsibility of identifying and treating those deviants whose supposed witchcraft had previously been handled by lawyers and priests. Executions sputtered on across continental Europe until the mid eighteenth century, while English juries remained superstitious enough to convict for two decades after Salem, but most judges now became sceptics – often pushing for acquittals, and invariably arranging reprieves for those found guilty. One of Sir Matthew Hale's successors as Lord Chief Justice, Sir John Holt, presided over some eleven not guilty verdicts in the late 1600s. By 1712, when Jane Wenham became the last person to be convicted by a jury – on a charge that she had conversed with Satan in the form of a cat – the scepticism from the bench was overwhelming. Sir John Powell ridiculed the evidence throughout, cheerfully observing at one point that there was no law against flying; and although he was sufficiently taken aback to ask the jurors if they *really* thought Wenham guilty of speaking to a satanic cat, he made sure to secure her a pardon. The final accusation came in 1717, when twenty-five informants asked a Leicester grand jury to indict three people who, they claimed, had floated like corks, remained bloodless when scratched, and caused them to vomit gravel, void immense stones from their bowels and exhale black bumblebees. The charges sound impressive enough, but even the jurors now refused to let the case proceed. The offence was finally abolished in 1735. Sixteen years later a Hertfordshire mob could still find the fear to drag Ruth Osborne from the church in which she had sought sanctuary and drown her in a stream; but it was the chimney sweep at its head who was hanged, and he died penitent, exhorting those around not to be so 'mad-brain'd' as to believe in witchcraft.

There was a nice irony about the 1735 statute. In the name of combating superstition, it did not just decriminalize witchcraft but made it an offence to 'pretend' to have magical powers – thus restoring Britain to the Dark Age orthodoxy that claims of sorcery were sinful even though sorcery itself did not exist. The law was deployed for the last time in early 1944 to prosecute a spiritualist called Helen Duncan in the naval town of Portsmouth. Duncan's promise to bring news from beyond the grave in return for twelve shillings and sixpence was doing little to boost morale at a time of war,* and a raid on one of her séances was followed by a charge that she had been 'pretending to conjure spirits'. Detective Inspector Ford and War Reserve Constable Cross testified that she had been manipulating a muslin sheet which, when seized, had been pulled away by someone in the audience. Duncan countered that that was no sheet, but ectoplasm that had dematerialized when touched by mortal flesh. The jury went with Ford and Cross, and she was sentenced to nine months in jail. She appealed on the basis that, far from 'pretending' to invoke spirits she had in fact been doing so, but the Court of Appeal ruled that the claim was all that counted. The contrary conclusion, it pointed out, would require that she be allowed to demonstrate the genuineness of her talents, and jurors could not be expected to assess the tangibility of ectoplasm in a dim light. It makes sense, even if the law had for several centuries asked them to do little less.

There has been no shortage of modern explanations for the witch-hunts. Neo-pagans, inspired by the discredited theories of a pre-war historian called Margaret Murray, still claim that they represented official attempts to suppress an ancient fertility cult that worshipped a great horned god. Some feminocentric writers have argued that they were a patriarchal holocaust. Others have pointed the finger at hard drugs, observing that rye – a staple food of the poor – was often contaminated by a hallucinogenic fungus called ergot and noting that some inquisitorial records contain recipes for mind-bending potions that would still make people think they could fly today. But a phenomenon that spanned two hundred years and five thousand miles, implicating peasants and princes and impelling countless women to send other women to their deaths, was underpinned by more than gender bias and really bad trips. If that ever needed proof, it came during the 1980s, when a campaign against satanic sexual abuse generated accusations of nocturnal flights, orgiastic sex, and ritual sacrifice that could have been drawn almost directly from the records of a sixteenth-century trial.

---

* That at least was the official reason for the prosecution. A legend within the spiritualist community has always insisted that the true motivation was panic within official circles that a loose-lipped spirit might tell Duncan the date of D-Day: see e.g. Alan E. Crossley, *The Story of Helen Duncan, Materialisation Medium* (Ilfracombe, 1975), pp. 66-8.

The case that would form the basis for all the others began on 12 August 1983, when Judy Johnson of Manhattan Beach, California, contacted the police to tell them that her 2½-year-old son had a sore 'bottom'. She was concerned that a teacher called Ray Buckey at his preschool might have assaulted him. At a time when it was becoming apparent that the abuse of children had been under-reported and under-investigated for decades, the allegations were taken very seriously – and they would get worse. By February 1984, Johnson would be telling investigators not just that the 25-year-old teacher had sodomized her son, but that his colleagues had plunged scissors into the boy's eye and stapled his ears, nipples, and tongue. Weirder events had also occurred. Although the teachers were all outwardly respectable Christian Scientists, they had supposedly taken him to a church where, by the light of black candles, Buckey's septuagenarian grandmother had played a piano and the child had been forced to insert his cut finger into the anus of a goat. Buckey's mother, Peggy McMartin, had sacrificed a baby, burned its brains, and given him blood to drink. Johnson's son had then been buried alive in a sealed coffin.

Johnson was a mentally disturbed alcoholic and the claims, which she was attributing to a toddler with no evident physical injuries, were as fantastic as they sound. But instead of wondering whether she might be wrong, the authorities proceeded from the outset on the assumption that she had to be right. The premises of the McMartin preschool, established by Ray Buckey's grandmother, Virginia McMartin, almost thirty years before, were searched and Buckey himself was arrested on 7 September 1983. He was promptly released for lack of evidence, but the police followed up by writing a day later to the parents of two hundred past and present McMartin pupils with a request for further information. In particular, they wanted to know if anyone had seen Buckey tie anyone up, or recalled having been fondled, subjected to oral sex, or sodomized by him.

The parents, not one of whom had ever previously heard any complaints of sexual abuse at the school, were understandably sent into a tailspin. Police advised them to contact the Children's Institute International, a clinic specializing in childhood trauma, where director Kee MacFarlane could provide assistance. But MacFarlane, though committed to the protection of abused children and the recipient of several awards for her work on their behalf, had no professional qualifications, and events would subsequently unfold with an inevitability that was as farcical as it was tragic. She subscribed to a theory then at the cutting edge of therapeutic thought – that children were literally incapable of lying about abuse – and had developed a whole series of informal interviewing techniques, involving mismatched clothes, non-standard language and the use of hand puppets and dolls with realistic sexual organs. At the behest of the police, she now began using the same methods to gather evidence. And just as inquisitors had once transformed their hunches about Satan's penis into evidence of congress with demons, she and fellow investigators would confect a case from theory and enthusiasm alone.

Using black dolls to represent the teachers and white ones for everyone else, they encouraged the children to place the puppets' breasts, penises and vaginas wherever whatever might have happened had happened. Some were advised to take out their anger by beating up the Ray Buckey puppet. Speaking through characters like Mr Alligator and Pac-Man, MacFarlane told her interviewees that it was now safe to tell the truth – or, as she put it, to reveal their 'yucky secrets' – because '[a]ll the mummies and daddies' already knew about 'all the touching, the sneaky games'. The parents were, she added, extremely pleased with those other children who had been honest with her. Anyone who responded with memories of their abuse was rewarded with praise and cuddles. Those less forthcoming were told, notwithstanding the notional need to believe them, that they were being forgetful, unhelpful, and – in at least one case – 'dumb'.

Although none had mentioned sexual abuse before coming to MacFarlane, many were soon speaking of little else. As they manipulated the dolls' genitalia, several recalled acts of athletic sex and penetration by objects. Encouraged by MacFarlane's enthusiasm, many added that the abuse had taken place in studios filled with floodlights and photographic umbrellas. Others described tunnels and secret chambers under their classrooms, through which teachers had whisked them away for escapades in car washes, zoos, aircraft cabins, and hot-air balloons. One had apparently been flushed down the school's toilets and through the sewer system for an abusive rendezvous before being cleaned up and returned in time for the home run. An increasing number also began to remember that very sinister rituals had often accompanied the sex. Some had seen Ray Buckey in a red robe. Others had been made to watch the slaughter of creatures ranging from horses to hamsters; one boy recalled that pupils themselves were provided with knives and hypodermics in order that they could kill beasts in class. For reasons unspecified, teachers had also taken some children to a local cemetery where, supervised by intoning priests and nuns, they had been given pickaxes, shovels, and pulleys and set to work disinterring corpses. By March 1984, MacFarlane had interviewed almost four hundred children, and her conclusions were as awful as could have been expected. All but thirty-one, she feared, had been subjected to acts of sexual violence by a cabal of satanic schoolteachers.

Her findings were corroborated, after a fashion, by one of her colleagues. Consultant paediatrician Dr Astrid Heger used a recently invented device to take and examine photographs of the genitalia of 150 children, and she detected signs that were 'consistent' with attempted sodomy, or the full act, in four-fifths of them. It was an impressive proportion, save that no research had yet been carried out anywhere in the world to establish what would definitely be *inconsistent* with it. After three centuries, the Devil's teat had been rediscovered.

Strenuous efforts were made to find something – anything – else. The sheriff's office hired archaeologists to search the school grounds for tunnels and indications of ritual slaughter, but although excavations unearthed fragments of a turtle shell and some chicken bones, subsequent analysis would disclose no signs of slaughter, ritual or otherwise. FBI agents perused reams of child pornography in the hope of finding a photograph taken at McMartin, but all in vain. The only material that would add any ballast at all to the prosecution case consisted of items removed from the Buckey household – and its weight was not great. The objects seized included several copies of *Playboy*, a graduation gown (later described as a satanic robe), and a rubber duck – seized on the grounds that it showed an 'interest in children'.

A juggernaut was rolling, however, and momentum alone would now keep it moving. A series of reports on Los Angeles KABC-Channel 7, heralded by full-page newspaper ads that showed a battered teddy bear with a missing eye, alerted the city to sinister goings-on at McMartin. District Attorney Robert Philibosian, then fighting a bitter re-election campaign, offered dubious reassurance by appearing on television himself to let it be known that he had just broken the biggest child pornography ring in American history. Los Angelinos responded by displaying bumper stickers declaring 'I believe the children'. Ray Buckey and

six other teachers, including his sister, mother, and 79-year-old grandmother, were meanwhile indicted in March 1984 on over a hundred
counts of sexual assault. The number soon doubled.

A preliminary hearing began in August. Such hearings, specific to
California, are held before a judge in order to weed out frivolous accusations, but the procedure's effectiveness in the McMartin case was limited. By
the time the inquiry came to an end eighteen months later – longer than
any previous preliminary hearing in California's history – the weaknesses in
the prosecution case had indeed become sufficiently apparent that charges
were dropped against five defendants. Ray Buckey and his mother were
ordered to stand trial, however, and although Peggy McMartin was finally
granted bail – after one and a half years in jail – her son was denied it. And
the public hearings, as so often before, had operated to magnify observers'
passions rather than dissipate them. Three-quarters of respondents to a
telephone poll thought that the five freed defendants had escaped justice.
One parent suggested that they might not do so for long. 'They'd be better
off with the trial,' observed Robert Currie. 'Otherwise I don't think they're
going to live.' Well over 90 per cent of those polled assumed Ray Buckey and
Peggy McMartin themselves to be guilty.

The trial proper, which would last for two and a half years, got underway in July 1987. It was one of the first ever televised in the United States
and ranks as one of the sorriest courtroom spectacles ever staged in
California, a state that has seen forensic farces aplenty. Judy Johnson died
of liver failure before it began and the trial judge decided that her son was
too disturbed to testify, with the result that the case came to rest on fourteen children handpicked on MacFarlane's advice as being most likely
to impress the jury. Of those, only ten eventually testified. One was
11-year-old Arthur, who recalled seeing Ray Buckey kill a horse on a
ranch with bare hands and baseball bat. Another was 13-year-old Billy,
who had watched his teacher hack a pony to pieces with a machete. Billy
also remembered an incident when Ray had sacrificed a rabbit on the altar
of the St Cross Episcopal Church, while he himself was being molested
by hooded, chanting, and atomically radiated mutants.

Prosecutor Lael Rubin shored up such claims with the meaningless
medical findings of Dr Heger, and the items seized from the Buckey
residence – up to and including the rubber duck. She also relied on the
testimony of a career criminal called George Freeman, who swore that Ray

Buckey had confided in him as they sat in jail about his proclivity to slaughter animals and commit ritualized sodomy. It soon turned out that Freeman had been placed in Buckey's cell at the DA's request, had previously informed on six other fellow cellmates, and had nine felony convictions and an untried murder allegation against his name. He had also committed perjury at least three times before.

The defendants testified wearily and angrily to their innocence, while their lawyers did their best to contradict those aspects of the prosecution case that were susceptible to verification. The owner of the ranch at which Buckey was said to have pummelled a horse to death told the jurors that none of her Arabian stallions had died during the three years in question. A bookkeeper at the St Cross Episcopal Church testified that she had never seen blood on its altar. Its priest denied that atomic mutants in hooded robes had even entered the building. He spent most of his time at the church, he explained, and if he left he made sure to lock the doors.

In January 1990, the jury found Peggy McMartin not guilty and acquitted her son of all but thirteen of the sixty-five charges against him. They were unable to agree on the remainder. Most jurors later explained that, although they thought that some of the children had been abused, they were not sure Ray Buckey was responsible and had found MacFarlane's interviews to be biased. It was a fair assessment after what had been the longest trial in American history. But Robert Philibosian's successor as Los Angeles' District Attorney, Ira Reiner, was now running for election as state Attorney-General and his office announced that it would proceed with a retrial. Only when the second jury also deadlocked, leaning strongly in favour of acquittal, did the DA's office decide – after a process that had cost over $15 million, reduced the McMartins to penury, and kept Ray Buckey in jail for five years – to throw in the towel. 'But', added a spokesperson, 'that does not mean he is not guilty.'

The source of the association between satanism and sexual abuse that assumed such force in the McMartin case is hard to pin down. Robert Currie, the parent who warned in 1986 that five defendants might not survive freedom, would later claim credit for identifying the connection. Others would trace it to a 1980 bestseller called *Michelle Remembers* in which the eponymous Michelle, assisted by her therapist (and co-author, and future husband), retrieved memories of horrendous assaults from not just diabolists but the Devil himself. Echoes from the work of men such as Heinrich Kramer and Pierre de Lancre suggest wellsprings even deeper. But whatever its origins, it tapped into fears that were pervasive.

Within months of Ray Buckey's arrest in September 1983 police in Jordan, Minnesota, had turned a simple sexual assault case into an investigation into satanism, yielding accusations that would soon see twenty-four people charged with having committed acts of ritualized abuse. The State Attorney-General's office would later accept that twenty-three had committed no crime at all, but the arrests marked the beginning of a national crisis. In September 1984, Kee MacFarlane warned a Congressional committee that the United States faced 'unthinkable networks of crimes against children', and in May 1985 ABC devoted a segment of its flagship *20–20* show to McMartin's 'sexual house of horrors'. Police officers from Toledo, Ohio, spent the summer solstice excavating a rubbish tip, hopefully but fruitlessly, having been told that it contained scores of dead children, and an unholy alliance of social workers, fundamentalists, and cult-busting cops meanwhile began to promote the anti-satanic gospel across the country. By September 1988, Patricia Pulling – whose specific concern revolved around the role-playing game *Dungeons and Dragons* – had calculated that the USA contained thirty thousand satanists, many in high places, and six months earlier she had estimated their number as a full three hundred thousand. Henri Boguet had, interestingly enough, reached precisely the same two figures when working out the extent of witchery in sixteenth-century France.

The fact that a child talks about monsters and witches hardly excludes the possibility that violent sexual assaults have occurred. It may well support it. But although official investigations have disclosed a handful of cases in which invented rituals were used by abusers to mystify children and frighten them into silence, none has ever found evidence of sexual violence being directed towards magical objectives. And although dozens of people were charged during the 1980s and early 1990s on the strength of accusations involving cannibalism and ceremonial slaughter, never once did such matters form the basis for a conviction after a contested trial.

There has been one person who pleaded guilty in such a case, but his confession is about as fragile a basis for asserting the reality of satanic abuse as can be imagined. In 1988 Paul Ingrams, a Protestant fundamentalist police officer from the state of Washington, was accused of sexual assaults by his two daughters and he was soon admitting that crime – and volunteering several others. Spurred on by the exhortations of his pastor, he began to recall images of robed diabolists and animal sacrifices, and the daughters were soon augmenting his memories with tales of infanticidal rituals during which they had been raped, nailed to the ground and penetrated by goats. Ingrams would later backtrack, claiming that he had admitted crimes that he could not actually remember for fear that Satan had erased them from his mind. The daughters themselves had recovered memories of the abuse only after one had been told of its existence by a charismatic faith healer. Medical examinations of both showed no relevant injuries, and excavation of a supposed satanic burial ground produced only an elk bone. But although most people familiar with the case – including a cult specialist first brought into it as a prosecution witness – came to regard both Ingrams and his accusers as fantasists, the court of appeals did not allow him to withdraw his plea. He served fourteen years before his release on parole in April 2003.

Anyone tempted to think that the satanic panic of the 1980s was a peculiarly American phenomenon would be wrong. A wave of prosecutions swept across the United Kingdom after 1989, and as rumours flew and child-protection conferences proliferated, similar cases would be seen throughout the English-speaking world. The allegations of diabolism were no more substantiated anywhere else than they had been against Ray Buckey, but any internet search will confirm that even today, it is not only American prosecutors and appellate judges who worry that satanic abusers stalk the earth. Only the fragile safeguards of the criminal process keep the fear within bounds.

Everyone can agree that the witch-hunts were 'irrational', but the lessons to be learned from that irrationality have always inspired controversy. Reactions to the 1953 Broadway opening of Arthur Miller's *The Crucible* are a case in point. The play premiered at a time of escalating fears of communist infiltration, a panic fostered by Senator Joseph McCarthy and the House Un-American Activities Committee, and it was immediately appreciated that Miller was drawing analogies between the seventeenth century and the twentieth. Several critics complained that the comparison was specious. Whereas Salem's witches had not existed, they pointed out, members of the American Communist Party certainly did.

Insofar as the objection was more than an opportunistic shot at Miller's liberal politics, it was misdirected. The key feature of the early modern witch-hunts was not that they focused on evils that did not exist. Their lunacy – and their lethality – arose because they allowed for punishment on the strength of panic alone. Individuals were called to account for vast events that they could never have prevented, because they seemed to be the kind of people who would have brought them about if they could. The absence of proof linking them to crime became a reason to intensify the search rather than to abandon it.

The mentality was not specific to witchcraft, and it revived during the first years of the Cold War just as it did during the 1980s. Those pursuing the accusations against Communists and satanic abusers thought that they were tackling real crimes and were inspired by the most unassailable of motives – whether a love of country or concern for children – but the righteousness of their cause compounded the irrationality instead of controlling it. And faith in the essential rationality of modern prosecution can still blind people to an aspect of criminal justice that has very little to do with objective realities and hard facts. For it is not the presumption of innocence, but the possibility of conviction, that fuels the criminal trial – and the urge to punish lies close to the heart of every prosecution.

A trial is not a whodunit. It has only one suspect – and the hope that the person accused will be proved guilty is generally far more compelling than the formal insistence that he or she may not be. There can certainly be pleasure in seeing innocence vindicated, but it only exceptionally matches the thrill of seeing the guilty go down. Evidence of that can be seen, or felt, during any high-profile trial. Popular reaction to the McMartin charges produced a particularly striking illustration of the rule. At the height of the hysteria, a *Los Angeles Times* poll of July 1985 showed three times as many people concerned that guilty abusers would not face trial than were worried about the dangers of making innocent citizens undergo one.

The reasons for the visceral appeal of punishment are obscure. A psychoanalyst might claim that people subconsciously identify with the desires of a wrongdoer even as they suppress them, and it is intuitively plausible that those who follow a trial are less concerned to explore the difference of the defendant than to punish the similarities that they fearfully detect. What is very clear, however, is that the restraint of prejudice is only one of the functions that prosecutions have historically served. They have often, like a rain dance, dispelled doubts using noise and movement alone. As the next chapter makes even clearer, some of the rituals have fallen only just short of sacrificial.

5

The Trials of Animals, Corpses, and Things

'He doesn't know the sentence?' . . . 'No', said the officer. 'It would be pointless telling him. He learns it on his body.'

FRANZ KAFKA, *In the Penal Colony*

In April 1545, the small Alpine village of St Julien was hit by crisis. Weevils had begun eating their way through its vineyards, and were threatening to destroy the local economy. The peasants turned for help to the Church. In an era when an Act of God was no mere accident, that is hardly surprising. Rather more noteworthy is that their pleas came not on bended knees in the parish church, but in the form of an application for relief to the episcopal court of the diocese.

The tribunal's willingness to entertain the complaint honoured a long Catholic tradition of resolving conundrums through open debate. By the mid 1500s, the Church had been engaging Jews, Muslims and heretics in disputations for the better part of a thousand years. Its faith in internal free speech remained firm during the Counter-Reformation – so much so that Pope Sixtus V in 1587 institutionalized the Devil's Advocate, an officer required to advance all those arguments that Satan himself might use against prospective saints. At a popular level, episcopal courts had preserved an accessibility that the tribunals of the papal and secular inquisitions had never even adopted. And the judge who heard the application of St Julien's communards certainly honoured Catholicism's open-minded traditions.

On receiving notice of the application, he appointed two lawyers to defend the weevils. After hearing arguments from both sides, he then bent over backwards to accommodate the insects. Noting that the fruits of the earth had been created not only for humans, he warned that it would be 'unbecoming to proceed with rashness and precipitation against the animals now actually accused and indicted'. Far better, he suggested, for the locals to turn to the Lord, repent of their sins, and carry Communion wafers around the afflicted vineyards, according to a complex schedule which he proceeded to set out in full.

The prescription was remarkably successful, at least if the local curate's records are to be believed, and for four long decades the cycle of harvesting, treading, and drinking resumed its ancient rhythm in the terraces of St Julien. But in 1587 a weevil, or perhaps more than one, was spotted again, and the villagers headed straight back to court to re-apply for the relief that had been refused their forefathers. The court instructed new lawyers, those previously instructed having all died, and adjourned to enable everyone to get up to speed. Within just a few weeks, the case was ready for trial.

Battle was joined on 6 June 1587 and Pierre Rembaud, the principal advocate on the beetles' two-man team, delivered a series of forceful submissions that showed him to be a champion worthy of his clients. God Himself had created and blessed the lower orders, he reminded those listening, and it had to be presumed that He had not done so in order that weevils would starve. Had He not, Rembaud demanded, expressly stated in the Book of Genesis that 'to every thing that creepeth upon the earth . . . I have given every green herb for meat'? He then suggested that it was absurd to invoke human laws against animals anyway, and – doubtless concerned not to end on a weak point – wrapped up with a vituperative attack on the character of his opponents. Quoting liberally from the Scriptures, he warned the people of St Julien that instead of launching judicial proceedings against a group of defenceless weevils, they should have fasted and donned sackcloth, for all the signs were that they faced imminent annihilation from God.

Rembaud had every reason to expect that the court would accord his submissions great respect. In a thirteenth-century action brought by

Mainz peasants against an infestation of bright green beetles, to take one of several possible examples, the insects' representative (who was appointed 'due to their small size and their status as minors') was not just heard with politeness. He was able to persuade the court to give the beetles a parcel of land, which was still being leased to them, by way of an annually renewed contract, several decades later. The St Julien drama would drag on for at least three more months and the records end somewhat inconclusively, but there are certainly indications that it had a similar outcome.

During one of several adjournments that punctuated the case, the villagers gathered in the local square at the suggestion of their lawyer and hammered out proposals for a settlement. The weevils were offered a nearby tract of land, described as a fertile place of oaks, planes, and cypresses, and were asked only to share its springs, give up any claim to its ochre deposits, and grant St Julien's residents shelter during wartime – 'without prejudice to the said Animals' rights of pasture'. The compromise does not sound unreasonable – not least because the Duke of Savoy was busily shuffling troops through the town and preparing to invade nearby Saluzzo – but it was not enough.

Whatever their clients' response might have been, their lawyers treated the offer with contempt. As soon as the soldiers had departed, Pierre Rembaud's colleague, Antoine Filliol, returned to court to assert that the land was in fact barren and wholly incapable of feeding the weevils. And instead of formulating alternative proposals he invited the court to dismiss the villagers' claim with costs. Sadly, it will never be known whether the hardball paid off. Shreds of the last page of the trial record reveal that experts were paid three florins to visit the site and report on its suitability, but the document's final words have been lost – destroyed, according to one historian, by vermin.

Weevils were not the only non-human defendants to be brought to justice in early modern Europe. For at least four centuries, beginning in the thirteenth, ecclesiastical tribunals would routinely, if theoretically, restrain the activities of inconvenient, recalcitrant, and rapacious creatures of all kinds. The lamprey of Lake Geneva were ordered to cease, desist or leave in 1451, when fishermen complained that the little suckers were molesting the local salmon. Glaciers around the village of

Chamonix had to reckon with exorcisms throughout the early 1600s. The jurisprudence even established a toehold in Catholicism's transatlantic empire, when in 1706 the Franciscan friars of St Anthony's cloister in Piedade no Maranhão, Brazil, proceeded against a colony of ants that had been eating their flour and tunnelling under their walls. The Portuguese chronicler of the dispute recorded that the case had ended very amicably indeed. The insects' lawyer won them alternative accommodation, and when the details were recited before their hills, the ants reportedly filed out in immense columns and marched in their millions to the field assigned.

The force of law was also brought to bear against animals that overstepped natural lines of decency and propriety. A Latin entry in the diary of Basel's fifteenth-century chaplain recounts, for example, the judicial comeuppance suffered in 1474 by a rooster that had laid an egg. Naturalists had long warned that so unnatural an occurrence heralded the hatching of a basilisk: a hybrid of cockerel and serpent that belched lethal fumes and was capable of killing by its glare alone. In an era keenly attuned to coincidence, the similarity between the words 'basilisk' and 'Basel' could only have added to the unease. The fowl was decapitated and disembowelled outside the municipal courthouse before a large crowd of onlookers, all presumably torn even more

A 17th century basilisk. 'Born by fermentation from a mixture of semens,' it inspired less fear than its predecessor and was exhibited for many years in the Boboli Gardens in Florence.

than usual between the urges to watch and to look away, and magistrates found two more eggs before incinerating the messy *corpus delicti*.

Animals that ignored their station by having sex with human beings were punished no less harshly. Only exceptionally did they receive treatment different from that given their human accomplices. A buggered mule from Montpellier had its hoofs severed at the stake in 1565, whereas its partner in crime went to his death with feet intact; but the amputation occurred only because the beast had proved 'vicious and inclined to kick'. When Guillaume Guyart escaped from custody and left his sodomized dog to burn alone at Chartres in 1606, the authorities did their best to minimize the injustice by nailing a painting of him to the gallows. The case of Jacques Ferron, convicted at Vanvres in 1750 for coupling with a female donkey, offers perhaps the most impressive illustration of judicial even-handedness. Man and beast faced certain execution until Ferron's neighbours and parish priest petitioned the court to show mercy. Unfortunately for Ferron, they vouched only for the good character of the animal. The signatories claimed to have known her for four years and affirmed that she was 'in word and deed and in all her habits of life a most honest creature'. Not a word was said about her co-defendant. The villagers' willingness to overlook the ass's moment of madness – which was probably motivated less by pathological sentimentality than by the hope of preventing a valuable communal asset from going up in flames – paid off. The donkey was spared; Ferron was burned alive.

Scores, and possibly hundreds, of animals would also be tried for the most heinous transgression of all – homicide. Prosecutions are first recorded in thirteenth-century France, but they would spread west and north and continue for another five hundred years. Most of those charged were swine, as might be expected of an age when peasants' pigs regularly bedded down alongside the family cradle; but bulls, cows, and horses all had their day in court.

Again the animals were treated with all the dignity that would have been due any penniless human criminal, and exceptional treatment served only to confirm that equality was the norm. The municipal executioner of Schweinfurt chose not to wait for a death warrant before hanging a pig that had nibbled off a child's ear and hand in 1576, but his disrespect to the town's magistracy was such that he was forced to flee, never to return. When judges at the Abbey of Moyen-Moutier ordered in May 1572 that a swine be led to its doom by a rope – in a region where prisoners customarily went unencumbered by anything at all – they were careful to inform the executing authorities that their precaution established no precedent. They noted that the Lord-Abbot had been accustomed for time out of mind to consign condemned criminals wholly naked, but that 'by reason of the fact that the said pig is a brute beast, [the court] delivers and leaves [it] with you . . . bound with a cord.' The Lord-Abbot's decision to do so was, however, an act of grace that was 'without prejudice to his aforesaid rights to hand such criminals over to you in the nude', just as he always had, and just as he always would.

Lawyers were denied to all animals facing criminal charges (as they ordinarily were to human beings), but judges listened to evidence and reached verdicts that were never entirely preordained. A case from 1457 illustrates that well. It arose out of the death of 5-year-old Jehan Martin, whose half-eaten body had been found near the Burgundy estate of Savigny, surrounded by a sow and six snuffling piglets. The porcine family was arrested. After hearing from eight witnesses the court imposed the duchy's customary sentence for homicidal pigs on the mother – condemning her to be hanged by the hind legs. It noted with some concern, however, that no evidence directly implicated the piglets. Their owner, Jehan Bailly, was asked to put up 100 sols to guarantee their good conduct while further inquiries were conducted. Since the creatures had been apprehended next to a mutilated body, bathed in blood, it is – in a sense – understandable that he declined to vouch for them. But by the time the case returned to court a month later, the danger had passed. The little swine were acquitted.

Legal proprieties were observed no less scrupulously after conviction. A 1408 document signed by Toustain Pincheon, royal jailer at Normandy's Pont de Larche prison, shows, for example, that he took receipt of four shillings and two pence to cover the costs of feeding a pig for twenty-five days on death row. Escorted to the execution ground by a baying mob, carried in a cart, or dragged upside down on a hurdle, the animals were also killed just as humanely as anyone else. That could, of course, be very inhumane indeed. A sow convicted at Falaise in 1386 of gnawing the face and arms of a 3-month-old baby was condemned not just to hang, but to be maimed in a way that would reflect its crime. At the market square, the public executioner duly donned a single white glove, for which he would later invoice the local viscount, and only slipped the noose around its neck after he had torn at its head and foreleg with a pair of pincers. A mural that was later painted in the village church showed the pig thrashing from the gallows to be dressed in human clothes.

Pragmatic justifications would always be advanced for the homicide trials. The first jurist to write about them, a thirteenth-century lawyer called Philippe de Beaumanoir, evidently regarded them as money-spinners, advising the nobles of Beauvais only to execute dangerous beasts – and sell their carcasses – and to confiscate donkeys and horses alive. Pierre Ayrault, writing three hundred years later, was more analytical but equally rational-minded: the trials, he argued, were designed to establish whether the owner of the beast deserved to lose it while the punishments were staged to discourage human negligence. 'When we see a pig hanged for having eaten a child in the cradle,' he wrote in 1591, 'it is to warn fathers and mothers, carers and servants, not to leave children by themselves, and to secure their animals so that they cannot do harm to the children.'

Seigneurial greed is certainly evident in some trial records. The effect of acquitting the six piglets of Savigny in 1457 was to make them liable to confiscation, and the 100 sols bail imposed on their owner was a sum sufficiently hefty to savour of extortion rather than precaution. The hope of deterrence was also present in many cases: at Senlis in 1567, for example, where a black-snouted swine that had eaten the head of a 4-month-old girl was hanged outside her village, and its inhabitants warned to control their beasts on pain of fines and corporal punishment. But records show countless more animals executed at a lord's expense than they do ones seized to his profit, and the rules that most closely approximate Beaumanoir's recommendations – the customary laws of nearby Burgundy – contain chilling confirmation that the rational arguments obscured deeper passions. For pigs were not the only prisoners to be hanged upside down. After providing for the confiscation of horses and oxen, Burgundy's customary code specified that 'if another animal, or a Jew' should be found guilty, the convict was to be suspended by the *piez derreniers* – or 'hind legs' – until dead. Courts that could confiscate piglets while hanging their mother by the heels were concerned with something other than human carelessness. And a jurisprudence that recognized the value of a horse while treating Jews like swine was certainly not inspired by economics alone.*

Appearances notwithstanding, the trials and punishments never depended on the notion that beasts or insects were morally responsible for their actions. Europe's theologians and lawyers always agreed that innocence and guilt depended on the rational exercise of free will, and although debate would long rage over precisely what that meant for human beings, no thinker of note ever argued that animals were morally obliged to obey man-made laws. Philippe de Beaumanoir was already stating the obvious when he observed in the late thirteenth century that 'punishment is lost on [animals]', and his contemporary, Thomas Aquinas, was recapitulating equally conventional wisdom when he explained why penalties could have no moral basis. Human laws applied only to those 'who know what they are about, and have the alternative of doing a thing or leaving it undone', qualities that were 'proper to the rational creature only'. Irrational ones were subject instead to natural law – which described how God's creations *did* act instead of prescribing how they *should* act – and just as planets naturally obeyed it by wandering around the earth, animals did so by, for example, eating, quacking, or howling. Even Satan's activities could not alter the legal position. Although he might well manifest himself as an animal, he could do nothing without the nod from God. Condemnation of non-human creatures was therefore vain at the very least, warned Aquinas. It might even be blasphemous, insofar as the brute concerned was going about God's mysterious business.

---

* In the same vein, Europe's laws for centuries treated sex across the religious divide as an offence akin to bestiality. One of England's first legal writers recommended in 1290 that '[t]hose who have connexion with Jews and Jewesses or are guilty of bestiality or sodomy' were to be buried alive. Joost de Damhouder, an adviser to the King of Spain, opined in 1554 that Jews and Muslims were legally and theologically equivalent to beasts. Towards the end of the seventeenth century, Jacob Döpler summarized the reason for burning sexually indiscriminate Christians as being that it was equally criminal 'whether someone slept with a Jewess or a dog'. See Selden Society, *Fleta. Volume II. Prologue, Book I, Book II*, ed. Henry G. Richardson and George O. Sayles (London, 1955), p. 90; Joost de Damhouder, *Praxis rerum criminalum* (Antwerp, 1554), p. 360 ('De peccato contra naturam'); Jacob Döpler, *Theatrum poenarum, suppliciorum et executionum criminalium*, 2 vols (Sonderhausen and Leipzig, 1693–7), 2: 154.

That was not quite the last word, however. The distinction between things that did happen and those that ought to happen would remain a philosophically fuzzy one for five more centuries. The Old Testament made clear in any event that God Himself sometimes expected firm action – in that Exodus and Leviticus between them required that murderous oxen be stoned to death and sexually errant animals be annihilated – and medieval scholars had already justified that to everyone's satisfaction. As was explained in 1095 by a canonical scholar called Ivo of Chartres, destruction of such creatures served to suppress even the memory of their shameful acts, and in pursuit of so great a goal the irrationality of the culprit was irrelevant. The Church also had longstanding traditions of standing up to bestial evils in a more practical sense. Senior clerics had been ordaining at least since AD 868 that homicidal bees should be suffocated and their honey abhorred, and Aquinas' own era had produced several notable animal exorcists: men like the already legendary Bernard of Clairvaux who, finding Foigny Abbey filled with gnats, had muttered a curse so potent that monks had needed shovels to scoop up the fallen.

With such precedents informing him, it is hardly surprising that Aquinas' bar on legal action was far from absolute. In his *Summa theologica* – a compendium of late thirteenth-century wisdom that would form the backbone of Western moral philosophy for the next three hundred years – he opined that vengeance could properly be visited on animals to punish their owners and in 'horror of sin'. And while recognizing that irrationality ruled out punishment, he made clear that God could be asked to curse, or anathematize, an unwitting agent of Satan. The only precondition was that it had to be made clear that the target was the demonic possessor rather than the possessed creature itself.

The notion that it was wrong to hold beasts to account but proper to avenge their sins and damn their deeds occupies an intellectual structure that no longer looks very secure. But at a time when bishops and secular judges were constantly at loggerheads and facing regular pressure from papal inquisitors, both theories represented the cutting edge of jurisprudential thought. Rationality had worked its magic once again. For quadrupedal deviants, airborne insects, and creepy-crawlies of every description, the age of impunity was over.

*   *   *

*'On the condemnation of livestock': from a criminal law textbook
published in the Netherlands in 1555.*

The idea implicit in the writings of Ivo of Chartres and Thomas Aquinas, that laws apply simply because they exist, has over the years inspired inflexibility, complacency and brutality on a tremendous scale. But it has also underpinned a form of legal conservatism that is considerably more benign: the belief that certain rights are inalienable. For civil liberties owe at least as much to natural law traditions as to any modern political theory – a point vividly illustrated during a series of events that took place in sixteenth-century Provence.

In around 1510, peasants from Autun petitioned its episcopal court to hear their complaint that rats were destroying their barley crop. Trumpets and proclamations were sounded at several crossroads to notify the rodents of their obligations to attend court, and when they failed to appear, the prosecutor moved for judgment. The bishop, aware that the creatures stood on the brink of 'total destruction and extermination', thought it necessary however to give them a lawyer, and he appointed one Bartholomew Chassenée. The young advocate, who was destined to end his career as one of the most distinguished jurists in France, would fight his clients' corner with a tenacity that could put several modern public defenders to shame.

The rats' disobedience was compounded by their bad reputation,

which constituted powerful evidence of guilt under canonical law, but
Chassenée immediately seized the initiative with a ferocious counterattack.
The plaintiffs' action, he pointed out, did not just touch the health or ruin
of a handful of rats. Every single rodent in Autun was imperilled – and
every single one was therefore entitled to make representations. They were,
however, spread so far and wide that the summons issued could not possibly have notified them all. The fact that it did not appear to have notified
any was a point he ignored, but it evidently caused the court equally little
concern. For Chassenée had saved the day. The bench ruled that the
summons had been defective and remitted the case for re-hearing, ordering that the rats now be warned to attend by way of sermons preached
from every pulpit in Autun.

The priests of the diocese obediently promulgated the summons and
the time eventually came for the court to reconvene. Lawyers, clerics and
peasants gathered in the courtroom to await the rats' arrival. History does
not record how long it was before they stopped waiting. The record shows
however that not a single rat turned up. A lesser lawyer might have yielded
gracefully, but Chassenée was made of stern stuff. After acknowledging
that his clients had ignored the summons, he claimed that they had been
given too little time. He went further. It was an ancient principle of customary law that no defendant was required to risk life or limb to come to
court, and Chassenée argued that his clients therefore had a cast-iron
excuse. They were rats – and on every highway and byway, there were cats.
No court purporting to observe natural law could reasonably condemn a

rat for fearing a cat. Ergo, their absence was justified. Autun's judges seem to have been impressed with the logic. So much so, indeed, that they adjourned the case. Chassenée had won yet another reprieve.

As with the weevils of St Julien, no record of the court's final verdict has survived and there is no way of knowing whether the dilatory rodents took advantage of all the efforts being made on their behalf. It seems unlikely, however, and the court's own precedents suggest that it would have condemned them to perpetual banishment. When it had ruled against a snail invasion in 1487, it had instructed every priest in Autun to lead parishioners in processions under the standard of the cross for three days, sprinkling holy water and clutching illuminated tapers as they went. '[Y]ou should warn and adjure the said snails', the clergy had been advised, 'that they should desist within three days time from [their] destruction and devastation . . . and transfer themselves to deserted places, where they shall not be able to damage creatures and the fruits of the earth, under threat of the divine majesty's anger and eternal curse.' If, however, the rats had displayed the seriousness that everyone else was showing, it is just conceivable that the judgment might have been more merciful. A community of moles in the Tyrolean town of Stilfs, accused by three witnesses in 1500 of 'burrowing and throwing up the earth so that neither grass nor green thing could grow', won significant concessions after their counsel pointed out that they also helped the harvest by consuming caterpillar pupae. Though exiled, each defendant was granted a safe conduct against dogs and cats, and those that were pregnant or of tender years were given fourteen extra days to depart.

Whatever the fortunes of Autun's rats, Chassenée's own career went from strength to strength, and in 1531, fresh from a triumphant result against a plague of locusts, he wrote the most authoritative guide to insect injunctions that would ever be published in Europe. He recognized, as he was bound to do, that it was wrong to punish irrational creatures for crimes, but argued that restraining future misconduct was an entirely different matter. Birds, beasts, and bees themselves often punished miscreants with corporal or capital punishment, he asserted, and humans could therefore quite properly appeal to God to prevent wrongdoing. But just as it would be 'intolerable tyranny' for a ruler to impose summary punishment on a human being, it would be entirely unjust to seek God's help against an animal that had not been given a hearing.

The argument built on legal principles that were already centuries old. Back in the mid twelfth century, when canonical lawyers were just beginning to reconcile Roman law with the Bible, several had noted that God Himself, on learning that one of His apples was missing, had strode into the Garden of Eden and yelled '*Adam, ubi es?*' – Where art thou? If even He wanted explanations, they had reasoned, a righteous human sovereign could do no less. Adam's response – that it was all Eve's fault and that God had created her anyway – had sparked off even bolder thoughts. Although God had found it all very unconvincing, the canonists recognized in Adam's plea an arguable defence and proposed that if God had refused to hear it, any sentence would have been invalidated. All hastened to add that it was literally impossible for God to reach an invalid decision, which led to the most far-reaching assumption of all: that the duty to hear a suspect was inherent within the nature of the universe itself.

Such thoughts were so commonplace by the early thirteenth century that Pope Innocent III joked to unruly delegates at the Fourth Lateran Council in 1215 that even Satan might have a right to be heard. Within a few decades canonists were honing solemn explanations of why that was indeed the case. Chassenée simply took their reasoning one step further, arguing in effect that the serpent deserved a trial because Adam and Eve did. And although that sounds suspiciously like the argument of a lawyer looking for work, there was a consistency to his stance – for the postscript to the case of Autun's rats involved human beings.

In November 1540, by which time Chassenée had been appointed president of the Provence court of appeals, a major campaign against Protestants in southern France saw his court issue a summons to about a dozen inhabitants of the town of Mérindol. After taking clandestine legal advice, all chose not to attend; whereupon the court ordered that the town's entire population, regardless of age or sex, be burned at the stake. Some eighty families stood at risk of death for the presumed faults of a handful of men, and even pious Catholics of the region began to express their disquiet. As soldiers were mobilized to enforce the judgment, the *seigneur* of Arles decided to mount a last-ditch plea on the town's behalf.

In a powerful speech, summarized by an anonymous author fifteen years later, he reminded Chassenée of the submissions that he had made as a young lawyer at Autun. If it had been wrong then to refuse rats the opportunity to be heard, he argued, it had to be unjust now to deny the same right to humans. A case against rodents might outwardly seem to be of little importance, the nobleman recognized, but the dexterity and piety of Chassenée's pleadings had rightly won him renown for 'reiterat[ing] the seriousness with which judges should proceed in criminal cases'.

Chassenée was moved. He not only called off the troops, but persuaded France's king to stay his judgment indefinitely. It seemed as though Mérindol had been saved. In 1544 however, he dropped dead, and it became apparent that his attitude towards legal integrity was not universal. A new president of the court, Jean Menier, arranged for enforcement of the sentence in the following spring and his disregard for precedent was total. As troops stood ready to fell the trees and torch the homes, Menier agreed to allow Mérindol's inhabitants free passage to Germany, only to renege on the deal. The men of the town were rounded up and cut to pieces. Its women and children were herded into a barn and burned alive.

The initial reprieve of Mérindol shows that legal formalities, even when founded on the rights of rodents, can have substance. Its eventual destruction points to a far darker aspect that the same formalities always possessed. Outwardly similar rituals have existed in many other times and cultures, but those observed in early modern Europe reflected the uniquely political character that law had come to assume there. The claim to hold unthinking creatures to account showed who was boss.

Humanity has often regarded the failure to avenge an animal attack as shameful. The fear of *miasma* inspired the Athenians to establish an entire court dedicated to the prosecution of inanimate and irrational killers. The people around Madagascar's Lake Itasy, to take one of countless possible examples from early twentieth-century anthropology, used to get even with the local crocodiles after a homicide by capturing, interrogating, and executing a culprit at random, secure in the belief that the gods would not allow an innocent reptile to die. Europe's rituals, though informed by a similar sense of moral contamination, operated very differently, however. Judges might condemn animals to be buried in seclusion, incinerated, or flushed away by rivers, but the next of kin only exceptionally played a positive role in prosecution – and often found themselves doubly victimized. The foster-parents of a girl eaten by a pig near Chartres in 1499, for example, were not simply bereaved and deprived of the family bacon; they were also imprisoned and fined eighteen francs for supposed negligence. Legal officials, meanwhile, pursued goals that were often entirely indifferent to the relatives' interests, as at Moisy in 1314 – when lawyers acting for local monks posthumously appealed on behalf of an executed bull, simply to establish that the Count of Valois had exceeded his powers by assuming jurisdiction over it.

The reason for the difference was that disputes over the right to punish a bull – like the assertion of an ability to put snails to flight, or to line a highway with rotting pigs – spoke of more than catharsis. Beginning at a time when bishops, lords, and kings were tussling over territory and peaking during Europe's sixteenth-century religious schizophrenia, they reflected the extent to which the right to judge served to express power. A mastery of the animal world was an easily understood symbol of dominion – at it had been since Rome's emperors would slaughter brutes in their thousands, just to show that they could – and the infliction of pain on beasts had an even more sinister aura. Even today, psychopaths stereotypically take their first faltering steps towards mass murder by torturing animals during childhood; everyone understands why a Mafia boss might tuck a horse's head into his enemy's bed; and anyone who kills chickens with his bare teeth is worth avoiding. Legal theories that could leave a bull dangling limp from gallows were designed to leave few doubts about who had the whip hand.

Further proof of the law's claim to omnipotence can be found in an even more obscure nook of the continental legal system, for the authority that Europe's courts asserted did not stop with the animal kingdom. It reached beyond the grave. Defunct defendants, from ex-heretics and traitors to sodomites and suicides, would, until the early nineteenth century, be subjected to procedures that barely acknowledged their indifference to the outcome. Someone who died awaiting trial in fifteenth-century Nuremberg, for example, would be carried before the judges, in manacles, and invited to appoint an advocate. As and when the body failed to do so, the judges would examine it, formally surmise that it was dead and appoint a lawyer on its behalf. The corpse's counsel would then demand their assistance, on the basis that his client was not in full possession of his faculties, before attempting to establish its innocence. If he succeeded, all well and good. If he failed, the prisoner would be sentenced, dragged, and executed as though death was just a dream.

The ultimate origins of the proceedings are as unknowable as those of any ritual. Nineteenth-century anthropologists speculated that they reflected ancient fears of the undead, and the rites of impalement, evisceration, and obliteration that always characterized European capital punishment certainly seem to speak of cultures that were not entirely convinced that those killed untimely would stay deceased for long. But whatever their source, the trials of corpses, like those of animals, were elevated from superstitions to convictions in order to express power.

The first trial on record is that of a pope, Formosus, who was charged with abusing his office in February 897 by a successor called Stephen VI. The two men had been bitter enemies – each championed by opposing factions in a feud that convulsed Rome's aristocracy for decades – and Stephen had decided that death should be no bar to justice for his erstwhile adversary. Formosus' vault at St Peter's was duly unsealed and his eight-month old corpse was brought to the Basilica of St John Lateran, where Stephen had assembled scores of Roman bishops, deacons, and priests.

The shroud was unwound and the cadaver re-clad in pontifical vestments, before being placed on a throne. Stephen's advocate put the charges, accusing it of all manner of mischiefs, and the pope himself then demanded with a scream: 'Why hast thou in thy ambition usurped the Apostolic seat, thou who wast previously only Bishop of Portus?' Answer came there none, and although a young deacon had been appointed as counsel for the corpse, his defence was not recorded. It was, in any event, unpersuasive. After hearing Stephen propose that Formosus' guilt was clear, all present supposedly cried 'So be it!', and guards then stepped forward to carry out the sentence. The three fingers that Formosus had once used to bestow his papal blessings were hacked from his right hand, and the corpse was stripped of its papal garb, dragged down the nave, and buried in a potter's field. Hopeful grave robbers then exhumed it and, finding nothing of interest, tossed it into the River Tiber.

Death had not begun well for Formosus. But back on dry land the wheel of papal fortune continued to spin, and Stephen VI was soon running into some serious problems of his own. The large proportion of

Rome's clerics who owed their posts to Formosus regrouped and staged a coup, sending Stephen into a dungeon where he was very soon strangled by persons unknown. Complex machinations eventually placed the keys of St Peter in the hands of Theodore II, whose credentials depended on the rehabilitation of his predecessor – and in November 897, he announced tidings both joyous and convenient. A monk, pottering along the banks of Rome's river, had supposedly stumbled upon the prodigal pontiff. Quite how he recognized Formosus, who had by now spent one and a half years outside the grave and approximately ten months bobbing on the Tiber, does not bear much thought but Theodore asked no questions. The body was squeezed into a new set of papal robes, exposed for several days of veneration at an incense-drenched altar at St Peter's, and buried for a third and final time. Theodore himself died before he could overturn Formosus' conviction, but posthumous justice was done, one last time, when his successor denounced Stephen's synod, incinerated its decrees, prohibited future trials of the dead, and called down a curse on the miscreants who had dared disinter the pontiff from his potter's field.

The turn of the tenth century was the nadir of the medieval papacy, and Stephen VI was a bad egg even by the lights of the many other lunatics, hustlers, and whoremongers who have frequented the Holy See over the years. But the idea of putting a corpse on trial would live on. Although popes and chroniclers would begin trying to play down the *Synod horrenda* almost from the moment that it occurred, the last official word on the prosecution of Formosus – admittedly, delivered in 904 by yet another of his mortal enemies – was that it was perfectly valid.

Of longer-term significance was the fact that the Church would forget that it had even banned posthumous proceedings: during its conquest of the Languedoc during the early thirteenth century the practice of burning disinterred heretics 'in detestation of so heinous an offence' was steadily adopted as standard inquisitorial procedure. One of the very first tasks undertaken by Arnold Catalan, an outrider for the Inquisition who entered the vanquished Cathar stronghold of Albi in the summer of 1234, was to condemn a dead, but allegedly impenitent, heretic. As the Dominican broke the cemetery's parched earth with his mattock, the watching crowd grew so enraged that Catalan was hauled towards a nearby river and very nearly rendered posthumous himself, but many others would follow his lead. Literally hundreds of bodies would be disinterred and incinerated over the following century. A Dominican proudly recorded the misfortunes of some that were punished at Toulouse in 1237. 'Their bones and stinking bodies were dragged through the town,' recalled Guillaume Pelhisson. '[T]heir names were proclaimed through the streets by the herald, crying, "Who behaves thus shall perish thus," and finally they were burned in the count's meadow, to the honour of God and the Blessed Virgin, His mother, and the Blessed Dominic.'

Such proceedings were so valuable an expression of sovereignty that considerable sums of money might be expended to carry them out. Rulers were always entitled to the property of a convicted felon or heretic – on the basis of a maxim that 'he who confiscates the body confiscates the goods' – but the costs incurred in maintaining legal proprieties would not always have been recoverable. In 1499, an Evreux woman who had hanged herself in jail, quite probably a woman of limited means, was carted off to the gallows where the executioner earned his wages by strangling her a second time. The costs of cremation could be especially exorbitant. It cost around two livres apiece to disinter, bag, and burn the remains of four dead heretics at Carcassonne in 1323. According to those who calculate such things, the incineration of a fully fledged corpse requires the energy of 24 gallons of oil.

The right to prosecute was nevertheless so prized that it sometimes inspired complex litigation. Thus in 1269, when the Seneschal of Carcassonne disinterred and burned ten accused heretics from land owned by the Marshal of Mirepoix, an outraged Mirepoix protested to the court of appeals in Paris. His concern was not, of course, that it was wrong to burn dead people; it was that if there was burning to be done, he was the one to do it. The court respectfully agreed, and on 20 March 1270 the men of Carcassonne handed those of Mirepoix a notarized deed and ten sacks of straw, a search for the ashes having proved fruitless.

Although few legal rituals ever left Europe's jurists short of a justification or three, even they seem to have been a little troubled by suspicions that trials of the dead were somewhat uncivilized. The continent's favoured source of legal authority, Justinian's *Digest*, offered them no support – for, although the Roman Emperor had authorized formal condemnations of dead convicts and traitors, his laws had positively required that even the vilest villain be returned to his family for burial. Suicide in

particular had been not merely unpunishable; it was, in the eyes of con-
templative folk such as the Stoics, a potentially sensible response to the
tribulations of life.

The views of Jean de Coras, the judge of a famous 1560 case at which
one Arnaud du Tilh had been convicted of criminally impersonating a
peasant called Martin Guerre, exemplify the lawyers' uncertainties. He
had sentenced du Tilh to burn after hanging, but acknowledged in a book
five years after the trial that some thought such penalties 'strange, barbaric and inhumane'. While arguing that they instilled the awe and fear
proper to any well-policed state, he recognized that burning a prisoner
alive was arguably no less effective. And ultimately the only justification
he could propose was a variation on that advanced by Ivo of Chartres to
explain why the Book of Leviticus required the destruction of perverted
animals – that incineration could erase 'the memory of so miserable and
abominable a person'.

The most valiant effort to dignify the proceedings came from Pierre
Ayrault, the same judge who had argued that animal trials were indirect
inquiries into their owners' guilt. In a 1591 treatise, the excellently entitled *On the Trials of Corpses, Ashes, Memory, Animals, Inanimate Things
and Absent Defendants*, he conceded that prosecutions might seem like 'a
battle against shadows' but argued that condemnation of the guilty after
death was no more pointless than posthumous exoneration of the innocent. The claim has a certain appeal, until one remembers the cadaver in
the courtroom; and even Ayrault had to admit that he had no idea why a
dead defendant had to attend in person. He was also mystified as to why
witnesses were expected to recite their evidence before the body. He was
particularly at a loss to explain why an advocate was appointed on its
behalf. His conclusion was eloquent comment on the limits of rational
analysis in early modern France. It would make far more sense, he proposed, if a painting of the deceased could be punished in place of the
corpse itself. France's judges had some way to go before they gave up their
claims to judge the dead.

Just how far became clear in 1670, when the country's regional laws
and customs were replaced with a national code of criminal procedure,
consolidating a statist tradition that has characterized France ever
since. The reform was enacted at a time when posthumous condemnations were falling into disuse. Only a handful of dead people had been

convicted in France over the previous half a century, and at least one –
a 74-year-old man who hanged himself because convinced that
someone was magically making him incapable of sex with his 20-year-
old bride – was spared physical humiliation.* But just as trials of the
dead looked set to expire, the 1670 code breathed fiery life back into
them. Every suicide, traitor, duellist, and dead prisoner, it now proclaimed, was liable to trial; and at the same time that it swept away the
last vestiges of a right to counsel for living defendants, it granted dead
ones the right to an advocate in all cases. Corpses of limited means
were even given legal aid.

The code inspired thousands of pages of commentary, and the
writers invariably made clear that the new regime for the dead was to
be enforced as punctiliously as any other aspect of the reform. François
Serpillon advised judges in 1767, for example, that it was no longer
acceptable to extend mercy to suicides who had acted out of depression; although it had become common merely to order an unsanctified
burial, the law now required a full trial in every case. If someone suspected of the crime was buried without court permission, the judge
should therefore order exhumation. Another influential jurist, Daniel
Jousse, noted with impeccable logic in 1771 that the reforms had not
only altered the legal status of the dead. Those who tried but failed
to take their lives deserved punishment just as much as those who
succeeded. Anyone who survived a suicide attempt should therefore be
executed.

The sound and fury did not in fact lead to a significant increase in the
number of trials, even when fortified in 1712 by a second ordinance,
passed because people were beginning to dump family suicides on streets
and in rivers in the hope of avoiding disinheritance. The Paris court of
appeal did, however, eventually have cause to pronounce upon the law in
December 1737. A thief by the name of Louis Martin had been found

---

* The Picardy court that convicted him also mitigated the usual penalty of forfeiture by awarding his widow 1500 livres from his estate. The fact that she
remarried a fortnight after his death, combined with the nature of his phobia,
suggests that this might have been an instance when a suicide had positively
been counting on posthumous confiscation. See *Journal des principales audiences du Parlement . . . depuis l'année 1622 jusqu'en 1660*, 7 vols (Paris, 1757),
1: 109–10.

hanged in his prison cell at Orléans, and municipal and royal judges were each jealously claiming the right to put him on trial. A preliminary issue was whether Martin – who was sitting out the hearing in a tower at Orléans – should attend in person. The court ruled that his presence was not required. Since he had expired two months before and had been responsible for a major typhoid outbreak in the local jail, the judges themselves would have had to be a little suicidal to decide otherwise. But they were uncompromising about the principle, if not the practice, at stake. As a general rule, they pronounced, dead criminals were always to be arraigned in person in order that they could 'bear the penalty due to so great a crime'.

The same court spelled out what that penalty was twelve years later, in the case of an accused, but dead, thief and murderer called Hubert Portier. After dismissing the representations of Portier's advocate, the judges ruled that his corpse was to be 'attached by the Public Executioner to a cart and dragged on a hurdle, upside down and face turned to the ground'. The body was then to be drawn 'across the town from the prison to the public square, where it should be hanged by the feet from a gibbet which should be set up there for that purpose'. And after it had been suspended for twenty-four hours, it was to be 'thrown into the municipal cesspit'.

Such rituals had a classical antecedent, but it lay some distance from the marbled forums of idealized Roman law. They recalled nothing so much as the awful revenge that Achilles had visited upon Hector at the end of the Trojan Wars, lashing him through the tendons and dragging him for twelve days from a chariot, his black hair streaming in the dust. But whereas *The Iliad* acknowledged the passions that inspired Achilles' brutality, telling how the hero had then repented and returned his foe for honourable burial, the lawyers of eighteenth-century France justified their procedures, cesspit and all, as a product of the well-run state at its most sophisticated. François Serpillon explained that the punishments served to 'inflict terror on the living', and 'to deter others from committing similar crimes by the horror of the spectacle'. In the absence of any clear theory about who was being deterred – suicidally inclined prisoners, despondent people in general, or the entire population of France – the logic was considerably more apparent than real. Daniel Jousse provided another rationale, in a passage that cloaked the savagery with metaphysical abstractions. Criminal justice could not occur without formalities, he explained lyrically, 'any more than shadow can exist without substance; order without apportionment; or an angle without a line'. Regular procedures were so essential 'that as soon as one begins to deviate from them, acts lose the name of justice and take that of force and violence . . . Criminal justice . . . consists more in the formality of actions than in the actions themselves.'

Even insofar as the formalities did succeed in instilling terror, the fear seems to have been internalized so efficiently as to make them counter-productive. At the very same time that France's posthumous trials were peaking, during the civil wars of the late sixteenth century, it became common for rioting mobs to stage mock trials and executions for those they had just killed. At Provins in October 1572 – to take just one of the more dramatic examples – about a hundred Catholic boys cut down a hanged Protestant called Jehan Crespin, subjected his body to a tug-of-war, and then held a trial to resolve whether he should go to the cesspit head- or feet-first. The youthful prosecutors, defenders and judges decided to drag him by the heels – and had such fun that they then convened a second hearing to decide whether his sentence had been unduly lenient in the first place. The judge, after hearing arguments, ruled that Crespin ought to have been burned rather than hanged. His body was duly placed onto bales of flaming straw, before the mob tired of its game and dropped Crespin into a nearby river.

At other times and places, the terror was no more effective. Writing after a visit to Germany in the early 1600s, an English traveller 'abhorred to remember' the sight of young men and children chasing a suicide as it was dragged towards its ignominious burial, hurling dirt, stones, and abuse while local magistrates roared with laughter. The sanctity of the dead remained so easily violable in late seventeenth-century France that the mourners of Jean-Baptiste Colbert, the hated author of legal reforms that had included the 1670 criminal code, were made to gather at night and form their cortège behind archers of the royal watch for his 1683 funeral. And in the 1730s, while the Paris court of appeal was solemnly requiring corpses to attend court and accept their punishments, an incident took place in the life of a Parisian printer called Nicolas Contat that probably best encapsulates the gap between the pretensions and the realities of French law. Contat's diary tells how he and his co-workers spent an evening hunting down all the cats they could find and then constituted themselves as guards, priests, and executioners. To unstoppable laughter, they had tried and condemned their prisoners, given them last rites, and strung them up from an improvised gallows. 'The whole episode', according to cultural historian Robert Darnton, 'stood out as the most hilarious experience in [his] entire career'.

By the time of one of Western Europe's last posthumous executions, at Erfurt in 1806, it was members of the public who were insisting on the spectacle while the German court itself went ahead only with the greatest reluctance. The convict concerned had killed himself rather than have his live body broken by a cartwheel, and although the court recognized 'that the sentence should be carried out . . . for the deterrence of others', it dispensed with many of the elaborate rituals that had traditionally accompanied such executions. The result was a riot among the thousand-strong crowd as members of the carpenters' and masons' guilds battled police officers for their traditional right to hoist the shattered corpse onto a pole.

There was no obvious cultural reason why England, born from the same Christian and barbarian superstitions and subject to equally unpleasant bouts of war and pestilence, should have been any less draconian than the rest of the continent. Its animals were certainly no better behaved. While prosecutions were getting under way in France, hungry beasts were so likely to be prowling around England's cradles that Edward I habitually issued certificates to wounded children attesting to the cause of their injury – a matter of some importance in an age when mutilation often signified criminal convictions. One of the country's few distinctive contributions to demonological theory three hundred years later was the notion that Satan might manifest himself as a small animal such as a frog or a ferret. Nor did England ever show much sympathy for the evil dead. Traitors were quartered and displayed around the realm for centuries, and the meaning of posthumous desecration was sufficiently clear to everyone in 1660 for the government of King Charles II to think it politic to disinter, drag, and then hang the decaying body of Oliver Cromwell.

Religious sensibilities did make for some judicial activity. A theoretical respect for the divine origins of life meant that suicides were staked through the heart prior to burial. The Old Testament disgust for bestiality was also given the occasional stamp of official approval: the animal concerned was sometimes hanged in England, and the shame-obsessed emigrants who settled seventeenth-century Massachusetts were even more fastidious. Their earliest laws, passed in 1641, condemned creatures that had fornicated with humans to be 'slain, and buried and not eaten', and the provision claimed its first victims just a year later. A teenaged servant called Thomas Granger was arrested by magistrates who demanded that he identify all his sexual partners. The list turned out to be a long one for a lad so young – indeed, for a lad of any age – and he went to the gallows only after the slaughter of a mare, a cow, two goats, two calves, five sheep, and a turkey. England and America exhibited legal attitudes that were very different from those on the continent however – for neither corpses nor animals ever faced a jury trial in either country.[*]

One reason was the historical weakness of canonical law in England, and it is notable that three exceptional condemnations – the incineration of a dead witch in 1279, a heretic in 1514, and two coffins during the 1560s – followed hearings before Catholic clerics in ecclesiastical courts. A considerably more significant factor, however, was the nature of the jury system itself. Every ordinary criminal charge in England's courts had to begin with an accusation, and if a grieving relative had ever tried to

---

[*] There is a citation in the official papers of Henry VIII suggesting that when he dissolved England's monasteries in 1538, he summoned the bones of Thomas Becket to appear before him and then ordered that they be burned for failing to do so. One of the grounds on which Pope Paul III soon afterwards excommunicated him was that Henry's actions had 'surpass[ed] the ferocity of any heathen people, who, even when they have conquered their enemies in war, are not accustomed to outrage their dead bodies'. It was a bold charge from a man whose predecessors had pioneered the legal art of outraging dead bodies; but although the true fate of Becket's bones has excited much scholarly interest over the years, the nineteenth-century editor of Henry's papers thought it 'pretty certain' that the summons was forged. See James Gairdner et al. (eds.), *Letters and Papers, Foreign and Domestic, of the Reign of Henry VIII*, 21 vols (London, 1862–1932), 13(2)A: 49; see also Arthur J. Mason, *What Became of the Bones of St. Thomas?* (Cambridge, 1920), pp. 132ff.; John Butler, *The Quest for Becket's Bones* (New Haven, 1995), pp. 117–33.

prosecute a pig, say, he or she would have had to persuade twenty-three grand jurors to issue an indictment. For a conviction to take place, a judge would then have had to allow the case to proceed and twelve more people would have had to agree, unanimously, that the pig deserved to die. On the continent, by contrast, one man could have initiated proceedings and very often, the only person he was legally bound to persuade was himself. Judicial obsessions were certainly sometimes able to flower before a jury, but in inquisitorial courts they could thrive like a tumour.

Some measure of the baleful impact of continental law comes from the experience of Scotland, for its quasi-inquisitorial courts saw the only secular trials of the dead in Britain. They occurred sporadically through the late sixteenth century, and the one most completely recorded was among the last: the condemnation of John, Earl of Gowrie, and his younger brother, 19-year-old Alexander Ruthven, who faced the justice of King James in 1600.

Their misfortunes began on 5 August 1600, when both brothers – whose father James had been beheaded over a decade before – were mysteriously killed during a confrontation with the king in their ancestral home at Perth, some forty miles north of Edinburgh. No one has ever been sure what actually happened there, but James himself was almost immediately providing his own version of events. On his account, Alexander had lured him back to his lodgings with talk of gold treasure trove, and led him through several locked chambers to a room where a man with a dagger had been standing in wait. The potential assassin had supposedly then trembled, for some time, while James had called for help, wrestled Alexander to the ground and stabbed him repeatedly. The Earl of Gowrie himself had then arrived, a sword in each hand and a retinue of servants in tow, but all were vanquished after a tremendous battle.

Whether James's tale was entirely or only largely spurious – and historians have spent several centuries mulling over the possibilities – almost none of his contemporaries took it at face value. The king was widely reputed to be a coward of some distinction, and many found it inconceivable that he would have wandered off alone with a hotheaded youth who knew James to be responsible for his father's death. Others, aware that their monarch had a penchant for pretty boys, whispered that his tale of reckless strolls and hand-to-hand combat with the bonny teenager was only too explicable. To add to the confusion, Queen Anne was rumoured to have had a very soft spot indeed for young Alexander. And no one overlooked the fact that James had owed John Gowrie £40,000 at the time of his death – a vast debt that would be extinguished by a formal finding of treason.

In any event, James returned to Edinburgh after his supposed brush with death to find a city sounding fireworks, bells, cannons and trumpets to celebrate his deliverance. But as the municipally-sponsored cacophony died down, the citizenry's doubts began to sound loud and clear. When he instructed his ministers to tell their congregations about his miraculous escape, they declared themselves 'all readie to have praised God for his Majestie's deliverie generally' but regretfully felt unable to 'descend into particulars, to qualifie what sort of danger it was'. Anne, meanwhile, fell into a great huff, and her servants are said to have grimly informed James that their lady would not join the celebrations, nor speak to him, nor, indeed, leave her bed. The king promptly accused his clergy of treason and engaged a French tightrope walker to mollify his wife with unspeci-fied 'supple tricks'; but he knew that high-wire acts of a very different order would be required to divert the masses. James probably had more faith in the potency of the judicial process than any other monarch in British history, and he now decided that his credibility problems would be solved in a courtroom. His privy councillors had already ordered the bailiffs of Perth on 7 August 1600 to preserve the bodies of John Gowrie and Alexander Ruthven 'until they understand further of his highness's will and pleasure thereunto'. Twelve weeks later, he made that will and pleasure known.

A carriage containing the pickled bodies of both men left Perth on the eve of Hallowe'en, and over the next two days, while Scotland burned bonfires and prayed for its dead, they trundled towards their doom. On arrival at Edinburgh, they were thrown into dungeons and two weeks later, they were brought into Holyrood House and set before James's judges. As an odour of whisky, vinegar and allspice filled the trial chamber, thirteen witnesses testified to their treachery, their bloodlines were declared corrupt and their estates forfeit, and every Ruthven in Scotland was ordered to change his or her surname on pain of death. Four days later, the brothers were drawn through heavy snowdrifts along the capital's High Street to its gallows, where they were hanged, quartered, and dismembered before a multitude of groaning Scots. The cuts were then set on spikes outside the city jail.

The wrath of James was not yet sated. The brothers' skulls, still grinning under the turrets, were joined eight years later by the head of a humble notary called George Sprot, who had been belatedly accused of conspiring with them against the king. One final defendant fell victim to the vendetta a year after that, when Sprot's master, Robert Logan, was convicted as the last accomplice to the Gowrie Conspiracy. He had been dead for three years, and judgment was pronounced at Holyrood after seven witnesses had testified against his reassembled skeleton.

There was just one corner of the English legal system in which approximations of such rituals were found and it was, predictably enough, a relic from an age when England's jurisprudence had not yet parted ways from that of the continent. The coroner, originally an official of eleventh-century Norman kings, was a one-man criminal investigator; and although he often appointed juries to assist him in his inquiries his court was always something of a personal fiefdom, in which countless legal peculiarities incubated and mutated. His primary duty was to investigate deaths, but he also paid out rewards for outlaws' heads and forwarded them to the county jail. If someone drowned in a well, it was his job to ensure that it was sealed for evermore. In the name of his royal employer, he followed up rumours of buried treasure and claimed any whale and sturgeon that came to land. Until 1823, he also had to arrange the funerals of suicides – who were taken in a carriage after dusk to a crossroads, where they were staked through the heart and buried by the official hangman. And there was one ritual stranger than any other – for he also had to convene a jury to consider the guilt of any object that had caused the death of a human being.

The ideas underpinning such condemnations dated back at least to the Dark Ages, when tribes across Europe had regarded weapons of death as things accursed and so worthy of punishment that they were formally placed at the mercy of the next of kin. The novelty in England was that the right to vengeance, instead of falling into disuse, was assumed for the king. Anything that was suspected of being the physical cause of a homicide – from swords and wild stags to leaky rowboats – was brought before a jury, which was required to consider whether it had 'moved to the death' of the deceased. If the jurors swore that it had, the object was declared a deodand ('gift to God'), and auctioned on behalf of local monks in order that they could sing masses for the departed in question. The dissolution of England's monasteries in the 1530s, which silenced the chantries, ought by rights to have killed the deodand, which was already several centuries beyond its spiritual sell-by date. But instead of abandoning the institution, the monarchy appropriated it – and Tudors were soon franchising out the powers to their rapidly expanding aristocracy. Handing a right of confiscation to a lord in sixteenth-century England was hardly likely to make it fall into disuse. Attempts to forfeit property became more common than ever.

Ripped from the framework of superstition that had supported its growth, the system lost any vestiges of predictability. Hearings turned into lotteries, at which jurors would often reach verdicts that were based on sympathy and instinct alone. Although the law in theory required strict proof that an item had 'moved to the death', rather than away from it, the rule was ignored as often as it was observed. Church bells were seized not only when they fell onto people's heads – a surprisingly common event during the seventeenth century – but also in the event that enthusiastic ringers found themselves fatally tugged up the belfry. When a ferryboat capsized because fifty-eight sheep stampeded to one end, the panicked creatures were assumed, a little counter-intuitively, to have been approaching their two drowned shepherds. Confronted with homicidal carts, jurors repeatedly pronounced verdicts against wheels alone, and often specified that it was only an axle or a rim that had moved to the death. One of the most impressively precise verdicts of all came from a Nottinghamshire jury in 1535. Called upon to consider the death of Anthony Wylde, suffocated when a huge haystack fell on top of him, the jurors – most of whom would have been fellow farmers – solemnly identified a small bale as having been solely responsible.

During the nineteenth century, with England's agrarian economy giving way to rapid urbanization, the contradictions that underlay the deodand finally reached breaking point. At a time when befuddled migrants were being regularly mangled and mown down by spinning jennies and steam engines, a system that compensated aristocrats while ignoring accident victims began to look not just like an anachronism, but an affront.

The discontent reached a head in early 1842, after nine people were killed and sixteen others injured in a train crash near Sonning, a small village to the west of London. It was the latest in a series of locomotive disasters, and the coroner's jury ordered that the directors of the Great Western Railway Company should pay a deodand of £1000 to the lord of Sonning manor, one Robert Palmer, if they wanted their train back. The jurors almost certainly expected that their award would benefit victims of the tragedy; and that belief could only have been strengthened when *The Times* declared a week later that it could 'positively assert' that Palmer would not take 'one farthing to his own use'. But whatever the source of its confidence, it was certainly not Palmer. He promptly dashed off a letter to the editor warning that the report was 'only calculated to create disappointment'. It was far too early to say that he would actually receive the £1000, he explained, and 'still more so' to say how he would spend it. It proved to be the last straw. The deodand was abolished four years later and despite the opposition of some aristocratic industrialists – who argued with impressive audacity that it was barbaric to measure human life in monetary terms – a statute simultaneously granted an automatic right of compensation to the next of kin after fatal accidents. It was the end of the line for a procedure that enriched a lord if he was lucky enough to host a train disaster, but no longer bought even a prayer for those who died in it.

Back in the late thirteenth century, Philippe de Beaumanoir, the Beauvais lawyer who had been first to write about the animal trials, had characterized accidental homicides as crimes that could authorize mercy rather than mishaps that required acquittal. Thomas Aquinas, in a careful analysis of the meaning of good luck and bad luck, had simultaneously warned that it was a grievous mistake to imagine that fate could ever be detached from the divine will. Dante, a few decades later, imagined fortune as a grim angel who would hand out and snatch back vast fortunes – according to a plan that, though apparently random, followed God's orders to the letter. Each man was seeing the world from a perspective very peculiar to their time. Earth – and the entire cosmos that surrounded it – was a place where everything had a reason, and the reason came from on high. An unlucky event was almost a contradiction in terms.

Europe's criminal trials, until well into the eighteenth century, were driven by a similar vision: continental judges put the world to rights by condemning the suicidal and the over-sexual, and juries pronounced on every untimely death, no matter how insentient its perpetrator. The fact that the objects of judicial interest were unable to defend themselves was no obstacle to a verdict. It was not the culprit's choices, but its existence, that was morally reprehensible.

The proceedings against animals, corpses and things did not then come to an end because of novel insights into the mental difficulties of the inanimate, or heightened empathy for the dumb and the dead. They ended because the ideas that took hold during the Enlightenment made enough people change their minds about what criminal courts were for in the first place. The philosophers and reformers who emerged after the late 1600s were determined to subject not just ideas, but human institutions, to rational scrutiny, and they argued, to increasing effect, that courts had often been focusing on the wrong thing entirely. Like their predecessors they thought that punishments should deter crime, but they argued that only those who were capable of conforming to the law could be deterred. It was a claim that took hold – and once judges began to address themselves to individual wrongdoers, rather than the natural order that they had wronged, it was a short step to another conclusion: that offenders should appreciate not just their crime, but the penalty imposed for it.

But although the change appealed to many minds, it also left a large hole at the law's heart. No longer were jurists making the reassuring, if mystifying, claim that laws were about recognising God's natural plan. The moral link between crime and vengeance, fundamental to criminal justice for over two thousand years was thrown into doubt. Legal traditions that had previously presumed their own omnipotence yielded to the sense that some evils were simply unresolvable. But as with every intellectual revolution, the older ways of thinking were not eradicated, but weakened – and the urge to condemn revived, with force, in the second half of the twentieth century.

Notwithstanding the relatively mild record of legal violence in common law countries, it was in the United Kingdom that the repackaging of righteous revenge, which came to be called 'retributivism', found its first modern champion. Lord Denning, probably the most celebrated English judge of recent times, led the charge in 1949 when he testified before a Royal Commission that was considering whether the death penalty should be abolished. '[T]he punishment inflicted for grave crimes should adequately reflect the revulsion felt by the great majority of citizens for them,' he claimed. 'It is a mistake to consider the object of punishment as being deterrent or reformative or preventive and nothing else . . . The truth is that some crimes are so outrageous that society insists on adequate punishment, because the wrong-doer deserves it, irrespective of whether it is a deterrent or not.' Denning was unable to stave off the abolition of hanging in Britain, which came in 1965, but his beliefs now occupy a perfectly respectable place in the country's intellectual mainstream. Prime Minister John Major expressed the credo with particular succinctness in February 1993, a few days after two 11-year-old children had been arrested on suspicion of killing a small child called James Bulger. 'Society needs to condemn a little more,' he declared, 'and understand a little less.'

But although the seeds of modern retributivism can be said to have emerged in the United Kingdom, it is in the United States that they have found the most fertile ground. Several US states still try children as though they were adults and sentence them to life without parole if convicted. People who plead insanity – effectively a claim that they should be hospitalized rather than tried – are meanwhile disbelieved even if their deeds shriek of lunacy. When Jeffrey Dahmer admitted fifteen homicides, committed in an apartment that he shared with a refrigerated head, a torso in the shower, and a shrine of human skulls, jurors gave him a clean bill of mental health after the prosecutor begged them not to be 'fooled'. Since those identified as insane are often held in secure hospitals for longer than their imprisoned counterparts, vindictiveness could rationally favour insanity verdicts, but juries that choose the label of mad to bad (which happens in less than a quarter of one per cent of cases) are liable to cause outrage. In the 1982 case of John Hinckley – the man who tried to kill President Reagan in the hope of winning Jodie Foster's love – the jurors' finding of insanity inspired fury more widespread than any other verdict until that of O. J. Simpson. It did no great favour to Hinckley, who was still in a secure hospital when Reagan passed away twenty-two years later, but Congress was moved to alter the definition of madness, and at least four states went on to abolish the defence entirely.

It is in the field of capital punishment that the revival of retributivism in the USA has been starkest. A majority of the Supreme Court upheld the constitutionality of executions in 1976 – by way of a decision that saw three judges quote Denning's remarks on the importance of outrage – and their ruling reflected a change in sentiment that was more widespread. Support for capital punishment had sunk to a twentieth-century low of 47 per cent in 1966, but during the 1970s it began a rise that would level out only in the early 1980s – by which time, three-quarters of Americans supported executions, a proportion that has remained stable ever since. Advocates of death argue as they always have, that condemned prisoners deserve the ultimate penalty, but the shift reopens the question of what 'deserve' means in the first place. And once again, it is often the harm that people cause rather than their knowledge of wrong that is determining whether they live or die.

Few unwitting convicts have been safe in recent years, no matter how deficient or unformed their capacity to recognize wrong. In the fourteen years after 1990, the USA collectively executed more people for crimes committed as juveniles than the rest of the world combined. State governors of both political stripes would meanwhile approve the death warrants of mentally retarded offenders whenever it seemed politic to do so. Bill Clinton interrupted his presidential campaign of 1992 to fly to Arkansas and sign away the life of Ricky Ray Rector, a double murderer with half a brain who so little appreciated his fate that he tried squirrelling away some pecan pie to eat after his lethal injection. Clinton's successor as president, George W. Bush, was at least as content to kill the ill. As governor of Texas, he approved or ordered the executions of at least four men with serious mental difficulties. The first was Mario Marquez, a brain-damaged rapist and killer with the functional capacities of a 6-year-old, who was strapped to the gurney in 1995 telling his lawyer that he was about to become God's gardener and would take care of heaven's animals.

There have been some recent signs of a counter-reaction. In the summer of 2002, the Supreme Court ruled by a majority that it was at least potentially unconstitutional to execute a mentally retarded prisoner. At the time of writing, another majority seemed likely also to declare it impermissible to execute people who had been children at the time of their offence. But the popular desire to punish is not about to abate any time soon. Suspicions of insanity claims are arguably stronger today than they were at the time of John Hinckley's trial. Whereas his jury deliberated for three and a half days, Texas jurors twenty years later took the same number of hours to find that Andrea Yates, a woman with a history of mental problems, had sanely drowned

her five children in a bathtub to save them from Satan. Some judges
and legislators have displayed a hunger to kill convicts that can seem
downright peculiar. A federal appeals court in 2003, bound by the
Supreme Court's then recent ruling that it was unconstitutional to
execute mentally incompetent prisoners, found that it was proper for
Arkansas to medicate one by force and kill him as soon as he became
well enough to understand what was happening. The state did just that,
to a man called Charles Singleton, in January 2004.

A legal system capable of curing men for just long enough to inject
them with poison validates emotions that verge on the sadistic. It can
inspire hearings of ritualized barbarism that echo the show trials of 1930s
Moscow that are examined in the next chapter. But the deeper longing to
eliminate an insane criminal or a wicked child is far from inexplicable.
Losing a loved one to the barrel of a loaded gun is presumably no easier
to accept than bereavement to the snout of a snorting pig, and courts that
promise to locate blame somewhere offer at least the hope of consolation.
They may even reflect a utopian vision, of a society so concerned to
defend human dignity that a wrong to one is a wrong to all.

The most articulate of modern retributivists is Supreme Court
Justice Antonin Scalia, and his views in the case that ended a state's
right to execute mentally ill prisoners constitute an appropriate conclusion to the legal journey traced in this chapter. The majority of the
Court's judges based their opinion on a claim that the national consensus had swung markedly against such executions. Scalia was the
most vehement of the three dissenters. While framing his decision in
the language of states' rights, he did little to conceal his personal
opinion that the appellant deserved to die. He described the crime in
detail, literally counting out the eight bullets that were fired into the
victim and itemizing the body parts that had been hit. '[S]ociety's
moral outrage', he thundered, 'sometimes demands execution of
retarded offenders. By what principle of law, science or logic can the
Court pronounce that this is wrong? There is none.'

On that point, at least, Scalia was right. The sense that knowledge is
somehow related to sin, venerable though it is, rests on foundations as
flimsy as any superstition. There is no self-evident reason to assess moral
responsibility by mental capacity, any more than there once was to link it
to the shape of the cranium. Insofar as people believe that the two are

connected, their assumption generally rests on the fact that lots of other people think the link exists – and the Supreme Court's own decision is vivid proof that the appeal to consensus is a shaky foundation on which to build any moral claim.

All that can be said with any real certainty about the retributivists' arguments is that they have history on their side. For Justice Scalia, like Lord Denning before him, draws on a tradition that stretches back to Ivo of Chartres and Thomas Aquinas. Proceedings against insects, animals, corpses and things once reflected the hope of a magically coherent universe in which divine anathemas could prevent famine, no misdeed would go unpunished, and an object's destruction might erase the evils it had done. The medieval 'horror of sin' is now called 'revulsion' or 'outrage'; submission to God's will has been replaced by a respect for communal anger; and new ways have been found to conceal the assertion of power behind claims of deference. But the vision remains the same. It is that the job of a court is to condemn terrible crimes and to mete out fitting punishments. The fact that the condemnation is incomprehensible to the person punished would seem to be no more relevant to judges like Scalia than the mental state of pigs and corpses once was to the men who hoped to obliterate the very memory of their crimes.

6

The Moscow Show Trials

> I welcomed so freely, with such conviction and such joy, the pun-
> ishment that came, a sight that must have moved the gods, and
> I felt the gods' emotion almost to the point of tears.
>
> FRANZ KAFKA, *Diaries,* 20 October 1921

On 19 August 1936, the doors opened to the October Hall of Moscow's
Trade Union House. Two decades after the revolution that had brought
the Communist Party to power, the former ballroom of the Club of
Nobles had fallen firmly into the hands of the self-proclaimed proletarian state. Crimson banners hung between its Corinthian columns, and
three hundred people, almost all clerks and typists with the Soviet secret
police, sat on rough wooden benches. On a dais at the far side of the
room sat three men, the senior of them a loyal member of the Party
called Vasily Ulrich. Although his bullish frame, cropped dome, and tiny
eyes gave him the look of someone who might have been better
employed controlling proceedings outside a bar, he was in fact presiding
over the Military Collegium of the Supreme Court of the USSR.* Sixteen
defendants faced him from a makeshift dock, watched by guards with

---

* Appearances were doubly misleading. He actually took such pride in his
  judicial work that he would, in his twilight years, drunkenly regale Moscow
  prostitutes with accounts of executions that he claimed to have personally conducted. See Arkady Vaksberg, *Stalin's Prosecutor. The Life of Andrei Vyshinsky*
  (New York, 1991), p. 337 n.8.

fixed bayonets. Most had until very recently been leading members of the regime of Joseph Stalin, and all stood accused, entirely falsely, of conspiring to overthrow that regime and betray ideals that they had professed throughout their adult lives.

The criminal trial is, by definition, the point where rule-maker meets rule-breaker, and arraignment in court has often operated to mark the passing of one dispensation and the birth of another. King Charles I was executed at the end of England's Civil War only after judges loyal to the victorious Roundheads convicted him of 'all the Treasons, Murthers, Rapines, Burnings, Spoils, Desolations, Damages and Mischief to this nation'. When France's revolutionary turn came, the charges were no less damning. King Louis XVI was publicly tried for seeking to 'establish . . . tyranny by destroying . . . liberty', while the accusations levelled against Marie Antoinette included the claim that she had taught her son how to masturbate. But no matter how spectacular the trial or fantastic the allegation, the defendants of earlier epochs had resisted degradation. King Charles, imperious in gold and black, had poured scorn on the indictment and told his judges that their only authority was that of the highwayman. Louis had defended himself at length. Marie Antoinette positively turned the tables on her accusers and won widespread support by refusing even to speak to the charge of incest because 'nature itself forbids a mother to answer such an accusation'

Those in the dock at Moscow in 1936 however, who included some of the most dedicated revolutionaries that Russia had ever produced, insisted on their guilt. Prosecutors treated them as evasive liars and subjected every hesitation to withering attack. The prisoners themselves demanded the harshest punishments. Such behaviour might in other contexts signify an arcane religious ritual or a grave mental illness. In the October Hall, it was the law.

It is perhaps unsurprising, and it is certainly appropriate, that the journey to the October Hall had begun with an assassination. In December 1934, a popular member of the Politburo called Sergei Kirov had been gunned down in Leningrad's Smolny Palace. The man who pulled the trigger was a disgruntled member of the Communist Party rank-and-file, and historians have debated for decades whether or not Stalin arranged the murder. None has ever doubted that he benefited from it. The Soviet leader was already tightening his control over the Party, having recently seen off the last serious attempt to mobilize against him that would ever take place, and the assassination allowed him to turn his grip into a stranglehold. On the day that it occurred, he telephoned through orders to shoot anyone thought to be responsible. The killer was swiftly eliminated, taking any secrets he may have had to the grave, and Stalin then persuaded two former arch-rivals, Gregory Zinoviev and Lev Kamenev, to accept that their previous political stances encumbered them with a 'moral responsibility' for Kirov's death. At a secret trial in January 1935, they pleaded guilty and were sentenced to ten and five years in jail respectively. But by March of the following year, Stalin had concluded that they bore a responsibility more than just moral. He informed his police chief, Genrich Yagoda, that they had actually organized the murder of Kirov, in conjunction with Leon Trotsky – the first and greatest of Stalin's enemies, by now exiled in Norway – and that other conspirators remained to be identified. Yagoda's job would be to gather the evidence.

Though Stalin was thus the instigator of the prosecution and Yagoda its facilitator, another man would give the trial its form: the state prosecutor, Andrei Yanuaryevich Vyshinsky. The bespectacled 55-year-old, thin-lipped and sparsely moustached, wore the perturbed expression of

an over-conscientious accountant, but the passionless exterior, like much else at the five-day trial, was deceptive. Vyshinsky had been a radical opponent of tsarist rule since long before the Russian Revolution – albeit part of a faction that was bitterly opposed to the Communist Party – and he had complemented his legal studies with the organization of several strikes and the murder of at least three police agents. He was also a consummate orator, with a destructive talent that recalled no one so much as Sir Edward Coke, chief prosecutor during England's own show trials of the late 1500s and early 1600s. The charisma was such that another lawyer, recalling a meeting with Vyshinsky eighteen years after the event, still flinched. 'He had hypnotic powers,' an agitated Ilya Braude told journalist Arkady Vaksberg. 'Looking into his eyes, I would start cringing like a rabbit before a snake.' The British Foreign Secretary, Ernest Bevin, had been less intimidated, but equally impressed. 'When I look him in the face,' he declared in late 1945, 'I feel as though any moment now the blood of thousands of his victims [might] start trickling out of his monster's maw.'

Vyshinsky's relationship with Stalin was as close as that assessment might suggest. They had first met in a prison cell in 1908, and the two men – the first born of Polish immigrants, the second a recent arrival from Georgia – had argued bitterly, but developed a mutual respect that would last a lifetime. Each then belonged to rival leftist movements, but the similarities that bound them would always transcend the allegiances that once divided them. Three years after the 1917 revolution that brought the Bolsheviks to power, Stalin saved his former cellmate's political bacon by arranging for his admission to the Communist Party. Vyshinsky, for his part, would always nurse resentment towards others who had chosen the winning side before him, but his loyalty to his benefactor would never waver – and by the 1930s, he was in a position to repay the favours. Lenin's promise to the early revolutionaries, that the state would 'wither away' as communism approached, had made legal theory distinctly unfashionable during the 1920s, but as Stalin made clear that the Soviet state would not be withering for a long while, Vyshinsky manufactured a jurisprudence fit for the times. A conjuror at the side of the national ringmaster, able to pull new principles from the air and make inconvenient ones disappear in a puff of ideological smoke, he would create the illusion of socialist justice – and simultaneously turn sporadic brutality into a killing machine.

One consequence was the development of a radically novel form of criminal process. Propagandistic trials had been staged in the Soviet Union since the 1920s, but previous defendants had been unrepresented and had almost always asserted their innocence or remained silent. Vyshinsky, though concerned to assert a residual right to 'annihilate [an enemy] without trial', now proposed that an open contest between defence and prosecution was integral to socialism, and that political cases were invariably best proved by public confession. The ideas, soon to be set out in a textbook that aimed to '[raise] the doctrine of proofs . . . to the level of a scientific theory', made for a model of criminal procedure that would hold for the next two decades. The tradition of open legal argument, cultivated in institutions as diverse as the Old Bailey and the Catholic Church, was thereby combined with the concern for self-condemnation that had been so characteristic of the inquisitorial process. The synthesis would make for a spectacle of unparalleled power.

As the spring of 1936 turned to summer, preparations for the trial accelerated. Kamenev was warned that his son would be arrested and made to condemn him from the dock if he refused to co-operate. Zinoviev, whose health was failing anyway, was advised that he should confess not just to save himself, but for the sake of all those 'thousands of oppositionists' associated with him. At the same time, other leading Bolsheviks were rounded up and imprisoned, alongside five secret police officers who had been promised promotion in exchange for helping to break their counter-revolutionary conspiracy. Outright torture was not used, but threats hung heavy in the air. Interrogators asked their prisoners menacingly about their families' well-being, and displayed on their desks a 1935 decree that had reduced the minimum age of execution to 12 years old. Resistance, it was explained, would be futile. Holdouts would simply be executed in secret.

The breakthrough finally came in July, when Kamenev and Zinoviev, sweltering in cells where the radiators had been set at top blast, let it be known that they were ready to confess. All they asked was that Stalin promise to spare their lives, along with those of their families and co-accused, and that he do so in front of the full Politburo. The Soviet leader is said to have beamed with delight on learning the news, stroking his right moustache, and he ordered that they be brought to the Kremlin. As the two men entered his presence, both expressed surprise that other members of the Politburo were not present, but Stalin was reassurance itself. 'We are Bolsheviks, disciples and followers of Lenin,' he reminded them. '[W]e don't want to shed the blood of old Bolsheviks, no matter how grave were their past sins.' A senior secret police officer who was present would later recall that Stalin's words had seemed to ring with 'deep feeling'.

The trial that opened a month later was not without glitches. The most serious came when one of the accused claimed to have taken instructions in 1932 from Trotsky's son at the Hotel Bristol in Copenhagen – a building which, Soviet government records notwithstanding, had been demolished in 1917. The gulf between the scale of the conspiracy alleged and the absence of actual crimes also required the plot's supposed master-minds repeatedly to assert their own incompetence. One had armed himself with a revolver and tried frequently to ambush the car of a senior Communist on his daily route to work, only to call off the plot, after six months of loitering, because his intended victim always drove past too quickly. When trying to kill a second man at Leningrad's May Day parade, he marched too far from the rostrum to get a clear shot. Another had attempted twice to shoot Stalin at Party congresses: the plot had been thwarted on the first occasion by the Soviet leader's absence, and on the second by the distance to his seat.

All the inconsistencies and improbabilities were, however, steam-rollered beneath the sheer force of contrition that emanated from the dock. When, for example, Vyshinsky asked Kamenev whether his previous protestations of loyalty to the Party had been 'deceitful', the defendant found the term hopelessly inadequate. '[W]orse than deception,' he replied. 'Perfidy?' suggested the prosecutor. 'Worse', he insisted. 'Worse than deception, worse than perfidy?' mused Vyshinsky, apparently astounded, before making one last suggestion: 'Treason?' Kamenev con-firmed the awful truth. 'You have found [the word].'

Such testimony was inspired in part by fear – but not entirely. Trotsky himself had avowed in 1924 that 'one cannot be right against the party . . . for history has not created other ways for the realization of what is right', and an unquestioning faith in the Party line had always been an essential quality in any Communist. Toeing that line was becoming about as easy as treading a Möbius strip by the mid 1930s, when Stalin's policies were char-acterized not just by U-turns but by Ws and figure-eights, but no self-respecting revolutionary could doubt that the effort had to be made. With militarism rampant in Germany, Italy, and Japan, it seemed entirely plausible that capitalism was in its death throes and that the world was speeding towards a communist nirvana. If so, it was a short step to the belief that anyone who stood in the way of history was an enemy of the people, whether aware of it or not. And the last loyal service that any unwitting traitor could perform was to embrace his condemnation.

The defendants were nothing if not loyal. Zinoviev, though feverish and wheezing, admitted that he had been the prime mover behind Kirov's murder and had conspired with Trotsky to assassinate Stalin. Lev Kamenev spoke from somewhere deeper. 'Twice my life was spared,' he told the court in a trembling voice. 'But there is a limit . . . to the magnanimity of the proletariat, and that limit we have reached.' His eyes bright with stanched tears, he addressed his final words to his children. 'No matter what my sentence will be, I in advance consider it just. Don't look back. Go forward. Together with the Soviet people, follow Stalin.' Even Judge Ulrich appeared moved as Kamenev collapsed into his seat and lowered his shaking head into his hands.

No defendant more poignantly personified the capitulation than Sergei Mrachkovsky. The 44-year-old, born in a tsarist prison, had organized a workers' uprising in the Urals during 1917 and had a love of Party so profound that it reduced even his interrogator to tears – after both men had stayed awake, talking, for some ninety hours. 'I brought him to the point where we began to weep,' the secret policeman later recounted. 'I wept with him when we arrived at the conclusion that all was lost, that there was nothing left by way of hope or faith, that the only thing to do was to make a desperate effort to forestall a futile struggle on the part of the discontented masses. For this the government must have public confessions by the opposition leaders.' Mrachkovsky obliged with a monologue of tragic proportions.

Recapitulating his entire life, he told of a Soviet citizen who could hardly have seemed more perfect. Hailing from a family that had already produced two generations of revolutionaries, he had dedicated himself to communism ever since his first arrest by the tsarist police at the age of 13. 'And here I stand before you', he told his audience, in a tone that seemed almost ironic, 'as a counter-revolutionary.' As tears spilled down his cheeks and he smashed his hand against the rail of the dock, it looked for a moment as though he might be about to depart from the script. Vyshinsky shot a worried glance towards the judges' dais and seemed about to rise to his feet, a prearranged signal that would incite hoots and catcalls from the audience. But the danger passed. Let his proletarian background be a lesson to all those watching, continued Mrachkovsky. The threat of counter-revolution came not just from generals, princes, and noblemen. Even a worker with his credentials could betray communism. According to the later recollection of one of those present, Judge Ulrich 'flashed a smile at Vyshinsky', who sank back into his chair with relief. Mrachkovsky trained his last round of revolutionary ardour against himself. He asked that he be credited for having 'spat out the vomit of counter-revolution' but made no plea for mercy. Quite the contrary. 'I depart as a traitor to my party,' he concluded, '– a traitor who should be shot!'

Given that Stalin's promise of clemency had been communicated to all the defendants, Mrachkovsky's zeal was technically beyond the call of duty. But it would turn out that even there, he had history on his side. Vyshinsky ended his own address with the demand 'that dogs gone mad should be shot – every one of them!', and Ulrich obliged with death sentences all round. The protocol in earlier trials had been that the capital sentences were followed by immediate commutation; but this time, the words of reprieve did not come. Silence filled the court, broken only when one of the secret police defendants, shrieking with desperate hope, screamed 'Long live the cause of Marx, Engels, Lenin and Stalin!' He was, to his permanent misfortune, a patsy as well as a stooge.

All the defendants in the dock were taken within hours to the cellars of the State Security headquarters at the Lubyanka, where the guards pulled revolvers from their coats and shot them in the head. Most died in a cacophony of shouts and blows and pistol cracks, at the hands of policemen who became as hysterical as their victims. Zinoviev fell to the ground and screamed for Stalin to keep his word. One defendant, so ill that he had been tried in his absence, would be shot later on a stretcher. Only Ivan Smirnov, who had larded his testimony with sarcasm after submitting to prosecution in the hope of saving his ex-wife's life, accepted the double-cross with dignity. 'We deserve this,' he reportedly said, 'for our unworthy attitude at the trial.' As Bolshevik killed Bolshevik for the first time in Soviet history, a taboo was transgressed – and Stalin's betrayal would be compounded. With the logic of the blood feud he now turned on his victim's relatives: almost every wife and child of those executed in the Lubyanka would be hunted down and murdered in turn over the coming years.

Many explanations can be advanced for the 1936 trial, but one of the simplest remains one of the most persuasive. Jealousy, vengeance, and paranoia swirled in Stalin's head, and the destruction of his opponents satisfied a visceral lust. As early as 1923, he had startled Kamenev by telling him about the pleasures of revenge. 'To choose one's enemy, to prepare every detail of the blow, to slake an implacable vengeance, and

then go to bed,' he had enthused. 'There is nothing sweeter in the world!'
Kamenev had, however, done nothing. And in the autumn of 1936, as
Stalin stood with dagger upraised, his fellow Communists did not think
to wrest it from his grasp. Instead, they clasped the handle.

Their malign stupidity is well illustrated by a celebratory dinner that
Stalin held at the end of the year. One of those present was a jovial fellow
called Karl Pauker, the head of his personal bodyguard, who enjoyed a position so privileged that he was the only man alive whom the Soviet leader
trusted to shave his pockmarked face. Pauker had witnessed the killings in
the Lubyanka cellars and to entertain the guests he now re-enacted the final
moments of Zinoviev. He began by miming terror, his eyes darting around
the hall. As the apparatchiks chuckled nervously, watching for Stalin's reaction, Pauker fell to his knees and shuffled forward, clinging to the legs of an
imaginary guard. 'Please, for God's sake, comrade,' he gasped, 'call Joseph
Vissarionovitch.' On hearing his first names, Stalin spluttered into giggles
and the diners, reassured, began roaring their approval. They then called for
an encore. Throwing his hands to the heavens, Pauker transformed the
Jewish-born Zinoviev into a peasant from the *shtetl*. 'Hear Israel,' he yowled,
'our God is the only God!' Laughter engulfed the room, while Stalin, who
always enjoyed a spot of Jew-baiting, was almost doubled up with mirth,
clutching his belly and signalling desperately for Pauker to stop. Some of
those slapping their thighs may have realized that matters were not quite as
funny as they were pretending. But none could have appreciated just how
unfunny they had become. Within six months, Pauker, himself born a Jew,
would be arrested as a Nazi spy. Less than a year after that, he would be
dead. So too would most of those in the room.

Preparations for a second prosecution were already well underway.
Testimony at the first trial had identified eight more senior Communists
as counter-revolutionaries, and even before Judge Ulrich had handed
down the verdicts Vyshinsky had thought it right to tell him that all the
men named were under active investigation. Their response was as swift
as it was self-destructive. Karl Radek, an erstwhile ally of Trotsky who had
transformed himself into a flamboyant Party hack, immediately submitted an article to *Pravda* demanding that Ulrich's court 'crush the vipers'.
Khristian Rakovsky requested that 'no quarter' be given and that the 'mad
dogs be shot'. Yuri Pyatakov went furthest of all. Informed that his relationship with his ex-wife had thrown him under suspicion, he publicly

called for the defendants to be 'destroyed like carrion' and privately asked
Stalin for permission to prosecute his former spouse – and then shoot
her. If it would be helpful, he could do the same with other defendants
and justify his actions in writing. Stalin put the proposal before the
Central Committee in December, but expressed misgivings. Pyatakov's
presence in the prosecutor's chair might, he suggested, turn a trial into 'a
comedy'. He also worried that it might look as though he was acting
under pressure. 'No one would believe that we hadn't forced him to do it,'
he observed. His comrades assented, to a man.

Stalin would instead assume personal responsibility for co-ordinating
the trial – and his directorial vision would be focused, if mercurial. As
people like Pyatakov and Radek were rounded up, interrogators were initially told that they made up a dormant 'reserve centre' of terrorists, who
had been awaiting activation by the defendants convicted at the first trial.
The job of extracting appropriate confessions had already begun when
Stalin received a report from his secret police chief, Genrich Yagoda,
warning that ordinary citizens seemed not to have been entirely convinced
by the first prosecution. Graffiti had even been spotted in Moscow factories
declaring it a pity 'that they didn't kill the Georgian reptile [too]'. Stalin
promptly decided that the idea of dormant terrorists was nowhere near
threatening enough. A new hypothesis was forwarded to every investigator.
Their prisoners, they were now informed, had not constituted a 'reserve
centre'. They had in fact formed a 'parallel centre'. And far from lying doggo,
they had been diligently following Trotsky's orders, relayed from Oslo, in
order to overthrow Stalin's regime, restore capitalism, and cede vast swathes
of the Soviet Union to Nazi Germany and Japan.

The change caused consternation. Even the relatively simple conspiracy
alleged at the first trial had necessitated colour-coded diagrams to coordinate the defendants' admissions, and the new plot required the
abandonment of several confessions in progress. Some interrogators, too
embarrassed to flip their scripts, chose to swap prisoners instead. But the
days when secret policemen could still be shamed were about to come to
an end. Stalin now dismissed Yagoda – ominously observing that his inadequacies had set back the cause of anti-terrorism by four years – and
appointed as his replacement a Goebbels-lookalike called Nikolai Yezhov.
While Stalin worked behind the scenes, secretly instructing local Party officials and security chiefs to formalize their use of torture, Yezhov now

became the public face of the Terror, and under the *yezhovschina*, a purge began to roll through the secret police force itself. Twenty thousand officers would eventually lose their lives, and as replacements rose through the ranks, skimmed whenever they failed to show enough zeal, only the most tenacious scum would survive.

Stalin spent several more weeks reworking his ideas and, though more than a little obsessive, he was not too proud to accept assistance. When Karl Radek proposed that his role be rewritten to include imaginary meetings with Nazi and Japanese diplomats, the changes so pleased Stalin that he added them to confessions that had already been drafted. Andrei Vyshinsky, meanwhile, communicated the manuscripts and revisions to Yezhov, who arranged for evidence to be extracted or adjusted as appropriate. Altering reality to fit the text was not the most disciplined of literary techniques, but no one was ever likely to tell Stalin that his fiction lacked plausibility. In the run-up to the trial, he also held regular meetings with Vyshinsky (who was simultaneously rehearsing with defence lawyers) to offer tips on how to conduct the case. 'Don't let [the accused] speak too much,' he urged. 'Shut them up,' he advised. 'Don't let them babble' was another suggestion. As though capturing the utterances of a prophet, Vyshinsky scribbled down every word.

In January 1937, Stalin's handiwork was finally ready for its critical debut. Seventeen men filed into the dock, and although it was public knowledge that all those convicted at the first trial had been shot, they would play their parts to perfection. Yuri Pyatakov, denied the chance to prosecute his ex-wife, had been given the opportunity to open the show instead and he was soon setting the scene with aplomb. His predilection for terrorism had crystallized into a firm political programme after December 1935, he revealed, when he had flown to Oslo for a clandestine meeting with Leon Trotsky. Ensconced in his Norwegian lair, Trotsky had supposedly told him that the German and Japanese governments were about to wage war on the Soviet Union and wanted a shadow government to wait in the wings. The oppositionist had agreed that he would front the puppet regime required. He had also offered the fascists the entire Ukraine and all the oil reserves of the Soviet Union. Pyatakov's personal role had been to organize cadres that could sow havoc on the home front, by way of political assassinations and guerrilla strikes against the Red Army.

It was a mixed start. The testimony pulled off the impressive feat of portraying the defendants as warmongers and defeatists at the same time, but Stalin's insistence on roping Trotsky into the plot had made him repeat the most glaring blunder of the first trial. Pyatakov's claim that he had flown to Oslo for the meeting with Trotsky constituted a verifiable assertion, and when the world's journalists found themselves confronted with a fact, straying past their crosshairs like a bewildered beast, they annihilated it instantly. For Oslo in the 1930s was no travel hub. Within two days, Norwegian newspapers were reporting that no civilian aeroplanes had landed in the capital during December 1935. Before the week was out, it had been established that not a single plane had landed there for the entire eight months after September. Trotsky then turned the knife by inviting the Soviet government to seek his extradition in a Norwegian court.

The result of Stalin's error was that the linchpin holding together the indictment had fallen away. But mere impossibility could not stop the show. Through sheer force of hot air, the balloon was soon aloft once again. Karl Radek stepped into the breach with a claim that he and Trotsky had often communicated by post, although he had taken the precaution of burning all the letters. Others confessed to nebulous acts of terrorism, all the more threatening because they had never come to light, or to acts of 'wrecking', a catch-all economic crime that suspended ordinary rules of causation and moral responsibility. Inspired by a nefarious slogan of Trotsky ('The worse, the better'), the wreckers had caused havoc. Two had organized explosions at chemical factories by ignoring safety regulations. Others had set collieries alight by introducing new mining methods. Five admitted sabotaging the Soviet Union's train network by turning a blind eye to timetables and neglecting track repairs. At one point defendant Ivan Knyazev tired of the charade. Subjected to a blistering assault from Vyshinsky about his role in setting up a tremendous locomotive disaster by failing to maintain the line, he wearily observed that, 'Railwaymen have a notion that if a rail splits no one on the road is to blame.' The prosecutor, as though struggling to comprehend a primitive superstition, paused to take stock of Knyazev's claim. '[T]hey attribute it to objective causes?' he asked wonderingly.

For his own part, Vyshinsky tried to plug the credibility gap with chutzpah alone. When Boris Norkin mentioned that he had only confessed after spending several months in custody, the prosecutor demanded repeatedly that he disclose the reasons for his admissions, as though it was the defendant rather than the Soviet state that had something to hide. Norkin temporized, evidently unwilling to make good on his hint of mistreatment, and Vyshinsky persisted. Had he confessed because he had been subjected to improper pressure? 'A man can be deprived of good food, deprived of sleep,' the lawyer explained. 'We know this from the history of capitalist prisons. He can be deprived of cigarettes.' Norkin, his bluff called, backed down. 'If that is what you are talking about, there was nothing like it,' he replied.

The prosecutor's final speech, closely edited by Stalin, lasted several hours. It included legal submissions in which Vyshinsky argued, rather redundantly, that circumstantial evidence alone would have made a conviction inevitable. But he knew better than to end with anything as prosaic as the facts or the law. Instead, he invoked the moral authority of a spectral horde of dead workers and soldiers. 'I am not the only accuser!' he chanted. 'I feel that by my side stand the victims of the crimes . . . on crutches, maimed, half alive, and perhaps legless . . . I do not stand here alone! The victims may be in their graves, but I feel they are standing here beside me, pointing at the dock, at you, accused, with their mutilated arms, which have mouldered in the graves to which you sent them!' Flanked by phantom legions of the undead, more necromancer than lawyer, he was impelled to a familiar conclusion. '[T]hese heinous criminals . . . deserve only one punishment – death by shooting!'

The speech culminated in protracted applause from the courtroom audience, and as show trials go, events could hardly have ended on a more ringing note. Others, however, did their best to sound one. Ilya Braude, the defence lawyer who would tremble years later at the mention of Vyshinsky, admitted that he found himself in an 'exceptionally difficult position'. Although formally required to represent the railway wrecker Ivan Knyazev, he had not been able to hear his client's testimony without imagining the 'crash of wrecked cars and the groans of dead and dying . . . men'. Braude, like the other defence counsel, would later earn a medal from Stalin for his contribution to the trial.

Karl Radek ended in particularly eloquent style. He had been cutting down his co-accused throughout the trial, ridiculing their lies whenever they were insufficiently untrue, and with all the humility of an exhausted gladiator, he now turned towards the bench. His testimony had been given willingly, he assured the judges. Nothing could be more ludicrous than the idea that he had been pressurized; indeed, far from being forced to confess, he had tortured his interrogator by refusing to come clean for two and a half months. There could be no question of someone as guilty as he was attempting to advance a defence. But he invited the judges to reflect upon one thing. His testimony, along with that of Pyatakov, was the only evidence that linked the defendants to Trotsky. He had to be a man of integrity, or their convictions would be unsafe. The attempt to clamber over his comrades' bodies was complemented by a salute to Stalin's economic genius – and a warning. The terrorism of out-and-out Trotskyites was not the only danger that the country faced. It was riddled with 'semi-Trotskyites, quarter-Trotskyites [and] one-eighth-Trotskyites', many of whom were not even aware of their counter-revolutionary potential. Such was the society that the Soviet Union had become: a place where a seven-eighths Stalinist was an ignorant sleeper, just biding time until the malevolent fraction was ready to burst forth.

Ulrich and his fellow judges sat into the early hours to hear such speeches. Hope still sprang in the breasts of the defendants, and all but one asked for their lives to be spared. The exception was Alexei Shestov, a salaried police officer who had been planted in the dock to lend ballast to the state's case. In anticipation of promotion after the trial, he had refused to beg for mercy, claiming just one desire: 'to stand with . . . calmness on the place of execution and with my blood to wash away the stain of a traitor to my country'. He would, needless to say, have his wish granted. At three o'clock in the morning, the judges returned with death sentences against him and all but four of his co-defendants.

Among those spared was Karl Radek, given just ten years in jail, who turned to his fellow accused and shrugged, smiling shyly as though happily confused by the turn of events. If so, he had every reason: until the day before, the judges had been under instructions to impose the death penalty uniformly. Stalin probably changed his mind only because one of Radek's friends, the German novelist Lion Feuchtwanger, was in Moscow to write a book on the strides that the Soviet Union was making towards earthly perfection. Not that it mattered much. Radek was murdered in his cell just over two years later, and the three others reprieved would all be dead by 1941.

Popular reaction to the verdicts varied. Some assumed that hypnosis or drugs must have been used. Others took them at face value. Most, whatever their view, began to develop the capacity for doublethink that would later become endemic in post-war eastern Europe. Countless folk

convinced themselves that Stalin knew nothing of the evil being perpetrated in his name, while citizens who privately whispered doubts and jokes publicly manifested loyal hatred towards the defendants. Tens of thousands of banner-clutching Muscovites flocked to Red Square to welcome the condemnations, in temperatures that sank to -27° F. In the days that followed, farms and factories across the Soviet Union allowed citizens to express their joy with shows of hands. 'Wipe the Trotskyite-Zinovievite band of murderers off the face of the earth' read the banners – '– such is the sentence of the working people!'

Most foreign observers were more sceptical, but there were many exceptions. Lion Feuchtwanger's book recalled the proceedings as 'less like a criminal trial than a debate', at which the only real drama had come when Boris Norkin had denounced Trotsky with such vehemence that he had become a little queasy. Feuchtwanger admitted to initial perplexity at the defendants' willingness to confess but had come to realize the solution to the mystery. Just as Britain's political system accommodated a party opposed to the government but loyal to the country, even traitors to the Soviet Union were driven by their love for it. Feuchtwanger's longing to believe in Soviet justice owed much to his background as a Jewish refugee from Nazi Germany, but Stalin's conspiracy theories had a wider appeal. Walter Duranty, special correspondent of the *New York Times*, suggested that anyone who thought the confessions false did not understand the

Russian soul and ought to read more Dostoevsky, an insight that sparked off an erudite exchange of letters in the *New Republic*. Winston Churchill would later characterize the purge as 'merciless, but perhaps not needless'. One of the most extraordinary plaudits of all came from Joseph Davies, US Ambassador to the Soviet Union. 'To have assumed that [it] was invented and staged,' he cabled back to Washington DC, 'would be to presuppose the creative genius of Shakespeare and the genius of a Belasco in stage production.' The communication probably raised a wry smile in Stalin as and when his spies intercepted it. Unhappily for most of those around him, the notion of trial as theatre had become horribly, hypernaturally true.

The bloodletting would not be limited to politicians. In May 1937, four months after the trial's conclusion, it was the Red Army's turn. Six of its most senior officers were hauled into jail, stripped of their chevrons, and made to confess to spying for Germany and Poland. Some historians have argued that they represented a genuine threat to Stalin, but the process used to condemn them does not instil confidence in the truth of the charges. Their admissions were beaten out with such force that rusty marks on one transcript were found decades later to be human blood; and although the defendants were not made publicly to recite their guilt, their secret condemnations were in many ways even more bizarre than the show trials. All were forced to implicate other serving officers, and as they stumbled into their closed courts martial they found themselves before a nine-judge panel that included four of their supposed accomplices. A total of five judges were destined to be shot for the same crimes that they were trying. A sixth would save himself: with secret police officers waiting at the door, Marshal Semyon Budenny placed a telephone call to Stalin and incredulously explained that a terrible mistake had evidently been made. Stalin chuckled, congratulated Budenny on his presence of mind, and cancelled the arrest warrant.

Over the stifling summer of 1937, the repression intensified. Countless secret police tribunals, known as troikas, were established to deal with the anti-Soviet criminals who, according to the Politburo, were 'still entrenched in both countryside and city'. Regional and municipal authorities were given quotas of wreckers – sometimes in the hundreds, often in the thousands – to find and shoot. Stalin further ordered that hundreds of public trials be staged with maximal press coverage across the Soviet Union. Vyshinsky, having already encouraged regional prosecutors to review their files and use 'political flair' to discover crimes previously overlooked, led by example with a group of peasants whose requisitioned grain had been infested with ticks. Four hundred years earlier, the villagers' French counterparts might have sought an injunction against the insects. In the brave new world of Vyshinskian jurisprudence, they were charged with wrecking and sentenced to death.

The contents of the crimes alleged became ever more ludicrous. The cutter of a Minsk clothing factory was accused of fomenting industrial discontent by designing work clothes with pockets that were too narrow. A Jewish engineer was accused of Nazi sympathies because a Z-shaped scientific institute which he had designed struck someone in authority as resembling half of a swastika, while a popular fabric print of the Ivanovo Textile Combine was discontinued when the manager detected Japanese helmets in its pattern. Linguists who had refused to accept that all human language derived from the sounds *rosh, sal, ber*, and *yon* – an eccentric theory to which Stalin had whimsically subscribed during the late 1920s – were picked up and shot.

Interrogators increasingly required prisoners not only to explain why they had been arrested – an intimidatory technique that dated back to the earliest days of the papal Inquisition – but also to draft their own confessions in intricate detail. Those who proved insufficiently imaginative might be left in rat-infested cells to recall their crimes if they were lucky, or have their heads plunged into phlegm-filled buckets and their intestines pulped with coshes if they were not. In police stations and prisons across the Soviet Union, the concentration camps of communism were taking shape. But to ordinary civilians, the words that streamed forth seemed like pure, black magic. Nadezhda Mandelstam later recalled that her poet husband Osip, who would himself die in the Gulag Archipelago in 1938, was awestruck by the willingness with which defendants were talking away their lives. 'Stalin doesn't have to cut heads off,' he marvelled. 'They fly off by themselves like dandelions.'

The Terror sliced most keenly of all through Moscow. While a solitary lamp burned through the night at the Kremlin, assuring Muscovites that the Great Helmsman's hand remained on the tiller, black saloons transported the condemned, zipping along the deserted avenues like hearses at a time of plague. An assistant to the director of the capital's zoo was hauled in on suspicion of wrecking its monkeys, when police learned that

16 per cent of them had recently died from tuberculosis. Stamp collectors were arrested for espionage, and the entire Esperanto Society was rounded up because someone decided that its name sounded counter-revolutionary. Fitzroy Maclean, the legendary British spy who was then stationed at the Moscow embassy, later recalled the city as a place of wraiths, where telephone calls were answered with whispers and anaemic officials would attend diplomatic receptions in silence, daring neither to stay away nor to speak. Yevgeny Yevtushenko, writing about the pall that simultaneously descended over literary life across the Soviet Union, conjured an image more macabre but also more beautiful. It was a time and a place, he would later write, when people might walk 'with death sentences shining inside them like white crosses'.

One of the most extraordinary sagas was the tragicomedy of the Soviet Union's ninety or so astronomers. At least twenty-nine were arrested and tried on charges of wrecking agricultural output by failing to predict solar eclipses and sunspots, and all were convicted. At least four were immediately executed. A story, reportedly true, which has been recounted by Russian playwright and historian Edvard Radzinsky, vividly conveys the background to those deaths.

Radzinsky tells how the director of the Moscow Planetarium received a telephone call, late one balmy evening during the deadly summer of 1937. The person at the other end stated that he was calling from Stalin's suburban dacha (where the Great Helmsman habitually hosted lugubrious soirées for those of his comrades whom he had not yet killed) and that a matter of great importance had arisen. Two members of the Politburo, sitting in the garden, had just fallen into a vodka-fuelled dispute about the name of a star, and Stalin had suggested that the director of the planetarium would be able to help . . . Said director replaced the handset, doubtless inhaling very deeply, and within minutes was heading towards to the home of his institution's most eminent survivor. The scientist was in no state to receive unexpected visitors, however. He had watched his colleagues evaporate over the previous months, and when he heard a car draw up outside his home his weak heart began to pound. As doors slammed and footsteps echoed up the stairwell, it accelerated. By the time the doorbell rang, it had stopped. The panic-stricken director headed for a second address. Astronomer Two had similarly lost his inclination to sleep, and when he saw the black car glide to a halt far below his high-rise apartment, he too concluded that his time had come. As his haplessly homicidal visitor rang the door, he left via the window. Only after a third trip did the director obtain the information he needed, and he finally called the dacha with the name of the star. By then of course, everyone had gone to bed.

'Anybody who breathes the air of terror is doomed,' wrote Nadezhda Mandelstam. 'Everybody is a victim – not only those who die, but also all the killers, ideologists, accomplices and sycophants who close their eyes or wash their hands.' Society fractured as denunciation boxes appeared in police stations across the country, just as they had appeared in the churches of Scotland and Italy during the sixteenth-century witch-hunts. Within the Party, pleading on behalf of a comrade or family member became tantamount to a confession of counter-revolution, a rule of etiquette that sometimes afforded Stalin particular pleasure. During a conversation with a pusillanimous character called Otto Kuusinen, whose son had just been picked up by the secret police, Stalin expressed his sympathies and inquired why Kuusinen had not take steps to get him released. 'Evidently there were serious reasons for his arrest,' came the response. Stalin grinned, and ordered that Esa Kuusinen be freed.

By 1938, the Soviet leader had only one serious rival left. Nikolai Bukharin was the type of person who had become a rarity by the end of the 1930s: a pleasant Communist. Cultured, witty, and zestful, with an easy smile and a mind that crackled, few were immune to his charm. Nadezhda Mandelstam credited him for arranging 'all the good things' that ever happened to her; the students he taught thought him a genius; and Lenin's sister was said to worship him. Even Viacheslav Molotov, a lackey who survived to fawn at Stalin's right hand for two decades, reminisced in old age on what a 'good, kind, decent man of ideas' Bukharin had been. Lenin, in a testament written shortly before his death in 1922, had praised the young revolutionary as 'a most valuable and major theorist', and 'the favourite of the whole Party'. In the same message he had called Stalin 'too rude' and advised his comrades to find another General Secretary. They ignored him but it seems safe to assume that if Stalin had not already marked Bukharin's card for destruction, he made a mental note to do so then.

His patience was, however, as great as his memory was long. A more immediate threat came from Kamenev and Zinoviev, then galvanizing the

Party with proposals for rapid industrialization, and in 1925 Stalin had allied himself with the man who was most clearly opposed to their policies – Nikolai Bukharin. The duo, contending that consolidation of Communist rule depended not on industry but on a well-to-do peasantry, saw off their challengers in 1927. Having won the battle for the Soviet Union's soul, Stalin switched sides. By the following spring, he was letting it be known that prosperous peasants, far from being the key to success, in fact needed 'liquidation as a class'. The volte-face shocked Bukharin. 'He is an unprincipled intriguer who subordinates everything to the preservation of his power,' he told one of his fellow Communists. 'He changes theories depending on whom he wants to get rid of at the moment' The man he was confiding in was Lev Kamenev. Bukharin's eyes were opening, just in time to glimpse his doom. The theoretician was about to be eclipsed by the tactician.

The crunch came in the autumn of 1928, when the harvest failed catastrophically across the Soviet Union. The temperamental divide that had always separated the two men opened into a political chasm. As towns ran out of food, Party officials began to confiscate grain supplies from farms – at gunpoint, when necessary – leaving entire villages to starve to death. Stalin, acting as though the peasants were profiteers, urged that force be used to the fullest extent, whereas Bukharin mounted a bitter attack on the 'policy of tribute'. Stalin noted his concerns with contempt. Bukharin 'recoils from extraordinary measures', he observed, 'as the Devil from holy water'. The last gasp of Bukharinism was heard in September, when Stalin warned that a final conflict with capitalism was looming and that the Soviet Union had to industrialize within ten years. 'Either we do it,' he prophesied, 'or they crush us.' It was not so much a reversal as a handbrake turn. Stalin was now promising a cornucopia of pistons and dynamos while Bukharin continued to propose nothing more exciting than a little more agriculture. It was no contest. The man whom Lenin had anointed as the Party's favourite just six years before was required by fellow Central Committee members in November 1928 to admit that his views had 'turned out to be mistaken'. Henceforth, promised Bukharin, he would wage a 'decisive struggle' against anyone who dared advance them.

Stalin's economic policies would, to their credit, build an industrial base that would one day help to defeat Hitler. To their debit, they would cause millions of people to starve to death. Whatever the imponderable meaning

of that balance sheet, the Soviet Union's course was set in 1928. A photograph from the following year shows Bukharin standing alongside his nemesis atop the Lenin Mausoleum, each man gazing in diametrically different directions, and over the next few years their lives diverged just as sharply. By the mid 1930s, with Stalin at the top of the heap, Bukharin was deep in the dustbin of history. It would not save him. As Stalin grew athirst, he decided finally to slake the vengeance that he had nurtured for so long.

An investigation into Bukharin's counter-revolutionary activity had been announced as early as the end of the first show trial, and in his playfully psychopathic way Stalin had already twice threatened open condemnation before stepping back from a showdown. In January 1937, however, one of Bukharin's students – himself under arrest – identified his professor as the leader of a network of Trotskyite terrorists that had been operating for almost a decade. Later that month, two of the defendants at the second show trial named him as one of their fellow conspirators. A helpless Bukharin, sensing the ground opening below him, went on hunger strike. His comrades took no notice. The thread of his fate had been cut, and at a Central Committee meeting in February 1937 he fell.

By 1937 gatherings of the Party executive were rational processes only in the most formal sense. Actual exchanges of ideas had ended years before, and although the participants followed agendas and delivered reports, they might as well have commenced with ululation and continued with tom-toms for all the difference that the words made. The typical meeting involved those around the table turning on one of their number and ripping him apart to prove their loyalty. Stalin would meanwhile remain silent or invite his boys to show some tolerance – once he had made known his preferred scapegoat. In February 1937, he pointed the victim stick at Bukharin.

A secret police report had been circulated prior to the meeting, detailing the accusations made by Bukharin's student, and moments after he began to defend himself, Stalin asked why his own pupil would lie.

Bukharin tentatively suggested that his arrest for treason might have had something to do with it, but Stalin, expressing more sorrow than anger, disagreed. He had met the young man and, notwithstanding his treachery, had found himself persuaded by 'his eyes, the tone of the story'. 'I may be wrong,' he added thoughtfully, 'but my impression . . . is that he is a sincere man.'

The observation was enough to draw blood – and the seventy circling comrades of the Central Committee lunged. By the end of the meeting, three days later, they were tearing at the tatters of Bukharin's political corpse and demanding the production of a physical one. Stalin, the sober voice of reason once again, persuaded all present that it was only fair to await the result of the ongoing investigations. Another year would pass before the case was ready for trial. But Bukharin left the room under arrest – and from deep within, the pale cross of death had begun to shine.

His trial, alongside that of twenty co-defendants, opened on a gloomy day in March 1938. Anyone who was anyone in Moscow – admittedly, no longer a very large category of people – had tickets to the show. Diplomats and journalists sat among the rows of secret police officers, chatting busily on the benches like theatre-goers before curtain-up. Fitzroy Maclean would later record that at one point the beam of an arc light swung across the hall, piercing a darkened window near the ceiling to reveal the moustachioed profile of Stalin himself. Just as King James had secretly attended the trials of his own traitors more than three centuries before, the impresario had come to watch his show.

As the judges entered the hall, an usher called for silence and the buzz turned to silence. Ulrich deposited his bulk into the central chair, invited the audience to retake their seats, and called for the indictment to be read. For over an hour, the allegations rang out. They told of a plot so far-reaching that it pre-dated the revolution, with a cast of perfidious poisoners, ruthless assassins, and cabals of wreckers, working in unison to dismember the Soviet Union at the behest of Trotsky and the combined intelligence services of Japan, Germany, Poland, and Britain. Bukharin himself was said not only to have directed sabotage and espionage, but to have conspired to murder both Stalin and Lenin. It promised to be prequel, sequel, and grand finale to all that had gone before; but its success, as always, would depend on the acting talents of the men in the dock. Within a couple of hours there were already signs of serious dissension in the troupe.

The drama within the drama began when the defendants were arraigned. Bukharin and two others entered guilty pleas, but when the fourth in line, Nikolai Krestinsky, was asked to plead he declared that he had not known about any conspiracies, was not a Trotskyite, and had committed no crime. 'All my previous statements were a deliberate perversion of the truth,' he declared in a high-pitched voice. 'I acted thus because I knew that otherwise my words would not reach the ears of the rulers of this country.' A flustered Judge Ulrich tried three times to persuade him that there had to be some mistake – but to no avail. Vyshinsky sat anchored in his chair while guilty pleas were taken from the remaining seventeen defendants. Ulrich then sprang to his rescue by calling a recess, but twenty minutes proved inadequate to make Krestinsky see the error of his ways, and the prosecutor returned to announce testily that he would begin his case with a defendant called Sergei Bessonov.

As his examination proceeded, a dialogue that had flowed effortlessly in earlier trials then began to jump and stutter. At one point Bessonov paused, clearly unable to recall what he was supposed to be admitting. 'Perhaps I can help you?' offered Vyshinsky. 'I think you can do it better than I,' came the deadpan reply. 'What coming from me . . . may sound insincere and unconvincing will sound real if it comes from you.' When Vyshinsky then tried to use Bessonov to discredit Krestinsky, he almost opened an entirely new can of worms. 'You heard [Krestinsky] say he was not a Trotskyite. Is that right or wrong?' he inquired. Bessonov smiled, and Vyshinsky asked why. 'I am smiling because the reason why I am standing here is that . . . Krestinsky named me the liaison man with Trotsky . . . And if Krestinsky had not spoken to me about this in December 1933, I would not be in the dock today.' The enigmatic statement, which Vyshinsky chose not to explore further, was another reminder that each defendant's presence in court concealed countless machinations and backstage betrayals. Under the klieg lights of the October Hall, the magnificent edifice of Stalinist justice was beginning to sway like a stage set that had been built too high.

Tensions only increased the next day, as Vyshinsky set out his case against Bukharin. One of the lesser defendants, Vladimir Ivanov, had been selected to land the first blow. He dutifully testified that Bukharin had let slip back in 1918 that he was arranging for the assassination of Lenin, and that he had been working full-time for the overthrow of the Soviet Union since 1928. Ivanov had assisted by hindering sawmill production, with a view to depriving Soviet schoolchildren of exercise books, and had conspired hand in glove with Bukharin right up to the moment of the senior man's arrest. As he concluded his testimony, Bukharin requested permission to put a question. Was it not right, he asked, that they had in fact not met for two years? When Ivanov responded that 'in my opinion' they had certainly met since then, Bukharin twice pressed him for details. Taken aback, Ivanov refused to provide them. '[W]e had so many conversations of all kinds', he explained, 'that you can't remember everything.'

The intervention was hardly a killer blow, but Vyshinsky, troubled by what it might mean, requested permission to put some questions out of turn to Bukharin. Ulrich granted it. Did he agree, asked Vyshinsky, that Ivanov had spoken to him about counter-revolutionary action in 1928? Bukharin affirmed that to be correct. Vyshinsky then proposed several other matters, none of which Bukharin seemed to deny, but each admission slipped away like smoke. It was true, he accepted, that he had once recommended 'open battles' against the Party, but he had meant only that people should disagree candidly with official policy. He had certainly formed an illegal organization to 'muster forces against the party' but that was not to say that he had fostered practical insurrection. The 'logic of the struggle' had meant that the prospect of violence existed, 'potentially, in embryonic form', but he had never ordered its use. The words spoke of a weighty guilt – but their meaning floated as evanescent as butterflies.

Vyshinsky evidently realized that it would not do to chase that meaning around the court, and abandoned the skirmish. He had a far less risky trick up his sleeve. Stalin had recently developed a fascination for what he slyly referred to as the 'eternally true' story of Judas Iscariot, and either the Soviet leader or Vyshinsky himself had prepared a vignette for the crowd. Turning to one of the minor defendants, the prosecutor asked for confirmation that, three decades earlier, he had spent six years working as a tsarist police agent and had twice been paid thirty roubles by a certain Inspector Vasilyev to betray his fellow Communists. It was duly given. 'Thirty pieces of silver?' asked Vyshinsky, before adding in a stage whisper: 'Twice as much as Judas received!' The crowd sniggered appreciatively, but Vyshinsky was not yet finished. 'Perhaps', he asked Judge Ulrich, 'you will allow me to call Vasilyev.' Ulrich, smiling mischievously, nodded his permission. A shrivelled old man with a vast moustache thereupon entered the October Hall and tottered along its central aisle. Though a little deaf, he was able to confirm that it was all true. He distinctly remembered that thirty roubles had been paid, twice, back in 1909. He also recognized the man in the dock, although he had looked a little younger. 'I should think so!' exclaimed Vyshinsky. 'You were younger then too!' Ulrich's great potato of a head broke into a grin, and members of the audience stamped the floor with pleasure.

Matters only improved further during the evening session when Krestinsky – the defendant who had pleaded not guilty the day before – volunteered an explanation of his behaviour. It had, after all, been a misunderstanding. '[U]nder the influence of a momentary keen feeling of false shame, evoked by the atmosphere of the dock and the painful impression created by the public reading of the indictment, which was aggravated by my poor health . . . instead of saying, "Yes, I am guilty", I almost mechanically answered, "No, I am not guilty."'

As the case proceeded through its third day, Vyshinsky continued to recover ground and Bukharin remained silent. But even as the case

appeared to be stabilizing, a powerful static was building. No one knew if Bukharin's earlier sally represented the posturing of an intellectual or the feints of a fighter, but it held the promise of extremely dramatic resolution – for the Soviet nation, as much as for Bukharin the man. In 1917, the American radical John Reed had watched the defendant, then 28 years old, address a Party meeting from the same building in which he was now sitting. Then, the flame-haired firebrand, in leather jacket and loose shirt, had 'stood up, savage, logical, with a voice which plunged and struck, plunged and struck . . . Him they listened to with shining eyes.' Twenty-one years later, the high forehead and grey goatee lent him a physical resemblance to Lenin that could only enhance the revolutionary aura. Vyshinsky meanwhile had a political pedigree as dubious as that of Bukharin was impeccable. A committed opponent of the Bolsheviks in 1917, he had demanded the arrest of Lenin, and only got round to joining his adversaries three years after their triumph. Bukharin's very existence represented a rebuke to his own. Bukharin, for his part, knew that his performance would become his epitaph. For a contest that was rigged, the stakes were high indeed.

The encounter between the two men began on the fourth day. Bukharin opened by briskly confirming that, by virtue of his erstwhile opposition to Stalin, he was deeply implicated in all manner of anti-Soviet activity. He had been behind a vast counter-revolutionary organization and was guilty of 'the sum total' of all its crimes. But when questioned about specifics, the details were as elusive as before. It was true that his activities had promoted the restoration of capitalism, but they had been inspired by a concern for the welfare of workers and peasants. He was in any event so guilty that it was irrelevant whether he had known about particular acts of violence or espionage. That said, as a matter of fact, he had known of none.

Vyshinsky, accustomed only to confessions and denials, initially found the tactic outlandish. He then found it infuriating. 'In short,' he snapped at one point, after Bukharin had spent quarter of an hour explaining how he had mistakenly come to favour democracy and the free market, 'you lapsed into outright rabid fascism.' The journal *Izvestia* was no less offended. 'He has a system,' it reported, as though alerting its readers to the activities of an ideological card sharp. '[H]is aim is to deflect all concrete charges from himself by wholesale declarations of his responsibility for everything.'

For two days the duo fought over the politics, history, and language of the revolution, in a struggle that was not so much a mismatch as a category mistake, the opposition of an intellectual prizefighter and a master of mental ju-jitsu. While Vyshinsky hammered his opponent for his criminal genius, Bukharin earnestly admitted that he had made some serious political mis-judgments. For hour after hour, haymakers landed on air as Bukharin ducked and chopped, and when the contest culminated, it was not amidst the clamour of accusation and counter-charge but in a flurry of pedantry.

After a lengthy explanation by Bukharin of why he had not wanted to overthrow the government in 1932, Vyshinsky wearily interrupted to tell him that the court was interested in events that had happened rather than

those that had not. Bukharin, a former philosophy professor, cautioned him
to remember Spinoza's dictum that 'every negation contains an affirmation'.
A little later, when Vyshinsky told Bukharin that he was 'not asking . . . about
conversations in general, but about this conversation', Bukharin reminded
him that, 'In Hegel's *Logic*, the word "this" is considered to be the most difficult word.' Vyshinsky angrily asked Judge Ulrich to remind Bukharin that
he was 'not here in the capacity of a philosopher, but a criminal', and
returned to 'that conversation'. Bukharin now raised a semantic objection to
the word 'that', and advised his adversary that he did not need to wave his
hands around to make his point. 'Accused Bukharin, do not forget where
you are now,' snarled Ulrich. Vyshinsky, doubtless enraged to have sunk so
low that a mere judge was presuming to come to his aid, abandoned the
last pretence of composure. 'I will be compelled to cut the interrogation
short', he spluttered. '[Y]ou apparently are following definite tactics and
do not want to tell the truth, hiding behind a flood of words, pettifogging,
making digressions into the sphere of politics, of philosophy, theory and
so forth . . . Therefore stop pettifogging. If this is the way you want to
defend yourself I shall cut the interrogation short.' Within minutes, Ulrich
had declared a half-hour adjournment and when the court reassembled
Vyshinsky switched his attention to Bukharin's co-defendants. It was not a
knockout – but for the very first time, the prosecutor had been battled to
a standstill.

Matters only worsened for Vyshinsky two days later, when the time
came for former secret police chief Genrich Yagoda to testify. Yagoda had
been arrested in March 1937 (accused of working for the tsarist police
since 1907, when he had been ten years old) and having coordinated the
first show trial, he had been profoundly disturbed by Stalin's decision to
make him a defendant at the third. The pallid character with lank hair and
bedraggled toothbrush moustache had come close to a nervous break-
down while awaiting trial, pacing his cell and pronouncing that his
downfall proved the existence of God, and now that his turn to commit
hara-kiri had come around, he finally cracked.

Asked to clarify details about his attempt to poison the son of novelist
Maxim Gorky – a subplot of the indictment that was surreal even by the
Twilight-Zone parameters of the October Hall – Yagoda denied that he had
ever done such a thing. In that case, asked Vyshinsky, why had he admitted
it to his interrogators? 'Permit me not to answer this question,' growled

Yagoda, staring pointedly at the lawyer. The inquiry, addressed to a former secret police chief who was teetering on a psychic precipice, betokens a certain recklessness, but Vyshinsky had not become Stalin's prosecutor for his timidity. He declined to drop the subject. Why had Yagoda admitted the murder if he had not committed it? In a low and deliberate tone, the defendant repeated himself. 'Permit me not to answer this question.' He had also been implicated by three of his co-defendants, Vyshinsky reminded him. Were they all liars? They were, said Yagoda, and he himself had made a statement during his interrogation that was not true. And why, demanded Vyshinsky, had he lied? Yagoda finally exploded. 'I told you,' he hissed, with a venom that made several members of the audience gasp. 'Permit me not to answer this question.' He turned to Judge Ulrich and, in a remark that would never find its way into the official report of the trial, was heard to say: 'You can drive me, but not too far. I'll say what I want to say . . . but . . . do not drive me too far.' By the time the court resumed for its evening session, the secret police had leaned – hard – on their former boss. According to Fitzroy Maclean, 'In a few hours he had aged by ten years. Before he had looked broken; now he looked crushed.'

But Vyshinsky had also been wounded. The rest of Yagoda's evidence was largely heard in camera, and although he would admit his guilt when asking for mercy at the end of the case, his grudging plea was as close to a denial as a confession can get. In an attempt to regain the initiative before the final speeches, Vyshinsky closed his case with a second moment of light relief. Addressing the defendant Rosengolts, he established that a piece of dry bread had been found sewn into his pocket on arrest, and that it had contained a piece of paper. On it had been written two verses from the Book of Psalms. 'Let God arise, let his enemies be scattered,' intoned Vyshinsky. 'Thou shalt not be afraid for the terror by night; nor for the arrow that flieth by day; nor for the pestilence that walketh in darkness; nor for that destruction that wasteth at noonday.' Pausing for effect, he inquired how the bread had found its way into Rosengolts' pocket. 'My wife put it [there] one day before I went to work,' came the embarrassed reply. 'She said it was for good luck.' The answer condensed a thousand tragedies from 1938 Moscow: a place where a husband left home in the morning unsure that he would ever return, and a wife sent him off with a hidden prayer against sudden death. But for Vyshinsky, it was the prologue to a punch line. Like an old pro, he turned to the audience. 'For good luck!' he repeated, with a smile and a wink. The crowd erupted into laughter, and the court was cleared for the day.

When Vyshinsky rose to make his closing address two days later, he seemed fully to have recovered his poise. No longer required to go through the motions of dialogue, he summarized the script as he wanted it remembered. Bukharin's attempt to redefine his crimes as mere disagreements was a charade. Had not two of his henchmen admitted to infecting 25,000 horses and many thousands of pigs with anaemia and plague? Another had adulterated butter with glass and nails, and had arranged for fifty carloads of eggs to go bad. Even his intellectual posturing had been terroristic. 'Caught red-handed in the act, Bukharin calls Hegel himself as witness, hurls himself into the jungle of linguistics, philology and rhetoric, mumbles some sort of learned words, so as to cover up the traces in one way or another . . . [T]his is the first instance in history of a spy and murderer using philosophy, like powdered glass, to hurl it into his victim's eyes before dashing his brains out with a footpad's bludgeon.' His disloyalty to Stalin reminded Vyshinsky of another betrayal – the greatest of them all. 'How many times', he demanded, 'has Bukharin kissed the great teacher with the kiss of Judas the traitor?' Abuse of the other defendants also plumbed new levels of invention. They were 'excrement', 'stinking carrion', and a 'foul-smelling heap of human garbage', whose testimony was pervaded by the 'chill and stench of death'. They 'barked', 'crowed' or 'grunted' as often as they spoke. By the time his diatribe reached its end, Vyshinsky was once again master of the forensic universe. 'May your verdict resound as [a] refreshing and purifying thunderstorm!' he cried. 'Our whole country, from young to old, is awaiting and demanding one thing,' he roared. The finale was so predictable that the audience could probably have shouted along. 'The traitors and spies who were selling our country to the enemy must be shot like dirty dogs!'

The defendants' final speeches still lay ahead however – and the tension was immense as Bukharin rose to address the hushed courtroom. As he began systematically to measure the allegations against the evidence, it became clear that the feature that had defined every previous trial in the October Hall – an abject acceptance of the prosecution case – would be absent. He had never ordered anyone to wreck anything, hurt anyone, or spy for any foreign power, he asserted. While agreeing with the legal proposition that every member of a criminal gang was responsible for its collective actions, he pointed out that gangs were ordinarily composed of people who knew each other. He, on the other hand, had never even met several of his co-defendants. Vyshinsky yawned ostentatiously, but his nervousness was evident. The temple of Stalinist justice had already tottered. Even if the verdicts could never be in any doubt, the court delivering them looked almost set to topple.

'I now conclude my objections to certain charges which the State Prosecutor brought against me,' announced Bukharin. His speech had reached its pivot, the moment when he would utter the words that would echo into history. And its twist was savage. 'I will now return,' he declared, 'to the crimes I actually did commit.'

Bukharin had not, after all, escaped the curse of the show trials. Having proved to his own satisfaction that Vyshinsky was less clever than he thought, Bukharin was ready at last to display his own ideological purity. His magnificent performance faded into a pathetic coda, as he outlined the full extent of his former support for policies that Stalin had jettisoned. A democracy might have characterized such a stance as principled opposition. Bukharin could not have disagreed more. 'The severest sentence would be justified, because a man deserves to be shot ten times over for such crimes.'

Bukharin ended by explaining why he had chosen to confess. He denied that he had been hypnotized or drugged, and briefly discussed Dostoevsky to scorn the notion that there was something essentially penitential about the Slavic soul. Unable to resist one last dig at Vyshinsky, he also ridiculed the theory that a confession was required to support a valid conviction: that was 'a medieval principle of jurisprudence'. But yet again, the mental acrobatics ended with Bukharin positioned precisely below the executioner's blade. Although a confession might have no bearing on his legal guilt, an 'internal demolition of the forces of counter-revolution' had been necessary. And the demolition in his case had been a thorough one.

> For three months I refused to say anything. Then I began to testify. Why? Because while in prison I made a revaluation of my entire past. For when you ask yourself: 'If you must die, what are you dying for?' – an absolute black vacuity suddenly rises before you with startling vividness. There was nothing to die for, if one wanted to die unrepented. And, on the contrary,

everything positive that glistens in the Soviet Union acquires
new dimensions in a man's mind. This in the end disarmed
me completely and led me to bend my knees before the party
and the country.

The claim to have genuflected before the gleaming machines of the Soviet
experiment evokes a powerful image, and it would soon inspire a disillu-
sioned Stalinist called Arthur Koestler to fictionalize the process that made
Bukharin surrender. His 1940 novel, *Darkness at Noon*, would in turn
become the prism through which many would regard the show trials. The
paradox of its protagonist – who annihilates his ideals by confessing for
their sake – is still so poetic that it becomes tempting to see in it the fate of
the entire generation that died in Stalin's Russia.

But just as that would be a travesty of countless truths, the reality of
Bukharin's submission was considerably more complex than his own
redefinition of it. He had in fact been tiptoeing a vanishingly narrow
space between self-respect, blindness and hypocrisy for years. In 1936, he
had welcomed the execution of Kamenev and Zinoviev by declaring
himself 'terribly glad . . . that the dogs have been shot'. By the time of his
last Central Committee meeting in February 1937, he clearly saw the hell
bubbling around him and gave his young wife, Anna Larina, a letter in
which he condemned Stalin's 'pathological suspiciousness' and the 'infernal machine' of repression that could turn any Party member into a
terrorist or spy overnight. Even then, however, his ultimate faith in that
Party remained undimmed. He recalled, with nostalgia, a time when it
had only used 'justified cruelty against its enemies' – and even hoped that
such days might yet return. For the message he gave to Anna Larina was
addressed to a 'new, young and honest generation of Party leaders', and
he asked her to memorize it in order that she could one day transmit it
to them. 'Know comrades', his testament concluded, 'that the banner you
bear in a triumphant march toward communism contains a drop of my
blood too.'

The saddest insight into Bukharin's mental turmoil comes from his
prison cell. While awaiting trial, he wrote forty-three times to Stalin, in
terms so vulnerable that the words sometimes read like the whispered
confidences of a lover. The last letter, written in December 1937, is the
most helpless of all. As though discussing a brilliant advance in Marxist

philosophy, he congratulated Stalin on the 'great and bold . . . political idea' of using a purge to consolidate his regime. He understood that his personal situation was dwarfed by Stalin's mammoth responsibilities, but he was nevertheless conscious of an 'agonizing paradox' – namely, that he was innocent. He would have felt so much more at peace, he explained, if he could be sure that his old friend did not actually believe him to be guilty. He even hoped that they could give their relationship another chance. If, 'contrary to expectation', he was to be spared his life, he would 'work like a dynamo' for the revolution. He was willing, if his wife consented, to suffer exile in the United States, where he could open an important new front in the battle against Trotsky. He concluded by expressing his 'boundless love' for Stalin, embracing him mentally, and begging for forgiveness – although only 'in your heart, not otherwise'.

The messy reality is that cowardice combined with courage in Bukharin, and perspicacity with delusion. His testament, like the plea to Stalin, spoke the language of a man who could still justify brutal means with noble ends. But long before he wrote either, he had come to recognize Stalin's monstrosity, and at least some of the pressure to confess came from sources other than Party loyalty: as Bukharin sat in jail, interrogators serving the man he was mentally embracing were threatening to murder his wife and child. Neither hero nor villain, he was the object and victim of circumstance. If Stalin had offered to spare him, he might have become the October Hall's most damning accuser of all. But if he had not had a young family to protect, he might, like Alice, have brought the entire house of cards tumbling down.

In his final letter to Stalin, Bukharin expressed a wish. 'If I am to receive the death sentence, then I implore you . . . by all that you hold dear, not to have me shot. Let me drink poison instead.' The request recalled another defendant who had submitted to his ideals. More than two thousand years earlier, Socrates had refused to escape from his condemned cell on the grounds that, right or wrong, Athens was the state to which he owed his life. But the parallels ended there. Whereas Socrates is remembered for ridiculing his judges' condemnation, Bukharin earned his place in history by affirming that his conviction was just. And while Socrates was given his hemlock, the Russian's request for poison did not even get a reply. There is no reliable account of Bukharin's execution, but a legend swiftly spread that he had stood proud and spat curses at Stalin until cut down by his killer. The Soviet Union of 1938 was a land sorely in need of heroes.

With the end of the third trial in March 1938, the Terror began at last to squeal to a halt. But even as the last few hundred thousand victims were being despatched, one final search for scapegoats was launched – targeting the very people who had just finished conducting the purges. In May, Vyshinsky convened a legal conference at which he publicly humiliated a prosecutor who admitted pursuing indictments that he had not read, and by July *Pravda* was reporting the trials of several supposedly over-zealous legal officials. Come November, Stalin abolished his secret troikas and sent written instructions to all local Party bosses to halt extra-judicial arrests, with immediate effect. The directive, stern though it sounded, had a subtext that positively rippled with Stalinist humour. The Party leadership, explained Stalin, had become aware of some serious errors in secret police procedures. Investigators were often making do with bare confessions and ignoring the need for corroborative evidence. Some interrogations were being recorded after the event, and others were not being set down on paper at all. The man who had been gaily writing and rewriting his victim's confessions since 1936 noted that it was even known for 'drafts of testimonies, written in pencil, corrected and crossed out by unknown hands' to be entered into the record. The most ironic note of all was sounded by the final words. '[T]he slightest violation of Soviet laws . . . by any official of the [secret police] . . . regardless of who the person is, shall be met with severe judicial penalties.'

A week later, Nikolai Yezhov – the man who had presided over the Terror since Genrich Yagoda's fall in late 1936 – was made to resign. It was at last his turn to fall beneath the wheel of the juggernaut. Within five months he was under arrest for espionage. At his secret trial in February 1940 he refused to accept the truth of the charge because that 'would only be a gift to the English lords and Japanese samurai', but even he offered up a confession of sorts. The *mea culpa* lacked the introspection of Bukharin, but its logic was no less contorted. With bitter confusion he insisted that he had 'used everything at my disposal to expose conspiracies' and expressed pride in the fact that he had eliminated fourteen thousand people. On reflection, however, he had to accept that he had made mistakes. In particular he had allowed his subordinates to exercise too much leniency. '[M]y great guilt', he concluded, 'lies in the fact that I purged so few of them.' There was only one man whom he absolved. 'Tell Stalin', he told his judges, 'that I shall die with his name on my lips.'

Back in August 1936, Yagoda had collected some mementoes from the Lubyanka cellars. They were the bullets used to despatch the victims of the first show trial, and he had had them engraved with the names of the dead men. By the time he was shot in March 1938, the souvenirs had passed to Yezhov. And now Yezhov's time to give them up had come. On 4 February 1940 he was executed, and the ammunition, tagged and marked, was finally laid to rest in his court file.

A Trotskyist newspaper's 1941 comment on Stalin's purge.

Every trial tells a story, but the fairy tales enacted in 1930s Moscow retold history. In a revolutionary state that was woefully short of traditions, leaders who could claim a Communist pedigree had been among the only heroes – and when the trials unmasked virtually all of them as traitors, the lustre of the one who remained shone as never before. And Stalin would only polish his image. Following Bukharin's execution in March 1938, he personally edited the trial transcript for publication, and later in the same year he approved publication of *The Short Course of the History of the All-Union Communist Party*, a work that would assume almost sacred status in the communist world. In its pages, the convolutions, realignments and disappearances of Soviet history could at last be smoothed into one seamless narrative, in which Stalin humbly assumed

Lenin's mantle and led the country's workers and peasants onward, ever onward. As layer upon layer of civil society sloughed away, purged from the Party, frogmarched from stamp collections and escorted from observatories, a new nation emerged that could barely remember when there had been no Great Helmsman to keep watch for enemies of the people.

That nation would endure for half a century. Although Stalin's Terror was denounced by Nikita Khrushchev in 1956, only a handful of its victims were declared innocent and – in a shabby compromise that would typify the later Soviet Union – the rehabilitations were kept secret. The thaw meant, however, that Anna Larina's exile finally came to an end, and upon her return to Moscow she grew increasingly convinced that Bukharin's vision of a renewed Communist Party was becoming a reality. In 1961, she finally dared to send a written copy of his appeal to one of the 'new, young and honest' generation of Party leaders. Leonid Brezhnev did not reply. Another quarter of a century would pass before she found her man; but in 1988, with Mikhail Gorbachev's *glasnost* in full swing, she finally won justice for the husband whom she had never ceased to adore.

The verdict of recent history has been less favourable to the two men most responsible for the trials, but neither would have to account for his actions on this side of the grave. Andrei Vyshinsky's star continued to rise, and he would play a major role after the Second World War in orchestrating the Soviet contribution to the Nuremberg trials. He ended his career as Ambassador to the United Nations and died in 1954 at his Park Avenue apartment, attended by a wife and daughter and surrounded by the acquisitions of a life comfortably traversed. Stalin's departure had come at his dacha a year before, and had been rather less gentle – so unpleasant in fact that, to paraphrase Oscar Wilde, only someone with a heart of stone could fail to smile. He slipped into a coma while asleep and lay in a pool of urine for several hours, watched by comrades who were too nervous – or too hopeful – to come to his aid. For an entire day he remained still, but when he breathed his last, by way of a death rattle that filled the room, his eyelids snapped open and fury contorted his face. Everyone watched, aghast, as his left arm rose as though on strings and pointed somewhere high above. Earthly justice would not claim Stalin, but it would at least be nice to think that, after a lifetime during which he had dealt with his problems by eliminating others, he was finally confronted by a demon with which he had to grapple.

*   *   *

'Vaterland'. Bukharin is the central pig, and Trotsky is,
fittingly, at far right.

There is much that is straightforward about the show trials. Staged at a time
when the government was promising plenty and delivering chaos, they
delineated a sinister, elusive, and extremely useful enemy. As far back as
1900, Lenin had written that: 'Before we can unite, and in order that we may
unite, we must first of all draw firm and definite lines of demarcation.' The
logic was circular then, and reason bent at least as readily in the dynamized
atmosphere of the October Hall, where prosecutions could prove the Party's
excellence simply by asserting the defendants' vileness. 'It is now clear why
there are interruptions of supplies here and there, why, with our riches and
abundance of products, there is a shortage first of one thing, then of another,'
declared Vyshinsky in March 1938. 'It is these traitors who are responsible for
it.' The disloyal pigs shown in *Izvestia* in the same month, fed swill by a Nazi
from a trough marked 'Fatherland', exemplified what was at stake. In a world
of us and them, the choice was simple.

The fact that the defendants were prepared to confess is also no surprise. A
willingness to do so was typically what made people eligible for public prosecution in the first place. Only about sixty thousand Soviet citizens were given

the dubious privilege of a show trial during the 1930s. Some three million others were shot or died in jail, after secret hearings or none at all.

The enduring fascination of the Moscow trials does not, however, spring from the motivations inspiring the prosecutions or the reasons for the submission. It arises out of the potency of the sight itself. The public declarations of guilt all but created their own reality. Stalin, at some psychotic tier of the subconscious, was able to confirm his world-view by hearing enemies recite fictions that he put into their mouths. Sceptics had to wonder if so much smoke could be generated without a fire smouldering beneath. Diehard cynics were left to face the most powerful fact of all: that Stalin could turn even the mightiest of men into marionettes.

It is all but inconceivable that a spectacle as stage-managed will ever be seen in a Western democracy, but its power reflects a feature of the criminal trial that is both ancient and enduring. The ritual has always operated to rebalance communities after someone has broken the rules, and whether it has allowed suspects back into the fold or expelled them from it, it has demanded that they make their acceptance of those rules manifest, through humility or remorse. The Athenians asked defendants to propose their own punishments, while Rome required that they come to court unshaved and in mourning dress. English jury trials from the outset made suspects enter their pleas while hatless and on their knees, and those who refused were, for five hundred years, subjected to thumbscrews or pressed to death.* Papal inquisitors had suspects explain the reasons for their own arrests, and their successors in early modern France insisted that 'wrongdoers . . . must if possible judge and condemn themselves'.

It remains an article of faith in modern Western societies that a submissive suspect is less dangerous and morally preferable to one who expresses neither respect nor penitence. The defendant who denies guilt but accepts that crime is bad is better than one who scornfully expresses contempt for the law itself. Unreserved contrition attracts shorter sentences and earlier parole. Those who refuse to affirm or acknowledge the rules – not even with lies, not even with anger – can, however, inspire deep unease.

Few cases illustrate the point better than that of Oklahoma City bomber Timothy McVeigh. Apart from his face – shrewd, sharp, and

---

* See p. 74.

mean – the only aspect of his existence that still lingers in the imagination is his refusal to show any contrition whatsoever. He sat out his trial in silence and greeted the imposition of his death sentence with a peace sign. After waiving his right to appeal, he was strapped to a gurney on 11 June 2001 while more than two hundred relatives of his victims, hoping to make sense of their grief, peered at him on closed-circuit television screens. He responded by staring at the ceiling and left behind only a mawkish poem that concluded with one final assertion of spiritual independence: 'I am the master of my fate; I am the captain of my soul.' Many later expressed their bewilderment that seeing McVeigh twitch and die had failed to provide the closure for which they had hoped. A word of regret – or a scream of defiance – might well have offered considerably more satisfaction.

The intensity of the desire to see contrition has also carried risks that the right to silence can only begin to control. Friedrich von Spee, the Jesuit critic of Würzburg's seventeenth-century witch-hunt, once noted that inquisitors often intensified the pressure on a suspect to provide a confession simply to justify their decision to seek one in the first place. '[J]udges think it a disgrace if they acquit,' he had observed, 'as though they had been too hasty in arresting and torturing the innocent.' The checks and balances of a modern democracy certainly make matters more inconvenient for monomaniacal officials, but there is little reason to think that the communal *desire* to see submission is any weaker today than it was then. At times of great fear it can inspire a demand for public displays of loyalty, as it notoriously did both within and outside the House Un-American Activities Committee in the anti-communist United States of the late 1940s. Democracies *in extremis* have even resorted to torture, and survivors often report, in terms that echo those of Spee, that the people who committed it seemed driven not by sadism, but by a moral belief that they were fighting fire with fire. The interrogators themselves justify the torture in such terms; never more eloquently than in 1962, when a veteran of the French Foreign Legion called Captain Estoup explained why good men had been capable of inflicting water torture and electric shocks on the militants fighting for Algerian independence. He explained that neither a propensity for violence nor the brutalizing effects of war had underpinned the mentality of the torturers. 'If you believe that, you have neither suffered nor inflicted real pain . . . [F]or the most part the true motive for their actions was a secret, silent, inward, gnawing determination not to have committed crime that achieved no object.'

The danger of overzealous enforcement is complemented by the well-known phenomenon that some individuals are only too eager to make false confessions. Inspired by a desire to conform, a longing for self-esteem or an amorphous sense of guilt, innocent people have been admitting fictitious offences for centuries, and the eagerness to hear remorse often overwhelms doubts that might otherwise exist about the confession's truth. One example will stand for the thousands of others. In 1666, a Frenchman called Robert Hubert came forward to admit that he had started the Great Fire of London, having been offered five pistols to do the job by an unidentified stranger. He was, by common consent, mentally retarded. Although it is theoretically conceivable that he did indeed destroy London's thirteen thousand houses and eighty-seven churches with a burning rag on a pole, as he claimed, it seems almost certain that the event's gravity overcame any uncertainty about whether he had brought it about. There was considerable speculation among commentators as to why Hubert had confessed. Some thought that it was because he 'had a mind to assume the glory of being hanged for the greatest villain'. Others believed that he was 'a poor distracted wretch weary of his life, and chose to part with it this way'. According to one, 'Neither the judges nor any present at the trial did believe him guilty.' And yet, in thrall to his confession, the jurors convicted the young man of arson, the judge condemned him to death, and he hanged without a pardon.

The confession's potential for injustice remains. A concern to extract admissions and then believe them sent dozens of innocent people to English jails during the 1970s,* while developments in DNA testing since the late 1980s have revealed that the position might be even more dire in the United States. In the fifteen years after 1989, over a hundred and fifty prisoners positively proved their innocence through scientific analysis of exhibits in their cases, and around a quarter of those exonerated were convicted on the strength of a confession that was untrue or non-existent. Several had spent years on death row. The laws of probability, if nothing else, suggest that other innocent people must have been executed.

---

* One of the most notorious of all such cases, that of the Birmingham Six, is described at pp. 310–17.

Events within the USA since September 11 2001 have produced a particularly notable illustration of just how completely the urge to believe in a community's morality can overwhelm the specifics of that morality at a time of crisis. As President Bush rallied the nation for a new kind of war, Harvard professor Alan Dershowitz began to champion a new kind of law to complement it. It might be time, he proposed, to amend the US Constitution to permit judges to issue torture warrants in cases when lives were at imminent risk. Dershowitz, once better known for supporting limits to governmental power than for proposing extensions to it, hypothesized about the crimes that might thereby be prevented – if, for example, the proverbial time bomb was defused – but seemed oddly indifferent to the possibility that the person tortured might be innocent. He carefully explained that he was only calling for a debate – and the fact that he was publicizing a book at the time means that there is little reason to doubt that – but he gave every indication that in his own head the debate had already been won. Asked by MSNBC journalist Chris Matthews to describe the kind of torture that he had in mind, he suggested that the insertion of needles under a suspect's fingernails was one possibility. '[P]ain', he explained, 'is overrated.'

The War Crimes Trial

'There's the bandage over the eyes, and here are the scales. But aren't there wings on the figure's heels, and isn't it flying?' 'Yes', said the painter, 'my instructions were to paint it like that; actually it is Justice and the goddess of Victory in one.'

FRANZ KAFKA, *The Trial*

On 20 November 1945, proceedings opened in a courtroom on the second floor of the Palace of Justice in Nuremberg. It was six months after Nazi Germany's unconditional surrender and the twenty-one men in the dock – senior businessmen, military officers, diplomats and propagandists from the defeated regime – stood charged of having launched an illegal war, and of having commited other crimes ranging from art theft to the extermination of millions. The bushel of spotlights that hung over their heads showed a crème de la crème that had curdled into a motley mixture indeed. Rudolf Hess, whose last public outing at Nuremberg had been at Hitler's right hand in 1934 during the filming of Leni Riefenstahl's *Triumph of the Will*, was either feigning insanity or slipping into it – barking with sporadic laughter into a book and brushing imaginary flies from his eyebrows. Publisher Julius Streicher was no more impressive: his *Der Stürmer* newspaper had incited anti-Semitism in Germany for two decades, but the mumbling old man who leered hungrily up the stenographers' skirts was now inciting nothing but repulsion. And next to Hess at the end of the front row sat Hermann Göring, once second only to Hitler, commander of the *Luftwaffe* and an instigator of the Final Solution.

Reconciling the notion of pure evil with real human beings is never easy, but the contrast between deeds and doers can rarely have been as stark. A great balloon in his Nazi prime, custody had deflated him by a third, accentuating his effeminacy and reducing his sneer to a pout. The prisoner adrift within a baggy air-force tunic, eyes sparkling and lips aquiver, looked no more monstrous than a drag queen in the wrong type of dress.

The Nuremberg dock. Hermann Göring is the defendant
closest to camera, Rudolf Hess is next to him and Julius
Streicher is eighth from left on the front row.

The opening speech of the chief United States prosecutor, Robert Jackson, was an oratorical triumph. It was, he declared, 'one of the most significant tributes that power has ever paid to reason' that 'four great nations, flushed with victory and stung with injury, stay the hand of vengeance and voluntarily submit their captive enemies to the power of the law'. The rhetoric of Attorney-General Sir Hartley Shawcross, head of the British legal team, soared to altitudes no less giddy.

> There are those who would perhaps say that these wretched men should have been dealt with summarily without trial by 'executive action' . . . But that was not the view of the British Government. Not so would the rule of law be raised and strengthened on the international as well as upon the municipal

plane . . . not so would the world be made aware that the waging
of aggressive war is not a dangerous venture but a criminal one.

The sentiments were noble ones. The expression of them was just short of
an outright lie.

The British and American governments had certainly given considerable thought about how best to deal with the most senior Nazis, but their
favoured solution had until very recently been summary execution.
Although content for Nazi subordinates to be tried at the scene of their
crimes, Prime Minister Winston Churchill had proposed on 9 November
1943 that a list of '50, or at the outside 100 . . . world outlaws' should be
'shot to death within six hours and without reference to higher authority'.
In the United States, although War Secretary Henry Stimson pursued a
lonely campaign for trials, President Roosevelt expressed no opposition to
that view. He was ready at one point to go further. In September 1944, he
backed a plan drawn up by his Treasury Secretary, Henry Morgenthau, that
proposed Germany's 'pastoralization' – by demolishing its factories, parti-
tioning its land, relocating millions of its people and shooting to death,
without trial, up to two and a half thousand former Nazis.

Both countries' leaders changed their minds, but the reasons owed
little to principle. For the shameful little secret of international criminal law
is that Nuremberg was conceived in Moscow and came into being despite
the wishes of the Western allies, rather than because of them. Stalin was the
first to propose prosecution of the Nazi leadership at a meeting with the
British Ambassador to Moscow in November 1942. Sir Archibald Clark
Kerr had tried to persuade him of Churchill's view that punishment should
rest on 'a political decision'. That would, he explained, allow for penalties
'just as [severe] and much more [prompt] than under any legal procedure'.
The two men got on well and Clark Kerr thought Stalin 'favourable' to the
argument in general, but the Soviet leader was not convinced. According to
the diplomat, he took the view that 'whatever happened there would have
to be a decision by some kind of court' so that it could not be said that
'Churchill, Roosevelt and Stalin were wreaking vengeance on their political
enemies'. Clark Kerr had wryly expressed confidence 'that the political decision [Mr Churchill] had in mind would be accompanied by all the necessary formalities', but the mordant wit he shared with Stalin would not be
enough to bridge the difference of outlook. The division would in fact

widen considerably – and when it reached breaking point, it was the stubbornness of the Soviet leader that tipped the balance in favour of a trial.

By late August 1944, the western Allies were still so committed to summary executions that War Secretary Henry Stimson was unhappily contemplating the legal protections that US soldiers would need before participating in the firing squads. Roosevelt then went to meet Churchill at Québec City – taking along the advocate of pastoralization, Henry Morgenthau, but leaving his opponent, Henry Stimson, behind – and the Western leaders reached agreement on several outstanding issues. One of them was what to do with the Germans. As well as deciding that their country should become 'primarily agricultural and pastoral in its character', they resolved to ask Stalin to approve a list of '50–100 . . . world outlaws' who were to be 'executed summarily on capture and without recourse to the method of trial, conviction and judicial sentence'. Vengeance seemed very much at hand.

But the outline of Henry Morgenthau's plans was then passed on to the Associated Press and published on the front page of the *New York Times*. Whoever leaked the story was careful to withhold his proposals for mass executions, which would have attracted considerable support if polls of the time are any guide; but the report caused sufficient disquiet to put hardliners on the defensive in Washington for the first time. And Stalin now made his most decisive contribution to the debate. For Churchill, travelling to Moscow in October, found that he had decided to lay down the law, literally. 'On major war criminals U[ncle] J[oe] took an unexpectedly ultra-respectable line,' he cabled the US president. 'There must be no executions without trial otherwise the world would say we were afraid to try them.' Although the British cabinet would continue to hanker for shootings at dawn until the spring of 1945 – when it resolved to forward to the USA one last statement of its objections 'to any formal procedure for trial or judicial procedure' – it was the final word.

Stalin's legalism was certainly not informed by a desire to differentiate the innocent from the guilty. He had been prosecuting rivals to death since 1936, and by the summer of 1943 Soviet officials were staging meticulously co-ordinated spectacles of judicial self-abasement in areas recently liberated from the Nazis. The extent to which politics underpinned his concern for trials is apparent from the circumstances in which he first insisted upon them. The meeting with Ambassador Clark Kerr in November 1942 was intended specifically to patch up a spat over Hitler's deputy, Rudolf Hess, who had been in British custody since parachuting into Scotland in May 1941 – and it was the failure to try him that was rankling Stalin. The reasons for Hess's flight remain obscure to this day, but Stalin had no doubt that he had been hoping to strike a separate Anglo-German peace and the Soviet leader wanted him publicly discredited. *Pravda* had just published a bitter complaint that his presence was 'converting England into a refuge for gangsters', and when Stalin made his proposals for a post-war prosecution to Clark Kerr, he was simultaneously demanding that the British try Hess. The concern was not with justice, but with its trappings.

Assessing the workings of a mind as labyrinthine as Stalin's has never been a precise science, but there is another incident that throws even more light on his attitude. It came, as moments of truth often do, in the form of a joke. At a wartime conference in Tehran in November 1943 attended by all three Allied leaders, he threw a birthday dinner for Churchill. As the liquor flowed, he proposed a toast to post-war justice. In particular, he raised a glass to the liquidation of 'at least fifty thousand and perhaps one hundred thousand' senior Germans. Coming less than three weeks after Churchill had proposed shooting '50, or at the outside one hundred' Nazis, the remark was a relatively unsubtle example of Stalinist levity and Roosevelt responded to it with the cheerful suggestion that forty-nine thousand murders would suffice. The British leader, perhaps a little the worse for wear, was apoplectic. He spluttered that he would prefer to take a bullet himself, and when Stalin followed up by wondering at his affection for the Nazis, he stormed from the table. The Soviet leader finally called a halt to the horseplay by following Churchill into a darkened room, where he clapped his arms around the Englishman's shoulders and made up with a grin.

All those present other than Churchill recognized that Stalin had been playing. But Uncle Joe's games were never less serious than the pawing of a tiger. He toyed with people to see if they flinched – as countless dead enemies had learned – and he was doubtless delighted to see Churchill, whom he regarded with the deepest mistrust,[*] swivelling on the horns of

---

[*] According to the wartime memoirs of Yugoslav Communist Milovan Djilas, Stalin later told him (in the summer of 1944) that 'Churchill is the kind of man who will pick your pocket of a kopeck if you don't watch him. Yes, pick your pocket of a kopeck! By God, pick your pocket of a kopeck! Roosevelt is not like that. He dips in his hand only for bigger coins. But Churchill? Churchill – will do it for a kopeck.' Milovan Djilas, *Conversations with Stalin* (London, 1962), p. 70.

a dilemma. For he had great hopes for a post-war prosecution. Soviet lawyers had been thinking big since 1937, when Andrei Vyshinsky, fresh from his triumph at the second Moscow show trial, had demanded that 'criminal law . . . be mobilized against war and against those who incite war'. Stalin would in due course appoint Vyshinsky to coordinate arrangements for the trial, and appoint as his judge Iona Nikitchenko, whose most relevant previous experience was to have sat alongside Vasily Ulrich at the first Moscow show trial of 1936. As far as he could have anticipated in November 1943, two choices remained open to his allies: to insist upon a bloodbath, or to join him in a judicial pageant more grandiose than any that he could have presumed to stage alone.

Such dreams were not to be. Although Roosevelt's administration initially did no more than yield to Stalin's wishes, the simple fact that it committed itself to legalism soon brought the very different legal traditions of the USA into play. War Secretary Henry Stimson told Roosevelt

in September 1944 that Nazi leaders should get 'at least the rudimentary aspects of the Bill of Rights', and a jurist then emerged with an attitude to criminal procedure that Stalin would have found puzzling, at least. On 13 April 1945, Supreme Court Justice Robert H. Jackson delivered a charged address, more manifesto than speech, to the American Society of International Law in Washington DC. Peace, he declared, presented challenges that called for international lawyers with 'fire in their belly'. The horror of modern warfare demanded legal co-operation and punishment on an international scale; and while he was prepared to accept that summary executions might, arguably, be sensible as a political or military expedient, he would not countenance their imposition by a sham tribunal. 'If you are determined to execute a man in any case, there is no occasion for a trial,' he told his audience. '[T]he world yields no respect to courts that are merely organized to convict.'

The view was not one that would ever commend itself to the Soviets, but largely on the strength of the speech, Harry Truman, who had just taken over the Presidency after Roosevelt's death in office, appointed Jackson to direct US preparations for the forthcoming trial. A collision course was set. The crunch came at a pre-trial conference held in London over the summer of 1945.

The head of the Soviet delegation was Iona Nikitchenko – the afore-mentioned ex-show trial judge – who set out his country's stance at the second session. The Nazi leaders, he declared, were not ordinary offend-ers but 'war criminals who have already been convicted . . . by the heads of the governments'. Organizations like the SS and the Gestapo were by definition criminal because they had been 'most definitely labeled so by the governments'. The gulf only widened over the following few sessions. When Jackson attempted to clarify the meaning of 'aggressive war' – a reasonable enough endeavour, given that it was about to become a capital offence – Nikitchenko objected on the grounds that their country's lead-ers had already defined Nazi policy in its entirety as aggressive. When Jackson incredulously demanded why they were then bothering to put individuals on trial at all, the Soviet lawyer explained that the proposed tribunal's function would be to 'determine the measure of guilt of each particular person and mete out the necessary punishment'. By late July Nikitchenko was demanding that the court's charter stipulate that aggres-sion was a crime that only Nazis could commit, while an infuriated Jackson was threatening that the USA might hold a separate trial. The British nudged both sides back together, however, and at a session held on 2 August 1945 the requisite compromises were finally struck. Aggressive war was made a crime of general application and it was agreed that the Nuremberg court would have jurisdiction over three types of offence.

The first, called 'crimes against peace', rested on the notion that states had shown so clear an intention to renounce warfare that bellicosity itself had become an international crime. The claim was deeply dubious, rest-ing on little more than a single treaty from 1928, but Jackson would always regard aggression as the reason for Nuremberg's existence, the 'crime that comprehends all lesser crimes', and he reserved its prosecution for the American and British legal teams. The second type of offence – war crimes – covered mistreatment of POWs and civilians. Jackson considered it to constitute 'small change', while the word 'genocide' – a category of war crime that had been coined a year earlier by a Polish-Jewish refugee to the USA – was one that no American lawyer would even utter into the record during the eleven-month trial. Jackson was similarly dismissive of a third class of offences known as 'crimes against humanity', which covered systematic murder, extermination, and deportation. His concern was to outlaw war, not to police it more effectively. As the runts of the Nuremberg litter, he was happy to leave both war crimes and crimes against humanity to the French and Soviet prosecutors.

Although Jackson's hierarchy was questionable, and would be virtually inverted in the popular imagination over subsequent years, the most common criticism of the Nuremberg offences – that they penalized behaviour after the event – has only limited merit. The claim that one optimistic pre-war treaty had turned aggression into an international crime was not, admittedly, a convincing one. But the section of the indictment that would most clearly address activities that were lawful when committed – the Nazi mistreatment of German Jews before the war – would be ruled unpunishable. Custom had in any event been restraining savagery since the days when warring Greek armies had routinely observed time-outs to allow each side to bury its dead, and the Nazi's own military code had stipulated that superior orders were no defence to criminal charges. The fact that the rules were violated did not prove their non-existence, any more than a murder would disprove the law against it. Nuremberg certainly pulled international criminal law up by its bootstraps. But the novelty of war crimes and crimes against humanity did not lie in the declaration of fresh moral principles. It lay in the assertion that those principles would be enforced against individuals.

Hermann Göring was unimpressed as the trial began. '[I]t's just a cut and dried political affair,' he had contemptuously told Gustave Gilbert, the official prison psychologist, on 11 November 1945. 'The victors are the judges. . . . I know what's in store for me.' The short retort was that victor's justice, Nazi-style, would have been considerably more cut and dried, but the complaint was not without some force. Several of the judges and prosecutors had helped to draft the charges that they were trying. They would repeatedly suppress defence attempts to prove that the Allies had committed acts similar to those charged, though such arguments should have been central to the inquiry of a court that had to decide what types of wartime behaviour were so pathological as to be criminal. And the tribunal that was preparing to pronounce on war crimes was sitting in a city devastated by indiscriminate Allied bombing, where some thirty thousand civilians still lay rotting under chlorinated rubble.

It was of course the Soviets, personified by the uniformed* figure of Judge Major Iona Nikitchenko, who did most to taint the trial. On Nikitchenko's insistence, the indictment had charged the defendants with the murder of some eleven thousand Polish POWs at Katyn Forest in September 1941 – a massacre that the Russian Federation would admit half a century later had in fact been committed by the Soviet secret police. Soviet prosecutors were also able to persuade their Western counterparts not to mention Stalin's secret agreement with Hitler in 1940 to invade and partition Poland. And the shadow of justice victorious never loomed darker over Nuremberg than at the end of the trial's first week, when Andrei Vyshinsky flew into town. He was honoured with three banquets and, emulating his master's fondness for post-prandial mischief, made sure that he was never forgotten. At a dinner organized by US prosecutors on 26 November, he sat alongside the judges in a pale blue general's uniform and concluded the evening with a witty speech and a jovial toast. To general merriment, all present raised their glasses and downed the contents. When the words were belatedly translated, the blood drained just as swiftly from the diners' faces. 'To the defendants!' he had proclaimed. 'May their paths lead straight from the courthouse to the grave!'

Vyshinsky's understanding of open justice notwithstanding, 1946 Nuremberg was destined, however, to be very different from 1936 Moscow. Several of the eventual verdicts were predictable, but they were not preordained. German lawyers, though accustomed to a legal system in which judges took the lead role in questioning witnesses, mounted spirited defences for their clients. Judge Nikitchenko was outvoted when he tried to deny the defendants the right to testify, and Soviet prosecutors found themselves unable to obey Vyshinsky's instructions to silence

---

* His fondness for his uniform was not, however, all that it might seem. Nikitchenko initially proposed that all the judges should wear black business suits, and it was the French judge, Henri Donnedieu de Vabres, who stood on his dignity by insisting on a gown. It was the absence of consensus that produced a sartorial free-for-all. See Telford Taylor, *Anatomy of Nuremberg* (New York, 1992), p. 122.

'anti-Soviet attacks' during the trial. Although defence lawyers would have their final speeches vetted by both judges and prosecutors, they repeatedly read revelations about Soviet skulduggery in Poland into the record, while the defendants themselves fought tooth and nail to deny their guilt. Only one, arrested by the Soviets, had been forced to confess prior to attending court. He was Hans Fritsche, and he went on not just to assert his innocence but to win an acquittal.

No one better illustrated the independence of the prisoners than Hermann Göring himself. As one of the most astute defendants, and the senior officer among them, he was able for three months to ensure that they maintained a relatively defiant front. Even after psychologist Gustave Gilbert fractured the solidarity by making them lunch in separate groups, causing some at last to display flickers of remorse, Göring wavered only between amusement and anger. German witnesses who showed signs of contrition were greeted with mutterings of contempt or shouts of 'Schweinehund', and although he toyed with the idea of refusing to recognize the court at all, he ultimately chose to regard it as the war's last battleground – and to go down fighting.

The evidence he gave to his own lawyer was unremarkably self-serving, but his mettle emerged when his cross-examination began on 18 March 1946. Robert Jackson, whose concern to prevent grandstanding by the defendants at trial often reached almost Soviet levels, had thought hard how best to open his questioning. According to his memoirs, he had initially intended to ask Göring about art that he had looted from occupied countries, for personal gain; and about his anti-Jewish activities – which had included a request to Reinhard Heydrich for a programme to achieve 'the desired Final Solution of the Jewish question'. Jackson anticipated that the German would be knocked off balance, and he would then be better able to reveal the criminally aggressive nature of the entire Nazi state. But at the last minute, he reversed the order of the topics in the hope of 'flattering' his witness into complacency – and the results were disastrous.

'You are perhaps aware that you are the only man living who can expound to us the true purposes of the Nazi Party and the inner workings of its leadership?' he began. 'I am perfectly aware of that,' purred Göring. Opening gently is a time-honoured way of tempting witnesses who are stupider than they think, but Göring's intellect matched his arrogance – and whereas he retained the combative instincts of a Nazi brawler, it soon became clear that Jackson's years on the bench had left his street-fighting skills rusty indeed. For several minutes, the American plodded on with inquiries about the early days of Nazi Germany, and Göring was soon returning the lobs with smashes, parsing the questions, correcting translations, and sounding more like a pugnacious historian than the chief henchman of a police state. Matters then worsened for Jackson when he tetchily prevented Göring from continuing an answer because 'Your counsel will see to that.' The US judge, Francis Biddle, was seen to whisper to his British colleague, Sir Geoffrey Lawrence, who nodded his agreement and looked up at the prosecutor. 'Mr Justice Jackson,' he said. '[T]he Tribunal thinks the witness ought to be allowed to make what explanation he thinks right in answer to this question.' Jackson duly invited Göring to have his say, but inwardly he was seething. For the rest of his life would remain convinced that Biddle had deliberately sabotaged his questioning. It was a sign of just how badly the cross-examination was already going – and it only got worse.

The first day ended with Jackson saved only 'by the gong', in the words of one American spectator, and he spent the second ricocheting between corner cushion and canvas. The nadir came when he thrust a document

 at Göring and demanded that the German accept that his country had been preparing to invade the Rhineland in 1935. The piece of paper had, however, been mistranslated, and Göring gleefully pointed out that it actually dealt with the dredging arrangements that might be required *if* military movements were to take place. Jackson, stammering, then demanded – as though it proved something – that Göring admit that no plans for military mobilization had been disclosed. 'I do not think I can recall reading beforehand the publication of the mobilization preparations of the United States,' replied Göring, a smile playing on his lips. Jackson furiously complained to the judges about the defendant's 'arrogant and contemptuous attitude', causing Lawrence only to suggest that proceedings be adjourned 'at this state'.

The slip of the tongue was tacit recognition of Jackson's difficulties – and quite how bad a state he was in became clear on the morning of the third day. He opened by demanding that Göring be permitted from now on to answer only 'yes' or 'no' to any question. 'The point is,' he explained, 'do we answer these things or leave them, apart from the control of the trial? And it does seem to me that this is the beginning of this trial's getting out of hand, if I may say so, if we do not have control of this situation. I trust the Tribunal will pardon my earnestness in presenting this. I think it is a very vital thing.' The judges disagreed that the thing was as vital as Jackson thought, and gently suggested that he carry on.

Jackson eventually recovered some ground with questions that he ought to have opened with – about Göring's role in repressing and murdering Jews and his systematic art thefts – but it was the Scottish head of the British team, Sir David Maxwell-Fyfe, who toppled the former *Reichsmarschall* from his throne. Several of those who met Göring would later comment on his chameleon-like demeanour – contemptuous, for example, of the French, jocular with Americans, and downright terrified of the Soviets – but the courtesy that he showed Maxwell-Fyfe would only highlight the evasiveness that it failed to conceal.

The barrister took over late on the afternoon of 20 March and immediately fired a barrage of questions about the shooting of fifty RAF prisoners of war in the spring of 1944 – the conclusion of an episode which, suitably Americanized, would one day be filmed as *The Great Escape*. The executions violated a pleasantly sporting tradition that permitted, and expected, POWs to attempt escape, and although Hitler had ordered the killings, Göring had failed to prevent them. To the former *Reichsmarschall*, an ex-commander of the Red Baron's air squadron who imagined himself heir to centuries of Teutonic chivalry, the questions cut to the quick. When the court adjourned, barely ten minutes later, he was glistening with sweat and gripping the sides of the witness box. By the following morning he had concluded that the matter was 'the most serious incident of the whole war'. Maxwell-Fyfe concluded with a few inquiries about another serious incident: the murder of some six million Jews. Göring, by now seriously ill at ease, claimed that he had known nothing of any extermination policy and asserted that 'not even [Hitler] knew the extent of what was going on'. The lawyer homed in. Did Göring still feel that he had to be loyal towards Hitler? It was the kind of no-win question that cross-examiners love, and Göring himself would later recall it as 'the most dangerous [one] in the whole trial'. 'I believe in keeping one's oath not in good times only, but also in bad times when it is much more difficult,' he replied hesitantly. Maxwell-Fyfe then read aloud a statement from Hitler in April 1943 that the Jews 'had to be treated like tuberculosis bacilli, with which a healthy body may become infected. . . . Nations which do not rid themselves of Jews perish.' Did Göring maintain that Hitler knew nothing about plans to exterminate Germany's Jews? He confirmed that he did. Maxwell-Fyfe thanked him politely, and sat down.

The contrasting approaches of Jackson and Maxwell-Fyfe signposted the direction of the next six decades of international humanitarian law. Whereas Jackson's focus on aggression had allowed Göring to pontificate with the assurance of any power-crazed politician, Maxwell-Fyfe's concentration on war crimes and crimes against humanity had reduced him to thief, liar, unrepentant anti-Semite, and mass murderer. The charge that Germany had planned to go to war all but vanished against the revelation that it had operated by the moral standards of a rapist and serial killer.

The phenomenon was seen again and again as the trial progressed. When footage of the walking cadavers of Belsen and Buchenwald flickered through the court on 29 November 1945, a previously ebullient Göring dipped into a brief depression while even Julius Streicher seemed,

Hartley Shawcross

in the words of Gustave Gilbert, to 'show signs of disturbance for the first time'. Perhaps most affecting of all was the final speech that Attorney-General Sir Hartley Shawcross delivered at the end of July 1946. Although Jackson had given the British the supposed privilege of helping him to prosecute aggressive war, Shawcross was, like all his British colleagues, a seasoned jury advocate who instinctively tacked to the changing wind. His two-day summation was peppered with instances of human suffering, which reduced each defendant in turn to tears, rage or ashen fear, and all but hypnotized everyone else in court. It ended not with abstract attacks on German aggression, but with an unforgettable description of the real meaning of genocide from a Ukrainian engineer called Hermann Graebe.

Graebe had watched Jewish families in early October 1943 being herded out of trucks by militiamen under the direction of a whip-wielding SS officer. They had quietly undressed next to a large mound of earth and placed their clothes on the ground in neat piles. He recalled one family in particular, all naked and saying goodbye for the last time.

> An old woman with snow-white hair was holding the one-year-old child in her arms and singing to it and tickling it. The child was cooing with delight. The couple were looking on with tears in their eyes. The father was holding the hand of a boy about ten years old and speaking to him softly; the boy was fighting his tears. The father pointed to the sky, stroked his head, and seemed to explain something to him . . . I well remember a girl, slim and with black hair, who as she passed close to me, pointed to herself and said, 'twenty-three'. I walked around the mound and found myself confronted by a tremendous grave . . . Some were lifting their arms and turning their heads to show that they were still alive. The pit was already two-thirds full. I estimated that it already contained about one thousand people.

His voice hushed in a courtroom that had itself turned silent as a grave, Shawcross asked the judges to remember Graebe's evidence – 'not in vengeance [but] in a determination that these things shall not occur again'. The defendants wriggled on their seats, according to journalist Rebecca West, 'while their faces grew old'.

The judgment and verdicts were delivered over two days in early October 1946. Eighteen defendants were convicted of at least one charge, and three were acquitted outright; three Nazi organizations (the SS, Gestapo, and Leadership Corps) were criminalized in their entirety. Jurists, journalists, and historians have spent long decades debating the justice of the individual decisions, but no serious person has ever contended that the results were predetermined. The judges in fact haggled over them at length, meeting at least eight times to argue their corners, and even Iona Nikitchenko joined the horse-trading until Stalin decided to call a halt to the madness and ordered his major to dissent on any decisions that remained deadlocked.

Eleven men were sentenced to death, and during the evening of 15 October workers sawed and hammered three gallows into place in the prison gymnasium. Göring was among those condemned to hang, but he had one final surprise for the victors who presumed to judge him. Shortly before midnight, a guard peered into his cell and saw him in spasms, poisoned by a cyanide capsule that he is thought to have obtained from a Texan guard with whom he had been flirting, in a guns-and-hunting kind of way, ever since reaching Nuremberg. Frantic efforts were made to revive him to kill him, but only ten men walked to the gallows the following morning. In their last moments, the aggressors were finally reduced to victims: bound by straps and blinded by hoods, most expressed their love for Germany, a hope for God's mercy, or a prayer for peace on earth. Only Julius Streicher died with indignity intact, screaming 'Heil Hitler' on the scaffold and spitting accusations of Jewish ritual murder at his guards as the hood was tugged over his head. The executions themselves were reportedly even more unpleasant than such things are supposed to be. Several of the men are said to have had their faces battered by the swinging trapdoor as they fell. Some thrashed around for up to fifteen minutes, throttling at the end of nooses that had been cut too short to snap their necks.

The aspirations underlying the trial of Göring and his companions dated back centuries. In the early fifth century St Augustine had told an apocryphal tale about a captured pirate, asked by Alexander the Great how he dared to plunder the high seas. 'Because I do it with a little ship I am called a robber,' replied the brigand. '[B]ecause you do it with a great fleet, you are an emperor.' Augustine had thought the answer both elegant and excellent, but his only concern had been to put emperors on notice that their crowns would offer no defence when they appeared before God's great judgment seat. No one would presume to try a king until England's Puritans arraigned Charles I in 1649, and Europe's monarchies were always reluctant to follow that precedent: thus, when nineteenth-century British and Prussian governments were considering how to dispose of Napoleon, the only options considered were exile and execution. Only after the First World War did anyone make serious proposals to set up an international tribunal, as demands intensified to hang the Kaiser, and only at Nuremberg did they materialize.

The effect was to secularize Augustine's dream. He had warned emperors that God would judge them by the same standards that He applied to a buccaneer. Nuremberg's claim was that if an entire state turned into a piratical den, everyone from the captain to the lookout could face an earthly trial as well.

It was a radical development, but the fact that it occurred does not answer what it achieved. As the rest of this chapter will show, the answers are far from straightforward. The trial of the senior Nazis certainly generated overwhelming evidence to show that they and many others exterminated millions, but emergence of the truth was an almost coincidental side effect. Defence lawyers, confronted with hundreds of thousands of pages of evidence, did not have time to examine most of it, and large amounts of untested material found its way into the record. The most notorious example was the Soviet claim that the Nazis had tried to make bars of soap from human fat – an assertion that got as far as the judgment – which was, in fact, one of the few Nazi atrocities that has never been unequivocally proved, as the archives director of Jerusalem's Yad Vashem Museum publicly acknowledged in 1990.

Another conventional justification for the Nuremberg trial, that it allowed individual responsibility to be sharply delineated from collective guilt, is equally unsatisfactory. Trials, by definition, focus on the person in the dock, but even if it were self-evident that courts should ignore the communal contribution to a person's guilt – which it is not – that principle was repeatedly flouted at Nuremberg. A sense that Germany was being judged permeated the proceedings. Prosecutors paid lip service to the principle of individualized guilt, but repeatedly damned the entire German people; while the judges' decision to criminalize three Nazi organizations left two million of the country's inhabitants potentially liable to execution. Several of the accused, for their part, conducted their defences in terms that barely distinguished between their shame and that of the nation. Hans Frank called thunder onto the land with a sombre declaration that, 'A thousand years will pass and [the] guilt of Germany will not have been erased.'* Baldur von Schirach took it upon himself to

---

* The statement was made on 18 April 1946. By the end of the trial, he had had second thoughts and asked to withdraw the statement on the basis that Germany's guilt had been 'completely wiped out' by the mistreatment of Germans at the hands of Russians, Poles, and Czechs. See *Blue Series*, 12: 13; 22: 385.

assert the innocence of German youth for 'all that Hitler has done to the Jewish and to the German people'. Even Julius Streicher – by common consent the most shameless of all the defendants – pleaded with the judges not to 'imprint the stamp of dishonour upon the forehead of an entire nation'.

Even more ironic was the fact that Germany itself seemed singularly unconcerned for the fate of its forehead, while the Allies showed very little interest in publicity shaming anyone beyond the confines of the court-room. Out of the 250 journalists accredited to cover the trial, only five were German. The radio devoted just fifteen minutes a day to events in court, and a post-war paper famine meant that the proceedings received just a few lines of coverage, twice a week, in the German press. The Tribunal did not even think to make seats available for ordinary citizens for almost two months. It rectified its omission only after Friedrich Bergold – a lawyer working not for the prosecution, but for the absent Martin Bormann – confidentially suggested that it might be a good idea to let some Germans see what was going on.

The Allied indifference to German participation throws revealing light on the nature of the Nuremberg process, and illuminates an often over-looked aspect of war crimes prosecutions in general. Although the trial was a show of sorts, as any public hearing is bound to be, the primary audience was not the defendants' compatriots. It was the societies that were doing the judging. Those conducting the trial were celebrating their own fairness, repeatedly pointing out that the defendants were being accorded a justice that they would never have granted their victims – a mantra that has been recited by their self-righteous successors ever since. The proceedings' impact within Germany was, by contrast, at least negligible and arguably counter-productive. Though often recalled as a staging post on the path to post-war recovery, the trial generated a political culture that was suspicious of its value, and sometimes contemptuous of the claim that it had any at all.

The verdicts and executions of October 1946 produced few expressions of sympathy or loyalty towards the men who had brought Germany to destruction, but even fewer Germans were minded to ponder abstractions like war guilt. Much of the population was living in rubble, trading pota-toes, cigarettes or sex to survive, and although relations between the Allies and locals were always relatively friendly in Nuremberg itself, the mood elsewhere was darker. Defence lawyer Friedrich Bergold, returning from a Christmas visit to his family in early 1946, reported (with some distress) that the trial was seen across Germany as a 'swindle' devoted to inventing and exaggerating atrocities. People felt no more touched by it, he said, than they would have been by 'something taking place on the moon'.

Over the next three years the alienation would only increase. The United States staged another twelve major trials, prosecuting almost two hundred of the most senior officials of the Nazi state, and the four occupying Allies arraigned thousands of lesser psychopaths before military tribunals. But even as the convictions mounted, the purpose of achieving them was increasingly lost. By mid 1948, the man in charge of the American zone, General Lucius Clay, was anticipating 'a mass execution of more than five hundred persons' and recommending wholesale commutation because it was 'difficult to adjust to the idea' of so many hangings. Germans would find it even harder to come to terms with.

The Americans began killing their condemned prisoners on 15 October 1948, and continued to do so every single Friday for the next four months, in batches of up to fifteen men at a time. The Western Allies collectively would eventually hang well over four hundred people, and each became a moment at which German conservatives drummed up hostility towards the entire war crimes programme. As bells tolled and communities mourned, Robert Jackson's opening promise – that the Allies had chosen to 'stay the hand of vengeance' – began to sound like the words of a liar or the prattling of a fool.

Geopolitics finally caused the Allies to give up entirely on judicial denazification. In September 1949, a year after Stalin had failed to blockade Berlin and a month after his considerably more successful test of a Soviet atomic bomb, the legislators of what would become West Germany elected Konrad Adenauer to the chancellorship by one vote. Adenauer had no brief for the Nazis, who had imprisoned him twice, but he was determined to protect his country from yet another moustachioed tyrant – and he depended on politicians and civil servants who were considerably more nostalgic for the era that had just died. In the United States, conservative Congressmen were meanwhile becoming increasingly vocal opponents of the trials – arguing, for example, that they were communist plots 'aimed directly at property rights', or, in the words of Mississippi Representative John Rankin, rituals of 'sadistic vengeance' from 'a certain racial minority'.

The combined effect was that all concerned were soon downplaying the importance of justice, concerned instead to build Germany into a reliable ally against the Soviets.

The major trials had already petered out by the time of Adenauer's election, the last having come to an end in April 1949, and in January 1951 the Americans reduced the penalties of all but nine of their eighty-seven prisoners and released a third of them immediately. Their less clement decision to execute five of the nine exceptions on a single day in June was no less significant. All of those hanged were SS *Einsatzcommando* executioners. One was Otto Ohlendorf, a former lawyer who acknowledged having supervised some 90,000 murders and accepted that he would have machine-gunned his own sister had he been so ordered. Within western Germany, however, what they had done during their lives aroused considerably less emotion than the Allied insistence on their deaths. Adenauer had just begun talks with the Western Allies on the creation of an independent German state, but several parliamentarians now threatened to defeat any deal that did not include a total war crimes amnesty.

Negotiations inched towards deadlock until, in March 1952, the chancellor was presented with a pile of political capital from an unexpected direction. Stalin, wearing his finest crocodile smile, let it be known that he had no objections to the reunification of Germany so long as it undertook to remain democratic, peace-loving – and neutral between the communist and capitalist camps. Adenauer, though immune to the charms of the Soviet leader, informed his Western allies that he now needed movement, quickly, on the question of war crimes. They caved in. The outcome was a series of agreements whereby the USA, UK and France assumed responsibility for the handful of prisoners who remained, while West Germany formally nullified the verdicts of every single Allied war crimes trial since 1945. The upshot was that none of the thousands of convictions imposed by the Allied tribunals, up to and including that of Hermann Göring, would ever be recognized as valid by the criminal justice system of the Federal Republic of Germany.

That is not to say that the country ignored the need to tackle its past, but the contribution of the law to its eventual rehabilitation was distinctly ambiguous. Official figures would show that it convicted over six thousand people of Nazi-era crimes between the end of the war and German reunification in 1992. That statistic, though widely publicized by successive West

German governments, always concealed rather more than it displayed however. Only about 20 per cent of the convictions happened after 1949, only 472 people were ever found guilty of participation in the Final Solution and the overwhelming majority of crimes charged were non-lethal ones. One category of offender, whose accountability was crucial if judicial denazification was to have credibility, would prove particularly elusive. Although West Germany's courts would convict many people who had denounced their spouses, friends, and enemies for capital crimes – an act defined as homicide by West Germany's penal code – one courtroom participant would never be found guilty of anything: the judges themselves.

Judges who had tried criminal offences under the Third Reich were almost by definition compromised. They were required by Nazi laws to punish not only acts defined as criminal but also misdeeds that were 'analogous' to crimes or were worthy of punishment in the light of 'healthy public opinion'. Over the twelve years of Nazi rule, they probably sentenced between forty and fifty thousand defendants to death, and around 80 per cent of those condemned went to the gallows. The Americans had prosecuted sixteen of the very top jurists in February 1947, but as West Germany stabilized into a Cold War ally the Nazi lawyers returned – and by 1959, at least eight hundred were in senior judicial positions. The effect was to lodge a virus in the immune system of the West German body politic.

Holding every judge to account would have been unworkable and might even have been unfair, but West Germany's courts went to the other extreme. The country's laws formally imposed criminal liability on those who had intentionally perverted justice; but although that could have worked to focus prosecutorial efforts on only the most zealous Nazis, the principle was soon interpreted to achieve exactly the opposite result. The more fanatical a Nazi judge, decided the courts, the more likely it was that he had intended not to pervert justice, but to see it done.

Typical was the case of Edmund Kessler, charged in 1952 over his decision nine years earlier to execute a Jew called Werner Holländer for having had sex with an Aryan woman. Holländer had initially been charged under the Nazi's Blood Protection Law, which did not provide for capital punishment, but Kessler had taken it on himself to turn to the Law on Dangerous Habitual Criminals – which did. He then ruled that the young man's history of philandering made his criminality both 'dangerous' and

'habitual', and thus made him eligible for execution. It was Nazi jurisprudence at its most inventive, displaying an ingenuity far beyond what
might have been expected from a less racist judge. After analysing his reasoning, the West German court concluded that, far from perverting justice, Kessler therefore may have believed that he was exercising 'a high
level of judicial achievement'. And because the possibility of a 'blindness
to injustice' could not be excluded, he was not guilty.

Such decisions rested on a jurisprudential tradition called legal positivism, which claimed that distinguishing between law and morality
would help produce greater efficiency in the legal sphere and greater
clarity in the moral one. The theoretical separation has never been easy to
achieve, and its realization in post-war Germany would prove chimerical.
The law did not remain neutral between good and evil; it elevated sincere
immorality to a watertight defence.

The nature of that defence would be most chillingly illustrated in
respect of the People's Court, a Nazi tribunal that annihilated some seven
thousand of the state's enemies. Its senior judge had been Roland Freisler,
once christened 'our Vyshinsky' by Hitler. The sobriquet was meant affectionately enough, but the Soviet prosecutor had in fact choreographed
spectacles of balletic elegance compared to the cacophonous *danses
macabres* presided over by Freisler. The trial of the July Plotters – a group
of German officers who detonated a bomb close to Hitler on 20 July 1944
– saw the unshaven defendants, deprived of dentures and belts, being
humiliated by the crimson-robed judge. 'You dirty old man!', he shrieked
at Field-Marshal von Witzleben at one point. 'Why do you keep fiddling
with your trousers?' On the sole occasion that it was thought necessary
to consult the criminal code, no copy could be found. After final
speeches during which the defence lawyers joined prosecutors in calling for convictions, all the defendants had been taken to Berlin's
Plötzensee Prison, where they were hoisted onto meat hooks and left to
die. The entire process was filmed, and it sickened even some of the
Nazi high command. The Minister of Justice, no stickler for due process, grimly informed Hitler's office that Freisler had 'totally lack[ed]
the kind of ice-cold authority and control such a trial requires' and had
'seriously undermined' the gravity and dignity of the proceedings. Josef
Goebbels almost fainted while watching the men's death throes – a
scene recorded primarily for Hitler's personal pleasure – and shelved

plans to release the courtroom footage as a celebration of Nazi law and order. The Propaganda Minister knew better than most that some spectacles were worse than none.

The generation of lawyers that followed would not, however, be quite as sure. Freisler himself died during a bombing raid in the final months of the war, but his second-in-command, Hans Joachim Rehse, was put on trial in 1967 in relation to seven of the 230-odd capital sentences that he had approved. He was initially convicted on the basis that his eagerness to stretch the law – notably, by holding that a priest had given 'aid and comfort to the enemy' by scribbling hostile thoughts about the Nazis into a diary – had taken him over the line separating judge from killer. But after a successful appeal, another judge acquitted him at his retrial in December 1968. Ernst-Jürgen Oske explained that, rightly or wrongly, the Nazi regime had always been legally entitled to execute traitors. He recognized that many people might think that treason had been too broadly defined by Rehse, and in particular they might feel that secret diary entries could offer neither 'aid' nor 'comfort' to an enemy of the state. Rehse's imaginative interpretations proved, however, just how strongly he had believed in the justice of his decision.

It was a triumph of legal positivism. But Rehse, who died in 1969, did not live long enough to hear the even more rigorous detachment of morality from law that was delivered on 12 March 1971 by the Berlin County Court in relation to the July Plotters case. Notwithstanding that Hitler had promised to make 'short work' of the defendants and hang them 'without the slightest pity', the court's six-year investigation concluded that the proceedings had been legally valid. Speaking of men who had been convicted on the urging of their own lawyers and then hanged from meat hooks, it found no proof that 'they had been murdered, or been sentenced to death in what was merely a show trial, or that their trial had failed to fulfil the minimal requirements of correct legal procedure'.

Although the actual prosecution of war crimes was far from smooth within West Germany, the development of the law underpinning them continued apace everywhere else. Much of the world agreed by treaty in 1948 that genocide should be prevented and punished whenever it occurred. A year later, a set of agreements known as the Geneva Conventions, eventually ratified by every major nation on earth, reiterated and amplified the most

long-standing laws of war, and again they obliged signatories to prosecute
the gravest types of war crime. The United Nations General Assembly in
1950 then recognized the principles underpinning the Nuremberg process
as part of customary international law. It was becoming possible for the
first time in Western history to envisage a system of trials that was detached
from the laws of nation states.

As the two sides of the Cold War embarked on the ideological staring
match that would keep them occupied for the next few decades, the
prospect of prosecutions before another multinational tribunal all but
vanished however. West Germany's experience, meanwhile, exemplified
the problems of leaving enforcement to the country where the crime
occurred. But there was an argument, arising logically out of Nuremberg
itself, that international crimes by their nature were capable of prosecution by any country. The claim was known as the theory of universal
jurisdiction – and it would be asserted first not by those who had
vanquished Nazism, but on behalf of the Nazis' most defenceless victims.

On the evening of 11 May 1960, seven Israeli Mossad agents
approached a man known as Ricardo Klement outside his house on
Garibaldi Street in Buenos Aires and bundled him into a car. Just over a
week later, he had been drugged, disguised as an El Al worker with con-
cussion and spirited back to Israel. Klement's real name was Adolf
Eichmann, and he was more deeply implicated in the Nazi attempt to
exterminate the Jews than anyone else on earth. Even before the war, he
had been responsible for considering how the Reich might efficiently rid
itself of its non-Aryans, and in late 1941, when Hermann Göring
demanded a 'Final Solution of the Jewish question', he had played a
central role in refining that solution's details. After minuting the Wannsee
Conference, at which it was decided to concentrate Jews in the East,
he had personally chaired meetings to deal specifically with mixed
marriages and forced sterilizations. In the last year of the war, he then
organized the transportation of well over 400,000 Hungarian Jews to the
death camps at Auschwitz-Birkenau.

The night and fog of wartime Europe clung to Adolf Eichmann. As at
Nuremberg however, the prosecution addressed the concerns of those
doing the judging at least as much as it investigated the guilt of the
person judged. For although the indictment asserted breaches of international law, the decision to send in a snatch squad pursued an agenda that

was very national indeed. From the moment that the Israelis learned of Eichmann's whereabouts (tipped off by the West German government), Prime Minister David Ben-Gurion specifically decided to stage a trial in order to boost internal and external support for his country. Two weeks after the kidnapping, he explained to a friend what he hoped to achieve. A prosecution would remind world opinion about the Holocaust, and educate Israeli youth, which 'has heard only faint echoes [about it]'. Both would also come to understand that Israel's neighbours were no different from the Nazis. '[T]here are scores and hundreds of Nazis, German and Arab, who . . . are now plotting the same thing for the nation of Israel . . .' he wrote. 'Public opinion . . . must be reminded whose disciples are those now planning Israel's destruction, and just who is aiding them, knowingly or unknowingly.'

The fifteen charges of war crimes and genocide included two involving gipsies and Czechs, but Israel's particular moral rights would structure the entire eight-month trial. When Eichmann's German lawyer, Dr Robert Servatius, argued that his client's kidnapping made the trial illegal, the judges declared the circumstances of arrest irrelevant – and although one ground given was that his crimes were global in nature, another was that Israel's status as Jewish homeland gave it a unique right to try him. Attorney-General Gideon Hausner also made clear from the outset in whose name he was prosecuting. 'When I stand before you here, judges of Israel . . . I am not standing alone,' he told the court as the trial opened on 11 April 1961. 'With me are six million accusers. But they cannot rise to their feet and point an accusing finger . . . Their blood cries out, but their voice is not heard.' For nine more hours he spoke, concluding with a eulogy to the lost communities of European Jewry and gratitude to the Israel that had preserved enough survivors to put Eichmann on trial. The defendant would now be granted the rights that he had denied so many others, promised Hausner – and, like a prophet of yore, he foresaw that 'the judges of Israel will pronounce true and righteous judgment'.

The political subtext of the trial was similarly reflected in the evidence that was called. Eichmann stipulated from the moment he entered his pleas that he contested his own guilt but did not deny that the atrocities described in the indictment had occurred. Testimony from the victims was therefore irrelevant, from a strictly logical point of view. It was, however, central to Ben-Gurion's hopes for the trial and, coincidentally or otherwise, the judges granted the prosecution leave to call scores of survivors who had much experience of suffering but nothing to say about Eichmann's personal guilt.

The stage-managed nature of the prosecution and the tendentiousness of Ben-Gurion's moral equations will always leave a question mark over that decision. Similar observations about political calculations could, however, be made in the context of countless other high-profile trials, and the fact that the witnesses' testimony was logically unnecessary is, in itself, an unpersuasive criticism. It ignores an aspect of the criminal process that has become fundamental to the Western understanding of why that process exists. Convenience is not justice – and justice means little unless it is publicly done.

It was certainly seen and heard within Israel. The testimony, broadcast by closed-circuit television into a packed hall near the court and transmitted live over national radio, stopped the country in its tracks. Stories that are now terribly familiar – the survivor of a mass execution who dug her way out of a pit of corpses; the prisoner who came across the bodies of his wife and two children while on burial duty – were told for the first time. Many who heard them had the mental defences of twenty years swept away. Others were suddenly made to realize what their friends and parents had kept secret for so long. Few, if any, were entirely unaffected. According to one writer, '[A]t crucial moments . . . one might walk along any street and listen to the proceedings pouring out of the open windows of every flat.'

While the evidence gripped Israel, Eichmann's very presence mesmerized the courtroom. The balding, bespectacled, and besuited German

had been enclosed in a plexiglass booth for his own safety, but the dock protected him only in the sense that a bullet-proof bowl would safeguard a fish. Hundreds of journalists would vie to encapsulate his extraordinary ordinariness before the trial was over. Attorney-General Hausner would go to the other extreme, telling the judges in his final address that Eichmann had been 'born a human being, but lives as a tiger in the jungle', perpetrating deeds that lay beyond 'that barrier which separates men from beasts'.

The truth was that he was a meagre man who had committed enormous crimes. Political philosopher Hannah Arendt famously saw in him the 'banality of evil', an ordinariness that terrified, and his hands were stained with ink as much as with blood. No Nietzschean superman, amoral to the end, he was a villain who paled at his crimes after capture – but committed them without compunction. The Final Solution that he described was more a force of nature than an act of mass murder, a phenomenon that had 'crystallized gradually' and 'resulted automatically' from Nazism. Even his use of the word 'I' in letters had been bureaucratic jargon and had 'nothing to do with Eichmann as a person'. Although the Nazi treatment of Jews had certainly been monstrous, he had been a soldier rather than a lawyer and had relied for moral guidance on his oath alone. When Reinhard Heydrich had told him that 'the Führer has ordered the physical extermination of the Jews', he had therefore felt no personal responsibility. In fact, after taking the minutes at the Wannsee Conference – the 1941 meeting that had set the Final Solution into motion – he had felt like Pontius Pilate because he had become 'a tool in the hands of others', and was therefore innocent 'from the point of view of my inner-self'. He had even been able to celebrate with 'a glass of brandy, or a couple of glasses of brandy – three, perhaps'

When asked eventually by one of the judges if he was prepared to accept any responsibility at all, Eichmann chewed his cheeks for long seconds before stating that in 'human terms' he was 'reflecting and judging' himself. Two decades earlier, he had been rather more candid. According to testimony given by one of his subordinates at Nuremberg, he had said that he would 'leap laughing into the grave because the feeling that he had five million people on his conscience would be for him a source of extraordinary satisfaction'.

Eichmann claimed to have voiced discontent about the genocide often, but only one example that he gave rang true. The occasion had come in Lwów, as he was returning to Germany from a tour of occupied Belarus, where he had witnessed an SS death squad at work. As he had watched the soldiers scything men and women with gunfire and unloading rosy corpses from mobile carbon-monoxide chambers, he had finally been struck by the reality of genocide. Unable to contain himself, he had confronted one of the commanding officers. 'This is terrible,' he had thundered. 'We [are] educat[ing] . . . young people to grow up as sadists . . . [O]ur own people.' No answer better encapsulates the malevolence and blindness that combined in Eichmann – someone who not only saw the butchers as victims, but thought that it might help his case to tell that to an Israeli court.

Eichmann's end was swift and complete. Throughout the trial, Israel's authorities were so anxious that he might die untimely, at the hand of an assassin or himself, that a guard was permanently stationed in his cell, watched through a peephole by another, who was kept under continuous observation by a third. But once the evidence had been heard judgment was swift. He received the first death sentence to be imposed by an Israeli court, and after an unsuccessful appeal, was hanged, cremated and scattered in international waters on 31 May 1962.

The trial drew its share of criticism. The fact that Eichmann was kidnapped led some to argue that the Israeli government was undermining as much as promoting the international rule of law. Hannah Arendt took countless swipes at Prime Minister Ben-Gurion's politicking and Attorney-General Hausner's taste for melodrama in her account of the case. Israeli philosopher Martin Buber argued that the prosecution was 'a mistake of historical dimensions', which individualized a guilt that properly belonged to all Germans. Few denied, however, that Eichmann had received a fair hearing, and the trial's impact on its intended audience – present and future supporters of Israel – was impressive. A US Gallup poll conducted in June 1961 suggested that around a third of non-Jewish Americans were more sympathetic towards the country at the trial's end than they had been at its beginning. Gideon Hausner let it be known that hundreds of Israeli youngsters had written to thank him 'for opening our eyes to learn what really happened there'. A cultural symposium convened by the newspaper *Maariv* promised even more far-reaching ramifications. Two out of four poets and novelists invited to consider why no one had yet given 'adequate literary expression to the great catastrophe of our generation' regarded Eichmann's trial as a watershed. It could only hasten the day, they felt, when an Israeli writer would forge a link between personal experience, national history and the Nazi attempt to exterminate Europe's Jews.

Expecting victims or victors to avoid disingenuity when punishing their enemies is always a tall order. The assumption of international criminal law, that some crimes are so heinous that individuals cannot escape responsibility by claiming national interests, carries an even greater challenge. Robert Jackson had recognized that much in the April 1945 speech that had propelled him towards the prosecutorial chair at Nuremberg. 'We cannot successfully co-operate with the rest of the world in establishing a reign of law unless we are prepared to have that law sometimes operate against what would be our national advantage,' he had observed.

States have, for good or ill, rarely displayed such selflessness. Israel's Supreme Court formulated the theory of universal jurisdiction, but its subsequent rulers have invariably cited the national interest when threatened by that jurisdiction. A recent illustration came in 2002–3, when quixotic moves by a Belgian court to indict Prime Minister Ariel Sharon for his careless failure to prevent the slaughter of a thousand Palestinians at the Sabra and Shatila refugee camps, twenty years before, inspired nothing but incredulity and abuse from Israeli officials.* The United States has been similarly reluctant to have its own citizens tried for war crimes. Only once, during the Civil War, has an American been tried in a US court for violation of the laws of war, and the specific offences defined at Nuremberg have never been prosecuted on the country's soil. Its army has, however, occasionally charged its soldiers with violations of US law – and one such case offers an object lesson in the double standards that have always bedevilled the concept of universal rights.

Just after 7.30 a.m. on 16 March 1968, the stillness around the South Vietnamese settlement of Son My began rippling to the thud of distant rotors. Helicopters were soon swarming, and while two companies – Alpha and Bravo – sealed off its northern and eastern boundaries, the

---

* The twenty-three survivors who brought the case alleged of course that he was more than merely careless, but the only allegation that has been proved – to the satisfaction of an official Israeli inquiry – was that the then General Sharon had made a 'grave mistake' by 'disregard[ing] . . . the danger of a massacre'. See Yitzhak Kahan et al., *The Commission of Inquiry into the Events at the Refugee Camps in Beirut* (1983), pp. 67–71.

hundred or so members of Charlie Company dropped onto a dry paddy field on its western edge. Rockets and tracer fire spurted from two accompanying gunships as they darted towards the perimetre ditches. The village they were entering was one of several that collectively made up Son My, and it had been the scene of two intense firefights in recent months. Army intelligence now reported that it was home to a battalion of crack Vietcong guerrillas. Charlie Company's task was to flush out the fighters, and then eradicate the huts, livestock, and wells. Its name was My Lai.

The men, who were on their first full combat mission, had reason to be jittery. It was almost literally the most violent moment of the conflict, smack in the middle of a six-month period during which some 60,000 US soldiers would be wounded and 10,000 killed. Although they had been in Vietnam for just twelve weeks, four of their number had already died and over a third had been injured by sniper fire or booby-traps. The promise of their commanding officer, 33-year-old Captain Ernest Medina, at a briefing the previous night – that they could expect 'a hell of a good fight' – offered reassurance that was at best equivocal. But the adrenalin coursing through the soldiers' veins was soon mixing with something much more toxic. They had been told that all innocent civilians would have gone to market. As they edged through the bamboo screens and banana plants, it became apparent that the only people *absent* from My Lai were its able-bodied young men. Even as danger receded, however, gunfire stuttered through the village – and the sporadic violence was soon turning to carnage.

Ignoring the presence of an official army photographer, Ronald Haeberle, the soldiers began perpetrating acts that could have earned them life sentences in almost any country of the world. Military investigators would later gather evidence sufficient to charge a third of the entire unit. Vernado Simpson would recall killing about twenty-five people. 'I cut their throats, cut off their hands, cut out their tongue, their hair, scalped them,' he recalled in the early 1990s. 'A lot of people were doing it and I just followed.' About twenty females were raped or sodomized, in one case by five different men. Half of them were girls under sixteen and the youngest was ten. Several had their genitals stabbed with bayonets, and one had a rifle fired into her vagina. Some who were killed had the ace of spades or Charlie Company's initials carved into their flesh. By midday, around five hundred people, all elderly men, unarmed women, or children, lay dead. The sole American casualty was a soldier who shot himself in the foot.

The movements of Captain Ernest Medina would never be satisfactorily established, but those of one of his platoon leaders, Lieutenant William L. Calley, would never be in any doubt. The Florida-born officer, a short and unprepossessing 24-year-old with the furtive expressions of a rodent, herded scores of villagers together and had them shot down. Known to Medina as Lieutenant Shithead and so unpopular that some of his men had put a bounty on his head, he commanded too little respect to delegate much of the work, but some were willing to assist. Most helpful of all was Paul Meadlo who, though reduced to tears, killed whenever Calley told

William Calley

him to do so. The strange duo, homicidal homunculus and killing cry baby, fired their M-16s in bursts long and short for about an hour, pausing only to change magazine clips, until their captives had been reduced to quivering heaps of flesh and blood.

An argument sometimes advanced against holding soldiers to account for crimes is that ordinary rules are somehow suspended in the heat of the battle. The claim has never been convincing on empirical grounds, in that most combat troops demonstrably resist the temptations of rape and torture, and even at My Lai 10 to 20 per cent of those present committed no crime at all. Several tended to the injured. Some disobeyed Calley's direct orders to machine-gun civilians. One man went further still.

Hugh Thompson, a 25-year-old helicopter pilot from Georgia, was assisting the ground assault from the air, zipping over the treetops in his glass bubble in search of hidden guerrilla forces. He and his two-man crew shot a single man fleeing with a gun, but soon realized that the village contained no more targets. They turned their attention instead to wounded civilians – hurt, they assumed, by accident – and spent much of the next hour signalling their positions with canisters of green smoke in order that they could receive medical treatment. Thompson then left to refuel. On his return, he saw that the plumes were no longer rising over the injured. They marked the dead.

It took some time for Thompson to grasp the magnitude of what was taking place beneath him. The first hint came as he hovered his helicopter above a wounded woman to indicate that she required assistance. An

Hugh Thompson

officer who would later turn out to be Captain Medina approached her, prodded her with his leg, and shot her. The airborne trio, circling smoke that was billowing from the torched village, then saw a group of GIs sunbathing and smoking next to a pile of twitching bodies. Thompson decided to land his craft. He made his way towards the senior officer on the scene, a sergeant, to point out that there were people yards away who needed help. The response was a cinematic cliché before its time. 'The only way of helping them', replied the soldier – presumably gazing into the middle distance – 'is to kill them.' Thompson's incomprehension was turning to anger, and he returned a cold stare. 'Why don't you see if you can help them?' he repeated. But the officer was as good as his word. As Thompson took off, the man began pumping gunfire into the ditch. He realized at last that he was witnessing a massacre.

Incandescent with rage – not least at his own reluctance to recognize the obvious – the pilot was about to take a step unprecedented in US military history. As he flew on, he spotted several soldiers running across a field towards about a dozen women, children, and old men who were scrambling into a bunker. Thompson landed again, planting his craft directly between the two groups. He then told his crewmen to train their M-60s on the troops. If they saw civilians being shot, he yelled, they were to open fire on the Americans. The teenagers, incredulous, asked for the order to be repeated. 'Open up on 'em!' screamed Thompson as he leapt from the cockpit. 'Blow 'em away!'

Thompson then strode towards the soldiers and demanded to know who was in charge. Calley stepped forward. A furious exchange between the two Southerners followed, during which Thompson demanded that the civilians be evacuated from the bunker. The only way to do that, replied Calley, was with a hand grenade. This time, Thompson did not leave, and the stand-off that ensued ended with the lieutenant skulking away. 'He doesn't like the way I'm running this show,' he told his radio operator, 'but I'm the boss here.' Thankfully, he no longer was.

Thompson radioed for emergency assistance to two gunships that were accompanying his flight. According to the later recollection of one of those he contacted, the 'enraged' pilot had told them that, 'if he saw the ground troops kill one more woman or child he would start shooting [them] himself'. The dumbfounded men thereupon landed their cumbersome craft – a manoeuvre both extraordinary and dangerous – and lifted the survivors to safety. Thompson's radio transmissions, monitored by officers co-ordinating the day's operations, were meanwhile causing such consternation that an order to stop killing civilians was issued to Captain Medina. And although no one would ever admit that the murders had been controllable, they ended as suddenly as they had begun.

My Lai contained one last surprise. As Thompson lifted off to leave the village, now a still heap of embers littered with bodies human and animal, his crew chief Glenn Andreotta called out that he had seen something move in one of the gullies. Thompson set down once again and Andreotta ran from the craft to lower himself into the pit. Wading through corpses, he found the source of the movement – a tiny child, uninjured and clinging in silence to its dead mother. Andreotta handed the infant up to door gunner Larry Colburn. No one said a word as they flew back to base. Tears were streaming down Thompson's cheeks.

The pilot immediately reported the massacre to anyone who would listen, from platoon commander to chaplain, but the lies of war were soon drowning him out. On receipt of his complaint, superior officers began a systematic cover-up that would eventually implicate officers up to the rank of major-general. An army press release meanwhile reported that a raid on the Vietcong 'stronghold' of My Lai had gone 'like clockwork' and that 128 enemy had been killed and three weapons captured, at the cost of just two American lives. The ratio of arms to casualties, far from raising eyebrows, inspired General William C. Westmoreland, supreme head of US forces in Vietnam, to send Charlie Company a telegram of congratulations. Thompson himself was awarded a Distinguished Flying Cross –

to honour his supposed rescue of fifteen children from 'the intense cross fire' at My Lai – and though sufficiently displeased to throw it away, he kept his head low, concerned by indications that he himself might face disciplinary action. All the while, statements were filed, boxed, and buried deep in the army's archives.

But just when the truth seemed to have been laid to rest, it punched its way out of the grave. A young veteran called Ronald Ridenhour, who had learned about My Lai from friends in Charlie Company, had been haunted by their accounts for months. On 29 March 1969 he sent a three-page letter summarizing what he believed had happened to thirty of the most senior politicians in the USA. 'Exactly what [occurred]. . . I do not know for *certain*,' he wrote, 'but I am convinced that it was something very black indeed.'

The wheels of military justice rapidly restarted, as witnesses who had been ignored for months were suddenly interviewed. Court martial inquiries were quietly commenced against several soldiers at the end of the summer, and towards the end of the year rumours of the allegations were leaking beyond the army. They entered the mainstream in early November, thanks to a *New York Times* story and an article by a young freelancer called Seymour Hersh. Towards the end of the month Paul Meadlo raised a storm with a television interview in which he admitted more murders than he could remember, and recalled that when shooting babies he had switched to single shots to save ammunition. A week later the country finally got to see what all the fuss was about. The 5th of December issue of *Life* magazine – then, a window to the world for much of middle America – published photographs taken by army photographer Ronald Haeberle: image after image of villagers huddled, sobbing, crawling, and dead.

Amidst the furore that now erupted, attempts to institutionalize the passions were redoubled. The House Armed Services Committee hurried to set up an investigative subcommittee while General Westmoreland, keenly aware that his telegram of congratulations to Charlie Company was not looking good, persuaded the Secretary of the Army to establish an inquiry into the cover-up. Even President Nixon felt the need to weigh in, though his views on the massacre were even more opaque than usual. In public he undertook to ensure that 'those who are charged, if they are found guilty, are punished, because if it is isolated it is against our policy and we shall see to it that what these men did – if they did it – does not smear the decent men that have gone to Vietnam in a very, in my opinion, important cause'. In private, he began covert surveillance of Ridenhour and Hersh and fulminated against the 'dirty rotten Jews from New York' who were behind it all.

As investigations progressed, however, those hoping for swift resolution were soon finding themselves on very awkward ground. The evidence uncovered was soon sufficient to prosecute one in every three members of Charlie Company, while efforts to identify what had turned the unit into a killing machine would reveal only that its age, educational qualifications, and racial composition were almost literally average. Inquiries also threatened to open up questions, better unasked, about whether there was something inherently violent about the entire US strategy in Vietnam. Brutality was becoming so routine that General Westmoreland had thought it important in October 1967 to instruct all commanders to prevent their men from severing human fingers and ears. The fact that My Lai had been within a so-called free-fire zone raised further problems. Such regions, also termed 'specified strike zones', were ones where soldiers were formally permitted to fire, without warning, at anything that moved – and the jargon arguably facilitated the atrocity as much as anyone who killed in reliance on it. Most unhelpfully of all, investigations were revealing that there had been a second massacre on 16 March 1968. At exactly the same time that Calley's men had been wiping out My Lai, a separate company under the command of Captain Thomas K. Willingham had been slaughtering between eighty and ninety civilians in the neighbouring settlement of My Khe. Punishing those who had overstepped the mark was all well and good, but over-strenuous efforts to locate that mark were beginning to seem increasingly undesirable.

The result was that moves towards justice were increasingly determined by their likely effect on public relations. The army's report into the cover-up, while candid and damning, would remain classified for four and a half years. The proposed trials themselves became the subject of secret discussions in the spring of 1970 between the Pentagon and the Justice Department. With a total of twenty-five soldiers facing courts martial and several demobilized men beyond military jurisdiction but under serious suspicion, there were some who argued that President Nixon should draw the venom by establishing a military tribunal to try everyone simultaneously. Others could think of little worse, and argued forcefully for individual trials. They would get their way, and at a time of growing popular unease about the Vietnam conflict, the proceedings would pull off an impressive balancing act. They would recognize that soldiers were not saints, but simultaneously show how exceptional atrocities were. The war's essential nobility would be proved and justice would be seen to be done – in processes that would operate not to explore questions, but to close them down.

The talk of a joint trial had barely been silenced when the individual charges began to fall away. All those suspected of involvement in the My Khe killings had claimed memory loss or a right to silence, and on 9 June 1970 the company's former commander, Thomas K. Willingham, learned to his great relief that charges against him were being dropped. The reason given, such as it was, was that 'based upon available evidence, no further action should be taken'. Several more cases were discontinued, in the supposed interests of justice, over subsequent months, and it was not until November 1970 that the first court martial opened at Fort Hood in Texas. The defendant was Sergeant David Mitchell – allegedly the man who had told Hugh Thompson that he could best help the wounded by killing them – and his fate suggested that the route to convictions would be far from smooth.

The case was holed at the outset, when the trial judge ruled that Thompson could not testify because a Congressional subcommittee (dominated by pro-war Representatives) was refusing to give the court transcripts of what he had told them. Mitchell himself informed the servicemen on the jury, in tears, that he was 'not sure what had happened or who was in my squad . . . [b]ut I'm positive that I did not shoot anyone'. The army's prosecutor produced three witnesses, only one of whom was prepared to say that Mitchell had definitely fired fatal shots, before confidently telling the jurors that, 'I feel I've proved my case.' They disagreed. After hearing defence counsel warn that the court martial was an attempt to destroy the army, and beg them not to betray a young man whose only crime was to fight for his country, they acquitted on all counts.

The outcome of William Calley's trial, which had started at Fort Benning in Georgia on 17 November 1970, three days before Mitchell's acquittal, would now be crucial. The officer, charged with the murder of 102 people, had come to personify the massacre in the popular imagination, and a second failed prosecution would make the pressure to drop the remaining cases all but irresistible. The chances of a conviction looked no more promising than they had in Mitchell's case. The jurors comprised five Vietnam veterans and a sixth career officer who had served in Korea. Calley's attorney was George Latimer, a decorated Second World War colonel and court-martial lawyer of legendary reputation. The responsibility for prosecution had meanwhile been placed in the hands of Captain Aubrey Daniel, a 28-year-old lawyer whose military experience consisted of two years in the courtrooms of Fort Benning. The imbalance was so stark that it almost seemed contrived.

If it was, however, the contrivers had made a serious miscalculation. Daniel, an idealist who had personally lobbied for prosecutions almost as soon as he had heard of My Lai, would deliver a performance as formidable as that of Latimer would be lackadaisical. Thirty-five witnesses, most of them members of Charlie Company, entered the low wooden courthouse over the next two weeks to place Calley squarely at the centre of an inferno. Several were themselves guilty of crimes that would never be punished, but only Paul Meadlo, the man who had wept as he killed, advanced any justifications. It was not one that did Calley any favours. He accepted that many of those whom he had shot had been children, but insisted that all had posed a threat. Even the babies, he claimed, might have 'attacked' him. Daniel, incredulous, asked what he meant. They might have been booby-trapped, he explained. He had feared that at any point their mothers could have lobbed them, like human hand grenades, from the ditches in which they were being killed.

The case advanced by Latimer swung between the counter-productive and the mystifying. One of his favoured cross-examination techniques was to suggest that everyone at My Lai had been homicidal – an assertion which, even if true, showed only that Calley had commanded a death squad. After Hugh Thompson testified, cautiously tiptoeing around the more dramatic details of his confrontation with US ground troops, Latimer slyly suggested to the jury that actions so 'questionable' could hardly be called heroic. As part of his own case, he then called a psychiatrist who asserted that the defendant was not guilty of murder because his intent had not been to kill but 'to waste'. Another proposed that Calley had been temporarily deranged as a result of passively smoking too much marijuana.

By the time the lawyer was done, however, two long months after he had begun, the structure of a defence had finally emerged from the mist.

Twenty-one members of Charlie Company had testified that Captain Medina's pre-operation briefing had come immediately after an emotional memorial service for a recently fallen comrade, and that he had made clear that My Lai would be their chance to get even. Their recollections of his words differed in particulars but dovetailed in general: they were to 'leave no living thing', 'kill anything that breathed', and 'destroy everything'. It did not make for the most attractive of pleas, coming perilously close to the defence of blind obedience that had been rejected when advanced by SS commandos at Nuremberg. Under US military law however, if the jury concluded that Calley might have been obeying instructions that he reasonably thought lawful, he would be entitled to an acquittal.

The verdict was always going to pivot on what the jury made of Calley himself, and on 22 February 1971, he finally stepped forward to give his own account. Outside court, he could be candid to a fault. He had already told psychiatrists that the Vietnamese had seemed like animals with whom he 'could not speak or reason'. He was privately telling the ghost-writer of his autobiography that anyone 'hung up' about his killing of babies should remember that those same babies might grow up to become murderous guerrillas. But on the witness stand, polite, small, and perfectly uniformed, he began not by justifying his homicides but by denying them entirely. He recalled seeing men firing into a ditch and admitted doing the same, but insisted that anyone he may have shot had seemed dead already. Under the avuncular guidance of Latimer he eventually added, however, that he had instructed Meadlo to 'waste' his prisoners. That had, he explained, been the order of the day at the 'Battle of My Lai', because commanding officers always wanted a high body count and normal procedure was to include 'everything . . . – V[iet]C[ong], buffalo, pigs, cows'. In response to one final nudge from Latimer, he let slip that Captain Medina had also been investigated and that he had said, 'Well, it looks like I am going to jail for twenty years.'

Latimer had barely reached the defence table, when Aubrey Daniel – whose eyes had remained fixed on Calley throughout – sprang to his feet. Within seconds he had launched a salvo of questions about the location and movement of various individuals on the morning of 16 March. Calley, too dim or too nervous to fake uncertainty, made clear that he had a panoramic recall of their whereabouts and then referred, once again, to the 'Battle of My Lai'. Daniel pounced. 'Did you receive any fire getting off the helicopter?' he snapped. Calley, suddenly rigid with fear, replied that he had 'no way to know'. 'Did you receive any fire?' insisted Daniel. 'No, sir,' came the mumbled response. 'Did you see any Vietnamese?' he continued. Calley replied that he had seen someone in a tapioca patch, and Daniel demanded to know what he had been doing. 'He was dead, sir,' muttered Calley. The next villager that he had seen had also been dead. It soon emerged that every Vietnamese person whom Calley had encountered at the 'Battle of My Lai' had been dead – excepting only those who were in the process of being killed.

Linguistic clumsiness and emotional crassness accompanied the evasions. He could recall nothing about the age or the numbers of people whom he had killed, and was unwilling to be specific about their gender because he did not want to 'discriminate'. He could not remember whether one of his men, having just forced a woman to give him oral sex, had pulled his pants up afterwards but observed – with a smirk – that 'he would look kind of funny if he hadn't'. When Daniel asked what he had meant by telling Hugh Thompson that he would 'evacuate' women and children from a bomb shelter using a hand grenade, Calley looked blank. 'I don't have any idea, sir,' he replied. 'It was a figure of speech.' And he did not even understand the question when asked whether he had reported his mass-executions back to Medina – the man whose orders he claimed to have been following. Daniel repeated it. 'That wasn't any big deal,' he replied.

The case closed three years to the day after the murders at My Lai. America's focus had wandered considerably, not least because most court reporters had chosen to winter in Los Angeles, where Charles Manson, a serial killer less prolific but more colourful than Calley, had been facing his own trial – but the journalistic corps now flocked back en masse. On 10 March 1971, Ernest Medina rebutted the claims made against him, staring Calley in the eye as he spoke and sharply saluting the judge as he left. Six days later came the speeches that closed the case, and after Aubrey Daniel had invited the jurors to be the conscience of the army and the nation, and Latimer had begged them not to second-guess Calley's battlefield decisions, they filed out of court. It was almost two weeks before they returned. The defendant, they declared on 29 March, was guilty of 22 of the 102 murders charged. Two days later, they had to decide on sentence. Latimer this time informed them that Calley had been a

'good boy until he got into that Oriental area', while Daniel, opposed to
the death penalty, asked simply for 'an appropriate punishment'. After a
short retirement, the jury handed down a term of life imprisonment.

The decisions were hardly a rush to judgment, but they electrified the
country. The murderous antics of the Manson Family were briefly
bumped off the front pages, and right-wing America promoted Calley
from martyr to saint. A bilious dirge called the *Battle Hymn of Lt. Calley*
– tracing his patriotic trajectory back to the days when he had marched
around his mother's kitchen with saucepan on head and flag in hand –
sold 200,000 copies in three days. Governor Jimmy Carter, displaying a
populist touch that would singularly desert him in later years, proclaimed an 'American Fighting Man's Day' and invited Georgians to
show their solidarity by driving during the daytime with car headlights
on. The greatest tribute of all came at a 'Rally for Calley' in Columbus,
Georgia, where the minister reminded the crowd that this was not the
first time that humanity had witnessed an injustice at Easter. 'There was
a crucifixion two thousand years ago of a man named Jesus Christ,' he
told them. I don't think we need another crucifixion of a man named
[William] Calley.'

The White House was no less concerned. President Nixon, though not
a man to take unnecessary decisions on issues of principle, was always
finely tuned to the popular mood – and it was favouring some decisive
action. He eventually received about a hundred thousand telegrams
about the case, 100–1 in favour of Calley, and a Gallup poll published the
following week would show disapproval of the verdict running at a rate
of 79 per cent. Washington National Airport simultaneously contacted
administration officials to tell them that a billy-goat, wearing a waistcoat
of red, white, and blue inscribed with Calley's name and the word
'SCAPEGOAT', had arrived as unaccompanied baggage from Atlanta,
addressed to Nixon. History does not record which, if either, tipped the
balance, but the president decided on 1 April 1971 that the interests of
justice and military morale required that Calley be removed from the
stockade to house arrest, pending the outcome of his appeal. Although
that appeal would fail, there he remained, cohabiting with a girlfriend,
tropical fish, and a mynah bird, until granted full parole on
27 February 1974. The effect was that he spent three days of his life
sentence behind bars.

Prosecutor Aubrey Daniel wrote a furious letter of protest. Five of the jurors, he reminded Nixon, were Vietnam veterans themselves. Aware that they had received hate mail and death threats, he demanded of his commander-in-chief:

> Have you considered those men in making your decisions? The men who, since rendering their verdict, have found themselves and their families the subject of vicious attacks upon their honor, integrity and loyalty to the nation. . . . I would expect the President of the United States, a man who I believed should and would provide the moral leadership for this nation, would stand fully behind the law of this land on a moral issue which is so clear and about which there can be no compromise.

Aubrey's conclusion was as unfounded as his expectation. There could be compromise. Although over two dozen men had been charged in relation to the massacre and cover-up, the last indictments were abandoned – in the 'interests of justice' – after five more trials all ended in acquittal. Captain Medina's own jury took less than an hour to find him not guilty. William Calley, like all the other murderers of My Lai and My Khe, returned to the obscurity that he might have eminently merited in a parallel universe, and now runs a jewellery store at the Cross Country Plaza Shopping Mall in Columbus, Georgia.

It would be three more decades before the United States was finally ready to make official concessions to the truth. In March 1998 Hugh Thompson and Larry Colburn – along with Glenn Andreotta, killed in action just weeks after he had climbed through corpses to save a child's life – were awarded the Soldier's Medal for their conduct at My Lai. Thompson's citation finally erased the stain of the Distinguished Flying Cross bestowed upon him in 1969, which had falsely recorded that he had rescued Vietnamese children from 'intense cross fire'. It stated that he had landed 'in the line of fire between fleeing Vietnamese civilians and pursuing ground troops to prevent their murder'. He had been 'prepared to open fire on those American troops' – an act of valour that reflected credit on him, and the US army.

It was a decent gesture. But although the United States proved belatedly able to honour the American heroes of My Lai, its decision to try the villains was a rare aberration. An optimist might argue that that reflected the essential goodness of soldiers in the field, but there were certainly some serious allegations that never came to trial. Even while Calley was being prosecuted, complaints from a serving sergeant sparked off an investigation of the Tiger Force platoon of the 101st Airborne Division, then conducting operations in the same province where My Lai was located. The inquiry would disclose that the platoon had killed and scalped hundreds of civilians during 1967, and hard evidence emerged against eighteen men. The administration of President Ford secretly squelched further action in 1975. More recently, former US Senator Bob Kerrey admitted to an investigative journalist in April 2001 that a seven-man SEAL unit under his command had killed at least thirteen women and children at the village of Thanh Phong on 25 February 1969. Although he accepted that the event was an 'atrocity' that could not be justified on moral or military grounds, he went on to excuse it on both levels. Most of the victims, he claimed, had been caught in crossfire, while the rest had died in a hut, unbeknownst to him, during mopping-up operations. The recollection of his senior subordinate, Gerhard Klann, was different. Klann claimed that Kerrey had helped him kill a woman and three children in a hut, had personally slit the throat of an old man, and had finally ordered that fifteen or so other captives, including a baby, be machine-gunned. After pondering Klann's account, Kerrey conceded that it was 'possible that a slight version of that happened. . . . Yeah, that's possible. But, boy, it's not my memory of it.' The story caused a mild rumpus during the dog days of 2001 but – even before the attacks of September 11 turned scrutiny of the military into an unpatriotic act across much of the United States – there was no official attempt to investigate whether criminal charges might be justified.

By the end of the 1980s international criminal law had reached an impasse. Nuremberg had asserted that some crimes were global, the Genocide and Geneva Conventions had required states to investigate and punish them, and the Eichmann prosecution had put into play the idea that they were triable anywhere. The only courts capable of doing so were, however, national ones;* and domestic concerns loomed large on those

---

* The World Court and regional tribunals like the European and Inter-American Courts of Human Rights, although entitled to consider breaches of humanitarian law, only proceed against states.

rare occasions that proceedings were commenced. But paradox then propelled the precedent established at Nuremberg back onto the front line. Yugoslavia erupted into Europe's first internal war since 1945 – and the return of crimes against humanity there revived the process that had been supposed to bring them to an end.

Yugoslavia, a federation of six separate republics, had been eroding since the early 1980s. The country had been established in 1919 in the hope of accommodating the nationalisms of Europe's southern Slavs – an aspiration as urgent as it was ambitious in a multi-ethnic region that had begun to spin apart as the Ottoman Empire had crumbled. Its leader after 1945, Josip Broz Tito, had then been particularly successful in neutralizing the ambitions of the two most powerful constituents, the Serbs and the Croats, by rallying both behind an anti-Soviet form of communism. He had died in 1980, however and separatist movements, long-simmering, were soon back on the boil. The nation's glue was about to give.

No single person would do as much to tear Yugoslavia apart as Tito had done to hold it together, but a Serb called Slobodan Milošević would come close. In 1984, fresh from five years at the helm of the state bank, the ambitious apparatchik became head of the Belgrade branch of the Communist Party and realized that his country was changing – and that his comrades were not. His moment came in April 1987 during a visit to Serbia's southern province of Kosovo, a trip that was ostensibly intended to repair deteriorating relations between its Serb minority and the Albanian-dominated Communist Party. At one meeting, a mob gathered outside the building and in an atmosphere of high tension, the nervous participants asked Milošević to calm the rock-throwing crowd. Erstwhile bureaucrat though he was, he possessed the recklessness of a roulette fiend – and he now span the wheel for all he was worth. Stepping into the mêlée, shadowed by a television crew, he sided not with the authorities but with the mob. 'No one should dare to beat you!' he bellowed. 'No one should dare to beat you!' The amazed crowd began a chant – 'Slobo! Slobo! Slobo!' – and overnight the lifelong Communist metamorphosed into a Serb hero. While Party hacks elsewhere in Europe were still flogging their dead horses, he had found a tiger to ride.

Thanks to Milošević, the beast was soon running wild. In a barnstorming campaign that he pursued throughout the summer of 1988, the former functionary launched a battle against bureaucracy, and under cover of that dependable smokescreen he played crowds against colleagues and turned the dilapidated structures of Yugoslavian communism into citadels of Serbian nationalism. His reward came on 8 May 1989, when he won the Serb presidency, and two months later he delivered a speech – again in Kosovo – that would define the next decade of Balkan history. On the 600th anniversary of an epochal defeat by the Ottoman Empire – a humiliation that Serbia always memorialized with gusto – he visited the site of the rout, known as the Field of Blackbirds, and warned a million-strong crowd that 'battles and quarrels' confronted Serbia once again. He recognized that the struggle was no longer armed, but in the hazy summer heat he proposed, to ecstatic cheers, that 'such things should not yet be excluded'. It would be on 29 June 1991 – two years later, minus one day – that the first shots of Yugoslavia's civil war were fired.

The opening skirmishes were fought in the small republic of Slovenia. The fighting, between separatists and Yugoslavian army units reporting to Milošević, lasted only ten days, but the televised images of central European men, zigzagging through suburban streets under crackling gunfire, rumbled with a peculiar resonance – and the flashbacks were about to get worse. Over in Croatia, the second largest Yugoslavian republic after Serbia, another nationalist champion had just been elected. President Franjo Tudjman had reinvented himself no less thoroughly than Milošević: a veteran anti-Nazi, he had become a Serb-hating apologist for Croatian fascism, and denied that Yugoslavia's substantial Muslim minority even merited recognition as an ethnic group. He was not the kind of leader who would let Milošević unilaterally destroy the country. He was the kind who would do it with him.

Their teamwork began a month after the Slovenian war, when federal army units mobilized alongside Serb insurgents across a swathe of Serb-populated Croatia known as the Krajina. The nature of the conflict that was about to engulf Yugoslavia was revealed at Kijevo, a village inhabited by Croats who refused to leave, which was reduced to rubble by a twelve-hour bombardment. Although the remains looked like a wasteland, both sides told journalists – in pride or in anger – that it had in fact been 'cleansed'. A new euphemism had been born. The spectre of genocide had risen from the grave.

The stakes rose in the new year, as the European Union recognized Croatian independence, and all eyes turned to Bosnia, situated squarely between the belligerents and the third largest of Yugoslavia's republics. With a population that was roughly a third Serb, a fifth Croat, and two-fifths Muslim, it would have been hard to invent somewhere more ethnically unclean. Imposing racial hygiene on the republic would be about as messy as unscrambling an omelette. Many on both sides were, however, eager to give it a go. The last hopes of avoiding a calamity evaporated in March 1992, when Bosnians voted for independence by a two-to-one majority. Serb gunmen fired on peace demonstrators in the capital of Sarajevo, while forces allied to them but owing allegiance to Milošević began rampaging through the republic's northern towns. Croat irregulars, backed by President Tudjman, meanwhile instituted a land grab of their own to the east. The Bosnian government, lacking armies, factories, and a coastline, were reduced to begging for international assistance as mosques were dynamited, thousands of women were raped, and communities that had been working, marrying, and mourning together for centuries disintegrated. Nowhere was the agony more protracted than in Sarajevo itself. Serb forces sealed off the cluster of minarets and spires and mansions in April 1992, and over the next twenty-two months a city as pretty as a postcard turned into a landscape as ugly as hell. From artillery positions in the mountains that girdled the town, shifts of *šljivovica*-swigging gunners sent half a million bullets and bombs splashing into the markets and streets, turning the municipal library into a furnace and countless gardens into graveyards. It would become the world's most emblematic siege since Leningrad. Then, in the summer of 1992, the Western media obtained and published images of skeletal captives gazing through the barbed wire fences of Serb prison camps in northern Bosnia. Five decades after scenes from Buchenwald and Belsen had first flickered through the courtroom at Nuremberg, it seemed as though the continent had begun, by some terrible magic, to tock and tick back through time.

As popular anger mounted across the Western and Muslim worlds, the United Nations Security Council procrastinated. Indeed, it did even less than nothing. Its first intervention had come in the form of an arms embargo imposed in September 1991, a step that hardly touched Serbia and Croatia, each with industry and porous borders aplenty, but condemned Bosnia to helpless death. Almost a year later, it authorized 'all measures necessary' to secure the delivery of humanitarian relief, a formula that unequivocally mandated military action under international

law. But although there was a legitimate government and a people on the
ground both pleading for help and willing to fight, members of the
Council on both sides of the Atlantic acted as though paralysed.

President George Bush Sr. had been cautioned by advisors that 'We
don't have a dog in that fight', and while he publicly condemned the
'horror' of the Serb camps he punctiliously specified that they were not
'genocidal' – aware that international law required intervention if he said
anything different. The British Prime Minister, John Major, was in many
ways even less inclined to take action. His government had taken the lead
in arguing for a weapons embargo and when an incoming administration, headed by the newly-elected President Clinton, tentatively proposed
in early 1993 that the time had come to arm the Bosnians and bomb Serb
forces, it was Major's ministers who did most to squash the idea. Foreign
Secretary Douglas Hurd was the most resolutely inactive of all. An urbane
and experienced diplomat, with all the gravitas that an education at Eton
and Trinity College, Cambridge, can instil, he had risen inexorably to the
apex of every institution he had graced; but there would be no challenge
in Yugoslavia from which he did not shrink.

The passivity of Hurd's Balkan policy has been well documented elsewhere, but it was encapsulated in his April 1993 response to an American
suggestion that Bosnians should be allowed to engage their killers on an
even playing field. Rearmament of the victims was actually, Hurd warned
in a letter to the *Daily Telegraph*, 'the policy of the level killing field'. It was
an elegant *jeu de mots*, of which he was reportedly proud;* but in the very
same month that he uttered it, the curtain rose on the worst instance of
unbalanced murder in the entire war. On 16 April 1993, the overwhelmingly Muslim inhabitants of Srebrenica in eastern Bosnia surrendered to
Serb forces, and the United Nations Security Council was soon solemnly
warning the victorious commanders that the town was now to be regarded
as a 'safe area'. Although no one knew precisely what the designation
entailed, blue-helmeted peacekeepers were sent to prove that it existed.

---

* Rather less proud of him was his former boss, Margaret Thatcher, whose commitment to the Bosnian cause was impassioned. She regarded their slaughter
  as tantamount to a second holocaust and reportedly complained to Hurd at
  one point: 'Douglas, Douglas, you would make Neville Chamberlain look like
  a warmonger.' See 'Atticus', *Sunday Times* (London), 2 May 1993, pp. 2–3.

They were still there in July 1995, when Serb troops systematically executed between seven and eight thousand of the town's disarmed men and boys. It was one massacre too many for the Clinton administration, which finally resolved to launch air strikes on Serb artillery positions. When the newly elected French government of Jacques Chirac expressed its support, Britain reluctantly agreed to join in. After three years of carnage that had claimed the lives of countless Muslims, Serbs, and Croats – perhaps 50,000, perhaps 200,000 – the guns fell silent within days.

Such was the background against which, in February 1993, the USA, the UK, and the Russian Federation had supported a French-sponsored resolution to establish a tribunal to try those who committed war crimes and crimes against humanity in the warring territories. The International Criminal Tribunal for the former Yugoslavia (ICTY) was the first international court since Nuremberg, and the sentiments expressed by Security Council members were suitably lofty. 'This will be no victor's tribunal,' declared Madeleine Albright for the United States. 'The only victor that will prevail in this endeavour is the truth.' Others were equally inspired by their own decision. It would send a clear message to the aggressors and do justice to the victims, said the French. The British noted that the world was angry and shocked, and hoped for a reckoning for all the perpetrators of war crimes. The Russians believed its creation would bring Yugoslavia's politicians to their senses and send a resounding warning to human rights abusers around the world.

The realities were rather less exalted. Although Albright and several State Department officials certainly believed in the court, taking the view that justice would be essential to lasting peace, its establishment replaced policy among observer nations as much as it complemented it – insofar as it was taken seriously at all. French and Russian support for prosecutions was never better than tepid, while John Major's government had positively worked to limit the likelihood of prosecutions since mid 1992, more concerned to facilitate negotiations between the ethnic cleansers of Yugoslavia than to hold them to account.

Underfunded and ignored, the court did little but limp along for a year and a half, but that began to change in July 1994, when South African President Nelson Mandela released a constitutional judge called Richard Goldstone to become chief prosecutor. Goldstone, the former head of South Africa's Truth and Reconciliation Commission, brought new energy that saw indictments issued by the end of the year, and the first trial was under way by April 1995. Duško Tadić, a former karate instructor and café owner from northern Bosnia, faced allegations arising out of his activities in 1992 around his hometown. After helping Yugoslav troops shell the Muslims with whom he had grown up, he had lazed away the summer in nearby prison camps, watching inmates being made to eat live pigeons, perform acts of oral sex, and in one case, bite off a prisoner's testicle. In May 1997, Tadić was convicted, by way of rulings that affirmed for the first time that war crimes and crimes against humanity were applicable to internal conflicts as well as wars between states, and that terrorists as well as officials could be tried for committing them.

After a trial that had lasted more than two years, ICTY had finally landed a war criminal and even made some new law but, monstrous minnow though Tadić was, the court needed to fry some considerably bigger fish if it was to justify its existance. The chances of that happening, however, depended on nabbing some more suspects – and although Goldstone had promised to target commanders and the court's statute had made heads of state liable to prosecution, every senior figure from the conflict remained at large. NATO-led troops had been occupying Bosnia since late 1995, but erstwhile psychiatrist and part-time poet Radovan Karadžić, the bouffant-haired supervisor of the siege of Sarajevo, could generally be found strolling around the Bosnian ski resort of Pale. General Ratko Mladić, a pioneer of ethnic cleansing at Kijevo and commander of Serb forces at Srebrenica, maintained an address in Belgrade. And the two men at the top – Slobodan Milošević and Franjo Tudjman – remained not just at liberty, but in power.

The inaction finally ended in the late 1990s. A change of government in the United Kingdom replaced the stultification of the Major government with the hyperactivity of Tony Blair's first administration, and NATO forces were soon smashing down doors and hotly pursuing suspects all over Bosnia. Trouble was meanwhile beginning to brew among Serbia's most substantial ethnic minority – Kosovo's Albanians – and Milošević mobilized to crack down on the unrest. The United States, the United Kingdom, and France, by now keely sensitive to charges of appeasement and emboldened by their belated success in Bosnia, this time demanded that Serb forces withdraw – albeit that Kosovo was a province of Serbia itself. Milošević was finally in their political sights.

On 24 March 1999, following the collapse of negotiations with the Serbian government, all three powers launched a sustained campaign of aerial bombing. Two months later, an indictment was issued by prosecutors at The Hague charging the Serbian president with having ordered or failed to prevent war crimes and crimes against humanity in Kosovo. The gambler was finally running out of chips. As Milošević lost control of the province, which was the traditional fount of Serb nationalism, domestic opposition to his rule mounted, and elections in September 2000 resulted in a defeat so immense that even his attempts to rig the result left him short of a majority. After one last attempt to brazen it out, he found himself under arrest. Serbia's new government, threatened with the loss of $1.28 billion in aid by the administration of President George W. Bush, then agreed to hand him over to ICTY. He arrived at The Hague's prison on 28 June 2001. Twelve years to the day after his speech at the Field of Blackbirds had heralded Yugoslavia's ethnic meltdown, Milošević walked from a blue-and-white UN helicopter across Scheveningen's floodlit yard to join about three dozen of the men who had done most to stoke its fires.*

The Tribunal had finally netted the biggest fish of all. It still had to reel him in, however, and the scale of the challenge soon became clear. Prosecutor Carla del Ponte gave a press conference the morning after his arrival at which she announced that: 'The Serbian people are not on trial here. The history of Serbia is not under examination.' Milošević entered court for the first time four days later, and from the moment he stood to address the judges, wearing a tie striped with Serbian red, white, and blue, he was determined to prove her wrong. When the senior judge, Richard May of the United Kingdom, suggested that he appoint a lawyer, his eyes sparkled like a burning fuse. 'I consider this tribunal a false tribunal and

---

* Relations within the jail were, needless to say, extremely cordial. Radislav Krstić, otherwise known as the Butcher of Srebrenica, had overcome the loss of a leg to establish himself as the unit's table-tennis champion. Dario Kordić, mastermind of Croatian ethnic cleansing in eastern Bosnia, had won renown as its best chef. Milošević would add to the bonhomie by befriending his neighbour, a Bosnian Muslim general, who became a regular chess partner. See Martin Fletcher, 'An Armistice Behind Bars', *The Times* (London), 23 February 2001, p. 28; Isabel Vincent, 'The trial of Slobodan Milosevic has shown a side of him unfamiliar to the Western world', *National Post* (Canada), 2 March 2002.

the indictment a false indictment,' he snarled in English. 'I have no need to appoint counsel to illegal organ.' His response to May's inquiry whether he wanted the indictment read was no friendlier ('That's your problem') and after twelve minutes of speechifying through microphones that were repeatedly disconnected, the session finished in shambles. At his second appearance, on 29 October 2001, May notified him that three lawyers would henceforth raise points on his behalf whether he liked it or not. '[T]wo teams working for the benefit of the same party,' he growled contemptuously. 'This can now be called Hague fair play.'

The strategy was transparent enough. Every hearing was being broadcast live in Serbia and, like any old crooner given an audience, he had convinced himself that the magic would work just one last time. He had kick-started his career by telling Serb rioters to defend themselves, consolidated it by warning Serbs that their genius was under threat, and would now stand up to an entire world that wanted only to kick sand in Serbia's face. The pose was more than a little distingenuous. Milošević had been amassing thousands of documents to use in his defence from the moment that he was indicted, and while he grumbled about the illegality of Judge May's organ, lawyers were busily filing motions on his behalf behind the scenes. But his claim of victors' justice was not entirely fantastic. When the Security Council had established ICTY, none of its members was at war in Yugoslavia and their most ulterior motive had been the hope that they might be able to avoid trials altogether. By the time he was indicted however, three of them were bombing Kosovo – and the allegations against him concerned Kosovo alone. Prosecutors would justify that with the claim that his Kosovan crimes were easier to prove, but they swiftly added allegations relating to Bosnia and Croatia once he had been brought into custody. Carla Del Ponte further rebuffed suggestions of bias by asserting that she had also drawn up charges against Franjo Tudjman, the Croatian leader, and abandoned them only because he died in December 1999. Given that he had been terminally ill since 1997, the claim had a strong whiff of damage limitation about it, and did little to dispel the odour of political calculation that still lingers around the circumstances of Milošević's indictment.

The trial proper opened on 12 February 2002. In the days following Milošević's arrest, it had become popular among journalists to note that the former president's parents had both killed themselves and significantly to wonder whether captivity might break his own will. It now became very clear, however, that any inclination towards self-destruction had been decisively cured by his half a year at Scheveningen. He had already declared he would be calling thirty-five witnesses, said by his lawyers to include Bill Clinton and Tony Blair, and the scale of the conspiracy to which they were allegedly party was soon turning out to be just as vast as might have been expected. Within a month, Milošević was asserting that NATO and al-Qaeda had fought in cahoots in Kosovo, the Westerners bombing from the air while their plucky fundamentalist allies mobilized resistance on the ground. In September 2002 he revealed that the thousands of murders at Srebrenica had been the work of rogue Serb mercenaries, hired by President Jacques Chirac to create a pretext for military intervention. Sarajevan politicians had connived in the slaughter of their compatriots. Indeed, 'this practice of killing their own people . . . was typical for the Muslim side during the war'.

Milošević's ability to wrong-foot the court has been as masterful as his defence has been imaginative. In April 2004, as he prepared to advance his own case, he let it be known that he would in fact be calling not thirty-five witnesses, but just over sixteen hundred. When the court then attempted to curb his exuberance by appointing lawyers to run his day-to-day defence, he went on strike, his witnesses went to ground and the lawyers concerned eventually asked to be discharged on the basis that their client would not talk to them. Insofar as Milošević has any concern to establish his legal innocence the strategy may prove less effective than the tactics, however. The case against him rests on the claim that he directed crimes or failed to take proper steps to prevent them, and the very obsessiveness with which he has advanced his wilder theories undercuts suggestions that he ever delegated much to subordinates. The performance of former presidents and prime ministers in the witness box, though potentially good news for the gaiety of nations, is similarly unlikely to help his cause. The more he harangues witnesses to remember how happy the West once was to deal with him, the more of a player he shows himself to be – and the more plausible becomes the argument that he controlled events on the ground.

Insofar as Milošević's concern is to reserve his niche in the pantheon of wronged Serb heroes, however, his performance is likely to prove far

more effective. Serbs used to joke that Milošević's most unforgivable war
crime was to keep losing them, but the corrupt loser whom they threw
out of office in late 2000 has been regaining hearts and minds ever since
his arrival at The Hague. In March 2002, a month after the beginning of
the trial, polls showed that most Serbs were unable, or unwilling, to name
a single place where their countrymen had committed war crimes – and
four out of ten gave their former President top marks for his first appearances. When Serbian state broadcasters then pulled the plug on trial
coverage, it was Milošević's own supporters who were infuriated. As far as
they were concerned, the sight of their leader repulsing a war crimes allegation could only work to their advantage, and general election results in
late 2003 suggested that they were right. Nationalists owing allegiance to
Vojislav Šešelj, another prisoner at The Hague, won more votes than any
other electoral contender; Milošević's party won enough votes to make
him eligible for a parliamentary seat.

The proceedings against Milošević also illustrate in a more nebulous
sense just how contingent the world's demands for justice can be. It is
no longer just the dock but the entire court that is bullet-proof,
screened from the world behind a sheet of two-inch thick glass, and the
event that it cocoons has an equivalent air of unreality. Within Serbia,
the trial has consolidated the national sense of victimhood at least as

Survivor of Srebrenica watching Milošević's first court
appearance on 3 July 2001.

much as it has assuaged it; and in the wider world, the Bush administration, once so determined to have Milošević arraigned that it threatened Serbia with economic sanctions, has found notoriously worse evildoers with whom to contend. That is not to say that the possibilities for justice have died on the ground. An eagerness to join the European Union, if nothing else, looks set at the time of writing to produce a spate of domestic war crimes trials in all of the major republics. But as The Hague's show unspools, addressing the global concerns of an era that has passed and raking the embers of a war that most observers have rewritten or forgotten, its own auditorium is all but empty.

The pragmatic justifications for war crimes trials have never been particularly compelling. The establishment of ICTY in 1993 was followed a year later by the slaughter of almost a million Tutsis in Rwanda, while the threat of indictment did nothing identifiable to restrain the killers of Srebrenica a year after that. The ability of international courts to discover truth is no more assured. Although testimony sometimes cuts through the fog of war, showing the corpses beneath the euphemisms, trials ignore countless facts – out of fairness to defendants if nothing else. The idealistic claim that prosecutions secure justice for victims is equally unsatisfactory. No trial can meet the expectations of every individual, and one that collectively satisfies one side of a conflict generally stokes the resentments of the other. Trials might even positively obstruct both truth and reconciliation. In 1998, The Hague's then senior prosecutor, Louise Arbour, found herself opposing the creation of a 'truth commission' to investigate the Bosnian war – at a time when all three parties claimed to want one – because it could have contaminated evidence and made it harder to win fair convictions.

One weakness has always underpinned all the others – the rarity of prosecution – since erratic enforcement has always been as likely to encourage aggression and conflict as to restrain it. The hope that prosecutions might become routine has consequently been built into international treaties since the late 1940s, but for decades the prospect seemed all but unattainable. As the Cold War came to an end however, many obstacles fell away, and much of the world co-operated through the 1990s to negotiate a permanent tribunal into existence. The teamwork bore fruit in 1998 when 160 countries gathered in Rome to establish an International Criminal Court (ICC), empowered to try war crimes and crimes against humanity.

The new court focused exclusively (as had ICTY) on the two categories of offence that Robert Jackson had regarded with some disdain at Nuremberg, but its passage nevertheless represented a culmination of the idealism that had inspired the American over half a century before. The Rome Statute was not however passed by acclamation – and among the seven opponents of the new court, standing shoulder to shoulder with China, India, Iraq, Israel, Libya, and Saudi Arabia, was the United States. US politicians then made it a priority to subvert the institution, and by late 2003, the administration of President Bush had persuaded more than three dozen nations to promise that they would ignore their obligations to the court as and when disobedience was deemed desirable. The complaint, summarized by Congress in the preamble to a 2002 statute called the American Servicemembers Protection Act, was that the ICC denied certain fundamental guarantees – in particular the right to jury trial – and was liable to interfere with efforts to deter global aggression. The same law gave Bush prior authority for several measures, potentially including the invasion of Holland, if required to rescue American suspects from the court's clutches.

Given that ICC officials could not even open an investigation unless they concluded that the United States had deliberately refused to do so, the stated concerns were more than a little speculative, but they reflected others that tapped deep into the nation's sense of self. The USA was created by anti-imperialist rebels, and a suspicion of the world beyond its shores has formed part of the nation's political discourse since 1796, when George Washington had warned in his farewell address against 'entangl[ing] our peace and prosperity in the toils of European ambition'. The USA inspired the League of Nations only to refuse to join it, has blown fiery and frigid towards the United Nations ever since its creation in 1945, and signed up to human rights treaties like the Genocide and Geneva Conventions only warily and belatedly. The fact that it now has over seven hundred military bases in thirty-eight countries, maintains an armed presence in over a hundred more, and exercises a cultural influence as great as that of any power in history makes the dream of isolation a little paradoxical. But the United States has always clung to its dreams.

The very belief in its uniqueness has, however, also pulled the USA in the opposite direction. It has been notoriously eager to export the ideological gifts with which it feels blessed, and a similar confidence has helped it to shape modern international law. Its lawyers have done more than those of any other country to whip the world into line over biological and chemical weapons. They have simultaneously ensured that the weapon of mass destruction most commonly favoured by Western democracies, namely bombs dropped from a great height, has never been regulated by treaty. International criminal law in its entirety was also, in many ways, an American creation. Had it not been for Henry Stimson and Robert Jackson, Nuremberg would have been a rubber stamp for the swifter justice that had been favoured by the United Kingdom and the Soviet Union. Such Americans would have been more likely to commandeer the ICC than to sabotage it.

The tension between isolationism and engagement in US foreign policy might have produced reactions to the ICC that ranged only from obstructive to manipulative. Events since September 11 2001, have, however, caused the two traditions to interact in a way that potentially threatens the entire consensus on which international human rights law depends. Instead of merely pushing for changes in that law, the USA has tried unilaterally to redefine it.

The new stance began to emerge very soon after the attacks the attacks on the World Trade Center and the Pentagon. The United States, boosted by an unprecedented wave of international support, swiftly obtained backing from the UN Security Council for military action against al-Qaeda leaders in Afghanistan. It very soon became clear, however, that it was less concerned with formal legitimacy in other fields. On 20 September 2001, President Bush informed Congress that America faced a war that would be fought not just with weapons, but with tools diplomatic, financial, and legal. While the country's armed forces geared up for 'Operation Infinite Justice' – swiftly renamed 'Enduring Freedom' lest anyone think that arrogant – it became clear that criminal justice was going to be on the front line. The government incarcerated over seven hundred domestic illegal immigrants (none of whom was ever charged with a terrorism-related offence) and imprisoned scores of others on the basis that they might have something interesting to tell a grand jury. It then declared in November 2001 that it was 'not practicable' to apply ordinary laws to foreigners who were suspected of terrorism. They would instead be detained indefinitely and tried by military tribunals, if at all.

Prisoners from Afghanistan were soon being airlifted into a detention centre at the military base in Guantánamo Bay, Cuba, and in March 2002 Defense Secretary Donald Rumsfeld announced the ground rules for any such trials. The judges would be chosen either by Rumsfeld or by a person appointed by him, who would pick a number – any number – between three and seven. Only serving or retired military officers would be eligible to serve. Defence attorneys would be accredited only if they agreed to the monitoring of their conversations with clients; the judges would be entitled to consider evidence regardless of its reliability; and defendants could be removed from their own trial – as could their lawyers – if the authorities thought that best. US courts for their part would have no right to question any decision reached by the tribunal, up to and including sentences of death. Rumsfeld pronounced his rules 'fair' and 'balanced', but Pentagon general counsel William Haynes III made clear that they were 'rules' only in a loose sense. 'If we had a trial right this minute, it is conceivable that somebody could be tried and acquitted . . . but . . . not . . . released', he explained. '[W]e may hold enemy combatants for the duration of the [war on terror].'

The administration went on to assert that its powers of indefinite detention extended to people who were already charged with ordinary criminal offences, and, indeed, to any US-born citizen whom it regarded as an enemy. With chutzpah, it swatted away the first legal challenges by telling federal judges, who humbly agreed, that they had no right to examine the complaints because scrutiny of the army's cells, brigs, and interrogation chambers would trespass onto presidential privileges and the sovereignty of Fidel Castro's Cuba. Less than two years after Congress had condemned the International Criminal Court for denying jury trial to suspected war criminals, more than six hundred of them – some senile and at least one just 13 years old – had been sent into a legal limbo in the name of Enduring Freedom. According to the Red Cross, twenty-one had tried to commit suicide by October 2003.

The fact that governments seize powers in emergencies is not news. Rulers have been redefining their rules at times of crisis ever since Pope Gregory IX sent inquisitors into the Languedoc during the 1230s. Innocent IV authorized torture as a temporary measure in 1252 and it would remain part of the continent's judicial arsenal for another five hundred years. In England, the ministers of Queen Elizabeth I dusted off the rack and thumbscrews to tackle the state's Catholic enemies during the 1570s, and their British successors in the 1970s introduced internment and juryless trials to deal with the paramilitaries of Northern Ireland. More recently, the government of Tony Blair responded to September 11 2001 by rushing through legislation declaring that the nation's very life was under threat and entitling it to imprison any foreigner, if sufficiently suspicious, without trial and without limit of time. US history offers some especially epic examples of executive overreaching: President Lincoln tried to close federal courts entirely during the Civil War, while Franklin Roosevelt ordered the indefinite detention of more than 100,000 Japanese-Americans following the attack on Pearl Harbor.

Military tribunals have a particularly rich tradition. France and Britain once relied on them to quell restive natives in troublespots from Algeria to Zululand, and they have been sporadically dispensing their summary justice in the USA for at least two centuries. Spies and deserters have been at the receiving end most frequently, but not exclusively. It was a military tribunal that facilitated the bloodiest execution of American history, when it convicted over three hundred Dakota Indians of capital offences after the Great Sioux Uprising of 1862. President Lincoln approved the death sentences of thirty-eight, and they were hanged simultaneously from a single wooden beam at Mankato, Minnesota, on 26 December 1862.

Such measures have generally come to be regarded as overreactions. That was the view taken by the UK judiciary of the Blair government's first attempt to legitimize post 9/11 panic, when the House of Lords ruled in December 2004 that the summary jailing of foreigners, even suspicious ones, was incompatible with the country's Human Rights Act. A similar fate may one day befall the jack-in-the-box jurisprudence of the US war on terror. But whether or not it does so, the legal changes enacted by the first Bush administration are significant for reasons that transcend their effect on the USA's internal criminal justice system. They represented a deliberate attempt to redesign the structure of international criminal law.

Since 1949, the third Geneva Convention has guaranteed 'prisoners of war' certain minimum standards of detention and trial. When the USA transported its first captives from Afghanistan to Guantánamo Bay in January

2002, however, Donald Rumsfeld announced that they were not POWs at all. They were 'unlawful combatants', and although his Pentagon planned to treat them 'for the most part' in accordance with the Convention, it did so out of choice rather than duty. The stance was not new, in that US administrations had argued for over a quarter of a century that irregular fighters ought not to be granted Geneva Convention protections. The assertion that the US view either represented customary international law or allowed the country to ignore that law was, however, entirely novel. It had never been advanced, let alone accepted, in any multinational court anywhere in the world. The only precedent was an Israeli draft statute from April 2000, and the Imprisonment of Illegal Combatants Law had caused such an outcry within and outside Israel that the government of Ehud Barak had abandoned it.* American courts, for their part, had only ever previously used the term 'unlawful combatant' to describe spies, saboteurs and mercenaries. But although there was, at the very least, a serious argument that the administration was wrong, it did not care. The Convention itself provides that 'any doubt' about a prisoner's status should be resolved in that prisoner's favour until determined by a court. A military attorney at the Pentagon explained that the provision was irrelevant, because President Bush had no doubts.

The US claim to enjoy exclusive jurisdiction over its soldiers and enemies has eminently authoritative antecedents. The proconsuls who upheld the *Pax Romana* would never have dreamed of handing over citizens to the wicker men and lotteries of barbarian justice, while savages crushed by the Empire were brought to Rome and made to trudge in rude finery behind the excreting beasts of their laurel-wreathed conquerors. As that implies, the power asserted is a quintessentially imperial one and North America's own history offers another, neat, illustration of the claim. Britain in the 1770s ruled that American rebels, along with any British troops who killed them, were triable only in the homeland – laws so egregious to Thomas Jefferson that he railed against them in the Declaration of Independence.

---

* Subsequent events suggest that the decision was inspired by a concern for appearances rather than a commitment to fairness, in that the proposals for internment were replaced by a policy of homicide, characterized as 'targeted assassinations'. Following the US lead at Guantánamo, the law was reintroduced by the government of Prime Minister Ariel Sharon and enacted in March 2002: Nina Gilbert, '"Dirani-Obeid" Law approved by Knesset', *Jerusalem Post*, 5 March 2002, p. 4.

The imperial nature of a power to judge and avoid judgment beyond national borders should be inconvenient for those many citizens within the USA who remain convinced that the country's destiny is to slay empires rather than to establish them. Such folk tend to be no more troubled by contradictions than ideologues anywhere, however – and the combination of nationalism and absolutism underlying their view has in any event produced a moral solipsism far more disturbing than simple incoherence could ever be.

The rage that built as the sadness ebbed after September 11, fortified by the rectitude of victimhood, created a legal climate in which nothing was certain except that the gloves were off. By the summer of 2002 it was becoming unclear whether the fight was bound by any rules at all. At a time when some US commentators had already called for constitutional amendments to permit torture within the USA, the country refused to sign up to an extension of the 1984 Torture Convention that would have opened detention facilities under its control to international inspection. Administration officials assured those few US media representatives who noticed that they were protecting the autonomy of individual states and the privacy rights of prisoners. Events that were simultaneously unfolding elsewhere suggest, however, that the stance reflected a widespread official culture that simply regarded the propriety of American actions as a matter beyond question.

In August 2002, just a month after the US refusal to sign the Torture Convention protocol, Justice Department lawyers secretly sent to White House Counsel, one Alberto R. Gonzales, a 50-page analysis of international law on the topic of aggressive interrogation. It explained how American soldiers could lawfully commit 'cruel, inhuman or degrading' acts, and explored how the president's powers as Commander-in-Chief might entitle him to authorize torture – a trick that essentially required only that the interrogator concerned act with sufficiently noble intentions at the time of inflicting the violence. By April 2003, Donald Rumsfeld was confidentially instructing officers at Guantánamo Bay to deploy interrogation techniques with names such as 'Fear Up Harsh', 'Dietary Manipulation', and 'Sleep Adjustment'. As the war on terror rolled into a new front with the launch of 'Operation Iraqi Freedom' in March 2003, the methods were exported to that newly liberated country. Rumsfeld seemed concerned about what people might think if they knew – to the extent that in November 2003 he ordered officers in Iraq to conceal the existence of one captive in case the Red Cross wanted to visit him – but others would be less ashamed. In the spring of 2004 a thousand or so photographs and videos emerged from the private collections of guards at Baghdad's Abu Ghraib prison, showing hooded and naked prisoners who had been humiliated, sexually violated and, in at least one case, beaten to death.

The USA continues to detain other enemies secretly in ships, bases and overseas prisons around the world, and time may reveal that the torture of nude prisoners at Abu Ghraib was unexceptional. It may not. In either event, the collective blindness that allowed the abuse to occur there represents an appropriate conclusion to the US administration's decision to treat international humanitarian law as an option rather than a commitment. When President Bush had appealed for the world's support in the aftermath of September 11 2001, global sympathy for the American people had soared to levels not seen since the Second World War. Nothing since racial segregation has done more to damage the international reputation of American justice, however, than the shackled and cowering captives of Abu Ghraib and Guantánamo Bay.

The second administration of President George W. Bush, still finding its feet at the time of writing, may row back from the legal extremes of recent years. The presidential claim to be able to imprison anyone incommunicado forever had already taken a hit in June 2004, when the Supreme Court denied that any such power existed. The government's argument that it should be treated as an outlaw in Guantánamo Bay was simultaneously dismissed, and one consequence might be that its prisoners will be transferred to a suitably conservative jurisdiction within the United States – a step that would placate the more hand-wringing critics of the executive while losing it nothing that it had not already lost. The administration will probably accept that federal courts have the right to question military tribunal verdicts – if only because the contrary stance would almost certainly fail before the Supreme Court – and it may even concede, under pressure of court rulings or reality, that the political costs of ignoring the Geneva Convention outweigh the benefits. But even if Bush's second administration reinvents its war on terror entirely, showing a subtlety that it has hitherto tended to ridicule, attempts to re-position the goalposts of criminal justice will continue – and trials will form part of the war.

Their continuing importance was seen when the revelations from Abu Ghraib in April 2004 inspired a suddenly vehement concern to hold someone to account. Notwithstanding all their secret memos on how best to conduct inhumane treatment and torture, the Defense and Justice Departments rediscovered the importance of publicly showing intolerance towards the few rogues who brought dishonour to US ideals. The curtain meanwhile looked set to rise on an even more splendid display of western justice by proxy. President George W. Bush had let it be known on 15 December 2003 that America's Iraqi allies would soon publicly prosecute the recently captured Saddam Hussein. He would at last be given the justice that he had 'defied [sic] . . . to the people of Iraq' for so long.

The ultimate ramifications of Operation Iraqi Freedom are as unguessable as they always were. The future stance of the UK government, itself responsible for torture and thus far incapable of seeing any reason to question transatlantic wisdom on questions of fairness and freedom, is also unclear. But however many show trials or no-trials the war on terror is destined yet to produce, the spectacle first seen at Nuremberg will never now disappear. Truth commissions may reveal and repair the breaches of a traumatized society more subtly than a prosecution. Indefinite detention and summary execution are certainly more efficient ways of waging a military campaign. But holding a living, breathing defendant to account has a magic that no amount of truth or efficiency can provide, and no *Realpolitik* entirely remove. It dramatizes some of the core beliefs of the Western moral tradition: that individuals have a choice, that bad things happen because people do them, and that a moral order remains capable of restoration.

The spotlight on the individual comes with many risks. A prosecution might lend the patina of martyrdom to mass murderers. It can divert attention from bad policies and worse people. A multitude of sinners can hide behind one designated scapegoat. But just as Cicero once claimed that, 'The law is silent when arms are drawn', prosecutions assert that once the weapons are re-sheathed, civilization takes over again. A man like William Calley is tried so that a man like Hugh Thompson can be admired – and so that everyone watching remembers that even on the battlefield, murder might be wrong.

8

The Jury Trial (2):
A Theatre of Justice

'It is not necessary to accept everything [the Law says] as true, one must only accept it as necessary.' 'A melancholy conclusion,' said K. 'It turns lying into a universal principle.'

FRANZ KAFKA, *The Trial*

Irrationality still riddles the jury system. Jurors no longer deliberate without evidence, but their verdicts are as unreasoned as ever. Their acquaintance with the defendant is no longer assumed; instead, prior relevant knowledge is supposed to be ignored. And the system's integrity rests, as it always has, on the most daring leap of faith. Only the touchstone has changed. It was once God who dealt out the cards and stacked the jury pack. In an age when few still believe in a deity who cheats at patience, it is to random chance and human wisdom that the hope of justice has been entrusted.

Yet despite all the illogic, the jury has thrived. Over the last three and a half centuries, it has been exported to almost every colony in which the British Empire ever laid its boot. Several abandoned it after independence, among them large democracies such as India and Malaysia, but it retains a presence in former dominions and dependencies from Australia and Hong Kong to Tonga. In the last years of the twentieth century, Spain and Russia actually restored to their citizens a share of the right to judge, and some form of jury exists today in over a quarter of the countries on earth.

In the two countries with the longest common law traditions – the United Kingdom and the United States – the institution is not just tolerated, but venerated. Defendants on both sides of the Atlantic have the right to be tried before their peers whenever they face the prospect of six months or longer in prison, and jury service is officially regarded as something close to a civic sacrament. Politicians often denigrate the system and popular support is far from unequivocal. Even idealists rarely emerge from a stint of jury service with their illusions entirely unchanged. But the ideals prevail. Lord Devlin once declared the jury to be 'the lamp that shows that freedom lives', an institution so inconvenient to tyranny that any competent dictator would be sure to abolish it. The general public and their elected representatives have never quite had the courage of their lack of convictions to disagree.

The jury trial has been a drama for centuries, and no nation has clung to the paraphernalia and props more tenaciously than England.* The courtroom described by Charles Dickens in *Bleak House*, a sepulchral chamber where eighteen wigs and gowns would undulate like swept piano keys whenever a remark fell from His Lordship's lips, still has its equivalents in halls and castles around the country. Even in the modern buildings that are now more typical, where the courts are strip-lit boxes adorned with plastic crests and plywood swords, everyone and everything has its proper place. Judges survey their domains from on high, clad in sashes of scarlet and purple, watching over corralled defendants, boxed jurors, and counsel who remain confined behind long wooden benches. Punctilious dress codes meanwhile identify who may and may not speak. Colours, collars, and waistcoats all have their significance, and the thrall of the horsehair wig remains so potent that any barrister who pleads without hairpiece in place still courts career meltdown.

Reforms are endured rather than embraced. In 1992, more than three centuries after London's lawyers adopted the Parisian periwig as a prudent cringe to the fashions favoured by the newly restored King Charles II, England's Bar Council began to wonder if it was time for a

---

* England and Wales make up a legal unit which, for historical reasons, remains entirely independent of Scotland. In this chapter, as elsewhere in this book, 'England' is used as shorthand for this jurisdiction.

makeover. In the spirit of a sage observation from Lord Donaldson that
there should be no haste about abolishing a tradition that was obsolete a
century ago, inquiries have been conducted ever since. All one can say is
that the wig might, one day, bow out of history.

Judicial theatricality in the United States has been more informal ever
since Thomas Jefferson pleaded with his fellow founding fathers to
'discard the monstrous wig which makes the English judges look like rats
peeping through bunches of oakum'. Advocates yell objections and roam
from jury box to bench with a licence at which their English counterparts
can only wonder. Respect for the presumption of innocence means that
defendants have always sat next to their lawyers, even if regard to the
possibility of guilt means that they might also be shackled to the desk.
The freedoms and liberties have historically been greatest of all in the
South. Spittoons, ashtrays and rifle racks were once part of the region's
judicial woodwork, and although health concerns have put paid to the
consumption of tobacco, the right to bear arms remains firm in some
states. Florida allows its judges to carry hidden handguns on the job, and
in July 2002 Kentucky extended a similar right to prosecutors. State
attorney Sandy McLeod, asked why she might need easy access to a concealed firearm, pointed out that courtrooms were full of criminals. 'We're
dealing with people who are violent offenders,' she explained. '[T]hey'll
kill you over a ham sandwich, if they have the opportunity.'

But wherever the shows are performed, far more unites them than
divides them. All come with the dependable plots and surprise endings
that might be expected of any long-running production. All proceed
according to rules of engagement that suspend reality even as they sim-
ulate it: combining the restraint of a packed elevator with the tension of
a showdown, the etiquette of the courtroom creates a world where witnesses are corkscrewed by courtesy and whispers can echo like screams.
The colourful cast, packed with familiar heroes and villains, is also universal – and at centre stage sits the defendant, whose role is perhaps the
most stylized of all.

The person accused, whether before an English or American court, was
only permitted to give sworn evidence for the first time in the nineteenth
century, and the suspect who can inspire hatred outside the courtroom
typically turns to cipher within it. England's most reviled twentieth-
century criminals, child murderers Ian Brady and Myra Hindley, received

threats so serious that the authorities constructed a bullet-proof dock for their 1966 trial – five years after the Israelis had introduced the precaution for Adolf Eichmann – but to those in court, they seemed more like taxidermal specimens than captured beasts. According to the judge, Justice Fenton Atkinson, 'One watched them day after day, looking for the smallest flicker of an expression indicating some shame or regret or realisation of the horror of what was being unfolded in the evidence, but it never came.' A similar vortex surrounded the notorious Jeffrey Dahmer. When he stood trial in Wisconsin in 1992, having admitted fifteen killings and acts of necrophilia, trepanning and cannibalism, many spectators found it hard to credit that he even looked human. A 19-year-old called Steve Skelton summed up the sense of incredulity. 'It's just kind of amazing that he was nobody special,' he breathlessly told a reporter. 'I figured there'd be some big aura or something like that, but he just kind of walked in and sat down and nothing really happened.'

Few cases better illustrate the strange redundancy of the defendant than that of John Scopes, a 24-year-old sports teacher from Dayton, Tennessee, charged in May 1925 with teaching evolution to his pupils. Specifically, he was said to have 'denie[d] the story of the divine creation of man as taught in the Bible', and taught instead 'that man has descended from a lower order of animals'. The American Civil Liberties Union (ACLU), convinced that the recently enacted prohibition violated the Constitution's guarantees of free speech and freedom from religious interference, had publicly asked for volunteers to break the law in order that it could be challenged. A group of Dayton citizens, assembled around the soda fountain of the town's drugstore, decided that a test case would do wonders for the local economy. Scopes, who had once taught biology for two weeks, was asked if he was game – and although he could not recall ever having mentioned evolution to his pupils, he affably agreed to be a defendant if anyone could 'prove' that he had broken the law. A telegram was duly despatched to the ACLU. Another was sent to William Jennings Bryan, a populist politician thrice-nominated for the presidency by the Democratic Party, who was widely regarded as the most articulate Protestant fundamentalist in the United States. Bryan quickly accepted the invitation to lead the prosecution, and when the ACLU briefed Clarence Darrow – no less renowned for his skills as a defence attorney and a proud agnostic, to boot – the stage was set for an incendiary conflict.

Seekers of sensation, attention, and journalistic copy converged on Dayton from across the United States. While a New Orleans construction company tried persuading the trial judge that he needed a new 20,000-seat stadium, WGN of Chicago made technical arrangements for America's first coast-to-coast wireless broadcast, and a press contingent that would swell to over two hundred began swarming in. H. L. Mencken of Baltimore's *Evening Sun*, whose bleak social Darwinism made for an outlook as unforgiving as that of any fundamentalist, produced the first of a series of blistering polemics against the town's 'yokels', 'buffoons' and 'dupes'; by early July the case was making waves even in faraway Britain, where several newspapers used it as a hook to run diatribes against the stupidity and hypocrisy of America, in general. On the streets hot-dog stands and watermelon vendors set up shop alongside the Anti-Evolution League, which was hawking pamphlets with titles like *Hell and the High Schools* and *God or Gorilla?*, while Deck Carter, self-proclaimed Bible Champion of the World, told anyone who would listen that he was the first person since Joan of Arc to have communicated directly with God. Holy Rollers colonized a church at the edge of town, holding nocturnal services at which they babbled and gyrated amidst kerosene

'Evolution in Tennessee': one 1925 cartoonist's view of the transformation that the Scopes case wrought on primitive Daytonians.

shadows, offering thanks to the Lord for having spared them the evils of newspapers and education. There was even a degree of evolutionary diversity. A 3½-foot dwarf with receding forehead, protruding jaw, plaid suit and brown fedora identified himself as the missing link, while primates came to town from as far afield as Coney Island. The most distinguished was a chimpanzee from Atlanta, Georgia, who perambulated through Dayton in spats, suit, felt hat, and walking stick and let it be known, via his owners, that he was willing to testify for the defence.

It was standing room only in the 700-seat Rhea County courthouse when proceedings began on 10 July 1925. Flies buzzed and dogs panted in the steamy heat, while journalists cranked movie cameras, exploded flash-bulbs and pounded muffled typewriters to record the moment. Judge John T. Raulston then called the throng to order with a reading of the first chapter of the Book of Genesis. It would have boded ill if anyone had been hoping for a fair trial. But they were not. Since Scopes himself had no recollection of breaking the law, the defence had no interest in dispassionate consideration of the evidence, and Darrow positively wanted a conviction in order that he could argue the constitutional issues on appeal. As a result, he now waved through jurors who, according to Mencken, 'glar[ed] at [Darrow] as if they expected him to go off with a sulphurous bang every time he mopped his bald head'. He also committed a more serious dereliction of professional duty. In order to compensate for the absence of prosecution evidence, he instructed three schoolboys to claim that Scopes had taught them evolution, and coached them to give perjurious testimony. To compound his deception – which could have resulted in disbarment had he been found out – he would tell the jury shortly before they retired that Scopes had not testified 'because he could not deny the statements made by the boys'.

Scopes' irrelevance would only increase as the week progressed. Darrow's concern was to put fundamentalism on trial, and he had lined up a dozen theologians and scientists to testify that religious literalism could not be squared with science, and that no sensible Christian would read the Bible literally anyway. Judge Raulston listened to just one – a zoologist who briefly outlined how the earth had changed over the previous six hundred million years – before ruling all the others irrelevant. The truth of evolution was not, he declared on Friday morning, relevant to whether Scopes had taught it. But his attempt to refocus the case was promptly countered by a virtual conspiracy between the lawyers. For Bryan was no more interested than Darrow in what Scopes had actually done. In the hope of proving the Book of Genesis – literally – he now accepted a challenge from Darrow to testify as a biblical expert himself.

Darrow (left) and Bryan (right)

Both lawyers informed Raulston of their agreement on the morning of Monday 20 July 1925, and the judge merely observed that, in view of the heat, it would make sense to conduct the cross-examination on the court-house lawn. Darrow, hoping finally to humiliate the rival whom he had had in his sights for twenty years, had spent the weekend preparing questions with his theological experts. The clash that now ensued would become one of the most famous encounters in American legal history.

Shaded by giant maples from the heat of a Tennessee dog day, Darrow, sweating in braces and homespun shirt, leaned his bulky frame forward and asked whether it was really true that the prophet Jonah had been swallowed by a whale. Bryan, bald and dark-eyed, smiled wryly and flapped his palm leaf fan. 'When I read that a big fish swallowed Jonah,' he declared, 'I believe it, and I believe in a God who can make a whale and can make a man and make both do what He pleases.' Did he also believe, asked Darrow, that Joshua had made the sun stop in the sky? Bryan con-firmed that he did, but refused to be drawn on whether it was the earth or the sun that had ceased orbiting. The Bible, he pointed out, did not say. It was the first sign of the strategy that Bryan intended to use – namely,

honest credulity – and he was about to learn that measured fundamentalism could sound at least as inane as the full-blooded variety. Bryan's own
co-counsel, realizing the risks, pleaded with Judge Raulston to rule the
questioning irrelevant; but like a turkey strutting towards a Thanksgiving
dinner, Bryan insisted that he be allowed to continue. 'They came here to
try revealed religion,' he declared to applause. 'I am here to defend it, and
they can ask me any questions they please.' It was not long before he
began to stumble. When Darrow asked for the precise date of the Flood,
Bryan told him that he had never tried to work it out. 'What do you
think?' demanded Darrow. 'I do not think about things I don't think
about,' replied Bryan. Quick as a flash, Darrow asked him if 'you think
about things you do think about?' 'Well . . .' – Bryan hesitated, as laughter
rippled through the court – 'sometimes'. He soon recovered a degree of
precision. The Tower of Babel had been constructed in the second half
of the 23rd century BC, he confirmed, and it was about a century later that
the Flood had destroyed every creature that did not get onto Noah's Ark,
with the possible exception of the fish. But he then equivocated again
when asked how old human civilization might be. Subjects like history
had, he explained, never interested him. Neither had comparative religion. Nor had science. Bryan's own ark was taking in dangerous amounts
of water by the late afternoon, as he tacked a lurching course between
judiciousness and ignorance, and it was finally overwhelmed when
Darrow asked if he believed that the earth had been created in six days.
'Not six days of twenty-four hours,' came the reply. The admission that
God might use figures of speech stunned almost everyone. Even Darrow
was reduced to momentary silence, while gasps filled the court and one
voice was heard to hiss, 'What does he want to say that for?' Bryan
explained, flustered, that different people might honestly disagree about
the length of a biblical day. His personal 'impression', however, was that
each might in fact have lasted millions of years.

The end came, appropriately enough, when Darrow turned to the
subject of the Fall. Bryan agreed that, following its temptation of Eve, the
serpent had been condemned by God to crawl upon its belly but refused
to contemplate how it had moved around before then. Darrow asked if it
might have walked on its tail. 'I have no way to know,' he declared. Visions
of pogoing pythons conjured a great whoop from the audience, and
even Bryan finally realized that it was time to shut up. '[T]his man, who

does not believe in a God, is trying to use a court in Tennessee [to slur at the Bible]', he bellowed, his voice rising to a shriek. Darrow responded by shaking his fist, and retorted that he was asking about 'fool ideas that no intelligent Christian on earth believes'. Raulston called a halt to the proceedings, and John Scopes would recall four decades later that Bryan was 'left alone on that green, spacious lawn, a forgotten forlorn man'. Before the bar of twentieth-century history, the case was over. All that remained was for Dayton's jurors to have their say. After hearing Darrow tell them that 'we cannot even explain to you that we think you should return a verdict of not guilty' they took nine minutes to convict Scopes.

The reverberations of the case have never quite stopped rumbling. Bryan would drop dead less than a week later, providing perfect dramatic resolution and giving birth to folk memories, later consolidated in an Oscar-nominated movie, *Inherit the Wind*, that enshrined the contest at Dayton as a triumph for rational progress. The truth was considerably less clear-cut. Bryan's expiration notwithstanding, he was in many ways victorious. A technical error in the fine of $100 imposed on Scopes resulted in his conviction being overturned on appeal, with the result that Darrow was unable to pursue the constitutional issues in a federal court. All mention of evolution was thereupon deleted from school textbooks throughout Tennessee. Only in 1968 did the Supreme Court finally declare it unconstitutional to forbid teaching the subject. The issue remains contentious, albeit that it has been reversed: fundamentalists are now complaining that science courses fail to give equal time to tales of miraculous creation. Even Bryan's intellectual legacy lives on. In January 2000, no less a figure than George W. Bush declared that 'the verdict is still out on how God created the earth'. But although the Scopes case crystallized a controversy that remains an issue of moment, the person at its centre was all but lost to history. From the moment that he entered his plea to the moment of his conviction, John Scopes had said not a single word.

The conduct of Darrow and Bryan at Dayton in 1925 does not just exemplify how lawyers hog the judicial limelight. It also shows how the arguments that they advance sometimes bear a connection that is at best coincidental to the facts supposedly in dispute: a problem that has been earing them a bad press for centuries. Those Athenians who prosecuted

public offences for a living were known as *sykophants*, and they were so
disdained that defendants often reminded jurors that an acquital would
serve to spite the meddlesome *sykophant* who had brought the case. Plato
proposed, in a similar vein, that too many trials were a sign of distemper
in the body politic, and idealists have been following his lead for more
than two millennia. Thomas More's Utopians found lawyers unnecessary;
the Puritans of colonial Massachusetts banned them; and Shakespeare's
Dick the Butcher famously fantasized that the first thing to do was to kill
them all. Plato also blasted the first rhetoricians, known as the Sophists,
for their boast that they could turn weak arguments into strong ones, and
dreamers of a better world have been making a similar complaints ever
since. Adolf Hitler put the objection with characteristic force. The legal
profession, he warned, is 'essentially unclean, for the advocate is entitled
to lie to the court'.

Historical examples of the finagling lawyer abound, but few finagled
with more panache than William Howe, one half of a legendary law firm
that thrived in the Lower East Side of New York City during the late nineteenth century. Over the course of a career during which he represented
more than six hundred accused murderers – a larger number than the rest
of New York's criminal bar combined – there was very little that he did
not do to defend the indefensible. Single clients, no matter how
Neanderthal, might find themselves in court with pretty wives and cheru-
bic children. Though fastidiously groomed and bulky as a walrus, Howe
once delivered an entire jury speech on his knees. Even his elegance was
eloquent. He would begin a case in jaunty style, glistening with jewellery
in a dove-grey suit and red tie, but as it progressed the demeanour would
darken. Watch chains, rings and tiepins would be daily discarded and
suits would descend through a spectrum of charcoals and blues until the
day of final submissions – when he invariably arrived at court sombre as
a pallbearer, with countenance to match.

Howe's oratory spanned only the short distance from flattery to
pathos, and its delivery came in an accent that regularly flitted back to his
birthplace in London's East End; but his control of the courtroom was as
alchemical as it was judicial. At least once, he literally terrified a jury into
submission. The story was later told, with great admiration, by Howe's
opponent in the 1891 case: prosecutor Francis L. Wellman. Ella Nelson
stood accused of shooting her lover and for most of Howe's summation,

the young woman sat sobbing in a chair while gloom enfolded the room. 'It was well on toward ten o'clock,' recalled Wellman, and '[e]verybody connected with the case was under a high nervous tension.' As Howe boomed towards his more or less irrelevant conclusion, he 'went behind [Nelson's] chair ... forced her hands from her face [and] ... dug his nails deep into her flesh. The unexpected movement of her lawyer, together with the sudden pain he inflicted, caused the woman to utter a piercing scream ... It would be impossible to describe [its] effect ...[but t]he jury seemed completely petrified . . . I saw the case was over from that moment.' Wellman acknowledged that there could be no rational basis for predicting the jurors' response, but Howe's instincts were vindicated. Ella Nelson, they found, had pulled the trigger of her gun by accident – not just once, not just twice, but four times.

Howe's most remarkable talent, a skill that won him plaudits from colleagues and hoodlums alike, was an apparent ability to weep at will. Although Wellman suspected that he used an onion-scented handkerchief to get in the mood, the ducts, once opened, flowed steady as a siphon, and never were they deployed more effectively than during his summation in 1887 for a client called Edward Unger. The trial had left Unger with not so much his foot on the scaffold as his neck in the noose. He had admitted his hatred of the victim, one August Bohle. He acknowledged battering him with a hammer, dismembering his body, and sending his limbs and trunk in a box to Baltimore. He also accepted that he had taken Bohle's head to Brooklyn and dropped it off an East River paddleboat. It was hard to identify any doubt, let alone a reasonable one, from the evidence. But as the handkerchief hit Howe's forehead and his eyes began to shine, an argument, if not quite a defence, swirled out of the maelstrom. Unger had three children, including two daughters who had been clinging to him throughout the trial, and – although Howe begged the jurors not to let that sight cloud their judgment – it was to their tragedy that he turned. For Edward Unger's only crime, he insisted, had been to spare the little ones the sight of death. He was no guiltier than the girl being dandled on his knee. 'It was his son that cut up his body,' he sobbed. 'It was that beautiful child that used the saw; it was the elder sister that throw [sic] the head in the river.' Reminding the jurors that there were no eyewitnesses to the killing, he pleaded with them not to make up that deficiency with logic. 'Did you leave your homes to hang a man upon inference or your reasoning?' he demanded. 'God forbid.' The point was, in every sense, a rhetorical one. Unger was found not guilty of murder.

The skill with which Howe could cry was exceptional, but the existence of his talent was not. At the same time that he was jerking tears from Manhattan jurors, the Tennessee Supreme Court had cause to consider the appropriateness of crying counsel more generally. It did not only reject a claim that the public displays of emotion were wrong; it affirmed that they might be positively desirable things. 'Tears have always been considered legitimate arguments before a jury,' it ruled in 1897. 'Indeed, if counsel has them at his command, it may be seriously questioned whether it is not his professional duty to shed them whenever proper occasion arises.'

Judicial weeping remains a vibrant tradition in parts of the United States, nowadays kept alive primarily by prosecutors, and courts of appeal remain almost as sympathetic as they were in 1897. In order to overturn a conviction, a defendant must show that the prosecutor's tears were deliberate or that they directly prejudiced the likelihood of an acquittal, and none has ever succeeded in doing so. The issue arises most often south of the Mason-Dixon line and was ruled upon most recently in January 2003, when Florida's Supreme Court declined to grant a retrial to Dusty Ray Spencer, who complained that his prosecutor had cried while asking the jury to convict him of capital murder. Its judges noted that the court below had found that she had only 'quavered' during her summation. She had in any event turned away and 'composed herself' before continuing. Because Spencer had produced no proof that she had physically shed a tear there was therefore no unlawful error, and his lethal injection could proceed.

An emotionally incontinent lawyer is rarely a pleasant sight, and a prosecutor who is unable or unwilling to keep the quavering under control when a man's life is at stake inspires even less admiration. But the simple fact that lawyers exploit jurors' feelings is a spurious basis for criticizing them. Independent advocates are important – as defendants from Salem to Moscow might have agreed – and any community that aims not just to do justice, but to show it being done, has to allow them to advance emotional claims as well as reasoned argument. Western legal systems have been doing so at least since the days when Athenian defendants would routinely parade their wives and children in court. Even Socrates, while loftily telling his judges that he would not flaunt his family before them, made sure to mention his three sons, two of whom were 'only children'. Three centuries later, Cicero concluded the speech conventionally regarded as his greatest, *Pro Milone*, by telling his judges through choked sobs: 'But I must stop now. I can no longer speak for tears – and my client has forbidden me from using tears in his defence.' Such ruses may seem cynical, and the personal motivations that underlie them might even *be* cynical – but the words uttered can also go to the heart of what justice means.

Examples are necessarily better spoken than recorded, but exceptions exist and one of the best comes, again, from the career of Clarence Darrow. Indeed, the speech concerned – his summation in a 1926 murder case that he took on immediately after the Scopes trial – has strong claim to be the finest forensic address of the twentieth century.

His client was a 22-year-old black student called Henry Sweet, and the charge arose out of the decision of his brother, Dr Ossian Sweet, to leave the overcrowded slums of Detroit's East Side for a new home in its leafy – and overwhelmingly white – suburbs. Ossian Sweet had studied in Vienna and Paris, but the journey across the colour bar was, in every sense but geographical, the longest that he would ever make. Detroit's black population had soared thirteenfold in just sixteen years as its booming automobile industry had sucked up Southern migrants, and the city's whites were turning violent. When Sweet took possession of his new house on the morning of 8 September 1925, a cross had recently been burned on the town hall steps; and he had personally received murder threats, directed not just towards him, but at his wife and baby daughter. A 'Waterworks Improvement Association' had meanwhile been set up by his neighbours to 'render constructive social and civic service' to the area. Sweet was under no illusions about what that meant. He left his child with her grandmother. He asked Henry Sweet, along with other friends and relations, to stay at the house for the first few nights. And among the first items that they unpacked were ten guns and 391 rounds of ammunition.

Sullen spectators, loitering on the street, dispersed without incident on the first night. But they drifted back during the following day – and by the late afternoon, the knots were coalescing. Ossian Sweet, who had spent the day at his medical surgery, whiled away the early evening playing cards with the others in the house until, as dusk fell, a missile crashed onto the roof. Everyone seized their guns, and the lights were turned out. A rock then hurtled through a window – at which point Henry Sweet arrived, almost falling in from the street, having just run a gauntlet of abuse and spittle from the surging crowd. The door was pulled behind him, and stones began to hail onto the wooden walls and roof. In the darkness, amidst screams and shouts, a fusillade of shots cracked out from the top floor, and Leon Breiner, one of the members of the mob, fell fatally injured to the ground. A group of police officers, who had been watching from a distance, was finally spurred to action. The rioters were pushed aside, and the eleven people in Dr Sweet's home were charged with murder.

When their trial ended in a hung jury, prosecutors chose to retry just Henry Sweet because he, unlike the others, had admitted to firing his rifle. Their hope was that a conviction would persuade everyone else to plead guilty without a fight, and by the time the evidence was in, they had good reason to anticipate success. In order to acquit him, the jury had to conclude that gunfire was, or might have been, a necessary and proportionate response to the dangers that Henry Sweet had faced, and supporting evidence was scant. He himself had not testified. Although the sheer number of prosecution eyewitnesses – seventy-one – undercut the state's theory that there had in fact been no mob outside the Sweet residence, all those who gave evidence had sworn to the tranquil atmosphere on the evening of 9 September. But the most formidable obstacle to acquittal transcended what any single witness did or did not say. From the moment that the twelve jurors were sworn, every one white, the crucial question was not whether they would be able to weigh up the testimony before assessing Henry Sweet's fears. It was whether they could appreciate his fears at all.

Everything hung on Darrow's powers of oratory, and on 18 May 1926, the 69-year-old leant on his lectern, scanned the jury box, and began a summation that he would later characterize as 'one of the strongest and most satisfactory arguments that I ever delivered'. A cardinal rule of rhetoric, as old as Aristotle, is that speeches should begin by making the audience receptive to the argument that it is about to hear. Most lawyers honour the prologue by complimenting jurors on their attentiveness or

lobbing them a joke. But Darrow's voice, harsh as gravel, was never well
suited to flattery, and gentleness was not his style. His way of softening up
listeners was to punch them in the stomach.

> I shall begin about where [the prosecutor] Mr. Moll began yester-
> day. He says lightly, gentlemen, that this isn't a race question. This
> is a murder case. We don't want any prejudice; we don't want the
> other side to have any. Race and colour have nothing to do with
> this case.

> I am going to try to be as fair as I can with you gentlemen [but]
> I insist that there is nothing but prejudice in this case. [I]f it was
> reversed and eleven white men had shot and killed a black while
> protecting their home and their lives against a mob of blacks,
> nobody would have dreamed of having them indicted. I know
> what I am talking about, and so do you. They would have been
> given medals instead.

> I want to put this square to you, gentlemen. I haven't any doubt
> but that every one of you are prejudiced against coloured people.
> You will overcome it, I believe, in the trial of this case. But they
> tell me there is no race prejudice, and it is plain nonsense, and
> nothing else.

Darrow then turned his attention to Leon Breiner, the victim in the case.
Several witnesses had claimed that he had been doing little more than
smoking his pipe and shooting the breeze on a late summer evening.
Although none of the claims was particularly convincing, a less confident
speaker than Darrow might have paid lip service to the niceties of respect-
ing the dead. He had already staked out high moral ground, however, and
was not about to cede an inch in favour of a man who had died part of an
incipient lynch mob. Instead of pussyfooting around his grave, Darrow
pissed on it.

> 'Mr. Moll says that I wiggled and squirmed every time they men-
> tioned Breiner. He said that I don't like to hear them talk about
> Breiner. I don't, gentlemen, and I might have shown it. I don't like

to hear the State's Attorney talk about the blood of a victim. It has
such a mussy sound. I wish they would leave it out. I will be frank
with you about it. I don't think it has any place in a case. I think
it tends to create prejudice and feeling and it has no place, and it
is always dangerous. And perhaps – whether I showed it or not,
my friend read my mind. I don't like it.

Now, gentlemen, as he talked about Breiner, I am going to talk
about him, and it isn't easy, either. It isn't easy to talk about the
dead, unless you slobber over them and I am not going to slobber over Breiner. Who was he? He was a conspirator in as foul a
conspiracy as was ever hatched in a community; in a conspiracy
to drive from their homes a little family of black people and not
only that, but to destroy these blacks and their home.

The summation lasted eight more hours. Darrow tore apart the testimony of the prosecution witnesses and then, watched by hundreds of
spectators, at least two-thirds of them black, he told a tale that had never
before been heard in an American court. Several of those present would
recall it as the most moving speech that they had ever heard. Judge Frank
Murphy, who would later be appointed to the Supreme Court, was one of
many who ended the afternoon in tears.

[The prosecutor] said that my client here was a coward. A coward,
gentlemen. Who are the cowards in this case? Cowards, gentlemen! Eleven people with black skins, eleven people, gentlemen,
whose ancestors did not come to America because they wanted
to, but were brought here in slave ships, to toil for nothing, for
the whites – whose lives have been taken in nearly every state in
the Union – they have been victims of riots all over this land of
the free. They have had to take what is left after everybody else
has grabbed what he wanted. The only place where he has been
put in front is on the battlefield. When we are fighting we give
him a chance to die, and the best chance. But, everywhere else, he
has been food for the flames, and the ropes, and the knives, and
the guns and hate of the white, regardless of law and liberty, and
the common sentiments of justice that should move men. Were

they cowards? No, gentlemen. They went in and faced a mob seeking to tear them to bits. Call them something else beside cowards. The cowardly curs were in the mob gathered there with the backing of the law.

He concluded with the simplest of appeals. Having set out the defence versions of the facts, and argued how to judge them, he could finally appeal to pure empathy.

Do you think [Henry Sweet] ought to be taken out of his school and sent to the penitentiary? All right, gentlemen, if you think so, do it. But if you do, gentlemen, if you should ever look into the face of your own boy, or your own brother, or look into your own heart, you will regret it in sackcloth and ashes. You know, if he committed any offence, it was being loyal and true to his brother whom he loved. I know where you will send him, and it will not be to the penitentiary. I have watched day after day, these black, tense faces that have crowded this court. To them it is life. Not one of their colour sits on this jury. Their fate is in the hands of twelve whites. Their eyes are fixed on you, their hearts go out to you, and their hopes hang on your verdict. I ask you, on behalf of this defendant, in the name of progress and of the human race, to return a verdict of not guilty in this case.

The jury were away for four hours. As they filed back into their box, Darrow stared hard at the ground. On hearing them pronounce Henry Sweet not guilty, he slumped so low that the prosecutor leaned over to check that he had not fainted. 'I'm all right,' he murmured. 'I've heard that verdict before.' He had in fact ended his speech confident, uncertain only about one man who had listened with a poker face throughout. 'I wonder if he is for us or against us?' Darrow had asked his co-counsel. It later turned out that the juror had lit a cigar and settled down with a book on entering the jury room, telling his eleven colleagues not to disturb him until they were ready to acquit.

While the criminal lawyer may have the best lines, star billing must go to the judge. Three centuries after judges lost their power to veto a jury verdict[*]

---

* See p. 93.

they remain the gatekeepers of the law – guarding its logical portals and counter-intuitive mysteries with the wisdom of a druid and the jealousy of an ogre. Abraham Lincoln once described an anecdotal judge who would 'hang a man for blowing his nose in the street . . . but . . . quash the indict-ment if it failed to specify what hand he blew it with', and life has produced countless obsessives who were only too real. There was Alabama Supreme Court Justice Roy Moore, so anxious in August 2001 to prove his humility that he surreptitiously installed a two-ton granite version of the Ten Commandments in the lobby of his courthouse. Judge Sheldon M. Schapiro of Florida's Broward County is another example: reprimanded in 2003 for over-exuberantly oppressive activities which had included inter-rupting one defence attorney in a sexual battery case with a device that simulated the sound of a flushing toilet. The possible examples are endless and it is, in fact, hard to imagine many steps that some US judge, some-where, has not taken to maintain decorum in court. None has yet killed for the sake of legal propriety, it is true, but that may only be a matter of time. In 1992, Judge J. Leonard Fleet became the second Florida judge in ten years to draw a revolver on an unruly defendant. 'I don't miss,' he warned.

Criminal trial judges undergo an election of some sort in over half the states of the USA, and as one might expect of a judiciary with democrat-ic mandates to win, the fierce independence has always been especially robust when handing down punishments. The conspiracy prosecution of the Chicago Eight, at which the country's most prominent deviants were accused of agreeing to disrupt the 1968 Democratic convention (inspir-ing Abbie Hoffman's memorable: 'Agreement? We couldn't agree on lunch') saw Judge Julius Hoffman issue 159 citations for contempt – 38 of them against defence lawyers – and at one point order that Black Panther Bobby Seale be gagged and tied to a chair. Judge J. Manuel Banales of Corpus Christi, Texas, hit the headlines in May 2001 after requiring four-teen convicted child molesters to display signs on their houses and cars reading 'Danger! Registered Sex Offender!' The revival of Elizabethan justice was as shameful as might have been hoped: the men's families were threatened, some lost jobs or homes, and at least one tried to kill himself. Arguably less cruel, but certainly more unusual, was the penalty imposed on Curtis Lee Robin Jr by another Texan, Judge Buddie Hahn, in March 2003. Robin had pleaded guilty to whipping his stepson with a car aerial, and it was said that the boy had also been locked out at nights – causing

Hahn to offer him the choice of thirty days in jail, or thirty nights in a used two-foot by three-foot doghouse. Robin's counsel mounted a protest of sorts, arguing that his client merited a larger and more luxurious model, but when the judge would not budge the defendant went for the kennel.

English judges, their fancy dress notwithstanding, have always been less inclined to make a splash. In their wily way they have, however, developed methods of courtroom domination that can make even the most trigger-happy US jurist look like an amateur. Several cantankerous, self-important and unhinged examples are legends in their own courtrooms, but only a handful have become emblematic of judicial obtuseness to a wider world. One who did make the leap was Michael Argyle, largely as a result of his conduct at one particular trial: the 1971 prosecution for obscenity and indecency of Jim Anderson, Felix Dennis, and Richard Neville, youthful publishers of an underground magazine called *Oz*.

The case arose out of an issue that the trio had delegated for editing to a group of schoolchildren. It contained several sexually explicit images,

and one that caused the authorities' particular concern showed Rupert the Bear – a distant and *déclassé* relative of Winnie the Pooh – equipped with an erection and eager to explore the genitalia of a comatose old woman. As with most experiments of the era, one presumably had to be there; but the authorities' decision to flatten the three publishers with a triple-barrelled indictment carrying a potential life sentence was more excessive than the magazine's contents could ever have been. In the heady atmosphere of 1971 London, culture and counter-culture were soon limbering up for a clash of civilizations. Conservatives hoped at last to drain the permissive society's swamp, while their opponents saw it as a watershed for sexual, artistic and emotional freedom – and each side had its champion. John Mortimer, a luminary of liberal Britain who would soon be scripting the first episode of *Rumpole of the Bailey*, headed the defence. The forces of orthodoxy had His Honour Major Michael Argyle – and his handling of the trial would make it one of the most notorious in modern British legal history.

Any prosecution in the Old Bailey is a solemn affair. The court has more peculiar customs than any other in England, and several were in evidence during the six weeks of the *Oz* trial. Bailiffs in tight breeches and patent leather boots regularly manifested themselves for no apparent reason. Judge Argyle once opened proceedings clutching a bunch of posies, at the head of a silent procession of sword-bearers and tipstaffs: a ritual still observed at the court several times each year, lest anyone forget the barristers and judges who contracted typhoid from unwashed prisoners below the building in 1750. But magnificently glum though such ceremonies could be, it was Argyle himself who did most to suppress spontaneity in court.

Argyle, an amateur boxer with a passion for breeding whippets, was never going to have much affinity for the defendants, whom he would later characterize as heroin addicts, drug peddlers, and professional pornographers. The repulsion was not, however, *entirely* instinctive. Throughout the trial, he continued to receive written death threats from the 'Friends of *Oz*', and although it would turn out that the author was the deranged wife of his own court clerk, the effect was to convince the powers-that-were that the dock contained some extremely dangerous men. Alsatians and three armed officers sat secretly stationed behind Argyle's bench whenever the court was in session, ready to pounce upon or shoot homicidal hippies as and when required. They guarded his family home during the weekend, and on nights during the week, when he made do with a suite in the Savoy, a fourth officer surveyed the surrounding airspace from the hotel roof to prevent a would-be assassin from abseiling through his windows. Even with such precautions, Argyle would eventually come to believe that a Friend of *Oz* had poisoned one of his whippets. The tensions were encapsulated by Detective Inspector Frederick Luff's account of how one defendant had concluded his interview with the words, 'Right on!' Argyle, who was taking a longhand note of the evidence, peered up from his pad. 'Write on?' he murmured suspiciously. 'But you had finished?' 'Not W-R-I-T-E, my Lord, but R-I-G-H-T,' explained Luff. 'It is', he added grimly, 'a *revolutionary* expression.'

Argyle was not opposed to levity in principle. He would once, for example, cheerfully moan to a jury that the absence of television coverage of a certain Test match between England and the West Indies was 'enough to make an Orthodox Jew want to join the Nazi Party'. But courtroom mirth always had to be on his terms, and those terms were tight indeed at the *Oz* trial. Such moments of light relief that occurred came at his expense, rather than his instigation. When jazz musician George Melly expressed his belief that women who received oral sex were not necessarily harmed by the experience, Argyle, puzzled by a Latin word that he had used, interjected. 'Well, pardon me,' he began. 'For those of us who did not have a classical education, what do you mean by the word *cunnilinctus*?' Melly smiled understandingly. 'I'm sorry, my Lord,' he apologized. 'I've been a bit inhibited by the architecture. I will try to use better known expressions in the future. "Sucking" or "blowing", your Lordship. Or "going down" or "gobbling" is another alternative. Another expression used in my naval days, your Lordship, was "yodelling in the canyon".' Laughter, in time-honoured fashion, erupted in the gallery, and Argyle, performing the role of pantomime villain no less on cue, threatened to have it cleared. At another point the subject of dildos arose and Argyle blanched when told what the word meant. 'We had better call it an imitation male penis,' he suggested softly. Richard Neville pricked up his ears. 'Your Honour,' he volunteered. 'I think the word male is unnecessary.'

The prosecutor, Brian Leary, was significantly more urbane than Argyle, but he too was determined to drain humour from the court – for professional reasons. His job was to prove that *Oz* was likely to deprave or corrupt its likely readers and possessed no artistic merit, questions that rested squarely on the sympathies of the jurors, and one of the criminal law's golden rules is that a laughing jury is not one that convicts. Leary duly decided to subject a magazine that was best viewed through prisms narcotic or hallucinogenic to microscopic analysis and, confronted with defence witnesses who were outraged by nothing so much as the very notion of indecency laws, he could usually rely on others to up the ante further. Jim Anderson's evidence provided some of the best, or worst, moments of all. Like all the most effective English prosecutors, Leary was ineffably polite, but could swivel from charm to savagery on the turn of a single miscalculation – and Anderson provided several. Asked, for example, to explain his use of the words 'youthful genius' on *Oz*'s editorial page to describe the cartoon of a priapic Rupert Bear, he began uncertainly to talk about 'the juxtaposition of two ideas ... the childhood symbol of innocence'. 'Making Rupert Bear *fuck*?' bellowed Leary. Anderson – as startled as anyone else – could respond only with a plaintive, 'Er . . . yes.' At another point, the prosecutor asked him if there was anything at all that he would consider indecent. Anderson, reluctant on principle to make concessions, eventually suggested that urinating in the courtroom might just qualify.* Leary tentatively proposed that masturbating in front of one's children might also do the trick. Anderson did not sound entirely sure. 'Well, I don't . . . it depends on the family circumstances,' he replied. 'The *what*?' yelled Leary, thumping his bench and turning with incredulity towards the jurors. For several long seconds, a phantom vision of Anderson, thwacking his tackle in front of a group of curious toddlers, billowed through the court – and only as it dispelled did Leary's gaze return to the witness box. 'May we have that reply again?' he asked quietly.

Only a handful of witnesses gave quite as good as they got, but disc jockey John Peel was one of them. Called to testify to the artistic merits of a music review, he used the phrase 'making love' at one point, and Leary pretended to be taken aback. 'Yes . . . I see you used the expression "making love" . . . So can we take it that you would consider it in bad taste to use the word "fuck"?' In his flat Liverpudlian accent, so monotonous that candour was indistinguishable from contempt, Peel did not miss a beat. 'I just felt because I was in court I should say "make love"', he explained dolefully. '[B]ut', he added, 'everybody else seems to say "fuck", so I will say "fuck" as well.'

For the same reasons that Leary wanted to avoid humour, the defence tried hard to introduce it, but the efforts came to naught. John Mortimer's eye for absurdity was keener than most, but irony could not be long maintained in a courtroom where three men potentially faced

---

* Interestingly enough, Anderson's answer happened to have some legal authority on its side. Chief Baron Pollock, considering an indecency case in 1848, recalled that when he was younger, judges would routinely relieve themselves in court, 'even in the presence of ladies', in a porcelain vase that was kept specifically for the purpose in one corner of the room. The practice would, he noted pensively, 'perhaps . . . be considered indecent now.' See *R. v. Webb* (1848), 2 Car. and K. 933 at 938, in Max A. Robertson and Geoffrey Ellis (eds), *The English Reports*, 176 vols (London, 1900–30), 175: 394.

life in jail for having printed some rude pictures. The joys of drugs and free love were analysed by various psychologists, while Professor Hans Eysenck came down from Oxford University to confirm wearily that *Oz* would have no harmful effects on its readers (except perhaps 'on their prose style'). Mortimer's own closing speech revolved around sombre assertions that laughter was a great cleanser and lamentations that Brian Leary had anaesthetized his best jokes. The lawyers' best chance of a deliberate laugh came courtesy of Geoffrey Robertson, a young law student who had volunteered his services to the defence. After toying with the possibility of calling Groucho Marx to give expert evidence, he asked a witness who was already on board, psychologist Edward de Bono, how they might best puncture the pomposity of Argyle's court. De Bono, who had just written a bestseller called *Lateral Thinking* about novel approaches to problem solving, returned with a brightly coloured clockwork bird. He had a plan. He would keep the bird in his pocket, fully wound, as he testified, and at a critical moment of his cross-examination would yank it out and set it flapping across the room. 'It always helps on solemn occasions,' he assured Robertson. 'I'll explain to the judge and jury how the surprise has worked to unlock their think-ing processes, to enable them to look at the evidence with a more open mind.' The impact on Argyle's mind would have been a wonder to behold, but it will always be one of legal history's great what-ifs. De Bono went on to give evidence with panache, expertly responding to questions from Brian Leary concerning, for example, why Rupert had such a large penis ('What size do you think would be natural?') but he never found the moment to let his bird fly.

At the end of the case, Argyle made his most decisive intervention of all. English judges, unlike those in the United States or Scotland, are required to summarize the evidence and permitted to comment on it – a power that allows them to augment the winks, smirks, and yawns deployed by judges everywhere with an open expression of their views. The summing-up invariably pays lip service to the principle of jury inde-pendence – typically, by ending a devastating criticism with the observation that, 'It is, of course, entirely a matter for you' – but its influ-ence is potentially huge, and Argyle spun it out for all it was worth. His seven-hour address dissected the defence case with observations that were accompanied with expressions of perplexity or pain, and each mention of

Oz itself brought on a display of undisguised repulsion. After lifting the magazine by his fingertips, as though unsavoury fluids might yet ooze from it, he let it drop limply to his desk, muttering, with obscure significance, 'Well. There you are.'

When the jurors, predominantly working class and with an average age of sixty, convicted the defendants on 28 July 1971 – albeit only by a 10–1 majority and only on the less serious charges – Argyle hoped to wreak some serious punishment. He remanded all three in custody, in order to wean them off the heroin to which he by now presumed them to be addicted and to obtain psychiatric assessments of their mental problems. On being advised that they were not psychotic, he imprisoned them for between nine and fifteen months and ordered that Richard Neville be deported to his Australian homeland.

But with the end of the trial, the spell that Argyle had cast for six weeks was suddenly shattered. Removed from the Old Bailey to jail, the defendants were released by other judges within days, pending their appeals, and his summing-up was soon ruled to have overstepped the mark differentiating legitimate comment from legal error. Felix Dennis, who had been given the shortest sentence on the basis that he was 'very much less intelligent' than the other defendants, would get a more personal revenge in 1995. Argyle, by then retired and devoting himself to occasional whippet breeding and full-time duties as president of Restore the Death Penalty International, decided to revisit the trial that had thrust him to national prominence. *Oz* had, he explained in an article for *The Spectator*, been more than just a smutty magazine. It had been a front for an immense criminal conspiracy, devoted to the importation of truckloads of continental pornography and the supply of drugs to 'state schools, youth clubs and such' across England. Although he was determined to have the last word, it no longer belonged to him. Dennis, who had overcome any intellectual disadvantages to establish an international publishing house worth several hundred million pounds, was able at last to turn the judicial tables and extract both an apology and substantial damages for libel.

The last participant in the jury trial consists of the twelve decision makers themselves. Their continued existence has inspired countless theories and thousands of articles, but whatever the jury's most fundamental function might be – and this chapter concludes with one suggestion – wisdom certainly falls far down the list of its attributes. Verdicts often seem to pivot on body language and the attractiveness of lawyers or witnesses, and jurors have slipped even further off the rational rails. One Newcastle juror was dismissed in 1998 when he asked for the defendant's birthday in order to draw up a horoscope. A Kentucky jury two years later resolved its doubts in a murder case by tossing a silver dollar. Perhaps the most demonstrably irrational jury of recent times was one that found itself sequestered in a Sussex hotel for a double murder case in 1994. Four of its members decided, several drinks into a bout of nocturnal deliberations, to consult a ouija board. They soon found themselves in communication with the spirit of one Harry Fuller, one of the victims in the case, who confirmed that the defendant had shot both him and his wife. As everyone present except the jury foreman broke down in tears, the tumbler then began to spell out Fuller's message: 'vote guilty tomorrow'. The advice was relayed over breakfast to the remaining eight jurors, who swiftly followed it, but one was sufficiently troubled then to contact the defendant's solicitors. Although prosecutors valiantly argued at the consequent appeal that there was nothing improper about a jury attempting to communicate with the dead, the Court of Appeal disagreed and ordered a retrial.* The defendant was reconvicted, on the basis of deliberations, or forces, that would this time stay hidden.

But any account of the jury that focuses on stupidity, superstition, and the influence of the paranormal risks misleading. Far more common is the jury that tries its hardest, but simply gets it wrong. There is, regrettably, no shortage of examples to prove the point. One particularly notorious case was that of the Birmingham Six, a set of Irish defendants

---

* To be precise, prosecutors relied on the fact that English law forbade jurors from disclosing their deliberations and argued that the Court of Appeal was therefore barred from investigating the ouija board session at all. The Court agreed that it could not hear evidence about deliberations, but circumvented any difficulties by finding that the seance had taken place during a *break* in those deliberations. The upshot was that English juries remained at liberty for several more years to invoke spirits, toss coins and cast horoscopes, so long as they did it within the confines of the jury room. Only in 2004 did the House of Lords overrule the earlier decision: *R. v. Mirza* [2004] 2 WLR 201.

who fell victim to one of the many miscarriages of justice that England produced during the 1970s.

On the evening of Thursday 21 November 1974, IRA bombs tore through two pubs in central Birmingham, leaving twenty-one people dead and more than a hundred and sixty injured. Although Britain was in the middle of a sustained IRA bombing campaign, the explosions were the first to be aimed at mainland targets with no military connection, and they unleashed panic. The Irish in 1970s England had an extremely tenuous social status anyway, just one step above the darker immigrants from southern Asia and the Caribbean who were at the bottom of the heap, and ordinary men and women now found themselves spat upon and abused. Several Irish-owned organizations and businesses were torched. In Birmingham itself car workers downed tools to demand the reintroduction of capital punishment, and the country at large saw anti-terrorist legislation rushed onto the statute book within eight days. Even *The Guardian*, England's traditional journalistic standard bearer for civil liberties, was overwhelmed. 'A liberal society cannot let its freedom, and its concern for the rights of the individual be abused in order that it shall be torn to pieces,' it warned. 'From now on anybody who complains that he is being harassed by the police bomb squad will find a less than sympathetic audience.' It was only too right.

Five Irishmen who had left Birmingham by train just before the bombs exploded were arrested at the ferry terminal of the small town of Morecambe. All had been en route to the funeral of a Birmingham IRA bomber who had been blown up by his own explosives a week before, and although nothing directly linked them to the pub blasts their movements were enough to arouse suspicion. Three carloads of detectives from the West Midlands Serious Crimes Squad, commanded by Detective Superintendent George Reade, were soon speeding through the night from Birmingham to take over the investigation. An experienced forensic scientist, Dr Frank Skuse, was simultaneously summoned to Morecambe, and on arrival he took swabs from the hands of the arrested men and tested them for the presence of nitroglycerine.

The men could not know it, but their luck had just taken a vertical nosedive. The Serious Crimes Squad would one day stand revealed as the most systematically brutal police unit ever to have existed in England, a force that was not so much corrupt as fanatical in its willingness to fight crime with crime. Frank Skuse's tests would one day turn out to have been far worse than useless. But on the morning of 22 November 1974, that day lay far, far in the future. As dawn broke, Skuse informed the Serious Crimes Squad team that at least two of the detainees had recently been handling explosives. Reade's officers promptly set about terrorizing confessions from the men whom they now presumed to be guilty. They would not stop for three days.

The first to crack was Billy Power, a softly spoken casual labourer whose father had once been a sergeant-major in the British army. He was repeatedly choked, kicked, and punched, and told that he would be thrown from a speeding car on the way back to Birmingham. His will to resist finally collapsed when officers suddenly broke off their questioning and hurled chairs aside in order to drag him to a window, while yelling to each other that even if the fall did not kill him, there was a mob outside that would tear him apart. Power, so terrified that he fouled his trousers, agreed to confess and, as he sat in his excrement, was made literally to speak his guilt. After he had admitted planting the bombs, the officer who had been composing his confession stared at him. 'Jesus, I'm sorry,' he intoned. 'Isn't that right?' Power looked confused, but nodded as the policeman silently raised a pair of handcuffs that he had been using as a knuckle-duster. 'Well, say it then!', screamed the officer. 'Jesus, I'm sorry,' whimpered Power. The confession he then signed ended with the words, 'Jesus, I am sorry. I wish this day had never come.'

The Serious Crimes Squad team set off back to Birmingham with their prisoners. A sixth man, an Irish friend who had waved them off from Birmingham's New Street train station, was arrested the following evening. After two more days – during which the men were deprived of sleep, shown nooses, held nose to snout against snarling dogs and subjected to mock executions with unloaded pistols – the police had four signed confessions. They had also recorded that, although the other two resolutely refused to put their signatures to paper, one had admitted planting the bombs and the other had broken down in tears as he begged God to forgive him for his crimes.

Their trial opened on 9 June 1975 in a vaulted chamber behind the 10-foot-thick walls of Lancaster Castle, about a hundred and fifty miles from Birmingham. The location had been chosen specifically to minimize the risk of jury bias against the men and it would contribute to a mood of almost soporific calm as proceedings unfolded over the next nine weeks. The fortress had, however, hosted England's first mass witchcraft trial in 1612, and echoes of the earlier panic were present from the outset. Alongside the six men sat three other suspected terrorists, none of whom was said to have been involved in the Birmingham bombings. In the tense atmosphere of 1975 England the republican connection had been sufficient to justify a joint trial. One of the three would claim to be an IRA infiltrator working for the police while another would, in true paramilitary style, refuse to recognize the court at all – generating a cloud of suspicion that would float above the dock until the end of the trial. Thirty-six policemen then filed through the witness box to tell the jury about the confessions, rebutting any suggestions that they had seen, heard, or committed violence against the defendants with the slightly hurt but stoical air traditionally adopted by officers who have resolved to lie through their teeth. The star of the show was explosives expert Frank Skuse. Although there were some odd discrepancies between his preliminary and final tests, he explained his methodology in a tone as confident as it was measured and assured the jurors that he had taken every step possible to avoid contamination of his samples. The upshot was that he could be 'ninety-nine per cent certain' that at least two of the defendants had been handling nitroglycerine.

Although no evidence placed the six defendants at the scene of the Birmingham explosions, their cases seemed flimsy by comparison. All were working-class Irish Catholics who moved in circles where anti-British feelings were rife, and there were some indications that their republicanism might have been more than merely sentimental. Five had been arrested on the way to the funeral of James McDade, a proven Birmingham bomber. One had even looked after a bag belonging to McDade which contained ammunition and bomb detonators, and he was said by neighbours to have taken delivery of several mysterious sacks late at night. Receipts seized from his home also suggested an unusual interest in alarm clocks and watches. The polished conclusions of Dr Skuse were meanwhile countered by a defence expert who admitted not only that he had carried out no tests of his own, but that he had never even set foot inside a forensic science laboratory.

When summing up the claims and counterclaims, Justice Bridge strained to sound fair, warning the jury not to let emotion cloud their judgment and emphasizing that suspicion, even if strong, fell far short of proof. But when it came to the most damning evidence – namely the confessions and the scientific analyses – he barely tried to conceal his contempt. The testimony of the six men, if true, would mean that the police were guilty of a conspiracy 'unprecedented in the annals of British criminal history'. And Dr Frank Skuse 'must have spent much of his professional life wasting his time' if his tests were unreliable. 'Do you think that Dr Skuse has been wasting most of his professional time?' he wondered aloud. 'It is a matter entirely for you.'

After a trial that had lasted over two months, the jury took six and a half hours to come back with their answer. On 15 August 1975, in a courtroom filled with over a hundred police and prison officers, journalists, and lawyers, but just half a dozen members of the public, they returned guilty verdicts on every one of the 126 murder counts. Justice Bridge finally lowered the mask of impartiality. Before imposing twenty-one life sentences on each of the six, he stated that he was 'entirely satisfied . . . that all the investigations were carried out with scrupulous propriety'. The evidence was, in fact, the 'clearest and most overwhelming' that he had ever heard.

English law insists that jurors take the secrets of their deliberations to the grave (ostensibly to encourage candour within the jury room and finality outside it), and their own explanation for the verdicts will probably never be revealed. Hatred of the IRA bombers and fear of future attacks presumably played a role, and the apparent authority of Skuse and the police in court were undoubtedly crucial.* The most significant feature of the jury's verdict would never be its rationale, however. It would be its existence. For the fact that twelve jurors had spoken would operate as a kind of legal fiction, and an entire generation of British judges would now keep the defendants in jail in its name. The men's appeals were dismissed, and when they subsequently mounted an indirect challenge to their convictions by suing the police, Lord Denning disallowed it. The

---

* Over the next year, at least eleven more people, including a 15-year-old child, would be wrongly convicted of IRA bombing and explosives charges on the basis of perjured testimony, worthless science and confessions extracted by violence. Five would spend more than a decade behind bars. One would die there. See *R. v. Richardson et al.*, *The Times* (London), 20 October 1989; *R. v. Ward* [1993] 1 WLR 619; *R. v. Maguire* [1992] QB 936.

jury had already decided that they lacked credibility, he ruled. And that was not all that flowed from its decision. On the integrity of the verdict, opined Denning, rested the entire edifice of English criminal justice – and the temple, no matter how rotten, could be kept standing by dumb faith alone.

> If the six men win, it will mean that the police are guilty of perjury, that they are guilty of violence and threats, that the confessions were invented and improperly admitted in evidence and the convictions were erroneous . . . This is such an appalling vista that every sensible person in the land would say that it cannot be right that these actions should go any further.

The complacency would continue. In 1987, the case was referred back to the Court of Appeal – largely as a result of pressure from the Irish government following signature of the 1985 Anglo-Irish agreement – and the men's lawyers produced considerable amounts of fresh evidence. Police witnesses now claimed to have been at Birmingham police station when the men were beaten up, while new scientific analyses cast serious doubt on Skuse's nitroglycerine tests. Most intriguing of all was a document, unearthed in Birmingham police station by independent police inspectors, which had been written thirteen years before by Detective Superintendent George Reade. Seven pages long, headed with the words 'MASTER COPY', and littered with cross-references and deletions, it was a schedule of all the men's police interviews. Among many other curious features, it detailed a fruitless attempt to obtain a confession from defendant Paddy Hill – an attempt that he had described at trial but which, according to the sworn evidence of several police officers, had never taken place. Reade claimed under cross-examination from barrister Michael Mansfield that he simply could not recall why it had been necessary to record a non-existent interview. His forgetfulness, like all the rest of the new evidence, would not trouble the judges, however. The senior of the three, Lord Chief Justice Geoffrey Lane, initially pretended not to understand Mansfield's point, and then ridiculed the suggestion that Reade had 'hoodwinked' everyone at the trial with a 'blueprint' for perjury. The sarcasm turned to anger as Mansfield stood his ground. '[S]peaking for myself,' said Lane, 'it does not seem to me that this is an indication of a master perjury plan.' The barrister asked what else it might be, so that he could put the possibility to Reade. 'You have heard,' snapped the judge. 'Ask the next question.' It would take Lane and colleagues five hours to recite their reasons for dismissing the appeal, but their conclusion was simple. The Court of Appeal had no right to substitute its own view of the trial for that of the jury, and the new evidence gave it no reason to do so. Indeed, 'the longer this hearing has gone on the more convinced this court has become that the verdict of the jury was correct'.

By the time the case reached the Court of Appeal for a third time in 1990, worms were finally tumbling from the can. The West Midlands Serious Crimes Squad had just been disbanded in disgrace, amidst revelations that it had for years systematically concocted evidence and used violence against suspects in its custody. The men's supposed confessions had been undermined further by a recently developed scientific technique known as electrostatic deposit analysis (ESDA) that allowed lost notebook entries to be recreated if the writer's pen had left imprints on the sheet of paper below. ESDA tests now proved beyond doubt that one of the supposed admissions could not have been recorded contemporaneously – directly contradicting the sworn evidence of every police officer who had testified on the matter. Detective Superintendent George Reade was asked before the appeal if he could provide an explanation. 'No I can't, not at this stage,' he replied. 'I'll give it a lot of thought . . . I will probably be able to, but not at this stage.' He never would. The last pillar of the prosecution case collapsed with new evidence concerning Dr Frank Skuse's 'ninety-nine per cent certainty' that he had found traces of explosives on several defendants. New research showed that countless innocent substances could in fact give a positive reading to his tests. Among them was the soap that he had used to clean his instruments.

On the afternoon of 14 March 1991, the men finally walked free. The Court of Appeal accepted at last that the evidence given at their trial had been deficient, but it emphasized, as all its predecessors had done, that it was no light matter to interfere with the verdict of the jury. It was 'a point of great constitutional importance' that, '[t]he task of deciding whether a man is guilty [fell] on the jury' rather than the Court of Appeal. The twelve people who had spoken at Leicester in 1975 had performed their final service in the case. Lord Denning had cited the respect owed to the jury as a reason to avoid reviewing the case. Lord Lane had relied upon its wisdom to explain why the men should stay in jail. And the Court of Appeal now identified its great constitutional importance to explain why they had remained there for sixteen years.

The six defendants outside the Old Bailey after their release. In the centre stands Chris Mullin, a journalist and MP who had spent years keeping their case in the public eye.

It is not just wrongful convictions that cause injustice. Jury acquittals, uncontrollable and unappealable, are capable of producing even more arbitrary results. The power to ignore the evidence, known as jury nullification, is often seen as a shield against over-mighty governments, and juries are often invited to exercise it by defendants with axes to grind, from euthanasia advocates to political malcontents. It is reassuring, in an anarchic kind of way, that the law allows for the arguments and the acquittals. But it only does so with extreme caution – generally making it an act of professional misconduct for a lawyer to remind the jury that it can ignore the evidence – and the power to nullify can have consequences as unpredictable as any ball of dynamite.

The dangers are magnified if a juror over-identifies with a defendant. A willingness to see things from the accused's point of view is certainly appropriate to jury service. The very first right enjoyed by defendants was to exclude anyone they thought unsympathetic from their jury, and jurors

were being drawn from the neighbourhood and rank of the accused long
before the notion of random selection was ever articulated. Cooks or
fishmongers might be summonsed to serve on a case that required their
expertise, while all-women juries were routinely convened to conduct
inquiries that required a feminine touch – to establish, for example, if a
supposedly pregnant capital offender should be hanged immediately or
later. Until the nineteenth century, ethnic minorities on both sides of
the Atlantic were entitled to be tried by a jury that included six of their
countrymen. It has never been enough, however, for jurors to feel a defendant's pain, and the jury system would collapse if compassion simply
trumped judgment.

The trick has always been to assemble a mixture of temperaments.
Jurisdictions in the United States continue to use a variation on the original jury system, allowing both prosecution and defence to disqualify a
specific number of jurors; England, which abolished the right of defence
challenges in 1988, now relies on randomness alone. But whichever
method is relied upon to achieve a balance, the integrity of the system still
rests on nothing more than a hope: that those sworn will reach a verdict
according to the evidence.

The risks that jurors will fail to do so have always been particularly
acute in racially charged cases, where the pull of empathy – towards
either defendant or victim – can easily overwhelm the ability to assess the
rights and wrongs of a case. The trial of Henry Sweet offers a stirring
reminder that people sworn to do justice can transcend their back-
grounds, but the verdict stands out precisely because it was so singular
an aberration from a system that enshrined racism for two centuries.
Black people were denied the right to sit on juries by three of America's
original thirteen states, including Virginia, the home of Thomas
Jefferson, James Madison, and George Washington. Despite the Civil War
that was fought to change that during the 1860s, all-white juries
remained the norm across the South for another century, thanks to officials who made sure to keep blacks off the electoral rolls. The injustice
was endemic – and never was it more poignant than in Mississippi
during the summer of 1955.

In the early evening of Wednesday 24 August, a 14-year-old black boy
called Emmett Till strolled into one of the three stores of a dusty Delta
town called Money, and asked the white cashier, 21-year-old Carolyn

Bryant, for two cents' worth of bubble gum. Till had arrived from Chicago to spend the summer with his uncle and cousins just a week before, and was in high spirits. He had been wowing the black youngsters of Money with tales of life up north, and although his mother had warned him that Mississippi played by very different rules, he had not listened hard enough. For he had entered the store on a dare. The challenge was that he ask Bryant on a date.

No one will ever know precisely what happened during the moments that Till spent behind the swinging screen doors. Carolyn Bryant herself would later claim that he had touched her waist and used language so foul

that she could not repeat it, but she was a southern belle with her honour at stake. All that seems certain is that, as several of his friends recalled, he bade goodbye with a wolf-whistle and the words, 'Bye baby'.

The indiscretion would cost him his life. In the early hours of Sunday morning, three white men clutching flashlights and Colt-45s, battered at the door of his uncle's cabin. Sixty-four-year-old Moses Wright knew why they had come. He had already whipped Till, he pleaded, and besides, he 'ain't got good sense. He was raised up yonder. He didn't know what he was doing.' Brushing him aside, the three men hauled the teenager from his bed and, after apparently showing him to the shadowy figure of a woman in their pickup truck, threw him into the back. He was found three days later in the warm shallows of the Tallahatchie River, feet upwards and neck bound with barbed wire to an industrial fan. The corpse was already so decomposed that Moses Wright could identify it only because it was wearing a ring engraved with the initials of Till's dead father.

The sight was so appalling that the sheriff of Tallahatchie County, Harold Clarence Strider, proposed an immediate burial. Mamie Till, telephoned by relatives with news of her son's death, disagreed. He would not stay in the state that had killed him – and he would certainly not bear the shame that belonged elsewhere. A black undertaker from Chicago called A. A. Rayner lent her the money to have the body transported, and both were there to receive the coffin at the city's Twelfth Street railway station. Orders signed by the Mississippi mortician stipulated that it was to remain sealed – but Mamie Till told Rayner that she would hammer open the bolts herself if he obeyed them. As the lid was lifted, she chose to look first at the body's feet. In a memoir written shortly before her death in 2003, she recalled the moment that her eyes began travelling upwards. 'The horror . . . was as overwhelming as the smell had been before all this, and the sight of the box before that. And it was not because this body looked like something out of a horror movie. It was because I was getting closer . . . to confirming . . . that this body had once been my son.'

What she beheld was unimaginable. Till had been a child of unusual elegance, but he had turned into a tumorous monster. A bullet wound ploughed across one side of its head, a bloated tongue lolled from its mouth and an eyeball was dangling on one of its cheeks. But the hairline and two teeth that remained were enough for Till to recognize her only child, and when Rayner offered to clean up the body, she declined. Her son would have an open-casket funeral instead. 'Let the world see what I've seen,' she declared. Thousands of men and women from Chicago's South Side filed past to pay their respects in person. And when the *Chicago Defender* and *Jet* magazine published close-up photographs of the corpse, the rest of the world also saw – and it took notice.

The murder set off shock waves of such intensity within northern black communities that ripples were soon rolling back even as far as Tallahatchie County. The concern among the authorities there was not of course that a black boy had been slain. It was that the killing would draw unwelcome attention at a time when white supremacy was coming under unprecedented pressure. Over a year earlier, the Supreme Court had declared Arkansas' racially segregated educational system to be unlawful and although federal authorities were reluctant to force a showdown, there were indications that marshals might soon be despatched to enforce the Court's ruling. Mississippi's racists knew that their own hopes of keeping Washington at bay required that the Magnolia State appear at least capable of upholding the rule of law. Police duly arrested

Roy Bryant and J. W. Milam, husband and brother respectively to
Carolyn Bryant, whom Moses Wright had identified as having been
among the trio who knocked at his door. The two men accepted that they
had abducted Till, but lackadaisically claimed to have set him free after
concluding – wrongly – that he was not the boy they were after. The
admissions led to their indictment for murder, and as their trial
approached a sense built that it would form a defining moment in
Southern history. Lynchings had been on a steep decline since the 1930s,
but the Supreme Court ruling was giving rise to fighting talk among
white conservatives. The verdict would either signal that segregationism
was on the turn – or show that the jury boxes would be among the last
redoubts of white supremacy.

Which it would be became apparent in the middle of September 1955
in a packed courthouse in the small town of Sumner. Every one of the
community's five lawyers had volunteered their services to the defendants, and four-fifths of the four hundred-odd spectators were white.
While white journalists and photographers were allocated three large
areas in which to work, the dozen or so black professionals – northern
reporters, lawyers, and one Congressman – were left to huddle around a
bridge table. Even then, the presence of so many black people with suits
and pens inspired consternation. One defence attorney discreetly asked
Sheriff Harold Strider to seat them among the whites, just to remind the
jury what of was at stake. Strider refused, because he opposed integration
in principle, but he would tickle his pistol and jovially greet them with
cries of 'Mornin' niggers!' throughout the trial. He was, in any event,
happy to assist the defendants in other ways. Outside court he had already
begun telling journalists that he thought Till was still alive, making vague
suggestions that the entire 'deal' was an elaborate put-up job by the
National Association for the Advancement of Colored People. Inside it, he
now falsely stated that he had never identified Emmett Till at all. The
corpse fished from the Tallahatchie, he told the jury, had in fact been that
of an unknown adult.

Amidst such murk, honesty could only flash and it never shone
brighter than when Moses Wright stepped onto the witness stand. Wright
had been warned he would be killed if he testified, and the last time a
black witness had testified against a white one in Mississippi, twenty years
before, he had been shot dead on the spot. But when asked to say who had

carried his nephew into the night, the tiny old man raised his finger to the 235-pound Milam. 'There he is,' he declared. The moment was surreptitiously frozen on film by one of the black journalists, but haunting though his image is, it only hints at the atmosphere that congealed beyond the witness stand. According to *New York Post* reporter Murray

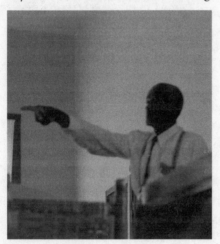

Kempton, Milam 'leaned forward, crooking a cigaret [*sic*] in a hand that seemed as large as Moses Wright's whole chest, and his eyes were coals of hatred'. The witness, whose bags were already packed for the train journey that would take him away from Mississippi for ever, stared right back – and turned towards the second defendant. 'And there's Mr Bryant,' he added. C. Sidney Carlton, one of the defence lawyers, then tried to lash him back into line, but Wright remained unfazed – smiling coldly and sitting back to absorb each roared question, before responding with terse answers that omitted the word 'sir'. He later recalled that he could feel 'the blood boil in hundreds of white people as they sat glaring in the courtroom. It was the first time in my life I had the courage to accuse a white man of a crime, let alone something [as] terrible as killing a boy. I wasn't exactly brave and I wasn't scared. I just wanted to see justice done.'

Others in court also displayed integrity. Judge Curtis Swango conducted the proceedings with consummate fairness throughout. Eighteen-year old Willie Reed, although almost paralysed with fear, identified Milam as one of six people with Till in a pick-up on the morning after the abduction, and recalled someone later screaming for mercy from a nearby tractor shed. Mamie Till held up with grace against defence innuendoes that she had misidentified an unknown body in order to cash in her son's life insurance policy. 'If I thought it wasn't my boy', she said, dabbing her eyes, 'I would be looking for him now.' But honesty and integrity would secure justice only if they were recognized in the jury box – and in a county that was 60 per cent black, the jurors comprised only white men.

Each side delivered its final addresses on 23 September 1955. Even the prosecutor, genuinely anxious to obtain a conviction, was concerned not to sound too sympathetic to the dead teenager. '[T]he very worst punishment that should have occurred', he told the jurors, 'was to take a razor strap, turn him over a barrel and whip him.' He was simply tailoring his arguments to his audience, but his opponents spoke from the heart. J. W. Kellum made the timeless appeal to American idealism: if Milam and Bryant were not let loose, he demanded, 'where under God's shining sun is the land of the free and the home of the brave?' John Whitten, who wrapped up the defence summations, delivered the most impassioned performance of all. Reiterating the speculations of Sheriff Strider, he theorized that civil rights activists had exhumed a 'rotting, stinking corpse' and then planted it in the Tallahatchie in the hope of fostering racial disharmony. He could only hope that 'every last Anglo-Saxon one of you men in this jury has the courage to set these men free'. It took the jurors just 67 minutes to pluck up the nerve – and their foreman later recalled that, 'If we hadn't stopped to drink pop, it wouldn't have taken that long.' He justified the not guilty verdicts to reporters on the basis that there had been no evidence to show that the body found was that of Emmett Till, and dismissed the suggestion that Mamie Till's identification had provided it. 'If she had tried a little harder,' he sneered, 'she might have got out a tear.'

Roy Bryant (left) and J. W. Milam (right). Carolyn Bryant
stands second from left.

The defendants themselves said little as they descended the courthouse steps, cigars clenched between rictal grins and wives' waists tightly clutched. They were silent only because they had been warned that they might yet face another trial, but a couple of months later, having appeared before a grand jury that declined to indict them on kidnapping charges, they gave a series of interviews to chequebook journalist William Bradford Huie. Bryant stayed off the record, but Milam now admitted that they had abducted Till and driven him to the Tallahatchie. They had made him take his clothes off and carry the fan that would anchor his corpse. In the cool dawn, at the lapping water's edge, they had then shot him in the head. Milam said nothing about his accomplices, and claimed that the original intention had been only to frighten Till. Matters had got out of hand only when the boy, naked at the Tallahatchie, had called them 'bastards' and bragged about his sexual prowess with white women. The only thing more offensive than the lies was that Milam and Bryant received $4000 for having told them.

Among white conservatives, the verdicts were an appropriate conclusion to the whole unhappy affair. The *Delta Democrat Times* and the *Jackson Daily News* both observed that the presumption of innocence had been vindicated, although they disagreed with each other on who emerged from the trial with most discredit. The former condemned the prosecution for proceeding on such flimsy evidence, while the latter was more troubled by the impudent northern Negroes who had created so strong an 'NAACP atmosphere in court'. The *Greenwood Morning Star* was content to note simply that the fairness of the proceedings reflected well on Mississippi.

Reactions elsewhere were different. The verdict made headlines across North America and Europe, and its impact on the black community is hard to overestimate. Saturation coverage in the minority press and movie footage broadcast on all three networks in New York ensured that it became not only a cause célèbre, but a moment that etched itself into the collective consciousness of black America. In the South, the effects were immediate. Anne Moody, then a 14-year-old maid in Mississippi, later recalled that her white employer had insisted on sitting her down to discuss the case. The housewife had explained that Till had been killed for 'getting out of his place with a white woman', and had then asked Moody pensively how old she was. 'Fourteen, I will soon be fifteen though.' 'See that boy was just fourteen too,' replied her employer. 'It's a shame he had to die so soon.' Moody had gone home trembling. 'Before Emmett Till's murder, I had known the fear of hunger, hell and the Devil. But now there was a new fear known to me – the fear of being killed just because I was black . . . I knew that once I got food the fear of starving to death would leave. I was also told that if I were a good girl, I wouldn't have to fear the Devil or hell. But I didn't know what one had to do or not do as a Negro not to be killed. Probably just being a Negro period was enough, I thought.' Others would respond less desperately. One of those who wept with fury when she saw the photograph of Till's corpse in *Jet* magazine was Rosa Parks. Two months after the acquittal of his killers, her refusal to give up a bus seat to a white passenger in Selma, Alabama, sparked off black America's modern civil rights movement.

Verdicts like that in the case of Milam and Bryant – delivered by an unrepresentative jury in a riven community – undermine the notion of good faith that the system depends on. The wrongness of a decision is not, however, a good reason to despise juries in general – because unpopularity is a necessary consequence of their existence. The point is well made by two cases, different in countless other ways, that occurred almost ten years apart at opposite ends of the United States.

The first is the 1987 prosecution of Bernhard Goetz. The 37-year-old electronics repairman stepped from obscurity to celebrity on the afternoon of 22 December 1984. Entering a downtown express at New York's 14th Street station, he found the carriage divided between two groups. At one end were four boisterous black teenagers. At the other were the remaining passengers, fifteen or twenty men and women who found the boys sufficiently unpleasant to give them a wide berth. Goetz, a scrawny and bespectacled white man, chose to sit with the teenagers. As the train picked up speed, 19-year-old Troy Canty, lying on a bench, pulled himself up and asked his new companion for five dollars. Goetz invited him to repeat his request. When the teenager did so, the older man reached under his windcheater and drew a handgun. Passengers dived for cover as shots exploded. All four youths were hit and incapacitated. According to admissions that Goetz would later make, he then leant over to examine Canty and contemplated gouging out his eyes with a bunch of keys, before approaching Darrell Cabey who was slumped in his seat. He peered at the 19-year-old. 'You seem to be doing all right,' he observed. 'Here's another.' In his confession he recalled then shooting him at point blank range with his fifth and last bullet. The injuries of three of the boys were superficial, but one of the two rounds fired into Cabey had severed his spinal cord. He would be permanently paralysed, and three weeks later would enter a coma and suffer brain damage from which he would never recover.

The case of the Subway Vigilante – as the *New York Post* dubbed Goetz on the day of his arrest – opened up social fault lines across the United States, and nowhere did the gulf yawn wider than in New York itself. Race relations in the city were sinking towards a nadir at the same time that the rate of violent crime was soaring towards its twentieth-century high. The

subway had meanwhile become the Big Apple's rotten core, a heart of darkness that saw thirty-eight felonies every single day. Opinions polarized. Some saw Goetz as a self-appointed and racist executioner. Many thought him a hero.

In such circumstances, the meaning of impartiality was elusive even in conceptual terms, and the challenge of achieving it in practice very soon became clear. Support for Goetz's actions was so widespread that the first grand jury to consider the evidence refused to indict him for shooting his gun at all. Another eventually found a case to answer, but about thirty of the three hundred people who were then assembled as potential trial jurors greeted him with applause when he entered court. So many had suffered from crime that the judge had to ask if they had *not* been victims rather than vice versa. Of the twelve who were eventually selected – ten whites, a young black woman, and an older black man – six had direct experience of crime, and two had actually been robbed on the subway.

After many false starts, the case finally got under way on 27 April 1987.

The indictment contained charges up to and including attempted murder, and the crucial issue was whether Goetz had been acting in self-defence. In legal terms, that required the jury to assess whether his actions were, or might have been, necessary and proportionate to resist Troy Canty's demand for five dollars. Cut to the bone, the question was whether he was better regarded as a helpless victim or a trigger-happy thug.

The answer was always going to turn on whether Goetz had taken a pause before firing a fifth shot into Darrell Cabey at point blank range, and the evidence was unclear. The only eyewitness who unequivocally said that he had done so would re-enact the shooting in a way that contradicted medical evidence that was undisputed by either side. However, Goetz himself had confessed to a very deliberate second shot – and there were plenty of other circumstances to trouble the jurors. He had pulled guns on would-be muggers twice before. His unlicensed pistol was worn on a quick-release holster and the ammunition he had fired on 22 December 1984 included three dumdum bullets – hollow-point shells designed to flatten on impact and maximize internal haemorrhaging. And the two-hour videotape of his police interview, which would be played in its entirety to the jurors, showed a shivering Goetz admitting that he had not just fired his gun intentionally at Cabey a second time, but that he had contemplated blinding Troy Canty. His main problem, he told them, had been that he had run out of bullets. 'I turned into a vicious animal . . . [I]f there's a God, God knows what was in my heart. And it was . . . sadistic and savage.'

The jurors consequently faced questions of almost impossible complexity. The prosecutor, Gregory Waples, opened by portraying Goetz as an 'emotionally troubled' man with a 'twisted . . . sense of right and wrong', but even if true, that was the beginning rather than the end of their inquiry. Although the defendant's police interview contained admissions that were clear, their legal significance depended on inquiries that anything but. New York's law of self-defence allowed for the use of deadly force only if it was both 'reasonably necessary' and accompanied by a 'reasonable belief' that the target had also been about to use lethal force. The question of 'reasonableness' was supposedly an objective one, but the law required that, in assessing it, juries should take account of a defendant's own perceptions of danger. Attempting to define a fact from someone else's point of view is the kind of riddle that several philosophers have spent lifetimes pondering, but the jury would have just days. The scale of their task was encapsulated by a part of Goetz's interview in which he explained that, when he pulled out his gun, he had not meant to kill the four boys but that, when he saw Troy Canty's bright, shining eyes and smile, 'I decided that I was going to kill them after all, murder them after all . . . They were going to have fun with me . . . enjoy me for a while, beat the shit out of me . . . You don't think, you act, speed is everything.' Goetz's words – mean, hateful, desperate and afraid – simply transcend the categories of the criminal law. He had felt an inexpressible fear, and simultaneously longed for four boys to die violently because of something he had detected in a smile. The jurors had to decide whether that was reasonable.

The strategy of defence attorney Barry Slotnick was simply to ignore the evidence against his client. As flamboyant as his opponent was sober (he would step from his limousine each morning and wade into court through a scrum of reporters, while Waples jogged past anonymously), his opening speech focused almost exclusively on the 'savages and vultures' whom his client had shot. The teenagers all had criminal records, and Slotnick told the jury that he and Waples 'might as well switch tables, because I'm going to prosecute those four . . . And you're going to convict them and acquit him.' The prosecutor just about clung on to his table, but he gave ground in every other direction as the case went on. He agreed to Slotnick's demand that a police officer refer to those shot as 'young men' rather than 'victims'. He yielded again when Slotnick insisted that Goetz's admissions be called a 'statement' rather than a 'confession'. And when it came to stagecraft, Slotnick was something of a sorcerer – while the wooden Waples was not so much an apprentice, as a broom.

Wooing a jury that included two black members, the defence lawyer knew better than to unveil the racial superstitions behind the case, but they loomed in the shadows from the outset. A month into the case he dramatically gave them flesh. The jurors were kept out of court for an hour on the morning of 28 May, and entered court to find that the outline of a New York subway car had been taped to the floor. With everyone wondering what it all might mean, Slotnick called a ballistics expert named Joseph Quirke to the witness stand, and informed the judge that he had secured four 'props' to assist with a re-enactment of the shootings.

A quartet of young men stepped forward from the back of the court. All were members of the Guardian Angels, a vigilante group that had vocally supported Goetz since his arrest, and on the secret but specific request of Slotnick, all were black. An incredulous Waples suddenly realized what was afoot and demanded that court officers be used instead, but Slotnick was able to persuade the judge that his props had been very carefully selected – because they were just the right height. They thereupon shuffled to the front of the court, swathed in baggy T-shirts and topped with baseball caps, where they sullenly jostled a fifth, white, prop while Quirke delivered a running commentary. The spectral subway carriage would remain taped to the floor until the end of the trial.

An even more decisive moment of the trial had come earlier in the same month, when Slotnick had cross-questioned one of Goetz's victims, James Ramseur. Ramseur had been arrested and convicted of a gang rape after being shot, and from the moment that he slouched into court, sporting prison dungarees and mumbling 'I refuse to take the stand', it was apparent that his contribution to the prosecution's case would be equivocal at best. Two weeks later he returned; but although he had decided to testify and wrapped himself in a coat and tie, he remained deeply disgruntled – and Slotnick was not the man to gruntle him.

Under New York law, questions about the rape were formally admissible only to persuade the jury that Ramseur was untrustworthy, but Slotnick knew that setting out the gory details would do infinitely more. And faced with a witness as volatile as an ammunition dump, he was soon flicking his questions like matches. Was it true, he wondered, that the victim had needed eighteen stitches in her anus? Was it right that Ramseur had been convicted after a not guilty plea, and had therefore already been found unworthy of belief by one jury? When had he last committed a crime? Ramseur occasionally tried to respond in kind, dismally oblivious to the protocol of courtroom abuse. When Slotnick asked him at one point to confirm that they had not met before, Ramseur skewered him with a stare. 'No,' he murmured, 'but I heard about you.' 'I hope it was nothing unpleasant,' responded Slotnick brightly. 'It was unpleasant,' he growled. 'I know about you, baby.' The aura of violence crystallized when three security guards, misinterpreting an attempt by Ramseur to tie his laces, leapt onto the witness stand – and Slotnick milked the menace for considerably more than it was worth. Addressing journalists at his regular evening press conference, he claimed that Ramseur had in fact been trying to remove his shoe to throw it. 'If he had a gun,' he added, 'he would have attempted to shoot me.' Their uneven duel ended the next day. Asked by Slotnick when he had last been with his friends before the subway shooting, Ramseur spat back, 'When was the last time you got a drug dealer off?' Pressed for an answer, Ramseur settled into a mute smile and refused to say another word. The result under New York law was that his testimony was struck from the record, and its minimal legal significance evaporated. Its odour remained.

The jury retired on Friday 12 June 1987, and returned with verdicts at the beginning of the following week. Its members found that Goetz had been in possession of the unlicensed Smith & Wesson that he had fired and was therefore guilty of the least serious of the thirteen charges against him. They acquitted him of all the others. The jurors later explained that, in their view, Goetz had fired all his bullets in such rapid succession that he had not had time to consider if the threat he faced was over. His admissions to firing a deliberate shot into an immobile Darrell Cabey were, or at least might have been, the recollections of a man too confused to remember the truth. Goetz received a six-month prison sentence from the trial judge, later increased by the Court of Appeals to one year, along with a fine and probation order.

The jurors, after lining up for Goetz's autograph, informed journalists that race had not figured in their deliberations, but it was a highly relevant factor everywhere else in New York. Polls soon suggested that less than half of the city's black inhabitants supported the verdict, compared to four out of five of its whites. Several black politicians declared the jury's decision 'inexcusable' and 'frightening', uttering the traditional prophecies of a long hot summer, while David Dinkins, then Manhattan Borough President, thought it 'a clear and open invitation to vigilantism' which ignored the fact that, 'In this country, we no longer employ firing squads.' The *New York Post* could hardly have disagreed more, and ran countless columns extolling the common sense of the jurors. Most typical, however, was a view expressed by Mayor Ed Koch. Though worried about the 'signal' that the jurors had sent out, he recognized that they had the final word. 'The law is the law,' he said. 'Under our American system of justice, I accept the verdict.'

Eight years later, that verdict, and the popular reaction to it, would find a mirror image in a double murder case on the other side of the United States. It began on the warm evening of 12 June 1994, when a 25-year-old man and 35-year-old woman were found dead in a garden in the Los Angeles suburb of Brentwood. While two children had slept undisturbed in an upstairs bedroom, the couple had faced a killer who had acted with the unhesitating ferocity of an animal. The man had crumpled against a metal fence, punctured by at least thirty stab wounds, while the woman lay on a terracotta walkway, felled by a slash to her neck so powerful that the blow had nicked her spine and drained 90 per cent of the blood from her body. Crimson footprints trailed away and then looped back, as though the killer had returned to wonder at his own monstrosity. The man was a waiter called Ron Goldman and his dead companion went by her maiden name of Nicole Brown. Alongside the footprints were five drops of blood that would later be found to belong to her estranged husband, retired football star Orenthal James Simpson.

The bodies were discovered when Nicole's distraught dog pulled neighbours to the scene. The police arrived shortly after midnight. Officers would later claim to have found a dark-blue woollen cap and a left-handed brown leather glove inside the garden. It was another five hours before they made the two-mile journey to Simpson's residence on Rockingham Avenue. When they received no reply to the doorbell, Detective Mark Fuhrman climbed over a wall and let the others into the property. Simpson himself was not present, but officers would find drops of Simpson's blood between the driveway and the foyer of the house, and a single drop in his bathroom. Even more significant was an item recovered by Fuhrman alone. After being told by Kato Kaelin, a houseguest, that there had been a loud crash near his bungalow at around 10.45 p.m., the detective wandered off and returned with a wet leather glove that he claimed to have retrieved near a perimeter wall. It was, if genuine, rather more damning than a smoking gun. It matched the glove recovered at the murder scene, and would prove to be saturated with not just the blood of Nicole Brown and Ron Goldman, but to contain traces of blood that almost certainly belonged to Simpson himself.

Simpson certainly had the motive to murder. His relationship with Nicole had always been tempestuous – to the extent that he had previously threatened to kill her – and their most recent reconciliation had fallen apart just three weeks before. He also had no alibi. He had flown to Chicago for business on the night of the killings, and at 10.25 p.m. – around the time of the murders – the driver of the stretch limousine that would take him to the airport had rung his doorbell. There had been no response, and he had returned to his car. The chauffeur would claim that he had then seen a well-built 6-foot-tall black man entering the house. When the driver then buzzed at the doorbell a second time, Simpson had answered and explained through the intercom that he had overslept, and was only just stepping from the shower. Soon afterwards, he emerged, carrying several pieces of luggage. One, a small duffel bag, would later disappear.

Telephoned by police at his Chicago hotel, Simpson returned immediately to Los Angeles. He waived his right to a lawyer and attended for interview at midday, barely twelve hours after the killings. Officers were particularly interested in a gash on his left index finger. In a series of halting responses, he explained that he had cut himself the day before and that, because he played 'golf and stuff' such injuries were not unusual. The wound had then reopened in Chicago when, stricken by anguish upon hearing that Nicole was dead, he had gone 'bonkers' and cut himself on a glass in his hotel bathroom. When told that red drops had been found at his house, he further recalled that his finger had been dripping blood as he had left for the airport. The explanation opened a hundred overlapping riddles – not least because four of the five blood drops at the murder scene were to the left of the footprints, suggesting that they had come from the killer's left hand – but the interview concluded after just thirty-two minutes. The police officers did not even bother to ask Simpson what he had been doing at the time of the murders. It was the first sign of just how comprehensively the case against him was going to be botched.

Simpson was informed within days that he was to be charged and agreed once again to surrender – but this time thought better of the decision. On 17 June 1994, the day he was due to give himself up, he left home in the passenger seat of a friend's Ford Bronco, leaving behind a suicide note but taking along $8750 in cash, a false goatee and moustache, and a passport. Whatever kind of afterlife he may have been anticipating on his departure, the plans changed after he took a call on his cellphone from a police detective. As patrol cars were scrambled, he told the officer that he had a gun to his head, that he had done whatever he had done for the love of Nicole, and that he wanted to 'go with' her and 'do it at her grave'. A leisurely chase ensued during which the Bronco drifted along the palm-fringed freeways of southern California, shadowed by helicopters and trailed by columns of police cruisers, before returning to Rockingham Avenue where Simpson was peacefully arrested. All the networks inter-rupted their schedules to cover the drive, and for two hours, ninety-five million Americans sat glued to the inaction. Never before in human history had so little been watched by so many for so long – and the spectacle had only just begun.

Simpson's move from prime suspect to sole suspect now caused his own role to be very publicly rewritten. News of his estranged wife's murder had been greeted with its share of suspicion and *Schadenfreude*, but he initial-ly seemed to have considerable reserves of goodwill on which to draw. O. J. – or The Juice, as he was affectionately known – had won hearts willy-nilly during his running-back career for the Buffalo Bills. Since his 1978 retirement he had been colour-blindly endorsing products and accepting B-movie parts, and with his good looks and affable manner he had become the kind of black man that white middle America has always trea-sured: living proof that sufficient talent and humour could bridge even its supposedly intractable racial divide. But the precariousness of that status now became apparent. His arrest made the cover of *Time* on 27 June, cap-tioned 'An American Tragedy' and illustrated by a deliberately darkened mug shot. The District Attorney's office – still smarting from a series of high-profile failures going back to the McMartin case described in Chapter 4 of this book – then leaked tapes of two 911 calls made by Nicole Brown, in which she was heard screaming as Simpson raged around their house. By 10 July the *New York Times* was sonorously pronouncing that murder exerted a 'primal fascination' and that Simpson – a man 'given great gifts' who had been 'brought to a grim pass by either fate or frailty' – fitted a 'fearsome pattern [of tragic hero] that lurks in our ancestral memory'. Tales of the slum kid with the fatal flaw, the self-doubting black man with a hunger for trophy blondes, were soon spawning. Orenthal was becoming Othello – and The Juice was turning rancid.

The media interest would grow exponentially. When Simpson attended court on 22 July 1994 – by which time he had recovered sufficient will to live to enter a plea of 'absolutely, one hundred per cent not guilty' – a hi-tech shantytown known as 'Camp OJ' was already taking shape in a nearby car park. Its nine antennae, scores of trailers and eighty miles of cable would generate ratings not seen since the first Gulf War, and the two thousand reporters who covered the case would not just sensationalize events; they often became part of them. The *National Enquirer* paid $12,500 for three witnesses' accounts of 'How I Sold A Stiletto to O. J. Simpson'; the jagged blade bought at their hardware store would eventually turn out to be pristine, but its image on the front pages threw prosecutors into a predictable tizzy. A woman called Jill Shively, who claimed to have encountered Simpson driving home furiously during the hour of the killings, was dropped as a prosecution witness after she falsely told a grand jury that she had not given any paid interviews. Attorneys, meanwhile, began using the press to spin their strategies and attack opponents, and in their mutual anxiety to seem on the ball they would lodge 16,000 objections with trial judge Lance Ito by the case's end – a level of complaint pathological even by the prolix standards of the legal profession. Although to himself would occasionally acknowledge that a world turned outside his courtroom – notably when he adjourned the trial for Election Day 'to allow the democratic electoral process to go forward' – he too was soon losing sight of where his courtroom ended and its televisual representation began. In the middle of jury selection, he gave an extended interview to a local news show, and at one point invited both legal teams into his chambers to show them a comedy routine about himself that had just aired on Jay Leno's *Tonight Show*.

But even if many would enjoy their moments in the spotlight, the coverage worked to polarize opinion along racial lines even before the trial began. The speed with which the national media was turning on Simpson encouraged many blacks to reclaim him as a prodigal – not least because there were eminently sensible grounds to distrust the record of the Los Angeles Police Department and District Attorney's office in racially charged cases. Just three years earlier, several LAPD officers had been videotaped unawares as they had delivered fifty-six baton blows on an unarmed black motorist called Rodney King, and a subsequent inquiry had established that racially motivated violence was systemic within the force. Those particular officers had nevertheless been acquitted by a jury on the basis that it had been reasonable for them to inflict brain and kidney damage on King. And the risk of popular prejudice remained real. A national poll conducted in July 1994, just a month after Simpson's arrest, showed that whereas 60 per cent of black Americans still gave him the benefit of the doubt, 68 per cent of whites were already presuming his guilt.

Race and publicity would, in combination, have a marked effect on the composition of the jury. Each side exercised peremptory challenges on racial lines, with the defence excluding five whites but just one black, and the prosecution rejecting eight blacks as against two whites. The dozen eventually selected, who were two-thirds female and three-quarters black, were fairly representative of downtown Los Angeles in demographic terms. Saturation coverage of the case had already made it very unlikely, however, that they would be typical in any other sense. DA Gil Garcetti had already cynically acknowledged the forces at play, when asked whether the leak of Nicole Brown's calls to the emergency services might have jeopardized Simpson's chances of a fair trial. He was 'confident', he assured the assembled journalists, that 'we can find twelve jurors who know very little if anything about [it]'. The jurors had indeed been selected largely because they had expressed a degree of unawareness or lack of interest acceptable to both sides – and to maintain their suitability, they were sequestered in a hotel from the moment that the trial proper began.

When it did so, on 24 January 1995, a series of almost incomprehensible decisions by lead prosecutor Marcia Clark suggested that she personally, or her twenty-five-strong prosecution team collectively, was cursed either by a serious lack of judgment or a critical lack of self–confidence. She chose not to introduce evidence of the Bronco chase – and thus not to reveal that Simpson had been carrying a passport, wads of cash, and a disguise – because the jurors might feel sorry for Simpson and believe his explanations. She positively opposed playing his police interview, because it included his claim to be innocent. Compounding the prosecutorial misjudgments was police incompetence. Evidence soon showed that LAPD employees had trampled through the murder scene unregulated and unrecorded for hours, and that blood samples had begun to degrade in the afternoon heat – because the only refrigerator they had brought with them was not working. Some senior officers meanwhile seemed unaware why evidence had to be accounted for at all. When

Detective Robert Riske was invited by Marcia Clark to tell the jury about his expertise in securing a crime scene, he simply looked blank. 'They kind of gloss over it,' came the eventual response. 'They don't really train you.'

The assistance that the police provided Simpson did only consist of things that they had failed to do; in one crucially important respect, they boosted his defence. For much of the trial, defence lawyers half-heartedly explored alternative explanations for the murders, and their hunches – that, for example, Brown and Goldman had been killed for unknown reasons by unknown drug dealers – were never very compelling. As the shoddiness of the LAPD investigation became apparent, they steadily homed in on the theory that Simpson had been framed. The path to an acquittal on that basis was, however, strewn with obstacles – and the most elephantine was that Simpson's blood had somehow dripped around the crime scene and got onto a glove that apparently belonged to the murderer. Explaining how the police could have laid their hands on stray bodily fluids belonging to Simpson might ordinarily have been tricky – but the LAPD came through for the defence.

Detective Philip Vannatter, an officer of twenty-six years' experience, recounted how a police nurse had given him a blood sample taken from Simpson on the morning after the killings. Instead of booking it into the refrigeration facility, which was a mile away, he had decided to register it with an officer at Simpson's house – twenty miles away. On the prosecution's own evidence, almost a quarter of the sample then went missing. The police nurse would eventually make a new statement, several months later, in which he suddenly remembered that he had actually taken a quarter less blood than he had previously stated. The picture would have been unimpressive whatever the nature of the case. In the context of one where the defence was alleging police misconduct and the planting of blood, it was disastrous.

The prosecution's presentation of scientific evidence only made matters worse. Its analysts claimed that the various bloody swatches lifted from the crime scene and Rockingham Avenue matched that of Simpson by odds of up to 6.8 billion to 1. Such matters were irrelevant if the issue was whether his blood had been deliberately planted. Insofar as it was not, prosecutors needed to explain just three things – that everyone's DNA profile is unique, that profiles are recoverable from blood samples, and that deterioration is not the same as contamination. They should have been able to do so within a week. But the experts in fact spent longer than a month on the stand, delivering testimony so mystifying that transcripts of their evidence are now all but impossible to decrypt. The defence responded with a character called Dr Henry Lee, who took just three days to identify dozens of bloodstains that had been overlooked or lost by LAPD investigators. Much of his testimony gave off more heat than light, but compared to a prosecution case that was failing to emit either, its impact was huge. His conclusion was delivered in broken English, but the import was so clear that several jurors would later recall it as decisive. 'Only opinion I can giving under this circumstance,' he said. '[S]omething wrong.'

Such matters were ultimately sideshows, however. The strongest evidence for the prosecution – and the greatest obstacle faced by the defence – was the glove that Detective Mark Fuhrman claimed to have found in Simpson's garden. It would give rise to a pivotal moment on 15 June 1995, when prosecutor Christopher Darden invited Simpson to try it on. Few trial attorneys would have taken such a gamble with the stakes so high – and Darden paid the price. Simpson gingerly probed it with his fingers and, wearing an expression that might almost have been surprise, found that it was too small. Grimacing, he tugged at it repeatedly before raising his hand to show the jurors that it did not fit. For over half a year, Simpson had sat on the sidelines and he would never testify in his own defence, but thanks to the prosecution, he had finally been allowed to assert his innocence – and hammy though the performance was, it could only help his case.

The bloody glove had one more surprise in store, the biggest of all. The defence needed to explain how it had found its way into Simpson's residence, if not on his murderous hand, and its theory was that Fuhrman had brought it. The detective certainly had the opportunity, having been at the murder scene earlier that night. He was also relatively familiar with the house, having gone there to deal with a domestic violence complaint from Nicole Brown nine years earlier. The crucial question was why he would have gone to such lengths to frame an innocent man. The defence claimed that the motive was pure and pathological racism.

The fate of Fuhrman would encapsulate like nothing else the inadequacies of the prosecution. Rumours that the officer was a racist had been circulating since the summer of 1994 when, in the week of Simpson's arraignment, the then head of the defence team, Robert Shapiro, had floated the notion of a fit-up to a journalist at the *New Yorker*. Fuhrman's LAPD personnel file, which Christopher Darden had seen by January 1995, further indicated that the policeman's bias was not simply unthinking prejudice: he had previously voiced fantasies of attacking and murdering non-whites. Darden had been concerned enough to call Fuhrman in for an interview; but although he would plaintively write after the trial that he had found 'something' about the officer 'eerie' and 'evasive', he had accepted his assurances that there was no reason to worry. Marcia Clark, for her part, ignored Fuhrman's own hints about the file. She then called him to the stand in March 1995. In a bravura performance that ended with Clark placing an arm around his shoulder, the officer confidently denied that he had framed Simpson, and rejected defence suggestions that he was a racist. The word 'nigger', he claimed, had never crossed his lips.

A timebomb had been set and the fuse fizzed for six months. It exploded on 5 September 1995. On that day, the defence produced taped interviews with a journalist in which Fuhrman had used the word 'nigger' forty-one times.* Two witnesses also recalled that he had expressed disgust at the idea of a white woman with a black lover and had talked of 'burn[ing] and

---

* The evidence gave rise to the single most extraordinary evidential ruling of the entire trial. Mark Fuhrman used the word 'nigger' forty-one times on the tape, but Ito ruled that the jury should be told about just two instances. Whether or not that was correct – and it was arguably unfair to the defence – it made the tape itself irrelevant. The head of Simpson's legal team, Johnnie Cochran, applied to play it in the absence of the jury nevertheless. He was only doing what any legal huckster might do, but instead of briskly dismissing the application, Ito granted it. The jury thereupon became the only people in the world denied the right to hear Fuhrman describe getting away with 'breaking' black suspects, turning their faces to 'mush', drenching a room with 'unbelievable' amounts of blood. and smashing one man's head so badly that he had needed seventy stitches. The defence was then allowed to recall Fuhrman, again in the absence of the jury, and ask him whether he had planted evidence against O. J. Simpson – a question that he refused to answer. The testimony was engrossing enough, but the fact that it was delivered to everyone *except* the jury indicates that Ito had finally lost sight of the dividing line between evidence and entertainment. See generally Paul Thaler, *The Spectacle* (Westport, Conn., 1997), pp. 237–43.

bomb[ing] niggers'. He had further declared that 'the only good nigger was a dead nigger'. The prosecutors watched with stunned embarrassment, as though they had been the victims of his deception rather than the facilitators of it. Marcia Clark would eventually seek to repair the damage by telling the jury that Fuhrman was a lying racist whom she wished had never been born – but that they could still trust him. The argument was tenable as a matter of logic. Emotionally, it stank.

The summation of lead defence attorney Johnnie L. Cochran Jr. constituted an appropriate end to the case. Structured around the moment when Simpson had tried on the glove and punctuated with the mantra, 'If it doesn't fit, you must acquit', it was a brutally effective demolition of the prosecution case. The oratory itself was inelegant, and occasionally preposterous. Fuhrman was promoted from racist perjurer to architect of genocide. He was like 'another man . . . who wanted to burn people'. In the case of that man, 'People didn't care. People said he's crazy. He's just a half-baked painter.' And yet, 'This man . . . became Adolf Hitler because people didn't care, didn't try to stop him . . . And so Fuhrman. Fuhrman wants to take all black people now and burn them or bomb them. That's genocidal racism. Is that ethnic purity? What is that? . . . Maybe you're the right people at the right time at the right place to say, "No more".' Cochran was no Clarence Darrow and the jurors themselves would later groan when recalling the hyperbole. For what it would be worth, at least two expressed no doubt that the glove had in fact fitted. But the lawyer needed neither to inspire, nor present a watertight defence. He only had to remind his audience of twelve that the prosecution case had been a shambles.

The jurors began their deliberations on the morning of Monday 2 October 1995. It was widely expected that they would be out for days if not weeks, but a collective opinion formed far sooner. Their first ballot disclosed a 10-2 split, and within four hours the dissenters – one black, one white – had come round to the majority view. Judge Ito, informed that they had a verdict, announced that he would not unseal it until the following morning. The decision sparked a frenzy. Many Los Angelinos assumed that Ito was giving the authorities the head start they had not had after the acquittal of Rodney King's assailants – when riots had left over fifty people dead and more than two thousand injured. The impression only intensified when evening news bulletins blithely showed hundreds of LAPD officers being issued with shotguns. Media critic Howard Kurtz, writing in the *Washington Post*, meanwhile told the rest of the world that it stood on the brink of 'the most dramatic courtroom verdict in the history of western civilisation'. He was of course entirely right. Socrates had been convicted before fewer people. The findings at Nuremberg had been more predictable. Even contemporaneous trials that might have merited more attention had been drowned out by the Simpson extravaganza – notably one that had ended in New York just the day before, when ten men were convicted on federal charges relating to the February 1993 bombing of the World Trade Center. Whether O. J.'s fate was not just more dramatic but also more important is a question that only history might answer, but Kurtz's bombast stands as a suitable epitaph to the story that his profession had promoted from two-bit tragedy to American epic in little more than a year.

Los Angeles the next morning seemed like a city on the brink of revolution. Helicopters circled a courthouse that had been festooned in yellow crime scene tape, while surging crowds were controlled by formations of mounted police and LAPD infantry in body armour, visors and shields. But at 10.22 a.m., the police fell still with the crowds. So too did 150 million other Americans, and at least as many elsewhere in the world. Radios and televisions hushed as the clerk of the court unsealed the envelope containing the verdict. 'We the jury in the above entitled action find the defendant Orenthal James Simpson not guilty . . .' The expression of the prosecutors disintegrated, while Cochran grasped his client's arm in apparent disbelief. Simpson himself clenched both fists and flashed a winning smile at the jury. Ron Goldman's sister delivered a terrible scream. From the streets rose a tremendous roar.

The responses elsewhere were no less divided, and in many ways recalled reactions to the verdict on Bernard Goetz in 1987. A poll soon showed that four out of five black Americans thought the jury fair while only a half of whites thought the same, ratings that almost precisely reversed the attitudes expressed by New Yorkers in a survey conducted eight years before. The Californian jurors claimed, just as their New York predecessors had done, that they had chosen to acquit not because they knew Simpson to be innocent, but because the prosecution had not persuaded them of his guilt. But notwithstanding the parallels, the predominant reaction could hardly have been more different. Whereas white commentators in 1987 had typically sympathized or empathized with the jurors who had assessed the guilt of Goetz, several were soon rounding like rattlesnakes on those who had had judged Simpson.

Simpson welcomes his acquittal, flanked by defence lawyers
F. Lee Bailey (left) and Johnnie Cochran (right).

The first sign of the attacks to come occurred just minutes after the verdict. Brenda Moran, a 45-year-old computer technician on the jury, was asked whether she would be able to 'live with her conscience'. She coolly asserted that 'we did the right thing' and was not challenged on the point, but others would soon have far more to say about the jurors' good faith. Their claim to have acted colour-blindly (rarely questioned by white commentators when asserted by the slightly less diverse Goetz jury) was typically dismissed, and the dozen workers and retirees, who included two whites and a Hispanic man, were soon being caricatured as a bunch of deluded, black, know-nothing racists. George Will in the *Washington Post* complained that they had 'abused their position' and had given credence to the view of those (other) people who had assumed that they would be incompetent and intellectually incapable. Vincent Bugliosi put the finishing touches to a polemic called *Outrage*, in which he ridiculed the prosecution for failing to recognize that it had to 'spoonfeed' the jurors to compensate for their lack of 'intellectual firepower'. Struggling to strike a note that might sound more sorrowful than instinctive, he also warned that some (other) people now thought blacks as a whole to be stupid and callous, and were liable to take their revenge by 'hurting' them through the ballot box. Tammy Bruce, president of the Los Angeles chapter of the National Organization for Women, preferred to regard the jurors as panderers to sexism. Inviting CNN viewers to recall 'the bodies of Ron and Nicole . . . rotting in their graves', she condemned the jurors' 'hatred and bigotry', which had made them 'an embarrassment to this city'. Ten had of course been women. At least one knew enough about domestic violence to have divorced her husband for inflicting it on her.

It was a peculiarly intense overreaction. The twelve people in the jury box had been forced to serve under threat of imprisonment. They had not been deprived of food, drink and fire like their eighteenth-century predecessors, but they had been isolated for 266 days and subjected to an 11 p.m. curfew and a 5.30 a.m reveille in the name of media freedom and public curiosity. Over the course of their incarceration, jurors and alternate jurors had suffered hardships ranging from acute depression to a heart attack. As their coach drove to court on the trial's last day, one had wondered whether the riot police were protecting them from vengeful crowds, and most would feel sick with worry as they delivered their verdict. And having done so, they now found themselves shouldering the blame for everything from gender conflict in Los Angeles to the future of racial integration in the United States.

Hindsight has shrunk the storm to the proportions of a teacup, but it certainly did not seem that way at the time – and that was no accident. The vilification heaped onto the Simpson jurors reached particularly grotesque proportions, but it exemplified why the system has lasted for eight centuries, and will last for some time yet. The primary role of the people in the jury box has never been to establish ultimate truths. It has been to carry the can. Ever since Aeschylus' *Oresteia* told how Pallas Athena had asked ten humans to assess Orestes' guilt, because the question was too complicated for a mere immortal like her, jurors have borne the same burden. The dozen men who tried the killers of Emmett Till were presented with a dilemma that was confounding Mississippi's racists, and when they whitewashed a murder, they were only lending legitimacy to what many others wanted to do. The jurors at the trial of the Birmingham Six were asked to reconcile panic, prejudice and the presumption of innocence, and their answer served for sixteen years as a fig leaf to cover the inadequacies of the English judicial system. Those judging Bernhard Goetz had a few days to solve issues that had perplexed

New York for two decades, whereupon Mayor Ed Koch could shrug his shoulders and observe that the law was the law.

Juries do not give reasons, because that would open up disagreements rather than close them down. Society meanwhile stands ready to vilify them if they go one way and to riot if they go the other. Small enough for collective liability but large enough to lose individual responsibility, they are pressed to serve as a forensic firing squad. By sealing a defendant's fate they release everyone else from the trial's burden and riddle: how to do justice without hurting either the injured or the innocent.

There are certainly ways to improve the system. Diversification of the jury pool, whether by drawing from sources beyond the electoral register or by minimizing the professions excluded from service, is essential to avoid its stagnation. Another reform that deserves to be more widespread is the practice, common in the USA but unknown in the UK, of swearing standby jurors to lessen the risk of a trial collapsing at the eleventh hour. Restricting the right of peremptory challenge across the United States – and reintroducing a limited version of it to the UK – might well strike a more appropriate balance between the shifting and conflicting demands of impartiality and diversity.

The age-old dream of perfect justice is, however, as mythical today as it was when ancient Egypt's gods weighed the hearts of the dead against the feather of truth. Juries are obviously fallible. Someone has to resolve the irresolvable, however, and the crucial question is whether any alternative is likely to command more confidence and respect. Both history and logic counsel caution in that regard. The inquisitorial system, honed by men far more learned than ever stepped into an English jury box, generated crazed jurisprudence that regularly brought werewolves, corpses, and animals to justice, and killed witches at a rate that dwarfed that of England. And although the nature of the superstitions may have changed, the risks of professionalizing justice remain. The questions most commonly disputed at a criminal trial are whether witnesses are credible and whether beliefs or doubts are reasonable, and such issues demand social legitimacy rather than fiendish cleverness. Reliance on professionals is therefore as much an act of faith as is confidence in the jury, simply because there is no copper-bottomed basis for asserting that they know the answers. The only comprehensive comparison of judges and juries, admittedly based on data that is now half a century old, showed that in three criminal trials out of four, each would have reached the same verdict. In the quarter of cases where they disagreed, judges were over six times as likely to support conviction, but the relative leniency of the jurors was only exceptionally based on outright mistakes of fact or law. It arose simply because they took a different view of the evidence, believed different witnesses, and, ultimately, were more inclined to give some defendants the benefit of the doubt. Only the assumption that more people should be convicted says that they were unreasonable to do so.

The ultimate justification for the jury system is that portrayed so compellingly in Sidney Lumet's *Twelve Angry Men* (1957). The film, shot in real time inside a New York jury room, concerns a murder charge against a young Hispanic defendant. At the beginning of the film, eleven jurors, eager to get home on the hottest day of the year, agree that he is clearly guilty. Only Henry Fonda insists on pausing before sending him to the electric chair. His colleagues explain why there is no point, with sorrow, anger or impatience, but even as they are doing so, their own failings become apparent. As the doubts multiply, clarity turns to doubt. One by one, they change their minds – until they conclude that the defendant is not just presumptively innocent, but actually not guilty. The movie appeals to sentiment rather than reality – so much so that barristerial legend in England credits it with bumping up acquittal rates whenever it is screened – but it contains a message of solid importance. Jurors may not be oracles, infallible and omniscient, but diversity allows their failings at least potentially to cancel each other out. The prejudices and stupidities of like-minded professionals are less likely to – and those of one judge never can.

Conclusion

The criminal trial is about as omnipresent as it has ever been. Although thousands no longer attend courts in person, millions stand ready to watch a noteworthy prosecution. Computer graphics and verbatim re-enactments are reducing legal limits on broadcast coverage to irrelevance and in the United States, where the Constitution has always guaranteed the media particular latitude, tawdry crimes routinely escalate into trials of the century. Perpetrators are promoted into the symbols of an age, their rapes a reminder of lost innocence, their frauds, molestations and murders signs of apocalypse to come. Fake trials are hardly less popular. Countless squabbles of spectacular insignificance are resolved by pseudo-judges in pretend courts, and criminals are shielded from the wrath of Judge Judy et al. thanks only to the technicalities of the Constitution – an impediment that producers may yet overcome. Legal fictions of yet another kind have also become a cinematic staple. Ever since Fritz Lang's *M* (1931) showed a loathsome but pitiful Peter Lorre having to defend his murderous paedophilia before a kangaroo court of beggars, cut-throats, and crooks, the celluloid courtroom has been tackling issues of moment. *Miracle on 34th Street* (1947) saw a sanity board convene to decide what to do with Kris Kringle, an old New Yorker who insisted he was Santa Claus. In *A Matter of Life and Death** (1946) a celestial hearing had to determine whether pilot David Niven, theoretically deceased but spared by a kink in the time–space continuum, could love a woman whom he had wooed while undead. Any televisual icon worth its semiotic salt has also undergone its own courtroom drama. Bart Simpson and *South Park*'s Cartman have confronted and deconstructed trial by media; Dr Who has been arraigned on

---

* US: *Stairway to Heaven*.

charges of cosmic interference; and *Star Trek* has logged prosecutions that span the final frontier itself, arising out of offences so intergalactic that they boggle the human mind even to describe.

Whether the defendant is a thief or a Time Lord, and whether his judges are angels or underworld scum, the ritual honoured by the popular interest enshrines a noble ideal: that people should pause before punishment and allow deliberation to prevail over instinct. The act of restraint quivers, however, with a far darker promise – that justice will take its price in pain – and the hope of protecting the innocent has always vied against a more visceral longing to convict the guilty. Appeals to the ideal have been camouflaging the urge to hurt at least since the time of Aeschylus, who portrayed the protagonists of the *Oresteia* repeatedly invoking the name of Justice while their hands dripped with blood. The ancient Hebrews' idea of even-handedness was to require both guilty defendants and wrongful accusers to suffer an eye for an eye and a tooth for a tooth. Europe's barbarians regarded their penalties as sacraments, as holy as the trials that preceded them, and honoured their gods by burning criminals alive in wicker men or strangling them from gallow-trees. And although modern trials rein in the instincts, each safeguard pays homage to an underlying impulse to punish. The principle that people are responsible only for deliberate acts fights against the gut feeling that some evils deserve punishment whether intended or not. The insistence that silence cannot prove guilt whispers the opposite, and struggles with the perennial desire to hear guilt confessed. The presumption of innocence is laden with the most powerful contradiction of all: the hope that the right person has been charged and that the world will have one less unsolved crime by the time the trial is over.

The two visions – one of hope, the other of fear – have alternated throughout Western history, but the last half a century in the United States has offered a striking illustration of how quickly the polarity can reverse. During the 1950s, as civil rights activists showed Americans that the Constitution was a lie for many Southern blacks, the Supreme Court began imposing uniform standards of criminal procedure across the nation for the very first time. In a flurry of decisions between 1963 and 1968, it then held that every serious charge came with rights – to silence, to call and confront witnesses, to effective counsel, and to a speedy jury trial – all of which states had previously been free to deny. But although those particular decisions still stand, the Court then began to switch. Satisfied that the complacency of a century had been swept away in five years, a bench that presidential appointments was shifting ever further to the right turned its attention towards rising crime figures – and the concern to prevent wrongful convictions became a worry about wrongful acquittals instead.

The new mood first manifested itself with a widespread reappraisal of the purpose of punishment. For several decades it had been conventional to regard its goal as the moral improvement of the wrongdoer, but that consensus now began giving way to an older absolutism, centring on the notion that every crime had its just desserts. A Supreme Court majority reaffirmed the constitutionality of capital punishment in 1976, and incarceration came increasingly to be seen as a form of human pest control. New York introduced laws in 1973 imposing draconian minimum jail sentences for drug offenders, setting in motion a trend that would culminate twenty years later, when the state of Washington passed what became known as the 'three-strikes' statute. It required that anyone who was convicted of a serious felony for a third time had to be given a life sentence, regardless of factors specific to the offence or offender. Similar provisions would soon be enacted in more than half of all states in the USA – often drawing little distinction between savage violence and minor theft – and they now underpin several thousand jail terms.

Although such laws theoretically have no effect on the process that decides whether someone is guilty in the first place, corresponding changes were soon transforming the trial as well. At the same time that state legislators were depriving judges of the prerogative of mercy, a power as old as judgment itself, the Supreme Court began to reconsider the relationship between prosecution and defence in the courtroom. And having spent two decades favouring individuals against states, the Court concluded that when it came to fighting crime, the states – and, more particularly, the attorneys who prosecuted suspects on their behalf – often knew best after all.

The Court's vote of confidence came in the field of plea-bargaining. The practice of trading guilty pleas for reduced sentences has a venerable history in the United States* that dates back over a century, and such negotiations are unavoidable and in many ways unobjectionable. There were certainly more trials in the past – up to a dozen a day – but only because defendants and prosecutors were both reluctant to compromise in an era of inflexible punishments and probable death sentences. Any modern system that did not reward guilty pleas would require either a return to similarly rough-and-ready standards, or spending more typical of defence budgets than legal-aid funds. But even if plea bargains might constitute an important component of modern criminal procedure, their worth as a guarantor of justice depends on each side having roughly equal bargaining power. In 1978, the Supreme Court considered for the first time precisely where the balance lay.

The appellant was Paul Hayes, who had been charged in Kentucky with writing a false cheque for $88. He had been offered a five-year sentence recommendation if he pleaded guilty, but was simultaneously told by the prosecutor that he would face an extra charge under the state's Habitual Criminal Act if he insisted on the 'inconvenience' of a jury trial. He did. When convicted he appealed, pointing out that he had a constitutional right to jury trial and arguing that it had been infringed by the prosecutor's threat. A majority of the Court disagreed. All that had happened, it found, was that Hayes had been presented with 'unpleasant alternatives'. That at least was uncontentious, in that the consequence of being convicted as a 'habitual criminal' meant that his $88 crime earned him a life sentence. The Court's decision in every other sense was, however, a tendentious one. Every plea bargain involves a gamble of sorts, but prosecutors suddenly found themselves with chips of unprecedented value.

The recalibration of the scales of justice has continued ever since. One of the most recent readjustments came in March 2003, when another 5–4 majority of the Supreme Court gave its blessing to California's 'three-strikes' laws, in a case involving one Leandro Andrade. Arrested twice in 1995 for stealing some children's video cassettes from a Kmart store, Andrade was a heroin addict with several previous convictions. The most significant were three burglaries, unarmed but residential, which he had

---

* Plea-bargaining has never been given legal recognition in England. Barristers nevertheless haggle over pleas and judges give 'indications' of their likely sentences almost every day in almost every court of the land.

committed some thirteen years before. Under Californian law, their exisence allowed the prosecutor to charge his Kmart thefts either as felonies – which would activate the minimum sentence laws – or as misdemeanours. He opted for the former course, and a crime worth $154 thereby attracted a sentence of fifty years to life. The Supreme Court rejected his claim that the penalty was so disproportionate as to be unconstitutional. Andrade, in his mid forties at the time of writing, will now stay in jail until 2046, unless he dies there first.

The declining fortunes of defendants and the rising stock of the prosecutor have also been reflected in the trajectory of American cinema. The courtroom drama came of age during the 1950s, and every significant movie of the era celebrated the glories of due process and the valour of the defence attorney. The defendant was typically the victim of hidden machinations or circumstance, while those who championed his corner were unalloyed heroes like Henry Fonda (*Twelve Angry Men*, 1957) or Jimmy Stewart (*Anatomy of a Murder*, 1959). No case was too dirty to deserve a defence. Charles Laughton could be manipulated in *Witness for the Prosecution* (1957) and Maximilian Schell might fight for a Nazi in *Judgment at Nuremberg* (1961), but both were doing no less than a man had to do. Even when the system was rotten, defence lawyers were not: Kirk Douglas and José Ferrer used courts martial to turn the tables on military corruption (*Paths of Glory*, 1957; *The Caine Mutiny*, 1954) while Gregory Peck stared down the entire segregationist South in *To Kill a Mockingbird* (1962). Television followed suit with series such as *The Defenders*, *Petrocelli* and, most famously of all, *Perry Mason* – a legal superhero, capable of vindicating a client with just minutes to spare, generally by reducing a lying witness to blubber or unmasking the true culprit in the public gallery.

The mood lasted into the 1970s, but in an era of post-Watergate cynicism the studios and networks, like the Supreme Court, began to change tack. If there was a single moment when mud entered the fountain of cinematic justice, it came with the 1979 release of *And Justice For All*. The star, a young Al Pacino, was a defence attorney with a clear sense of right and wrong, but that now put him at odds with a legal system that operated with the self-respect of a psychopath and the ethics of an abacus. Pacino himself begins the movie in a cell, having punched a judge who is capriciously keeping his client imprisoned, and ends it reluctantly defending the same judge on a justified charge of rape – redeeming himself only through a timely act of professional suicide. Four years later, *The Star Chamber* depicted a cabal of judges who were themselves so perturbed by the law's shortcomings that they regularly hired hit-men to take out the vermin who wriggled through its loopholes. Although the movie left Michael Douglas aware that looking guilty is not always the same as being it, the moral hazards of criminal defence were soon multiplying exponentially. In *Jagged Edge* (1985), former prosecutor Glenn Close agreed to take on a defence brief for the first time – only to fall for the accused Jeff Bridges and learn the hard way that representing an alleged knife-wielding maniac is the kind of job that gives decent folk sleepless nights. Two years later, Cher was another inadequate female defender in *Suspect*, overworked, underpaid, and so stymied by corruption that establishing her client's innocence required that she turn a blind eye to professional ethics and a flirtatious one towards a male juror. Defence lawyers as gullible sap or ethical basket case were soon stock characters – figuring in movies such as *Just Cause* and *Primal Fear*, to take two impressive examples from 1996 – and they were joined by figures considerably more grotesque. *Law and Order* dominated televisual drama throughout the nineties, and the structure of each episode – showing New York's finest arresting suspects and plucky prosecutors then pursuing them through court – resembled that used in a sixties show called *Arrest and Trial*. But the earlier version had showcased the defence lawyer, whereas the defenders in *Law and Order* were generally shysters of the lowest sort, displaying a tireless devotion to injustice and a zealous concern to abet their clients' crimes. By the time Al Pacino reprised the legal career he had abandoned in 1979, the fall was irredeemable. In *Devil's Advocate* (1997), he was Satan himself, moonlighting as the senior partner of a Manhattan law firm, while Keanu Reeves was a legal acolyte who gave up nothing more than the shreds of his soul for a supernatural power to win acquittals on behalf of child molesters.

Movie corporations and directors can still be found to sanctify the actually innocent, so long as their tale is safely historical (*In the Name of the Father*, 1993; *Murder in the First*, 1994; *Amistad*, 1997; *The Hurricane*, 1999). Reasonable doubts still pass muster if the accused's crime is one that Hollywood respects, such as the slaying of racist paedophiles (*A Time to Kill*, 1996). Marines remain on the side of the angels even if they murder tell-tales down in Guantánamo Bay (*A Few Good Men*, 1992) or machine-gun riotous Arabs for love of America (*Rules of Engagement*, 2000). Otherwise, however, the defensible defendant has become a very rare bird, and the righteous defence attorney has been virtually written out of the script. Joe Pesci played the role for laughs in the excellent *My Cousin Vinny* (1992), and Diane Lane should have done the same in the abysmal *Judge Dredd* (1995); but the only memorable straight specimen in recent years was Raul Julia in *Presumed Innocent* (1990) – and his client was a prosecutor.

The shift in sympathies towards the prosecution has been a little less pronounced in the United Kingdom. All else being equal, which it admittedly never is, UK citizens are more willing than their US counterparts to accept that an accused person might be an innocent underdog rather than unconvicted villain. English barristers who represent alleged scum are as likely as American defenders to inspire perplexity and suspicions of moral bankruptcy, but lawyers who would punish are typically mistrusted at least as much as those who would defend. And whereas the defence attorney as hero has imploded under the pseudo-moral gravity of modern US cinema and television, Britain's sole contribution to twentieth-century courtroom drama – *Rumpole of the Bailey* – was a bedraggled old hack who would barely have known how to untie the white ribbons of a prosecution brief.

Conventional wisdom teaches, however, that in any significant field of human endeavour Britain lags only a few years behind the USA, and there are plenty of indications that an official redefinition of fair play is proceeding apace. Governments have been introducing watered-down versions of minimum sentences and three-strikes provisions since the late 1990s, and although politicians still generally think it sensible to express suspicions of plea-bargaining – typically, if disingenuously, by deploring its American strangeness – they have been piling the pressure on defendants for years. Successive statutes have steered an ever increasing volume of serious crime towards magistrates, who are at least 10 per cent more likely than juries to convict. The United Kingdom has also found itself able to discard several venerable, but inconvenient, defence rights with an ease that the state and federal constitutions of the USA would never permit. The rule that silence could not prove guilt, incorporated into the Fifth Amendment of the US Constitution, was abolished by the UK Parliament in 1994. The rule that no one could be tried twice for the same crime, already ancient when America's revolutionaries borrowed it for the double jeopardy clause of the Bill of Rights, was tossed aside in 2003 – by a law that made no exceptions even for people acquitted decades before its enactment.

The increasing pressures to convict on both sides of the Atlantic are not necessarily wrong. The ritualistic claim to be 'rebalancing' justice in favour of victims, typically advanced when votes are in the air, can be cynical in the extreme, but history, if nothing else, shows that there is nothing absolute about the ground rules used to address guilt or innocence. A heightened sensitivity to social disorder – whether burglaries, racist violence, sexual abuse or anything else – might arguably be good reason to reconsider some of the rules. But all the activity, whatever its merits, comes with a peculiar paradox. While legislators and judges have been increasing prosecutorial powers, while those powers have been exercised ever more aggressively, and while virtual trials have filled the ether, the proportion of cases actually resolved at trial has hovered only just above statistical insignificance. Back in 1839, about three-quarters of felony charges in New York ended in a trial, but the figure in US state and federal cases is now just over 5 per cent. In the UK, the comparable statistic is probably even lower, down from over 95 per cent in the 1830s. At the same time, it remains all but impossible to imagine the extinction of the struggle between prosecution and defence. The courtroom contest has always presented a potent spectacle – and whatever the sight might have meant in the past, each trial now means it more than ever.

Social scientists have long argued that the exposure of criminals to communal vilification serves an important function. The first to do so was the nineteenth-century founder of sociology, Émile Durkheim, who argued that rules logically presupposed rule-breakers, and that a community without wrongdoers was therefore literally inconceivable. 'Imagine a society of saints, a perfect cloister of exemplary individuals,' he wrote in 1895. 'Crimes, properly so called, will there be unknown; but faults which appear venial to the layman will create there the same scandal that the ordinary offense does in ordinary consciousnesses. If, then, this society has the power to judge and punish, it will define these acts as criminal and will treat them as such.' Durkheim's claim – essentially that if crimes did not exist, people would have to make them up – was pleasantly provocative. It was also sufficiently devoid of substance that thinkers of both left and right would find it a useful springboard for their own theories. One whose intellectual legacy has been claimed by both sides – but whose views fall squarely into the authoritarian category – was psychologist Carl Gustav Jung. His perspective, though somewhat peculiar, opens up a particularly illuminating perspective on the modern criminal trial.

Jung is usually remembered as a gentle sage with an eye for archetypes and a nice line in dream analysis, but he was also a rabid disciplinarian. His respect for irrationality was such that he once justified capital punishment on the basis that it recalled Aztec traditions of tearing out human hearts, and he was always insistent that a community's well-being depended on its willingness to condemn its mischief makers. Attempting to reform them was tantamount to nurturing a disease, and individuals were betraying themselves if they failed to hate those who did wrong.

That said, Jung's penchant for unreason made him fond of paradox, and he simultaneously accorded the criminal the stature of tragic hero. 'There must be some people who behave in the wrong way,' he told his audience at a 1935 London lecture. '[T]hey act as scapegoats and objects of interest for the normal ones. Think how grateful you are . . . that you can say, "Thank heaven, I am not that fellow who has committed the crime; I am a perfectly innocent creature." You feel satisfaction because the evil people have done it for you. This is the deeper meaning of the fact that Christ as the redeemer has been crucified between two thieves. These thieves in their way also were redeemers of mankind, they were the scapegoats.' And for Jung, wrongdoers did not just perform their services to the community from the heights of a crucifix. He also hankered for a simpler past – a time when, before they were solemnly escorted to their deaths, criminals had been given the 'dignity of [their] merit . . . a long trial with judges in wigs and gowns'.

The theory that trials defined people as bad to establish what was good, flexibly circular as it was, then became popular among a very different type of theoretician in the decades after the Second World War. Ethnographers, increasingly concerned to analyse cultural differences by standards that were value-neutral, began to notice how stick fights among west African tribes, say, or singing contests between disputing Eskimos resembled, in their own different way, the Western trial. Several sociologists and historians of a leftist bent helped along by advancing complex analyses to show that all was not as it seemed in the courtroom – that the formalized degradation of deviants served, for example, to prop up capitalism and distract the masses from various more important things.* The speculations, whether illuminating or mystifying, all cut across the assumption that trials inquire into guilt while punishments are subsequently visited upon it. Since that assumption has been fundamental to the Western legal tradition for most of a millennium, it is perhaps not surprising that they made little headway into the actual practice of law. But in 1980, support for the sociologists and anthropologists came from a surprising source – the then Chief Justice of the US Supreme Court, Warren Burger. And it did so in the context of a decision that has helped to define the modern trial: a ruling that the media should have unrestricted access to any criminal prosecution.

Ever since the witchcraft and treason trials of sixteenth-century England inspired the first court reports, publicity has been potentially able to exaggerate a case's prominence and prejudice a jury. The integrity of the process was historically protected by legal limits on media freedom, and English law continues to control press reporting and ban broadcasters from trials. The US Supreme Court imposed similar restrictions after the introduction of radio following free-for-alls such as the 1925 Scopes trial, and for almost half a century states were obliged to curtail coverage when necessary to guarantee a fair trial. But in 1980, it declared that the public interest in openness in fact always trumped a defendant's rights,

---

* The era's most emblematic radical, historian Michel Foucault, regarded the courtroom in this light. His classic work on criminal justice focused exclusively on penalties, noting of trials only that they attracted attention that would once have been focused on punishments (*Surveiller et punir* [Paris, 1975], p.15; *Discipline and Punish*, tr. Alan Sheridan [London, 1977], p. 9), but he had had more to say about courts three years earlier. Asked by a group of Parisian Maoists in 1972 whether he approved of their plans to stage a people's trial of the Parisian police force, he warned of serious risks. Recalling the French revolutionaries' kangaroo courts of September 1792 (see pp. xi–xiii of this book), he worried that the eagerness to mimic bourgeois justice might derail the Maoists' enterprise. He expressed no qualms about the sansculottes' bloodthirstiness but was very concerned by their decision to place a table between themselves and those whom they were judging. 'Can we not see the embryonic, albeit fragile form of a state apparatus reappearing here?', he wondered. See Michel Foucault, *Power/Knowledge: Selected Interviews and Other Writings, 1972–1977*, ed. and tr. Colin Gordon (New York, 1980), p. 2.

paving the way for another ruling later in the same year that would permit states to allow television cameras into court. The reasoning of Burger, who wrote the Court's primary opinion, was instructive.

Burger barely mentioned two of the most common arguments for open justice: that transparency can educate the outside world about the workings of the legal system and keep participants on their toes. His decision hinged instead on the claim that publicity operated to maintain popular confidence in courts. The idea that justice should be seen to be done was hardly novel, but Burger supported it with a sociological perspective seen less often in legal judgments. After a lengthy survey of the history of openness in the Anglo-American criminal justice system, he asserted that, 'long before there were behavioral scientists . . . to frame the concept in words' people were widely aware that public trials had 'significant community therapeutic value'. He then observed that shocking crimes were often followed by 'a community reaction of outrage and public protest'. As a result, he argued, the media's access to courtrooms should be guaranteed because only a state power to allow them into criminal trials could meet the public's 'fundamental, natural yearning to see justice done – or even the urge for retribution'.

The claim put a dynamic spin on some very venerable jurisprudence. Thinkers from Aeschylus to Aquinas had regarded judgment and punishment as a process through which the community secured revenge for crime's individual victims. Burger was proposing, however, that the trial itself could – and should – offer spectacular retribution to the public at large. It was a radical assertion. Although countless judges had previously asserted that their sentences were intended to reflect popular anger at guilty defendants, none of note had ever argued that trials ought to accommodate the rage even before a verdict was returned. The traditional position was expressed succinctly in 1957 by a reflective legal writer called Henry Weihofen (in a work that Burger oddly named in support of his argument albeit that, when read, it entirely undermines it). 'The function of the law is to hold the brute forces of hate and vindictiveness in check,' wrote Weihofen, 'not to encourage them.'

In 1980 it may have seemed possible that unrestricted coverage would only depict reality. More than two decades on, few would doubt that it has transformed it. Since the 1991 launch of Court TV, the threshold of the acceptable, set by nothing more restrictive than broadcasters' competitiveness and viewers' hunger for novelty, has sunk ever lower. Primetime in 2002, to take a representative recent year, hosted the testimony of countless distraught victims, the perplexities of a mentally disturbed female killer in Texas, and the embarrassments of four pubescent homicides in Florida. Not a moment of the trial or an inch of the courtroom remains out of bounds. In early 2002 an Arizona court allowed ABC television to film and broadcast jurors' deliberations in five criminal cases that were then broadcast in a docudrama series called *State v.* Later in the same year, Texas Judge Ted Poe permitted a crew to record jury discussions *after* conviction – in a case where the question was whether to condemn a mentally subnormal 17-year-old boy called Cedric Harrison to death by lethal injection. A majority of the court of appeals stepped in to overrule him, but not since the closure of imperial Rome's arenas had a populace come quite as close to having a life-and-death decision served up as entertainment. The thumbs-up and the thumbs-down may yet return, to screens across the nation.

Trials have been the only public ritual of Western criminal justice since executions disappeared behind prison walls during the mid nineteenth century, and it is tempting to draw parallels between people's appreciation of the courtroom spectacle and the attention their predecessors once paid to outdoor hangings. Sensationalist commentators profit like the pamphleteers of old Tyburn. Respectable ones, like the equally responsible reporters of yesteryear, lament the prurience while feeding it. And just as it was abolitionists who most vehemently opposed the concealment of capital punishment, some of those most in favour of publicity have been convinced that it can expose defects in the process. It was prosecutors who appealed against Judge Ted Poe's decision in the case of Cedric Harrison – while the would-be broadcasters were from PBS's high-minded *Frontline* show, and Harrison's own counsel asked that cameras be allowed in the jury room.

Trial broadcasts are, however, more pernicious than public executions ever were. Abolitionists wanted to keep hangings visible because the sight of men and women going to their deaths, roaring with defiance or defecating with fear, was as likely to disgust as to amuse. Events around the gallows were so volatile that the death penalty itself looked threatened for a time. But for all the ferocity that occasionally coalesces around a lengthy case such as that of O. J. Simpson, the sound bites and highlights that are broadcast into the comfort of viewers' homes overwhelmingly operate to defuse tension rather than foster it. It is even arguable that the broadcasts are slowly, but surely, skewing criminal justice in favour of conviction. Although routine transparency is an excellent safeguard against corruption and stupidity, selective coverage generates expectations of even-handedness that can undermine the presumption of innocence itself. As lawyers are promoted to celebrities outside court they turn to gladiators inside it, and restrictions on the prosecution come to seem like unfair handicaps rather than the centuries-old methods of avoiding mistakes that they are. Trials thereby become battles between champions – and when innocent victims and the public interest are on one side, an individual defendant may sometimes win the battle, but the rights of defendants in general can only lose the war.

The risks are obvious. Although no system of justice worth the name could ever be neutral towards the horror of crime or towards victims, focusing on either during a trial risks turning an inquiry into a memorial service – and the unhappy results of that litter legal history. As far back as 1580, Jean Bodin warned that witchcraft was 'so obscure and its mischiefs so hidden' that 'not one out of a thousand . . . would be punished' unless lawyers circumvented obstacles to conviction. His concern for victims' rights sparked off Europe's most ferocious decades of witch-hunting, and although witches are as thin on the ground today as they were then, the logic of demonology lives on. It emerged on dozens of occasions in 1970s England, when fears of IRA terrorism and hatred of terrorists inspired policemen to extract fantastic confessions, which judges then believed and juries then relied upon. Its power was seen again when the federal prosecutors of al-Qaeda sympathizer Zacarias Moussaoui argued in late 2003 that photographs of the three thousand-odd people murdered on September 11 2001 could help a jury decide if he had intended to kill them. At a time of great fear, however, when legal safeguards sometimes seem no more secure than the chaos they theoretically subordinate, the eagerness to partake, painlessly, of the agonies of the injured is likely only to grow. Evildoers, whether accused or actual, can probably expect even less sympathy than usual over the next few years.

Lest anyone think that an unequivocally good thing, the death rows of the United States offer a particularly striking example of how the hatred of crime can short-circuit the ability of rational men and women to judge

criminality. During the quarter of a century that followed the reintroduction of the death penalty in 1976, one capital offender had a conviction
overturned on appeal for every seven who were executed. In fourteen of
those cases – along with 137 non-capital ones – innocence was established
by DNA analysis of stored trial exhibits. Prosecutors in Florida and
several other states did not respond by trying to work out what they
might have been doing wrong. They argued instead that, in the interests
of 'finality' and sensitivity towards victims, those exhibits that remained
untested should be destroyed.

It is hard to imagine a more inefficient method of resolving crime than the
modern criminal trial. Even the most routine case is characterized by
counter-intuitive rules of evidence and aggressive argument rather than a
co-operative search for truth. An elaborate one can cost millions, last years,
and conclude with a guilty defendant walking free, costs in hand. Those that
take place, whatever their complexity, are in any event just a dwindling fraction of the total number of allegations, selected for trial on a basis that few
outsiders ever learn. While they form popular perceptions of what law and
order is all about, the interests of suspects and victims alike are meanwhile
determined far from the public gaze, as prosecutors pursue convictions and
drop charges as principle, personal inclination or public mood takes them.

And yet to judge trials in terms of their efficiency makes not much more
sense than it would to assess a wedding or a funeral by its accuracy.
Prosecutions have been pursuing goals more intangible than efficiency

since the days when Athenians convened to dispel the *miasma* of a murderer and Europe's advocates debated the rights of caterpillars and corpses. Exploitable though the spectacle has always been, it possesses qualities that no system of negotiated pleas will ever rival, no matter how cheap and no matter how fair. For each time a defendant comes to court and contests his or her guilt, a process unfolds that reiterates precepts that are central to the self-image of modern democracy. It asserts that individuals bear the burden of their sins, and that a community can always outlast the sinners in its midst. It portrays a state that is sufficiently self-controlled to prevent public officials from unilaterally deciding anyone's fate, and humble enough to trust its citizens to watch justice – even, sometimes, to do it. Perhaps most potently of all, the criminal trial literally enacts the meaning of human dignity, showing a civilization that treats its most despicable enemies with respect – presuming them innocent, confronting them as equals, and giving them a champion to argue their cause.

As the sword and scales give way to the stick and carrot, many of the claims can sound either quaint or naive. The ideal of equality before the law regularly loses out to the reality of racial, sexual, and financial bias. Shrill calls for law and order routinely drown out the plea for fairness. Courtrooms at their worst epitomize nothing more exalted than hypocrisy. But each trial re-enacts the dream – and as even Carl Jung would have agreed, a community forgets its dreams at its peril.

It is only our conception of time that makes us call the Last Judgment by that name; in fact it is a permanent court martial.

FRANZ KAFKA, *Aphorisms*

Further Reading

Narrative accounts and original sources relating to all the trials covered in this book are contained in the notes that follow, and a full bibliography can be found on a website that accompanies this book: www.thetrial.net. Many legal sources, which have been traditionally encrypted by references and concealed in inaccessible tomes, are now widely available on to the internet. A search for any given case will almost certainly produce at least some information, and quite possibly a transcript. The endnotes include website addresses where they contain an electronic version of the work cited; those who want to dabble further might find the following addresses suitably surfworthy.

The best site on trials in general, called simply Famous Trials, is run by Doug Linder at the University of Missouri-Kansas City: www.law. umkc.edu/faculty/projects/ftrials/ftrials.htm. It contains transcripts, evidence and commentary relating to dozens of the proceedings covered in this book, including those of Ray Buckey, William Calley, John Scopes, Socrates, O.J. Simpson and Henry Sweet. A vast collection of older texts, ranging from the Code of Hammurabi to the complete laws of Emperor Justinian and the collected writings of Thomas Jefferson, is contained at the Constitution Society's Liberty Library: www.constitution.org/ liberlib.htm. Another site that merits exploration, containing articles on legal history, sociology and crime fiction, is the University of Texas Law School's Tarlton E-Text Collection: http://tarlton.law.utexas.edu/lpop/etext.

War crimes trials are well reported on the internet. Transcripts of the first Nuremberg trial (along with much else) can be found via the Yale Law School's Avalon site at www.yale.edu/lawweb/avalon/imt/imt.htm. Full or edited records from the later Nuremberg trials are available at several locations, notably www.mazal.org and sites maintained by the

University of the West of England (www.ess.uwe.ac.uk/genocide/trials.htm) and Harvard Law School (www.law.harvard.edu/library/digital/digital_projects.htm). The complete records of the Eichmann Trial are searchable at www.nizkor.org; while transcripts from the prosecution of Slobodan Milošević are posted on www.un.org/icty. Developments at the International Criminal Court can be followed via the court's official site: www.icc-cpi.int.

Current judgments are available at no charge from a number of sources. The United States Supreme Court publishes its own decisions at www.supremecourtus.gov, and a large archive of US cases, along with links to many more American legal sites, can be found at Findlaw: www.findlaw.com/casecode. The UK judiciary runs official websites at www.parliament.uk/judicial_work/judicial_work.cfm (House of Lords) and www.privy-council.org.uk (Privy Council). Further decisions, taken from the Court of Appeal, the High Court and other parts of the judicial machine in and beyond the United Kingdom, can be found at the British and Irish Legal Information Institute (www.bailii.org). Even more rulings, including those of several inferior tribunals, are published on www.courtservice.gov.uk.

International materials, along with links to legal institutions in virtually every country in the world, are available at sites run by the American Society of International Law (www.asil.org/resource/Home.htm), the Institute of Advanced Legal Studies (http://ials.sas.ac.uk/links/eagle i.htm), and New York University (www.law.nyu.edu/library/foreign_intl/foreign_search.html).

The text of all new federal statutes is available via the US Government Printing Office (www.gpoaccess.gov/index.html). UK statutes can be found at Her Majesty's Stationery Office (www.legislation.hmso.gov.uk/acts.htm#acts).The US Department of Justice maintains a site devoted to federal criminal law at www.ojp.usdoj.gov/bjs, and equivalent state materials can be found at www.ncsconline.org. The Department for Constitutional Affairs in the United Kingdom deals with criminal matters at www.dca.gov.uk/criminal/crimfr.htm, and the Home Office maintains a site at www.homeoffice.gov.uk. Official UK statistics and reports are available via the HMSO site at www.official-documents.co.uk/index.html.

Notes

The quotations from Franz Kafka that head each chapter are taken from the
following editions of his writings: *The Great Wall and other Short Works*, tr.
Malcolm Pasley (Harmondsworth, 1991), which contains the aphorisms; *The
Trial*, tr. Willa and Edwin Muir (London, 1937); and Max Brod (ed.), *The
Diaries of Franz Kafka 1914–23*, tr. Martin Greenberg and Hannah Arendt
(New York, 1949). The passage from *In the Penal Colony* (*In der Strafkolonie*)
is translated by the present author.

Introduction

xi: *soon over*' . . . Simon Schama, *Citizens* (New York, 1989), p. 628.

xi: *walls of Paris*' . . . Ibid., p. 630.

xi: *a sword*' . . . Alfred Bougeart, *Marat. L'Ami du peuple*, 2 vols (Paris, 1865),
2: 85.

xi: *had survived* . . . See the eyewitness account of Jean Claude Hipolite Méhée
(Méhée de Latouche) in G. Lenotre (pseud.), *The September Massacres*
(London, 1929) ['Lenotre'], at pp. 143–4; cf. the account of one of those in
the carriages, the Abbé Sicard, at p. 277.

xii: *tried first* . . . Pierre Caron, *Les massacres de Septembre* (Paris, 1935),
pp. 29–39.

xii: *darkened chamber* . . . This account is taken from François Jourgniac de
Saint-Méard, *Mon agonie de trente-huit heures* (Paris, 1792), translated as
My Agony for Thirty-Eight Hours (London, 1792).

xii: *70-year-old man* . . . Saint-Méard states that he was about sixty, but see
Thomas Carlyle, *The French Revolution*, 3 vols (London, 1837) ['Carlyle'],
3: 49.

xiii: *citizenry alike* . . . See Lenotre, pp. 44, 121–2, 141; Oscar Browning (ed.),
The Despatches of Earl Gower (Cambridge, 1885), pp. 227–8; Carlyle, 3: 42.

xiv: *Jesus Christ* . . . Asher Maoz, 'Historical Adjudication: Courts of Law,
Commissions of Inquiry, and "Historical Truth"', 18 *Law and History
Review* 559 (2000) at pp. 559–60.

xvii: *properly convicted* . . . The first four sections of Hammurabi's Code prescribed execution for anyone who failed to make out an accusation: see Godfrey R. Driver and John C. Miles, *The Babylonian Laws*, 2 vols (Oxford, 1952–5), 1: 58–68.

xvii: *who agreed* . . . I Kings 3: 16–28.

xvii: *to oblivion* . . . See Siegfried Morenz, *Egyptian Religion*, tr. Ann E. Keep (London, 1973), pp. 126–7; see also Adolf Erman, *Life in Ancient Egypt* (London, 1894), pp. 139, 309.

xvii: *his innocence* . . . See 'Charge of Murder. Prisoner's Evidence', *The Times* (London), 8 March 1909, p. 5.

xviii: *invisible substance* . . . Edward Marjoribanks, *For the Defence: The Life of Sir Edward Marshall Hall QC* (New York, 1929), pp. 256–64.

Chapter 1: From Eden to Ordeals

1: *King Hammurabi* . . . See Amélie Kuhrt, *The Ancient Near East c.3000–330 BC*, 2 vols (London, 1997), 1: 111; for the code's text, see Godfrey R. Driver and John C. Miles, *The Babylonian Laws*, 2 vols (Oxford, 1952–5).

1: *Mount Sinai* . . . Exodus 31: 18.

1: *from Zeus* . . . Plato, *Laws* 624a–625a.

2: *common people* . . . Numbers 35: 24; Joshua 20: 6–9.

2: *722 BC* . . . See Richard E. Friedman, *Who Wrote the Bible* (New York, 1987), pp. 89–100, 188ff.

2: *Greek mythology* . . . All English quotes that follow in the text from are taken from Aeschylus, *The Oresteia*, tr. Robert Fagles (Harmondsworth, 1977).

4: *vote for Orestes* . . . 'Eumenides' 737–46. Athena's speech is in fact ambiguous in the original Greek, and can be read to mean simply that in the event of a tie, Orestes is to be acquitted. The preponderance of scholarly opinion is, however, that her casting vote broke what would otherwise have been a tie. See Walter G. Headlam and George Thomson, *The Oresteia of Aeschylus*, 2 vols (Cambridge, 1938), 2: 298–300; Robert J. Bonner and G. Smith, *The Administration of Justice from Homer to Aristotle*, 2 vols (Chicago, 1930), 1: 127–8.

4: *all things* . . . See generally George B. Kerferd, *The Sophistic Movement* (Cambridge, 1981), pp. 85ff.

4: *twelve Gods* . . . For other treatments of the myth of Orestes, see *Odyssey*, Books I and III; Euripides, *Orestes* 1650; Demosthenes, *Against Aristocrates* 66 and 74.

5: *accursed at worst* . . . See Humphrey D. F. Kitto, *The Greeks* (London, 1991) ['Kitto'], p. 244.

5: *lesser sins* . . . For examples of paired sin and burnt offerings, see Numbers 6: 10, Leviticus, 9: 2, 15: 15. For examples of the sacrifice/release ritual, see Leviticus 14: 7, 14: 53 and 16: 8–34.

5: *man's misdeeds* . . . Hesiod, *Works and Days* 225, 240.

6: *of contamination* . . . See Robert Parker, *Miasma. Purification and Pollution in Early Greek Religion* (Oxford, 1983), pp. 269–71.

6: *hail of stones* . . . Jan Bremmer, 'Scapegoat Rituals in Ancient Greece', 87 *Harvard Studies in Classical Philology* 299 (1983).

6: *the sea* . . . On the *bouphonia* ritual, see Walter Burkert, *Homo necans. The Anthropology of Ancient Greek Sacrificial Ritual and Myth*, tr. Peter Bing (Berkeley and London, 1983), pp. 136–43; Dennis D. Hughes, *Human Sacrifice in Ancient Greece* (London and New York, 1991), at p. 86.

6: *thousand and one* . . . See Christopher Carey, *Trials from Classical Athens* (London and New York, 1997) ['Carey'], pp. 2–7, 22 n.20.

6: *seventy silent per cent* . . . See Simon Hornblower and Antony Spawforth (eds), *The Oxford Classical Dictionary*, 3rd edn (Oxford and New York, 1996), pp.451–2 (entry for 'democracy, Athenian').

6: *great pain* . . . On the legal status of Athenian women, see Carey, pp. 7–8. On that of slaves, see ibid., pp. 16–17.

7: *misty as any myth* . . . No one knows how earlier generations of Greeks regarded homicide. E. R. Dodds pointed out that the *miasma* was unknown to the seventh- or eighth-century author of the *Iliad* and the *Odyssey*, and argued that manslaughter must have been perceived as a relatively unremarkable event by people of the era: see E. R. Dodds, *The Greeks and the Irrational* (Berkeley and Los Angeles, 1951), p. 21 n.37, pp. 35–7. Cf. Robert Parker, *Miasma. Purification and Pollution in Early Greek Religion* (Oxford, 1983), pp. 130ff., who minimizes the discontinuity between the two eras. See also Douglas M. MacDowell, *Athenian Homicide Law in the Age of the Orators* (Manchester, 1963) ['MacDowell, *Homicide*'], *passim*.

7: *not sunk* . . . See Antiphon, 'On the Killing of Herodes' 11, 82–4, in Carey, pp. 44, 57.

7: *like a slave* . . . See Antiphon, 'On the Chorister' 4, in Carey, p. 64.

7: *murderous objects* . . . Demosthenes, *Against Aristocrates* 76; Aristotle, *Constitution of Athens* 57; MacDowell, *Homicide*, pp. 85–9.

7: *circumspect distance* . . . See MacDowell, *Homicide*, pp. 82–4, and sources cited therein.

7: *obtain vengeance* . . . See Antiphon, 'On the Chorister' 6, in Carey, p. 64; and see Antiphon's *Tetralogies* as translated by J. S. Morrison in Rosamond K. Sprague, *The Older Sophists* (Columbia, S.C., 1972), pp. 136–63.

7: *to stand trial* . . . Numbers 35: 11–33, Joshua 20: 6–9, Deuteronomy 19: 2–13.

8: *right or wrong* . . . On the unquestionable nature of a wrongful conviction, see Antiphon, 'On the Chorister' 3, in Carey, pp. 63–4. For an overview of the *polis* in Greek thought, see Victor Ehrenberg, *The Greek State* (Oxford,

1960), pp. 28–102; and on its juristic importance, see especially pp. 77–80.

8: *called Xenophon* . . . Xenophon wrote two works on the subject: an account of Socrates' speech to the jury and a selection of memories about Socrates' character: see his 'Apology of Socrates to the Jury' (tr. Andrew Patch) in Robert C. Bartlett (ed.), *The Shorter Socratic Writings* (Ithaca, NY, 1996), pp. 9ff., and *Memorabilia*, tr. Amy L. Bonnete (Ithaca, NY, 2001) ['*Shorter Socratic Writings*' and '*Memorabilia*' respectively].

8: *demolishing its walls* . . . See Xenophon, *A History of My Times*, tr. Rex Warner (Harmondsworth, 1978) ['*Hellenica*'], pp. 107–8 (2.2.20–3).

9: *ten years of war* . . . Aristotle, *Constitution of Athens* 35.4; *Hellenica*, p. 129 (2.4.21).

9: *Critias himself* . . . See *Memorabilia*, pp. 7ff. (1.2.12ff.); on Plato's lineage, see G. C. Field, *Plato and His Contemporaries* (London, 1930), pp.4–5

9: *comedy,* The Clouds . . . On Socrates' sympathies for Sparta, see also Plato, *Crito* 52e; Aristophanes, *The Birds* 1281.

9: *time in power* . . . See Plato, *Apology* 32c–d; *Memorabilia*, pp. 11–12 (1.2.31ff).

9: *as a soldier* . . . Plato, *Apology* 28e and 32b. Xenophon, *Hellenica*, p. 88 (1.7.15); see also Plato, *The Symposium* 219e–221b.

10: *wanted to die* . . . Xenophon, *Shorter Socratic Writings*, p. 9.

10: *earthenware jars* . . . The pebbles were different colours, only one of which would count for the result: see Carey, p. 17. Two balls, one solid and one hollow, would later be used: see Aristotle, *Constitution of Athens* 68.

11: *his own sentence* . . . Some offences had fixed penalties, whereas others did not: Carey, pp. 7, 61.

11: *suggest anything* . . . Xenophon, *Shorter Socratic Writings*, p. 15.

11: *anyone but God'* . . . The translation comes from Plato, *The Last Days of Socrates* (Harmondsworth, 1969), p.76.

11: *mass murder* . . . See Kitto, p.153; cf. Dodds, p.190 (who emphasizes the religious aspect of the prosecution, while recognising the importance of its political component). On the trial in general, see also I. F. Stone, *The Trial of Socrates* (Boston, 1988), though the work is flawed by the author's apparent belief that all would have been well if only Athens had possessed the First Amendment.

11: *private persons?'* . . . Ibid., p.90. For the dialogue itself, see Plato, *Crito*.

12: *[of our time]* . . . Plato, *The Last Days of Socrates* (Harmondsworth, 1969), p. 183 ('Phaedo' 118).

12: *conquered city'* . . . Sigmund Freud, *Civilization and its Discontents* (New York, 1961), p. 84.

13: *mourning dress* . . . See Arnold H. M. Jones, *Criminal Courts of the Roman Republic and Principate* (Oxford, 1972), p. 14; introduction to *Cicero: Defence Speeches*, tr. D. H. Berry (Oxford, 2000), p. xxix.

13: *took a breather* . . . K. M. Coleman, 'Fatal Charades: Roman Executions Staged as Mythological Enactments', 80 *Journal of Roman Studies* 44 (1990); see also Thomas Wiedemann, *Emperors and Gladiators* (London, 1992), pp. 68–92.

13: *permutation thereof* . . . See Edward Gibbon, *The History of the Decline and Fall of the Roman Empire*, 6 vols (London, 1776–88), 4: 400–2 and sources cited therein.

14: *stamp of the feet* . . . Cicero, *On the Ideal Orator* (ed. James M. May and Robert Wisse, New York and Oxford, 2001) ['Cicero, *De Oratore*'], p. 292, 294 [3.217, 3.220].

14: *with it exactly* . . . 'On Duties (II)' in Cicero, *On the Good Life*, tr. Michael Grant (Harmondsworth, 1971), at p. 147.

14: *judges' eyes* . . . Quintilian, *The Orator's Education. Books 1–2*, (*Institutio oratoria*), (ed. Donald A. Russell, Harvard, 2001), p. 387 [2.17.21]; Plutarch, *Life of Cicero* 25.

14: *to a trial* . . . Cicero, *Laws* (*De legibus*) 1.15.42, available in Cicero, *De re publica. De Legibus*, tr. Clinton W. Keyes (London and New York, 1928), pp.343–5.

14: *in 63 BC* . . . On Cicero's role in suppressing the Catiline conspirators see Anthony Everitt, *Cicero. A Turbulent Life* (London, 2001), pp. 102–7.

14: *orator's tongue* . . . Cassius Dio Cocceianus, *Dio's Roman History*, tr. Earnest Cary, 9 vols (London, 1914–27), 5: 130–3 [47.8.4].

15: *ever penned* . . . See S. P. Scott (ed.), *The Civil Law Including The Twelve Tables, The Institutes of Gaius, The Rules of Ulpian, The Opinions of Paulus, The Enactments of Justinian, and The Constitutions of Leo*, 17 vols (Cincinnati, 1932), vols. 2–11.

15: *mid 530s* . . . See Mike Baillie, *Exodus to Arthur: Catastrophic Encounters with Comets* (London, 1999), *passim*; David Keys, *Catastrophe: An Investigation into the Origins of the Modern World* (London, 1999), *passim*.

16: *royal leg* . . . See Frederic Austin Ogg (ed.), *A Source Book of Mediæval History. Documents Illustrative of European Life and Institutions from the German Invasions to the Renaissance* (New York, 1907) ['Ogg'], p. 172.

16: *squarely on the gods* . . . For an overview of the transition see the three-part essay by J. S. Taylor-Cameron, 'Roman Law in the Early Middle Ages', in 7 *Juridical Review* 241 (1895), 8 *Juridical Review* 118 (1896), and 10 *Juridical Review* 438 (1898).

16: *processes of criminal justice* . . . Ordeal by fire does, however, appear once in Greek literature: Sophocles, *Antigone* 264–7.

16: *propitiate their gods* . . . Julius Caesar gave an account of the Druidic rituals in a work he wrote about his victories in western Europe: see *The Conquest of Gaul*, tr. S. A. Handford (Harmondsworth, 1951), pp. 31–3.

16: *god of war* . . . See Tacitus, *Germania* caps. 7, 10, 12.

16: *while they died* . . . See James G. Frazer, *The Golden Bough*, 3rd edn, 12 vols (London, 1907–15) ['Frazer'], part 4.1 ('Adonis, Attis, Osiris'), p. 290.

17: *killing the survivor* . . . Joseph F. Tuso (ed.), *Beowulf*, tr. E. T. Donaldson (New York, 1975), pp. 42–3 [§§34–5].

17: *shadowlands of Hel* . . . See Frazer, part 7.1 ('Balder the Beautiful'), pp. 101–2.

18: *regardless of intention* . . . See generally John H. Wigmore, 'Responsibility for Tortious Acts: Its History', in Ernst Freund et al. (eds), *Select Essays in Anglo-American Legal History*, 3 vols (Boston, 1909), 3: 474.

18: *for a nobleman* . . . Title XXX of the Salic Law: see Ernest F. Henderson (ed.), *Select Historical Documents of the Middle Ages* (London, 1910), p. 181; Laws of Æthelbert, No. 82, in Benjamin Thorpe (ed.), *The Ancient Laws and Institutes of England* (London, 1840) ['Thorpe, *Ancient Laws*'], p. 181; Karl August Eckhardt and Albrecht Eckhardt (eds), *Lex Frisionum* (Hanover, 1982) ['Eckhardt, *Lex Frisionum*'], pp. 34–7, Tit.1, §§1, 11.

18: *tied them to trees* . . . Paul Bohannan, *Justice and Judgment Among the Tiv* (London, 1957), pp.142–4; *Social Anthropology* (New York, 1963), pp. 290–3; Norbert Rouland, *Legal Anthropology*, tr. Philippe G. Planel (London, 1994), pp. 261–2.

18: *small twigs* . . . Norbert Rouland, *Legal Anthropology*, tr. Philippe G. Planel (London, 1994), p. 261.

18: *and a bull* . . . Demosthenes, *Against Aristocrates* 68–9; see generally MacDowell, *Homicide*, pp. 90–100.

18: *bisected calf* . . . Jeremiah 34: 18–19. Cf. Genesis 15: 10.

18: *body parts of saints* . . . Relics were used to support judicial oaths until the thirteenth century: see Esther Cohen, *The Crossroads of Justice* (Leiden, 1993) ['Cohen, *Crossroads*'], p. 69.

19: *swear to their cause* . . . A suspect caught red-handed could be summarily judged and punished, however: see Adhémar Esmein, *A History of Continental Criminal Procedure* (Boston, 1913) ['Esmein'], p. 61.

19: *confirm her chastity* . . . Henry C. Lea, *Superstition and Force* (New York, 1968, reprint of 1870 edn) ['Lea, *Superstition*'], p. 36. See generally ibid pp. 28ff.

19: *Dark Age Wales* . . . Aneurin Owen (ed.), *Ancient Laws and Institutes of Wales* (London, 1841), p. 399.

19: *special privileges* . . . Lea, *Superstition*, pp. 21–2.

19: *their accusers* . . . S. P. Scott (ed.), *The Visigothic Code* (Boston, 1910), p. 41, Book 2, Title 2.6.

19: *knew of a case* . . . See Lea, *Superstition*, pp. 55–7.

19: *were non-clerical* . . . Ibid., pp. 24–5.

20: Burnt Njal . . . The account that follows in the text is drawn from *Njal's Saga*, tr. M. Magnusson and H. Pálsson (Harmondsworth, 1960) and more specifically from pp. 265–323.

21: *provisions every year* . . . Jón Jóhannesson, *A History of the Old Icelandic Commonwealth*, tr. Haraldur Bessason (Winnepeg, 1974) ['Jóhannesson'], pp. 47–8.

24: *the fourteenth century* . . . See Esmein, pp. 56–7; Cohen, *Crossroads*, pp. 62–6.

24: *to take hold* . . . Jóhannesson, pp. 46–7.

24: *dwarfish proportions* . . . See generally Ian Wood, 'How Popular was Early Medieval Devotion', 14 *Essays in Medieval Studies* (1997), available online via www.luc.edu/publications/medieval.

25: *'the dispute ended'* . . . Gregory's account is translated in Ogg, pp. 198–200.

25: *woes of the accused* . . . See e.g. 'The Breviary of Eberhard of Bamberg', translated in University of Pennsylvania, *Translations and Reprints from the Original Sources of European History*, 6 vols (Philadelphia, 1894–1900), 4.4: 7; §28 of the laws of King Æthelstan (AD 924–39) in Thorpe, *Ancient Laws*, p. 96.

26: *combination of the two* . . . See Ernest F. Henderson (ed.), *Select Historical Documents of the Middle Ages* (London, 1910), pp. 314–17; §28 of the laws of King Æthelstan in Thorpe, *Ancient Laws*, p. 96; Lea, *Superstition*, pp. 230, 237.

26: *asked to begin* . . . See University of Pennsylvania, *Translations and Reprints from the Original Sources of European History*, 6 vols (Philadelphia, 1894–1900), 4.4: 13; Lea, *Superstition*, pp. 233–4.

26: *Peter Bartholomew* . . . See Raymond d'Aguilers [*sic*], *Historia Francorum qui ceperunt Iherusalem*, tr. J. H. Hill and L. L. Hill (Philadelphia, 1968), pp.100–8; other sources cited in Lea, *Superstition*, p. 241, n.1.

26: *with luck, resuscitated* . . . See Ogg, pp. 200–1; see generally Lea, *Superstition*, pp. 246ff.

27: *choking to death* . . . See Robert Brady, *A Complete History of England* (London, 1685), p. 66; Lea, *Superstition*, pp. 263–6.

27: *dropped dead* . . . See e.g. Roger of Wendover, *Flowers of History*, tr. J. A. Giles, 2 vols (London 1849), 1: 311; see generally Lea, *Superstition*, p. 265.

28: *rock in a sack* . . . Lea, *Superstition*, p. 120; see also Hermann Knapp (ed.), *Das Rechtsbuch Ruprechts von Freising* (Leipzig, 1916, reproducing 1328 original), pp. 73–4.

28: *than their accuser* . . . Eckhardt, *Lex Frisionum*, pp. 58–61 (Tit. XIV, §§4–7).

28: *delivered it* . . . See Lea, *Superstition*, pp.102, 104–7; see also Cohen, *Crossroads*, p. 63.

29: *believe in them* . . . Lea, *Superstition*, p. 301.

29: *cold water instead* . . . Robert Brady, *A Complete History of England* (London, 1685), p. 65.

29: *might sometimes work* . . . John W. Baldwin, 'The Intellectual Preparation for the Canon of 1215 Against Ordeals', 36 *Speculum* 613 (1961) ['Baldwin'], at pp. 614 n.9, 618.

29: *mantle of churches'* . . . Rudolfus Glaber, *Historiarvm libri qvinqve. The Five Books of the Histories*, ed. John France (Oxford, 1989), pp. 115–17 [3.2].

30: *coalesced in Bologna* . . . For a detailed account of legal developments in Europe between the collapse of the Western Roman Empire and the intellectual renaissance of the twelfth century, see Manlio Bellomo, *The Common Legal Past of Europe 1000–1800* (Washington DC, 1995), pp. 34–77.

30: *to do with it* . . . See Baldwin, pp. 626ff.

30: *suspicious of the system* . . . See for example the story told of King William Rufus of England reprinted in R. C. van Caenegem (ed.), *English Lawsuits from William I to Richard I* (London, 1990), p. 122. Another indication of royal scepticism comes from an English law of 1166, which provided that people with particularly evil reputations who were acquitted through compurgation had to depart the realm within eight days on pain of outlawry: §14 of the Assize of Clarendon, translated in Ernest F. Henderson (ed.), *Select Historical Documents* (London, 1892), pp. 16–20.

31: *the early 1130s* . . . Walter L. Wakefield and Austin P. Evans (eds), *Heresies of the High Middle Ages* (New York, 1991) ['Wakefield, *Heresies*'], pp.107–21; Malcolm Lambert, *Medieval Heresy*, 3rd edn (Oxford, 2002) ['Lambert'], pp. 52–5.

31: *ethereal perfection* . . . Lambert, op. cit., offers a good account of the dualist origins of Catharism, the different strands of Cathar theology, and its relationship to other heresies; see also Wakefield, *Heresies*, pp. 41–50. For translated primary sources, including tracts by and against the Cathars, see ibid., pp. 301–73, 447–630; and see Edward Peters, *Heresy and Authority in Medieval Europe* (Philadelphia, 1980) ['Peters'], pp. 103–37.

31: *love of the Lord* . . . Eusebius, *The History of the Church from Christ to Constantine*, tr. G. A. Williamson (New York, 1966), pp. 247–8.

31: *hoary myths* . . . The classic analysis of the genesis and development of these myths is Norman Cohn, *Europe's Inner Demons* (London, 1993).

31: *annual dragnet* . . . Episcopal inquisitorial procedures were established by Lucius III in his decretal 'Ad abolendum' of 1184: see Peters, pp. 170–3.

32: *than the reflecting* . . . Jacques-Paul Migne (ed.), *Patrologiæ cursus completus*, 221 vols (Paris, 1844–64) ['Migne'], 214: 377.

32: *eighteen-year pontificate* . . . See Ralph H. C. Davis, *A History of Medieval Europe* (London, 1957), p. 342; see also pp. 306, 346.

32: *dumb to bark* . . . See e.g. the letters from 1200 and 1206 reprinted in Migne, 214: 903 and 215: 819.

33: *contemporary account* . . . William of Tudela, *The Song of the Cathar Wars, a History of the Albigensian Crusade*, tr. Janet Shirley (Aldershot, 1996), p. 13.

33: *broke through* . . . Ibid., pp. 20–1.

33: *'God will know His own'* . . . Caesarius of Heisterbach, *The Dialogue on*

Miracles, tr. H. von E. Scott and C. C. Swinton Bland, 2 vols (London, 1929), 1: 343 [5.21]. The words are hearsay, but Arnold's subsequent report to Innocent suggests that they would not have been out of character. He informed him, with evident joy, that twenty thousand people had been slaughtered, 'sparing neither rank, nor age nor sex': Migne, 216: 139.

33: *exterminating them personally* . . . Migne, 216: 159.

33: *almost certainly* . . . His public pronouncements on the subject of ordeals before 1215 were ambivalent: see Baldwin, p.615 n.13.

34: *Church disciplinary cases* . . . Lea, *Superstition*, pp. 62–3.

34: *Sodom and Gomorrah* . . . See James A. Brundage, *Medieval Canon Law* (London and New York, 1995), pp. 147–9.

34: *abuses unaddressed* . . . For English text of the decrees approved at the Fourth Lateran Council, see H. J. Schroeder (ed.), *Disciplinary Decrees of the General Councils: Text, Translation and Commentary* (St. Louis and London, 1937), pp. 236–96. A description of events by one of those present can be found in S. Kuttner and A. Garcia y Garcia, 'A New Eye-Witness Account of the Fourth Lateran Council', 20 *Traditio* 115 (1964).

34: *pointy-toed shoes* . . . Canons 15–16. The same provisions prohibited the wearing of red or green.

34: *noticed the difference* . . . Canon 68.

34: *unhallowed ground* . . . Canon 21.

35: *worked the magic* . . . See Joachim John Monteiro, *Angola and the River Congo*, 2 vols (London, 1875), 1: 65.

36: *the first time* . . . Frederick Pollock and Frederick W. Maitland, *The History of English Law Before the Time of Edward I*, 2nd edn, 2 vols (Cambridge, 1898), 2: 598.

36: *done in ignorance'* . . . St Anselm, *Proslogium; Monologium; An Appendix In Behalf of the Fool by Gaunilo; and Cur Deus Homo*, tr. Sidney N. Deane (Chicago, 1903), p. 264.

37: *a person thought* . . . See Jacques Le Goff., *The Birth of Purgatory*, tr. Arthur Goldhammer (London, 1984), p. 214; James A. Brundage, *Medieval Canon Law* (London and New York, 1995), pp. 171–2.

37: *some civil disputes* . . . See Lea, *Superstition*, pp. 67–84.

37: *until 1819* . . . See *Ashford v. Thornton* (1818) 1 B. & Ald. 405 in Max A. Robertson and Geoffrey Ellis (eds), *The English Reports*, 176 vols (London, 1900–30), 106: 149; 59 Geo. III, c.46 (1819).

37: *identify the murderer* . . . See Lea, *Superstition*, p. 283.

Chapter 2: The Inquisition

39: *a leopard'* . . . Thomas L. Kington, *History of Frederick the Second, Emperor of the Romans*, 2 vols (London, 1868), 2: 117.

39: *papal Inquisition* . . . On the genesis of the papal Inquisition, see Edward Peters, *Heresy and Authority in Medieval Europe* (Philadelphia, 1980) ['Peters'], pp. 190–1; Malcolm Lambert, *Medieval Heresy*, 3rd edn (Oxford, 2002) ['Lambert'], p. 108; H. C. Lea, *A History of the Inquisition of the Middle Ages*, 3 vols (New York, 1888) ['Lea, *Inquisition*'], 1:322; Michael Costen, *The Cathars and the Albigensian Crusade* (Manchester and New York, 1997), pp.163–74.

39: *than the sun* . . . For a detailed explanation of the relationship between Conrad and Pope Gregory IX see Lea, *Inquisition*, 2: 329ff.; see also Jeffrey B. Russell, *Witchcraft in the Middle Ages* (Cornell, 1972), pp. 160–1. Lea states that the heretics concerned were a sect known as the Luciferans, but Norman Cohn persuasively argues that they were Waldensians: see *Europe's Inner Demons* (London, 1993), p. 48.

40: *person he summonsed* . . . On the life, career and death of Conrad and company, see Lea, *Inquisition*, 2: 34–5.

41: *pig entrails* . . . See Jean, Sire de Joinville, *Saint Louis, King of France*, tr. James Hutton (London, 1868), especially at pp. 10, 205–9.

41: *royal control over southern France* . . . See Franz Funck-Brentano, *The Middle Ages*, tr. Elizabeth O'Neill (New York, 1923) ['Funck-Brentano'], p. 296; see also Adhémar Esmein, *A History of Continental Criminal Procedure* (Boston, 1913) ['Esmein'], pp. 96–7.

41: *impose his will* . . . See Charles Petit-Dutaillis, *The Feudal Monarchy in France and England from the Tenth to the Thirteenth Century* (London, 1936), p. 298.

41: *Old Testament* . . . See Kenneth Pennington, *The Prince and the Law, 1200–1600* (Berkeley & Oxford, 1993), pp. 143–4, 156–7.

42: *similarly eroded* . . . See Richard H. Helmholz et al., *The Privilege Against Self-Incrimination* (Chicago, 1997), pp. 26–8.

42: *alleged against them* . . . See Peters, p. 199; Michael Costen, *The Cathars and the Albigensian Crusade* (Manchester and New York, 1997) ['Costen'], p. 166; Lea, *Inquisition*, 1: 444–5; Bernard Gui, 'The Conduct of the Inquisition of Heretical Depravity' (1323–4), reprinted in Walter L. Wakefield and Austin P. Evans (eds), *Heresies of the High Middle Ages* (New York, 1991) at p. 397.

42: *every word* . . . For a vivid example of entrapment by papal inquisitors, see the depositions translated in Walter L. Wakefield, *Heresy, Crusade and Inquisition in Southern France* (London, 1974), pp. 242–7.

42: *matter of course* . . . Leviticus 14: 45; see generally Lea, *Inquisition*, 1:481–3. The destruction of heretics' homes predated the papal Inquisition: see §21 of the Assize of Clarendon 1166, in Ernest F. Henderson (ed.), *Select Historical Documents*, (London, 1892), pp. 16–20; Pope Innocent III's 'Cum ex officii nostri' of 1207; Canon 6 of the Council of Toulouse, 1229, in Peters, p. 194.

42: *'with rejoicing'* . . . 'The Chronicle of William Pelhisson', in Walter L. Wakefield, *Heresy, Crusade and Inquisition in Southern France 1100–1250* (London, 1974), p. 207, at pp. 215–16.

42: *centuries subsequent* . . . 'Ad extirpanda', §26, reprinted in the Church of Rome's *Bullarum diplomatum et privilegiorum sanctorum Romanorum pontificum Taurinensis editio*, 25 vols (Rome, 1857–72) ['*Bullarum diplomatum*'], 3: 556; see also H. C. Lea, *Superstition and Force* (Greenwood, 1968, reprint of 1870 edition) ['Lea, *Superstition*'], p.375; Lea, *Inquisition*, 1: 421–2. On Justinian's employment of torture, see S. P. Scott (ed.), *The Civil Law Including The Twelve Tables, The Institutes of Gaius, The Rules of Ulpian, The Opinions of Paulus, The Enactments of Justinian, and The Constitutions of Leo*, 17 vols (Cincinnati, 1932) ['Scott, *Civil Law*'], 11: 9 (*Digest*, Book 48, Title 18). On its use by barbarians, see Lea, *Superstition*, pp. 343–64; Esmein, pp. 108–10.

43: *work so required* . . . See the Bull 'Ne inquisitionis negotium' of 4 August 1262, reprinted in *Bullarum diplomatum*, 3: 694. Other measures to extend the powers and discretions of the papal inquisitors, which were regularly reiterated and amplified over this period, are contained in the same volume.

43: *names be disclosed* . . . 'A Manual for Inquisitors at Carcassonne' (1248–9), reprinted in Peters, p. 200.

43: *decade or two* . . . On the penances imposed by inquisitors, see Lea, *Inquisition*, 1: 459–500; Costen, pp. 172–4.

43: *spilling blood* . . . See e.g. Canon 27 of the Third Lateran Council (1179) and Canon 18 of the Fourth Lateran Council (1215) in H. J. Schroeder (ed.), *Disciplinary Decrees of the General Councils: Text, Translation and Commentary* (St. Louis and London, 1937), pp.234, 258; see also Book III, Title 49, §5 of the 1234 'Decretalia Gregorii' in Robert S. Mylne, *The Canon Law* (London, 1912) ['Mylne'], p. 74.

43: *'moderate' in its sentence* . . . See Lea, *Inquisition*, 1: 534; 'Form of Relaxation to the Secular Arm', translated in University of Pennsylvania, *Translations and Reprints from the Original Sources of European History*, 6 vols (Philadelphia, 1894–1900), 3.6: 15.

44: *liable to condemnation* . . . See e.g. 'A Manual for Inquisitors at Carcassonne' (1248–49), translated in Peters, p. 205.

44: *burned to death* . . . The 'Schwabenspiegel', translated in Peters, p. 209.

44: *the recalcitrant* . . . On the preference of the Inquisition for mundane penance over execution, see Lea, *Inquisition*, 1: 484–95, 549–51. On the need to give heretics an opportunity to repent, see e.g. Thomas Aquinas, *The 'Summa Theologica' of St Thomas Aquinas* . . . *Literally Translated by Fathers of the English Dominican Province*, tr. Laurence Shapcote, 2nd edn, 22 vols (London, 1921?–32), 9: 155–8 (Part 2.2, Q.11, Art. 4).

44: *heretical in itself* . . . See the decretal 'Ad abolendum' of 1184 in Peters, pp. 171–2; cf. the Council of Tarragona, 1242, ibid., p. 198.

45: *questions on oath* . . . See Esmein, pp. 105–7, 136.

45: *followed suit* . . . Ibid., pp. 96–7; see also Peters, pp. 210–1.

46: *become ubiquitous* . . . Esmein, p.137, 157–8; Lea, *Superstition*, p. 382.

46: *centuries of disunity* . . . See Ralph H. C. Davis, *A History of Medieval Europe* (London, 1957), p. 382.

46: *as pontiffs go* . . . For a biography of Boniface, see Thomas S. R. Boase, *Boniface VIII* (London, 1933) ['Boase'].

46: ipso facto *excommunicated* . . . See the bull 'Clericis laicos' of 25 February 1296, translated in Ernest F. Henderson (ed.), *Select Historical Documents of the Middle Ages* (London, 1892) ['Henderson, *Documents*'], at pp. 432–4.

47: *powerful social class* . . . See Funck-Brentano, pp. 361–3.

47: *promptly did* . . . See Pierre Dupuy, *Histoire du differend d'entre le Pape Boniface VIII. et Philippes le Bel Roy de France* (Paris, 1655) ['Dupuy'], at p. 8 of introduction; Boase, pp. 238–9.

47: *Satan incarnate* . . . Boase, pp. 299–300.

47: *eternity in hell* . . . See his bull 'Unam sanctum' of 18 November 1302, translated in Henderson, *Documents*, at pp. 435–7.

48: *neglect of fasts* . . . Boase, pp. 333–4.

48: *fists in his mouth* . . . See Dupuy, at p. 24 of his introduction; see also Boase, pp. 350–1.

48: *burned at the stake* . . . See Boase, pp. 357–63.

49: Digest's *various recommendations* . . . See Scott, *Civil Law*, 5: 232 (*Digest*, Book 22, Title 5).

49: *lawyers then turned to* . . . 'Decretalia Gregorii IX', in Mylne, p. 53 (Book 2, Title 20); Esmein, p. 623 n.3.

49: *proved – conclusively* . . . See Esmein, p. 60.

49: *needed to convict them* . . . Louis' 1254 reforms provided that torture could not be imposed on the word of a single witness, except where the accused was a person of bad character (*mala fama*): Esmein, pp. 111–2; Lea, *Superstition*, pp. 378ff.

50: *guarantor of guilt* . . . By the mid fourteenth century the absence of torture was exceptional: Esmein, pp. 136–41, Lea, *Superstition*, p. 389. See generally John H. Langbein, *Torture and the Law of Proof* (Chicago and London, 1977), pp. 3–60.

50: *divine law* . . . Moses Ben Maimūn (Maimonides), *The Code of Maimonides. Book Fourteen. The Book of Judges*, tr. Abraham M. Hershman (New Haven, 1949), pp. 52–3.

50: *unhallowed burial* . . . Canon 21 of Lateran IV, reprinted in H. J. Schroeder (ed.), *Disciplinary Decrees of the General Councils: Text, Translation and Commentary* (St. Louis and London, 1937), pp. 259–63.

50: *presence of a priest* . . . See H. C. Lea, *History of Auricular Confession and Indulgences in the Latin Church*, 3 vols (Philadelphia, 1896), 1: 168ff.

St Augustine, though famously willing to admit his shortcomings, never once claimed that confession was a necessary penance, while John Chrysostom specifically denied that it was required for salvation.

50: *considerable resistance* . . . Ibid., 1: 233–4.

50: *their patients* . . . 'Decretalia Gregorii IX', in Mylne, p. 97 (Book 5, Title 37, §13).

51: *the undead* . . . Caesarius of Heisterbach, *The Dialogue on Miracles*, tr. H.von E. Scott and C. C. Swinton Bland, 2 vols (London, 1929) ['Caesarius'], 1: 126 (3.3); 1: 130 (3.6); 1: 153 (3.21); 1: 146 (3.15); 1: 161 (3.26); 1: 157 (3.24).

51: *repeated three times* . . . Esmein, p. 114. On the increasing flexibility of the theoretical restrictions, see Lea, *Superstition*, pp. 404, 425ff; Esmein, pp. 139, 157–8.

51: *'continued' indefinitely* . . . André Morellet, *Abrégé du manuel des inquisiteurs*, ed. Jean-Pierre Guicciardi (Grenoble, 1990), pp. 131–2.

52: *abhorred infinity* . . . Lea, *Superstition*, p. 426, citing Martin Bernhardi, *Diss. Inaug. de Tortura*, c.1, §11.

52: *without cause'* . . . Quoted in Esmein, pp. 129–30.

52: *outright acquittal* . . . Henri Duplès-Agier (ed.), *Registre criminel du Châtelet de Paris du 6 Septembre 1389 au 18 Mai 1392*, 2 vols (Paris, 1861–4). For examples of cases in which a defendant would not confess but was punished regardless, see ibid., 1: 507 (Berthaut), 2: 53–4 (Joesne d'Espaigne), 2: 147 (Thévenin de Braine).

52: *Gilles de Rais* . . . For a detailed account of the case, including transcripts of the original trial records, see Eugène Bossard, *Gilles de Rais, dit Barbe-Bleue* (Paris, 1886) ['Bossard']. For a translated collection, see George Bataille, *The Trial of Gilles de Rais* (Los Angeles, 1991) ['Bataille'].

53: *to the English* . . . Reginald Hyatte, *Laughter for the Devil* (Rutherford, 1984), p. 19.

53: *human blood* . . . Bataille, pp. 219–20.

53: *King Herod* . . . Bossard, pp. 61–2.

54: *in late July* . . . Bataille, pp. 126, 155.

54: *some 140 children* . . . Ibid., pp. 162–5.

54: *refused to speak* . . . Ibid., pp. 163–4.

55: *read to him* . . . The witness statements are reproduced ibid., at pp. 209–40.

55: *scrutinize the truth'* . . . Ibid., p. 190.

55: *a full confession* . . . The confession is reprinted ibid., at pp. 194–204.

56: *church of choice* . . . Ibid., p. 283.

57: *expiate guilt* . . . For such an argument (referring specifically to Gilles de Rais' confession), see Michel Foucault, *Histoire de la folie à l'âge classique*

(Folie et déraison) (Paris, 1961), pp.177–8, translated as *Madness and Civilization* (London, 1967), pp. 66–7.

57: *by contrition* . . . Caesarius of Heisterbach had assumed in the early thirteenth century that confession was useless unless made with the intention of avoiding future sin: see Caesarius at e.g. 1: 174–5, 1: 190–1 (3.34, 3.35, 3.52).

57: *his 'motives'* . . . Bataille, pp. 188–9.

57: *end nor intention'* . . . Ibid., p. 193.

58: *of which [I am] guilty* . . . Ibid., p. 237; see also p. 278.

58: *or torture them* . . . Pierre Ayrault, *De l'ordre et instruction iudiciaire, dont les anciens Grecs & Romains ont vsé en accusations publiques, conferé á l'usage de nostre France, etc.* (Paris, 1588) ['Ayrault, *Ordre et instruction*'], p. 341a; Esmein, pp. 151–4. See also Lea, *Superstition*, pp. 400ff.

58: *after 1670* . . . See Esmein pp. 159, 227–9, 275; John H. Langbein, *Prosecuting Crime in the Renaissance* (Harvard, 1974), pp. 236, 245.

59: *honest and reasoned* . . . Ayrault, *Ordre et instruction*, pp. 314b, 326b, 345b, 349a, 358a.

59: *Jacques Roulet* . . . For the case records – which were, admittedly, set down by an obsessive witch-hunter over twenty years after the event – see Pierre de Lancre, *L'incredulité et mescreance du Sortilege plainement convaincue* (Paris, 1622), pp. 785–90.

60: *people into wolves* . . . Jean Bodin, *De la Demonomanie des Sorciers* (Paris, 1680), pp. 94b–104a.

60: *fellow demonologists* . . . For more sceptical views see Henry Boguet, *Examen of Witches*, tr. E. Allen Ashwin (London, 1929), pp. 136ff. (see also his *Discours des Sorciers* [Lyons, 1608], pp. 332–74); Nicolas Rémy, *Demonolatry*, tr. E. Allen Ashwin (London, 1930), p. 111 (2.5); Martín del Rio, *Investigations into Magic*, tr. P. G. Maxwell-Stuart (Manchester, 2000), pp. 98–100. For a medical refutation, see Jean de Nynauld, *De la Lycanthropie, Transformation, et Extase des Sorciers* (Paris, 1615); for one written by a Franciscan friar, see Claude Prieur, *Dialogue de la Lycanthropie, ou Transformation d'Hommes en Loups* . . . (Louvain, 1596).

60: *condemn themselves'* . . . Ayrault, *Ordre et instruction*, p. 16a. Two centuries later Daniel Jousse reiterated his predecessor's opinion: see Daniel Jousse, *Traité de la justice criminelle de France*, 4 vols (Paris, 1771), 1: viii.

60: *could be false* . . . Ayrault, *Ordre et instruction*, pp. 319a–21a.

61: *towns and principalities* . . . See Brian Levack, *The Witch-Hunt in Early Modern Europe* (London and New York, 1995), p. 94. The number of criminal jurisdictions may have been even higher: see Richard J. Evans, *Rituals of Retribution* (London, 1997) ['R.J. Evans, *Rituals*'], p. 42 ('nearly two thousand different state authorities . . . all of them enjoying full legal powers to punish . . . ').

61: *be established* . . . Heinrich Brunner, *Deutsche Rechtsgeschichte*, 2 vols (Leipzig, 1906), 1: 254; Heinrich Brunner, 'Die Klage mit dem toten Mann und die Klage mit der toten Hand', 31 *Zeitschrift der Savigny-Stiftung für Rechtsgeschichte, Germanistische Abteilung* 235 (1910); Hans Schreuer, 'Das Recht der Toten', 34 *Zeitschrift für vergleichende Rechtswissenschaft, einschliesslich der ethnologischen Rechtsforschung* 1 (1916).

62: *from a gallows* . . . This specific illustration of the judgment ritual comes from 1812 Heidelberg (see R. J. Evans, *Rituals*), but it reflected customs that were already well established by 1532: see Arts. 81–96 of the Carolina, reprinted in, John H. Langbein, *Prosecuting Crime in the Renaissance* (Harvard, 1974) ['Langbein, *Prosecuting Crime*'], pp. 288–92; Fynes Moryson, *An Itinerary* (Amsterdam and New York, 1971 reprint of 1617 London edition), part 3, p. 206; and see Esmein, pp. 307–8.

62: *pushed the epicentres* . . . On the development and spread of the myth, see Christopher Ocker, 'Ritual Murder and the Subjectivity of Christ: A Choice in Medieval Christianity', 91(2) *Harvard Theological Review* 153 (April 1998).

63: *had they said?'* . . . Raphael Straus, *Urkunden und Aktenstücke zur Geschichte der Juden in Regensburg, 1453–1738* (Munich, 1960), pp. 72–3.

63: *imaginary murder* . . . See R. Po-chia Hsia, *The Myth of Ritual Murder. Jews and Magic in Reformation Germany* (New Haven and London, 1988) ['Hsia'], p. 74.

63: *fully recorded* . . . Ibid., p. 12. For the Endingen records themselves, see pp. 17–41.

64: *for circumcision* . . . Ibid., p. 21, translating from Karl von Amira, *Der Endinger Judenspiel* (Halle, 1883), p. 97.

64: *as was routine* . . . R. J. Evans, *Rituals*, pp. 32, 55–6.

64: *two hungry dogs* . . . Guido Kisch, 'The "Jewish Execution" in Mediaeval Germany', 5 *Historia Judaica* 103 (1943); see also *A Hangman's Diary. Being the Journal of Master Franz Schmidt, Public Executioner of Nuremberg, 1573–1617*, tr. Calvert and Gruner, ed. A. Keller (London 1928), p. 60.

64: *well into the 1800s* . . . See R. J. Evans, *Rituals*, pp. 90–8, 194, and sources cited therein.

65: *far back as 1401* . . . Joshua Trachtenberg, *The Devil and the Jews* (Philadelphia, 1983) ['Trachtenberg'], pp. 148–9.

65: *first time at Endingen* . . . This is asserted ibid., at p. 149.

65: footnote. For Catherine's own description of her visions see *The Letters of Catherine of Siena*, tr. Suzanne Noffke, ongoing (Tempe, Arizona, 2000–), especially at 1: 147 and 2: 595. On the theological significance of Christ's foreskin see James Bentley, *Restless Bones: The Story of Relics* (London. 1985), pp. 138–42. For Maimonides' discussion of circumcision see Moses ben Maimūn (Maimonides), *The Guide of the Perplexed*, tr. Shlomo Pines

(Chicago and London, 1963), p. 609, and for that of Isaac Ben Yedaiah see Marc Saperstein, *Decoding the Rabbis* (Harvard, 1980), pp. 97–8.

65: *involved theories* . . . See e.g. Ernest A. Rappaport, *Anti-Judaism. A Psychohistory* (Chicago, 1975) ['Rappaport'], *passim*; Hyam Maccoby, *The Sacred Executioner* (London, 1982), *passim*.

65: *along the Rhine* . . . See Hsia, pp. 17, 22–3, 41, 79; Trachtenberg, p. 149.

65: *inquisitors in Baden* . . . Hsia, pp. 34–6; Trachtenberg, p. 149–51.

65: *into the nineteenth* . . . Trachtenberg, pp.149–51; Hsia, p. 37.

66: *in 1967* . . . Rappaport, p. 110.

66: *'proximate indication'* . . . See Esmein, pp. 291–2.

66: *more than usual* . . . See e.g. François Serpillon, *Code Criminel*, 2nd edn, 2 vols (Lyons, 1784) ['Serpillon'], 2: 165, citing a 1590 source. All citations to Serpillon refer to this work rather than the original 1767 edition.

66: *gaze of their judge* . . . Henri Boguet, *Discours des Sorciers* (Lyons, 1608) at p. 14 of the supplementary 'Instruction pour un Iuge en faict de Sorcelerie'. A different edition has been translated as Henry [*sic*] Boguet, *An Examen of Witches*, tr. E. Allen Ashwin (London, 1929): see pp. 223–4.

66: *the Carolina* . . . On the code's origins, see Langbein, *Prosecuting Crime*, pp. 155–66; Esmein, pp. 305–6.

66: *customary laws however* . . . See the preamble to the Carolina, reprinted in Langbein, *Prosecuting Crime*, p. 267.

67: *at the crime scene* . . . Arts. 18–44, reprinted ibid., pp. 272–9.

67: *spiritual needs* . . . See Lea, *Superstition*, pp. 412–13.

67: *already overwhelming* . . . Carolina, Art. 69, reprinted in Langbein, *Prosecuting Crime* at p. 285.

67: *otherwise ensue* . . . See Lea, *Superstition*, p. 428.

67: *a Bamberg statute* . . . Esmein, p. 308.

67: *for want of [it]'* . . . Fynes Moryson, *An Itinerary* (Amsterdam and New York, 1971 reprint of 1617 London edition), part 3, p. 204.

67: *body of the accused'* . . . Pierre François Muyart de Vouglans, *Institutes au droit criminel* (Paris, 1757), p. 341. See also his 'Réfutation du Traité des Délits et Peines', in Pierre François Muyart de Vouglans, *Les Loix Criminelles de France* (Paris, 1780) ['*Les Loix Criminelles*'], at p. 824.

67: *short of death* . . . See Lea, *Superstition*, pp. 405–6; *Les Loix Criminelles*, p. 60.

67: *suitably proportioned punishment* . . . *Les Loix Criminelles*, p. 824.

68: *for life instead* . . . See Esmein, p. 265; cf. p. 60.

68: *among civilized nations'* . . . Muyart de Vouglans, *Les Loix Criminelles*, p. 814.

68: *a powerful attack* . . . Cesare Beccaria, *Dei delitti e delle pene* (Livorno, 1764). The author restructured the book prior to its French publication in 1766 and it then appeared in English as *An Essay on Crimes and Punishments*, *translated from the Italian; With a Commentary Attributed to Mons. de Voltaire, Translated from the French* (London, 1767).

68: *removed with pincers* . . . Serpillon, 2: 162–3.

69: *a man to his death* . . . François Marie Arouet de Voltaire, *Commentaire sur le livre Des Délits et Des Peines* (Geneva?, 1766), pp.100–1, available in translation in *An Essay on Crimes and Punishments* (London, 1767), op. cit., at p. lxxvi.

69: *accomplices after conviction* . . . Esmein, p. 382.

69: *duty to judge them* . . . See ibid., pp. 402ff.

69: *a law code* . . . See ibid., pp. 462ff.

69: *thing of the past* . . . In modern France, police and prosecutors commence the investigation of a serious offence and examining magistrates, known as *juges d'instruction*, then take over the process. Although their inquiries are initially confidential (Art. 11, *Code de Procédure Pénale*, available online via www.legifrance.gouv.fr), the dossier is available to the defendant's lawyers and interested civil parties, and the trial itself is presumptively public (Art. 306, ibid.). See also Bron McKillop, 'Anatomy of a French Murder Case', 45 *American Journal of Comparative Law* 527 (1997); and see generally Neil Vidmar (ed.), *World Jury Systems* (Oxford, 2000).

Chapter 3: The Jury Trial (1)

71: *fill them up* . . . Punitive incarceration was not unknown but it was exceptional: see Ralph B. Pugh, *Imprisonment in Medieval England* (Cambridge, 1968) ['Pugh, *Imprisonment*'], pp. 1–25.

71: *of each case* . . . Frederick W. Maitland, *Pleas of the Crown for the County of Gloucester . . . in . . . 1221* (London, 1884) ['*Gloucester Pleas*'], pp. xxxviii–xxxix.

71: *property-owning neighbours* . . . On early property requirements, see James S. Cockburn and Thomas A. Green (eds), *Twelve Good Men and True* (Princeton, 1988) ['*Twelve Good Men and True*'], pp. 31, 68, 83.

71: *quartet was hanged* . . . Roger D. Groot, 'The Early Thirteenth Century Criminal Jury', in *Twelve Good Men and True*, at pp. 17–18.

72: *judged certain offences* . . . See generally Arnold H. M. Jones, *Criminal Courts of the Roman Republic and Principate* (Oxford, 1972), pp.45–90.

72: *a peace treaty* . . . Benjamin Thorpe (ed.), *The Ancient Laws and Institutes of England* (London, 1840), pp. 66–7.

72: *later jurists* . . . See e.g. Edward Coke, *The First Part of the Institutes of the Lawes of England: or, A Commentary upon Littleton,* 4th edn (London, 1639) ['Coke, *Institutes (1)*'], p. 155a. Note, however, that although twelve and multiples thereof figure conspicuously in early records, other numbers were also used. Several modern jurisdictions in the USA allow for juries of eight or six in modern felony trials, and the majority do so in relation to misdemeanour charges.

72: *rather than their friends* . . . See Henry C. Lea, *Superstition and Force* (Greenwood, 1968, reprint of 1870 edition), p. 44. Independent jurors were also seen in other areas of the law by the late twelfth century. The Assize of Clarendon of 1166, §1, instituted the jury of presentment, the prototype of the grand jury, which became responsible for vetting individual accusations and issuing indictments: see Ernest F. Henderson (ed.), *Select Historical Documents* (London, 1892), pp. 16–20. Juries were first used to decide the merits of cases in certain land disputes after 1179, pursuant to a statute that has now been lost: see R. C. van Caenagem, *The Birth of the English Common Law* (Cambridge, 1973), p. 80. At around the same time, an appellee became eligible to buy a jury to decide if he had been accused from 'hate or spite': see Roger D. Groot, 'The Jury of Presentment Before 1215', 26 *American Journal of Legal History* 1 (1982), p. 8.

73: *only testimony required* . . . See *Gloucester Pleas 1221*, p. xli; Roger D. Groot, 'The Early Thirteenth-Century Criminal Jury' in *Twelve Good Men and True*, at pp. 18ff; Edward Powell, 'Jury Trial at Gaol Delivery in the Late Middle Ages: The Midland Circuit, 1400–1429', ibid., p. 78; J. B. Post, 'Jury Lists and Juries in the Late Fourteenth Century', ibid., p. 65.

73: *considered perjurious* . . . See Percy H. Winfield, *The History of Conspiracy and Abuse of Legal Procedure* (Cambridge, 1921), pp. 189, 196; Anon, *The Peoples Ancient and Just Liberties Asserted, in the Tryal of William Penn, and William Mead* (London, 1670), p. 21.

73: *lose their souls* . . . See generally Richard H. Helmholz et al, *The Privilege Against Self-Incrimination* (Chicago, 1997), pp. 26–8, 82–108.

73: *divine judgment* . . . See the observations of Frederick W. Maitland in *The Constitutional History of England* (Cambridge, 1908), p. 130.

73: *nothing of the deed'* . . . George E. Woodbine (ed.), *Bracton on the Laws and Customs of England*, tr. Samuel E. Thorne, 4 vols (Harvard, 1968–77), 2: 387; see also Selden Society, *Fleta. Volume II. Prologue, Book I, Book II*, ed. H. G. Richardson and G. O. Sayles (London, 1955), p. 79.

74: *immediately released* . . . *Gloucester Pleas*, pp. 31, 43, 55 (cases 111, 161, and 229); Groot in *Twelve Good Men and True*, at pp. 26–30.

74: *unceremoniously hanged* . . . Groot in *Twelve Good Men and True*, at pp. 30–1.

74: *right hand raised* . . . See William Eden, *Principles of Penal Law*, 3rd edn (London, 1775) ['Eden, *Principles*'], p. 186. Although Eden was writing in the late eighteenth century, the custom was ancient. Britton prescribed in the early thirteenth century that homicides be arraigned without cap, belt, or boots and required verbally to consent to trial: Francis M. Nichols (ed.),

Britton: The French Text Carefully Revised with an English Translation, Introduction and Notes, 2 vols (Oxford, 1865) ['Britton'], 1: 35 (1.6).

74: *until they died* . . . The procedure was put on a statutory footing in the case of indictments by 3 Edw. I Westm. I, c.12 (1275) (the Statute of Westminster), though its origins were older: see Britton, 1: 26–7 (1.5); see also Edward Coke, *The Second Part of the Institutes of the Lawes of England* (London, 1642), p. 177; Groot in *Twelve Good Men and True*, p. 20 n.71. The practice had its equivalents in parts of France: see *Gloucester Pleas*, p. xxxix.

74: *until 1772* . . . See Daines Barrington, *Observations on the More Ancient Statutes*, 4th edn (London, 1775) ['Barrington, *Observations*'], pp. 82–3. Although commentators have often explained the resistance on the basis that it allowed defendants to avoid the disenfranchising of heirs that ordinarily followed convictions for felony or treason, confiscation was rarely enforced by the 1700s: see J. M. Beattie, *Crime and the Courts in England, 1660–1800* (Oxford, 1986) ['Beattie, *Crime*'], p. 338. Refusals to plead were deemed guilty pleas in 1772 (12 Geo. III, c.20), and only after 1827 were they treated as denials of guilt (7 & 8 Geo. IV, c.28).

74: *for their lives* . . . Counsel were traditionally denied to all traitors and felons except where the case gave rise to a debatable point of law: see Edward Coke, *The Third Part of the Institutes of the Laws of England* (London, 1644) [Coke, *Institutes (3)*'], p. 137; William Hawkins, *A Treatise of the Pleas of the Crown*, 2 vols (London, 1716–21), 2: 401. The exception was narrow, but a defence lawyer appears in the reports as early as 1309–10: see Herman Cohen, *A History of the English Bar and Attornatus to 1450* (London, 1929), p. 210. The classic description of a (hypothetical) trial in this period is in Thomas Smyth's *De Republica Anglorum* (London, 1583), at p. 80 (2.23). See generally John H. Langbein, 'The Criminal Trial Before the Lawyers', 45 *University of Chicago Law Review*, 263 (1978) ['Langbein, 'Criminal Trial Before Lawyers'']; John H. Langbein, 'The Privilege and Common Law Criminal Procedure: The Sixteenth to the Eighteenth Centuries', in Richard H. Helmholz et al, *The Privilege Against Self Incrimination* (Chicago, 1997) ['Langbein, 'Privilege and Common Law'], pp. 82–108.

74: *until the early 1500s* . . . See John H. Langbein's essay in Antonio P. Schioppa (ed.), *The Trial Jury in England, France, Germany 1700–1900* (Berlin, 1987), at pp. 30, 32; and that by Thomas A. Green at p. 44. On witnesses, see p. 73 and accompanying note.

75: *unbiased men* . . . John Fortescue, *On the Laws and Governance of England*, tr. Shelley Lockwood (Cambridge, 1997), pp. 29–47 (caps. 20–32).

75: *eighty-one torture warrants* . . . John H. Langbein, *Torture and the Law of Proof* (Chicago and London, 1977), pp. 81ff; see generally David Jardine, *A Reading on the Use of Torture in the Criminal Law of England* (London, 1837).

75: *thought of man'* . . . Quoted in Frederick Pollock and Frederick W. Maitland, *The History of English Law Before the Time of Edward I* , 2nd edn, 2 vols (Cambridge, 1898), 2: 474–5.

75: *until the 1700s* . . . See Barrington, *Observations*, pp. 144–5.

76: *a sixpence* . . . Treason Act, 1352 (III Edward 25, Stat. 5, c. 2), set out by Edward Coke in *Institutes (3)*, pp. 1ff.

76: *and quartered* . . . 25 Hen. VIII c.22 (1534); 28 Hen. VIII c.7 (1536); 35 Hen. VIII c.1 (1544).

77: *positive gratitude* . . . See the bull 'Regnans in Excelsis' of 25 April 1570, reprinted in Church of Rome's *Bullarum diplomatum et privilegiorum sanctorum Romanorum pontificum Taurinensis editio*, 25 vols (Rome, 1857–72), 7: 810; J. E. Neale, *Queen Elizabeth* (London, 1934), p.251.

77: *London Bridge* . . . William B. Rye, *England as Seen by Foreigners in the Days of Elizabeth and James the First* (London, 1865), pp. 9, 192 n.22.

77: *name of their crime* . . . See Catherine Drinker Bowen, *The Lion and the Throne* (Boston, 1957) ['Bowen'], p. 112.

77: *nostrils* . . . 5 Eliz. c. 14, set out in William Blackstone, *Commentaries on the Laws of England*, 3rd edn, 4 vols (Oxford, 1768–9) ['Blackstone, Commentaries'], 4: 245.

77: *right wrist* . . . William Camden, *Annales. The True and Royall History of the famous Empresse Elizabeth* (London, 1625), Book 3, pp. 15–16.

78: *reply to this'* . . . John Hawarde, *Les Reportes del Cases in Camera Stellata 1593 to 1609*, ed. William P. Baildon (London, 1894), pp. 36–8.

78: *sown the seeds* . . . On Henry VIII's exploitation of the trial process, see Geoffrey Elton, *Policy and Police: The Enforcement of the Reformation in the Age of Thomas Cromwell* (Cambridge, 1972), pp. 263–326.

78: *contradict the defendant* . . . David Jardine, *Criminal Trials*, 2 vols (London, 1832) ['Jardine, *Criminal Trials*'], 1: 324, 353.

78: *domestic and European* . . . On the propagandistic intent and effect of the trials, see e.g. ibid., 2: 4–5, 2: 235; Bowen, pp. 94, 163–4; George S. Kitson Clark, *The Critical Historian* (London, 1967), p. 87.

79: *blood before God'* . . . C[hristopher] B[arker] *A True and plaine declaration of the horrible Treasons, practised by William Parry the Traitor* (London, 1585); Jardine, *Criminal Trials*, 1: 246ff; and see Lacey Baldwin Smith, *Treason in Tudor England* (London, 1986), pp. 11–19.

79: *Sir Walter Raleigh* . . . The account of Raleigh's trial in this book is derived, except where otherwise specified, from sources collected and transcribed in Jardine, *Criminal Trials*, 1: 400ff. A less accurate version of the proceedings is contained in Thomas B. Howell et al. (eds), *A Complete Collection of State Trials*, 33 vols (London, 1816–26), 2: 1ff.

79: *return trip away* . . . See generally Robert Lacey, *Sir Walter Ralegh* (New York, 1974) [Lacey, *Ralegh*']; see also Walter Ralegh, *The Discoverie of the*

Large, Rich, and Bewtiful Empire of Guiana. With a relation of the Great and Golden Citie of Manoa (which the Spanyards call El Dorado) (London, 1596), pp. 69ff.

80: *grace-and-favour mansion* . . . Bowen, p. 394.

80: *two thousand lives a week* . . . Ibid., p. 187.

80: *sentenced to death* . . . See Jardine, *Criminal Trials*, 1: 457, 465.

81: *those they know not'* . . . Bowen, p. 188.

81: *are a guide* . . . The peers at the Earl of Essex's trial were said by the French Ambassador to have made themselves 'silly' by smoking: see Lacey, *Ralegh*, p. 90. In 1606 the eight Gunpowder Plotters, fresh from thumbscrews and soon to be eviscerated, castrated, and decapitated, whiled away half an hour in the Star Chamber prior to trial in Westminster Hall, 'taking tobacco, as if hanging were no trouble to them': see 'The Arraignment and Execution of the late Traitors . . . Printed 1606', in John Somers, *A Collection of scarce and valuable Tracts*, ed. Walter Scott, 2nd edn, 13 vols (London, 1809–15), 2: 113.

81: *other major trials* . . . According to a letter dated soon after the trial of the Gunpowder Plotters, 'the Queen and Prince were in a secret place by to hear, and some say the King in another': Jardine, *Criminal Trials*, 2: 115. James attended another major trial, that of the Jesuit Superior Henry Garnet on 28 March 1606, in an antechamber of Westminster Hall 'with a vast assemblage of courtiers': ibid., 2: 238.

81: *the mirror image* . . . On Coke's appearance and background, see (Lord) John Campbell, *Lives of the Chief Justices*, 3 vols (London, 1849) ['Campbell'], 1: 344; Bowen, p. 121; Cuthbert W. Johnson, *The Life of Sir Edward Coke*, 2 vols (London, 1837), 1: 11.

82: *than to attend them* . . . It was said that Coke neither read nor saw a play in his life and never once met an actor: Campbell, 1: 243.

82: *out of their lives'* . . . Jardine, *Criminal Trials*, 1: 321.

83: *law of the time* . . . See ibid., 1: 514.

84: *had already told the jury* . . . Ibid., 1: 415.

84: *confuse the jury.* . . Ibid., 1: 427. Popham's precise concern was that the jury would be 'inveigled'.

85: *by its end* . . . Quoted by Sir Dudley Carleton: ibid., 1: 466.

85: *greatest pity'* . . . Ibid, 1: 461.

85: *something daunted'* . . . S[tate]P[apers] 14/6, p. 82, at the Public Record Office in London.

86: *king's pleasure* . . . Thomas Overbury, *The Arraignment and Conviction of Sr Walter Rawleigh* (London, 1648), p. 25; William Oldys, *The Life of Sir Walter Raleigh from his Birth to his Death on the Scaffold* (London, 1740), p. 576.

86: *times far away* . . . See Jardine, *Criminal Trials*, 1: 478ff.

87: *wherein they abide'* . . . Ibid., 1: 499.

87: *the curtain* . . . Jardine, *Criminal Trials*, 1: 509; Bowen, p. 416.

87: *upon his scaffold* . . . Jardine *Criminal Trials*, 1: 474; see also 1: 466–8, 517–18.

88: *second trial, with witnesses* . . . Ibid., 1: 497.

88: *into compassion*' . . . Bowen, p. 415; cf. Jardine, *Criminal Trials*, 1: 485ff.

88: *from his deathbed* . . . Jardine, *Criminal Trials*, 1: 487.

88: *after convicting him* . . . Anon, *Observations Upon Some particular Persons and Passages in a Book lately made publick; Intituled A Compleat History of the Lives and Reignes of Mary Queen of Scotland, and Her Son James* (London, 1656), p. 9; Francis Osborne, *Traditional Memoirs*, in Walter Scott, *Secret History of the Court of James the First*, 2 vols (Edinburgh, 1811), 1: 161.

88: *if at all* . . . King James, *The True Lawe of free Monarchies* (Edinburgh, 1598), pp. D1–D2.

89: *down to size* . . . On Coke's influence among America's revolutionaries, see Bowen, pp. 513–14; see also *Klopfer v. North Carolina*, 386 US 213 (1967) at pp. 225–6.

89: *widely agreed* . . . See e.g. Coke, *Institutes (1)*, p. 155b.

89: *and fire* . . . On jury deference and independence during the late sixteenth and early seventeenth centuries, compare the essays by Cockburn and Green in *Twelve Good Men and True*.

89: *into the jury room* . . . *Welcden v. Elkington* (1576), in Edmund Plowden, *Les Commentaries, ou Reportes de Edmunde Plowden* (London, 1578), pp. 519–20.

89: *forty shillings* . . . *Mounson and West's Case* (30 Eliz.) 1 Leonard 133 in Max A. Robertson and Geoffrey Ellis (eds), *The English Reports*, 176 vols (London, 1900–30), 74: 123.

90: *violating the statute* . . . See Hugh Barbour, *The Quakers in Puritan England* (New Haven and London, 1964) ['Barbour'], pp. 224–33.

90: *to his credit* . . . Henry J. Cadbury (ed.), *George Fox's 'Book of Miracles'* (Cambridge, 1948) ['Fox, *Miracles*'], p. ix.

90: *while at prayer* . . . See H. Larry Ingle, *First Among Friends. George Fox and the Creation of Quakerism* (New York and Oxford, 1994), p. 54; Barbour, pp. 99–102.

90: *raise the dead* . . . See Fox, *Miracles*, pp. 5–6, 12–15, 20.

90: *wooden shack* . . . Donald Rumbelow, *The Triple Tree. Newgate, Tyburn and the Old Bailey* (London, 1982), p. 68.

90: *a magnificent show* . . . The following account draws from a transcription published very soon after the trial's conclusion: *The Peoples Ancient and Just Liberties Asserted, in the Tryal of William Penn, and William Mead* (London, 1670). Although most libraries credit it to Penn, he denied authorship (while recognizing its accuracy): see William Penn, *Truth Rescued from*

Imposture (London, 1670), pp. 6–7. Starling wrote *An Answer To the Seditious and Scandalous Pamphlet, Entituled, The Tryal of W. Penn and W. Mead* . . . (London, 1671), in which he also substantially accepted the truth of the account. See generally Mary M. Dunn & Richard S. Dunn, *The Papers of William Penn*, 5 vols (Philadelphia, 1981–7), 1:171-80; 5:118-128. There is no surviving estimate of the numbers in court, but Penn informed his father that there were 'about one hundred people' present at a pre-trial hearing of 15 August: ibid., 1:173.

92: *at Lincoln's Inn* . . . Penn claimed that he had been 'banisht' from the 'hellish darkness and debauchery' of Oxford: see *An Account of W. Penn's Travails in Holland and Germany* (London, 1694), p. 182. For further details of his troubles at university, along with his character and life more generally, see Catherine O. Peare, *William Penn* (Philadelphia and New York, 1957).

92: *perfunctory affair* . . . An Old Bailey jury would typically resolve between twelve and twenty cases a day in the late 1600s: see Langbein, 'Criminal Trial Before Lawyers', p. 277.

92: *becoming unusual* . . . Beattie, *Crime*, pp. 395–9. By the early nineteenth century, it was even rarer. Juries typically gathered around the foreman and spent just two or three minutes debating their verdict: see Charles Cottu, *On the Administration of Criminal Justice in England and the Spirit of the English Government* (London, 1822) ['Cottu'], p. 99.

93: *died awaiting trial* . . . Court records from Guildford in 1598, where conditions are unlikely to have been significantly worse than in seventeenth-century Newgate, showed a pre-trial mortality rate of 12 per cent: see Cecil L'Estrange Ewen, *Witch Hunting and Witch Trials* (London, 1929), p. 27. See generally Pugh, *Imprisonment*, pp. 331–3

94: *force of his understanding'* . . . 'Case of the Imprisonment of Edward Bushell' [*sic*], in Thomas B. Howell et al. (eds), *A Complete Collection of State Trials*, 33 vols (London, 1816–26), 6: 999 at 1006.

94: *the next few decades* . . . On the right to call defence witnesses – which was granted accused traitors in 1696, and felons in 1701 – see James B. Thayer, *A Preliminary Treatise on Evidence at the Common Law* (London, 1898), pp.157–61. Defence counsel began to appear in ordinary English criminal trials during the 1730s, and by the last two decades of the century were doing so in 20–50 per cent of all Old Bailey cases: Stephen Landsman, 'The Rise of the Contentious Spirit: Adversary Procedure in Eighteenth Century England', 75 *Cornell Law Review* 497 (1990) ['Landsman'], at p.533. They were given the right to address the jury only in 1836 however. Several American colonies denied defendants professional lawyers until the late eighteenth century: see Francis H. Heller, *The Sixth Amendment to the Constitution of the United States* (New York, 1969 reprint) ['Heller, *Sixth*

Amendment'], pp. 17ff. See generally Langbein, 'Criminal Trial Before Lawyers'.

94: *admissibility and exclusion* . . . On the development of rules of evidence after the late eighteenth century, see John H. Wigmore, 'A General Survey of the History of the Rules of Evidence', in Ernst Freund et al., *Select Essays in Anglo-American Legal History*, 3 vols (Boston, 1907–9), 2: 695.

94: *promoted to axiom* . . . Old Bailey juries were being directed on the standard of proof, and implicitly on the burden, by the 1780s, while Massachusetts records show similar directions a decade earlier: Langbein, 'Privilege and Common Law', in Richard H. Helmholz et al., *The Privilege Against Self-Incrimination* (Chicago, 1997), p. 234 n.43. The importance of caution before conviction had been recognized for over a thousand years: see Book 48, Title 19 of Justinian's *Digest* in S. P. Scott, *The Civil Law Including The Twelve Tables, The Institutes of Gaius, The Rules of Ulpian, The Opinions of Paulus, The Enactments of Justinian, and The Constitutions of Leo*, 17 vols (Cincinnati, 1932), 11: 110; the Council of Narbonne, c.23, in Michael Costen, *The Cathars and the Albigensian Crusade* (Manchester and New York, 1997), p. 166; John Fortescue, *On the Laws and Governance of England*, tr. Shelley Lockwood (Cambridge, 1997), p. 41 [c.27]; see also César de Saussure, *A Foreign View of England in the Reigns of George 1 and George II*, ed. and tr. Mme van Muyden (London, 1902) ['Saussure'], p. 119.

94: *nation's liberties* . . . Blackstone, *Commentaries*, 4: 342–4.

95: *commonplace across colonial America* . . . On the early history of jury trial in America see John M. Murrin, 'Trial by Jury in Seventeenth-Century New England', in David D. Hall et al. (eds), *Saints and Revolutionaries: Essays on Early American History* (New York and London, 1984), pp.152–206; Harold M. Hyman and Catherine M. Tarrant, 'Aspects of American Trial History', in Rita J. Simon (ed.), *The Jury System in America: A Critical Overview* (Beverly Hills and London, 1975); Heller, *Sixth Amendment*, pp. 15ff.

95: *in every case* . . . Article VIII of Pennsylvania's first Frame of Government of 25 April 1682, in Francis Newton Thorpe (ed.), *The Federal and State Constitutions, Colonial Charters, and Other Organic Laws of the States, Territories, and Colonies Now or Heretofore Forming the United States of America*, 7 vols (Washington DC, GPO, 1909), 5: 3060.

95: *as their English counterparts* . . . Leonard W. Levy, *Emergence of a Free Press* (New York and Oxford, 1985), pp. 38–44. The claim made on Zenger's behalf – that a jury could properly disagree with a judge about not just facts but law – was even more radical than that upheld in Bushel's case.

95: *Edward Coke* . . . On Blackstone's popularity in North America, see *Schick v. United States*, 195 US 65, 66 (1904); on Coke see pp. 8–89 of this book and accompanying note.

95: *England's political struggles* . . . The prohibition on retrospective laws and executive punishment (Art I, §9) and the narrow definition of treason (which included the two-witness rule that Sir Walter Raleigh had attempted to rely upon: see Art III, §3 [1]) were examples of the English influence. The Fifth Amendment's protection of due process and the privilege against self-incrimination also borrowed from old English ideas. The Eighth Amendment's prohibitions on excessive bail and cruel and unusual punishment directly reproduced §10 of England's Bill of Rights of 1689: see Anthony F. Granucci, '"Nor Cruel and Unusual Punishments Inflicted": The Original Meaning', 57 *California Law Review* 839 (1969).

95: *existed in 1776* . . . See Albert W. Alschuler and Andrew G. Deiss, 'A Brief History of the Criminal Jury in the United States', 61 *University of Chicago Law Review* 867 (1994), at p. 870. See also *Singer v. United States* 380 US 24, 28–31 (1965).

95: *'rebellion or invasion'* . . . Art. 1, §9, cl. 2; see also Article III, §2.

95: *gunshots and murders* . . . See James S. Cockburn, *A History of English Assizes 1558–1714* (Cambridge, 1972), pp.109–10.

96: *floor to collapse* . . . Ibid.

96: *became regulars* . . . See e.g. Saussure, pp. 120–2; and see the accounts in Thomas A. Green, *Verdict According to Conscience* (Chicago, 1985), pp. 285–8; Leon Radzinowicz, *A History of English Criminal Law*, 5 vols (London, 1948–86) ['Radzinowicz'], 1: 699-726

96: *would sometimes interrupt* . . . Douglas Hay, 'Property Authority and the Criminal Law' in Douglas Hay et al., *Albion's Fatal Tree* (London, 1988) ['Hay, 'Property'], p. 33.

96: *can have access'* . . . Barrington, *Observations*, p. 144.

96: *javelin-wielding officials* . . . Cottu, p. 43.

96: *through the night* . . . See John Howard, *The State of the Prisons in England and Wales* (London, 1777), pp. 27–9.

96: *black cap of death* . . . See Hay, 'Property', p.27; Cottu, p. 106.

97: *ecclesiastical courts* . . . See e.g. Pierre Darmon, *Le tribunal de l'impuissance* (Paris, 1979), pp. 96–101.

97: *called Satan* . . . Anon, *The examination and confession of certaine Wytches at Chensforde* (London, 1566).

97: *pedlar's cart* . . . On the 'dozens' of chapbooks published from the late sixteenth century onwards, 'mostly Jacobean but a few earlier', see John H. Langbein, *Prosecuting Crime in the Renaissance* (Harvard, 1974), pp. 45–54. Several four-page pamphlets from the early 1680s, detailing sittings at the Sessions House of the Old Bailey, are collected together in a British Library collection of tracts, catalogue number 1480.c.25. For examples from mid-eighteenth-century Sessions Papers, see John H. Langbein, 'Shaping the Eighteenth-Century Criminal Trial: A View from the Ryder Sources',

50 *University of Chicago Law Review* 1 (1983) [Langbein, 'Ryder Sources'], pp. 15–16. For a thoughtful account of how the media came to perceive trials as newsworthy stories in their own right, which also examines the historical development of crime fiction and courtroom architecture, see Jonathan H. Grossman, *The Art of Alibi. English Law Courts and the Novel* (Baltimore and London, 2002).

97: *call out their name* . . . Peter Lake, 'Deeds Against Nature . . .', in Kevin Sharpe and Peter Lake, *Culture and Politics in Early Stuart England* (Basingstoke, 1984), p. 271.

97: *to the gallows* . . . Anon., *The horrible Murther of a young Boy of three Yeres of age, whose Sister had her tongue cut out* (London, 1606); Anon, *The most cruell and bloody Murther committed by an Innkeepers Wife, called Annis Dell* (London, 1606).

97: *within days of a verdict* . . . Langbein, 'Ryder Sources', pp. 3, 10.

97: *proceedings be published* . . . *An Account of the Proceedings Against Capt Edward Rigby* (London, 1698).

97: *with a dog* . . . *A Compleat Collection of Remarkable Tryals, of the most Notorious Malefactors, at the Sessions-House in the Old Baily*, 4 vols (London, 1718–21), 2: 94.

98: *public gaze* . . . See Beattie, *Crime*, pp. 470–83. The practice of sending convicts to the colonies had begun in the early seventeenth century, but a statute of 1718 regularized it.

98: *in 1810* . . . Radzinowicz, 1: 3–5.

98: *unwanted cadaver* . . . Ibid., 1: 168ff; V. A. C. Gatrell, *The Hanging Tree* (Oxford, 1994) ['Gatrell'], pp. 52, 83; Roy Porter, *London. A Social History* (London, 2000), p. 185.

98: *removed and buried'* . . . Saussure, pp. 125–6.

99: *'pious perjury'* . . . Blackstone invented the term: see Blackstone, *Commentaries*, 4: 239. One legal historian has estimated that it may have been at work in a quarter of all English cases by the 1750s: see Langbein, 'Privilege and Common Law', pp. 82, 93. It may, however, have been on the decrease by the early nineteenth century: Gatrell, p. 524. Pious perjury was also seen in colonial New York: see Philip E. Mackey, *Hanging in the Balance: The Anti-Capital Punishment Movement in New York State, 1776–1861* (New York, 1982) ['Mackey, *Hanging in the Balance*'], p. 33.

99: *under twenty-one* . . . Gatrell, pp. 616–18. Radzinowicz, 1: 14; see also Landsman, p. 606.

99: *were being commuted* . . . Gatrell, p. 616.

99: *to help me'* . . . Quoted in Hay, 'Property', p. 29; see also Langbein, 'Ryder Sources', pp.118–19.

99: *bathed in tears'* . . . Johann Wilhelm von Archenholz, *A Picture of England*, 2 vols (London, 1789), 2: 22.

99: *repeatedly struck* . . . For the accounts of some foreign visitors, see Radzinowicz, 1: 720.

100: *employment prospects* . . . See e.g. Eden, *Principles*, p.59 (marking offenders with lasting and visible stigma was 'contrary both to humanity and sound policy' because it habituated them to their status, made them lose their shame and made it impossible for them to associate with virtuous people); 5 Anne, c.6 (branding on the cheek for theft 'hath not had the desired effect, by deterring such offenders from the further committing such crimes and offences, but on the contrary, such offenders being rendered thereby unfit to be entrusted in any honest and lawful way, become the more desperate').

100: *drafted a law for Virginia* . . . 'A Bill for Proportioning Crimes and Punishments in Cases Heretofore Capital', in *The Papers of Thomas Jefferson*, ed. Julian P. Boyd (Princeton, 1950–), 2: 492–507.

100: *criminals' corpses* . . . See J. S. Cockburn, 'Punishment and Brutalization in the English Enlightenment', 12 *Law and History Review* 155 (1994) at p.170.

100: *with an axe* . . . James Boswell, *The Hypochondriack*, ed. Margaret Bailey, 2 vols (Stanford, 1928), 2: 283–4.

101: *one writer had warned* . . . Bernard Mandeville, *An Enquiry into the Causes of the Frequent Executions at Tyburn etc.* (London, 1725), p. 37.

101: *surgeons present* . . . See Pieter Spierenburg, *Spectacle of Suffering* (Cambridge, 1984) ['Spierenburg'], pp.100–9; see also Gatrell, pp. 61 n.21, 99–100; J. S. Cockburn, 'Punishment and Brutalization in the English Enlightenment', 12 *Law and History Review* 155 (1994) at p.170.

101: *outside Newgate* . . . Gatrell, pp. 52–4, 602–4.

101: *before their eyes'* . . . Henry Fielding, *An Enquiry into the Causes of the Late Increase of Robbers* (London, 1751), pp. 189–96.

101: *would influence legislators* . . . See Radzinowicz, 1: 401–2 (it 'met with immediate success and . . . [had] a deep impression on public opinion').

102: *turn of the century* . . . See Mackey, *Hanging in the Balance*, pp. 36–78. On the shift in English sensibilities, see Michael Ignatieff, *A Just Measure of Pain* (London, 1978); Gatrell, pp. 325ff. The spread of the penitentiary movement in France was the subject of a particularly influential work by Michel Foucault, *Surveiller et punir: Naissance de la prison* (Paris, 1975), subsequently translated as *Discipline and Punish*, tr. Alan Sheridan (London and New York, 1977). For an overview of the change across Western Europe, see Spierenburg, pp. 183–99.

102: *abolition of capital punishment'* . . . Mackey, *Hanging in the Balance*, p. 117; see also Philip E. Mackey, *Voices Against Death* (New York, 1976), p. xx.

102: *to be outmanoeuvred* . . . For a survey of the debate in England, see Radzinowicz, 4: 343–53. He states (at 4: 350) that, 'By this time some of those who wanted to retain capital punishment, at least for murder, were already realizing what the abolitionists had realized from the first. To put a stop to public executions could reduce the revulsion felt against the punishment, could become a major stabilising factor in its retention.'

102: *behind prison walls* . . . 'The Execution of Barrett', *The Times* (London), 27 May 1868, p. 9; Capital Punishment Amendment Act 1868.

102: *sacrificial rite* . . . See p.16.

102: *two hundred years ago* . . . Support for capital punishment stabilized in the early 1980s at around 70 to 75 per cent: see Hugo Adam Bedau (ed.), *The Death Penalty in America* (New York and Oxford, 1997), p. 90.

103: National Police Gazette . . . For a potted history of the journal, see Elliott J. Gorn, 'The Wicked World: The *National Police Gazette* and Gilded-Age America', 6 *Media Studies Journal* 1 (1992).

103: *across the country* . . . Richard J. Evans, *Rituals of Retribution* (London, 1997), pp. 264–6, 305-15, 471-5.

103: *judging criminal cases* . . . See Adhémar Esmein, *A History of Continental Criminal Procedure* (Boston, 1913), pp. 408 ff.

103: *next three-quarters of a century* . . . Lay assessors would, during the nineteenth and early twentieth century, assume a role in the criminal trials of Austria, Belgium, Czechoslovakia, Germany Greece, Italy, Poland, Portugal, Russia, Scandinavia, Spain, and Switzerland: see Neil Vidmar, 'The Jury Elsewhere in the World', in Neil Vidmar (ed.), *World Jury Systems* (Oxford, 2000), at pp.429–32. In modern France, serious offences are still tried before nine members of the public and three professional judges and a two-thirds majority (i.e. eight) is required for a valid conviction: Code de Procédure Pénale, Arts. 296, 359, available online via www.legifrance.gouv.fr; and see Bron McKillop, 'Anatomy of a French Murder Case', 45 *American Journal of Comparative Law* 527 (1997); Stephen C. Thaman, in Vidmar, op. cit., p. 338. In modern Germany, jurors sit on all but the most serious cases, which are tried by five professional judges: see Royal Commission on Criminal Justice, *Criminal Justice Systems in Other Jurisdictions* (London, 1993), pp. 98–100; Nigel G. Foster, *German Legal System and Laws*, 2nd edn (London, 1996), pp. 221–2.

103: *in the Western world* . . . France's final public execution was that of 31-year-old Eugene Weidmann, who was beheaded on 17 June 1939 before about a thousand people: see 'France Guillotines Head of Murder Ring', *New York Times*, 17 June 1939, p. 5; 'No Public Executions in France', *The Times* (London), 26 June 1939, p. 13. The last to occur in the United States came just three years before, when thousands gathered at dawn to watch one Rainey Bethea die: see '10,000 See Hanging of Kentucky Negro', *New York Times*, 15 August 1936, p. 30.

103: *reported in the newspapers'* . . . François Marie Arouet de Voltaire, *Histoire d'Elisabeth Canning et de Calas* (London, 1762), p. 3. For similar observations by other foreigners, see Radzinowicz, 1: 699–726.

104: *that of Doubs . . . Observations des tribunaux criminels sur le projet de Code criminel* 6 vols (Paris, Imprim. impériale, an XIII), 2: 7–8, cited in Esmein, p. 473.

104: *absence could demand . . .* For an examination of the new architecture with specific reference to the Troppmann trial (below), see Katherine F. Taylor, *In the Theater of Criminal Justice* (Princeton, 1993) ['Fischer'].

105: *admission passes . . . The Times* (London), 30 December 1869, p. 8.

105: *one of the deceased . . .* John T. Morse, *Famous Trials* (Boston, 1874), p. 320; see Fischer, *passim*.

105: Le Petit journal . . . Thomas Grimm, 'Emotions Judiciaires', *Le Petit journal* (27 December 1869), p. 1, cited in Fischer, p. 27.

105: *only with shame . . .* 'The Pimlico Mystery. The Judge's Summing Up', *Weekly Despatch*, 25 April 1886, p.10.

106: *forty-eight hours . . .* Paul Aubry, *La Contagion du meurtre, 3rd edn,* (Paris, 1896), p. 107.

106: *with the* femmes . . . See the concluding remarks of René de Pont-Just's report in *Le Figaro*, 1 January 1870, p. 2.

106: *fourteen years before . . .* For an examination of early Russian jury trials see Girish N. Bhat, 'The Moralization of Guilt in Late Imperial Russian Trial by Jury: The Early Reform Era', 15 *Law and History Review* 77 (1997).

106: *slender pink ribbon . . .* Fyodor Dostoyevsky, *The Brothers Karamazov*, tr. David McDuff (London, 1993), pp. 760–1.

106: *act of parricide . . .* Ibid., p. 791.

106: *right-thinking folk everywhere . . .* Examples of the distaste are ubiquitous in the *Daily News, News of the World* and *Weekly Despatch* during the 1880s. For a specific complaint about 'tumblers, footless wine glasses, tea cups and other picnic effects' see 'The Pimlico Poisoning Case', *Daily News*, 19 April 1886, p. 5. For an example of French criticisms, see Maxime du Camp, *Paris, ses organes, ses fonctions et sa vie dans la seconde moitié du XIXe siècle*, 6th edn, 6 vols (Paris, 1869–76), 3: 223–4.

107: *acquittal in 1907 . . .* See Harry Hodge and James H. Hodge, *Famous Trials* (Harmondsworth, 1984), pp. 204–5.

107: *long before sunrise . . .* See e.g. *Weekly Despatch*, 9 September 1917.

107: *on a dish . . .* 'The Crippen Trial', *The Times* (London), 20 October 1910, p. 4; Hodge, op. cit., p. 76.

107: *drifted home . . .* See '5 A.M. Queue For To-Morrow's Malcolm Trial. Tickets Refused Even to the Morbid Rich', *Weekly Despatch*, 9 September 1917, p. 2.

Chapter 4: The Witch Trial

108: *hundred thousand people* . . . Compare the estimates of Brian P. Levack, *The Witch-Hunt in Early Medieval Europe*, 2nd edn, (London and New York, 1995) ['Levack'], pp. 24–5 and Anne L. Barstow, *Witchcraze: A New History of the European Witch Hunts* (London, 1995), p. 23.

109: *familiar spirit'* . . . Exodus 22: 18; Leviticus 20: 27.

109: *beasts and birds* . . . St Augustine, *The City of God Against the Pagans*, tr. R. W. Dyson (Cambridge, 1998), pp. 842–5 (18: 18).

109: *tenth-century canon* . . . This was the 'Canon episcopi': see Norman Cohn, *Europe's Inner Demons* (London, 1993) ['Cohn, *Demons*'], pp. 167ff.

109: *far more benign* . . . See generally Henry C. Lea, *Materials Toward a History of Witchcraft*, 3 vols (Philadelphia, 1939) ['Lea, *Witchcraft*'], 1: 101–3.

109: *a rapist* . . . Roger of Wendover, *Flowers of History*, tr. J.A. Giles, 2 vols (London, 1849), 2: 464–5.

109: *at the stake* . . . Caesarius of Heisterbach, *The Dialogue on Miracles*, tr. H. von E. Scott and C.C. Swinton Bland, 2 vols (London, 1929), 1: 338–41 (5.18).

110: *call in his due* . . . Thomas de Cantimpré, *Les exemples du 'Livre des abeilles': une vision médiévale*, ed. Henri Platelle (Brepols, 1997), p. 246 (*Bonum universale de apibus* 2. 56).

110: *debt unredeemed* . . . See Desmond Seward, *The Hundred Years War* (New York, 1978), p. 214.

110: *Johann Faust* . . . See generally Philip M. Palmer and Robert P. More, *The Sources of the Faust Tradition from Simon Magus to Lessing* (New York, 1936).

110: *in the process* . . . On the natural malice of demons, see Thomas Aquinas, *The 'Summa Theologica' of St Thomas Aquinas . . . Literally Translated by Fathers of the English Dominican Province* tr. Laurence Shapcote, 2nd edn, 22 vols (London, 1921?–32) ['Aquinas, *Summa theologica*'], 3: 146–8 (Part 1, Q.63, Art. 1). On the nature of incubi and succubi, see ibid., 3: 21–5 (Part 1, Q.51, Art. 3); see also Thomas Aquinas, *On the Power of God*, 2 vols (London, 1932), 2: 208–12 (6.8), Thomas Aquinas, *Quodlibet* (Part 11, Q.9, Art. 1), translated in Walter Stephens, 'Witches Who Steal Penises: Impotence and Illusion in *Malleus maleficarum*', 28 (3) *Journal of Medieval and Early Modern Studies* 495 (1998), at p.504.

111: *pact with hell* . . . Thomas Aquinas, *Summa theologica*, 11: 198–200 (Part 2.2, Q.95, Art 4). For more of Aquinas' thoughts on the risks that magicians ran when invoking demons, see *Of God and his Creatures: An annotated translation, with some abridgement, of the Summa contra Gentiles of Saint Thos. Aquinas*, tr. Joseph Rickaby (London, 1905), p. 269 (3.107).

111: *at the stake* . . . Paulin Paris (ed.), *Les grandes Chroniques de France, selon que elles sont conservées en l'eglise de St Denis en France*, 6 vols (Paris, 1836–8), 5: 269.

112: *until cockcrow* . . . For detailed accounts of these early prosecutions see Lea, *Witchcraft*, 1: 230–60; see also Cohn, *Demons*, pp. 202ff; Levack, pp. 35–9, 50–1.

112: *a full report* . . . See his 1484 bull 'Summis desiderantes affectibus' in Heinrich Kramer (aka Institoris) and Jacob Sprenger, *Malleus maleficarum*, tr. Montague Summers (London, 1928) ['*Malleus*'], pp. xliii–xlv.

112: *itself a heresy* . . . *Malleus*, pp. 1–11 (Part I, Q.10); see also p. 56 (1.8).

112: *human sense anyway* . . . See e.g. ibid., pp. 7–8 (1.1), pp. 63–5 (1.10).

113: *human flesh* . . . Lea, *Witchcraft*, 1: 146; Homer, *Odyssey*, Book 10; Cohn, *Demons*, pp. 162–75.

113: *to fly* . . . *Malleus*, pp. 41–8, 66, 107, 111–14, 140–4 (1.6, 1.11, 2.1.3, 2.1.4, 2.1.13).

114: *parish priest'*' . . . Ibid., p. 121 (2.1.7); see also pp. 58–61 (1.9). For a detailed discussion of Kramer's concerns, see Walter Stephens, 'Witches Who Steal Penises: Impotence and Illusion in *Malleus maleficarum*', 28 (3) *Journal of Medieval and Early Modern Studies* 495 (1998).

114: *turned black* . . . *Malleus*, p. 119 (2.1.7).

114: *next four decades* . . . Geoffrey R. Quaife, *Godly Zeal and Furious Rage* (London, 1987), p. 23.

114: *eternal damnation* . . . *Malleus*, p. 228 (3.15).

114: *four-fifths of those charged* . . . Levack, pp. 133–5.

114: *procedure and evidence* . . . Ibid., pp. 94–9, 215–16, 219–21, 231–2.

114: *instability* . . . See ibid., pp. 114–20; Geoffrey R. Quaife, *Godly Zeal and Furious Rage* (London, 1987), pp. 12–14.

115: *once done* . . . For an overview of the relationship between the Reformation and the witch-hunts, see Levack, pp. 100–24; for a detailed study of southwestern Germany, where Catholic judges held almost twice as many trials and executed 3.6 times as many people than their Protestant counterparts, see H. C. Erik Midelfort, *Witch-Hunting in Southwestern Germany 1562–1684* (Stanford, 1972), p. 33.

115: *continent combined* . . . Levack, pp. 22, 24, 193.

115: *accomplices in France* . . . Jean Bodin, *De la Demonomanie des Sorciers* (Paris, 1580) ['Bodin'], at the fourth page of his preface.

116: *prior to questioning* . . . Ibid., p. 171b.

116: *support a conviction* . . . Ibid., p. 186b.

116: *in a garden'* . . . Henry [*sic*] Boguet, *An Examen of Witches*, tr. E. Allen Ashwin (London, 1929) ['Boguet, *Examen*'], pp. xxxii–xxxiv.

116: *fear and dread'* . . . Ibid., p. 116.

116: *touch alone* . . . Ibid., p. 213.

116: *break its hold* . . . Ibid., pp. 214, 217.

116: *pre-pubescent* . . . Ibid., p. 234.

117: *their throats* . . . Nicolas Rémy, *Demonolatry*, tr. E. Allen Ashwin (London, 1930) ['Rémy'], pp. 174–5, 164.

117: *excruciating torments* . . . Martín Del Rio, *Investigations into Magic*, tr. P. G. Maxwell-Stuart (Manchester, 2000) ['Del Rio'], p. 217.

117: *in no time* . . . Ibid., pp. 217–18.

117: *but satanic* . . . Bodin, p. 194a.

117: *fifteen pounds* . . . See Henry C. Lea, *Superstition and Force* (Greenwood, 1968 reprint of 1870 edition) ['Lea, *Superstition*'], p. 255; see also Lea, *Witchcraft*, 2: 892–3.

117: *thunderstorm* . . . Rémy, pp. 84–5.

117: *at their feet* . . . Del Rio, p. 197.

118: *hallmark of witchcraft* . . . *Malleus*, pp. 99–104 (2.1.2).

118: *repulsive fashion* . . . Del Rio, pp. 92–3. For another description of the sabbath, see Boguet's *Examen*, pp. 55–61 (cf. his *Discours des Sorciers* (Lyons, 1608), pp. 129–43).

118: *to the stake* . . . A factual account (in French) of De Lancre's campaign can be found in the introduction to a modern reissue of his work: see Pierre de Lancre, *Tableau de l'inconstance des mauvais anges et démons*, ed. Nicole Jacques-Chaquin (Paris, 1982), p. 11.

118: *and tigers* . . . Pierre de Lancre, *Tableau de l'inconstance des mauvais anges et démons* (Paris, 1612) ['De Lancre, *Tableau*'], pp. 202–11.

119: *forehead* . . . Ibid., p. 72.

119: *covered in scales* . . . Ibid., pp. 222–3; see also 132–6.

119: *scream so much* . . . Ibid., p. 225.

119: *those of the Franche-Comté* . . . Ibid.; cf. Henri Boguet, *Discours des Sorciers* (Lyons, 1608), p. 69.

120: *never see you again'* . . . For the background to Junius' case and a translated transcript of his letter in full, see Lea, *Witchcraft*, 3: 1175.

121: *over that night'* . . . Ibid., 2: 707–10.

121: *in the heavens* . . . On English superstitions of the period, see Keith Thomas, *Religion and the Decline of Magic* (London, 1978) ['Thomas, *Religion*'], *passim*.

121: *executed in Germany* . . . On execution figures in England, see Cecil L'Estrange Ewen, *Witch Hunting and Witch Trials* (London, 1929) ['Ewen, *Witch Hunting*'], pp. 31, 112; for those on the continent, see Levack, pp. 21–6. On gender bias, see Quaife, p.107; Levack, p. 134.

121: *late 1600s* . . . See John H. Langbein, 'The Origins of Public Prosecution at Common Law', 17 *American Journal of Legal History* 313 (1973), at pp. 315–17.

121: *forward at all* . . . For a thorough survey of the grand jury's history, see

Helene E. Schwartz, 'Demythologizing the Historic Role of the Grand Jury', 10 *American Criminal Law Review* 701 (1972).

122: *or his councillors* . . . See p.75 of this book and accompanying note.

123: *suck with a little blood* . . . For an overview of the distinction between the English and continental witchcraft traditions, see Thomas, pp. 519ff. Statistics analysed by one historian, drawn from over five hundred indictments tried at Essex Assizes between 1560 and 1680, suggest that about 98 per cent of the cases there alleged actual damage to people or property: see Alan Macfarlane, *Witchcraft in Tudor and Stuart England* 2nd edn (London, 1999) ['Macfarlane, *Witchcraft*'], pp. 25–8.

123: *set on murder* . . . Anon, *The Apprehension and confession of three notorious Witches. Arreigned and by Justice condemned and executed at Chelmesforde* (London, 1589).

123: *per witch* . . . Ewen, *Witch Hunting*, p. 62; Christina Larner, *Enemies of God. The Witch-hunt in Scotland* (London, 1981) ['Larner, *Enemies of God*'], p. 115.

123: *to visit her* . . . The art of watching was described by John Gaule in his *Select Cases of Conscience touching Witches and Witchcrafts* (London, 1646), at pp. 78–9.

124: *almost certainly hanged* . . . Another nine are known to have died of disease in jail, and only one was definitely acquitted: see Macfarlane, *Witchcraft*, pp. 135–42.

124: *invented them* . . . Matthew Hopkins, *The Discovery of Witches* (London, 1647), pp. 2–3.

124: *and Glasgow* . . . Peter Stein, 'The Influence of Roman Law on the Law of Scotland', 23 *Studia et Documenta Historiae et Iuris* 149, 151 (1957); see generally O. F. Robinson et al. (eds), *European Legal History: Sources and Institutions*, 2nd edn (London, 1994), pp. 224–41.

124: *parish church* . . . Bodin, pp. 168a–b.

124: *recited aloud* . . . See I. D. Willock, *The Origins and Development of the Jury in Scotland* (Edinburgh, 1966) ['Willock'], p. 201.

125: *simply academic* . . . On James's appearance and character, see the sources collected in Robert Ashton (ed.), *James I. By His Contemporaries* (London, 1969), pp. 1–21. On his demonological activities, see Christina Larner, 'James VI and I and Witchcraft', in Alan G. R. Smith (ed.), *The Reign of James VI and I* (London, 1973) ['Larner, "James and Witchcraft"'], pp. 74–90; Larner, *Enemies of God, passim*.

125: *Firth of Forth* . . . James Melville, *Memoirs*, ed. A. Francis Steuart (London, 1929) ['Melville, *Memoirs*'], pp. 327–8.

125: *three hundred* . . . David Calderwood, *The History of the Kirk of Scotland*, ed. Thomas Thomson, 8 vols (Edinburgh, 1842–9) ['Calderwood'], 5: 67.

125: *in the snow* . . . Ethel Carleton Williams, *Anne of Denmark* (London,

1970) ['Williams'], p. 21. For a (translated) Danish account of the wedding see David Stevenson, *Scotland's Last Royal Wedding* (Edinburgh, 1997).

126: *misfortunes* . . . Williams, p. 38; see also Larner, 'James and Witchcraft', p. 232 n.20.

126: *Anne's ship* . . . Williams, p. 38. Torture to extract confessions was, however, formally forbidden in Denmark: Jens Christian V. Johansen, 'Denmark: The Sociology of Accusations', in Bengt Ankarloo and Gustav Henningsen (eds), *Early Modern European Witchcraft: Centres and Peripheries*, (Oxford, 1990), at p. 340.

126: *their husbands* . . . Melville, *Memoirs* p. 327.

126: *made them better* . . . See Anon, *Newes from Scotland, Declaring the Damnable Life and Death of Doctor Fian* (London, 1591) ['*Newes from Scotland*']. The author of this unpaginated pamphlet is not identified, but he may have been one James Carmichael, the then Minister of Haddington: see Melville, *Memoirs*, p. 353.

126: *almost two years* . . . Comprehensive sources, including transcripts of many original documents, can be found in Robert Pitcairn (ed.), *Criminal Trials in Scotland*, 3 vols (Edinburgh, 1833) ['Pitcairn, *Criminal Trials*'], 1(2): 209ff.

127: *had to say* . . . *Newes from Scotland*.

127: *vagina* . . . Ibid.

127: *in the process* . . . See No. 40 of the indictment, or 'dittay' in Scotch, in Pitcairn, *Criminal Trials*, 1(2): 236–7.

127: *one version* . . . i.e. *Newes from Scotland*.

127: *order of things* . . . See the accounts of the satanic convention ibid., and in James Melville, *Memoirs* (London, 1929), p. 353.

127: *and returned home* . . . See No. 50 of the dittay in Pitcairn, *Criminal Trials*, 1(2): 239.

127: *taking the register* . . . See counts 14–16 of his dittay ibid., 1(2): 212.

127: *as might bee'* . . . *Newes from Scotland*.

128: *continental counterparts* . . . See Willock, pp. 198–200. On continental rules, see pp. 51–2 of this book.

128: *thirty-two women* . . . Calderwood, 5: 116. In this context, it is interesting that the instigator of the proceedings, David Seaton, accused Fian of breaking into his house (see para. 10 of his dittay, Pitcairn, *Criminal Trials*, 1[2]: 211–2). Given the rumours of promiscuity that evidently surrounded Fian, it is conceivable that the teacher was clandestinely courting Gillis Duncan, the servant of Seaton whose arrest sparked off the hunt.

128: *scores executed* . . . See Larner, 'James and Witchcraft', p.79.

128: *to tell the truth* . . . John H. Burton and David Masson (eds), *The Register of the Privy Council of Scotland*, 1st series, 14 vols (Edinburgh, 1877–98), 4: 680.

128: *evil spirits* . . . 1 Jac. I, c.12 (1604), reprinted in Barbara Rosen (ed.), *Witchcraft in England*, 1558–1618 (Amherst, 1991), pp. 57–8.

128: *next four years* . . . Ewen, *Witch Hunting*, p. 31.

128: *the first time* . . . The sabbath's debut was, however, a flop. Grace Sowerbutts told a jury at Lancaster Castle in 1612 that four of the accused had hammered nails into a little baby and boiled it up into a magical ointment; and that she had attended a meeting where she had danced and had sex with a black thing which had the gait of a man but not the face of one. The meagre tale of hanky-panky with a dark stranger left the judge so mystified that he investigated her claims further – and it emerged that she had been coached by a Jesuit priest, educated on the continent and anxious to revenge himself against lapsed Catholics: see Thomas Potts, *The Trial of the Lancaster Witches, A.D. MDCXII,* ed. George B. Harrison (London, 1929), pp. 86–107. Ten defendants nevertheless went to their deaths: pp. 162–6.

129: *in a sieve* . . . *Macbeth*, I. iii. 7–10 and IV. i.; on the likely date and location of first performance, see the introduction to the Penguin edition of 1967 at p. 29.

129: *of his own* . . . Ewen, *Witch Hunting*, p.31.

129: *particulars against them'* . . . John H. Burton and David Masson (eds), *The Register of the Privy Council of Scotland*, 1st series, 14 vols (Edinburgh, 1877–98), 5: 409.

129: *across the country* . . . George L. Kittredge, *Witchcraft in Old and New England* (Harvard, 1929), pp. 322–3. The author states that only five more people were hanged in England in the remaining nine years of James's reign.

129: *that of England* . . . See Levack, p. 202; on execution figures in Scotland generally, see Larner, *Enemies of God*, pp. 62–3.

130: *or the evidence* . . . See Cecil L'Estrange Ewen, *Witchcraft and Demonianism* (London, 1933) ['Ewen, *Witchcraft and Demonianism*'], p. 125.

131: *belong to God'* . . . Matthew Hale, *Historia placitorum coronæ: The History of the Pleas of the Crown*, 2 vols (London, 1736), 1: 429.

132: *of her Crutches* . . . Anon, *A Tryal of Witches at the Assizes Held at Bury St Edmunds* (London, 1682), pp. 11–12.

132: *what awaited her* . . . Anon, *The Tryal, Condemnation and Execution of Three Witches . . . Arraigned at Exeter on the 18th of August 1682* (London, 1682). Considerably more detailed is Frank J. Gent's *The Trial of the Bideford Witches* (Bideford, 1982) ['Gent, *Bideford Witches*']. A certain Alice Molland was convicted of witchcraft at Exeter two years later, but her death sentence seems to have been commuted: see Gent, p. 17.

132: *but believe them'* . . . Letter of 19 August 1682 reprinted in F. H. Blackburne Daniell (ed.), *Calendar of State Papers, Domestic Series, January 1st to December 31st, 1682*, (London, 1932), p.347.

132: *and Essex* . . . See Kai T. Erikson, *Wayward Puritans* (Boston, 1966), p. 37.

133: *through the world'* . . . John Winthrop, 'A Modell of Christian Charity', *Winthrop Papers*, 5 vols (Boston, 1929–47) 2: 295.

133: *familiar spirits* . . . §94(2) of the Body of Liberties 1641; cf. 'Capital Lawes' in the Massachusetts Laws and Liberties of 1649. Both are reprinted in William H. Whitmore (ed.), *The Colonial Laws of Massachusetts* (Boston, 1889), pp. 55, 128.

133: *since 1656* . . . John Putnam Demos, *Entertaining Satan* (Oxford and New York, 1982), pp. 401–9.

134: *guilty of Witchcraft'* . . . Increase Mather, *Essay for the Recording of Illustrious Providences* (Boston, 1684), pp. 140, 142–55.

134: *as witchcraft is'* . . . Cotton Mather, *Memorable Providences, Relating to Witchcrafts and Possessions* (Boston, 1689), at p. 10 of 'A Discourse on Witchcraft'.

134: *their urine* . . . John Hale, *A Modest Enquiry into the Nature of Witchcraft* (Boston, 1702) ['Hale, *Modest Enquiry*'], pp. 23–4. The entire work is reprinted in George L. Burr, *Narratives of the Witchcraft Cases 1648–1706* (New York, 1914) ['Burr'], pp. 399–432.

134: *one beating* . . . Robert Calef, *More Wonders of the Invisible World* (London, 1700) ['Calef'], p. 91.

135: *be anyone* . . . See Paul Boyer and Stephen Nissenbaum (eds), *The Salem Witchcraft Papers. Verbatim Transcripts of the Legal Documents of the Salem Witchcraft Outbreak of 1692*, 3 vols (New York, 1977) ['Boyer'], 3: 747–55.

135: *outside the hall?* . . . Ibid., 1: 248–54; and see Deodat Lawson, *A True Narrative of Some Remarkable Passages relating to sundry Persons afflicted by Witchcraft at Salem Village*, reprinted in *A Further Account of the Tryals of the New-England Witches* (London, 1693) ['Lawson'], p. 3.

135: *as its source* . . . Lawson, p. 6; see also Boyer, 2: 351–3.

135: *of her life* . . . See Frances Hill, *The Salem Witch Trials Reader* (Cambridge, Mass., 2000) ['Hill, *Salem Reader*'], p. 295.

136: *broke his cane* . . . Calef, p. 100.

136: *remain standing* . . . Ibid., pp. 95–7.

136: *pivotal moment* . . . Miller identified the moment when he read Samuel Parris's record of the confrontation as the point when 'the thousands of pieces I had come across were jogged into place': see Arthur Miller, 'Why I Wrote "The Crucible"', *New Yorker*, 21 and 28 October 1996, p. 158. The play was, incidentally, highly ahistorical, centring on a fictional love affair between protagonists who were in reality 11 and 60 years old.

136: *animal scream* . . . Boyer, 1: 661.

136: *fifty people in jail* . . . Thomas Brattle's letter of 8 October 1692, transcribed in Burr, pp. 169–90, at p.173.

136: *put in irons* . . . Calef, p. 95.

136: *and Anus'* . . . Boyer, 1: 107. For Bishop's trial generally, see ibid., 1: 83–109; and see Cotton Mather, *The Wonders of the Invisible World* (Boston, 1693) ['Mather, *Wonders*'], pp. 104–14.

137: *obnoxious to God* . . . *The Return of several Ministers consulted by his Excellency*, reprinted as part of a postscript to the London edition of Increase Mather, *Cases of Conscience Concerning Evil Spirits Personating Men* (London, 1693).

137: *blood to drink'* . . . Calef, pp. 101–3.

138: *a cane* . . . Ibid., p. 106. On the practice of pressing unco-operative defendants, see p. 74 of this book. There are at least two other possible instances of its occurrence in colonial America, but it fell into disuse there considerably earlier than in England: see Cecil Geek, 'Drug Control and Asset Seizures: A Review of the History of Forfeiture in England and Colonial America', in Thomas Mieczkowski (ed.), *Drugs, Crime and Social Policy: Research, Issues, and Concerns* (Boston, 1992), at pp. 121–2.

138: *had not committed* . . . Calef, pp. 106–8.

138: *hell hanging there'* . . . Ibid., pp. 109–10.

138: *evil eye* . . . Ibid., p. 108; cf. Thomas Brattle's letter of 8 October 1692, transcribed in Burr, at pp. 180–2.

139: *mind overnight* . . . Hale would write his *Modest Enquiry into the Nature of Witchcraft*, op. cit., an extended *mea culpa* in which he analysed and repudiated the mentality that had generated the witch-hunt.

139: *should be Condemned'* . . . Increase Mather, *Cases of Conscience Concerning Evil Spirits Personating Men* (London, 1693), preface and p. 38.

139: *his own wife had been accused* . . . Calef, p. 154.

139: *upon mee'* . . . The original letter is in the Public Record Office in London (CO 5/857, pp. 87–8). It is transcribed in Burr, pp. 196–8.

139: *she was a witch* . . . Calef, pp. 141–2.

139: *the Countrey'* . . . Ibid., p.141.

139: *within two years* . . . Richard Weisman, *Witchcraft, Magic and Religion in 17th-Century Massachusetts* (Amherst, 1984), p. 182.

140: *shoulders of Satan* . . . See Calef, pp. 143–5; 'The Confession of Ann Putnam' (1706), reprinted in Hill, *Salem Reader*, p. 108.

140: *fifteen capital offences* . . . See § 94 of the 1641 Body of Liberties and 'Capital Lawes' in the *Lawes and Liberties* of 1648–9, reprinted in William H. Whitmore (ed.), *The Colonial Laws of Massachusetts* (Boston, 1889), pp. 55, 128.

140: *put together* . . . See John Putnam Demos, *Entertaining Satan* (Oxford and New York, 1982), pp. 11–13, 401–9. The author's data disclose sixteen witchcraft executions prior to those at Salem.

140: *or against it* . . . See generally Hill, *Salem Reader*, pp.117–76.

140: *particularly blameworthy* . . . See Howard Schweber, 'Ordering Principles:

The Adjudication of Criminal Cases in Puritan Massachusetts, 1629–1650, 32 *Law and Society Review* 367 (1998), at p. 371.

140: *tore it apart* . . . See generally Kai T. Erikson, *Wayward Puritans* (Boston, 1966); on the role of Samuel Parris specifically, see Hill, *Salem Reader*, pp. 117–76. For a survey of ritual and atonement in colonial New England, see David D. Hall, *Worlds of Wonder, Days of Judgment* (Harvard, 1990), pp. 166–212. A good general account of the Salem witch-hunt can be found in Frances Hill, *A Delusion of Satan* (London, 1996).

140: *ten years before* . . . Gent, *Bideford Witches*, pp. 7–8.

140: *relied upon* . . . One Salemite claimed in 1693 that 'at least 6 or 7' of ' 14 or 15' features found in the Bury St Edmunds case had been present at Salem: see Lawson, p. 9. Cotton Mather included a summary of the earlier trial in a pseudo-apology for the Salem prosecutions that he wrote soon after their conclusion: see Mather, *Wonders*, pp. 83–93. See also Hale, *Modest Inquiry*, pp. 51–2, 77–8.

141: *the late 1600s* . . . Ewen, *Witchcraft and Demonianism*, p. 46.

141: *her a pardon* . . . Wallace Notestein, *History of Witchcraft in England 1558–1718* (Washington DC, 1911), pp. 324–8; Ewen, *Witchcraft and Demonianism*, pp. 384–9. Notestein observes that the earliest surviving record of Powell's supposed comment about flying dates from the early 1800s, but that it tallies with Jonathan Swift's assessment of the judge: 'an old fellow with grey hairs, who was the merriest old gentleman I ever saw, spoke pleasing things, and chuckled till he cried again.'

141: *final accusation* . . . Ewen, *Witch Hunting*, pp. 68, 314.

141: *believe in witchcraft* . . . 21 *The Gentleman's Magazine* (1751), pp. 186, 198, 375, 378.

142: *mortal flesh* . . . See the defence case transcribed in Gena Brealey and Kay Hunter, *The Two Worlds of Helen Duncan* (London, 1985), pp. 127ff.

142: *dim light* . . . R v. Duncan [1944] KB 713, at p.715.

142: *horned god* . . . Margaret Murray's thesis, set out in *The Witch-Cult in Western Europe* (Oxford, 1921), has been comprehensively discredited: see Cohn, *Demons*, pp. 152ff; see also Quaife, pp. 9–10, 66ff., Thomas, pp. 614–15. Some persecutions may however have been inspired by attempts to suppress pre-Christian rituals and traditions, as Carlo Ginzburg has well demonstrated: see e.g. *Ecstasies*, tr. Raymond Rosenthal (London, 1990), *passim*.

142: *patriarchal holocaust* . . . See e.g. Andrea Dworkin, *Woman Hating* (New York, 1974), p. 130 ('In Europe, women were persecuted as witches for nearly four hundred years, burned at the stake, perhaps as many as nine million of them').

142: *fly today* . . . See Linnda R. Caporael, 'Ergotism: The Satan Loosed in Salem?', *Science* 192 (2 April 1976), p. 21; Quaife pp. 201–4; Levack, pp. 17–18, 48–9.

143: *sealed coffin* . . . These facts and those which follow are taken, except where otherwise specified, from Edgar W. Butler et al., *Anatomy of the McMartin Child Molestation Case* (Lanham, Md, 2001) ['Butler'], and Paul Eberle and Shirley Eberle, *The Abuse of Innocence: The McMartin Preschool Trial* (Buffalo, NY, 1993) ['Eberle'].

143: *sodomized by him* . . . For the letter's text, see Butler, p. 14.

143: *professional qualifications* . . . Although possessed of a degree in social work and practical experience in the fields of child abuse and psycho-analysis, Kee MacFarlane admitted under cross-examination that she was not licensed as a social worker in California, and had no licence to practise as any type of therapist, psychotherapist, or other medical professional in any state in the US: see Butler, pp. 72–3 citing the transcript of 7 September 1984, pp. 24–5.

144: *sexual organs* . . . See Kee MacFarlane and Sandy Krebs, 'Techniques for Interviewing and Evidence Gathering', in Kee MacFarlane and Jill Waterman with Shawn Conerly et al., *Sexual Abuse of Young Children* (London, 1986), pp. 67–100; see also Debbie Nathan and Michael Snedeker, *Satan's Silence* (New York, 1995) ['Nathan'], pp. 77–8.

144: *happened had happened* . . . Eberle, pp. 153, 191–2.

144: *'yucky secrets'* . . . Butler, p. 70.

144: *'dumb'* . . . See Butler, pp.170–4; Eberle, pp.187–99.

144: *none had mentioned* . . . Robert D. Hicks, *In Pursuit of Satan* (Buffalo, NY, 1991) ['Hicks'], p. 191.

145: *disinterring corpses* . . . Butler, p. 87.

145: *satanic schoolteachers* . . . Ibid., p. 193.

145: inconsistent *with it* . . . Nathan, pp. 190–1; Hicks, pp. 192–3.

145: *chicken bones* . . . Mark Arax, 'McMartin Parents Spur Action by Authorities. Officials Search Lot for Abuse Evidence', *Los Angeles Times*, 18 March 1985, p. 2; Hicks, p.193.

145: *photograph taken at McMartin* . . . Butler, p. 19.

145: *'interest in children'* . . . Eberle, pp. 140, 175–6.

145: *missing eye* . . . Thomas B. Rosenstiel, 'Lurid News: Are Victims Exploited?', *Los Angeles Times*, 11 May 1984, I-1.

145: *in American history* . . . Eberle, p. 21.

145: *believe the children'* . . . Butler, p. 58.

146: *soon doubled* . . . See Butler, pp. 16–18 for the genesis and mutation of the charges.

146: *to be guilty* . . . Butler, p. 45; for Currie's comment, see '5 Freed in Sex-Abuse Case; Parents Urge State Action', *Chicago Tribune*, 18 January 1986, p.3.

146: *disturbed to testify* . . . Butler, p. 168.

146: *baseball bat* . . . Eberle, p. 149.

146: *mutants* . . . Ibid., p. 171.

146: *rubber duck* . . . Lois Timnick, 'Boxes of Evidence Enliven McMartin Trial', *Los Angeles Times*, 30 April 1988, pp. 2–3.

147: *three times before* . . . Eberle, pp. 95–105; Butler, pp. 177–81.

147: *three years in question* . . . Eberle, p. 241.

147: *lock the doors* . . . Ibid, p. 236; Butler, p. 220.

147: *to be biased* . . . Butler, pp. 198–202.

147: *longest trial in American history* . . . Albert W. Alschuler and Andrew G. Deiss, 'A Brief History of the Criminal Jury in the United States', 61 *University of Chicago Law Review* 867 (1994) at p.925.

147: *throw in the towel* . . . Carol McGraw, 'In the End, Jury Gave in to Confusion', *Los Angeles Times*, 28 July 1990, p. 1; 'McMartin Jury Deadlocks; Buckey Won't Be Retried', *Los Angeles Times*, 29 July 1990, A1.

147: *he is not guilty'* . . . Butler, p. 251.

147: *identifying the connection* . . . Hicks, p. 194.

148: *no crime at all* . . . Thomas L. Feher, 'The Alleged Molestation Victim, The Rules of Evidence and the Constitution: Should Children Really Be Seen and Not Heard?', 14 *American Journal of Criminal Law* 227 (1987), at pp.239–40; Arthur Lyons, *Satan Wants You* (New York, 1988) ['Lyons, Satan'], p.143.

148: *crimes against children'* . . . Nathan, p. 91.

148: *house of horrors'* . . . Butler, pp. 30–3.

148: *across the country* . . . Jeffrey S. Victor, *Satanic Panic* (Chicago and La Salle, Il., 1993), pp. 19–20; Lyons, *Satan*, pp. 2–3, 143–6.

148: *three hundred thousand* . . . Hicks, p. 292.

148: *sixteenth-century France* . . . See p. 116 of this book.

148: *magical objectives* . . . Jean S. La Fontaine, *The Extent and Nature of Organised and Ritual Abuse. Research Findings* (London, 1994) reported (at p. 30) that in three out of eighty-four cases, supposedly mystical rituals had been used to encourage abuse victims to remain silent. There was no evidence, however, of 'sexual or physical abuse . . . directed to a magical or religious objective'. Two federal reports produced in the USA during the early 1990s also concluded that tales of organized abuse by satanic cults were fictions: see Nathan, p. 230.

148: *a contested trial* . . . See Jean S. La Fontaine, *Speak of the Devil* (Cambridge, 1998), p. 5 and sources cited therein; John Johnson and Steve Padilla, 'Satanism: Skeptics Abound', *Los Angeles Times*, 23 April 1991, A1.

149: *withdraw his plea* . . . A detailed account of the case can be found in Lawrence Wright, *Remembering Satan: A Case of Recovered Memory and the Shattering of an American Family* (London, 1994). See especially pp. 134–46, 176–8, 186–7.

149: *English-speaking world* . . . See Jean S. La Fontaine, *Speak of the Devil* (Cambridge, 1998), especially at pp.12, 163.

149: *certainly did* . . . See Arthur Miller, 'Why I Wrote "The Crucible"', *New Yorker*, 21 and 28 October 1996, p.158.

150: *undergo one* . . . Lois Timnick, 'Children's Abuse Reports Reliable, Most Believe', *Los Angeles Times*, 26 August 1985, p.1 (61 per cent to 21 per cent, with 12 per cent saying both dangers worried them equally).

150: *suppress them* . . . For a straightforward Freudian exposition of such views, see Henry Weihofen, *The Urge to Punish* (London, 1957); for postmodern varieties, see e.g. René Girard, *Things Hidden Since the Foundation of the World* (London, 1987); Jacques Derrida, 'Force of Law: The "Mystical Foundation of Authority"', in Drucilla Cornell et al. (eds), *Deconstruction and the Possibility of Justice* (London and New York, 1992), pp. 3–67.

Chapter 5: The Trials of Animals, Corpses, and Things

152: *of the diocese* . . . Léon Camille Ménabréa, *De l'origine de la forme et de l'esprit des jugements rendus au Moyen Âge contre les animaux* (Chambéry, 1846), pp. 7–24. Ménabréa reprints the trial records at pp. 148–61. An English account of the case is contained in Edward P. Evans' minor classic, *The Criminal Prosecution and Capital Punishment of Animals* (London, 1906) ['E. P. Evans'], at pp. 37–50. The work was reprinted by Faber in 1987, omitting the transcript of this trial (which can be found at pp. 259–84 of the 1906 edition).

152: *prospective saints* . . . See the bull 'Immensa aeterni Dei', reprinted in Church of Rome's *Bullarum diplomatum et privilegiorum sanctorum Romanorum pontificum Taurinensis editio*, 25 vols (Rome, 1857–72), 8: 985.

154: *several decades later* . . . Émile Agnel, *Curiosités judiciaires et historiques du moyen âge* (Paris, 1858) ['Agnel'], p. 30.

154: *by vermin* . . . E. P. Evans, p. 49; but see Ménabréa, pp. 23–4.

155: *the local salmon* . . . Agnel, pp. 29–30; E. P. Evans, p. 27.

155: *the early 1600s* . . . Jean Delumeau, *Catholicism between Luther and Voltaire: A New View of the Counter Reformation*, tr. Jeremy Moiser (London, 1977) p. 168.

155: *field assigned* . . . Manoel Bernardes, *Nova Floresta*, 5 vols (Lisbon, 1706–47), 1:270-3; c.f. Agnel, pp. 41–6.

155: corpus delicti . . .Wilhelm Vischer and Heinrich Boos, *Basler Chroniken*, 2 vols (Leipzig, 1880), 2: 102.

156: *to kick'* . . . E. P. Evans, p. 146; see also Daniel Jousse, *Traité de la Justice Criminelle de France*, 4 vols (Paris, 1771) ['Jousse'], 4: 123.

156: *to the gallows* . . . E. P. Evans, pp. 148, 344–5.

156: *Jacques Ferron* . . . Ibid., pp. 150–1.

156: *day in court* . . . See Agnel, pp. 13–15; E. P. Evans, pp. 160–1, 358–9; Jousse, 1: vi (bulls); E. P. Evans, p.169 (a cow); ibid., p.162 (a horse).

156: *never to return* . . . E. P. Evans, p. 147.

157: *he always would* . . . Jean Bouvier (Lionnois), *Histoire de villes vieille et neuve de Nancy* . . . , 3 vols (Nancy, 1805–11), 2: 375.

157: *swine were acquitted* . . . E. P. Evans, pp. 153–4, 346–51.

157: *on death row* . . . Ibid., pp. 340–1.

157: *on a hurdle* . . . See e.g. Louis Tanon (ed.), *Registre criminel de la justice de Saint-Martin-des-Champs à Paris au XIVe siècle* (Paris, 1877), p. 227.

158: *local viscount* . . . E. P. Evans, p. 335.

158: *human clothes* . . . Ibid., p. 141.

158: *horses alive* . . . Philippe de Beaumanoir, *Coutumes de Beauvaisis*, ed. Amédée Salmon, 2 vols (Paris, 1899), 2: 481, alternatively available as *The Coutumes de Beauvaisis of Philippe de Beaumanoir*, tr. F. R. P. Akehurst (Philadelphia, 1992), p. 712.

158: *harm to the children* . . . Pierre Ayrault, *Des proces faicts au cadaver, aux cendres, a la memoire, aux bestes brutes, choses inanimées, & aux contumax* (Angers, 1591) ['Ayrault, *Des proces* '], pp. 24b–25a, 27a–28a.

158: *corporal punishment* . . . E.P. Evans, pp.160, 356–7.

158: '*hind legs' – until dead* . . . Charles J. B. Giraud, *Essai sur l'histoire du droit francais au moyen âge*, 2 vols (Paris, 1846), 2: 302.

159: *lost on [animals]'* . . . Beaumanoir, op. cit.

159: *rational creature only'* . . . Thomas Aquinas, *Of God and His Creatures*, tr. Joseph Rickaby (London, 1905), p. 276 (3.114).

159: *mysterious business* . . . Thomas Aquinas, *Summa Theologica* 3: 146–8 (Part 1, Q.63, Art. 1)., tr. Laurence Shapcote, 2nd edn, 22 vols (London, 1921?–32) ['Aquinas, *Summa theologica*'], 10: 312–13 (Part 2.2, Q. 76 Art. 2).

160: *be annihilated* . . . Exodus 21: 28–9; Leviticus 20: 15–16.

160: *was irrelevant* . . . Ivo of Chartres, 'Decretum', Part 9, Cap. 108, in Jacques-Paul Migne, *Patrologiæ cursus completus*, 221 vols (Paris, 1844–64), 161: 686.

160: *honey abhorred* . . . Canon 64 of the Council of Worms, AD 868, reprinted in Joannes Dominicus Mansi, *Sacrorum conciliorum nova et amplissima collectio*, 55 vols (Florence, Venice, Paris, Arnhem and Leipzig, 1759–1962), 15: 880. The distrust of killer bees evidently has earlier origins, for it appears in the Penitential of Theodore, Archbishop of Canterbury between 668 and 690: see John T. McNeill and Helena M. Gamer, *Medieval Handbooks of Penance* (New York, 1938), p.208.

160: *the fallen* . . . William of Thierry et al., *St Bernard of Clairvaux. The Story of his Life as recorded in the* Vita Prima Bernardi, tr. Geoffrey Webb and Adrian Walker (London, 1960), p. 71.

160: '*horror of sin'* . . . Aquinas, *Summa theologica*, 12: 71–5 (Part 2.2, Q.108, Art. 4).

160: *possessed creature itself* . . . Ibid., 11: 161–2 (Part 2.2, Q.90, Art. 3).

161: *sixteenth-century Provence* ... The case that follows is first mentioned in the anonymous *Histoire mémorable de la persécution & saccagemēt du peuple de Merindol & Cabrières & autres circōuoisins, appelez Vaudois* (1556), pp. 35–7. This appears to have been the source for Jean Crespin, *Histoire des martyrs* (Geneva, 1582), pp. 132–42, and Jacques-Auguste de Thou in his *Historiarum sui temporis* ..., published in various editions in the early 1600s and later translated as *Histoire universelle ... depuis 1593 jusqu'en 1607* (London, 1734) (see pp. 413ff.). Chassenée's nineteenth-century biographer indignantly protested that his subject would have never done anything so frivolous as to defend rats, but that seems to speak more of his assumptions than those of the sixteenth century; he also dates the story's origins to 1597, apparently unaware of the almost contemporaneous 1556 source: see J.-Henri Pignot, *Barthélemy de Chasseneuz* [*sic*] ... *Sa vie et ses œuvres* (Paris, 1880) ['Pignot'], pp. 315–20.

163: *and eternal curse'* ... Esther Cohen, *The Crossroads of Justice* (Leiden, 1993) ['Cohen, *Crossroads*'], p. 131, translating from Chassenée's *Consilium primum ... De excommunicatione animalium insectorum* (1531).

163: *extra days to depart* ... Erwin Bonkalo, 'Criminal Proceedings Against Animals in the Middle Ages', 3 *Journal of Unconventional History* 25 (Winter 1992), at pp.28–9; see also E. P. Evans, pp. 111–13, 259–60.

163: *given a hearing* ... Chassenée's *Consilium primum ... De excommunicatione animalium insectorum* (1531), summarized in Pignot, pp. 212–27 and in Evans at pp. 21–7, 31–6.

164: *Where art thou?* ... Genesis 3: 9.

164: *was indeed the case* ... On the development of due process by canonical lawyers see Kenneth Pennington, *The Prince and the Law, 1200–1600* (Berkeley and Oxford, 1993), especially at pp. 142–3, 162–3. On Satan's legal status see Clarence Gallagher, *Canon Law and the Christian Community* (Rome, 1978), p. 160. For Innocent III's joke, see Stephan Kuttner and Antonio García y García, 'A New Eyewitness Account of the Fourth Lateran Council', 20 *Traditio* 115 (1964), lines 107–10.

165: *burned alive* ... Anon, *Histoire mémorable de la persécution & saccagemēt du peuple de Merindol & Cabrières & autres circōuoisins, appelez Vaudois* (1556). The exchange between the *seigneur* and Chassenée is at pp. 35–7.

165: *irrational killers* ... See p. 7 of this book.

165: *reptile to die* ... James G. Frazer, *The Golden Bough*, 3rd edn, 12 vols (London, 1907–15), vol. 5.2 ('Spirits of the Corn and of the Wild'), pp. 214–16.

166: *supposed negligence* ... E. P. Evans, pp. 304–5.

166: *jurisdiction over it* ... Agnel, p. 14.

167: *establish its innocence* ... See the introduction by C. Calvert to Albrecht Keller (ed.), *A Hangman's Diary. Being the Journal of Master Franz Schmidt,*

Public Executioner of Nuremberg 1573–1617, tr. C. Calvert and A.W. Gruner (London 1928), p. 35.

167: *fears of the undead* . . . See Cohen's discussion in *Crossroads*, pp. 135ff.

167: *Formosus* . . . For accounts of the trial and sources see Ferdinand Gregorovius, *History of the City of Rome in the Middle Ages*, 2nd edn, 8 vols (London, 1900–9) ['Gregorovius'], 3: 224–32; Henry H. Milman, *History of Latin Christianity*, 3rd edn, 9 vols (London, 1864) 3: 242–4. On the more general jurisdiction asserted by the Church over the dead, see Henry C. Lea, *A History of the Inquisition of the Middle Ages*, 3 vols (New York, 1888) ['Lea, *Inquisition*'], 1: 230–2 (note, however, that Lea mistakenly asserts that Formosus himself was posthumously tried twice).

168: *perfectly valid* . . . Gregorovius, 3: 244.

168: *standard inquisitorial procedure* . . . See e.g. the 'Manual for Inquisitors at Carcassonne 1248–49', translated and reprinted in Edward Peters, *Heresy and Authority in Medieval Europe* (Philadelphia, 1980), pp. 200, 205–6.

168: *posthumous himself* . . . 'The Chronicle of William Pelhisson' ['Pelhisson'], in Walter L. Wakefield, *Heresy, Crusade and Inquisition* (London, 1974), at pp. 226–8; see also p. 211.

169: *the following century* . . . Some indication of the scale of posthumous condemnations comes from the fact that of the 636 cases that came before the inquisitor Bernard Gui in the fourteen years between 1308 and 1322, at least 67 defendants – over 10 per cent – were dead: see Lea, *Inquisition*, 1: 495.

169: *Blessed Dominic'* . . . Pelhisson, p. 224.

169: *confiscates the goods'* . . . See e.g. Bartholo a Chasseneo [*sic*], *Commentariorum in consuetudines ducatus Burgundiae* (Paris, 1528), p. 54b.

169: *a second time* . . . Cohen, *Crossroads*, p. 142.

169: *Carcassonne in 1323* . . . Lea, *Inquisition*, 1: 553.

169: *gallons of oil* . . . See Paul Barber, *Vampires, Burial and Death* (New Haven, 1988), pp. 76–7.

169: *having proved fruitless* . . . Lea, *Inquisition*, 1: 537–8.

169: *family for burial* . . . S. P. Scott (ed.), *The Civil Law Including The Twelve Tables, The Institutes of Gaius, The Rules of Ulpian, The Opinions of Paulus, The Enactments of Justinian, and The Constitutions of Leo*, 17 vols (Cincinnati, 1932), 11: 129 (Book 48, Title 21) and 11:137 (Book 48, Title 24); see also A. H. J. Greenidge, 'The Conception of Treason in Roman Law', 7 *Juridical Review*. 228 (1895), 239.

170: *tribulations of life* . . . For a good discussion of Stoic attitudes to suicide, see John M. Rist, *Stoic Philosophy* (Cambridge, 1969), pp. 233–55.

170: *abominable a person'* . . . Jean de Coras, *Arrest memorable du parlement de Tolose* (Lyons, 1565), pp. 146–7.

170: *the corpse itself* . . . Ayrault, *Des proces, passim,* but especially at pp. 3a, 9a, 16a–17b, 19a–20a.

171: *legal aid* . . . On the changes made by the statute to legal representation for the living see Esmein, pp. 227–9, 275. For its effect on the rights of the dead, see François Serpillon, *Code Criminel,* 2nd edn, 2 vols (Lyons, 1784) ['Serpillon'], 2: 219, 226. The latter work was originally published at Lyons in 1767.

171: *in every case* . . . Ibid., 2: 214.

171: *exhumation* . . . Ibid., 2: 218.

171: *therefore be executed* . . . Jousse, 4: 134–5. Serpillon suggested leniency in such cases: see 2: 214 n.7.

171: *avoiding disinheritance* . . . Pierre François Muyart de Vouglans, *Les Loix Criminelles de France* (Paris, 1780), p. 185.

172: *municipal cesspit'* . . . Serpillon, 2: 220–3.

172: *horror of the spectacle'* . . . Ibid., 2: 212, 221, 226.

173: *the actions themselves'* . . . Jousse, 1: viii.

173: *a nearby river* . . . Claude Haton, *Mémoires de Claude Haton,* 2 vols (Paris, 1857), 2: 704–6. See generally Natalie Zemon Davis, *Society and Culture in Early Modern France* (Stanford, 1975), pp. 163, 179; and see V. H. H. Green, *Renaissance and Reformation* (London, 1964), pp. 257, 259.

173: *roared with laughter* . . . *Shakespeare's Europe – Unpublished Chapters of Fynes Moryson's Itinerary,* ed. Charles Hughes (London, 1903), p. 265.

173: *his 1683 funeral* . . . Jacques Boulanger, *The Seventeenth Century* (London, 1920) p. 345.

174: *[his] entire career'* . . . Robert Darnton, *The Great Cat Massacre and Other Episodes in French Cultural History* (New York, 1985), p. 77.

174: *onto a pole* . . . Richard J. Evans, *Rituals of Retribution* (London, 1997), p. 205.

174: *cause of their injury* . . . V. H. H. Green, *Medieval Civilization in Western Europe* (New York, 1971), pp. 232–3.

174: *Oliver Cromwell* . . . Thomas B. Howell et al. (eds), *A Complete Collection of State Trials,* 33 vols (London, 1816–26), 5: 1335ff.

175: *prior to burial* . . . See p.178 and accompanying note.

175: *hanged in England* . . . See e.g. Keith Thomas, *Man and the Natural World* (London, 1983), p. 98; see generally V. A. C. Gatrell, *The Hanging Tree* (Oxford, 1994), p. 283.

175: *and not eaten'* . . . §94(7) of the Body of Liberties in William H. Whitmore (ed.), *The Colonial Laws of Massachusetts* (Boston, 1889), p. 55.

175: *and a turkey* . . . William Bradford, *Of Plymouth Plantation,* ed. Samuel Eliot Morison (New York, 1963), pp, 320–1.

175: *corpses nor animals* . . . King Alfred's laws repeated the requirement of the Book of Exodus that homicidal oxen be stoned to death (see Benjamin

Thorpe, *The Ancient Laws and Institutes of England* [London, 1840], p. 22), but England's first great jurist, Henry Bracton, made clear in the mid 1200s that 'animals which lack reason cannot be said to commit *injuria* or felony': see George E. Woodbine, *Bracton on the Laws and Customs of England*, tr. Samuel E. Thorne, 4 vols (Harvard, 1968–77), 2: 379 and see 2: 384, 2: 424. E. P. Evans refers to two cases from England – a dog in Chichester in 1771 and a cock in Leeds sometime before 1861 – but one of his sources refers to a third-hand and no longer extant report while the other is incomplete. Even if those trials took place, it seems incredible that they would have occurred before a jury (rather than, for example, an eccentric magistrate), without being remarked upon elsewhere. See E. P. Evans, pp. 333–4; citing Karl von Amira, 'Thierstrafen und Thierprocesse', 12 *Mittheilungen des Instituts für oesterreichische Geschichtsforschung* 545 (1891), at p.559 and volume 2 of the *Allegemeine Deutsche Strafrechtszeitung* (Leipzig, 1861).

175: *ecclesiastical courts* . . . See Frederick Pollock and Frederick W. Maitland, *The History of English Law Before the Time of Edward I*, 2nd edn, 2 vols (Cambridge, 1898), 2: 554 (a witch from 1279); Simon Schama, *A History of Britain*, 3 vols (London, 2000–2), 1: 284 (an account of the case of Richard Hunne); *A briefe treatise concerning the burnynge of Bucer and Phagius at Cambrydge, in the tyme of Quene Mary, with theyr restitution in the time of our moste gracious souerayne Lady that nowe is*, tr. Arthur Goldyng (London, 1562) (two coffins).

176: *occurred sporadically* . . . For an overview of posthumous proceedings in Scotland, see Robert Pitcairn, *Criminal Trials in Scotland*, 3 vols (Edinburgh, 1833) ['Pitcairn, *Criminal Trials*'], 2: 277–8; and see William K. Dickson, 'The Scots Law of Treason', 10 *Juridical Review* 243 (1898) at p.244.

176: *the possibilities* . . . The debate is comprehensively re-examined in two articles by William F. Arbuckle: 'The "Gowrie Conspiracy" – Part I', 36 *Scottish Historical Review* 1 (1957), 'The "Gowrie Conspiracy" – Part II', 36 *Scottish Historical Review* 89 (1957).

177: *soft spot indeed* . . . See Pitcairn, *Criminal Trials*, 2: 316.

177: *£40,000* . . . William F. Arbuckle, 36 *Scottish Historical Review* 1 (1957), p.3.

177: *danger it was'* . . . David Calderwood, *The History of the Kirk of Scotland*, ed. Thomas Thomson, 8 vols [Edinburgh, 1842–49]) ['Calderwood'], 6: 56–7.

177: *leave her bed* . . . Ethel Carleton Williams, *Anne of Denmark* (London, 1970), p. 63. Note, however, that Williams' citation (p. 326 of James Melville, *The Autobiography and Diary of Mr James Melville*, ed. Robert Pitcairn, 2 vols [Edinburgh, 1842]) does not support the anecdote.

177: *'supple tricks'* . . . James Melville, *The Autobiography and Diary of Mr James Melville*, ed. Robert Pitcairn, 2 vols (Edinburgh, 1842) 2: 488 n.1.

177: *will and pleasure thereunto'* . . . Pitcairn, *Criminal Trials*, 2: 233.

177: *Hallowe'en* . . . Ibid., 2: 247.

177: *allspice* . . . The recipe for the preservatives is not, it must be admitted, recorded. The ingredients mentioned were used in the case of the Earl of Huntley however, prior to his own trial in 1562: John H. Burton, *History of Scotland*, 2nd edn, 8 vols, (Edinburgh, 1873) 4: 51.

177: *pain of death* . . . Pitcairn, *Criminal Trials*, 2: 247; Calderwood, 6: 99.

178: *against the king* . . . Pitcairn, *Criminal Trials*, 2: 276.

178: *reassembled skeleton* . . . Ibid., 2: 276ff.

178: *came to land* . . . Roy F. Hunnisett, *The Medieval Coroner* (Cambridge, 1961), pp. 34–5, 81; Paul Matthews (ed.), *Jervis on the Office and Duties of Coroners*, 12th edn (London, 2002), pp. 9–10.

178: *official hangman* . . . See Barbara T. Gates, *Victorian Suicide. Mad Crimes and Sad Histories* (Princeton, 1988), pp. 3, 6.

178: *next of kin* . . . See Frederick Pollock and Frederick W. Maitland, *The History of English Law Before the Time of Edward I*, 2nd edn, 2 vols (Cambridge, 1898), 2: 472–4.

179: *expanding aristocracy* . . . For a summary of the deodand's history, told with a distinctly anti-Catholic slant, see William Blackstone, *Commentaries on the Laws of England*, 3rd edn, 4 vols (Oxford, 1768–9) ['Blackstone, *Commentaries*'], 1: 300.

179: *the belfry* . . . Teresa Sutton, 'The Deodand and Responsibility for Death', 18(3) *Journal of Legal History* 44 (1997), pp. 44–5.

179: *two drowned shepherds* . . . Roy F. Hunnisett (ed.), *Sussex Coroners' Inquests 1558–1603* (Kew, 1996), pp. 37–8.

179: *or a rim* . . . See e.g. Roy F. Hunnisett (ed.), *Calendar of Nottinghamshire Coroners' Inquests 1485–1558* (Thoroton Society, 1969): for wheels, see cases 188, 332, 214, 277, 331; for an axle, see case 47, for a rim, see case 112. See also Blackstone, *Commentaries*, 1: 301–2.

179: *solely responsible* . . . Roy F. Hunnisett (ed.), *Calendar of Nottinghamshire Coroners' Inquests 1485–1558*, case 140. See also case 276, involving a similar finding against certain sheaves of rye.

180: *to his own use'* . . . *The Times* (London), 7 January 1842, p. 3.

180: *would spend it* . . . *The Times* (London), 11 January 1842, p. 5.

180: *monetary terms* . . . Hansard (HL), 24 April 1846 *per* Lords Campbell and Brougham. On the decline of the deodand, see generally H. Smith, 'From Deodand to Dependency', 11 *American Journal of Legal History* 389 (1967); Jacob J. Finkelstein, 'The Goring Ox: Some Historical Perspectives on Deodands, Forfeitures, Wrongful Death and the Western Notion of Sovereignty', 46 *Temple Law Quarterly* 169 (1973). There is no evidence that the institution ever found its way across the Atlantic. E. P. Evans claims at p. 187 that a homicidal tree was confiscated by a Maryland jury on 31 January 1637, but the state archives which he cites nowhere mention the case. The Tennessee Supreme Court once asserted (albeit without any sup-porting historical evidence) that English colonists abandoned the deodand on arrival in America: see *Parker-Harris Co. v. Tate*, 188 S.W.54 (Tenn.1916), at p.55. ('At the base of the doctrine was superstition deemed to be so repugnant to our ideas of justice as not to be included as a part of the common law of this country').

180: *that required acquittal* . . . Philippe de Beaumanoir, *Coutumes de Beauvaisis*, ed. Amédée Salmon, 2 vols (Paris, 1899), 2: 478–92, also avail-able as *The* Coutumes de Beauvaisis *of Philippe de Beaumanoir*, tr. F. R. P. Akehurst (Philadelphia, 1992), pp. 710–19; see generally Naomi D. Hurnard, *The King's Pardon for Homicide before A.D. 1307* (Oxford, 1969), pp. 68ff.

180: *the divine will* . . . Aquinas, *Summa theologica*, 5: 168–74 (Part I, Q.116); see also Thomas Aquinas, *Of God and His Creatures*, tr. Joseph Rickaby (London, 1905), p.18 (1.23).

180: *to the letter* . . . Dante Alighieri, *The Divine Comedy: Inferno*, Canto 7.

182: *deterrent or not'* . . . Royal Commission on Capital Punishment, *Minutes of Evidence taken before the Royal Commission on Capital Punishment* (London, 1949–52), p. 207. On the shift towards retributivism generally, see John M. Kelly, *A Short History of Western Legal Theory* (Oxford and New York, 1992), pp. 448–50.

182: *a little less'* . . . Jonathan Holborrow, 'Major on criminals: "We should condemn a little more, understand a little less" – The prime minister sets out his values for the nineties', *Mail on Sunday*, 21 February 1993.

182: *to be 'fooled'* . . . Don Davies, *The Milwaukee Murders* (London, 1992), p. 283.

182: *their imprisoned counterparts* . . . See Eric Silver, 'Punishment or Treatment? Comparing the Lengths of Confinement of Successful and Unsuccessful Insanity Defendants', 19 *Law and Human Behavior* 375 (1995). His data from seven states showed that defendants found to be insane spent more time in jail than sane counterparts in California and New York but were released sooner in Georgia and Ohio, while the type of verdict made no difference in three states: p. 386.

182: *quarter of one per cent* . . . This figure applies specifically to felonies. See Lisa A. Callahan et al., 'The Volume and Characteristics of Insanity Defense Pleas: An Eight-State Study', 19(4) *Bulletin of the American Academy of Psychiatry and the Law* 331 (1991).

182: *the defence entirely* . . . On the Hinckley trial, see William F. Lewis, 'Power, Knowledge, and Insanity. The Trial of John W. Hinckley, Jr.', in Robert Hariman (ed.), *Popular Trials: Rhetoric, Mass Media, and the Law* (Tuscaloosa, 1993), pp. 114–32. The states which have abolished the plea are Idaho, Kansas, Montana and Utah: see Christopher Slobogin, 'The

Integrationist Alternative to the Insanity Defense: Reflections on the Exculpatory Scope of Mental Illness in the Wake of the Andrea Yates Trial', 30 *American Journal of Criminal Law* 315 (2003) at pp. 339–41. An attempt in Nevada to do the same was struck down on constitutional grounds: *Finger v. State,* 27 P.3d 66 (2001).

182: *three judges quote* . . . See the plurality judgment of Stewart, Powell and Stephens in *Gregg v. Georgia*, 428 US 153 (1976), at p. 184 n. 30.

183: *stable ever since* . . . Phoebe C. Ellsworth and Samuel R. Gross, 'Hardening of the Attitudes: Americans' Views on the Death Penalty' in Hugo Adam Bedau (ed.), *The Death Penalty in America* (New York and Oxford, 1997), at pp. 90–1.

183: *the world combined* . . . See Amnesty International's figures, as updated at www.internationaljusticeproject.org/juvworld.cfm.

183: *his lethal injection* . . . Sharon LaFraniere, 'Governor's Camp Feel His Record on Crime Can Stand the Heat', *Washington Post,* 5 October 1992, A6.

183: *heaven's animals* . . . See the recollection of his lawyer, Robert McGlasson, quoted in Texas Defender Service, *A State of Denial: Texas Justice and the Death Penalty*, p. 67, available online via www.texasdefender.org. Bush also signed warrants for Terry Washington, Oliver David Cruz, and Johnny Paul Penry.

183: *time of their offence* . . . *Roper v. Simmons* (No. 03-633). The case, argued in October 2004, followed a decision of the Missouri Supreme Court that had ruled such executions unconstitutional.

184: *save them from Satan* . . . Paul Duggan, 'Texas Mother Convicted of Murder. Verdict Is Swift in Bathtub Drownings', *Washington Post*, 13 March 2002, A1.

184: *Singleton, in January 2004* . . . Steve Barnes, 'One Execution Held; One is Stayed', *New York Times*, 7 January 2004, A17.

184: *There is none'* . . . *Atkins v. Virginia*, 536 US 304 (2002), at p. 351.

Chapter 6: The Moscow Show Trials

186: *with the Soviet secret police* . . . Alexander Orlov, *The Secret History of Stalin's Crimes* (New York, 1953) ['Orlov'], p. 158.

187: *to this nation'* . . . *King Charls His Tryal at the High Court of Justice sitting in Westminster Hall* . . . 2nd edn (London 1650), p.18.

187: *by destroying…liberty* . . . David P. Jordan, *The King's Trial* (Berkeley and London, 1979), p. 109.

187: *how to masturbate* . . . Gérard Walter (ed.), *Le Procès de Marie-Antoinette* (Brussels, 1993), p. 60.

187: *the highwayman* . . . *King Charls His Tryal at the High Court of Justice sitting in Westminster Hall* . . . , op. cit., p.20.

187: *such an accusation'* . . . See Walter, op. cit., p. 61.

188: *jail respectively* . . . Orlov, p. 24; Robert Conquest, *The Great Terror. A Reassessment*, (Oxford and New York, 1990) ['Conquest'], pp.48–9.

188: *three police agents* . . . Arkady Vaksberg, *Stalin's Prosecutor. The Life of Andrei Vyshinsky* (New York, 1991) ['Vaksberg'], p. 17.

189: *before a snake'* . . . Ibid., p. 117.

189: *monster's maw'* . . . Ibid., p. 283.

189: *last a lifetime* . . . Ibid., pp. 20–1.

189: *arranging for his admission* . . . Ibid., p. 30.

189: *without trial'* . . . Quoted ibid., p. 192.

189: *by public confession* . . . See Peter Solomon, *Soviet Criminal Justice Under Stalin* (Cambridge, 1996)['Solomon'], pp. 177, 362–3.

189: *a scientific theory'* . . . George Katkov, *The Trial of Bukharin* (New York, 1969), pp. 102–3, citing A. Vyshinsky, *Teoriya sudebnych dokazatelstv v sovetskom prave* [i.e. *Theory of Judicial Evidence in Soviet Law*], 3rd edn (Moscow, 1950), pp. 215ff. The latter work was first published in 1941: see Solomon, p. 362. Vyshinsky had already laid the ground with a 1938 work that was translated into English ten years later: *The Law of the Soviet State*, tr. Hugh W. Babb (New York, 1948).

190: *refused to co-operate* . . . Orlov, p. 118.

190: *associated with him* . . . Ibid, pp. 120–1.

190: *12 years old* . . . Ibid., p. 41.

190: *the full Politburo* . . . See Conquest pp. 85–7; for extracts of letters sent by Zinoviev to Stalin from prison, see Edvard Radzinsky, *Stalin* (New York, 1997) ['Radzinsky'], pp. 338ff.

190: *'deep feeling'* . . . Orlov, pp. 126–9.

191: *demolished in 1917* . . . Ibid., pp. 55–8.

191: *to his seat* . . . People's Commissariat of Justice of the USSR, *Report of Court Proceedings. The Case of the Trotskyite-Zinovievite Centre* (Moscow, 1936) ['*1936 Report*'], pp. 103–5, 114.

191: *Vyshinsky asked Kamenev* . . . Ibid., p. 68.

191: *what is right'* . . . Quoted in Leonard Schapiro, *The Communist Party of the Soviet Union* (London, 1960) ['Schapiro'], p. 284.

191: *to assassinate Stalin* . . . *1936 Report*, p. 170.

192: *we have reached'* . . . Ibid., pp. 169–70.

192: *into his hands* . . . Orlov, p. 166.

192: *secret policeman later recounted* . . . Quoted in Walter G. Krivitsky, *I Was Stalin's Agent* (London, 1939) ['Krivitsky'], pp. 224–5.

192: *with relief* . . . Orlov, p. 165.

193: *should be shot!'* . . . *1936 Report*, p. 166.

193: *to all the defendants* . . . Orlov, p. 159.

193: *every one of them!'* . . . *1936 Report*, p. 164.

193: *Lenin and Stalin!'* . . . Orlov, pp. 167–8; Conquest, p. 83.

193: *on a stretcher* . . . The defendant's name was Gaven. His execution occurred two weeks after the others: Conquest, p. 104.

193: *attitude at the trial'* . . . Victor Serge, 'De Lenine à Staline', *Crapouillot* (Paris, January 1937), p. 50, subsequently translated as Victor Serge, *From Lenin to Stalin* (London, 1937) (see p. 145).

193: *the coming years* . . . See Conquest, pp. 104–5.

193: *sweeter in the world!'* . . . Orlov, p. 25.

194: *pockmarked face* . . . Ibid., p. 344.

194: *would be dead* . . . For the account of the dinner, see ibid., p. 353. For Pauker's fate, see People's Commissariat of Justice of the USSR, *Report of Court Proceedings in the Case of the Anti-Soviet 'Bloc of Rights and Trotskyites'* (Moscow, 1938) ['*1938 Report*'], pp. 556, 571.

194: *under active investigation* . . . *1936 Report*, pp. 115–16.

194: *'crush the vipers'* . . . See People's Commissariat of Justice of the USSR, *Report of the Court Proceedings in the Case of the Anti-Soviet Trotskyite Centre* (Moscow, 1937) ['*1937 Report*'], p. 485.

194: *'mad dogs be shot'* . . . Quoted in Vaksberg, p. 83.

195: *'destroyed like carrion'* . . . See *1937 Report*, p. 487.

195: *to a man* . . . Vadim Rogovin, *1937 – Stalin's Year of Terror*, tr. Frederick S. Choate (Oak Park, Mich., 1998), pp. 69–70, Conquest, p. 141; J. Arch Getty and Oleg V. Naumov, *The Road to Terror* (New Haven and London, 1999) ['Getty'], pp. 282–3.

195: *Georgian reptile [too]'* . . . Orlov, p. 173.

195: *Nazi Germany and Japan* . . . See ibid., pp. 171–3.

195: *colour-coded diagrams* . . . Ibid., p. 107.

195: *swap prisoners instead* . . . Ibid., p. 172.

195: *by four years* . . . See Getty, pp. 274–7, 433–5.

195: *use of torture* . . . See Conquest, pp. 121–2, 279–80.

196: *lose their lives* . . . Ibid., p. 279.

196: *already been drafted* . . . Orlov, p. 199; Krivitsky, p. 226.

196: *with defence lawyers* . . . See Vaksberg, p. 117, for details of one such rehearsal.

196: *scribbled down every word* . . . Ibid., p. 79.

196: *against the Red Army* . . . *1937 Report*, pp. 21–77.

197: *after September* . . . Orlov, pp. 184–5.

197: *Norwegian court* . . . Ibid., p. 186.

197: *burning all the letters* . . . *1937 Report*, pp. 85ff.

197: *'The worse, the better'* . . . Ibid., p. 206.

197: *ignoring safety regulations* . . . Ibid., pp. 410, 436, 446–8.

197: *new mining methods* . . . Ibid., pp. 257–8.

197: *neglecting track repairs* . . . The five were Livshits, Knyazev, Turok, Serebryakov and Boguslavsky. See their testimony ibid., *passim*.

197: *he asked wonderingly* . . . Ibid., p. 378.

198: *like it', he replied* . . . Ibid., p. 288.

198: *closely edited by Stalin* . . . Vaksberg, p. 79.

198: *death by shooting!'* . . . *1937 Report*, p. 516.

198: *protracted applause* . . . Vaksberg, p. 98.

198: *dying . . . men'* . . . *1937 Report*, pp. 517–18.

198: *a medal* . . . Vaksberg, p. 102.

199: *counter-revolutionary potential* . . . *1937 Report*, p. 550.

199: *traitor to my country'* . . . Ibid p. 563. On Shestov's role at the trial, see Orlov, pp. 173–4.

199: *turn of events* . . . Orlov, p. 204; Lion Feuchtwanger, *Moscow 1937* (London, 1937) ['Feuchtwanger'], p. 147.

199: *dead by 1941* . . . Conquest, p. 165.

200: *of the working people!'* . . . For reactions to the Terror, see e.g. Victor Kravchenko, *I Chose Freedom* (New York, 1946), pp. 206–83; Frederick Beck and W. Godin (pseud.), *Russian Purge and the Extraction of Confession* tr. D. Porter (New York, 1951) ['Beck and Godin'], p. 34; Veronique Garros et al. (eds), *Intimacy and Terror.* (New York, 1995), pp. 350–1; Sheila Fitzpatrick, *Everyday Stalinism: Ordinary Life in Extraordinary Times: Soviet Russia in the 1930s* (New York and Oxford, 1999), pp. 212–17.

200: *love for it* . . . Feuchtwanger, pp. 145, 150, 155.

201: *read more Dostoevsky* . . . His advice was cited in 'Another Russian Trial' (editorial), *The New Republic*, 3 February 1937, p.400; see also Sally J. Taylor, *Stalin's Apologist. Walter Duranty: The New York Times's Man in Moscow* (New York and Oxford, 1990), pp. 267–9.

201: *perhaps not needless'* . . . Winston Churchill, *The Second World War*, 6 vols (London, 1948–54), 1: 225 ('The Gathering Storm').

201: *in stage production'* . . . Joseph Davies, *Mission to Moscow* (London, 1942), p. 139.

201: *human blood* . . . Conquest, p. 200.

201: *the arrest warrant* . . . Vaksberg, p. 104.

201: *across the Soviet Union* . . . Getty, pp. 454–62; see also Sheila Fitzpatrick, 'How the Mice Buried the Cat: Scenes from the Great Purges of 1937 in the Russian Provinces', 52(3) *The Russian Review* 299 (July 1993).

202: *and sentenced to death* . . . Solomon, pp. 239–41; Conquest, pp. 283–4.

202: *too narrow* . . . Roy A. Medvedev, *Let History Judge* (New York, 1972) ['Medvedev'], p. 352.

202: *a swastika* . . . Beck and Godin, p. 114.

202: *in its pattern* . . . Radzinsky, p. 403.

202: *picked up and shot* . . . Conquest, p. 297.

202: *in intricate detail* . . . On arrest, see Ante Ciliga, *The Russian Enigma* (London, 1979), pp. 141–2. On confessions, see Beck and Godin, pp. 42–4.

202: *like dandelions'* . . . Nadezhda Mandelstam, *Hope Against Hope* (New York, 1976) ['Mandelstam'], p. 298.

203: *from tuberculosis* . . . Ivanov-Razumnik (pseud.), *The Memoirs of Ivanov-Razumnik*, tr. Peter S. Squire (London, 1965), pp. 305–6.

203: *sounded counter-revolutionary* . . . Medvedev, p. 352.

203: *nor to speak* . . . Fitzroy Maclean, *Eastern Approaches* (London, 1949) ['Maclean'], p. 26.

203: *like white crosses'* . . . Yevtushenko's introduction to Andrei Platonov, *The Fierce and Beautiful World* (London, 1971), p. 8.

203: *immediately executed* . . . Robert A. McCutcheon, 'The 1936–1937 Purge of Soviet Astronomers', 50 *Slavic Review* 100 (Spring 1991), at pp. 110–13.

204: *gone to bed* . . . Radzinsky, p. 402.

204: *wash their hands'* . . . Mandelstam, p. 297.

204: *across the country* . . . Medvedev, p. 354.

204: *Kuusinen be freed* . . . Ibid., p. 309.

204: *Bukharin had been* . . . Mandelstam, p. 250; Felix Chuev (ed.), *Molotov Remembers* (Chicago, 1993), pp. 131, 118.

205: *at the moment'* . . . Stephen F. Cohen, *Bukharin and the Bolshevik Revolution* (New York, 1975) ['Cohen, *Bukharin*'], p. 286; see also pp. 290–1.

205: *'policy of tribute'* . . . Ibid., p. 320.

205: *from holy water'* . . . Ibid., p. 321.

205: *dared advance them* . . . Ibid., p. 335.

205: *Central Committee meeting* . . . For a full account of the session, including transcripts, see Getty, pp. 367–419.

207: *a sincere man'* . . . Ibid., p. 372.

207: *Stalin himself* . . . Maclean, pp. 119–20.

208: *committed no crime* . . . *1938 Report*, p. 36.

208: *of this country'* . . . 'Confessions in Moscow. Only One Pleads "Not Guilty". Treason Charges', *The Times* (London), 3 March 1938, p. 14.

208: *comes from you'* . . . *1938 Report*, p. 44.

208: *the dock today'* . . . Ibid., p. 49.

209: *remember everything'* . . . Ibid., p. 127.

209: *Judas Iscariot* . . . He had in January 1937 complimented Lion Feuchtwanger on the invention by 'you Jews' of the 'eternally true legend' of Judas Iscariot: see Feuchtwanger, p. 128. References to 'Judas-Trotsky' (an insult coined by Lenin in 1912) were ubiquitous in the Soviet press of the 1930s: see Jeffrey Brooks, *Thank You, Comrade Stalin* (Princeton, 2000) ['Brooks'], p. 143.

210: *floor with pleasure* . . . *1938 Report*, pp. 144–50; Maclean, pp. 91–3.

210: *I am not guilty'* . . . *1938 Report*, pp. 157–8.

210: *shining eyes'* . . . John Reed, *Ten Days that Shook the World* (New York, 1919), p. 253.

211: *arrest of Lenin* . . . Vaksberg, p. 25.

211: *The encounter began* . . . *1938 Report*, pp. 369ff.

211: *for everything'* . . . Quoted in Medvedev, p. 178.

212: *interrogation short'* . . . *1938 Report*, p. 423.

212: *existence of God* . . . Orlov, p. 260.

213: *official report* . . . For the authorized version of the exchange, see *1938 Report*, pp. 527–30.

213: *drive me too far'* . . . Quoted in Walter Duranty, *The Kremlin and the People* (London, 1942), p. 85.

213: *looked crushed'* . . . Maclean, p. 103.

214: *cleared for the day* . . . *1938 Report*, pp. 622–3; Maclean, pp. 106–7.

214: *like dirty dogs!'* . . . For Vyshinsky's speech, see *1938 Report*, pp. 625–97.

214: *hushed courtroom* . . . For Bukharin's speech, see ibid., pp. 767ff.

216: *actually did commit'* . . . Ibid., p.775.

215: *principle of jurisprudence'* . . . Ibid., p. 778.

216: *party and the country* . . . Ibid., p. 777.

216: *welcomed the execution* . . . Vaksberg, p. 82.

216: *my blood too'* . . . Anna Larina, *This I Cannot Forget* (London, 1993), pp. 343–5.

217: *not otherwise'* . . . The letter is translated in Getty, pp. 556–60.

217: *wife and child* . . . Orlov, p. 281; Medvedev, p. 187.

217: *a legend* . . . See Victor Kravchenko, *I Chose Freedom* (New York, 1946), p. 283.

218: *over-zealous legal officials* . . . Solomon, pp. 253–4.

218: *severe judicial penalties'* . . . Getty, pp. 531–7.

219: *on my lips'* . . . For Yezhov's statement to the court, see ibid, pp. 560–2.

219: *his court file* . . . Radzinsky, p. 345.

219: *edited the trial transcript* . . . Ibid., p. 384.

219: *the communist world* . . . See Schapiro, pp. 470–1; see also Brooks, pp. 78–9.

220: *were kept secret* . . . Conquest, pp. 479–80.

220: *to adore* . . . Anna Larina's own account is in *This I Cannot Forget* (London, 1993) at pp. 343–51.

220: *high above* . . . Svetlana Alliluyeva, *Twenty Letters to a Friend* (Harmondsworth, 1968), p. 17; see also Radzinsky, *Stalin*, pp. 566ff.

221: *demarcation'* . . . Vladimir Il'ich Lenin, *Collected Works*, 47 vols (Moscow, 1960–80), 4: 354.

221: *responsible for it'* . . . *1938 Report*, p. 675.

222: *none at all* . . . See Getty, pp. 470, 588, 591–2; Conquest, pp. 485–6.

222: *into their mouths* . . . See generally Robert C. Tucker, *Stalin in Power* (New York and London, 1990), pp. 475–8.

222: *their own arrests* . . . Bernard Gui, 'The Conduct of the Inquisition of Heretical Depravity' (1323–24), reprinted in Walter L. Wakefield and Austin P. Evans (eds), *Heresies of the High Middle Ages* (New York, 1991) at p. 397.

222: *condemn themselves'* . . . See p. 60 and accompanying note.

223: *they had hoped* . . . See Pam Belluck, 'Calm at Execution Site and Silence by McVeigh Prove Unsettling for Some', *New York Times*, 12 June 2001, A27; Paul Duggan, 'Too Easy for Him. For Witnesses in Oklahoma City, A Long Day Brought Little Relief', *Washington Post*, 12 June 2001, A1.

223: *torturing the innocent'* . . . See p. 120 and accompanying note.

224: *no object'* . . . Pierre Vidal-Naquet, *Torture: Cancer of Democracy* (Harmondsworth, 1963), p. 154. On the use of torture in Algeria, see generally Henri Alleg, *The Question*, tr. John Calder (London, 1958), *passim*; Pierre-Henri Simon, *Contre la torture* (Paris, 1957), *passim*.

224: *the confession's truth* . . . Freud was among those who emphasized the risks of treating confessions as reliable expressions of fact: see 'Psycho-Analysis and the Ascertaining of Truth in Courts of Law' (1906) in Sigmund Freud, *Collected Papers*, tr. Joan Riviere, 2 vols (New York, 1959), 2:23; see also Theodore Reik, *The Compulsion to Confess* (New York, 1959), pp. 193–356.

224: *eighty-seven churches* . . . For this statistic, see Roy Porter, *London. A Social History* (London, 2000), p. 109.

224: *without a pardon* . . . Accounts of Robert Hubert's trial can be found in Thomas B. Howell et al. (eds), *A Complete Collection of State Trials*, 33 vols (London, 1816–26), 6: 807–66.

224: *or non-existent* . . . Adam Liptak, 'Fewer Death Sentences Being Imposed in U.S.', *New York Times*, 15 September 2004, A16 (151 DNA exonerations); Barry Scheck, Peter Neufeld and Jim Dwyer, *Actual Innocence*, (New York, 2001), pp. 120, 318 (22 per cent of exonerations based on false confessions, as of 2000).

225: *at imminent risk* . . . He went public with his proposal on *Sixty Minutes* (CBS), 20 January 2002.

225: *publicizing a book* . . . See *Shouting Fire: Civil Liberties in a Turbulent Age* (New York, 2002), published on 9 January 2002. He later expanded his arguments in *Why Terrorism Works* (New Haven, 2002): see especially pp. 131–63.

225: *overrrated'* . . . *Hardball* (MSNBC), 29 January 2002.

Chapter 7: The War Crimes Trial

226: *a book* . . . Joe Heydecker and Johannes Leeb, *The Nuremberg Trial*, tr. E.A. Downie (London, 1962) ['Heydecker and Leeb'], p. 77.

226: *skirts* . . . Telford Taylor, *Anatomy of Nuremberg* (New York, 1992) ['Taylor, *Anatomy*'], p. 228.

227: *a third* . . . His weight declined from about 275 pounds to 153: Eugene Davidson, *The Trial of the Germans* (New York, 1966) ['Davidson'], p. 59.

227: *power of the law'* . . . *The Trial of German Major War Criminals. Proceedings of the International Military Tribunal sitting at Nuremberg, etc.*, 23 vols (London, 1946–51) ['*Blue Series*'], 2: 99 (21 November 1945).

228: *a criminal one* . . . Ibid., 3: 1 (4 December 1945).

228: *higher authority'* . . . Winston Churchill, 'The Punishment of War Criminals', War Cabinet Paper W.P. (43) 496, 9 November 1943 in PREM 4/100/10, pp. 622–3; CAB 66/42. Other members of the War Cabinet thought the Prime Minister's proposals 'open to grave objection' however, and no formal decision was taken: PREM 4/100/10, at p. 621. These documents, like others with similar references in the next few notes, are available at the Public Record Office in London.

228: *expressed no opposition* . . . Gary J. Bass, *Stay the Hand of Vengeance* (Princeton, 2000) ['Bass, *Stay the Hand*'], pp. 166, 182; Tom Bower, *Blind Eye to Murder* (London, 1997) ['Bower'], p. 78; Taylor, *Anatomy*, p. 30.

228: *former Nazis* . . . Bass, *Stay the Hand*, pp. 157–9, Bower, p. 144.

228: *any legal procedure'* . . . Clark Kerr was referring to the view set out by Churchill in a telegram of 3 November 1942: FO 371/30922 ('United Nations Commission for investigating war crimes, 1942').

228: *got on well* . . . See Donald Gillies, *Radical Diplomat. The Life of Archibald Clark Kerr, Lord Inverchapel, 1882–1951* (London and New York, 1999), p.125ff.

228: *necessary formalities'* . . . Telegram from Clark Kerr to Churchill of 6/7 November 1942 in FO 371/30920 ('Parliamentary Statement on Rudolf Hess, 1942').

229: *firing squads* . . . Bass, *Stay the Hand*, p. 153, citing preparatory notes made by Stimson on 25 August 1944 for a meeting with Roosevelt.

229: *judicial sentence'* . . . See the telegram to the British ambassador to Washington of 6 November 1944 in FO 371/39005 ('War Criminals: Treatment of, 1944') and in PREM 4/100/10, p. 535. Churchill suggested (on 2 October 1944) a six-hour interval between identification and execution, after initially proposing that a single hour would suffice: see PREM 4/100/10, p. 546.

229: New York Times . . . 'Morgenthau Plan on Germany Splits Cabinet Committee', *New York Times*, 24 September 1944, p. 1.

229: *polls of the time* . . . See George H. Gallup (ed.), *The Gallup Poll. Public Opinion 1935–1971*, 3 vols (New York, 1972). Questioned on 22–27 September 1944 about the proper fate of 'Hitler, Himmler, Goering and other Nazi leaders', 53 per cent of US respondents proposed execution,

25 per cent were in favour of 'exile', and 22 per cent supported 'other pun-ishment (mainly torture)'. There was also overwhelming approval for a draconian policy towards post-war Germany: 80 per cent supported 'a hard peace' as opposed to just 8 per cent who approved a 'soft peace'. See 1: 463–4. See also William J. Bosch, *Judgment on Nuremberg* (Chapel Hill, N.C., 1970) ['Bosch'], pp. 87–93.

229: *afraid to try them* . . . Telegram of 22 October 1944 in PREM 4/100/10, p. 539 ('Treatment of major war criminals 1942 Jun.–1944 Oct.').

229: *judicial procedure'* . . . CAB 65/50, W.M. (45) 43 (War Cabinet meeting of 12 April 1945).

229: *judicial self-abasement* . . . See George Ginsburgs, *Moscow's Road to Nuremberg. The Soviet Background to the Trial* (The Hague, 1996) ['Ginsburgs'], pp. 45–57.

230: *refuge for gangsters'* . . . Telegram of 6/7 November 1942 in FO 371/30920. For details of the clash, which was sparked off by a leading article in *Pravda* on 19 October 1942, see FO 371/33036 ('Soviet criticisms of British policy towards Hess 1942').

230: *with a grin* . . . Winston Churchill, *The Second World War*, 6 vols (London, 1948–54), 5: 330 ('Closing the Ring').

230: *had been playing* . . . Stalin's words were minuted by the only Russian-speaking Westerner present, US diplomat Charles (Chips) Bohlen, who remarked on the Soviet leader's 'entirely friendly . . . obviously teasing' atti-tude: see US Department of State, *The Conferences at Cairo and Tehran 1943* (Washington DC, 1961), p. 554. President Roosevelt's son, who was also at the dinner, was no less sure of the humorous intent: see Elliott Roosevelt, *As He Saw It*, (New York, 1946), pp. 188–90. In his memoirs, Churchill accepted that Stalin may have been pulling his leg, though he remained 'not . . . fully convinced that all was chaff': *The Second World War*, 6 vols (London, 1948–54), 5: 330 ('Closing the Ring').

231: *who incite war'* . . . Quoted in A. N. Trainin, *Hitlerite Responsibility Under Criminal Law*, ed. A. Y. Vishinski [*sic*], tr. Andrew Rothstein (London, 1945), p. 12.

231: *appoint Vyshinsky* . . . Arkady Vaksberg, *Stalin's Prosecutor. The Life of Andrei Vyshinsky* (New York, 1991) ['Vaksberg'], pp. 258–9.

231: *Bill of Rights'* . . . Bass, *Stay the Hand*, p. 165.

231: *organized to convict'* . . . Speech of 13 April 1945, printed in 39 *American Society of International Law Proceedings* 10 (1945). See generally Telford Taylor, 'The Nuremberg Trials', 55 *Columbia Law Review* 488 (1955).

231: *strength of the speech* . . . See Telford Taylor, 'The Nuremberg Trials', 55 *Columbia Law Review* 488 (1955) at p.495 n.37.

232: *heads of the governments'* . . . US Department of State, *Report of Robert H. Jackson United States Representative to the International Conference on*

Military Trials (Washington DC, 1949) [*'Jackson Report'*], p. 105 (29 June 1945). On the conflict between Soviet and Western negotiators generally, see Ginsburgs, pp. 95–108.

232: *labeled so by the governments'* . . . *Jackson Report*, p. 107 (29 June 1945).

232: *the necessary punishment'* . . . Ibid., p. 303 (19 July 1945).

232: *only Nazis could commit.* . . Ibid., p. 387 (25 July 1945).

232: *a separate trial* . . . Telford Taylor, 'The Nuremberg Trials', 55 *Columbia Law Review* 488 (1955), p.501.

232: *three types of offence* . . . For the minutes of the final 2 August session of the London Conference, see *Jackson Report*, pp. 399–419. For the final agreement and charter, see ibid., pp. 420–9.

232: *a single treaty from 1928* . . . This was the Kellogg–Briand Pact. The Tribunal's eventual judgment would also refer to the Versailles Treaty of 1919 and the Locarno Treaty of 1925: *Blue Series*, 22: 459–61.

232: *all lesser crimes'* . . . Ann Tusa and John Tusa, *The Nuremberg Trial* (London, 1995) ['Tusa'], p. 73; see generally Taylor, *Anatomy*, pp. 54–5; Bass, *Stay the Hand*, p. 174.

232: *'small change'* . . . Robert H. Jackson, *The Reminiscences of Robert H. Jackson*, 9 vols (Chicago, 1955). This transcript of several interviews recorded by Jackson in 1952 is part of the University of Chicago's Oral History Project, and is held (along with the tapes themselves) at the law school (R. H. Jackson collection).

232: *coined a year earlier* . . . Raphaël Lemkin, *Axis Rule in Europe* (Washington, DC, 1944), pp. 79–95.

233: *into the record* . . . This can be established by checking any of the several searchable versions of the Nuremberg transcripts that are available online: see e.g. www.yale.edu/lawweb/avalon/imt/imt.htm.

233: *French and Soviet prosecutors* . . . See Tusa, p. 102.

233: *ruled unpunishable* . . . *Blue Series*, 22: 498; see also Taylor, *Anatomy*, pp. 76, 583.

233: *bury its dead* . . . See Coleman Phillipson, *The International Law and Custom of Ancient Greece and Rome*, 2 vols (London, 1911), 2: 275; see also Yvon Garlan, *War in the Ancient World* (London, 1975), pp. 57–62.

233: *no defence to criminal charges* . . . Article 47 of the German Military Penal Code, cited by Jackson in his opening (*Blue Series*, 2: 150).

233: *store for me'* . . . Gustave M. Gilbert, *Nuremberg Diary* (London, 1948) ['Gilbert'], pp. 7–8.

233: *draft the charges* . . . Two of the eight judges – Nikitchenko and Falco – helped to draft the Nuremberg Charter and the indictment: Tusa, p. 74. Jackson and Maxwell-Fyfe also contributed: Tusa, p. 95. Biddle, in his capacity as US Attorney-General, also played a part in drafting the Charter and advised prior to trial that certain Nazi leaders and organizations were to be regarded as criminal, albeit that this was one of the matters to be decided at trial: see Bass, *Stay the Hand*, p. 176, Davidson, pp. 6, 16.

233: *similar to those charged* . . . The Tribunal ruled the issue of Allied crimes irrelevant when Dr Stahmer tried to raise it on behalf of Göring: see *Blue Series*, 9: 684–8. Judges in later cases reiterated that the Nazi–Soviet pact could have no bearing on the finding that Germany had launched an aggressive war: see *United States of America vs. Otto Ohlendorf et al., Case No. 9* ('The Einsatzgruppen Case') in *Trials of War Criminals before the Nuremberg Military Tribunals under Control Council Law No. 10*, 15 vols, (GPO, Washington DC, 1949–53) ['*Green Series*'], 14: 322; *United States of America vs. Ernst von Weizsaecker et al.* ('The Ministries Case'), ibid., 4: 457. Evidence of Allied submarine warfare practice (in the form of an affidavit from US Admiral Chester Nimitz) was however admitted in Dönitz's defence: an account of this is given in Davidson, p. 421.

234: *chlorinated rubble* . . . Rebecca West, *A Train of Powder* (London, 1984) ['West'], p. 10.

234: *Soviet secret police* . . . Edvard Radzinsky, *Stalin*, tr. H. T. Willetts (New York, 1997), p. 499.

234: *partition Poland* . . . Vaksberg, p. 259; Taylor, pp. 192–3.

234: *to the grave!'* . . . Taylor, *Anatomy*, p. 211; see also Bass, *Stay the Hand*, p. 202.

234: *questioning witnesses* . . . On the conflict between the Anglo-American common law and the post-inquisitorial legal structures of the continent, see Taylor, *Anatomy*, pp. 63–4; Tusa, pp. 75–8.

234: *the right to testify* . . . Taylor, *Anatomy*, p. 321.

234: *Vyshinsky's instructions* . . . Vladimir Abarinov, *The Murderers of Katyn* (New York, 1993), p. 250; Vaksberg, p. 260.

235: *speeches vetted* . . . See Tusa, pp. 412, 416.

235: *into the record* . . . The lawyer representing Rudolf Hess and Hans Frank, for example, obtained a copy of the Hitler–Stalin pact and read its secret protocols into the public record on 1 April 1946 and 21 May 1946: *Blue Series*, 10: 311 and 14: 283.

235: *in separate groups* . . . Gilbert, pp. 93–5.

235: *recognize the court at all* . . . Ibid. p. 113.

235: *the Jewish question'* . . . Göring's order to Heydrich, dated 31 July 1941, was exhibited as 710-PS.

235: *into complacency* . . . Taylor, *Anatomy*, p. 335.

235: *he began* . . . *Blue Series*, 9: 417.

236: *sabotaged his questioning* . . . See Taylor, *Anatomy*, p. 336.

236: *'by the gong'* . . . Selkirk Panton, 'Goering, defiant, laughs at American accuser', *Daily Express*, 19 March 1946, p.3.

237: *he carry on* . . . *Blue Series*, 9: 510–12.

237: *art thefts* . . . See ibid., 9: 545ff.

237: *chameleon-like demeanour* . . . See Bruce M. Stave and Michele Palmer, with Leslie Frank, *Witnesses to Nuremberg. An Oral History of American Participants at the War Crimes Trials* (New York, 1998) ['Stave'], pp. 115–16, 197; see also Davidson, pp. 59–96.

237: *took over* . . . See *Blue Series*, 9: 571ff.; see also Selkirk Panton, 'Goering pales, admits that he lied', *Daily Express*, 22 March 1946, p.3; Tusa, p. 285; Taylor, p. 344.

238: *in the whole trial'* . . . Gilbert, p. 127.

238: *Jews perish'* . . . *Blue Series*, 9: 617 (Ex. GB-283; Document No. D-736).

238: *and sat down* . . . Ibid., 9: 619.

238: *for the first time'* . . . Gilbert, pp. 29–30.

238: *changing wind* . . . On the skill of the British lawyers, see Stave, pp. 184, 197, 207.

239: *one thousand people* . . . *Blue Series*, 19: 508.

239: *faces grew old'* . . . West, p. 22; and see Tusa, p. 423.

239: *verdicts were delivered* . . . *Blue Series*, 22: 411–589.

240: *remained deadlocked* . . . Tusa, pp. 456–82.

240: *reaching Nuremberg* . . . See Taylor, *Anatomy*, pp. 618–24.

240: *snap their necks* . . . Tusa, pp. 485–7; Taylor, *Anatomy*, pp. 610–11.

240: *you are an emperor'* . . . St Augustine, *The City of God Against the Pagans*, tr. R. W. Dyson (Cambridge, 1998), p. 148 (4.4).

240: *exile and execution* . . . Bass, *Stay the Hand*, pp. 37ff.

240: *hang the Kaiser* . . . See e.g. 'Kaiser Must Be Tried', *Daily News*, 30 November 1918, p. 1. Britain and France also forced Germany and Turkey to hold a series of farcical trials after the First World War, but they were theoretically domestic in nature: see Bass, *Stay the Hand*, pp. 78ff., 124ff.

241: *untested material* . . . According to Jackson's post-trial report to President Truman, about 100,000 captured documents and 25,000 pho- tographs were screened by the prosecution, but only about 10,000 and 1,800 (respectively) were produced as exhibits: *Jackson Report*, p. 433. The Soviets tried to convince the court of a theory that it should accept as fact any document produced before it (Ginsburgs, pp. 102–3), while US lawyers made equally audacious attempts to submit 'self-proving briefs': Taylor, *Anatomy*, pp. 172–7.

241: *acknowledged in 1990* . . . 'No Nazi Soap, Archivist Says', *Los Angeles Times*, 24 April 1990, p. 2; 'Jewish soap tale "was Nazi lie"', *Daily Telegraph*, 25 April 1990, p. 11.

241: *collective guilt* . . . See Karl Jaspers, *The Question of German Guilt*, tr. E. B. Ashton (New York, 1947), p. 58. A second distinction, between collective guilt and collective responsibility, later became equally conventional: see L.

May and S. Hoffman (eds), *Collective Responsibility: Five Decades of Debate in Theoretical and Applied Ethics* (Savage, Md., 1991), *passim*.

241: *entire German people* . . . See e.g. *Blue Series*, 2: 154; 19: 434 and 19: 528.

242: *and to the German people*' . . . Ibid., 14: 432.

242: *forehead of an entire nation*' . . . Ibid., 22: 387.

242: *only five were German* . . . Heydecker and Leeb, p. 74.

242: *the German press* . . . Hans Fritzsche, *The Sword in the Scales* (London, 1953), p. 99.

242: *what was going on* . . . Taylor, *Anatomy*, pp. 234–5. See also Stave, p. 156.

242: *abstractions like war guilt* . . . According to one German interviewed at the beginning of the trial by the US army newspaper *Stars and Stripes*, 'We are too hungry to think about legalistics. Death is too good for the swine, but we are not interested.' See *Stars and Stripes*, 21 November 1945 (German edition, Frankfurt), quoted in Tusa, p. 121.

242: *in Nuremberg itself* . . . See Stave, pp. 67–8, 81; West, pp. 3–77.

243: *on the moon*' . . . Taylor, *Anatomy*, p. 234.

244: *so many hangings* . . . Jean Edward Smith (ed.), *The Papers of General Lucius D. Clay: Germany 1945–1949*, 2 vols (Bloomington, Ind., 1974), 2: 658–9.

243: *fifteen men at a time* . . . Bower, p. 315.

243: *four hundred people* . . . John Teschke, *Hitler's Legacy: West Germany Confronts the Aftermath of the Third Reich* (New York, 1999) ['Teschke'], p. 242. The Soviets tried an estimated 45,000 Germans and executed about 10,000: ibid.; cf. Davidson, p. 30; and for a survey of the political steps taken to denazify East Germany, see Timothy R. Vogt, *Denazification in Soviet-Occupied Germany: Brandenburg 1945–48* (Harvard, 2000).

243: *'a certain racial minority'* . . . Bosch, op. cit., pp. 82–5. For other criticisms within the United States, see ibid. pp. 73ff., 132–3.

244: *third of them immediately* . . . Frank M. Buscher, *The US War Crimes Trial Program in Germany, 1945–55* (Westport, Conn., 1989) ['Buscher'], pp. 63–4, 175–8.

244: *had he been so ordered* . . . *United States of America vs. Otto Ohlendorf et al., Case No. 9* ('The Einsatzgruppen Case'), in *Green Series*, at 4: 269–73, 308–10.

244: *capitalist camps* . . . See John L. Gaddis, *We Now Know. Rethinking Cold War History* (New York, 1997), pp. 125–9.

244: *Federal Republic of Germany* . . . On Göring's good character, see Jörg Friedrich, 'Nuremberg and the Germans', in Belinda Cooper (ed.), *War Crimes: The Legacy of Nuremberg* (New York, 1999) ['Cooper, *War Crimes*'], at p.102; on the political machinations surrounding the end of the trials and negotiations for West German independence see ibid.; see also Peter Maguire, 'Nuremberg: A Cold War Conflict of Interest' in

Cooper, *War Crimes*, pp. 67–82; Buscher, pp. 69–86, 115–27, 131–53.

245: *non-lethal ones* . . . Dick De Mildt, *In the Name of the People* (London and The Hague, 1996), pp. 20–1, 403–4; Bower, p. 437.

245: *the judges themselves* . . . Ingo Müller, *Hitler's Justice. The Courts of the Third Reich*, tr. Deborah L. Schneider (Harvard, 1991) ['Müller'], pp. 274–83; Bower, pp. 198–202; David Binder, 'Germany: When the Nazi Judges Are Judged', *New York Times*, 29 December 1968, E7.

245: *'healthy public opinion'* . . . Müller, p. 74.

245: *to the gallows* . . . Ibid., p. 196.

245: *in February 1947* . . . *United States of America v. Alstoetter* et al., in *Green Series*, vol. 3. The prosecution, known as 'The Justice Case', was later dramatized as the Oscar-winning *Judgment at Nuremberg* (1961).

245: *senior judicial positions* . . . Committee for German Unity, *We Accuse: 800 Nazi Judges – Bastions of Adenauer's Militarist Regime* (Berlin, 1959); see generally Müller, *passim*; Teschke, pp. 27–32; Bower, pp. 430ff.

246: *he was not guilty* . . . Müller, pp. 112–13, 222, 277, 285.

246: *'our Vyshinsky'* . . . William L. Shirer, *The Rise and Fall of the Third Reich* (New York, 1960) ['Shirer'], p. 1070.

246: *trial of the July Plotters* . . . For the account that follows in the text, see Müller, pp. 148–51.

246: *men's death throes* . . . Shirer, p. 1071.

247: *justice of his decision* . . . Teschke, pp. 322–5; Müller, pp. 280–3; 'Acquittal is Won by Ex-Nazi Judge', *New York Times*, 7 December 1968, p. 7.

247: *slightest pity'* . . . Shirer, p. 1070, Müller, p. 148.

247: *correct legal procedure'* . . . Jörg Friedrich, *Die Kalte Amnestie* (Frankfurt, 1984), pp. 289–90.

247: *whenever it occurred* . . . Convention on the Prevention and Punishment of the Crime of Genocide 1948.

248: *customary international law* . . . On the background to the the Nuremberg Principles, see 'Formulation of the Nurnberg Principles', in United Nations, *Yearbook of the International Law Commission 1950*, vol. 2, pp. 181–95.

248: *Jewish question'* . . . See p.235 and accompanying note.

248: *Auschwitz-Birkenau* . . . Lucy S. Dawidowicz, *The War Against the Jews 1933–45* (London, 1975), pp. 138, 382.

249: *tipped off* . . . Isser Harel, *The House on Garibaldi Street*, 2nd edn (London, 1997), pp. xviii, 276.

249: *knowingly or unknowingly'* . . . David Ben-Gurion, *Israel: A Personal History* (London, 1972), pp. 574–5.

249: *fifteen charges* . . . The indictment can be found in Adolf Eichmann [*sic*], *The Attorney-General of the Government of Israel v. Adolf, the Son of Adolf Karl Eichmann*, 6 vols (Jerusalem, 1961–2) ['*The Eichmann Trial*'], 1: 1–14.

249: *unique right to try him* . . . For Dr Servatius' objection, see ibid., vol. I, Session 1 (11 April 1961). For the court's rulings see paras. 31–8 and 41–52 of the District Court judgment and paras. 12–3 of the Supreme Court judgment, ibid., vol. 6.

249: *voice is not heard'* . . . Shabtai Rosenne (ed.), *6,000,000 Accusers. Israel's Case Against Eichmann* (Jerusalem, 1961), p. 29.

249: *righteous judgment'* . . . Ibid., pp. 168–75.

250: *hall near the court* . . . Jacob Robinson, *And the Crooked Shall be Made Straight* (New York, 1965) ['Robinson'], p. 137.

250: *on burial duty* . . . Testimony of Yivka Yosselevska (8 May 1961) and Michael Podklebnik (5 June 1961) in *The Eichmann Trial*, vol. 2, Session 30 and vol. 3, Session 65.

250: *every flat'* . . . Robinson, p. 137.

251: *men from beasts'* . . . *The Eichmann Trial*, vol. 5, Session 120 (13 December 1961).

251: *'banality of evil'* . . . Hannah Arendt, *Eichmann in Jerusalem* (London, 1994) ['Arendt'], p. 252.

251: *automatically' from Nazism* . . . This translation of Eichmann's phrasing is taken from the documentary *The Specialist* (dir. Eyal Sivan, 1999).

251: *Eichmann as a person'* . . . Ibid.

251: *three, perhaps'* . . . *The Eichmann Trial*, vol. 5, Session 106 (21 July 1961).

251: *reflecting and judging' himself* . . . *The Specialist*, op. cit.; see also *The Eichmann Trial*, vol. 5, Session 106 (21 July 1961).

251: *extraordinary satisfaction'* . . . This was said by Dieter Wisliceny: *Blue Series* 4: 371 (3 January 1946). Eichmann accepted that he had made the statement but anxiously contradicted the Attorney-General's assertion that he had referred specifically to Jews: see *The Eichmann Trial*, vol. 4, Session 88 (7 July 1961).

252: *[Our] own people'* . . . *The Eichmann Trial*, vol. 1, Session 10 (19 April 1961); see also Arendt, pp. 88–9.

252: *observation by a third* . . . Jochen von Lang (ed.), *Eichmann Interrogated* (New York, 1999), p. xxxiii.

252: *belonged to all Germans* . . . See Arendt, *passim*, for her own views; for those of Martin Buber, see ibid., p. 251; Robinson, p. 134.

252: *Gallup poll* . . . Irving Crespi, 'Public Reaction to the Eichmann Trial', 28 *Public Opinion Quarterly* 91 (1964), at p. 95.

252: *really happened there'* . . . Robinson, p. 138.

253: *to exterminate Europe's Jews* . . . Moshe Bar-Natan, 'The Authors and the Party', *Jewish Frontier* (New York), November 1963, pp. 4–7.

253: *he had observed* . . . 39 *American Society of International Law Proceedings* 10 (1945) at p.18.

253: *from Israeli officials* . . . See e.g. Herb Keinon and Dan Izenberg, 'FM

Netanyahu charges Belgium with "blood libel"', *Jerusalem Post*, 14 February 2003, A1. The jurisdiction was being exercised pursuant to a statute that expressly allowed for universal jurisdiction, and a chastened Belgium amended the law into ineffectiveness in April 2003: see Andrew Osborn, 'Sharon made safe by Belgian vote on war crime law', *Guardian*, 3 April 2003.

253: *laws of war* . . . Captain Henry Wirz, the Swiss-born Confederate commander of a prison camp at Andersonville, was tried by military commission for violation of the laws of war and hanged on 10 November 1865.

254: *My Lai* . . . The background given in the text is largely drawn from Seymour Hersh, *Cover-Up* (Clinton, Mass., 1972) ['Hersh, *Cover-Up*'] and Michael Bilton and Kevin Sims, *Four Hours in My Lai* (New York, 1992) ['Bilton']. Many original sources are reproduced in James S. Olson and Randy Roberts, *My Lai. A Brief History with Documents* (Boston, 1998) ['Olson'] and in Joseph Goldstein, Burke Marshall and Jack Schwartz, *The My Lai Massacre and its Cover Up: Beyond the Reach of Law?* (New York, 1976) ['Goldstein'].

254: *and 10,000 killed* . . . The relevant casualty statistics, collated by the Office of the Assistant Secretary of Defense, are available on a website run by Eric Weil at www.angelfire.com/al2/vietnamops/.

254: *or booby traps* . . . Hersh, *Cover-Up*, p. 55.

254: *of a good fight'* . . . Richard Hammer, *The Court Martial of Lt. Calley* (New York, 1971) ['Hammer'], p. 307.

254: *a third of the entire unit* . . . Bilton, p. 323.

254: *I just followed'* . . . Quoted in Bilton, p. 130. His memory, or perhaps his sense of guilt, had magnified his crime over the years: he initially admitted killing eight people when questioned by US Army CID officers, and when interviewed by NBC on 25 November 1969 he claimed to have been 'personally responsible' for the deaths of ten: see Olson, pp. 89, 166.

254: *youngest was ten* . . . Olson, pp. 89, 99–102.

254: *into their flesh* . . . Bilton, pp. 129–32, 334.

254: *five hundred people* . . . Hersh, *Cover-Up*, p. 7.

254: *in the foot* . . . Olson, p. 81.

255: *bounty on his head* . . . Bilton, pp. 83–4.

256: *and shot her* . . . Medina would later admit prodding and killing the woman, but claimed that he had acted out of an instinctive sense of self-defence. According to a statement made to Army CID officers, he 'caught a glimpse out of the corner of my eye of something in her hand' after nudging her, and immediately thought, 'You dumb bastard, you are dead'. He then 'span around' and shot her two or three times. See Olson, p.94; cf. p.130. As noted at p.265, he was never proved guilty of murder beyond a reasonable doubt.

256: *gunfire into the ditch* . . . Olson, p. 90.

256: *'Blow 'em away!'* . . . Bilton, p. 139.

257: *a hand grenade* . . . The account given is based largely on Thompson's recollection, which Calley substantially accepted at his trial: see Hammer, p. 106.

257: *the boss here'* . . . Ibid., p. 132.

257: *shooting [them] himself'* . . . Dan R. Mullians, quoted in William Wilson, 'I Had Prayed to God That This Thing Was Fiction', *American Heritage*, February 1990, p.44, reprinted in Olson, at p. 159.

257: *issued to Captain Medina* . . . William R. Peers, *Report of the Department of the Army Review of the Preliminary Investigations into the My Lai Incident, Volume 1* (Washington DC, 1974) ['*Peers Report*'], pp. 10–6–10-7.

257: *down Thompson's cheeks* . . . Bilton, p. 140; see also William Wilson, 'I Had Prayed to God That This Thing Was Fiction', *American Heritage*, February 1990, p.44, reprinted in Olson, at p. 159.

257: *systematic cover-up* . . . *Peers Report*, 10-11 – 10-16; Hersh, *Cover Up*, pp.118ff.; Olson, pp. 113–32.

257: *just two American lives* . . . Olson, p. 27; see also Hammer, p. 18.

257: *telegram of congratulations* . . . Olson, p. 32.

258: *'the intense cross fire'* . . . Hersh, *Cover Up*, pp. 212–13.

258: *throw it away* . . . Trent Angers, *The Forgotten Hero of My Lai* (Lafayette, La., 1999) ['Angers'], p. 19; cf. Hersh, *Cover-Up*, p.213.

258: *very black indeed'* . . . For the text of the letter, see Hammer, pp. 23–8; on the response to it, see Hersh, *Cover-Up*, pp. 215ff.

258: *rapidly restarted* . . . See Angers, pp. 154–7. Colonel William Wilson, assigned to the Office of the Inspector-General in Washington, was charged with investigating Ridenhour's allegations and wrote an article twenty-one years later that described his reactions: see 'I Had Prayed to God That This Thing Was Fiction', *American Heritage*, February 1990, pp. 44–53, reprinted in Olson, pp. 152–63.

258: *to save ammunition* . . . The interview is transcribed at p.16 of the *New York Times*, 25 November 1969.

258: *crawling, and dead* . . . 'The Massacre at My Lai', *Life*, 5 December 1969, p. 36. On the emergence of the story generally, see Seymour M. Hersh, *My Lai: A Report on the Massacre and its Aftermath* (New York, 1970), pp. 128–43.

258: *not looking good* . . . For Westmoreland's own account of his actions, which includes an explanation as to why it would be wrong to view him as a war criminal, see his memoirs: *A Soldier Reports* (New York, 1976), at pp. 375–80.

259: *opinion, important cause'* . . . Goldstein, pp. 484–5.

259: *behind it all* . . .Bilton, pp. 321–2; Seymour Hersh, *Kissinger: The Price of Power* (New York, 1983), p. 135.

259: *literally average* . . . See Bilton, p. 51.

259: *fingers and ears* . . . Guenter Lewy, *America in Vietnam* (New York, 1978) ['Lewy'], p.329.

259: *anything that moved* . . . Ibid., pp. 105–7.

259: *My Khe* . . . For details of these killings and Willingham's role as commander of Bravo Company, see *Peers Report*, 7-1 – 7-16, 12-32; Hersh, *Cover-Up*, pp. 9–25, 243–6.

259: *four and a half years* . . . See Goldstein, pp. 2, 20, 22.

259: *for individual trials* . . . Hammer, p.38. Henry Kissinger was among those who supported such a course, advising Nixon in an undated memo that investigations should remain within the army's court-martial system, and that there should be no general commission of inquiry: Bilton, pp. 324–5.

260: *should be taken'* . . . Fred Farrar, 'One Freed in My Lai Army Case', *Chicago Tribune*, 10 June 1970, 1-3; see also *Peers Report*, 7-2, 7-9; Hersh, *Cover Up*, p. 256; Hammer, p. 39.

260: *had told them* . . . See Angers, p. 171. The author proposes that two southern Democrats, L. Mendel Rivers (D-South Carolina) and F. Edward Hebert (D-Louisiana.) deliberately conducted the hearings with a view to undermining the chances of successful subsequent courts martial: see ibid., pp. 160, 164–76.

260: *acquitted on all counts* . . . 'My Lai allegations "plot against Army"', *The Times* (London), 21 November 1970, p. 4; Hammer, pp. 40–1; Bilton, p. 329.

260: *of 102 people* . . . For the charges, see Hammer, pp. 46–7. Two additional specifications, alleging the murder of groups of four and three people, were dropped.

261: *lobbied for prosecutions* . . . See ibid., pp. 30–2, 52.

261: *they were being killed* . . . Ibid., pp. 161–2.

261: *called heroic* . . . Ibid., p. 107.

261: *too much marijuana* . . . Ibid., pp. 215–17, 234–8.

262: *'destroy everything'* . . . Ibid., pp. 187–9; Bilton, pp. 98–101.

262: *entitled to an acquittal* . . . For the judge's instructions to the jury, see Hammer, pp. 351–2. The directions were upheld on appeal: see *United States v. William L. Calley Jr.*, 22 U.S.C.M.A. 534 (1973), reprinted in Goldstein, pp. 520–34. Cf. *United States of America vs. Otto Ohlendorf et al., Case No. 9* ('The Einsatzgruppen Case'), in *Green Series*, 4: 470–88.

262: *speak or reason'* . . . Bilton, p. 336.

262: *become murderous guerrillas* . . . William Calley, *Body Count: Lieutenant Calley's Story as told to John Sack* (London, 1971), p. 102.

262: *seemed dead already* . . . Hammer, p. 251.

262: *for twenty years'* . . . Ibid., pp. 253, 258, 259.

262: *sprang to his feet* . . . The account of Calley's cross-examination that follows is drawn from ibid., pp. 260–82.

263: *rebutted the claims* . . . See ibid., pp. 300–23.

264: *Oriental area'* . . . Ibid., p. 366.

264: *in three days* . . . Bilton, p. 340.

264: *car headlights on* . . . 'Judgment at Fort Benning', *Newsweek*, 12 April 1971, at p. 29.

264: *'Rally for Calley'* . . . Bilton, p. 340.

264: *79 per cent* . . . 'Judgment at Fort Benning', *Newsweek*, 12 April 1971, p. 27.

264: *addressed to Nixon* . . . Bilton, p. 345.

264: *the president decided* . . . For Richard Nixon's own explanation of his actions, see his *Memoirs* (New York, 1978), at pp. 449–50.

265: *death threats* . . . Bilton, p. 341; Hammer, pp. 375–6.

265: *no compromise* . . . Hammer, p. 386.

265: *ended in acquittal* . . . Bilton, p. 309.

265: *Medina's own jury* . . . Ibid., pp. 347–9, 383; Lewy, pp. 359–62.

265: *Thompson's citation* . . . For the full citation, see Angers, p. 230.

265: *a rare aberration* . . . During the period between 1 January 1965 and 25 July 1975, US army investigators investigated 241 reports of war crimes other than those at Son My, found evidence to justify a trial in 78 cases, and prosecuted 36 of them. A total of 20, involving 31 servicemen, resulted in convictions. See Lewy, op. cit., pp. 347–50; cf. George S. Prugh, *Law at War: Vietnam 1964–1973* (Washington DC, 1975), p. 74.

266: *further action in 1975* . . . See the Pulitzer Prize-winning reports printed between 19 and 22 October 2003 in the *Toledo Blade*.

266: *my memory of it'* . . . Gregory L. Vistica, 'What Happened in Thanh Phong', *New York Times Magazine*, 29 April 2001, p. 50.

267: *to beat you!'* . . . See Laura Silber and Allan Little, *The Death of Yugoslavia*, rev. edn (London, 1996) ['Silber'], p. 37.

268: *yet be excluded'* . . . Ibid., p. 72.

268: *'cleansed'* . . . Ibid., p. 171.

269: *two-fifths Muslim* . . . 1991 census figures: Branka Magaš and Ivo Žanić (eds), *The War in Croatia and Bosnia-Herzegovina* (London, 2001), map 8 (p. xliv).

269: *two-to-one majority* . . . Silber, pp. 206–12, 226ff; Michael P. Scharf, *Balkan Justice* (Durham, 1997) ['Scharf, *Balkan Justice*'], p. 27. Most Serbs boycotted the poll.

269: *disintegrated* . . . On the extent of rape by Serb forces, see Aryeh Neier, *War Crimes* (New York, 1998) ['Neier'], pp.175ff; see also the 'Rape Camp' case (Judgment of Trial Chamber II in the Kunarac, Kovac and Vukovic Case), available via the ICTY website at www.un.org/icty. For accounts of the war in Bosnia generally, see Silber, pp. 222ff.; Noel Malcolm, *Bosnia. A Short History* (London, 2002), pp. 234–71.

269: *half a million* . . . Silber, p. 310.

269: *arms embargo* . . . UN Security Council Resolution 713 of 25 September 1991.

269: *humanitarian relief* . . . UN Security Council Resolution 770 of 13 August 1992.

270: *dog in that fight'* . . . Silber, p. 201, quoting Brent Scowcroft's recollection of a comment by James Baker.

270: *said anything different* . . . See Samantha Power, *A Problem From Hell* (London, 2003), p. 288; Michael Scharf, *Balkan Justice*, p. 31; Michael Scharf and William A. Schabas, *Slobodan Milošević on Trial: A Companion* (London & New York, 2002) ['Scharf & Schabas'], p. 24.

270: *a weapons embargo* . . . See Paul R. Williams and Michael P. Scharf, *Peace with Justice? War Crimes and Accountability in the Former Yugoslavia* (Lanham, Md, 2002) ['Williams & Scharf'], p. 93.

270: *well documented elsewhere* . . . Brendan Simms, *Unfinest Hour: Britain and the Destruction of Bosnia* (London, 2002) ['Simms'].

270: *level killing field'* . . . Douglas Hurd, 'Official wisdom on Serbia' (letter), *Daily Telegraph*, 5 April 1993, p.18.

270: *'safe area'* . . . UN Security Council resolution 836 of 4 June 1993.

271: *disarmed men and boys* . . . The authorities of Republika Srpska, the Serb-run section of Bosnia, officially accepted in November 2004 that almost 8,000 people were killed in the town: see Nicholas Wood, 'Bosnian Serbs Apologise for Srebrenica Massacre', *New York Times*, 11 November 2004, A4. See also Richard Holbrooke, *To End a War*, rev. edn (New York, 1999) p. 70, who cites the slightly lower Red Cross figure of 7,079 killed between 12 and 16 July 1995.

271: *to join in* . . . Simms, pp. 324ff.

271: *and crimes against humanity* . . . Aggressive warfare was not made indictable under ICTY's statute.

271: *sentiments expressed* . . . Williams & Scharf, p. 99. See also Scharf, *Balkan Justice*, p. 54; Power, p. 326.

271: *Underfunded and ignored* . . . See Williams & Scharf, pp.91ff.; Bass, *Stay the Hand* . . . , pp.214ff. On attempts by the United Kingdom to undermine the court after its creation, see Scharf, *Balkan Justice*, pp. 32, 44–7; Simms, pp. 62–4, 147–8; Bass, *Stay the Hand*, pp. 211–13.

272: *for committing them* . . . *Prosecutor v. Dusko Tadic a/k/a/ 'Dule'*, available via the ICTY website at www.un.org/icty. The most important legal rulings arose out of a preliminary hearing at which Tadić challenged the court's right to try him: Appeals Chamber Decision on the Tadic Jurisdictional Motion, Case No. IT-94-1-AR72, 2 October 1995. A detailed examination of the trial is contained in Scharf, *Balkan Justice*. See also Geoffrey Robertson, *Crimes Against Humanity* (London, 1999), p. 211; Neier, pp. 143–5; Diane Orentlicher, 'Internationalizing Civil War', in Cooper, *War Crimes*, p. 154.

273: *$1.28 billion in aid* . . . Martin Woollacott, 'Milošević's transfer was the price that had to be paid: Serbia awaits a second pay-off with a rescheduling of its debts', *The Guardian*, 6 July 2001, p. 18.

273: *not under examination'* . . . Rory Carroll and Andrew Osborn, 'Government collapse splits Yugoslavia', *The Guardian*, 30 June 2001, p. 1.

274: *finished in shambles* . . . See transcript of 3 July 2001. It is available, along with full records of all the proceedings, via the ICTY website: www.un.org/icty.

274: *Hague fair play'* . . . Transcript for 29 October 2001.

274: *amassing thousands of documents* . . . Tim Judah, 'Serbia backs Milošević in trial by TV: Alarm as former president gains the upper hand in war crimes tribunal', *The Observer*, 3 March 2002, p.23.

274: *would justify that* . . . See the interview with Nancy Paterson in Ed Vulliamy, Rory Carroll and Peter Beaumont, 'How I trapped Butcher of the Balkans', *The Observer*, 1 July 2001, p. 17.

274: *Del Ponte further rebuffed* . . . See Christiane Amanpour's report for CNN on 27 April 2001 ('Del Ponte urges war crimes arrest'), archived at www.cnn.com.

274: *circumstances of Milošević's indictment* . . . See generally Williams & Scharf, pp. 127, 130–1; Scharf & Shabas, p. 102.

275: *Clinton and Tony Blair* . . . 'Milošević in tribunal outburst' (BBC report), 9 January 2002, archived at www.bbc.co.uk.

275: *resistance on the ground* . . . See his cross examination of Sabit Kadriu on 8 March 2002.

275: *slaughter of their compatriots* . . . Testimony of 27 September 2002.

275: *Muslim side during the war'* . . . Quoted in Gary J. Bass, 'Milošević in the Hague', 82(3) *Foreign Affairs*, May/June 2003, at p. 91.

275: *over sixteen hundred* . . . Chris Stephen, 'Milošević trial mired in swamp of troubles', *The Observer*, 18 April 2004, p.21.

276: *had committed war crimes* . . . Jonathan Steele, 'Email', *The Guardian*, 4 March 2002, p. 18.

276: *his first appearances* . . . Timothy Garton Ash, 'A Nation in Denial' , *The Guardian*, 7 March 2002, p. 19.

276: *who were infuriated* . . . Tanjug news agency report from Belgrade of 8 March 2002, as monitored and translated by the BBC in Record Number 0F23325E2AAABBC2, available via Global NewsBank (www.newsbank.com).

277: *to win fair convictions* . . . Williams & Scharf, p. 126.

278: *gathered in Rome to establish* . . . Rome Statute, reprinted in Mark Lattimer and Philippe Sands, *Justice for Crimes Against Humanity* (Oxford and Portland, Or., 2003), pp. 430–93. For background and analysis, see M. Cherif Bassiouni, 'The Permanent International Court', in Lattimer & Sands, ibid., pp. 173–211; Donna K. Axel, 'Toward a Permanent International Criminal Court', in Cooper, *War Crimes*, pp. 311–22.

278: *disobedience was deemed desirable* . . . '7 nations agree to court exemption', *Chicago Tribune*, 2 November 2003, p.18.

278: *deter global aggression* . . . American Servicemembers Protection Act 2002, §2002(7-9).

278: *the court's clutches* . . . Ibid., §2008.

278: *refused to do so* . . . Article 17(1)(a) and (b) of the Rome Statute.

278: *of European ambition'* . . . Felix Gilbert, *To the Farewell Address: Ideas of Early American Foreign Policy* (Princeton, 1961), p. 145. The stance had broad support among Washington's contemporaries: see Charles Kupchan, *The End of the American Era: U.S. Foreign Policy and the Geopolitics of the Twenty-first Century* (New York, 2002), pp. 164–6.

278: *over a hundred more* . . . Chalmers Johnson, *The Sorrows of Empire* (New York, 2004), p. 154.

279: *regulated by treaty* . . . Although attempts were made during the 1920s and 1930s to limit or prohibit aerial bombardment, none assumed the status of a treaty: see J. M. Spaight, *Air Power and War Rights*, 3rd edn (London, 1947), pp. 244–81. Post-war proposals for legal revision (see e.g. 43 *Proceedings of the American Society of International Law* [1949], at pp. 102ff.), were simply ignored by the 1949 Geneva Convention.

279: *financial, and legal* . . . 'President Bush's Address on Terrorism Before a Joint Meeting of Congress', *New York Times,* 21 September 2001, B4.

279: *terrorism-related offence* . . . US Department of Justice, Office of the Inspector-General (Glenn A. Fine), *The September 11 Detainees: A Review of the Treatment of Aliens Held on Immigration Charges in Connection with the Investigation of the September 11 Attacks* (April 2003), available via www.fas.org/irp/agency/doj/oig.

279: *to tell a grand jury* . . . They were held as 'material witnesses' pursuant to 18 USC 3144. See generally Steve Fainaru and Margot Williams, 'Material Witness Law Has Many In Limbo. Nearly Half Held in War On Terror Haven't Testified', *Washington Post*, 24 November 2002, A1.

280: *if at all* . . . 'Military Order: Detention, Treatment, and Trial of Certain Non-Citizens in the War Against Terrorism', in 66 Fed. Reg. 57831-57836 (16 November 2001).

280: *any such trials* . . . 'US Department of Defense Military Commission Order No. 1, Procedures for Trials by Military Commissions of Certain

Non-United States Citizens in the War Against Terrorism', 21 March 2002, available online via the 'Press Resources' link at www.defenselink.mil.

280: *conversations with clients* . . . Katharine Q. Seelye, 'U.S. Seeking Guantanamo Defense Staff', *New York Times*, 23 May 2003, A16.

280: *of the [war on terror]* . . . Katharine Q. Seelye, 'Pentagon Says Acquittals May Not Free Detainees', *New York Times*, 23 March 2002, A13.

280: *regarded as an enemy* . . . Eric Lichtblau, 'Bush Declares Student an Enemy Combatant', *New York Times*, 24 June 2003, A15; John Mintz, 'Al Qaeda Suspect Enters Legal Limbo; Few Precedents Available for Case, Experts Say', *Washington Post*, 11 June 2002, A10.

280: *Fidel Castro's Cuba* . . . See *Coalition of Clergy v. Bush*, 189 F. Supp 2d 1036 (C.D. Cal, 2002), *Rasul v. Bush; Al Odah et al. v. US*, 215 F. Supp. 2d 55 & 321 F.3d 1134 (D.C. Cir, 2003). Note that the Supreme Court eventually ruled that federal courts did have jurisdiction over Guantánamo Bay: see *Rasul v. Bush; Al Odah et al. v. US*, 542 US ___.

280: *by October 2003* . . . Scott Higham et al., 'A Holding Cell in War on Terror Guantanamo Bay Prison Represents a Problem That's Tough to Get Out Of', *Washington Post*, 2 May 2004, A1.

281: *Algeria to Zululand* . . . See Frederick B. Wiener, *Civilians Under Military Justice. The British Practice Since 1689 Especially in North America* (Chicago and London, 1967), pp. 219–26; Frederick B. Wiener, *A Practical Manual of Martial Law* (Harrisburg, Pa., 1940), pp. 127–34; Pierre Vidal-Naquet, *Torture: Cancer of Democracy* (Harmondsworth, 1963), *passim*.

281: *on 26 December 1862* . . . On the history of military tribunals within the US, see Colonel Frederick Bernays Wiener, *A Practical Manual of Martial Law* (Harrisburg, Pa. 1940), pp.103–42; on their use in Mankato specifically, see Carol Chomsky, 'The United States-Dakota War Trials: A Study in Military Injustice', 43 *Stanford Law Review* 13 (1990); Duane Schultz, *Over the Earth I Come. The Great Sioux Uprising of 1862* (New York, 1992), pp. 246ff.

281: *Human Rights Act* . . . A(FC) and others (FC) v. Secretary of State for the Home Department [2004] UKHL 56.

281: *of detention and trial* . . . Geneva Convention (III) 1949 Relative to the Treatment of Prisoners of War, Articles 84 and 105.

282: *choice rather than duty* . . . Katherine Q. Seelye, 'First "Unlawful Combatants" Seized in Afghanistan Arrive at U.S. Base in Cuba', *New York Times*, 12 January 2002, A7. Two days before Rumsfeld's statement, Deputy Assistant Attorney-General John Yoo and Special Counsel Robert J. Delahunty had set out the claim in a legal memo. President Bush then made a formal decision that the Geneva Convention did not apply on 18 January 2002, and Alberto R. Gonzales, then White House

Counsel, retrospectively backed it up with a memo of his own on 25 January 2002.

282: *US administrations had argued* . . . This was one of the grounds on which the United States refused to sign up to the first Protocol to the Geneva Conventions. For a discussion of the status of irregular fighters under Articles 44 and 45 of that Protocol, see Yves Sandoz, Christophe Swinarski and Bruno Zimmerman (eds), *Commentary on the Additional Protocols of 8 June 1977 to the Geneva Conventions of 12 August 1949* (Geneva, 1987), pp. 519–59.

282: *spies, saboteurs and mercenaries* . . . *Ex parte Quirin*, 317 US 1 (1942), at p.35.

282: *Convention itself provides* . . . Art. 5.

282: *had no doubts* . . . James Meek, 'Welcome to Guantanamo. The people the law forgot', *The Guardian*, 3 December 2003, p.1 (Features).

282: *Declaration of Independence* . . . Jefferson condemned King George III for, among many other things, 'protecting [British soldiers], by a mock Trial, from Punishment for any Murders which they should commit on the Inhabitants of these States' and 'For transporting us beyond the seas to be tried for pretended Offences': *The Papers of Thomas Jefferson*, ed. Julian P. Boyd (Princeton, 1950–), 1: 417–33.

283: *to international inspection* . . . Barbara Crossette, 'U.S. Fails in Effort to Block Vote On U.N. Convention on Torture', *New York Times*, 25 July 2002, A7; William Orme, 'US Fails to Block Torture Inspections', *Los Angeles Times*, 25 July 2002, A3.

283: *a 50-page analysis* . . . The memo, by Assistant Attorney-General Jay Bybee, was sent to the then White House Counsel, Alberto R. Gonzales. See *Wall Street Journal*, 7 June 2004; Kate Zernike and David Rohde, 'Forced Nudity of Iraqi Prisoners Is Seen as a Pervasive Pattern, Not Isolated Incidents', *New York Times*, 8 June 2004, A1; Richard Cohen, 'A Plunge From the Moral Heights', *Washington Post*, 10 June 2004, A19; Michael Hirsh, John Barry and Daniel Klaidman, 'A Tortured Debate', *Newsweek*, 21 June 2004; 'The White House Papers', New *York Times*, 24 June 2004, A1.

283: *confidentially instructing* . . . 'Memorandum For The Commander, US Southern Command (Subject: Counter-Resistance Techniques in the War on Terrorism), 16 April 2003', disclosed by the Department of Defense in a press release of 22 June 2004 and archived online at www.dod.gov.

283: *methods were exported* . . . The use of interrogation techniques including unmuzzled dogs was approved for use at Abu Ghraib by General Ricardo Sanchez, borrowing from Guantánamo practices, in September 2003: see R. Jeffrey Smith and Josh White, 'General Granted Latitude At Prison Abu Ghraib Used Aggressive Tactics', *Washington Post*, 12 June 2004, A1.

284: *wanted to visit him* . . . Eric Schmitt and Thom Shanker, 'Rumsfeld Issued an Order to Hide Detainee in Iraq', *New York Times*, 17 June 2004, A1.

284: *any such power existed* . . . *Hamdi v. United States, Rasul v. Bush, Rumsfeld v. Padilla,* 542 US ___ (2004).

284: *outweigh the benefits* . . . The possibility of a judicial ruling to this effect came a step closer on 8 November 2004, when US District Judge James Robertson ruled that the executive was required to determine whether or not Salim Ahmed Hamdan, a Guantánamo detainee, was a POW under the Geneva Convention: see Carol D. Leonnig and John Mintz, 'Judge Says Detainees' Trials Are Unlawful' , *Washington Post,* 9 November 2004, A1.

285: *for so long* . . . Dana Milbank, 'Bush Says Iraqis Will Try Hussein. President Opposes International Tribunal For Captured Dictator', *Washington Post,* 16 December 2003, A1.

285: *when arms are drawn'* . . . Cicero, *Pro Milone* 11 (*'Silent enim leges inter arma'*).

Chapter 8: The Jury Trial (2): The Theatre of Justice

286: *countries on earth* . . . See Neil Vidmar (ed.), *World Jury Systems* (Oxford, 2000) ['Vidmar, *World Jury Systems*'], pp.3, 319-51, 432-6.

287: *longer in prison* . . . The constitutional position in the United States was set down by the Supreme Court in *Baldwin v. New York,* 399 US 66 (1970). On the growth of summary jurisdiction in England and Wales, see Penny Darbyshire, 'An Essay on the Importance and Neglect of the Magistracy', [1997] *Criminal Law Review* 627.

287: *that freedom lives'* . . . Patrick Devlin, *Trial by Jury* (London, 1956), p. 164.

288: *obsolete a century ago* . . . Frances Gibb, 'Wigs to Stay on For Now', *The Times* (London), 29 April 1992, p. 3; on the sartorial preferences of the British legal professions in general, see Charles M. Yablon's excellent 'Judicial Drag: An Essay on Wigs, Robes and Legal Change', *Wisconsin Law Review* 1129 (1995).

288: *oakum'* . . . Quoted in Benjamin Harrison, *The Constitution and Administration of the United States of America* (London, 1897), p. 320.

288: *next to their lawyers* . . . Charles Dickens observed even in the mid nineteenth century that an American defendant was likely to be found not in the dock, but 'lounging among the most distinguished ornaments of the legal profession, whispering suggestions in his counsel's ear, or making a toothpick out of an old quill with his pen-knife': *American Notes For General Circulation,* 2 vols (London, 1842), 1:127.

288: *Spittoons* . . . See ibid., 1: 272-3 ('In [all American] courts of law, the judge has his spittoon, the crier his, the witness his, and the prisoner his; while all the jurymen and spectators are provided for . . .'); see also Theo Wilson, *Headline Justice* (New York, 1996), pp. 56–7.

288: *have the opportunity'* . . . Lisa Brones, 'Guns Inside the Courtroom', www.whas11.com, 26 July 2002.

288: *to give sworn evidence* . . . For the historical shift that allowed defendants to testify – a right denied in Georgia until 1962 – see *Ferguson v. Georgia*, 365 US 570 (1961); Albert W. Alschuler, 'A Peculiar Privilege in Historical Perspective', in Richard H. Helmholz et al, *The Privilege Against Self-Incrimination* (Chicago, 1997), pp. 181–204.

289: *it never came'* . . . Quoted in *R. v. Secretary of State for the Home Dept.*, ex p. *Hindley* [1998] QB 751 at p. 760.

289: *really happened'* . . . Jim Romenesko, 'Scenes from a Courthouse', *Milwaukee Magazine*, April 1992.

289: affably agreed . . . John T. Scopes and James Presley, *Center of the Storm* (New York, 1967) ['Scopes'], pp. 58–60.

290: *20,000-seat stadium* . . . L. Sprague de Camp, *The Great Monkey Trial* (New York, 1968) ['Sprague, *Monkey*'], p. 108.

290: *wireless broadcast* . . . Ibid., p. 95.

290: *over two hundred* . . . 'Weird Adventures of 200 Reporters at Tennessee Evolution Trial', *Editor & Publisher*, 18 July 1925, p. 1.

290: *'buffoons' and 'dupes'* . . . H. L. Mencken, 'Homo Neanderthalensis', *Evening Sun* (Baltimore), 29 June 1925.

290: *America, in general* . . . Several British news reports are summarized in John W. Owens, 'Monkey Case Treated As Joke of Century by British Press', *The Sun* (Baltimore), 11 July 1925, p. 1; see also '"Monkey Case" Times Progress of Thought', *The Sun* (Baltimore), 12 July 1925, p. 10.

290: *On the streets* . . . Sprague, *Monkey*, pp. 160–5; Scopes, pp. 98–9.

291: *newspapers and education* . . . H. L. Mencken, 'Yearning Mountaineers' Souls Need Reconversion Nightly, Mencken Finds', *Evening Sun* (Baltimore), 13 July 1925; Allene M. Sumner, 'The Holy Rollers on Shin Bone Ridge', *The Nation*, 29 July 1925, p. 137; see also Scopes, p. 96; Arthur Garfield Hays, *Let Freedom Ring* (New York, 1937) ['Hays'], pp.39–40.

291: *Coney Island* . . . 'Two Apes and "Link" Arrive at Dayton', *New York Times*, 15 July 1925, p. 1; Frederick Lewis Allen, *Only Yesterday. An Informal History of the Nineteen-Twenties* (New York, 1931), p. 204; Archibald T. Robertson, *That Old Time Religion* (Boston, 1950), p. 96.

291: *from Atlanta, Georgia* . . . Sprague, *Monkey*, pp. 259–61.

291: *of the Book of Genesis* . . . National Book Company, *The World's Most Famous Court Trial. Tennessee Evolution Case* (Cincinnati, Ohio, 1925) ['*World's Most Famous Court Trial*'], pp. 5–6.

291: *his bald head'* . . . H. L. Mencken, 'Mencken Likens Trial To a Religious Orgy, with Defendant A Beelzebub', *Evening Sun* (Baltimore), 11 July 1925.

291: *perjurious testimony* . . . Charles F. Potter, 'Ten Years After the Monkey Show I'm Going Back to Dayton", *Liberty*, 28 September 1935, p. 36;

Charles F. Potter, *The Preacher and I* (New York, 1951) ['Potter, *Preacher*'], p. 293; Sprague, *Monkey*, pp. 432–3. Scopes himself later recorded that he had encouraged one pupil to 'go ahead and testify to what he had been told to say' but was 'sure' that the boys had not perjured themselves: see Scopes, pp.105, 134.

291: *made by the boys'* . . . *World's Most Famous Court Trial*, p. 311.

291: *whether Scopes had taught it* . . . Ibid., pp. 201–3. For explanation of the constitutional structure of the case, see Robert Hariman (ed.), *Popular Trials: Rhetoric, Mass Media, and the Law* (Tuscaloosa, 1993), ['Hariman'], pp. 62–70.

292: *biblical expert himself* . . . Scopes, p. 165; Potter, *Preacher*, pp. 275–6; Hays, p. 71.

292: *for twenty years* . . . Hariman, p. 60; Sprague, *Monkey*, p.79.

292: *most famous encounters* . . . The cross-examination is transcribed in *World's Most Famous Court Trial*, pp. 284–304, and in Arthur Weinberg (ed.), *Attorney for the Damned* (Chicago and London, 1989 reprint) ['Weinberg, *Attorney*'], pp. 192–228.

293: *say that for?'* . . . Sprague, *Monkey*, p. 403; see also Scopes, p. 178.

293: *whoop from the audience* . . . Potter, *Preacher*, p. 287.

294: *forgotten forlorn man* . . . Scopes, p.183.

294: *Darrow tell them* . . . *World's Most Famous Court Trial*, p. 311.

294: *technical error* . . . Tennessee law required fines over $50 to be set by the jury. On the immediate fallout from the trial, see Samuel Walker, *In Defense of American Liberties* (New York and Oxford, 1990), p. 74; Sprague, *Monkey*, pp. 468–71.

294: *textbooks throughout Tennessee* . . . Sprague, *Monkey*, p. 454.

294: *Supreme Court finally declare* . . . *Epperson v. Arkansas*, 393 US 97 (1968).

294: *how God created the earth'* . . . Laurie Goodstein, 'Conservative Church Leaders Find a Pillar in Bush', *New York Times*, 23 January 2000, p. 16.

294: *a single word* . . . Scopes, pp. 136, 187; Potter, p. 288.

295: *had brought the case* . . . Several such arguments are contained in Christopher Carey's *Trials from Classical Athens*: see e.g. Demosthenes' 'Reply to Eubolides' 34 (p.223) and 'Against Neaira' 43 (p.191); Antiphon, 'On the Killing of Herodes' 78 (p. 57). See generally Paul Cartledge et al. (eds), *Nomos: Essays in Athenian Law Politics and Society* (Cambridge, 1990), pp. 83–121; Robert J. Bonner, *Lawyers and Litigants in Ancient Athens: The Genesis of the Legal Profession* (Chicago, 1927), pp. 63–71.

295: *in the body politic* . . . Plato, *The Republic* 405a.

295: *kill them all* . . . Thomas More, *Utopia*, ed. George M. Logan and Robert M. Adams, rev. edn (Cambridge, 2002), p. 82; Massachusetts Body of Liberties 1641 §26 in William H. Whitmore (ed.), *The Colonial Laws of Massachusetts* (Boston, 1889), p. 39; *Henry VI, Part II*, IV. ii.

295: *into strong ones* . . . See e.g. Plato, *Gorgias* 455a; *Theætetus* 172c–73b.

295: *lie to the court'* . . . Hugh Trevor-Roper (ed.), *Hitler's Table Talk* (London, 1953), p. 132.

295: *criminal bar combined* . . . 'Decadence of New York's Criminal Bar', *New York Times*, 7 September 1902, p. 34.

295: *countenance to match* . . . Francis L. Wellman, *Gentlemen of the Jury* (New York, 1924) ['Wellman, *Gentlemen*'], pp. 100–1; Francis L. Wellman, *Luck and Opportunity* (New York, 1938) ['Wellman, *Luck*'], p. 27.

296: *but four times* . . . Wellman, *Gentlemen*, pp. 105–6; see also *New York Herald*, 19 June 1891, p. 3, and 20 June 1891, p .4; 'William F. Howe, Dean of Criminal Bar, Dead', *New York Times*, 3 September 1902, p. 9.

296: *in the mood* . . . Wellman, *Gentlemen*, p. 101; Wellman, *Luck*, p. 27.

297: *Unger was found not guilty* . . . This account is taken from the *New York Times* and *New York Herald* reports published between 15 February 1887 and 20 February 1887; see also 'William F. Howe, Dean of Criminal Bar, Dead', *New York Times*, 3 September 1902, p. 9.

297: *proper occasion arises'* . . . *Ferguson v. Moore*, 39 S.W. 341, 343 (Tenn. 1897).

297: *succeeded in doing so* . . . See *Coburn v. State of Indiana*, 461 N.E.2d 1154 (Ind. App. 2 Dist. 1984); *Hill v. State of Arkansas*, 977 S.W.2nd 234 (Ark. App. 1998); *Gibbins v. State*, 495 S.E. 2d 46 (Ga. App. 1997). Convictions have also been upheld on the basis that errors can be cured by jury instructions from the judge to disregard emotional appeals: see e.g. *Agee v. Wyrick*, 414 F. Supp. 435 (1976); *State v. Green*, 730 P.2d 1350 (Wash., 1986).

297: *injection could proceed* . . . *Spencer v. State of Florida*, 842 So. 2d 52 (Fla. 2003), at p. 75.

298: *'only children'* . . . Plato, *Apology* 34d.

298: *tears in his defence'* . . . Cicero, *Pro Milone* 105.

298: *in just sixteen years* . . . [Anna] Marcet Haldeman-Julius, *Clarence Darrow's Two Great Trials. Reports of the Scopes Anti-Evolution Case and the Dr. Sweet Negro Trial* (Girard, Kan., 1927) ['Haldeman-Julius'], p. 68.

298: *rounds of ammunition* . . . Ibid., p.56.

299: *had not testified* . . . Ibid., p. 70; Phyllis Vine, *One Man's Castle: Clarence Darrow and the American Dream* (New York, 2004) p. 253.

299: *seventy-one* . . . Haldeman-Julius, p. 58.

299: *I ever delivered'* . . . Clarence Darrow, *The Story of My Life* (New York, 1932), p. 311. The account given here is freely edited (without ellipses) from the full speech, which was published verbatim as a 36-page pamphlet by the NAACP immediately after the case: see Clarence Darrow, *Argument of Clarence Darrow in the Case of Henry Sweet* (New York, 1927). The full transcript is reprinted in Weinberg, *Attorney*, pp. 229–63.

301: *two-thirds of them black* . . . Haldeman-Julius, p. 51.

301: *in tears* . . . Phyllis Vine, *One Man's Castle. Clarence Darrow and the American Dream*, op. cit., pp. 257, 304; see also Sidney Fine, *Frank Murphy: The Detroit Years* (Ann Arbor, 1975), pp. 165–6.

302: *ready to acquit* . . . Irving Stone, *Clarence Darrow for the Defense* (New York, 1941), pp. 485–6.

303: *he blew it with'* . . . Benjamin Cardozo, 'Law and Literature', in *Selected Writings of Benjamin Nathan Cardozo* (ed. Margaret E. Hall, New York, 1947), p. 427.

303: *lobby of his courthouse* . . . Stan Bailey, 'Moore Puts Commandments Monument in Court Building', *The Birmingham News*, 2 August 2001.

303: *flushing toilet* . . . Ann W. O'Neill, 'Supreme Court reprimands judge; the Broward Circuit judge who so often belittled attorneys, was told to apologise', *Orlando Sentinel*, 11 April 2003, B4.

303: *'I don't miss', he warned* . . . 'Florida Judge Brandishes a Gun at an Unruly Defendant in Court', *New York Times*, 17 May 1992, p. 30.

303: *over half the states* . . . Stephen B. Bright and Patrick J. Keenan, 'Judges and the Politics of Death: Deciding Between the Bill of Rights and the Next Election in Capital Cases', 75 *Boston University Law Review* 759 (1995), pp. 776–80. The authors also found that judges were elected in thirty-two of the thirty-eight states that retained the death penalty.

303: *tied to a chair* . . . Jason Epstein, *The Great Conspiracy Trial* (New York, 1970), pp. 254–69, 408–19.

303: *to kill himself* . . . Ross E. Molloy, 'Texas Judge Orders Notices Warning of Sex Offenders', *New York Times*, 29 May 2001, A10.

304: *for the kennel* . . . Mark Babineck, 'Abuser gets 30 days in doghouse', *Chicago Tribune*, 14 March 2003, p.14.

305: *in 1750* . . . Tony Palmer, *The Trials of Oz* (Manchester, 1971) ['Palmer'], p. 80; John Pringle, *Observations on the Diseases of the Army* (London, 1752), pp. 346–9.

305: *his own court clerk* . . . See Geoffrey Robertson, *The Justice Game* (London, 1998) ['Robertson, *Justice*'], p. 34; Richard Neville, *Hippie, Hippie, Shake* (London, 1995) ['Neville'], p. 352.

305: *abseiling through his windows* . . . Michael Argyle, 'No John! No John! No John! No!', *The Spectator*, 20 May 1995, p. 27.

305: *poisoned one of his whippets* . . . Neville, p. 352.

306: revolutionary *expression'* . . . Robertson, *Justice*, p. 24.

306: *Nazi Party'* . . . *The Guardian*, 22 February 1986, p. 2.

306: *have it cleared* . . . Robertson, *Justice*, p. 28.

306: *male is unnecessary'* . . . Neville, p. 291.

307: *'Er . . . yes'* . . . Palmer, pp. 103–4.

307: *he asked quietly* . . . Palmer, p. 106; Neville, pp. 313–14.

307: *"fuck" as well'* . . . Robertson, *Justice*, p. 29; cf. Neville, p. 307.

308: *their prose style*' . . . Neville, p. 305.

308: *his best jokes* . . . See Palmer, pp. 206–7.

308: *Groucho Marx* . . . Neville, p. 282.

308: *more open mind*' . . . Robertson, *Justice*, p. 31.

308: *would be natural?*' . . . Ibid., p. 26; Palmer, p. 146.

308: *The summing-up* . . . See generally Vidmar, *World Jury Systems*, pp. 41–2.

309: *There you are.*' . . . Palmer, pp. 238–61; Robertson, *Justice*, pp. 38–9.

309: *10–1 majority* . . . The requirement that juries be unanimous was abolished in England in 1967, and verdicts can now be delivered by qualified majorities. In the United States, only Oregon and Louisiana allow majority verdicts in felony trials. Scotland seems always to have allowed a simple majority of its fifteen-member juries to reach a verdict, though they also have the option of a not-proven verdict. Australia, Canada, and New Zealand still require unanimity. See Valerie P. Hans and Neil Vidmar, *Judging the Jury* (New York, 1986), pp. 171–6; Vidmar, *World Jury Systems*, pp. 26, 31.

309: *from legal error* . . . *R. v. Anderson* (1972) 1 QB 304.

309: *article for* The Spectator . . . Michael Argyle, 'No John! No John! No John! No!', *The Spectator*, 20 May 1995, p. 27; see also Robertson, *Justice*, p. 46.

309: *damages for libel* . . . 'Oz Defendant Wins Drug Slur Award', *The Guardian*, 26 July 1995, p. 5.

310: *lawyers or witnesses* . . . For research supporting this anecdotal assertion, see Nora K. Villemur and Janet S. Hyde, 'Effects of Sex of Defence Attorney, Sex of Juror, and Age and Attractiveness of Victim on Mock Juror Decision Making in a Rape Case', 9 *Sex Roles* 879 (1983).

310: *a silver dollar* . . . Paul Wilkinson, 'Juror Wanted to Find Truth in the Stars', *The Times* (London), 9 July 1998, p. 3; Michael Ellison, 'Heads it's Murder, Tails it's Not', *The Guardian*, 26 April 2000, p. 16.

310: *ordered a retrial* . . . *R. v. Young (Stephen)* (1995) QB 324.

311: *sympathetic audience*' . . . 'Savagery and the Law', *The Guardian*, 22 November 1974, p. 14. See also Chris Mullin, *Error of Judgement*, 3rd edn (Dublin, 1990) ['Mullin'], pp. 7–8. Mullin's book and his personal belief in the innocence of the Birmingham Six, pursued first as a journalist and then from the floor of parliament as an MP, were instrumental in keeping the case in the news during the 1980s.

312: *been handling explosives* . . . Mullin, pp. 44–7.

312: *had never come*' . . . Denis Faul and Raymond Murray, *The Birmingham Framework* (Armagh, 1976), p. 48.

312: *for his crimes* . . . This account of the men's mistreatment is drawn from their later statements to defence lawyers, reprinted ibid., pp.16–46.

313: *soporific calm* . . . See John Chartres, 'Britain's biggest mass murder trial may cost £200,000', *The Times* (London), 16 August 1975, p. 2.

313: *handling nitroglycerine* . . . Mullin, pp. 165–7.

313: *clocks and watches* . . . Ibid., pp. 47, 148–50, 195.

314: *entirely for you'* . . . Quoted in *R. v. McIlkenny* (1991) 93 Cr App R 287, at p. 297.

314: *members of the public* . . . John Chartres, 'Six Birmingham bomb murderers get life sentences', *The Times* (London), 16 August 1975, pp. 1, 2.

314: *had ever heard* . . . Mullin, p. 206.

314: *finality outside it* . . . *R. v. Mirza* [2004] 2 WLR 201, at pp. 209–10.

315: *go any further* . . . *McIlkenny v. Chief Constable* (C.A.) [1980] QB 283, at p. 323.

315: *Anglo-Irish agreement* . . . See Bob Woffinden, *Miscarriages of Justice*, pp. 315–17.

315: *never taken place* . . . See Mullin, pp. 99–100, 272, 278.

316: *the next question'* . . . Ibid., pp. 277–9.

316: *was correct'* . . . Stewart Tendler, 'New witnesses are branded unconvincing liars', *The Times* (London), 19 January 1988, p. 5; Mullin, p. 310.

316: *amidst revelations* . . . See generally Tim Kaye, *Unsafe and Unsatisfactory? The report of the independent inquiry into the working practices of the West Midlands Police Serious Crimes Squad*, (London, 1990).

316: *not at this stage'* . . . *R. v. McIlkenny* et al., 93 Cr.App.R. 287 (1991) ['*McIlkenny (2)*'], p.304.

316: *clean his instruments* . . . *McIlkenny (2)*, p. 299. On Skuse's incompetence, see also *R. v. Ward* [1993] 1 WLR 619, 677 ('Dr Skuse's evidence was wrong and demonstrably wrong, judged even by the state of forensic science in 1974').

316: *it emphasized* . . . *McIlkenny (2)*, p. 311.

318: *six of their countrymen* . . . Vidmar, *World Jury Systems*, pp. 23–5; Anon, *The Complete Juryman* (London, 1752), pp. 160–1; Albert W. Alschuler and Andrew G. Deiss, 'A Brief History of the Criminal Jury in the United States', 61 *University of Chicago Law Review* 867 (1994) ['Alschuler and Deiss'] at p.880.

318: *on randomness alone* . . . §118(1) of the Juries Act 1988. On English jury selection, see Sally Lloyd-Bostock and Cheryl Thomas, 'The Continuing Decline of the English Jury', in Vidmar, *World Jury Systems*, at pp. 68–77; Scotland abolished peremptory challenges seven years later: see Criminal Justice (Scotland) Act, 1995, §8. On the USA, see Nancy J. King, 'The American Criminal Jury, ibid., at pp. 108–14. For a comparative view of jury challenges, see Vidmar's introductory essay at pp. 32–6.

318: *original thirteen states* . . . See Alschuler and Deiss, p. 877.

319: *'Bye baby'* . . . On the events of 24 August, see Stephen J. Whitfield, *A Death in the Delta* (Baltimore, 1988) ['Whitfield'], pp. 16–19; see also William Bradford Huie, *Wolf Whistle and Other Stories* (New York, 1959), now scarce but reprinted in Christopher Metress (ed.), *The Lynching of Emmett Till* (Charlottesville and London, 2002) ['Metress'], at pp. 242–3.

320: *she recalled* . . . Mamie Till-Mobley and Christoper Benson, *Death of Innocence* (New York, 2003) ['Till-Mobley'], p.139.

320: *she declared* . . . Ibid.

320: *photographs of the corpse* . . . *Jet*, 15 September 1955, pp. 8–9; *Chicago Defender*, 17 September 1955, p. 19.

321: *since the 1930s* . . . Robert L. Zangrando, *The NAACP Crusade Against Lynching 1909–50* (Philadelphia, 1980), p. 4 and see the table of statistics at pp. 5–7.

321: *a bridge table* . . . Harry Marsh, 'Judge Swango is Good Promoter for South', *Delta Democrat-Times*, 21 September 1955, reprinted in Metress, p. 60; Juan Williams, *Eyes on the Prize: America's Civil Rights Years, 1954–1965* (New York, 1987) ['Williams, *Eyes*'], p. 51.

321: *an unknown adult* . . . Metress, pp. 36–8, 91.

321: *on the spot* . . . Williams, *Eyes*, p.45; on legal disabilities historically imposed on black witnesses in the South generally, see Randall Kennedy, *Race, Crime and the Law* (New York, 1997), pp. 37–8.

322: *omitted the word 'sir'* . . . Murray Kempton, 'He Went All the Way', *New York Post*, 22 September 1955, p. 5; John N. Popham, 'Slain Boy's Uncle on Stand at Trial', *New York Times*, 22 September 1955, p.64.

322: *see justice done'* . . . Williams, *Eyes*, p. 48.

322: *nearby tractor shed* . . . 'Whistle Killing May Go to Jury Today 2d Negro Accuses Two Defendants', *New York Post*, 23 September 1955, p. 3; John Popham, 'State Rests Case in Youth's Killing', *New York Times*, 23 September 1955, p. 15.

322: *life insurance policy* . . . Murray Kempton, 'The Future', *New York Post*, 23 September 1955, pp. 3, 40.

323: *looking for him now'* . . . Whitfield, p. 43.

324: *got out a tear'* . . . Accounts of the summations and juror comments are drawn from Charles Greenberg, 'Jury Tells Why It Acquitted – "Shocking", Says NAACP', *New York Post*, 25 September 1955, p. 3; John N. Popham, 'Mississippi Jury Acquits 2 Accused in Youth's Killing', *New York Times*, 24 September 1955, pp. 1, 38; Dan Wakefield, 'Justice in Sumner. Land of the Free', *The Nation*, 1 October 1955, at p.285. See also Till-Mobley, p. 188; Whitfield, pp. 41–2.

324: *having told them* . . . William Bradford Huie, 'Approved Killing in Mississippi', *Look*, 24 January 1956. Huie later expanded his article and published as a chapter in *Wolf-Whistle and Other Stories* (New York, 1959), op. cit. On his payment (of 'between $3600 and $4000'), see Whitfield, p. 53.

324: *reflected well on Mississippi* . . . Metress, pp. 115–17, reprinting 'Acquittal', *Delta Democrat-Times*, 23 September 1955; 'The Verdict at Sumner',

Jackson Daily News, 25 September 1955; 'Fair Trial Was Credit to Mississippi', *Greenwood Morning Star*, 23 September 1955.

324: *consciousness of black America* . . . On the media coverage, see Metress, p. 3; on the impact within the black community, see ibid., pp. 225–88.

325: *enough, I thought'* . . . Anne Moody, *Coming of Age in Mississippi* (New York, 1968), pp.125–6.

325: *was Rosa Parks* . . . Douglas Brinkley, *Rosa Parks* (New York, 2000), pp. 101–2.

326: *severed his spinal cord* . . . The background given here is drawn largely from George Fletcher, *A Crime of Self-Defense* (New York, 1988) ['Fletcher'].

326: *dubbed Goetz* . . . 'Subway Vigilante Gives Himself Up', *New York Post*, 1 January 1985, p. 2.

326: *twentieth-century high* . . . See FBI Uniform Crime Reports data as collated at www.disaster.center.com.

326: *every single day* . . . 'Under the Apple', *Time*, 8 April 1985, p. 38.

326: *when he entered court* . . . Mark Lesly, *Subway Gunman* (New York, 1988) ['Lesly'], p. 2.

326: *robbed on the subway* . . . Fletcher, pp. 90–1.

327: *by either side* . . . Ibid., pp. 123–6.

327: *twice before* . . . Lesly, pp. 150–1.

327: *three dumdum bullets* . . . 'A Troubled and Troubling Life', *Time*, 8 April 1985, p. 38.

327: *sadistic and savage'* . . . Quoted in Lesly, p. 149.

327: *right and wrong'* . . . Fletcher, p. 103.

327: *contained admissions* . . . See the extracts quoted by the Court of Appeals in *People v. Goetz*, 68 N.Y.2d 96 (1986).

328: *perceptions of danger* . . . See New York Penal Law, § 35.15, as interpreted ibid., at p. 114.

328: *and acquit him'* . . . Quoted in Lesly, p. 34.

328: *rather than a 'confession'* . . . Fletcher, p. 113.

329: *end of the trial* . . . Ibid., pp. 128–30, 207–8; Lesly, pp. 198–9.

329: *was untrustworthy* . . . Fletcher, p. 107.

330: *say another word* . . . Mike Pearl and Doug Feiden, '"Toss Out Ramseur Ravings". Goetz lawyer's plea after court uproar', *New York Post*, 21 May 1987, p. 7; Fletcher, p. 132. Juror Mark Lesly subsequently expressed certainty that Ramseur had not been intending to throw the shoe: see Lesly, p. 176.

330: *all the others* . . . See Fletcher, pp. 180–97; Mike Pearl and Doug Feiden, 'Bernie Goetz Off The Hook', *New York Post*, 17 June 1987, p. 2.

330: *jurors later explained* . . . Ann Bollinger et al., 'Proud Jurors Insist: He Couldn't Retreat', *New York Post*, 17 June 1987, p.5; Fletcher, pp. 194–6; Lesly, pp. 270–313.

330: *in their deliberations* . . . Mike Pearl and Doug Feiden, 'Bernie Goetz Off The Hook', *New York Post*, 17 June 1987, p. 2; Ann Bollinger et al., 'Proud Jurors Insist: He Couldn't Retreat', *New York Post*, 17 June 1987, p.5; Fletcher, p. 203.

330: *of its whites* . . . Barbara Whitaker, 'City Supports Goetz Verdict. Whites Back Acquittal 9–1; Blacks Almost Evenly Split', *Newsday*, 28 June 1987, p. 3.

330: *firing squads'* . . . David E. Pitt, 'Blacks See Goetz Verdict as Blow to Race Relations', *New York Times*, 18 June 1987, A1, B6.

330: *accept the verdict'* . . . Ransdell Pierson and Leo Standora, 'City Leaders Sharply Divided on Case', *New York Post*, 17 June 1987, p. 21.

331: *Orenthal James Simpson* . . . This narrative is drawn from several sources, primarily the works by Bugliosi, Thaler and Toobin detailed below.

332: *chauffeur would claim* . . . This was the testimony of the driver, Allan Park, given on 28 March 1995. Transcripts of his evidence, along with the other testimony and speeches cited below, can be found online at www.simpson.walraven.org.

332: *attended for interview* . . . For a transcript of the interview, see Vincent Bugliosi, *Outrage. The Five Reasons Why O. J. Simpson Got Away with Murder* (New York, 1996) ['Bugliosi'], pp. 291–305.

332: *suicide note* . . . The note, dated 15 June 1994, is transcribed ibid., pp. 306–8.

333: *his 1978 retirement* . . . On his background and life prior to 12 June 1994, see Jeffrey Toobin, *The Run of His Life. The People v. O. J. Simpson* (New York, 1996) ['Toobin, *Run of His Life*'], pp. 44 ff.; Jewelle Taylor Gibbs, *Race and Justice* (San Francisco, 1996) ['Gibbs'], pp. 121–39.

333: *darkened mug shot* . . . *Time*, 27 June 1994.

333: *raged around their house* . . . See Paul Thaler, *The Spectacle. Media and the Making of the O. J. Simpson Story* (Westport, Conn., 1997) ['Thaler'], pp. 25, 35–6.

333: *ancestral memory'* . . . *New York Times*, 10 July 1994, p. 14.

334: *first Gulf War* . . . Thaler, pp. 83–5.

334: *predictable tizzy* . . . Toobin, *Run of His Life*, p.139; Thaler, p. 119.

334: *any paid interviews* . . . See Marcia Clark, *Without a Doubt* (New York and London, 1997) ['Clark'], pp. 62–5; Thaler, pp. 39–40.

334: *16,000 objections* . . . Bugliosi, p. 79.

334: *to go forward'* . . . Thaler, p. 85.

334: *Jay Leno's* Tonight Show . . . Ibid., p. 91.

334: *was systemic* . . . Toobin, *Run of His Life*, pp. 26–30; Gibbs, pp. 76–83.

335: *damage on King* . . . See Gibbs, pp. 28–53.

335: *presuming his guilt* . . . Marty Baumann, 'Blacks, whites differ on Simpson case', *USA Today*, 6 July 1994, 2A.

335: *as against two whites* . . . Gilbert Geis and Leigh B. Bienen, *Crimes of the Century* (Boston, 1998), p. 192.

335: *demographic terms* . . . On the jury's composition, see Armanda Cooley, Carrie Bass and Marsha Rubin-Jackson, *Madam Foreman: A Rush to Judgment?* (Beverly Hills, 1995) ['Cooley'], pp. 215–8.

335: *anything about [it]'* . . . Quoted in Thaler, p. 37.

335: *his claim to be innocent* . . . Clark, pp. 398–401; see also Toobin, *Run of His Life*, pp. 374–5; Bugliosi, pp. 97, 111.

335: *was not working* . . . Testimony of Dennis Fung (12 April 1995).

336: *really train you'* . . . Testimony of Robert Riske (9 February 1995).

336: *twenty miles away* . . . Testimony of Philip Vannatter (21 March 1995).

336: *he had previously stated* . . . See Toobin, *Run of His Life*, pp. 341–3; Bugliosi, pp. 125–7.

336: *6.8 billion to 1* . . . Toobin, *Run of His Life*, p. 345.

337: *[S]omething wrong'* . . . Testimony of Dr Henry Lee (25 August 1995).

337: *nine years earlier* . . . See Mark Fuhrman's testimony of 9 March 1995.

338: *journalist at the* New Yorker . . . See Toobin, *Run of His Life*, pp. 144–57; and see Jeffrey Toobin, 'An Incendiary Defense', *New Yorker*, 25 July 1994, p. 56.

338: *no reason to worry* . . . Christopher Darden, *In Contempt* (New York, 1996), pp. 191–9, 271–7.

338: *about the file* . . . Clark, pp. 110–11, 341–53.

338: *crossed his lips* . . . See Mark Fuhrman's testimony of 15 March 1995.

339: *a dead nigger'* . . . See the testimony of Laura McKinny, Kathleen Bell, and Natalie Singer (5 September 1995).

339: *still trust him* . . . See Marcia Clark's summation of 26 September 1995.

339: *to say, "No more"* . . . See the concluding day of Johnnie Cochran's summation (28 September 1995).

339: *would later groan* . . . Cooley, pp. 138–9.

339: *had in fact fitted* . . . Ibid., p. 126.

339: *to the majority view* . . . Ibid., pp. 151–65; Bugliosi, p. 19.

339: *two thousand injured* . . . Michael Meyers et al., 'Path of Destruction', *Los Angeles Times*, 10 May 1992, A31.

340: *issued with shotguns* . . . See Thaler, pp. 269–73.

340: *of western civilization'* . . . Howard Kurtz, 'And the O. J. Verdict Is . . . You Name It. As Nation Holds Its Breath, Media Go On Speculating,' *Washington Post*, 3 October 1995, B1.

340: *World Trade Center* . . . 'Sheik and Nine Followers Guilty of a Conspiracy of Terrorism', *New York Times*, 2 October 1995, A1.

340: *almost precisely reversed* . . . According to a *Newsweek* telephone poll taken between 4 and 6 October, 80 per cent of blacks thought the jury was fair and impartial; 50 per cent of whites thought the same, while 37 per cent thought the opposite: *Newsweek*, 16 October 1995, pp. 30, 34. Eight years before, 83 per cent of whites but only 45 per cent of blacks had supported the Goetz verdict: Barbara Whitaker, 'City Supports Goetz Verdict. Whites Back Acquittal 9–1; Blacks Almost Evenly Split', *Newsday*, 28 June 1987, p. 3.

340: *persuaded them of his guilt* . . . See Cooley, pp. 124, 131, 177, 193–4; see also Gibbs, pp. 222–3.

341: *the right thing'* . . . Gibbs, pp. 222–4.

341: *intellectually incapable* . . . George F. Will, 'Circus of the Century', *Washington Post*, 4 October 1995, A25.

342: *the ballot box* . . . Bugliosi, pp. 19, 278–80.

342: *embarrassment to this city'* . . . Kimberlé Williams Crenshaw, 'Color-blind Dreams and Racial Nightmares: Reconfiguring Racism in the Post-Civil Rights Era', in Toni Morrison and Claudia B. Lacour (eds), *Birth of a Nation'hood* (New York, 1997), pp. 97, 144. Bruce's stance was later condemned by NOW's national president, Patricia Ireland: ibid. For further criticisms of the jury, see generally Gibbs, pp. 217–18, 333.

342: *inflicting it on her* . . . Cooley, p. 128.

342: *a heart attack* . . . Tracy Hampton was hospitalized with depression after her dismissal from the jury, on 2 May 1995: ibid., p. 216. Lionel (Lon) Cryer was rushed to hospital with a mild heart attack on 27 July 1995: Gibbs, p.175. Tracy Kennedy, dismissed in March 1995, attempted suicide two months later: Lance Morrow, 'A Trial For Our Times', *Time*, 9 October 1995, at p. 35. See generally S. M. Kaplan and C. Winget, 'The Occupational Hazards of Jury Duty', 20 *Bulletin of the American Academy of Psychiatry and the Law* 325 (1992).

342: *delivered their verdict* . . . Cooley, pp. 8–10, 175–6.

343: *avoid its stagnation* . . . Reforms abolishing most exceptions to jury service were introduced in New York in 1996: see 'Keep Moving on Jury Reform' (editorial), *New York Times*, 3 January 1996, A14. England has recently followed suit: see §321 and Schedule 33 of the Criminal Justice Act 2003.

343: *only comprehensive comparison* . . .See Harry Kalven and Hans Zeisel, *The American Jury* (Boston, 1966), especially at pp. 55–117. Attempts to carry out similar studies in England have been hampered by the judiciary's traditional suspicion of such activities: see ibid., pp. 514–15 and see Valerie P. Hans and Neil Vidmar, *Judging the Jury* (New York, 1986), pp. 118–20, and sources cited therein.

Conclusion

346: *even to describe* . . . See 'Bart the Murderer' (Season 3: 1991); 'Cartman's Silly Hate Crime' (Season 4: 2000); *Dr Who: The Trial of a Timelord* (1993).

For Star Trek trials, see 'Court-Martial' and 'The Menagerie' from the original series, *Star Trek VI: The Undiscovered Country* (1991), *Next Generation*'s 'The Drumhead', *Deep Space Nine*'s 'Rules Of Engagement'.

346: *tooth for a tooth* . . . Deuteronomy 19: 18–19, 21; see also Exodus 21: 23–5 and Leviticus 24: 20.

347: *a speedy jury trial* . . . *Gideon v. Wainwright*, 372 US 335 (1963); *Malloy v. Hogan*, 378 US 1 (1964); *Pointer v. Texas*, 380 US 400 (1965); *Klopfer v. North Carolina*, 386 US 213 (1967); *Washington v. Texas*, 388 US 14 (1967); *Duncan v. Louisiana*, 391 US 145 (1968).

348: *a venerable history* . . . See Albert W. Alschuler, 'Plea Bargaining and its History', 79 *Columbia Law Review* 1, 16ff. (1979).

348: *'unpleasant alternatives'* . . . *Bordenkircher v. Hayes*, 434 US 357 (1978), at p.365.

348: *Leandro Andrade* . . . *Lockyer v. Andrade*, 538 US 63 (2003).

351: *10 per cent more likely* . . . This estimate is based on figures given in charts 4 and 9 of recent Crown Prosecution Service Annual Reports, available online via www.archive.official-documents.co.uk. They show Crown Court conviction rates between 2000 and 2003 to be 55.7 per cent, 58 per cent, and 61.9 per cent, and the equivalent figures at summary trials to be 70 per cent, 69 per cent, and 70.1 per cent.

351: *in 1994* . . . Criminal Justice and Public Order Act 1994, §§34–7.

352: *before its enactment* . . . Criminal Justice Act 2003, part 10; see also House of Commons Standing Committee B, 16 January 2003, cols. 9–25.

352: *about three-quarters* . . . Raymond Moley, 'The Vanishing Jury', 2 *Southern California Law Review* 97 (1928) at pp. 107–9.

352: *5 per cent* . . . Bureau of Justice statistics for state and federal trials can be obtained via www.ojp.usdoj.gov.

352: *in the 1830s* . . . The nineteenth-century figure is based on the proportion of cases resolved by trial at the Old Bailey: see Malcolm M. Feeley, 'Legal Complexity and the Transformation of the Criminal Process: The Origins of Plea Bargaining', 31 *Israel Law Review* 183 (1997), at p. 187. It is extremely hard to estimate the precise modern equivalent. Official statistics are issued for England and Wales rather than the UK as a whole, and other distinct issues arise in Scotland, because an absolute right to jury trial exists only in very serious cases: see Neil Vidmar (ed.), *World Jury Systems* (Oxford, 2000) ['Vidmar, *World Jury Systems*'], pp. 11–12. Matters are further complicated by the fact that, whereas almost every criminal offence was tried by jury in the early 1800s, England/Wales now has a very large category of 'either-way' offences (equivalent to US 'wobblers') that, though relatively serious in nature, are triable by magistrates. All that can be said for sure is that many offences that would be eligible for jury trial in the USA go before magistrates in England. One writer has calculated that 'under 1 per

cent of defendants to criminal charges have their guilt or innocence determined by a jury' and that magistrates conduct four times as many trials as
Crown Courts: Penny Darbyshire, 'An Essay on the Importance and Neglect
of the Magistracy', [1997] *Criminal Law Review* 627, at p. 629.

352: *treat them as such* . . . Émile Durkheim, *The Rules of Sociological Method,*
8th edn, (Chicago, 1938), pp. 68–9.

353: *those who did wrong* . . . See Carl G. Jung, *Nietzsche's Zarathustra. Notes
of a Seminar given in 1934–39,* ed. James L. Jarrett, 2 vols (Princeton, 1989)
['Jung, *Nietzsche's Zarathustra*'], 1: 484–7.

353: *the scapegoats'* . . . Carl G. Jung, *Fundamental Psychological Conceptions.
A Report of Five Lectures,* ed. Mary Barker and Margaret Game (London,
1936), p. 116.

353: *wigs and gowns'* . . . Jung, *Nietzsche's Zarathustra,* 1: 472.

353: *Ethnographers* . . . A survey of the development of legal anthropology
over the last century can be found in John Bossy, *Disputes and Settlements:
Law and Human Relations in the West* (Cambridge, 1983), pp. 1–24; see
also Norbert Rouland, *Legal Anthropology,* tr. Philippe G. Planel (London,
1994).

354: *ban broadcasters from trials* . . . On juries and pre-trial publicity in
England, see Sally Lloyd-Bostock and Cheryl Thomas, 'The Continuing
Decline of the English Jury', in Vidmar, *World Jury Systems,* at pp. 78–80.

354: *to guarantee a fair trial* . . . See e.g. *Estes v. Texas,* 381 US 532 (1965);
Sheppard v. Maxwell, 384 US 333 (1966).

355: *another ruling* . . . *Chandler v. Florida,* 449 US 560 (1981).

355: *urge for retribution'* . . . *Richmond Newspapers Inc. v. Virginia,* 448 US 555
(1980) at pp. 570–2.

355: *crime's individual victims* . . . See e.g. Thomas Aquinas, *The 'Summa
Theologica' of St Thomas Aquinas* . . . *Literally Translated by Fathers of the
English Dominican Province,* tr. Laurence Shapcote, 2nd edn, 22 vols
(London, 1921?–32), 11: 1–4 (Part 2.2, Q.80). The first jurist systematical-
ly to criticize the notion that revenge was a proper function of punishment
was Hugo Grotius in the 1620s: see *On the Rights of War and Peace,* ed.
William Whewell (London, 1853), pp. 223–30 (Book 2, Chapter 20,
§§4–10).

355: *to encourage them'* . . . Henry Weihofen, *The Urge to Punish* (London,
1957), p. 140.

356: *called* State v. . . . See Hal Hinson, 'Just the Reality, Your Honour, and
Nothing but the Reality', *New York Times,* 16 June 2002, pp. 2, 3.

356: *to overrule him* . . . Adam Liptak, 'Bid to Tape Deliberations by Texas Jury
Is Rejected', *New York Times,* 13 February 2003, A24.

357: *Jean Bodin warned* . . . See p. 116 of this book.

357: *intended to kill them* . . . See Justice Brinkema's opinion of 2 October 2003 in *United States v. Zacarias Moussaoui* (Criminal No. 01-455-A), especially at p. 13 n. 22.

358: *stored trial exhibits* . . . Barry Scheck, Peter Neufeld and Jim Dwyer, *Actual Innocence* (New York, 2001), pp. 281–2; Adam Liptak, 'Fewer Death Sentences Being Imposed in U.S.', *New York Times*, 15 September 2004, A16.

358: *should be destroyed* . . . Adam Liptak, 'Prosecutors Fight DNA Use for Exoneration', *New York Times*, 29 August 2003, A1.

Illustrations

Index

The notes to this book are not indexed, but several contain additional information relevant to the subject concerned.